Lecture Notes in Computer Science 14239

Founding Editors

Gerhard Goos
Juris Hartmanis

AF900820

Editorial Board Members

Elisa Bertino, *Purdue University, West Lafayette, IN, USA*
Wen Gao, *Peking University, Beijing, China*
Bernhard Steffen, *TU Dortmund University, Dortmund, Germany*
Moti Yung, *Columbia University, New York, NY, USA*

The series Lecture Notes in Computer Science (LNCS), including its subseries Lecture Notes in Artificial Intelligence (LNAI) and Lecture Notes in Bioinformatics (LNBI), has established itself as a medium for the publication of new developments in computer science and information technology research, teaching, and education.

LNCS enjoys close cooperation with the computer science R & D community, the series counts many renowned academics among its volume editors and paper authors, and collaborates with prestigious societies. Its mission is to serve this international community by providing an invaluable service, mainly focused on the publication of conference and workshop proceedings and postproceedings. LNCS commenced publication in 1973.

Joachim R. Daduna · Gernot Liedtke ·
Xiaoning Shi · Stefan Voß
Editors

Computational Logistics

14th International Conference, ICCL 2023
Berlin, Germany, September 6–8, 2023
Proceedings

Springer

Editors
Joachim R. Daduna
Hochschule für Wirtschaft und Recht Berlin
Berlin, Germany

Xiaoning Shi
Deutsches Zentrum für Luft- und Raumfahrt (DLR)
Berlin, Germany

Gernot Liedtke
Deutsches Zentrum für Luft- und Raumfahrt (DLR)
Berlin, Germany

Stefan Voß
University of Hamburg
Hamburg, Germany

ISSN 0302-9743 ISSN 1611-3349 (electronic)
Lecture Notes in Computer Science
ISBN 978-3-031-43611-6 ISBN 978-3-031-43612-3 (eBook)
https://doi.org/10.1007/978-3-031-43612-3

© The Editor(s) (if applicable) and The Author(s), under exclusive license
to Springer Nature Switzerland AG 2023

This work is subject to copyright. All rights are reserved by the Publisher, whether the whole or part of the material is concerned, specifically the rights of translation, reprinting, reuse of illustrations, recitation, broadcasting, reproduction on microfilms or in any other physical way, and transmission or information storage and retrieval, electronic adaptation, computer software, or by similar or dissimilar methodology now known or hereafter developed.
The use of general descriptive names, registered names, trademarks, service marks, etc. in this publication does not imply, even in the absence of a specific statement, that such names are exempt from the relevant protective laws and regulations and therefore free for general use.
The publisher, the authors, and the editors are safe to assume that the advice and information in this book are believed to be true and accurate at the date of publication. Neither the publisher nor the authors or the editors give a warranty, expressed or implied, with respect to the material contained herein or for any errors or omissions that may have been made. The publisher remains neutral with regard to jurisdictional claims in published maps and institutional affiliations.

This Springer imprint is published by the registered company Springer Nature Switzerland AG
The registered company address is: Gewerbestrasse 11, 6330 Cham, Switzerland

Paper in this product is recyclable.

Preface

For decades, logistics tasks were of minor importance in economics as well as in business practice; the basic functions transportation, transshipment and warehousing were regarded as necessary factors, but not essential from a market-related as well as a competitive point of view. Discussions about logistics were mainly related to the military sector, from which, however, the key impact for a fundamental rethinking came at the end of the 1940s. The employment of qualified former military personnel with leadership and management experience in the civilian economy resulted in a transfer of essential logistical principles into operational planning and control, the importance of which increased steadily with the internationalization and, in particular, the globalization of the economy.

In the context of further developments, it became clear that logistics is not everything, but without logistics, everything is nothing. It became increasingly obvious that the mobility of goods is and will continue to be an essential prerequisite for ensuring satisfactory efficiency in service provision processes organized on the basis of the division of labor within the framework of spatially decentralized structures, which increasingly determined the industrial sector as well as retail trade. Linked to this was the necessity to install suitable external and internal information management for the continuous monitoring and control of a globally connected cooperation.

The essential importance of reliable and efficient flows of goods and information has become apparent to the general public. This holds especially as a result of the consequences of the Covid-19 pandemic and the effects of the Russian war against Ukraine. But even singular events, such as a well-observed accident in the Suez Canal not too long ago, can lead to serious disruptions in logistical processes, combined with significant negative economic consequences. Even despite increasing de-globalization and backshoring, efficiency and costs must not be the only key objectives; ensuring resilient logistics structures must also be included. Ultimately, this also means that efficient logistics must be seen as a necessary core competence for the economic success of companies, especially in the manufacturing and retail trade sectors.

In recent years, far-reaching progress has been made in logistics as well as in information and communication technology, for example in the areas of theoretical foundations, the available technical systems and also in operational realizations. In the foreground were the development and improvement of algorithms, the increased automation in transport and warehousing up to autonomous systems, the use of processes from the field of artificial intelligence as well as the development of new materials and manufacturing processes and also advances in communication technology. This results in the mandatory necessity of a problem-adequate and object-oriented combination of logistical functions, quantitative solution procedures and methods for decision support with elements of efficient information management in theory and practice. To push these developments is the central aim of the International Conferences on Computational Logistics (ICCL), which have been held worldwide for 13 years now.

Starting as a joint endeavor between Hamburg and Shanghai the ICCL was held in Shanghai (China) in 2010 (as well as in 2012), followed in 2011 by Hamburg (Germany), 2013 Copenhagen (Denmark), 2014 Valparaiso (Chile), 2015 Delft (The Netherlands),

2016 Lisbon (Portugal), 2017 Southampton (UK), 2018 Salerno (Italy), 2019 Barranquilla (Colombia), 2020 as well as 2021 Enschede (The Netherlands (online)) and 2022 Barcelona (Spain). The 14th ICCL conference, which took place in Berlin (Germany) in September 2023, also aimed to bring together representatives from fields of research and development as well as from practice with the objective of an intensive exchange of knowledge and experiences. Presentations and discussions of current research results as well as developments in various areas of logistics were at the foreground. The main topics of this conference were grouped into five streams as follows:

1. **Computational Logistics**
   Starting from observing the recent trend of using generative artificial intelligence tools, the first paper provides an insight into this regarding logistics. Moreover, among others, this group of papers considers issues of recommendation systems and logistics platforms, internal hospital logistics, cybersecurity aspects for synchromodal freight operations, as well as an emprical study regarding cross-border e-commerce.
2. **Maritime Shipping**
   The largest group of papers, extending a major focus of the ICCL conferences right from the start, concerns maritime shipping, including considerations of inland waterways. Specifically, the included papers span a wide area from developing digital twins in seaports, tramp ship routing, liquified natural gas (LNG) delivery programs, conventional as well as roll-on roll-off (RORO) stowage planning up to problems regarding the allocation of shore-side electricity for grouped container terminals, among others.
3. **Vehicle Routing**
   Vehicle routing problems make up the core of many logistics considerations. Beyond the inclusion of advances in classical vehicle routing, we encounter quite a few practical applications using a variety of modeling approaches. In more detail, we have works dealing with the vehicle routing problem with time windows, a truck-drone routing problem, risk and uncertainty considerations, e.g., in humanitarian logistics as well as an e-waste collection problem. An interesting twist are novel applications including the snow grooming routing problem, which is an extension of an arc routing problem with profits. The problem arises in cross-country skiing facilities when scheduling the grooming of track networks.
4. **Traffic and Transport**
   This volume extends the interest in public transport works, compared to earlier ones. This includes papers on rolling stock circulation planning as well as robust bus driver rostering with uncertainty, but also the prediction and analysis of travel times for transit ferries and ridesharing issues in rural areas with autonomous electric vehicles. The usability of public transport regarding health care services in rural areas as well as questions regarding the combination of public transport and freight transport are considered, too.
5. **Combinatorial Optimization**
   While many of the above problems might be considered as combinatorial optimization problems, there is more. Applications relate to location planning, job shop scheduling, but also various path planning problems and rich lot-sizing problems.

The editors thank all the authors for their submissions as well as the program committee and the reviewers for their helpful support and important feedback which have made a significant contribution to the realization of this book. Reviewing was single blind with 33 full papers accepted out of 71 submissions. Each paper was assigned to at least two reviewers and the average number of reviews received per submission was 2.42. Finally, we would like to express our thanks to Julia Bachale for her comprehensive support and assistance during the preparation of the conference and also the manuscript. We trust that the present volume supports the more important advances within computational logistics and inspires all participants and readers to further research activities.

September 2023

Joachim R. Daduna
Gernot Liedtke
Xiaoning Shi
Stefan Voß

Organization

Program Committee Chairs

Daduna, Joachim R.	Berlin School of Economics and Law, Germany
Liedtke, Gernot	German Aerospace Center (DLR) Berlin, Germany
Shi, Xiaoning	German Aerospace Center (DLR) Berlin, Germany
Voß, Stefan	University of Hamburg, Germany

Program Committee and Reviewers

Amirghasemi, Mehrdad	University of Wollongong, Australia
Armas, Jesica de	Pompeu Fabra University, Spain
Bearzotti, Lorena	Pontifical Catholic University of Valparaiso, Chile
Bell, Michael	University of Sydney, Australia
Boysen, Nils	University of Jena, Germany
Bubalo, Branko	KPMG Berlin, Germany
Cerulli, Raffaele	University of Salerno, Italy
Colak, Merve	University of Hamburg, Germany
Cuerebal, Ahmet	University of Hamburg, Germany
Daduna, Joachim R.	Berlin School of Economics and Law, Germany
Festa, Paola	University of Naples, Italy
Heilig, Leonard	University of Hamburg, Germany
Gonzalez, Rosa	University of the Andes, Chile
Hartl, Richard	University of Vienna, Austria
Hill, Alessandro	California Polytechnic State University, San Luis Obispo, USA
Ji, Zhe	University of Hamburg, Germany
Jovanovic, Raka	Hamad bin Khalifa University, Qatar
Lalla-Ruiz, Eduardo	University of Twente, The Netherlands
Lau, Hoong Chuin	Singapore Management University, Singapore
Mattfeld, Dirk	TU Braunschweig, Germany
Maturana-Ross, Javier	Pontifical Catholic University of Valparaiso, Chile
Mazza, Rina Mary	University of Calabria, Italy
Mazzulla, Gabriella	University of Calabria, Italy
Mes, Martijn	University of Twente, The Netherlands

Møller Jensen, Rune	IT University of Copenhagen, Denmark
Negenborn, Rudi	Technical University of Delft, The Netherlands
Neugebauer, Julian	University of Hamburg, Germany
Nourmohammadzadeh, Abtin	University of Hamburg, Germany
Pacino, Dario	Technical University of Denmark, Denmark
Pahl, Julia	University of Southern Denmark, Denmark
Paias, Ana	University of Lisbon, Portugal
Paternina-Arboleda, Carlos	San Diego State University, USA
Radojicic, Nina	University of Hamburg, Germany
Ramalhinho Lourenço, Helena	Pompeu Fabra University, Spain
Rössler, David	Free University of Berlin, Germany
Salazar Gonzalez, Juan Jose	University of La Laguna, Spain
Sarhani, Malek	Al Akhawayn University, Morocco
Schulte, Frederik	Delft University of Technology, The Netherlands
Schwartz, Frank	University of Hamburg, Germany
Shi, Xiaoning	German Aerospace Center (DLR) Berlin, Germany
Tierney, Kevin	University of Bielefeld, Germany
Ulmer, Marlin	University of Magdeburg, Germany
Voß, Stefan	University of Hamburg, Germany
Xie, Lin	University of Twente, The Netherlands
Yu, Jingjing	University of Hamburg, Germany

Contents

Computational Logistics

Successfully Using ChatGPT in Logistics: Are We There Yet?

Stefan Voß(✉)

Institute of Information Systems, University of Hamburg,
Von-Melle-Park 5, 20146 Hamburg, Germany
stefan.voss@uni-hamburg.de

Abstract. ChatGPT is among the recent most-commonly discussed artificial intelligence systems. While many success stories as well as misuses are exemplified in different fields like, e.g., education, the usefulness in various academic disciplines with very close ties to practical applications still needs to be proven. In this paper we explore the use of this artificial intelligence (AI) tool within the logistics domain. As a lesson learned, one has to be careful. That is, answers cannot always be granted as being correct. Beyond diving into related literature, we explore the use of ChatGPT regarding an as yet underexplored (even without consulting generative AI tools) logistics problem, that is, the stochastic vehicle routing problem with uncertainty in the number of available vehicles.

Keywords: Generative artificial intelligence · ChatGPT · Computational logistics · Artificial intelligence · Stochastic vehicle routing problem with uncertain number of vehicles · Right-hand-side uncertainty

1 Introduction

After more than 40 years [48], artificial intelligence (AI) is gaining rejuvenated popularity based on powerful computational environments as well as advances in information systems research. Acronyms and phrases like *deep learning*, *machine learning*, or *generative AI* currently make it into the popular press implying hopes and fears all around the globe. Generative AI can be a system using AI techniques being able to generate text, software, images, or other types of files/documents in response to prompts, questions or requests; see, e.g., [41]. At the core of these systems we see comprehensive language models being able to produce data based on appropriately trained systems using possibly large data sets (making this a big data application).

Popular generative AI systems include ChatGPT, a chatbot (a chatbot may be seen as a computer program that simulates and processes human conversation) built by OpenAI using a large language model like GPT-3 or GPT-4.[1]

[1] See, e.g., https://openai.com/blog/chatgpt; last access 30 April 2023.

© The Author(s), under exclusive license to Springer Nature Switzerland AG 2023
J. R. Daduna et al. (Eds.): ICCL 2023, LNCS 14239, pp. 3–17, 2023.
https://doi.org/10.1007/978-3-031-43612-3_1

Other systems include Bard, which is related to the company Google[2], Perplexity[3], Bing[4], as well as the Chinese counterpart Ernie available on Baidu [42,50]. A gentle introduction can be found at different places, e.g., in [19].

Generative AI has potential applications across a wide range of industries and domains, including software development, marketing, and fashion [4]. Most remarkable in the open public seems to be the discussion regarding its use in education (see, e.g., [25]).

Notable examples regarding the use of ChatGPT in logistics include [47] with a focus on Industry 5.0 and [52] concentrating on potential transportation applications. Other examples reaching out towards logistics in specific domains as well as supply chain management are [6,17]. In a subsequent companion paper, we focus on issues of bus bunching and bus bridging (see, e.g., [9]) in public transport and also compare answers from ChatGPT with those from Bing [45]. In general, however, the logistics domain has not yet been comprehensively covered regarding the description of using generative AI systems. Moreover, while attempting to showcase the opportunities and future applications, the limitations regarding content also need to be exemplified. In this paper, we aim to provide some insights regarding the use of ChatGPT in the logistics domain and exemplify possible limitations by investigating a specific problem in stochastic vehicle routing which has not yet been comprehensively covered in the academic literature, indicating that even large language models might face some difficulties for handling it, possibly due to the missing academic considerations in related works.

The remainder of the paper is structured as follows. First, we provide a literature review and problem description regarding the specific vehicle routing problem (VRP) to be considered. Moreover, we provide some entries towards using ChatGPT and generative AI to conduct academic studies and establish related reports. Then, in Sect. 3, we utilize ChatGPT in an attempt to gain insights regarding the advancements of a specific problem, namely the stochastic VRP with an uncertain number of vehicles. Parts of the paper are using results from ChatGPT where practical.[5] Finally conclusions are drawn and selected future research needs are exemplified.

2 Problem Exposition and Literature Review

We distinguish two important parts regarding this paper, i.e., vehicle routing and generative AI. Note that some application-oriented works are subsumed in the second part.

---

[2] See, e.g., https://blog.google/technology/ai/bard-google-ai-search-updates/; last access 30 April 2023.

[3] https://www.perplexity.ai/; last access 22 June 2023.

[4] https://www.bing.com/new?setlang=en&sid=081BEF962AF260422C13FCAE2BCC615F; last access 22 June 2023.

[5] All entries have been conducted or reconfirmed on 30 April 2023 using the release from 23 March 2023; see https://help.openai.com/en/articles/6825453-chatgpt-release-notes.

2.1 Vehicle Routing

In this paper, we refer to problem settings leading towards a specific VRP as well as some vehicle scheduling issues. Therefore, we start gently by introducing the general problem settings before becoming specific.

> "The vehicle routing problem (VRP) is a combinatorial optimization problem that involves finding the best set of routes for a fleet of vehicles to service a set of customers or locations. In the VRP, each customer or location has a demand for goods or services, and the goal is to determine the most efficient set of routes for the vehicles to deliver the goods or provide the services to the customers. The VRP is a complex problem that can be formulated in many different ways, depending on the specific constraints and objectives of the problem." (ChatGPT)

Asking ChatGPT about important references on the VRP gives five meaningful entries including the following (plus one reference that could not be found in popular databases): [11,43].

VRPs are among the most studied problems in operations research and discrete applied mathematics with quite a few textbooks and well-known compendiums devoted to the problem with a most recent one being [12]. Also surveys seem to be a dime a dozen including those focusing, e.g., on specific issues such as logistics distribution [18], reverse logistics [36] or stochastic VRPs [32].

Related to the VRP (and our research focus; see below) is also the topic of *vehicle scheduling* where the basic idea is to cover a given set of trips by means of a set of vehicles. To be more specific and choosing a specialized problem setting, given a set of timetabled trips and a fleet of vehicles the *integrated vehicle and duty scheduling problem* seeks to find minimum-cost vehicle blocks (the schedule of a vehicle) and valid driver duties such that each active trip is covered by one block, each active trip segment is covered by one duty, and each deadhead, pull-in, and pull-out trip used in the vehicle schedule is also covered by one duty. That is, a vehicle performs a feasible sequence of trips from the time it leaves a depot until it returns to the depot. Example references include [7,8,21].

Using different words, this can be described as follows:

> "The integrated vehicle and duty scheduling problem (IVDSP) is a combinatorial optimization problem that involves scheduling a set of vehicles and their drivers over a planning horizon to fulfill a given set of trips or duties. The objective of the IVDSP is to minimize the total cost, which typically includes the cost of vehicle operations, driver labor, and penalties for violations of operational constraints.
> The IVDSP is a challenging problem due to its complexity and the large number of decision variables involved. The problem involves simultaneously scheduling vehicles and drivers, considering factors such as vehicle capacity, driver skills, rest and work regulations, and travel times. Additionally, the problem often includes uncertain demand, which further complicates the planning process." (ChatGPT)

A specific area of research in the VRP domain is related to stochastic VRPs where it seems important to first distinguish between stochastic and dynamic VRPs. In the dynamic VRP (DVRP), also referred to as real-time or online VRP, some input data are (only) revealed during the execution of the plan (aka a solution). Examples for such input data can be knowledge about specific customers and/or their demands. More specifically, this can refer to new customer requests, real-time traffic information, knowledge about disturbances like vehicle breakdowns, weather conditions, capacity changes or even customer cancellations on a short notice.

The stochastic VRP (SVRP) is any VRP where at least one parameter is stochastic, i.e., some future events are random variables with a known probability distribution. Examples include the time required to serve customers where different customers may require different service times due to the specific nature of the service provided or varying order complexities. There might also be a probability distribution for vehicle breakdowns or failures during the routing process which can affect the availability of vehicles and require adjustments to the routes.

After an older survey by Gendreau et al. [10], there are quite a few more recent surveys on stochastic vehicle routing including [3,31,32,35,39]. While these surveys seem to be quite comprehensive, a wealth of specific additional works is available.

When emphasizing the SVRP, among the issues receiving general attention in recent scientific literature on logistics and transportation are the topics of robustness and uncertainty. This becomes especially important in the context of disaster relief problems like the January 2023 earthquake in Turkey and Syria or other "prominent" disasters of the last decades like the hurricane Katrina in New Orleans, USA (2005) or the Fukushima disaster in Japan (2011). Related VRP research in this respect might be concerned about an uncertain number of available vehicles, though, this seems to be limited to very few papers; see, e.g., [38]. Of course, not necessarily focusing on disaster relief issues in logistics, specific types of problems reveal the mentioned uncertainty per se, such as the investigation of the concept of crowdsourced delivery in [37]. Here, the crowdsourced couriers are not employed by the platform and this has fundamentally changed the planning and execution of the delivery of goods as the number of available drivers and vehicles is not known a priori. A related body of references exists on agent-based models and transport simulations, where the number of vehicles can vary like in taxi or ride-hailing systems; see, e.g., [49]. Actually, issues regarding a shortage of drivers are commonly discussed in logistics leading to quite some uncertainty in the spirit of what was mentioned above (see, e.g., [27]).

Interestingly enough, there seems to be no consideration in the abovementioned survey papers regarding an uncertain number of vehicles available. Usually, the number of vehicles can be a given constant or a decision variable [10]. However, an explicit consideration of an uncertain number of vehicles can hardly be found with [38] being an exception, as pointed out in the previous paragraph.

The above considerations open up the avenue towards formulating and investigating an SVRP or a vehicle scheduling problem with an uncertain number of vehicles. Regarding mathematical formulations, this relates to issues of right-hand-side (RHS) uncertainty. Note that in mathematical programming, RHS uncertainty refers to the uncertainty in the values of the right-hand side coefficients of a linear programming or mixed-integer programming model. To exemplify, we may consider RHS uncertainty in the context of SVRPs as well as integrated vehicle and crew/duty scheduling problems and show that these problem domains may actually be treated in a way that allows for deriving reasonable solution approaches as well as opening up for future research efforts [8]. The consideration of an uncertain number of vehicles may not only be motivated by means of disaster relief issues but also be motivated by means of electric vehicles having a restricted usable time of the battery, possibly making them unavailable after some time.

2.2 Generative AI

As mentioned above, generative AI can be a system using AI techniques being able to generate text, software, or other types of documents in response to questions or requests; see, e.g., [41]. ChatGPT has been widely discussed in the open public and, according to popular search engines, there are already thousand of articles with ChatGPT in their titles or mentioning it in their abstracts as emphasized in the review from [51]. This also includes quite a few more or less critical commentaries judging upon challenges and opportunities of ChatGPT; see, e.g., [16]. In Europe, a High-Level Expert Group on Artificial Intelligence had presented some Ethics Guidelines for what they call Trustworthy AI [1]. A collection of possible guidelines at German universities, if available, can be found in [40].

It seems important to both understand the technology as well as their limitations and even imagine possible misuses. A comprehensive study comparing human answers to ChatGPT answers can be found in [13]. That is, linguistic analyses of ChatGPT-generated content compared with that of humans can be found and is well documented in that source.[6] Various areas of research received commentaries and initial studies regarding the use of ChatGPT including, e.g., environmental research [53] and history [20]. The latter study is interesting as the author claims to see some political bias in what is presented by the system. While we do not comment on the specific result, we echo the need to be careful regarding possible misuses of ChatGPT.

The discussion of using generative AI is closely related to *cognitive intelligence* which is referred to as human mental ability and understanding developed

[6] The dataset, code, and models are publicly available at https://github.com/Hello-SimpleAI/chatgpt-comparison-detection; last access 30 April 2023.

through thinking, experiences and senses [29]. It is the ability to generate knowledge by using existing information (as is also a common and well-known issue in information management; see, e.g., [44]). We do not claim that ChatGPT and generative AI tools are able towards successfully pursuing this generation, but the fear of related claims is there.

Finally, we should note that comparative studies of different chatbots may also be conducted but are still rare; see, e.g., [28]. This is seen in front of what happened during the last 20 years regarding the use of chatbots especially in supply chain management where simple tasks such as tracking shipments or managing inventory are accompanied by related tools. Marrying natural language processing and optimization is also on the horizon with first efforts being on the way [34].

3 Example Explorations

First of all, we can put forward the core focus of our paper to ChatGPT in asking "Successfully Using ChatGPT in Logistics: Are We There Yet?" leading to the following answer.

> "Some of the potential use cases of ChatGPT in logistics include:
> - Customer Support: ChatGPT could assist with addressing customer queries, tracking shipments, providing order status updates, and resolving basic support issues.
> - Route Optimization: By analyzing data and understanding logistics constraints, ChatGPT could help in optimizing delivery routes to improve efficiency and reduce costs.
> - Inventory Management: ChatGPT could aid in managing inventory levels and predicting demand, leading to more effective stock management.
> - Supply Chain Visibility: By processing vast amounts of data, ChatGPT could provide insights into the supply chain, identifying potential bottlenecks or issues.
> - Natural Language Data Entry: ChatGPT could enable users to input data through natural language, simplifying data entry processes.
> - Forecasting and Decision Making: By analyzing historical data, ChatGPT could assist in making predictions and suggesting optimal decisions for logistics operations."
>
> (ChatGPT)

Current studies on ChatGPT are mostly reporting on experiences by asking questions and providing as well as discussing the answers. This will be surveyed in Sect. 3.1. Based on this, we perform a somewhat difficult selftest in Sect. 3.2.

3.1 Experiences from Literature

Examples from the available literature focusing on logistics issues performing related tests are [17] and [6], as mentioned above. Note that the latter reference also includes links to quite a few blog entries and related sources providing additional insights and discussions. The area of intelligent vehicles may have a major influence regarding autonomous vehicles in the future. In [5] this area is considered. Technically relevant questions might be answered in a superficial way firstly, but once quite a bit of knowledge has been disseminated towards the system, answers may become more meaningful.

Other examples touching the logistics domain include [46]. Also logistics service providers discuss the use of generative AI tools in logistics with [24] being an example. In [45] the concentration is on specific areas within the public transport domain.

3.2 A Selftest on a Stochastic Vehicle Routing Problem

Earlier, we already used ChatGPT for providing answers to commonly known aspects of the VRP. That is, ChatGPT provided a meaningful and practical characterization of what the VRP is about. Next, we go a few steps further and elaborate on the SVRP considering an uncertain number of vehicles (with other input data like demands kept constant). One might assume a lower and an upper bound on the overall number of available vehicles within a system, where the specific number of them is uncertain. In this specific problem area the literature (according to our understanding) should be much more comprehensive than it is. This seems important regarding the use of a generative AI tool for its treatment as there are very few references to copy from.

Various ideas for handling robustness with respect to uncertainties on some specified coefficients in mathematical programming models have been proposed. The different approaches can roughly be divided into two distinct categories, depending on whether the underlying uncertainty model refers to possible fluctuations on the row vectors of the constraint matrix ("rowwise uncertainty"), or on column vectors (we call this "columnwise uncertainty"). RHS uncertainty may refer to a special case of columnwise uncertainty namely the subclass of robust models with uncertainty limited to the RHS only. In the settings mentioned above, and they are also adaptable to the SVRP with an uncertain number of vehicles, we assume a constraint where the number of vehicles n_v is an uncertain value on the RHS. That is, the number of used vehicles according to the problem settings is constrained in a way that an uncertainty set is used for n_v. A first attempt can be seen in [8].

Thus, the following prompt is input into the ChatGPT interface: "How to solve stochastic vehicle routing problems with an uncertain number of vehicles?"

> "Solving stochastic vehicle routing problems with an uncertain number of vehicles is a challenging task, as it involves dealing with both stochasticity and combinatorial optimization. Here are some possible approaches to tackle this problem:

Stochastic Integer Programming: One way to address this problem is to use stochastic integer programming (SIP) techniques, which combine stochastic optimization with integer programming. SIP models explicitly consider the stochasticity in the decision-making process and can incorporate different sources of uncertainty, including demand, travel times, and the number of vehicles. To model the uncertain number of vehicles, one can use integer variables to represent the number of vehicles used in each scenario, and then solve the problem by minimizing the expected value of the objective function over all scenarios. SIP models can be solved using various methods, including scenario generation, sample average approximation, and stochastic dynamic programming.
Robust Optimization: Another approach is to use robust optimization techniques to handle the uncertain number of vehicles. Robust optimization aims to find solutions that are optimal under a set of possible scenarios, by minimizing the worst-case objective function value over all scenarios. To model the uncertain number of vehicles, one can use uncertain parameters that represent the upper and lower bounds on the number of vehicles, and then solve the problem using robust optimization methods. Robust optimization can be applied to both deterministic and stochastic programming problems and has been shown to be effective in dealing with right-hand-side uncertainty.
Simulation Optimization: A third approach is to use simulation optimization techniques, which involve simulating different scenarios and then optimizing the objective function based on the simulated results. To model the uncertain number of vehicles, one can use a range of possible values for the number of vehicles and then simulate different scenarios for each value. The objective function can then be optimized based on the simulated results, using techniques such as response surface methodology, genetic algorithms, or simulated annealing.
Some references on solving stochastic vehicle routing problems with an uncertain number of vehicles include:
Marianov, V., Perez, J. A., & Gutierrez, J. M. (2007). A stochastic vehicle routing problem with a varying number of vehicles. European Journal of Operational Research, 183(1), 492–508.
Wang, H., & Ceder, A. (2013). Stochastic programming with a varying number of vehicles for vehicle routing problems. INFORMS Journal on Computing, 25(3), 542–557.
Gajpal, Y., & Bansal, A. (2019). An integrated approach for stochastic vehicle routing problem with uncertain number of vehicles. Computers & Operations Research, 109, 77–87.
Wu, X., Ouyang, Y., & Yang, Y. (2019). A robust optimization model for the stochastic vehicle routing problem with uncertain number of vehicles. Journal of Advanced Transportation, 2019.
These references provide an overview of different approaches to solving stochastic vehicle routing problems with an uncertain number of vehicles and offer insights into solution methods and applications." (ChatGPT)

The answer seems good despite the fact that the given references do not seem to exist. It is an experience.

To be more specific, the mentioned authors exist and have worked on similar problems but they have not published those specific papers. The titles of those papers seem to be invented and they cannot be found with popular search engines (including Google Scholar). The journals exist, but they have other works in the mentioned issues and page numbers.

Now, let us focus on a specific issue in mathematical programming for solving the SVRP with an uncertain number of vehicles.

Question: What is right-hand-side uncertainty?

"In mathematical programming and optimization, the right-hand side (RHS) uncertainty refers to the uncertainty associated with the values of the parameters or data that appear on the right-hand side of the constraints or objective function in a mathematical optimization problem.
In a typical optimization problem, the decision variables are chosen to minimize or maximize an objective function subject to a set of constraints. These constraints typically involve parameters or data that are known with certainty, such as the number of customers, the capacity of a vehicle, or the duration of a task. However, in many real-world optimization problems, these parameters may be subject to uncertainty, such as demand fluctuations, unexpected events, or incomplete information." (ChatGPT)

Question: What is right-hand-side uncertainty in the vehicle routing problem and how can we solve it?

"Right-hand-side uncertainty is a type of uncertainty that affects the values of the parameters or data that appear on the right-hand side of the constraints or objective function. For example, in a vehicle routing problem, the demand for a customer may be uncertain, and the capacity constraint for a vehicle may be affected by this uncertainty.
To deal with right-hand-side uncertainty, several techniques can be used, such as stochastic programming, robust optimization, and scenario-based optimization. These techniques involve modeling the uncertainty using probability distributions or a set of scenarios and incorporating them into the optimization problem to find a robust or probabilistically optimal solution." (ChatGPT)

RHS uncertainty is considered, e.g., in [22,23,30,33]. Asking ChatGPT about references on this topic in different forms provides references on uncertainty and alike, but not specifically on RHS uncertainty. It reveals the following:

"These references provide an overview of different aspects of right-hand-side uncertainty in optimization problems, including robust optimization, uncertainty sets, and conditional value-at-risk. They cover both theoretical and practical aspects of the problem and offer insights into solution methods and applications." (ChatGPT)

As we found papers by Minoux [22,23] as being relevant to the topic of RHS uncertainty, we give that name to ChatGPT asking whether Michel Minoux has worked on RHS uncertainty.

> "Yes, Michel Minoux has worked on right-hand-side uncertainty in mathematical programming. He is a well-known expert in the field of optimization and has made significant contributions to the theory and applications of mathematical programming.
> In particular, Minoux has contributed to the development of robust optimization methods for handling right-hand-side uncertainty in linear and nonlinear optimization problems. He has also worked on stochastic programming and chance-constrained optimization, which are related to right-hand-side uncertainty." (ChatGPT)

Then, however, we get four references that are non-existing (or can not be found at the places/journals that they are claimed to be cited from). That is, ChatGPT tends to generate "hallucinated" information beyond the given knowledge; see, e.g., [2] for a related consideration. Hallucinations are factual inaccuracies, but they seem to appear as scientifically plausible (at least at first sight). Of course this is problematic because given references may give a false impression of existing work that does not exist.

In a yet not comprehensible form, we have worked on RHS uncertainty for the integrated vehicle and duty/crew scheduling problem. Again, the aim is to build minimum cost vehicle and daily crew schedules and rosters that cover a given set of timetabled trips as well as all daily crew duties incorporating a predefined days-off pattern. Details of the problem setting and a modeling approach can be found in [7,8,21], where the first puts up the overall problem while the latter extend in various dimensions especially including delay propagation and uncertainty in the number of vehicles. Those works had been done without using ChatGPT, and even attempting to let ChatGPT rejuvenate written code in Python towards solving the problem failed. Though, when we go back to a simple VRP or even further towards using it to provide code to input instances of the traveling salesman problem to a commercial solver like CPLEX, we might succeed.[7]

4 Conclusions

In this paper, we attempted to investigate the use of a specific generative artificial intelligence system, widely discussed even in the open public with quite a bit of media coverage. If generally known issues are considered, ChatGPT, the system

[7] Question: Can you write code to input a problem instance of the traveling salesman problem to CPLEX?
Answer: "Yes, I can provide a code snippet in Python to input a TSP instance to CPLEX. Here is an example code that reads a TSP instance from a file in the TSPLIB format, creates a CPLEX model, and solves it: ... " (ChatGPT).

exemplified, can provide meaningful answers. However, it needs quite a bit of care not to be used without *thinking*. In addition, there are quite a few ethical issues that have to be covered as emphasized, e.g., in [14].

Even if our conclusions deem to be close to *handwaving* (that is, they might be more specific), they may be used to better understand the issues. Regarding the specific problem settings considered in this paper, the following lessons may be learned. Once domain knowledge is available, generative AI tools like ChatGPT can be used to expedite the writing of a study. Nevertheless, the natural language processing domain, generative AI and related fields still need to go a long way, to become useful tools in practice. Once widely known terms can be utilized[8] we can envisage successful use cases. This also holds, once enabling technologies for automatization are well understood as, e.g., in intelligent transport systems or smart port developments (see, e.g., [15]). To simplify, in the latter case ChatGPT may help truck drivers to enter an unknown terminal even in a language that they usually do not utilize (e.g. supporting the avoidance of disturbances in executable plans of the above-mentioned dynamic or stochastic vehicle routing problems). This, however, needs additional work as ChatGPT as an AI language model currently has no access to real-time data or specific information about things happening in real time. However, once married with other systems, like e.g. sensors, or digital twins as virtual representation of a physical system (like a container terminal) plus related environment and processes the power of those tools may be utilized. Looking at use cases of digital twins (see, e.g., [26]), this is part of future research but one may envisage almost immediate application as technology development seems quite fast.

In general, research issues are related to different language models and related translation issues (also aiming to compare different tools from different providers as well as in different hemispheres like the United States and China). Moreover, the predictive power to enhance given knowledge needs to be improved. Most importantly, however, the systems should be advanced so that obviously wrong answers should be (more easily) checked and ruled out. To summarize, we most probably have some disruptive technology at hand open for further innovation and research. Beyond the mere of generative AI applications, we may also ask how combinations with the metaverse may support further advances of knowledge dissemination.

Generative AI tools are becoming popular and one of the future issues relates to the development of a process model regarding the use of such tools. To accommodate such a model, quite some preliminaries need to be clarified to make it meaningful. This not only relates to the focus of a study but also the reception level of the respective user. A "handwaving" notion could incorporate a learning curve which incorporates gaining experience based on issues that are well known to the user. Given references could be checked at the journals mentioned.

[8] Examples might be the use of INCOTERMS in logistics; see, e.g., https://iccwbo.org/business-solutions/incoterms-rules/incoterms-2020/; last access 30 April 2023.

A specific task that might be conducted as future work could be an attempt to provide ChatGPT with some detailed examples as inputs (including tables and code).

The general issue of right-hand-side uncertainty needs more research not only regarding the stochastic vehicle routing problem with an uncertain number of vehicles. This holds for generic versions of the stochastic vehicle routing problem as well as specific problems like integrated vehicle and duty or crew scheduling problems.

References

1. AI HLEG: Ethics Guidelines for Trustworthy AI. European Commission, Brussels (2019). https://digital-strategy.ec.europa.eu/en/library/ethics-guidelines-trustworthy-ai. High-Level Expert Group on Artificial Intelligence. Accessed 22 June 2023
2. Bang, Y., et al.: A multitask, multilingual, multimodal evaluation of ChatGPT on reasoning, hallucination, and interactivity (2023). https://doi.org/10.48550/arXiv.2302.04023. Available on Arxiv
3. Berhan, E., Beshah, B., Kitaw, D., Abraham, A.: Stochastic vehicle routing problem: a literature survey. J. Inf. Knowl. Manag. **13**(3), 1450022 (2014). https://doi.org/10.1142/S0219649214500221
4. Castelli, M., Manzoni, L.: Editorial: generative models in artificial intelligence and their applications. Appl. Sci. **12**(9), 4127 (2022). https://doi.org/10.3390/app12094127
5. Du, H., et al.: Chat with ChatGPT on intelligent vehicles: an IEEE TIV perspective. IEEE Trans. Intell. Veh. **8**(3), 2020–2026 (2023). https://doi.org/10.1109/TIV.2023.3253281
6. Frederico, G.F.: ChatGPT in supply chains: initial evidence of applications and potential research agenda. Logistics **7**(2), 26 (2023). https://doi.org/10.3390/logistics7020026
7. Ge, L., Kliewer, N., Nourmohammadzadeh, A., Voß, S., Xie, L.: Revisiting the richness of integrated vehicle and crew scheduling. Public Transp. (2022). https://doi.org/10.1007/s12469-022-00292-6
8. Ge, L., Nourmohammadzadeh, A., Voß, S., Xie, L.: Robust optimization for integrated vehicle and crew scheduling based on uncertainty in the main inputs. In: The Fifth Data Science Meets Optimisation Workshop at IJCAI-2022, Vienna (2022). https://sites.google.com/view/ijcai2022dso/. Accessed 30 Apr 2023
9. Ge, L., Voß, S., Xie, L.: Robustness and disturbances in public transport. Public Transp. **14**, 191–261 (2022). https://doi.org/10.1007/s12469-022-00301-8
10. Gendreau, M., Laporte, G., Séguin, R.: Stochastic vehicle routing. Eur. J. Oper. Res. **88**, 3–12 (1996). https://doi.org/10.1016/0377-2217(95)00050-X
11. Golden, B., Raghavan, S., Wasil, E. (eds.): The Vehicle Routing Problem: Latest Advances and New Challenges. Springer, New York (2008). https://doi.org/10.1007/978-0-387-77778-8
12. Golden, B., Wang, X., Wasil, E.: The Evolution of the Vehicle Routing Problem. Springer, Cham (2023). https://doi.org/10.1007/978-3-031-18716-2
13. Guo, B., et al.: How close is ChatGPT to human experts? Comparison corpus, evaluation, and detection (2023). https://doi.org/10.48550/arXiv.2301.07597. Available on Arxiv

14. Haman, M., Školník, M.: Using ChatGPT to conduct a literature review. Account. Res. 1–3 (2023). https://doi.org/10.1080/08989621.2023.2185514
15. Heilig, L., Lalla-Ruiz, E., Voß, S.: Digital transformation in maritime ports: analysis and a game theoretic framework. NETNOMICS **18**, 227–254 (2017). https://doi.org/10.1007/s11066-017-9122-x
16. Kasneci, E., et al.: ChatGPT for good? On opportunities and challenges of large language models for education. Learn. Individ. Differ. **103**, 102274 (2023). https://doi.org/10.1016/j.lindif.2023.102274
17. Kim, J., Lee, J.: How does ChatGPT introduce transport problems and solutions in North America? Findings (2023). https://doi.org/10.32866/001c.72634. Entry 72634
18. Konstantakopoulos, G., Gayialis, S., Kechagias, E.: Vehicle routing problem and related algorithms for logistics distribution: a literature review and classification. Oper. Res. Int. J. **22**, 2033–2062 (2022). https://doi.org/10.1007/s12351-020-00600-7
19. Lin, H.Y.: Large-scale artificial intelligence models. Computer **55**(5), 76–80 (2022). https://doi.org/10.1109/MC.2022.3151419
20. McGee, R.W.: How would American history be different if LBJ had lost the 1948 election? A ChatGPT essay (2023). https://doi.org/10.2139/ssrn.4413418. Available at SSRN
21. Mesquita, M., Moz, M., Paias, A., Pato, M.: A decomposition approach for the integrated vehicle-crew-roster problem with days-off pattern. Eur. J. Oper. Res. **229**, 318–331 (2013). https://doi.org/10.1016/j.ejor.2013.02.055
22. Minoux, M.: Robust linear programming with right-hand-side uncertainty, duality and applications. In: Floudas, C., Pardalos, P. (eds.) Encyclopedia of Optimization, pp. 3317–3327. Springer, Boston (2008). https://doi.org/10.1007/978-0-387-74759-0_569
23. Minoux, M.: Two-stage robust LP with ellipsoidal right-hand side uncertainty is NP-hard. Optim. Lett. **6**(7), 1463–1475 (2012). https://doi.org/10.1007/s11590-011-0341-z
24. Möller, P. (ed.): ChatGPT and the Like: Artificial Intelligence in Logistics. DHL (2023). https://dhl-freight-connections.com/en/trends/chatgpt-and-the-like-artificial-intelligence-in-logistics/. Accessed 10 May 2023
25. Mollick, E.R., Mollick, L.: Using AI to implement effective teaching strategies in classrooms: five strategies, including prompts (2023). https://doi.org/10.2139/ssrn.4391243. Available at SSRN
26. Neugebauer, J., Heilig, L., Voß, S.: Digital twins in seaports: current and future applications. In: Daduna, J., et al. (eds.) ICCL 2023. LNCS, vol. 14239, pp. 202–218. Springer, Cham (2023)
27. Nourmohammadzadeh, A., Voß, S.: An effective matheuristic approach for robust bus driver rostering with uncertain daily working hours. In: Daduna, J., et al. (eds.) ICCL 2023. LNCS, vol. 14239, pp. xx–yy. Springer, Cham (2023)
28. O'Leary, D.E.: An analysis of three chatbots: BlenderBot, ChatGPT and LaMDA. Intell. Syst. Account. Finance Manag. **30**(1), 41–54 (2023). https://doi.org/10.1002/isaf.1531
29. Otero, I., Salgado, J.F., Moscoso, S.: Cognitive reflection, cognitive intelligence, and cognitive abilities: a meta-analysis. Intelligence **90**, 101614 (2022). https://doi.org/10.1016/j.intell.2021.101614
30. Ouorou, A.: Robust models for linear programming with uncertain right hand side. Networks **68**(3), 200–211 (2016). https://doi.org/10.1002/net.21693

31. Oyola, J., Arntzen, H., Woodruff, D.L.: The stochastic vehicle routing problem, a literature review, part II: solution methods. EURO J. Transp. Logist. **6**(4), 349–388 (2017). https://doi.org/10.1007/s13676-016-0099-7
32. Oyola, J., Arntzen, H., Woodruff, D.L.: The stochastic vehicle routing problem, a literature review, part I: models. EURO J. Transp. Logist. **7**(3), 193–221 (2018). https://doi.org/10.1007/s13676-016-0100-5
33. Özaltın, O.Y., Prokopyev, O.A., Schaefer, A.J.: The bilevel knapsack problem with stochastic right-hand sides. Oper. Res. Lett. **38**(4), 328–333 (2010). https://doi.org/10.1016/j.orl.2010.04.005
34. Ramamonjison, R., et al.: NL4Opt competition: formulating optimization problems based on their natural language descriptions (2023). https://doi.org/10.48550/arXiv.2303.08233. Available on Arxiv
35. Ritzinger, U., Puchinger, J., Hartl, R.F.: A survey on dynamic and stochastic vehicle routing problems. Int. J. Prod. Res. **54**, 215–231 (2016). https://doi.org/10.1080/00207543.2015.1043403
36. Sar, K., Ghadimi, P.: A systematic literature review of the vehicle routing problem in reverse logistics operations. Comput. Ind. Eng. **177**, 109011 (2023). https://doi.org/10.1016/j.cie.2023.109011
37. Savelsbergh, M., Ulmer, M.: Challenges and opportunities in crowdsourced delivery planning and operations. 4OR **20**, 1–21 (2022). https://doi.org/10.1007/s10288-021-00500-2
38. Shi, Q., Yang, W., Yang, Z.M., Zhao, Q.C.: Relief materials vehicles planning in natural disasters. IEEE/CAA J. Automatica Sin. **5**(2), 595–601 (2018). https://doi.org/10.1109/JAS.2017.7510850
39. Soeffker, N., Ulmer, M.W., Mattfeld, D.C.: Stochastic dynamic vehicle routing in the light of prescriptive analytics: a review. Eur. J. Oper. Res. **298**, 801–820 (2022). https://doi.org/10.1016/j.ejor.2021.07.014
40. Solis, T.: Die ChatGPT-Richtlinien der 100 größten deutschen Universitäten (2023). https://www.scribbr.de/ki-tools-nutzen/chatgpt-universitaere-richtlinien/. Accessed 22 June 2023
41. Stokel-Walker, C., Van Noorden, R.: The promise and peril of generative AI. Nature **614**, 214–216 (2023). https://doi.org/10.1038/d41586-023-00340-6
42. Sun, Y., et al.: ERNIE: enhanced representation through knowledge integration (2019). https://doi.org/10.48550/arXiv.1904.09223. Available on Arxiv
43. Toth, P., Vigo, D.: Vehicle Routing: Problems, Methods, and Applications, 2nd edn. SIAM, Philadelphia (2014)
44. Voß, S., Gutenschwager, K.: Informationsmanagement. Springer, Berlin (2001). https://doi.org/10.1007/978-3-642-56878-7
45. Voß, S.: Bus bunching and bus bridging: what can we learn from generative AI tools like ChatGPT? Sustainability **15**(12, article #9625) (2023). https://doi.org/10.3390/su15129625
46. Wang, D., Lu, C.T., Fu, Y.: Towards automated urban planning: when generative and ChatGPT-like AI meets urban planning (2023). https://doi.org/10.48550/arXiv.2304.03892. Available on Arxiv
47. Wang, F.Y., Yang, J., Wang, X., Li, J., Han, Q.L.: Chat with ChatGPT on Industry 5.0: learning and decision-making for intelligent industries. IEEE/CAA J. Automatica Sin. **10**(4), 831–834 (2023). https://doi.org/10.1109/JAS.2023.123552
48. Winston, P.H.: Artificial Intelligence. Addison-Wesley, Boston (1992). (1st edn. in 1977)

49. Xiong, C., Chen, X., He, X., Lin, X., Zhang, L.: Agent-based en-route diversion: dynamic behavioral responses and network performance represented by macroscopic fundamental diagrams. Transp. Res. Part C Emerg. Technol. **64**, 148–163 (2016). https://doi.org/10.1016/j.trc.2015.04.008
50. Yang, Z.: The bearable mediocrity of Baidu's ChatGPT competitor. MIT Technology Review (2023). https://www.technologyreview.com/2023/03/22/1070154/baidu-ernie-bot-chatgpt-reputation/. Accessed 10 May 2023
51. Zhang, C., et al.: One small step for generative AI, one giant leap for AGI: a complete survey on ChatGPT in AIGC era (2023). https://doi.org/10.48550/arXiv.2304.06488. Available on Arxiv
52. Zheng, O., Abdel-Aty, M., Wang, D., Wang, Z., Ding, S.: ChatGPT is on the horizon: could a large language model be all we need for intelligent transportation? (2023). https://doi.org/10.48550/arXiv.2303.05382. Available on Arxiv
53. Zhu, J.J., Jiang, J., Yang, M., Ren, Z.J.: ChatGPT and environmental research. Environ. Sci. Technol. (2023). https://doi.org/10.1021/acs.est.3c01818

When Routing Meets Recommendation: Solving Dynamic Order Recommendations Problem in Peer-to-Peer Logistics Platforms

Zhiqin Zhang[1], Waldy Joe[1], Yuyang Er[2], and Hoong Chuin Lau[1(✉)]

[1] School of Computing and Information Systems, Singapore Management University, Singapore, Singapore
{zqzhang.2020,waldy.joe.2018}@phdcs.smu.edu.sg, hclau@smu.edu.sg
[2] AI Singapore, Singapore, Singapore
yuyang@aisingapore.org

Abstract. Peer-to-Peer (P2P) logistics platforms, unlike traditional last-mile logistics providers, do not have dedicated delivery resources (both vehicles and drivers). Thus, the efficiency of such operating model lies in the successful matching of demand and supply, i.e., how to match the delivery tasks with suitable drivers that will result in successful assignment and completion of the tasks. We consider a Same-Day Delivery Problem (SDDP) involving a P2P logistics platform where new orders arrive dynamically and the platform operator needs to generate a list of recommended orders to the crowdsourced drivers. We formulate this problem as a Dynamic Order Recommendations Problem (DORP). This problem is essentially a combination of a user recommendation problem and a Dynamic Pickup and Delivery Problem (DPDP) where the order recommendations need to take into account both the drivers' preference and platform's profitability which is traditionally measured by how good the delivery routes are. To solve this problem, we propose an adaptive recommendation heuristic that incorporates Reinforcement Learning (RL) to learn the parameter selection policy within the heuristic and eXtreme Deep Factorization Machine (xDeepFM) to predict the order-driver interactions. Using real-world datasets, we conduct a series of ablation studies to ascertain the effectiveness of our adaptive approach and evaluate our approach against three baselines - a heuristic based on routing cost, a dispatching algorithm solely based on the recommendation model and one based on a non-adaptive version of our proposed recommendation heuristic - and show experimentally that our approach outperforms all of them.

Keywords: Crowdsourced delivery · Data-driven optimization · Recommendations system

© The Author(s), under exclusive license to Springer Nature Switzerland AG 2023
J. R. Daduna et al. (Eds.): ICCL 2023, LNCS 14239, pp. 18–35, 2023.
https://doi.org/10.1007/978-3-031-43612-3_2

1 Introduction

Peer-to-Peer (P2P) transportation platforms, such as Uber, Lyft, and Food-Panda, have been gaining popularity in recent years with greater adoption of internet technology (such as e-commerce and mobile apps) and the growing demand for more efficient urban mobility. These platforms include ride-hailing or ride-sharing and crowdsourced delivery service providers where the former provide transportation services for people while the latter for goods. The key feature of such platforms is that the platform owners do not own the physical assets (fleet of vehicles) nor employ the transport operators (drivers or riders, used interchangeably) unlike the traditional taxi companies or logistics service providers. Thus, the efficiency of such P2P transportation model lies in the successful matching of demand and supply, i.e., how to match the delivery tasks (or orders or jobs, used interchangeably) with the appropriate drivers that will result in successful assignment and completion of the jobs. This is an interesting research challenge as unlike in the traditional routing problems, the drivers have a choice to accept or reject the jobs.

The work presented in this paper is motivated by a real-world problem scenario involving a P2P logistics platform uParcel[1], where new delivery tasks are being recommended throughout the day in the form of a ranked list (also known as menu) to individual crowdsourced drivers who have already existing pre-scheduled delivery tasks. This problem is essentially a combination of a user recommendation problem [23] and a Same-Day Delivery Problem (SDDP) which is a variant of a Dynamic Vehicle Routing Problem (DVRP) [5]. For a successful matching of delivery tasks to drivers, the recommendations need to take into account not only the platform's profitability (which in classical SDDP is determined by how good the delivery routes are), but also the drivers' preferences for the tasks recommended.

Both, the user recommendation problem and the SDDP have been widely studied and researched in their respective fields. However, there is a great potential for synergy between the two research domains in addressing the problem presented in this paper. The traditional Recommender Systems (RS) are only able to capture users' general personal preferences [29] while the Sequential Recommender Systems (SRS) go one step further by taking into account the sequential dependencies of user-item interactions for more accurate recommendation [7]. Although an SRS takes into account the existing state of a user, it is only able to recommend the user's next action, i.e., in the context of e-commerce, the item that he or she will purchase next. This is insufficient in addressing the problem in this paper which is akin to recommending a new product given that users have purchased a list of items (pre-scheduled orders) and that they are planning to purchase another list of items in the future (new orders that arrive dynamically). Meanwhile, current works in solving the SDDP assume that the drivers

[1] uParcel is a Singapore start-up company which offers on-demand delivery and courier services for business and consumers. See https://www.uparcel.sg/ (last access date 02 July 2023).

will *always* accept the assigned delivery tasks [27,28], which is not the case in a crowdsourced setting.

To address this gap, we bring together two key ideas from Reinforcement Learning and Recommender Systems. More precisely, we propose an adaptive recommendation heuristic (ARH) that incorporates reinforcement learning (RL) to learn the parameter selection policy within the heuristic and a RS model called xDeepFM [15] to predict the driver's probability of accepting an order based on their preference. ARH relies on a linear scalarization function that takes into account both routing information and order-driver interaction in generating the recommendation, and the RL-trained policy is utilized to adaptively determine the exact weightages of this linear function at a given pre-decision state.

2 Related Works

Same-Day Delivery Problem. There are two broad categories of approaches for solving SDDP or DVRP in general namely offline or pre-processsed decision support and online decision [24]. In offline approaches, policies or values for decision-making are computed prior to the execution of a plan. Here, the problem is usually formulated and solved as an Markov Decision Process (MDP). Unfortunately, MDP-based approaches (specifically tabular-based ones) fall into the curse of dimensionality and hence are not suitable for most real-world problems [19]. Approximate Dynamic Programming (ADP) approaches [20] are commonly used to tackle the scalability issue, and one such ADP method for the DVRP is Approximate Value Iteration (AVI) [1]. Increasingly, there also have been many recent works that addressed to solve the DVRP using RL [6,8,13,14]. Meanwhile, lookahead approaches have been applied successfully to solve dynamic and stochastic routing problems. These are commonly termed as rollout algorithms, e.g., [25], the pilot method, e.g., [17] and Multiple Scenario Approach (MSA), e.g., [4,28]. The approaches proposed in these works are not directly applicable to our problem since we are dealing with crowdsourced drivers; however, like many current works that use RL to solve the DVRP, we utilize RL to learn a policy to guide our recommendation heuristic.

Recommender System. There are two broad approaches to recommender systems, namely collaborative filtering methods and content-based methods. Collaborative filtering methods rely on past-recorded interactions between users and predict through similar user patterns to produce new recommendations. One such example is Factorization Machines (FM) [22]. Meanwhile, content-based methods use item features to recommend other items similar to what the user likes and based on their previous action or explicit feedback. One such example is linear models with Follow-the-Regularized-Leader (FTRL) [16]. Lately, Deep Neural Networks have been utilised to learn high-order interactions [15]. To combine the strength of a wide linear model (i.e., Generalized Linear Models) and a deep neural network for recommender systems, Google proposed a framework called *Wide & Deep* [9]. Subsequently a wide and deep architecture of DeepFM that integrates the Factorization Machine (the wide component) and the Multi-Layer Perceptron (the deep component) was proposed in [11]. xDeepFM, an extension of the DeepFM that can jointly model explicit and implicit feature interactions was proposed in [15]. In this paper, we select xDeepFM to predict drivers' probability of selecting an order as it combines both content-based and content filtering (hybrid approach) and mitigates the cold start and data sparsity issues by relying on the factorization of the sparse user-item matrix.

Dynamic Matching Problem. [3] introduced the concept of dynamic order matching in a Peer-to-Peer (P2P) logistics platform, which shares similarities with the problem addressed in this paper. The authors framed the problem as a two-stage decision problem and proposed a multiple scenario approach that involved sampling various driver selection scenarios and solving an integer program for each scenario to generate the final menu. However, it should be noted that the authors of [3] considered a simplified version of the DORP where drivers are only allowed to select one order, and no time windows or capacity constraints are imposed. Furthermore, the authors modeled the drivers' preferences using a pre-determined utility function. In contrast, the problem addressed in this paper takes into account real operational constraints and incorporates drivers' preferences based on historical data, making it a more realistic and comprehensive representation of the DORP.

3 Problem Description and Model

3.1 Problem Description

We assume that dynamic orders are generated throughout the planning horizon, and at a predetermined frequency, the platform consolidates the newly arrived dynamic orders and any unassigned orders and generates a personalized order recommendation list for the crowdsourced drivers. The dynamic orders consist of pickup and delivery tasks, order size, time window requirements for both pickup and delivery, and an expiration time. If a driver arrives at the pickup or delivery location earlier than the specified time window, a waiting time will be incurred. In the event that no driver accepts an order and arrives at the pickup location after the specified time limit, the order will be automatically canceled. A simple illustration of the proposed problem can be found in the supplementary materials[2].

The objective of the problem is to maximize the number of orders fulfilled within the given planning horizon, specifically, a full working day. This objective can be achieved by ensuring that the order recommendation list considers both the driver's preference and routing considerations. The driver's preference ensures that they have a high probability of selecting at least one of the recommended orders, while the routing considerations ensure that drivers with optimal delivery routes can fulfill more orders while minimizing delivery costs.

[2] https://anonymous.4open.science/r/iccl2023-7ADC/SupplementaryMaterials.pdf.

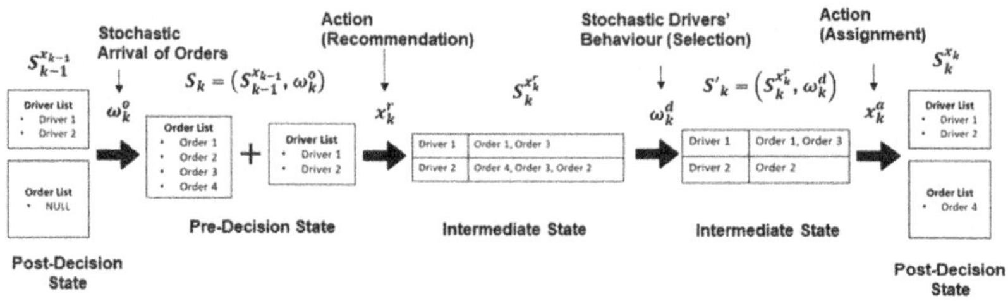

Fig. 1. Sequential decision process of a DORP.

3.2 Model Formulation

This problem can be modeled as a sequential decision process with stochastic information [20]. A visual depiction of the entire decision process is presented in Fig. 1. Here, we present an MDP formulation of the problem.

Decision Epoch. The decision epoch in our model is time-based. We discretize the planning horizon (e.g., a day) into multiple time periods. Here, we use $k = 1, 2 \ldots, i, i+1 \ldots, n$ to represent each decision point.

State. As shown in Fig. 1, a state consists of two parts, pre-decision state S_k and post-decision state $S_k^{x_k}$. Both states are represented by the same tuple $\langle d_k, o_k \rangle$ where d_k denotes the list of drivers and o_k denotes the list of unassigned orders. The list of drivers can be further broken down as follows: $d_k = \{d_k^1, \ldots, d_k^{m_k}\}$, where m_k denotes the number of the active drivers at decision epoch k. We assume the drivers are active when they arrive at pickup or delivery nodes within this decision time slot. Each element in d_k consists of the following features: the last reported location, vehicle capacity and the route of the remaining orders. Similarly, the list of unassigned orders is denoted as $o_k = \{o_k^1, \ldots, o_k^{n_k}\}$, where n_k denotes the number of the unsigned orders at decision epoch k. Each element in o_k consists of the following features: pickup and delivery locations, time windows for pickup and delivery, and size of the order.

Action/Decision. The decision in this model refers to the action of generating personalized order recommendation lists for each driver. Although in reality, the platform needs to execute an assignment action once drivers make their selections (see Fig. 1), we assume that this assignment is governed by a predetermined rule and we treat this step as part of the environment. We denote our decision variable as $x_k = \{x_k^1, \ldots, x_k^{m_k}\}$, where m_k still denotes the number of the riders available in this time slot. Each element x_k^i in x_k contains a subset of unassigned orders a sorted in descending order of suitability for driver i. Note that each order may be recommended to more than one driver and each driver can have more than one recommended order.

Transition. There are two main transitions in this model. Firstly, the transition occurs from the previous post-decision state, denoted as $S_{k-1}^{x_{k-1}}$, to the pre-decision state, represented as S_k. This transition is triggered by the realization of new dynamic orders, denoted as ω_k. The second transition takes place from the pre-decision state to the post-decision state, which occurs after executing the action x_k. However, this second transition introduces additional complexity due to multiple uncertainties that influence the outcome of the action taken. Specifically, there are two intermediate states that arise from two sources of uncertainty, namely the selection behaviors of the drivers and the assignment rule.

Reward/Objective Function. The reward $R(S_k, x_k)$ of an action x_k is defined as the total number of orders fulfilled for the decision epoch k. The solution to this Markov Decision Process (MDP) is a policy that generates the menus at each state. The optimal solution is the policy that maximizes the current reward and the total expected rewards for future states.

4 Solution Approach

Generating the personalized order recommendation lists directly based on the model formulation presented in the previous section will involve an enumeration of all possible permutations of unassigned orders of variable length for each driver. Even if we limit the length of the lists, the action space will still be combinatorial. Thus, to address the curse of dimensionality, we design a heuristic approach to generate the recommendation lists.

The remaining part of this section is organised as follows. We first introduce how our proposed ARH generates the recommendation lists. We then explain the two key components within the ARH, namely how RL is used to train the weightage selection policy for this heuristic; and how the drivers' preference is modelled and learnt from historical data by using xDeepFM.

4.1 Adaptive Recommendation Heuristic

In DORP, the state space and action space are too large to enumerate for large-scale problems. Compared with most dynamic same-day delivery problems such as [10,12] where a decision involves the assignment of one dynamic order to one rider, our problem involves a multi-order multi-driver matching, which leads to a very large state space. In addition, the action space also faces the "curse of dimensionality". Unlike the action space in [3], the recommendation lists for riders in DORP need to be sorted by the relevance (rider-order relevance) which contributes to a larger action space. This task is even made more challenging as decisions need to be done in real-time. Thus, we propose a heuristic solution approach to aggregate the action space.

Heuristic Scoring Function. In our heuristic, the key idea is to compute a driver-order pair score based on the routing cost and riders' personal preference. For a given rider-order pair score, the higher this score is, the more suitable for this rider to serve this order by our consideration. The recommendation list for each rider is then generated by these scores. The function to calculate the driver-order score is given as follows:

$$score(d_i, o_j) = \alpha H_1 + (1 - \alpha) H_2 \quad (1)$$

where α and $1 - \alpha$ are the weights on H_1 and H_2, respectively. The value H_1 is the estimated cost for inserting this order to this rider's route, calculated by the distance of the pickup location of this order to the nearest location of the remaining orders carrying by this rider (referred to as D_n) and normalized between 0 and 1:

$$H_1 = \frac{D_{max} - D_n}{D_{max}} \quad (2)$$

where D_{max} is the largest distance value for any two locations in a given problem instance.

The value of H_2 is the probability of the prediction for this rider's preference for this order, and computed using our proposed xDeepFM model where the details will be presented in Sect. 4.3.

Balancing Platform Objective and Driver Preferences. As a recommender system, the challenge is in calibrating the values of α adaptively over decision epochs, as the environment changes, in order to ensure good profitability (jobs served) on one hand, and good acceptance rate by drivers on the recommended jobs on the other.

From the point of view of the logistics platform, the efficiency of the dynamic routing plan hinges on timeliness of deliveries which in turn is measured by the physical measures such as the routing cost, as proposed in the SDDP and DVRP literature. On the other hand, from the drivers' point of view, they would like to serve orders of their preferences. For instance, the drivers may be more willing to serve the orders in the region which they are more familiar with, even though the locations may be a little far away from their current location and/or the locations of their pre-scheduled orders. If the heuristic generates the menu based on the preferences of the riders, it will not only improve the acceptance of these orders but also the user experience for drivers.

To achieve a good balance of these two potentially conflicting measures, we propose our ARH. The key idea is that we dynamically adjust the weights for each selection criterion based on the current state when making the decision. Intuitively, if the delivery resources are insufficient in some time period, the heuristic should assign orders to focus on the operational efficiency. Otherwise, we want to recommend preferred options to riders, hoping that the orders recommended are more likely accepted by riders (according to their personal preference). In the following, we present a Reinforcement Learning approach to obtain the parameter values (weights) for balancing these two selection criteria.

Finally, we present our heuristic approach, ARH, to calculate driver-order scores that take into account both driver preferences and routing costs at every decision epoch.

ARH consists of the following components:

- Driver's predicted preference score to represent the drivers' selection behaviour based on historical data.

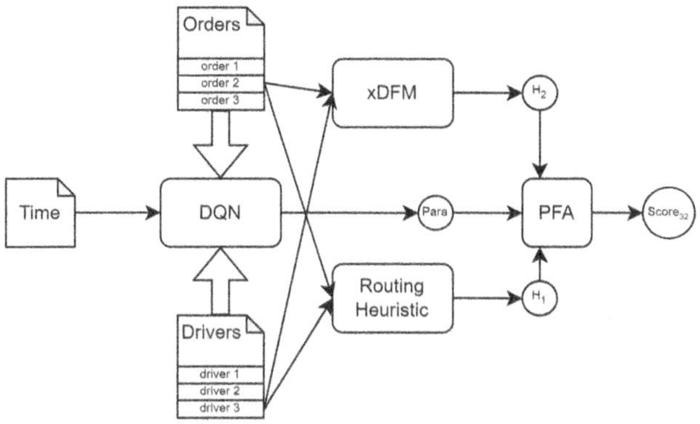

Fig. 2. Overview of the proposed Adaptive Recommendation Heuristic approach.

- A routing heuristic to calculate the cost for a given driver to serve a given order.
- RL-trained policy to determine the weights attached to each objective at a given pre-decision state.

Our proposed heuristic is based on a Policy Function Approximation (PFA) approach [21]. Traditional PFAs are analytical functions by which information in the state variable is mapped directly to a decision. The information of the state in this problem includes two perspectives: platform and drivers. This PFA applies Eq. 1 to calculate the pair scores to generate the final decision, namely the recommendation lists.

The overview of ARH can be found in Fig. 2. The two hollow arrows represent the input of all orders and drivers' data into the Deep Q-Network (DQN), while the other solid arrows signify the transfer of a single value. More details about the algorithm showing how the ARH generates the recommendation lists in a given decision epoch can be found in supplementary materials.

4.2 RL for Selection in ARH

In order to select a proper heuristic for a given decision epoch, we propose an RL approach. Before we elaborate this approach, we describe the MDP formulation for the new decision problem after introducing our proposed heuristic.

MDP Reformulation with State and Action Space Aggregation. The state of this new MDP is an aggregated state. Then we use handcrafted features to calculate the rider-order score. To condense the new state to a set of features, we select the following state information for our new MDP:

- Current time t for this decision epoch k. As the authors of [6,26] select the current point of time of this decision epoch, we also include this feature in our representation of state.

- Total number of unassigned orders n_k and active drivers m_k in this time slot (or decision epoch). We select these two features because it can help to capture how dense the supply/demand in the current time slot is. Combined with the current time, these two features can provide the information to learn the policy for making decisions not only on the current decision epoch but also looking further in terms of supply/demand ratio.
- Information about riders. We do not need all the rider's information in the original MDP. Here we consider to use the remaining orders (or carrying orders) of riders. Based on the remaining orders, we can calculate the distance and time-related information of a given new order to those remaining orders. These are main features to capture the power of supply in the near future time slots. For example, for driver i, the committed delivery time of carrying orders is denoted as vector $\boldsymbol{to_i}$. Then the average bottleneck time for all drivers tb can be calculated by

$$tb = \frac{1}{m_k}\sum_{i=1}^{m_k}(\|\boldsymbol{to_i}\|_{-\infty} - t) \tag{3}$$

  where the negative infinite norm can give the earliest committed delivery time of all the on-going orders of a given driver.
- Information about orders. Apart from the total number of the unassigned orders to calculate the ratio of supply/demand, we also consider average remaining time to obtain the information of the demand. To be more specific, the average remaining time tr is the average of the differences between the expired time te_j for a given order j and the current time t.

$$tr = \frac{1}{n_k}\sum_{j=1}^{n_k}(te_j - t) \tag{4}$$

The action is to select one heuristic to calculate the rider-order pair score for this current decision epoch. To be more specific, we use five parameters in our proposed heuristic. These five values of α are 0, 0,25, 0.5, 0.75 and 1, respectively.

The transition and reward function remain the same as the original MDP. Then, we formulate this problem and use a RL approach to train a policy to select a proper heuristic to calculate the rider-order score in each decision epoch. By these scores, we can directly generate the personalized recommendation lists to riders.

Deep Q-Learning for Weight Selection. For a given state S_k, the action x_k is to select the most proper heuristic to generate the personalized recommendation lists for riders. Thus, the solution of the DORP is to learn a policy $\pi \in \Pi$ that selects the action for each state. The optimal solution $\pi*$ can maximize the total reward. Q-learning [30] learns a value $Q(S_k, x)$ for each state and each action pair. This Q-value can estimate the immediate reward plus the expected future rewards if the action x is taken to the state S_k. Definitely, we cannot calculate and learn all these state-action pairs due to the size of the state and action space (even after aggregation). Thus, we use the DQN approach to estimate this value.

We applied the DQN with experience replay approach in [18]. To calculate the loss function to train this Q-network, the reward function is defined as the proportion of accepted jobs in a specific decision epoch (time slot). The hyper-parameters we used can be seen in the supplementary materials.

4.3 xDeepFM for Preference Prediction

In this subsection, we introduce xDeepFM to predict the job-driver preference score which will be used by the ARH presented above.

Similar to a typical RS problem, the task is to recommend delivery jobs to drivers. The role of the xDeepFM model is to generate the value of H_2, a score for each driver-job pair that indicates the probability that driver $d_k^{m_k}$ will accept job $o_k^{n_k}$. This probability will subsequently be used by the ARH to take into account the driver's preference in selecting a job.

Architecture. The architecture of xDeepFM can be broken down into four parts: (1) embedding layer, (2) linear/FM using the raw input features, (3) Deep Neural Network (DNN) using the dense feature embeddings, and (4) Compressed Interaction Network (CIN) using the dense feature embeddings.

The output of parts (2) to (4) jointly contribute to a shared sigmoid output. The embedding layer takes in the FM inputs and represents them as lower-dimensional vectors. Linear/FM uses matrix factorization to learn the low-dimensional representations and then learns the linear regression weights for the FM layer. For higher-order interactions, these are captured by DNN and CIN where DNN learns implicit high-order feature interactions at the bit-wise level while CIN learns explicit high-order feature interactions fashion at the vector-wise manner. CIN and plain DNNs can complement each other to make the model stronger by combining these two structures. In addition, xDeepFM is customizable as it can be configured as a classical FM model by enabling the linear part and the FM part only if the dataset does not require high-order feature interactions. The architecture of xDeepFM can be seen in supplementary materials. See [15] for more details.

Feature Engineering. The features used for training the xDeepRM model are presented in supplementary materials.

In DORP we face two key challenges involved in the learning task, namely, data sparsity and highly dynamic input features. The data is sparse because the platform only records positive samples, i.e., the accepted orders but not orders that are rejected. In addition, some important input features such as the current location of the drivers and the current capacity of the vehicle are highly dynamic and play an important role in determining whether a driver will accept or reject an order. We address these challenges as follows.

Distance-Based Feature. The current location of a driver plays an important role in determining whether he or she will accept an order. Thus, inclusion of distance-based features would improve the model's performance. These features capture the distance from the driver's current location to the pickup point and from the pickup point to the dropoff point. The challenge is the former. Unlike in typical RS, this feature is highly dynamic. The main challenge lies in calculating this value in real time as there could be some error in calculating expected versus actual values since such highly dynamic data may not be available or accurate. If it is not handled properly, these errors could accumulate over time, resulting in incorrect predictions. To overcome this, we propose to use a proxy feature, i.e., last known location to represent the current location of the driver in order to calculate the distance of the current location to the pickup location. During training, the last known location of a driver is defined as the location at the time point when jobs have last been accepted by this driver.

Negative Sampling. The given dataset consists of historical jobs accepted by individual drivers (item features), as well as a list of drivers (user features). For training the model, the accepted jobs form the positive training samples. As the platform does not allow drivers to reject jobs, all non-accepted jobs are automatically considered implicit negative samples. Hence most samples recorded are positive use cases. Thus, implicit negative samples are generated to ensure a more balanced data during model training. However, not all negative samples are useful and they may in turn introduce noise, hence negative sampling was used to decrease the amount of negative use cases. The chosen approach is by filtering within a time window and computing distance relative to the driver's most recent job/known location. We made the assumption that an active driver who accepted order(s) or performing a job at a given time window is likely to have seen and "rejected" the non-accepted jobs at the same time window.

5 Experiments

We evaluate our proposed approach using a real-world dataset that we collected from a local logistics platform. We ensure that the problem settings and input data closely resemble the real-world scenario.

5.1 Benchmark Algorithms

We present three baseline algorithms as benchmarks: one based solely on routing cost, one based solely on the driver's preference, and one that is a linear combination of these two aspects with equal weightage.

- *RH.* The first baseline algorithm is a routing heuristic (RH), which is similar to the order dispatching algorithm which uParcel currently adopts. This algorithm only considers the distance between the driver's current location and the new order location. This can be done by setting the $\alpha = 1$ in Eq. 1.
- *DP.* The second baseline algorithm is one which solely relies on the driver's preference (DP). This is similar to a typical recommender system which learns driver-order score to represent the driver's preference over a certain order. Section 4.3 describes how this preference score is computed. Then, we set the $\alpha = 0$ in Eq. 1 to ensure that the order dispatching is solely based on the drivers' preference.

- *FWH.* The third baseline algorithm is considering both aspects in a fixed weight. This is done by setting α in Eq. 1 as fixed value, (e.g. setting it as 0.5 as the third baseline algorithm). Thus, this model is a fixed weight heuristic (FWH) model where we assume a 'balanced' consideration.

5.2 Experiment Design

Data. In this experiment, we use a total of 894,794 rows of pickup-delivery tasks collected from 2021 to 2022 provided by uParcel. To train the xDeepFM model and the DQN, we generate two datasets from the raw data. More details about the dataset can be found in the supplementary materials.

xDeepFM Module. As mentioned in Sect. 4.3, we use the xDeepFM model to predict preference of the drivers. Here, we describe the detailed of our implementation of this model.

xDeepFM Training. The challenge of training the xDeepFM in this problem context lies in the sparsity of data and the dynamicity of the problem. Unlike in the typical RS, recommendation or preference scores need to be computed quickly and sometimes the input features change dynamically and may not be available at the moment of inference. This is because xDeepFM is customizable depending on the nature of the data used. We conducted an ablation study to ascertain which customized architectures of xDeepFM are effective in predicting drivers' preference. In addition, given that the current location of a driver plays an important role in determining how likely an order will be accepted, we include a distance feature to act as a proxy to determine how far the driver is from the order. Here, we use a proxy of the driver's real location because in practice, the exact location of a driver may not be available or be updated in the system due to the highly dynamic nature of this feature. See Table 1 for the list of customized models evaluated.

Model and Training Setup. The xDeepFM model that we implemented includes a DNN with 4 layers and a CIN with 3 layers. We use optuna [2] to tune the number of nodes in each layer. Apart from these hyperparameters, the training epochs is set as 500, the batch size is 128 and the learning rate is 0.001. To train the model for binary classifications, we use the following loss function:

$$\mathcal{L} = -\frac{1}{N}\sum_{i=1}^{N} y_i log\hat{y_i} + (1-y_i)log(1-\hat{y_i}) \tag{5}$$

where N is the number of total training instances, y_i and $\hat{y_i}$ is predicted value 0 or 1 (accept or not) and the related label.

Metrics. To evaluate the performance of the various baseline models, we use Precision@k and Recall@k where k refers to the top-k order recommendations given to a driver. To be more specific, the precision@k is defined as the number of recommended orders at top-k that are accepted by a given driver divided by k which is the number of top-k orders the model recommended to this driver.

$$Precision@k = \frac{\#\ of\ recommended\ orders\ @k\ that\ are\ accepted}{\#\ of\ recommended\ orders\ @k} \tag{6}$$

The recall@k is the proportion of accepted orders found in the top-k recommendations.

$$Recall@k = \frac{\#\ of\ recommended\ orders\ @k\ that\ are\ acceptd}{total\ \#\ of\ accepted\ orders} \quad (7)$$

We choose $k = 3$ and 5 as these are realistic lengths of a recommendation list that are both not too long (difficult to make decision) but at the same time give drivers enough options to choose.

RL Module. As mentioned in Sect. 4.2, we train a DQN to select the weights for our proposed solution method, Adaptive Recommendation Heuristic. Here, we show the details related to this module.

RL Environment. To conduct the experiments, we build a simulator for the DORP environment which simulates the selection behavior of riders. Here, we use a multi-attribute utility model similar to the one proposed in [3]. There are two attributes in this multi-attribute utility model namely detoured distance and drivers' preference, which are two considerations in decisions for our proposed DORP. In addition, we also introduce a discount factor to reflect the position of the recommended order in the list:

$$v_{i,j} = \gamma_p(\delta_1 D_{i,j} + \delta_2 P_{i,j}) \quad (8)$$

where $v_{i,j}$ is the utility value of order j to driver i. γ_p is the position discount factor. This number from large to small represents the position of the order appearing in the menu from top to bottom. δ_1 and δ_2 are two weights of the two attributes mentioned above and they sum up to one. To capture the difference of the driver selecting behavior, we uniformly randomize these two figures from driver to driver. $D_{i,j}$ is the estimated detoured distance for driver i to serve order j. Here we use the H_1 value to estimate the routing cost value. $P_{i,j}$ is the predicted probability that driver i will accept order j, which can be estimated by our trained xDFM model. A high value for $v_{i.j}$ indicates high willingness of driver i to serve the order j. To conduct the experiments, we also borrow the idea from [3] to set a threshold (0.5 in this environment to get a reasonable results by the similar current algorithm implemented in the logistics platform). Other experiment setups can be seen in the following paragraph.

Experiment Setup. The hyperparameters of the DQN can be found in supplementary materials. We train the DQN for ARH on the two-month dataset and test the performance of the ARH on the two-week dataset. More details related to the dataset can be found in supplementary materials. We define each day (or each instance) as an "episode" in the training and testing because the problem we consider is same-day delivery. We split each episode into 144 time steps (or decision epochs), where each step is 10 min.

Metrics. We evaluate our proposed ARH against the three baseline algorithms based on the test dataset and we use the order fulfill rate to compare the performance. The order fulfill rate can be calculated by:

$$order\ fulfill\ rate = 1 - \frac{\#\ canceled\ order}{\#\ total\ order} \quad (9)$$

Table 1. xDeepFM model with additional distance features outperforms the other baseline models in both precision and recall measures.

Model	Precision@3	Precision@5	Recall@3	Recall@5
FM only	0.431	0.436	0.109	0.110
FM + DNN	0.469	0.489	0.335	0.336
FM + CIN	0.468	0.478	0.095	0.095
FM + CIN + DNN	0.491	0.506	0.336	0.324
FM + CIN + DNN w/distance	**0.557**	**0.578**	**0.352**	**0.349**

5.3 Experiment Results and Discussion

Firstly, we show the evaluation results of the prediction model. Then, we compare the results of our ARH method with three baseline models described in Sect. 5.1.

xDeepFM. Figure 3 visualizes the convergence of the models with different components. In each graph, the horizontal axis is the epochs, while the vertical axis is the log loss. The blue and orange lines show the loss in the training data set and test data set, respectively. From these graphs, we can find that the FM model cannot predict a good result as the loss on test data set converge to about 1.25 to 1.5 after training. If introducing the DNN, the test loss of the prediction model will reduce to about 0.6 but it is not stable, comparing with the FM and the CIN model. The final prediction model, xDeepFM with all components can get the best results as the test loss converge to the smallest value.

Table 1 also shows the results that xDeepFM with the full suite of components outperforms the classical FM or FM with the subsets of the components. In addition, inclusion of distance-based feature improves the prediction.

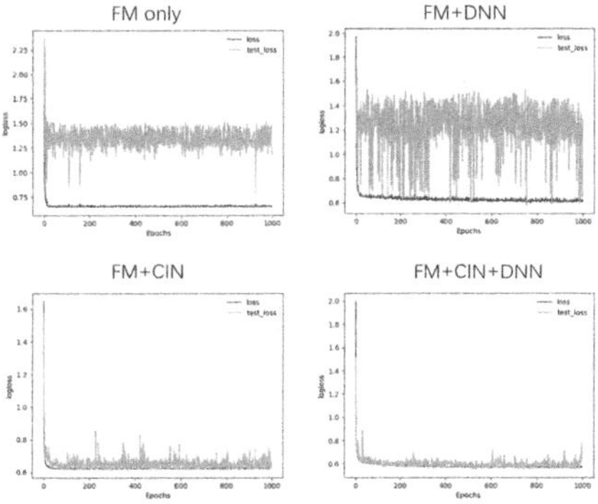

Fig. 3. Convergence of different prediction models. (Color figure online)

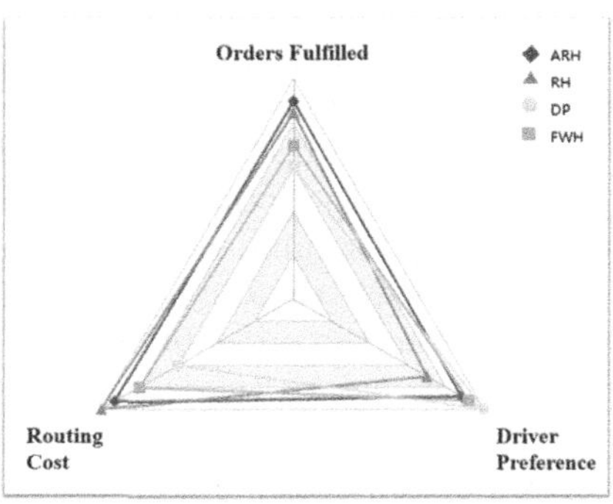

Fig. 4. Summary of the performance of different algorithms.

Table 2. Experiments results of test data set.

Instance	RH	DP	FWH	ARH
Instance 1 (912)	**93.97%**	84.87%	86.51%	93.86%
Instance 2 (383)	97.91%	98.17%	98.43%	**98.69%**
Instance 3 (779)	89.47%	83.44%	85.49%	**95.25%**
Instance 4 (467)	79.87%	72.38%	76.45%	**90.15%**
Instance 5 (453)	**100%**	**100%**	**100%**	**100%**
Instance 6 (435)	98.39%	94.48%	96.55%	**98.62%**
Instance 7 (1065)	85.45%	78.87%	80.01%	**91.27%**
Instance 8 (920)	94.02%	86.09%	87.61%	**97.83%**
Instance 9 (887)	93.46%	86.70%	87.15%	**94.59%**
Instance 10 (752)	99.20%	89.89%	90.69%	**99.34%**
Instance 11 (782	93.61%	86.57%	90.41%	**97.31%**
Instance 12 (384)	**97.14%**	**97.14%**	**97.14%**	96.89%
Instance 13 (440)	**90.68%**	87.73%	90.23%	90.23%
Instance 14 (424)	83.19%	**86.56%**	86.08%	84.67%
Avg.	92.59%	88.06	89.49%	**94.91%**
Var.	0.39%	0.57%	0.47%	**0.20%**

ARH. After having trained 200 episodes (one episode includes 144 epochs) on the training dataset, our proposed ARH with the trained DQN policy can achieve better results on most test datasets. Table 2 shows the results of the performance of our proposed ARH and three baseline algorithms. The entries are the order fulfilled rate defined as Eq. 9, so larger numbers represent better performance. The first column is instances in the two weeks data set. The number in the brackets represents the total number of the dynamic orders in one instance. Columns two to four are the results of three baseline models described in Sect. 5.1. The fifth column shows the best results among these three baselines. The last column shows the performance of our proposed ARH. From this table, we can observe that our proposed ARH can get the best results in 10 instances. ARH is the worst only in instance 12 with a slight difference. For the remaining instances, the ARH can outperform some of the baselines. As the statistical results shows, the average order fulfill rate of the ARH on the test dataset is the highest and the its variance is the smallest.

Apart from the order fulfill rate, we present a summary of the comparison on two other metrics (namely, the total routing cost and the driver preference measured by the probability of the driver accepting the order recommended to him/her based on the driver's historical data). Figure 4 shows that for routing cost, RH (i.e., solely considering routing cost) achieves the best performance compared with the other three algorithms (which is expected). Similarly, DP performs best in terms of driver preference compared with the other three approaches. Interestingly, our approach ARH achieves the best performance in terms of number of orders fulfilled, while not compromising by a large margin in terms of the other two conflicting metrics.

All in all, the results demonstrate that our proposed framework effectively dispatches more dynamic orders for P2P platforms, thereby enhancing customer satisfaction for both riders and customers. This positive impact translates into increased profitability for the platform in both the short and long term.

Acknowledgements. This research project is supported by the National Research Foundation, Singapore under its AI Singapore Programme (Award No: AISG2-100E-2021-089). We like to thank uParcel and AI Singapore for data, domain and comments, the ICCL PC chairs and reviewers, with special mention of Stefan Voss, for suggestions and meticulous copy-editing during the review process.

References

1. Agussurja, L., Cheng, S.F., Lau, H.C.: A state aggregation approach for stochastic multiperiod last-mile ride-sharing problems. Transp. Sci. **53**(1), 148–166 (2019). https://doi.org/10.1287/trsc.2018.0840
2. Akiba, T., Sano, S., Yanase, T., Ohta, T., Koyama, M.: Optuna: a next-generation hyperparameter optimization framework. In: Proceedings of the 25th ACM SIGKDD International Conference on Knowledge Discovery & Data Mining, pp. 2623–2631 (2019). https://doi.org/10.1145/3292500.3330701
3. Ausseil, R., Pazour, J.A., Ulmer, M.W.: Supplier menus for dynamic matching in peer-to-peer transportation platforms. Transp. Sci. **56**(5), 1304–1326 (2022). https://doi.org/10.1287/trsc.2022.1133
4. Bent, R.W., Van Hentenryck, P.: Scenario-based planning for partially dynamic vehicle routing with stochastic customers. Oper. Res. **52**(6), 977–987 (2004). https://doi.org/10.1287/opre.1040.0124
5. Berbeglia, G., Cordeau, J.F., Laporte, G.: Dynamic pickup and delivery problems. Eur. J. Oper. Res. **202**(1), 8–15 (2010). https://doi.org/10.1016/j.ejor.2009.04.024
6. Chen, X., Ulmer, M.W., Thomas, B.W.: Deep Q-learning for same-day delivery with vehicles and drones. Eur. J. Oper. Res. **298**(3), 939–952 (2022). https://doi.org/10.1016/j.ejor.2021.06.021
7. Chen, X., et al.: Sequential recommendation with user memory networks. In: Proceedings of the Eleventh ACM International Conference on Web Search and Data Mining, pp. 108–116 (2018). https://doi.org/10.1145/3159652.3159668
8. Chen, Y., et al.: Can sophisticated dispatching strategy acquired by reinforcement learning? In: Proceedings of the 18th International Conference on Autonomous Agents and MultiAgent Systems, pp. 1395–1403 (2019). https://doi.org/10.48550/arXiv.1903.02716
9. Cheng, H.T., et al.: Wide & deep learning for recommender systems. In: Proceedings of the 1st Workshop on Deep Learning for Recommender Systems, pp. 7–10 (2016). https://doi.org/10.1145/2988450.2988454
10. Dayarian, I., Savelsbergh, M.: Crowdshipping and same-day delivery: employing in-store customers to deliver online orders. Prod. Oper. Manag. **29**(9), 2153–2174 (2020). https://doi.org/10.1111/poms.13219

11. Guo, H., Tang, R., Ye, Y., Li, Z., He, X.: DeepFM: a factorization-machine based neural network for CTR prediction. arXiv preprint arXiv:1703.04247 (2017). https://doi.org/10.48550/arXiv.1703.04247
12. Hou, S., Gao, J., Wang, C.: Optimization framework for crowd-sourced delivery services with the consideration of shippers' acceptance uncertainties. IEEE Trans. Intell. Transp. Syst. **24**(1), 684–693 (2022). https://doi.org/10.1109/TITS.2022.3215512
13. Joe, W., Lau, H.C.: Deep reinforcement learning approach to solve dynamic vehicle routing problem with stochastic customers. In: Proceedings of the International Conference on Automated Planning and Scheduling, vol. 30, pp. 394–402 (2020). https://doi.org/10.1609/icaps.v30i1.6685
14. Li, X., et al.: Learning to optimize industry-scale dynamic pickup and delivery problems. In: 2021 IEEE 37th International Conference on Data Engineering (ICDE), pp. 2511–2522. IEEE (2021). https://doi.org/10.1109/ICDE51399.2021.00283
15. Lian, J., Zhou, X., Zhang, F., Chen, Z., Xie, X., Sun, G.: xDeepFM: combining explicit and implicit feature interactions for recommender systems. In: Proceedings of the 24th ACM SIGKDD International Conference on Knowledge Discovery & Data Mining, pp. 1754–1763 (2018). https://doi.org/10.1145/3219819.3220023
16. McMahan, H.B., et al.: Ad click prediction: a view from the trenches. In: Proceedings of the 19th ACM SIGKDD International Conference on Knowledge Discovery and Data Mining, pp. 1222–1230 (2013). https://doi.org/10.1145/2487575.2488200
17. Mendoza, J.E., Castanier, B., Guéret, C., Medaglia, A.L., Velasco, N.: Constructive heuristics for the multicompartment vehicle routing problem with stochastic demands. Transp. Sci. **45**(3), 346–363 (2011). https://doi.org/10.1287/trsc.1100.0353
18. Mnih, V., et al.: Human-level control through deep reinforcement learning. Nature **518**(7540), 529–533 (2015). https://doi.org/10.1038/nature14236
19. Pillac, V., Gendreau, M., Guéret, C., Medaglia, A.L.: A review of dynamic vehicle routing problems. Eur. J. Oper. Res. **225**(1), 1–11 (2013). https://doi.org/10.1016/j.ejor.2012.08.015
20. Powell, W.B.: Approximate Dynamic Programming: Solving the Curses of Dimensionality, vol. 842. Wiley, Hoboken (2011)
21. Powell, W.B.: Designing lookahead policies for sequential decision problems in transportation and logistics. IEEE Open J. Intell. Transp. Syst. **3**, 313–327 (2022). https://doi.org/10.1109/OJITS.2022.3148574
22. Rendle, S.: Factorization machines. In: 2010 IEEE International Conference on Data Mining, pp. 995–1000. IEEE (2010). https://doi.org/10.1109/ICDM.2010.127
23. Resnick, P., Varian, H.R.: Recommender systems. Commun. ACM **40**(3), 56–58 (1997)
24. Ritzinger, U., Puchinger, J., Hartl, R.F.: A survey on dynamic and stochastic vehicle routing problems. Int. J. Prod. Res. **54**(1), 215–231 (2016). https://doi.org/10.1080/00207543.2015.1043403
25. Secomandi, N.: A rollout policy for the vehicle routing problem with stochastic demands. Oper. Res. **49**(5), 796–802 (2001). https://doi.org/10.1287/opre.49.5.796.10608
26. Ulmer, M.W., Thomas, B.W.: Meso-parametric value function approximation for dynamic customer acceptances in delivery routing. Eur. J. Oper. Res. **285**(1), 183–195 (2020). https://doi.org/10.1016/j.ejor.2019.04.029

27. Ulmer, M.W., Thomas, B.W., Mattfeld, D.C.: Preemptive depot returns for dynamic same-day delivery. EURO J. Transp. Logist. **8**(4), 327–361 (2019). https://doi.org/10.1007/s13676-018-0124-0
28. Voccia, S.A., Campbell, A.M., Thomas, B.W.: The same-day delivery problem for online purchases. Transp. Sci. **53**(1), 167–184 (2017). https://doi.org/10.1287/trsc.2016.0732
29. Wang, S., Hu, L., Wang, Y., Cao, L., Sheng, Q.Z., Orgun, M.: Sequential recommender systems: challenges, progress and prospects. In: 28th International Joint Conference on Artificial Intelligence, IJCAI 2019, pp. 6332–6338 (2019). https://doi.org/10.24963/ijcai.2019/883
30. Watkins, C.J., Dayan, P.: Q-learning. Mach. Learn. **8**(3), 279–292 (1992). https://doi.org/10.1007/BF00992698

A Reactive-Periodic Hybrid Optimization for Internal Hospital Logistics

Ebrahim Ehsanfar[1,2](✉), Farzaneh Karami[3,4], and Tim Kerkenhoff[1]

[1] Fraunhofer Institute for Material Flow and Logistics (IML), Dortmund, Germany
{ebrahim.ehsanfar,tim.kerkenhoff}@iml.fraunhofer.de
[2] Faculty of Mechanical Engineering, TU Dortmund, Dortmund, Germany
[3] Department of Computer Science, KU Leuven, Ghent, Belgium
[4] DeltaQ, Brussels, Belgium
farzaneh.karami@deltaq.io

Abstract. Internal hospital logistics (IHL) involves the scheduling of materials and patient transportations employing a fleet of transporters. The problem of collecting and delivering these items within a hospital can be modeled as a Pickup and Delivery Problem with Time Windows (PDPTW). This paper proposes a hybrid dynamic optimization to address the IHL problem based on a two-step heuristic. This algorithm combines reactive and periodic optimizations to assign logistic's transports to the most suitable transporters while considering the urgency of each transport. To conserve resources, this algorithm addresses logistics transports with higher urgency reactively and handles less urgent transports periodically. The initial assignment is constructed using the earliest due date first (EDDF) assignment method. To further improve the efficiency of the procedure, a ruin and recreate heuristic is developed and tested. Computational experiments have been conducted utilizing hospital data from a large hospital with approximately 2100 beds located in Germany to evaluate the performance of the proposed dynamic hybrid optimization. Results show that the hybrid policy outperforms the baseline reactive policy used in the hospital in terms of service quality and cost efficiency.

Keywords: Internal Hospital Logistics · Dynamic Optimization · Dynamic Pickup and Delivery Problems · Ruin & Recreate Heuristics

1 Introduction

Recently, many developed countries have experienced a significant rise in their healthcare costs. This is due to higher demands to strengthen the foundations of

---

This research was conducted at the Fraunhofer Institute for Material Flow and Logistics as part of the KIK-Dispo project, funded by the Federal Ministry of Education and Research of Germany (Grant No. 01IS19041B). The responsibility for the content lies with the authors.

© The Author(s), under exclusive license to Springer Nature Switzerland AG 2023
J. R. Daduna et al. (Eds.): ICCL 2023, LNCS 14239, pp. 36–55, 2023.
https://doi.org/10.1007/978-3-031-43612-3_3

health systems, which results in guaranteeing higher levels of health services for a major part of the population. According to data from 1980 onwards, in most OECD[1] countries the percentage of GDP spent on health has increased over time [9]. Where, for example, Germany in 2020 allocated 12.5% of its GDP for healthcare, with approximately 30% of that expenditure being directed towards hospital services [18]. Logistics operation among different hospital activities is responsible for 20% to 40% of total hospital cost [11]. Therefore one of the interesting topics for researchers is investigating efficient algorithms for reducing the costs of logistics services.

In order to enhance the efficiency of hospital logistics, a crucial part of the cost, Internal Hospital Logistics (IHL) optimization must be prioritized. Effective management of IHL has been a longstanding challenge. Recently, the COVID-19 pandemic has added additional challenges to IHL operations by placing a heavy burden on their processes. Developing efficient IHL operations frees up valuable transport resources, particularly when hospitals face strict distancing guidelines and limited transport resources. In such circumstances, hospitals may need to quickly expand intensive care capacities to ensure continued care in the event of increased patient numbers. Additionally, there has been a significant increase in demand for protective equipment and hygiene products. Logistics management must therefore implement fast, pragmatic solutions to prevent such bottlenecks within hospitals.

IHL's timely transport services are typically planned between different locations within the hospital with an intention of maintaining continuous care. As such, the problem of collecting and delivering patients and materials (e.g., medical equipment and consumables) within hospitals can be considered as the Pickup and Delivery Problem with Time Windows (PDPTW) [8]. However, in real-world IHL problems, uncertainty in the transport data (e.g. unknown arrival times or time windows) makes it challenging to solve such a dynamic problem, efficiently.

To effectively handle the dynamic PDPTW challenges, several steps need to be taken. One crucial step is collecting and arranging transports for optimization. This involves determining how to collect data on new transports, how to integrate them with existing ones, and how to prioritize them. Another step is selecting an appropriate algorithm that can handle the dynamic nature of the PDPTW. The algorithm should rapidly and efficiently re-optimize schedules when new transports arrive or conditions change. Finally, it is essential to implement the schedules produced by the algorithm. This can be achieved using an automated transport management system that assigns transports to transporters, tracks their progress, and updates schedules in real-time. Addressing all these steps is crucial for providing high-quality services at a minimal cost.

Like many other optimization problems, the PDPTW can be solved using exact and heuristic methods. These methods are mostly differentiated by their

[1] The OECD (Organisation for Economic Co-operation and Development) is an international organization made up of 38 member countries. These member countries are generally considered to be developed, industrialized economies with relatively high levels of economic growth, stability, and well-being.

ability to generate optimal solutions and their computational demands. Exact algorithms produce optimal solutions; however, they are computationally expensive and memory-demanding. According to Rais et al. [13], it takes three hours to calculate routing and scheduling in a midsize hospital, which is not practical given the limited time available to conduct their logistics services, especially for vital and urgent transports. Heuristics on the other side can produce high-quality solutions within a reasonable computation time for large-scale problems.

The majority of research on the PDPTW employs heuristic solutions [12,19]. There are two types of heuristics as single-phase-based and two-phase-based heuristics. Single-phase-based heuristics, such as insertion heuristics, construct a feasible solution by adding pickup or delivery services to the transporter schedule one at a time. On the other hand, two-phase-based heuristics [5,7,17] generate the transports' schedule by first constructing a solution (e.g. by insertion) and then improving this solution iteratively. A few examples of two-phase-based heuristics introduced as route-first-cluster-second heuristic [4], the XOR-based heuristic [14], and two-phase simulated annealing [1]. Recently, a ruin and recreate (R&R) based heuristic [3] has been introduced as a state-of-the-art two-phase heuristic.

A common policy known as reactive optimization assigns services to a transporter as soon as they are received. Employing this policy allows immediate reactions without losing decision time and ensures that the quality of service is not compromised. In IHL operation, particularly for emergency transports, it is important to guarantee service quality. Another policy is the periodic optimization [7] which makes decisions only after a set of predefined criteria have been met. The periodic optimization policy schedules the transports in periods and re-optimizes the schedule after each period, enabling adjustments and reassignments of transports to transporters as necessary. It is especially beneficial when managing limited resources, such as transporters and vehicles, in an efficient manner. In [6], they have studied and compared these two approaches and investigated the circumstances under which one may be more effective than the other. However, this paper identifies a method to achieve the advantages of both policies. Therefore, a hybrid policy is developed that uses a ruin and recreate heuristic algorithm to provide high-quality services while minimizing route costs consistently. The term *optimization* is used for the pursuit of efficient solutions within the inherent complexities of the IHL. It does not imply the achievement of globally optimal solutions.

2 Definitions and Preliminaries

To enhance comprehension of the hybrid scheduling algorithm, the following definitions and preliminaries are presented:

Transport: Movement of a specific item from its pickup location to its delivery location.

Transport type: Mode of transportation used for each transport, e.g., wheelchairs or hospital beds for patients, or trolleys for medicines and equipment.

Transport locations: Specific locations where a transport begins or ends.

Time window: Each transport must start and be completed within a specified time window. Transports cannot be scheduled before the start of their time window but can be scheduled after the end of the time window.

Priority: Categorizes each transport by its level of importance or urgency.

Transporter: Logistics personnel responsible for transporting items within the hospital locations.

Shift: The period of time during which a transporter is working continuously.

Tour: Collection of all transports to be completed by a single transporter during their shift.

According to a study [2], a hospital with 1000 beds typically requires approximately 750 transportations daily. Transports are requested by clinical and executive staff and conducted by transporters. In this paper, data from a pilot hospital in Germany with approximately 2100 beds is utilized. This data is collected from specialized software designed for logistics and services management. The software facilitates the hospital in acquiring data pertaining to new transportation requests, assimilating them with the already existing ones, and classifying them based on critical factors such as urgency and proximity. The average statistics for transports and tours in this hospital are presented in Table 1.

In order to enhance the efficacy of IHL transport operations, medical institutions often implement management software systems, which facilitate the recording, processing, and handling of all transportation operations while also furnishing electronic assistance for manual dispatch and automatic scheduling. Automated scheduling software allows hospitals to distribute transport services based on current demand and available resources. In the daily operations of hospitals, medical staff members enter transport orders into the logistic management software. These orders contain information about each transport's pickup and delivery locations, time windows, transport type, and priority. Logistic managers then assign these transports to available transporters based on their skills and availability.

2.1 Hospital Internal Graph and Travel Time Calculation

A hospital's internal layout can be represented by a graph of several locations, where each vertex corresponds to a location within the hospital, such as patient rooms, labs, and pharmacies, and each edge represents the connections between two vertices. Even for small hospitals, the resulting graph can be large and complex, making scheduling and logistics management challenging.

Table 1. The average daily statistics for transports and tours in the pilot hospital.

Transports		Tours	
Number or Transports	1900	Number of Tours	122
Completed Transports	1500	Tours at Night Shifts	26
Emergency Transports	40	Tours at Day Shifts	96
Patient Transports	1100	Average Duration	550 min
Cito Transports	220	Average Number of Transports	19
Material Transports	570		

To accurately represent the transport times between locations within the hospital, this paper employs a data-driven approach that uses historical data based on the time required to travel between different locations. While Euclidean distance is one of the most commonly used methods to calculate these distances, it does not always reflect the actual travel time between locations, as factors such as stairways and the layout of the hallways can significantly influence the travel time. Thus, using time as an index, rather than distance, helps to obtain a more accurate representation of transport times between different locations. The travel time matrix is the set of the travel times between all locations of the hospital.

To create a more realistic travel time matrix for internal hospital logistics, it is important to consider the varying speeds of different transport types, such as wheelchairs and beds. The travel time for each transport type can vary greatly based on the nature of the task, such as the transportation of a patient on a bed versus a wheelchair. We also calculate the travel time for empty paths between locations, where the transporters travel without carrying any patient or object. Additionally, the accuracy of the travel time matrix can be improved by considering the time of day. Hospital corridors may be less crowded at night, leading to shorter travel times between locations compared to the day. This variability in transport times is factored into the travel time matrix, providing a more accurate representation of the actual travel times. The travel time matrix provides a valuable tool for optimizing total travel time in internal hospital logistics operations. Each element of the matrix is calculated as the 60th percentile of all travel time records between similar pickup and delivery locations for each hour and transport type. While the median is a commonly used measure of central tendency in such situations, we chose the 60th percentile to account for calculation errors and ensure that our data is closer to realistic. Prior to this calculation, the data was subjected to a cleaning procedure to remove any anomalous values that may have adversely affected the validity of the results.

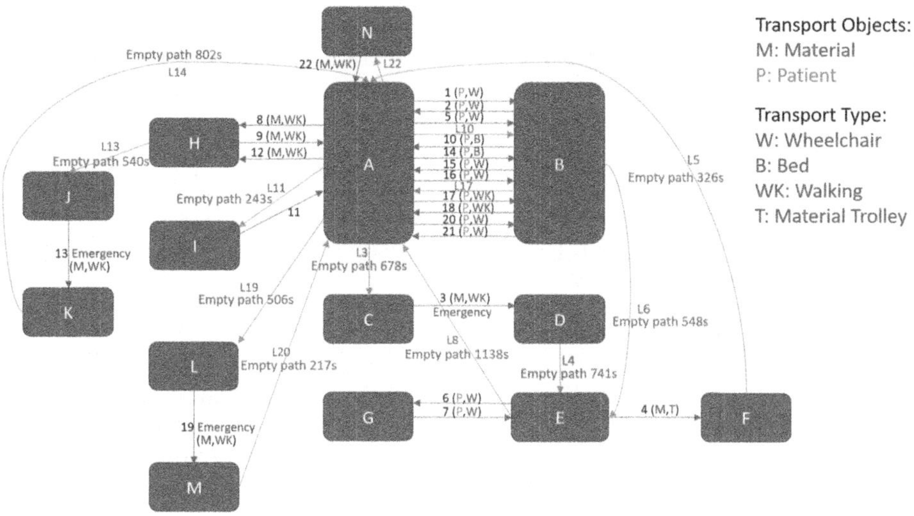

Fig. 1. Example of a transport tour based on real data collected from a hospital. The tour consists of 22 transports that were performed between 14 locations. (Color figure online)

Figure 1 shows an example of a transport tour performed by a single transporter, based on real data collected from a hospital. The blue boxes indicate hospital locations, the blue arrows indicate completed transports, and the red arrows indicate empty transports when the transporter is traveling without any equipment. The tour illustrates that when either material or a patient is assigned to a transporter, transporters sometimes need to walk to reach the pickup location. Some of these empty travels may take a considerable amount of time.

2.2 Problem Definition

From the perspective of hospitals, reducing logistic costs and improving transport service quality are two critical objectives. Providing high-quality service means ensuring that each transport service is provided within its predefined time window. Longer travel times result in higher costs for the hospital, particularly for skilled transporters who are paid more per hour of work. As a result, hospitals aim to efficiently utilize these valuable resources. Minimizing the total travel time of transporters helps to meet the hospitals' demand for cost reduction and efficient resource utilization, while also ensuring that transport services are provided within the designated time windows.

The problem involves assigning each transport to a transporter with the necessary skill and determining the sequence of transports to minimize the total travel time for all transporters. The objective of the current paper is to minimize the sum of the lateness of all transports and the total travel time for all transporters while also considering the various constraints and characteristics of the transport and transporters. For example, each transport should be assigned to a transporter with the necessary skill, and it is necessary to ensure that each transport is conducted within its given time window.

3 Algorithm

The dynamic and complex nature of hospital logistics has resulted in an increased demand for efficient algorithms that can quickly adapt to unexpected changes to maintain high-quality patient care services. In response, a novel algorithm is presented in this section, which consists of a pre-processing phase followed by a two-step heuristic solver.

3.1 Pre-processing

The pre-processing phase is a critical stage in the algorithm that prepares input data by combining suitable transports. Combining two or more transports implies that they can be accomplished by the same transporter during a single tour. Specifically, in this stage, transports that share the same time windows and have identical pickup or delivery locations are combined, provided that a combination is possible and allowed. The combined transports are then assigned to the same transporter in the subsequent stage. However, certain combinations may be forbidden under specific circumstances. For example, it may not be possible to transport a blood sample and a patient on a bed simultaneously due to health regulations. However, this depends on the specific regulations in place. Another example is that transporting more than one bed at the same time may not be possible for a single transporter.

To determine the best transport combination, subsets of transports are generated that can be combined based on their time windows and transport type. The objective is to create the largest possible subset that covers all transports, and then calculate the permutations of elements of each subset to find the best tour with the least travel time. The pre-processing step is given by Algorithm 1, which reduces the search space for the heuristic, leading to improved efficiency and transport quality.

Algorithm 1. Combine Transports

```
Input: A set T of n transports and a lateness threshold ϵ
Output: A covering set C_T ⊆ P(T) of T with minimum cardinality such that each
  transport in T is in exactly one element of C_T
function CombineTransports(T)
    found ← false
    for k = 1 to N_T do                    ▷ Initialize the covering set as C_T = {T}
        for Any covering set C_T with cardinality k do
            for each subset S of C_T do
                for each permutation P_S of S do
                    if Any Forbidden Combinations in P_S then
                        continue
                    end if
                    if Lateness (P_S) > ϵ then ▷ Lateness(P_S) = Sum of lateness for
  all consecutive t ∈ P_S
                        continue
                    end if
                    found ← true
                end for
            end for
        end for
        if found then
            return C_T
        end if
    end for
    return t : t ∈ T      ▷ No valid covering set found, return set of singletons (no
  possible combination)
end function
```

3.2 Heuristics Algorithm

To address the IHL problem, the scheduling starts with creating two separate service pools based on priority: urgent and non-urgent transports. Transport that exceeds the priority threshold is categorized as urgent and placed in the corresponding urgent transports pool, while non-urgent transports are stored separately. The proposed heuristic algorithm assigns transports stored in each pool individually. To illustrate, the paper begins by discussing urgent pool scheduling, followed by an explanation of how the non-urgent pool is scheduled. Finally, an overview of the entire heuristic algorithm is provided.

Urgent Pool: To schedule transports from the urgent pool, the algorithm follows a reactive scheduling policy, which focuses on urgent transports. We classify the urgent pool based on their priority level as either emergencies or highly urgent transports. Emergencies have the highest priority and must be handled immediately without any combination with other transports. Examples of emergency transports include emergency medical supplies for the operating room, moving patients who have suffered accidents, or transporting critical patients from the emergency department to the intensive care unit. As soon as the system identifies an emergency, it assigns the best available transporter, i.e., the available skilled transporter closest to the pickup location. The process of assigning the best transporters to each transport is shown in Algorithm 2.

Algorithm 2. Find Best Transporter

Input: A transport t and a set of available transporters P
Output: The best transporter p in P to carry out transport t
function FINDBESTTRANSPORTER(t, P)
    $T_t \leftarrow$ transport time of t
    $d_{\min} \leftarrow$ very large number
    $p_{\text{best}} \leftarrow$ None
    for each transporter p in P **do**
        $L_p \leftarrow$ last seen location of p
        $A_p \leftarrow$ next availability time of p
        $TravelTime_p \leftarrow$ empty travel time between L_p and pick-up location of t
        if $A_p + TravelTime_p + T_t < d_{\min}$ and p has the required skills for t **then**
            $d_{\min} \leftarrow A_p + TravelTime_p + T_t$
            $p_{\text{best}} \leftarrow p$
        end if
    end for
    return p_{best}
end function

Algorithm 3. Reactive Assignment Algorithm

Input: A set of transports T and a set of transporters P.
Output: A set of pairs Re with elements (t_i, p_j), where t_i is in T and p_j is in P. $\bigcup_{t_i \in T} t_i = T$.
procedure REACTIVEASSIGNMENT(T, P)
    $Re \leftarrow \emptyset$
    Sort T in ascending order based on the delivery time.
    for $t_i \in T$ **do**
        $p_j \leftarrow$ FINDBESTTRANSPORTER(t_i, P)   ▷ Find the best transporter for t_i (Algorithm 2)
        $Re \leftarrow Re \cup (t_i, p_j)$ ▷ Add the pair (t_i, p_j) to Re
    end for
    return Re
end procedure

After assigning the emergency transports employing Algorithm 2, there may still be other highly urgent transports in the pool, such as pharmacy transportation to patient rooms. For these transports, first, their possible combination is examined. If it is determined that the combination will result in lateness, they are scheduled separately with no combination. If it is possible to combine multiple transports without incurring any lateness, the system will roll them out as a single transport, using the same transporter. For each transport after the pre-processing phase, the system will assign a transporter based on the earliest

Algorithm 4. Urgent Pool Assignment

Input: A set of transports T and transporters P.
Output: A set of pairs Re with elements (t_i, p_j), where t_i is in T and p_j is in P. $\bigcup_{t_i \in T} t_i = T$.
procedure URGENTPOOLASSIGNMENT(T, P)
    $Thr \leftarrow$ threshold urgency factor
    $T_{not} \leftarrow \{t_i \in T \mid$ urgency factor $(t_i) \leq Thr\}$ ▷ Emergency transports
    $T_{urg} \leftarrow T \setminus T_{not}$ ▷ Urgent transports
    $P_{not} \leftarrow P$ ▷ Initialize Emergency transporter set
    $Re_{not} \leftarrow$ REACTIVEASSIGNMENT(T_{not}, P_{not}) ▷ Reactive Assignment for Emergency transports
    for $(t_i, p_j) \in Re_{not}$ **do**
        Update P_{not} based on the availability and last location of p_j
    end for
    $T_{urg} \leftarrow$ COMBININGTRANSPORTS(T_{urg}) ▷ Combine transports for urgent transports (Algorithm 1)
    $P_{urg} \leftarrow P \setminus P_{not}$ ▷ Urgent transporter set
    $Re_{urg} \leftarrow$ REACTIVEASSIGNMENT(T_{urg}, P_{urg}) ▷ Reactive Assignment for urgent transports
    $Re \leftarrow Re_{not} \cup Re_{urg}$ ▷ Combine emergency and urgent assignments
    return Re
end procedure

delivery time and proximity. If no transporter is available to perform a transport without incurring lateness, the algorithm will assign the transporter with the least amount of lateness to each transport. The whole process is shown in Algorithm 3.

Algorithm 4 outlines the process of scheduling the urgent pool and selecting the efficient transporters for handling emergencies and highly urgent transports using a reactive scheduling policy. Each transport that is scheduled will be removed from the pool. Additionally, each transporter that is assigned to a transport will receive a new availability time, which will be after the end of the delivery of the assigned transport. The transporter's last available location will be the delivery location of the assigned transport. The transporter's availability at this time and location for later assignments should be taken into account.

Non-urgent Pool: The proposed algorithm adopts a periodic scheduling policy, whereby a fixed duration of time (r minutes) is observed before scheduling transports from the non-urgent pool. Subsequently, each scheduling is executed after every r minutes. This policy is designed to optimize the tours by minimizing the total transporters' travel time while guaranteeing that they receive their due services within the stipulated period. At each scheduling step, the algorithm first checks if it is possible to combine any transports. If so, the pool is updated accordingly. The transports in the pool are then sorted based on their due date in ascending order, which represents the deadline for their delivery. The periodic assignment Algorithm 5 has two main steps as follows:

Step 1 - Earliest due date first (EDDF) Algorithm 6: The earliest due date first algorithm is employed to optimize tours considering the service due date such that transports with earlier due dates are assigned first. As a result of step 1, a set of tours is constructed as the initial solution.

Step 2 - R&R algorithm: The R&R algorithm is applied to improve the initial solution. This algorithm is repeated several times to optimize tours while minimizing total service lateness. The number of transports to be reassigned and the number of iterations at each iteration can be adjusted based on the transports pool size and the desired solution quality. In the next part, we will discuss R&R in general and the algorithm in more detail.

Algorithm 5. Periodic Assignment Algorithm

Input: Size of optimization periods r, set of transports T and set of transporters P in each loop
Output: Assignments, updated set of transports and updated set of transporters in each loop
procedure PERIODICASSIGNMENT(r) ▷ r: size of optimization periods in minutes
  while true **do** ▷ Loop until stopped. e.g. the end of working day
    Get (T, P) ▷ T : set of transports, P : set of transporters
    $initialAssignments \leftarrow$ EDDF(T, P)
    $refinedAssignments \leftarrow$ RUINRECREATE($initialAssignments$)
    Execute refined assignments
    Update (T) ▷ the assigned transports are removed from T
    Update (P) ▷ the next availability and location of the transporters get updated
    Wait for r minutes
  end while
end procedure

Algorithm 6. Earliest Due Date First Assignment (EDDF)

Input: A set of transports T and transporters P.
Output: The list of assignments in the initial step
procedure EDD(T, P)
  $Assignments \leftarrow$ Empty DataFrame
  $Sorted\_transports \leftarrow$ SORT$(T, key = \lambda t : t.$earliest_due_date$)$ ▷ Sort transports by earliest due date
  for i in 1 to $|Sorted\_transports|$ **do**
    $t \leftarrow Sorted\_transports[i]$
    $p \leftarrow$ FINDBESTTRANSPORTER(t, P)
    $Assignments$.append($[t, p]$)
  end for
  return $Assignments$
end procedure

Algorithm 7. Ruin & recreation algorithm (R&R)

```
Input: Transport pool T, List of tours P
Output: List of updated tours
procedure RUIN(T, P)
    TourEmptyFactors ← Calculate empty travel factor for each tour in P
    SelectedTour ← Tour with the highest empty travel factor from TourEmptyFactors
    RemovedTransports ← All transports from the selected tour in P
    TransportPool ← Add the removed transports back to the transport pool T
    return RemovedTransports, TransportPool        ▷ Removed transports and updated transport pool
end procedure
procedure RECREATE(T, P, RemovedTransports)        ▷ Transport pool T, List of tours P, Removed transports
    LatenessBefore ← Calculate the overall lateness of P
    for all transport in RemovedTransports do
        LatenessBest ← ∞
        InsertionTour ← None
        for all tour in P do
            LatenessInsert ← Calculate the lateness of inserting transport into tour
            if LatenessInsert == 0 then
                Insert transport into tour and return
            end if
            if LatenessInsert < LatenessBest then
                LatenessBest ← LatenessInsert
                InsertionTour ← tour
            end if
        end for
        Insert transport into InsertionTour
    end for
    LatenessAfter ← Calculate the overall lateness of P
    if LatenessAfter < LatenessBefore then
        return P                                   ▷ Recreated tours
    else
        return None                                ▷ Recreate failed, return None
    end if
end procedure
```

3.3 Ruin & Recreation (R&R) Algorithm

Many studies show that R&R is an effective algorithm for solving complex optimization problems such as PDPTW. The basic principle of R&R is to first "ruin" a large part of the initial solution by randomly selecting a certain number of transports and removing them from their assigned routes, and then "recreate" a new solution by reassigning the removed transports to routes in a way that improves the overall solution quality. For the first time, the R&R algorithm was proposed by Schrimpf et al., [16] for solving traveling salesman problems and has since been extensively studied and improved by researchers in the field. For example, Ropke and Pisinger [15] developed various ruin methods such as random, worst, cluster, or history-based, and then a greedy algorithm was used to recreate the solution. Later, Pisinger and Ropke [10] proposed an R&R algorithm that employs adaptive large neighborhood search. More recently, the state-of-the-art R&R algorithm has been proposed for the Vehicle Routing Problem with Time Windows (VRPTW) [3].

The R&R algorithm is particularly effective in dealing with complex and "discontinuous" problems, where small changes in the solution can result in large differences in quality. This is often the case in the VRPTW, where solutions must meet a variety of constraints and a small change in the scheduled transportation can cause a solution to become infeasible [3]. Using a large number of transports to remove from the solution can significantly enhance the performance of the R&R algorithm, allowing it to explore a larger solution space and increase the likelihood of finding high-quality solutions [3].

This paper optimizes scheduled transportation by employing the R&R algorithm (Algorithm 7). The algorithm begins by calculating an empty travel factor for each tour, which represents the total empty travel duration of each transporter divided by the total tour duration. This factor indicates the amount of time each transporter spends traveling between locations without performing any services. Tours with higher empty travel factors are more likely to benefit from improvement.

The R&R algorithm sorts tours based on their empty travel factor and attempts to reduce the empty travel duration by reassigning transports to other transporters.

Ruin: The iterative R&R algorithm initiates by identifying the tours with the highest empty travel time factor. At each iteration, the tours are sorted based on this factor, and the tour with the highest score is chosen to be ruined. Ruining the chosen tour involves removing all transports from the tour and reintroducing them back into the transport pool.

Recreation: The recreate step has two sub-steps: (1) inserting the removed transports into another existing tour or (2) creating a new tour with an empty transporter. When deciding on the insertion location for a removed transport, a simple criterion of minimizing the overall lateness caused by the insertion can be taken into account.

When determining the insertion location for a removed transport, the insertion is accepted into the existing tour if it adds zero lateness. If there is a lateness, the tour is continued to be built, and the overall lateness is compared to the previous overall lateness. If the new tour has less lateness, the new insertion is accepted. From an operational perspective, it is crucial to acknowledge that transporters have limited knowledge of their future transports, usually, they are only aware of a small number of upcoming ones. Therefore, the creation of new tours during rescheduling does not present significant challenges. This is mainly because the rescheduling process and the generation of new tours occur seamlessly in the background, ensuring a streamlined and effective workflow for the transporters. Therefore, the system can adapt to changes in real-world situations, making single modifications when needed while preserving efficient operational performance.

3.4 Overview of the Hybrid Algorithm in Practice

The hybrid algorithm proposed in this paper is illustrated in Fig. 2. The implementation of the hybrid algorithm starts with creating a list of transporters that includes their names, availability, and the last seen location of each. If a transporter has conducted any transport previously, the last location is considered as the delivery location of the last transport. Otherwise, it is assumed that the transporters begin their shift from the logistics center of the hospital.

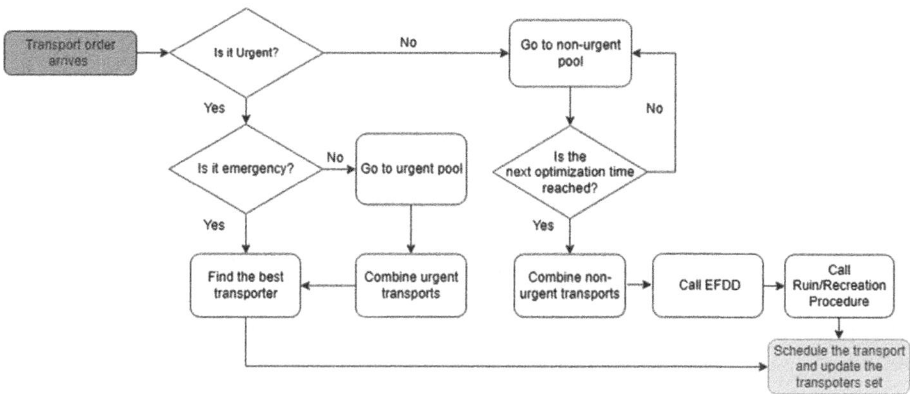

Fig. 2. Flow chart of hybrid algorithm

Upon receiving a transport order, the algorithm initially evaluates whether it corresponds to an urgent or non-urgent transport. For urgent transports, the algorithm checks again if the transport is an emergency. If it is, then the algorithm assigns the best available transporter to handle the transport with minimal delay. This is accomplished by identifying the transporter with the lowest travel time to the pick-up location of the transport. For highly urgent transports that are not emergencies, the process is the same, with the addition of a combination step (in case there is no lateness caused by the combination) before assigning the best transporter to the transport. This combination step is not usually necessary, unless there are multiple urgent transports announced at the same time. If there is only one urgent transport, then the pool contains only one at the same time as the assignment process is very fast, and the assignment will happen before the next transports are received by the algorithm.

After scheduling the transport, the table of transporters is updated to reflect their new availability and locations. If the transport request is non-urgent, the periodic policy is implemented, which includes the pre-processing step to combine transports and the two-step procedure that uses the EDDF and R&R algorithms. The transports are then assigned, and the list of transporters is updated accordingly to reflect the changes.

4 Computational Experiment

A set of computational experiments was conducted based on real-world hospital data. The hospital in question has an average of 42 transporters per working shift, with facilities located on different campuses, buildings, levels, and rooms, totaling 364 locations. The computational experiments involved simulating 6 months of logistic planning, from January 1st, 2019 to June 30th, 2019, based on actual historical data. All transport orders and schedules were stored in the hospital's logistic management systems. Transporter route schedules were assigned manually by logistic operators or automatically by a greedy algorithm. The transport orders were sorted based on their arrival time to ensure chronological processing. The list of available transporters was obtained from the historical data, and this information was used to create shifts for each transporter. Table 2 summarizes the primary features of the ILH data. The optimization period was set to 10 min. Therefore, the system waits for 10 min for re-optimization and then optimizes the non-urgent transports. We conducted the experimental results using a machine with 40 CPU cores and 187 GB of RAM. In all cases, the process of reactive assignments occurred within a matter of milliseconds, while periodic assignments, including the ruin & recreate phase, took a maximum of 1.43 s per period.

Table 2. The primary features of the historical data and their respective types

Feature Name	Feature Type	Description
Entry Time	Timestamp	The first time the transport is known in the database
TransportID	Real	The unique ID for each transport
Time Window	Time Interval	Including the earliest scheduled time for pickup and the latest scheduled time for delivery
PriorityID	Real	A number from set {1, 500, 1000, 1010, 1100, 1200}, smaller number indicates higher priority. 1 indicates emergencies, 500 indicates other urgent transports
Pickup	String	The pickup location identifier in the hospital
Delivery	String	The delivery location identifier in the hospital
Transporter	String	A transporter who has carried out the transport
Real Begin & End	Time Interval	the realised pick-up and delivery time in the database
Empty Path	Float	The time (in seconds) that the transporter was walking to reach the pickup location
TransportType	String	The type of transport, e.g. transport bed, wheelchair, etc. (16 types of transport in total)

To create shifts, the first timestamp that a transporter appeared in the data was set as the start time of the shift, and the last timestamp was set as the end time of the shift. This allowed for the assignment of transports to specific transporters based on their availability during their shifts. A loop was used to feed each transport into the hybrid algorithm, and each was assigned to the most suitable transporter. The waiting time for each transporter was considered the same as the real data to ensure accurate simulation. Once tours were scheduled, lateness and travel time were recorded.

To assess the performance of the hybrid algorithm, the results were compared to the actual historical data. The evaluation metrics consisted of the total lateness for both emergency and non-emergency services, the total transporters' travel time, the percentage of emergency transports delivered on time, and the travel time balance index ($TTBI$) among transporters. A higher $TTBI$ value indicates an uneven distribution of travel time among the transporters. The $TTBI$ is calculated using the following formula:

$$TTBI = (max\_travel\_time - min\_travel\_time)/(average\_travel\_time)$$

where max_travel_time is the total travel time taken by the transporter with the highest workload, min_travel_time is the total travel time taken by the transporter with the lowest workload, and $average\_travel\_time$ is the average travel time taken by all the transporters. A higher $TTBI$ indicates an uneven travel time distribution among the transporters.

It was observed that weekends and holidays had an average of 423 daily transports per day, whereas workdays had an average of 2070 daily transports. Therefore, two types of days were defined in hospital operations: busy and non-busy days, where non-busy days were considered those with less than 500 transports per day. Table 3 presents the average daily evaluation parameters for both busy and non-busy days, where the results of the hybrid algorithm are compared with the hospital records. Additionally, the benchmarks for each day of the week from Monday to Sunday were evaluated and presented in Tables 4, 5, 6, 7 and 8. The results indicate that the approach was effective in optimizing scheduled tours for different days and transport volumes.

5 Results and Discussion

In this section, the results of the evaluation of the hybrid algorithm for emergency and non-emergency transport operations are presented and compared to the historical data. Firstly, the lateness for emergencies was evaluated, and the average results are reported in Table 4. These results confirm that the proposed algorithm offers almost the same results as the historical data. The reactive policy followed by the hospital shows the main reason for such similarity. Therefore, the hybrid algorithm performs as well as the existing operations for emergencies in the hospital in most cases. However, in situations where the number of transports is low e.g. in non-working days and weekends (resulting in a reduced availability of transporters), some urgent transports may experience slight delays. This is primarily due to improved resource planning for non-emergency orders, where periodic assignments are incorporated for enhanced management. As a result, a few transporters may still be occupied when an emergency is announced, causing a minor delay in their availability. Nonetheless, the overall benefit lies in the considerable reduction of delays observed in non-emergency cases, justifying the tradeoff.

Furthermore, Table 5 reports the percentage of on-time delivery performance for emergencies. This result is also very similar to the historical data. Additionally, the results reported in Table 6 show that the workload balance of the proposed hybrid algorithm is very similar to the historical results. The main improvement provided by the hybrid algorithm was for non-emergency transports, as reported in Table 7. The hybrid algorithm reduces the lateness of these transports by employing a periodic policy, which allows transports to be combined and assigned to transporters more efficiently. This leads to saving time and resources, as well as more effective assignment of transporters, resulting in fewer empty tours. Moreover, the total transporters' travel time, as shown in Table 8, indicates that the hybrid algorithm performs slightly better than the historical hospital operations. The reduction of empty travel distances and the benefits of combining these transports may also contribute to the reduction of total travel time.

Table 3. The average daily evaluation parameters for days with less than and more than 500 transports during the six-month period of historic hospital operation data. The results of the hybrid algorithm are compared with the hospital records

Parameter	Transports (>500)			Transports (<500)		
	Historical Data	Hybrid Algorithm	Gap (%)	Historical Data	Hybrid Algorithm	Gap (%)
TTBI	0.25	0.21	16	0.29	0.32	−10.34
Lateness Emergencies	7.83	7.66	2.17	1.25	1.43	−14.4
On-Time Emergencies (%)	91	90	1.1	98	97	1.02
Lateness Non-Emergencies	579.87	214.67	62.97	70.04	27.55	60.66
Total Travel Time	13177	10786	18.12	2891	2002	30.75

Table 4. The average daily sum of lateness, in minutes, for emergency transports on weekdays within the experience horizon, as obtained from the results of the hybrid algorithm and hospital records

Parameter	Mon	Tue	Wed	Thu	Fri	Sat	Sun
Lateness Emergencies Historic Data	7.83	7.70	7.65	7.87	8.05	1.27	1.20
Lateness Emergencies Hybrid Algorithm	7.64	7.45	8.11	6.98	7.04	1.56	1.32

Table 5. The average on-time delivery percentages of emergency transports for weekdays within the experience horizon, comparing the results of the hybrid algorithm with hospital records.

Parameter	Mon	Tue	Wed	Thu	Fri	Sat	Sun
On-time Emergencies Historic Data (%)	91%	89%	90%	92%	96%	99%	98%
On-time Emergencies Hybrid Algorithm (%)	90%	90%	93%	92%	94%	97%	98%

Table 6. The average daily TTBI parameter for weekdays within the experience horizon for the results of the hybrid algorithm and the hospital records.

Parameter	Mon	Tue	Wed	Thu	Fri	Sat	Sun
TTBI Historic Data	0.25	0.22	0.19	0.18	0.19	0.28	0.29
TTBI Hybrid Algorithm	0.25	0.24	0.19	0.20	0.20	0.26	0.26

Table 7. The average daily sum of lateness, in minutes, for non-urgent transports on weekdays within the experience horizon, as obtained from the results of the hybrid algorithm and hospital records

Parameter	Mon	Tue	Wed	Thu	Fri	Sat	Sun
Lateness Non-Emergencies Historic Data	567.2	545.8	543.1	512.0	487.2	222.3	204.4
Lateness Non-Emergencies Hybrid Algorithm	198.4	200.2	214.8	186.3	215.4	67.9	72.6

Table 8. The average daily sum of total travel time, in minutes, on weekdays within the experience horizon, as obtained from the results of the hybrid algorithm and hospital records

Parameter	Mon	Tue	Wed	Thu	Fri	Sat	Sun
Total Travel Time Historic Data	13749	13876	10174	13543	13001	2812	2945
Total Travel Time Hybrid Algorithm	10653	10431	10111	10056	10399	1988	2061

6 Conclusion and Future Works

This paper presents a hybrid dynamic optimization approach for internal hospital logistics (IHL). This approach utilizes a two-step heuristic to assign logistic transports to transporters in a way that considers both urgency and resource conservation. The experiments show that the proposed method outperforms the baseline reactive policy used in the hospital in terms of service quality, resulting in less lateness. Additionally, the approach offers improved cost efficiency, resulting in less travel time.

While the proposed hybrid dynamic optimization approach has shown promising results in addressing the IHL problem, further research can be conducted to enhance its overall performance and impact. In particular, there are several areas where the incorporation of predictive analytics could be beneficial.

First, predictive analytics could be utilized to forecast the IHL workload based on various factors such as time of day and location within the hospital. This would allow for better scheduling decisions that take into account potential fluctuations in demand, ultimately leading to more efficient use of resources and increased service quality. Additionally, predictive analytics could be used to forecast the occurrence of urgent cases, allowing transporters to be reserved specifically for such cases, further enhancing service quality.

Second, the use of AI can further improve the proposed approach by adapting the size of periods and waiting strategies dynamically based on the workload and urgency of transports. This would enable more flexible scheduling and allow for better resource allocation to meet the demands of the hospital.

Lastly, the deployment of the proposed approach in a real-time scenario within a hospital could provide valuable insights into its performance and effectiveness. On-site evaluations that consider several other factors such as patient satisfaction, transporter workloads, and overall hospital efficiency could provide a more comprehensive assessment of the approach's impact and potential for implementation in practice.

Overall, the incorporation of predictive analytics and AI has the potential to significantly enhance this research. By utilizing these tools to forecast workload, adapt scheduling policies, and identify areas for improvement, the service quality and efficiency of IHL operations can ultimately be improved, enhancing patient care.

References

1. Bent, R., Van Hentenryck, P.: A two-stage hybrid algorithm for pickup and delivery vehicle routing problems with time windows. Comput. Oper. Res. **33**(4), 875–893 (2006). https://doi.org/10.1016/j.cor.2004.08.001
2. Bredehorn, T., Johow, L.: KI in der Krankenhaus-Transport-Disposition (2020). https://publica.fraunhofer.de/handle/publica/265840
3. Christiaens, J., Vanden Berghe, G.: Slack induction by string removals for vehicle routing problems. Transp. Sci. **54**(2), 417–433 (2020). https://doi.org/10.1287/trsc.2019.0914

4. Garside, A.K., Laili, N.R.: A cluster-first route-second heuristic approach to solve the multi-trip periodic vehicle routing problem. Jurnal Teknik Industri **20**(2), 172–181 (2019)
5. Gendreau, M., Guertin, F., Potvin, J.-Y., S'eguin, R.: Neighborhood search heuristics for a dynamic vehicle dispatching problem with pick-ups and deliveries. Transp. Res. Part C Emerg. Technol. **14**(3), 157–174 (2006). https://doi.org/10.1016/j.trc.2006.03.002
6. Karami, F., Vancroonenburg, W., Vanden Berghe, G.: Periodic vs. reactive scheduling for internal hospital logistics. Available as TR, KU Leuven (2019)
7. Karami, F., Vancroonenburg, W., Vanden Berghe, G.: A periodic optimization approach to dynamic pickup and delivery problems with time windows. J. Sched. **23**, 711–731 (2020). https://doi.org/10.1007/s10951-020-00650-x
8. Karami, F., Vancroonenburg, W., Vanden Berghe, G.: A buffering-strategy-based solution method for the dynamic pickup and delivery problem with time windows. In: The 12th International Conference on the Practice and Theory of Automated Timetabling, Vienna, Austria, 28–31 August 2018, pp. 256–272. PATAT (2018). http://patatconference.org/patat2018/files/proceedings/paper37.pdf
9. OECD. Health expenditure and financing (2020). https://stats.oecd.org/viewhtml.aspx?datasetcode=SHAlang=en#
10. Pisinger, D., Ropke, S.: A general heuristic for vehicle routing problems. Comput. Oper. Res. **34**(8), 2403–2435 (2007)
11. Poulin, E.: Benchmarking the hospital logistics process: a potential cure for the ailing health care sector. CMA Manag. **77**(1), 20–23 (2003). https://doi.org/10.1016/j.cor.2005.09.012. CMA, Canada
12. Psaraftis, H.N., Wen, M., Kontovas, C.A.: Dynamic vehicle routing problems: three decades and counting. Networks **67**(1), 3–31 (2016). https://doi.org/10.1002/net.21628
13. Rais, A., Alvelos, F., Figueiredo, J., Nobre, A.: Optimization of logistics services in hospitals. Int. Trans. Oper. Res. **25**(1), 111–132 (2018). https://doi.org/10.1111/itor.12370
14. Renaud, J., Boctor, F.F., Ouenniche, J.: A heuristic for the pickup and delivery traveling salesman problem. Comput. Oper. Res. **27**(9), 905–916 (2000). https://doi.org/10.1016/S0305-0548(99)00066-0
15. Ropke, S., Pisinger, D.: An adaptive large neighborhood search heuristic for the pickup and delivery problem with time windows. Transp. Sci. **40**(4), 455–472 (2006). https://doi.org/10.1287/trsc.1050.0135
16. Schrimpf, G., Schneider, J., Stamm-Wilbrandt, H., Dueck, G.: Record breaking optimization results using the ruin and recreate principle. J. Comput. Phys. **159**(2), 139–171 (2000). https://doi.org/10.1006/jcph.1999.6413
17. van Lon, R.R.S., Ferrante, E., Turgut, A.E., Wenseleers, T., Vanden Berghe, G., Holvoet, T.: Measures of dynamism and urgency in logistics. Eur. J. Oper. Res. **253**(3), 614–624 (2016). https://doi.org/10.1016/j.ejor.2016.03.021
18. Visa Guide. Statistics about the German health care system (2020). https://visaguide.world/international-health-insurance/germany/healthcare-statistics
19. Zhang, J., Van Woensel, T.: Dynamic vehicle routing with random requests: a literature review. Int. J. Prod. Econ. **256**, 108751 (2022). https://doi.org/10.1016/j.ijpe.2022.108751

Cybersecurity Considerations for the Design of an AI-Driven Distributed Optimization of Container Carbon Emissions Reduction for Freight Operations

Carlos Paternina-Arboleda(✉), Alexander Nestler, Nicholas Kascak, and Morteza Safaei Pour

Department of Management Information Systems, San Diego State University, San Diego, CA 92182, USA
cpaternina@sdsu.edu

Abstract. The transportation industry is a vital component of the global economy, responsible for the movement of goods between different locations. The intermodal freight transportation system involves the use of different modes of transportation, such as trucks, trains, and ships, to move freight containers. However, this system is loaded with inefficiencies due to the poor availability of real-time coordination and disruptions, causing delays, increased costs, and thus, higher carbon emissions. AI has the potential to improve the intermodal freight transportation system's efficiency by optimizing operations in real-time and self-evolving the models to make better/faster decisions. While both policymaking and business operations would benefit from using real-time optimization models, the implications and applications of these models are different in each context. In policymaking, real-time optimization models are used to improve public services, reduce overall network costs, and setting regulations for sustainable management of the network. The system can consider real-time traffic conditions, weather, and other factors to optimize the routing of the trucks, reducing transportation costs, improving delivery times, maintaining resiliency, and managing emissions. This work aims to contribute with a better understanding on how these information systems can be protected from cyberthreats, while performing the optimization of freight synchromodal transportation operations in real-time in terms of efficiency, cost-effectiveness, and carbon emissions reduction, considering the dynamic nature and heterogeneity of the intermodal freight system.

Keywords: Cybersecurity · Digital Twins · Transportation · AI-Driven Optimization · Environmental Impact

1 Introduction

If anything, the last three years have taught the maritime industry that the supply chain is vulnerable and very much dependent on global events. Ports around the world have witnessed some of the biggest cargo congestion challenges in modern history. This

© The Author(s), under exclusive license to Springer Nature Switzerland AG 2023
J. R. Daduna et al. (Eds.): ICCL 2023, LNCS 14239, pp. 56–84, 2023.
https://doi.org/10.1007/978-3-031-43612-3_4

congestion, driven by a continuous increase in the gap between consumer demand and logistics supply, exacerbated by supply-chain disruptions (among which, cybersecurity breaches are a main concern), is negatively impacting the maritime footprint, despite large investments by the industry to streamline, modernize, and reduce supply chain carbon emissions. Consumer demand for goods shipped across the world is set to be steady or increase. Major ports around the world are witnessing similar trends, leading to a rise in regional congestion and emissions at bottlenecks, whether in the port, at port gates, or in dray corridors. Saxon and Stone (2017) build on the container disruption of the shipping business and how the industry unfolds in the next 50 years. They suggest that by 2067, the annual growth of global trade of containers will range from 1.9% to 3.2% in the high case scenario. This equates to an increase from 182M TEUs (2016) to 464M TEUs and 858M TEUs by 2067 respectively for low and high. Every year, container ships plying the world's waterways spew about 1 billion metric tons of CO2 into the air (about 3% of global greenhouse gas emissions). Transportation stakeholders must continue to invest and develop groundbreaking solutions that monitor, track, and reduce cargo's carbon footprint.

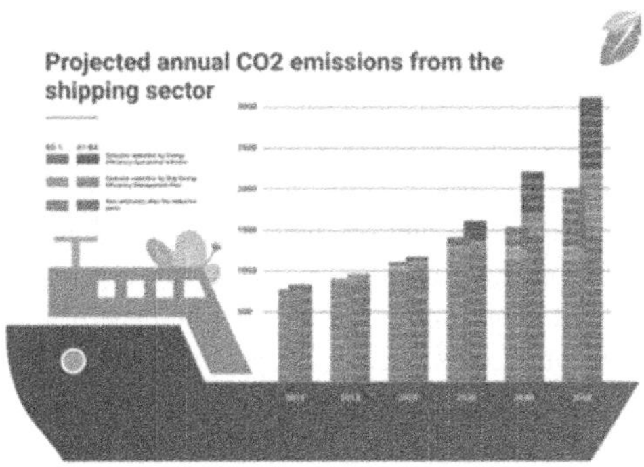

Fig. 1. Projected CO2 emissions, shipping

The increase of a global cargo movement, coupled with the added complexity of equipment and systems that are deployed to optimize the movement of goods, pose a new challenge of measuring the impact of intermodal container travel. This comes at a critical time as private sectors and government agencies are seeking reliable measurement sources to accurately assess carbon neutrality and drive decarbonization. Despite many efforts to measure carbon impact, there continue to be a lack of standardization and discrepancies among the metrics deployed to measure GHG emissions and their impact. The goal is to accurately measure GHG emissions and levelized costs of Mt-km (LCOTKM) analyzing the multi-variation by modes of energy and goods transportation and compare to projected values. Figure 1 shows a shipping emissions projection.

To control carbon emissions, we first need to accurately measure their impact. We propose a Digital-Twin enabled, AI-driven RT Distributed Optimization Platform, based upon a system level view of the intermodal network, mapping energy consumption, and calculating emissions, and offering suggestions for route and mode switching of containers, which could greatly improve those metrics. Due to the diversity and complexity of data this Platform would depend upon, success requires a massive data ingestion from hundreds of data sources while combining extensive data modeling, AI processing, and algorithms along with simulation. Investing in a high-fidelity simulation Platform such as Argonne's POLARIS simulation (Auld et al., 2016), and proven optimization meta-modeling information systems (Velasquez-Bermudez, 2020), is more beneficial and rewarding in the long run, as real-time Intermodal efficient mode switch is essential for these systems to convey good results. Jubiz-Diaz et al. (2021) modeled the Colombia Intermodal Transportation Network, and examine the relationship between infrastructure investment, freight accessibility, and GDP, with a data-driven geospatial approach, targeting investments with greatest GDP impact.

A digital twin is a virtual model designed to accurately reflect a physical object by using real-time data (IBM, n.d.). According to IBM, there are four types of digital twins depending on the level of magnification. To successfully implement a digital twin infrastructure capable of real-time coordination and reduce carbon emissions for intermodal freight transportation systems in the United States, several sources of data and information will need to be integrated to form various component twins.

An AI-driven real-time distributed optimization (RT-DO) system is deployed, considering the dynamic nature of the intermodal freight transportation system. The model uses real-time data and analytics to optimize operations, reducing costs and carbon emissions. The system considers real-time data on transportation routes, cargo volumes, and costs. The modeling methodology is based on the concepts of advanced parallel, and distributed analytics, as support to "artificial brains," the decision support systems in the era of Industry 4.0. The system is deployed at different levels. The first level presents real-time distributed optimization mathematical models for cargo routing which are used to determine the most efficient/sustainable path for traffic flow in a transportation network, considering a wide range of factors such as intermodal switching, traffic, and demand resource limitations. Intermodal switching refers to the transfer of cargo between different modes of transportation, such as from a ship to a truck or from a train to a waterway. We base our RT Optimization modeling framework in Large-Scale Optimization theories, such as Benders/Lagrangean decomposition, and a novel Event-Driven Real-Time modeling structure described in Abril et al. (2023). Paternina-Arboleda et al. (2008) show an integrated simulation-optimization framework for logistical systems.

The main contribution of the research paper entitled "Cybersecurity Considerations for the Design of a Digital Twin Enabled AI-Driven Real-Time Distributed Optimization of Container Carbon Emissions Reduction for Synchromodal Freight Operations" lies in highlighting and addressing the crucial cybersecurity considerations associated with the design and implementation of a digital twin-enabled AI-driven real-time distributed optimization system for synchromodal freight operations.

The paper identifies the specific cybersecurity challenges that need to be taken into account when designing such a system, including securing the data flow, ensuring the security of digital twin models, and safeguarding the system against cyber-attacks. It proposes practical solutions to address these challenges, such as implementing encryption mechanisms, access control policies, anomaly detection systems, and other cybersecurity measures.

From the cybersecurity perspective, Wang and Liu (2022) discusses the increasing application of cyber-physical systems (CPSs) in the rail industry and the corresponding rise in cyber threats that can cause significant failures and consequences. The authors propose a risk management methodology for addressing cyber security risks in rail CPSs, focusing on proactive identification, clear definition, and proper handling of these risks. Beaumont (2018) presents a case study of automated maritime container terminals (CTs). It has the aim of demonstrating that the risks derived from the use of technology associated with the Fourth Industrial Revolution (4IR) are both real and dangerous. In the shipping industry, the four largest shipping lines in the world have been hit by cyber-attacks since 2017 (Song, 2021). Cybersecurity is significant in maritime transportation because the costs of cyberattacks can be vast and the consequences fatal. For instance, digital navigation systems could be manipulated so that they sheer off or run aground, which would endanger the lives of the crew, people at sea and on land. The financial effects on shipowners and ship operators would also be immense (Tsvetkova et al., 2021). Woschank et al. (2020) mentions that AI may be used also in higher-level processes to detect fraud, prevent cybersecurity threats, and generally optimize higher-level processes for Smart Logistics in the future. De la Peña-Zarzuelo et al. (2020), present Internet of Things and sensing solutions, cybersecurity, horizontal and vertical system integration, cloud computing, 3D printing and additive manufacturing, big data and business analytics, augmented reality and simulation and modeling are the pillars of Industry 4.0. From all viewpoints, cybersecurity is a top concern for all AI-driven digital systems of today's logistics industry.

The paper emphasizes the critical importance of protecting the integrity, confidentiality, and availability of data in a digital twin-enabled AI-driven system. It underscores the potential risks and vulnerabilities that can arise in the transportation industry, especially when leveraging advanced technologies for real-time optimization and carbon emissions reduction. This paper is significant as it sheds light on the importance of cybersecurity in the context of digital twin-enabled AI-driven systems for synchromodal freight operations. It provides valuable insights for researchers, practitioners, and decision-makers in the transportation industry, offering a foundation for the development and implementation of secure and resilient systems that can effectively reduce carbon emissions, optimize operations, and improve sustainability.

2 Decision Support System Description

2.1 LCA and GHG Emissions

The first step is to define the system boundaries, which determine processes and activities that will be included in the analysis. The next step is to collect data on the energy source and the processes included in the system boundary. This involves data from suppliers, manufacturers, and energy producers, as well as conducting on-site measurements and calculations. Using the collected data, the GHG emissions associated with each process and activity are calculated. This involves using emissions factors or equations that estimate GHG emissions based on energy consumption, fuel use, and production processes. The GHG emissions calculated for each process and activity are then aggregated to determine the total GHG emissions associated with the low carbon energy source. This will become either an objective function or a constraint in our optimization models. We use a modified version to the framework proposed by Guo et al. (2022). In their article, the authors present a methodology for estimating carbon emissions in hinterland-based container inter-modal networks. Their study focuses on a specific intermodal network in China to show the application of the methodology which involves an estimation model that considers factors such as distance traveled, mode used, cargo type, and considers energy consumption of different modes and emissions associated. The study found that carbon emissions can be reduced by optimizing the network, including increased use of rail, reduced distance traveled, and use of clean energy sources.

The network estimation model evaluates carbon emissions in a specific period. Paternina-Arboleda et al. (2023), show an estimation of SO2 emissions derived from ships when hoteling and maneuvering, and cruising in the port, showing predictive modeling of port emissions inventories. The data relates to vessel's AIS, and Port's IoT environmental sensor network. Cammin et al. (2023) also present a similar approach to the one above mentioned (Fig. 2).

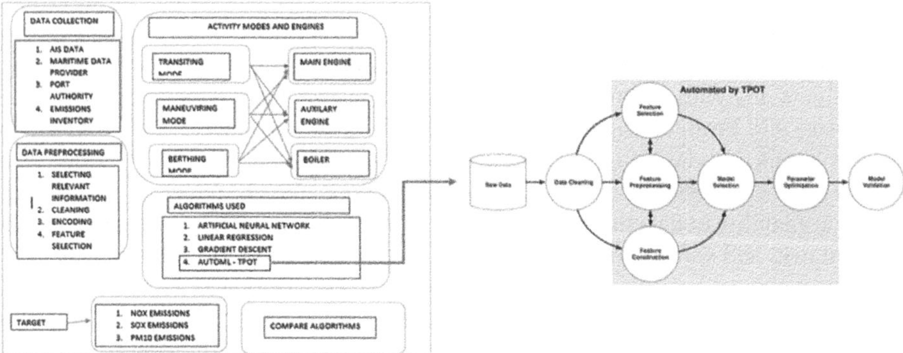

Fig. 2. Methodology for predicting Emissions Inventories (an example for Port Emissions), Paternina-Arboleda et al. (2023)

We are expanding the methodology to account for geospatial emissions for the intermodal network to be optimized based on the predicted metrics, with valuable insights to improve environmental practices and foster sustainable development.

2.2 Disruption Management

The system is designed to implement level metrics to assess the resiliency of a given "sustainable transportation network." These metrics provide a way to measure the ability of a transportation system to withstand and recover from disruptions/stresses, while still providing reliable and efficient transportation services to users.

A resilient transportation network should (a) have enough capacity to handle expected traffic volumes, while also being able to adapt to changes in demand and unexpected disruptions, (b) have high travel time reliability, to expect consistent travel times even in the face of disruptions, (c) be adaptable, to quickly adjust to changing circumstances and provide reliable and efficient services, (d) have an appropriate level of redundancy, to have multiple options for reaching their destination in the event of disruptions, and (e) be environmentally sustainable (Yang et al., 2023). The global resiliency metric of a system depends on the resiliency of each individual transportation mode within because a transportation system is made up of multiple modes, each of which has its own characteristics and vulnerabilities. The mode switching optimization models must be tightly coupled with the disruption models. Some metrics proposed for our system are:

- System capacity as a measure of the ability to handle traffic volumes during normal/peak periods, considering number/capacity of lanes, number/frequency of vehicles, availability of modes.
- Travel time reliability as a measure of the predictability of travel times of a network. This metric considers i.e., congestion, incidents, and weather conditions that can cause delays or disruptions.
- System adaptability as a measure of the ability of a transportation network to adapt to changes in demand, technology, or other factors that can impact services. This metric considers factors such as new technologies, flexibility to adjust based on demand, and respond to disruptions.
- System redundancy as a measure of availability of alternative routes or modes in the event of disruptions to the primary network. This metric considers factors such as number and location of alternative routes, availability of transit or other modes, and ability to switch between modes.
- Environmental impact as a measure of the sustainability, which takes into consideration factors such as energy consumption, emissions, and the impact on local ecosystems.

The resiliency of each transportation mode is influenced by a range of factors, including quality and age of infrastructure, availability of alternative transportation modes, the level of investment in research and development, and the degree of coordination and communication between transportation providers and policymakers (Trucco and Petrenj, 2023). Understanding resiliency of individual transportation modes is critical to developing strategies for enhancing resiliency of whole transportation systems. Our proposed solution is designed to determine the sensitivity to inputs such as routes, low carbon infrastructure rollout, GHG reductions, and other variables that can help foster resiliency in several ways. The solution can help identify vulnerabilities in the transportation system by simulating the effects of various input scenarios on system performance via a digital twin. We can simulate the impact of a disruption to a key route or a delay in the rollout of low carbon infrastructure and help identify areas where the system is most vulnerable.

We could prioritize investments in infrastructure and other resources based on the potential impact on system performance (identify most critical investments to enhance resiliency of the system and reduce vulnerability to disruptions), while testing strategies to enhance the resiliency of the system. It provides a visual representation of the system's performance under different input scenarios to help understand the potential impact of actions and decisions on the resiliency of the system to promote more effective collaboration. Intermodal logistics can be impacted by a range of disruptions (local and global). Some examples are: (a) natural disasters, (b) labor strikes, (c) disruptions in the supply chain, (d) global trade disruptions, (e) Pandemics, (f) Network Congestion, and the focus of this article, (g) **Cybersecurity threats**. Effective management of disruptions requires a comprehensive understanding of the system's vulnerabilities, as well as proactive planning and response strategies to mitigate the impact of disruptions and maintain the resiliency of the transportation system.

2.3 Full Synchromodal System Optimization

Intermodal transportation systems are an essential component of modern logistics and supply chain management. The complexity of these systems presents significant challenges in terms of optimizing routes, minimizing costs, and ensuring deliveries. Real-time (RT) optimization is a promising approach to address these challenges by leveraging advanced data analytics and optimization algorithms to make informed decisions in real-time. It allows transportation planners to respond quickly to unexpected events, such as traffic congestion or delays in shipments, and make necessary adjustments to routes and schedules to ensure efficient and timely delivery. Zhang et al. (2018), present an approach to RT optimization for transportation networks which discusses a method for optimizing the dynamic stowage of cargo at highway freight stations. They propose an algorithm that considers the cargo, the available space on the trucks, and the order in which the cargo is loaded and unloaded using a combination of dynamic programming and branch-and-bound techniques. They also use simulation to test the effectiveness of the algorithm under different scenarios.

The proposed system is designed to implement a framework for Autonomous Real-Time Distributed Optimization (ARTDO), as described in Velasquez-Bermudez et al. (2020). It enables autonomous optimization of transportation logistics in real-time, using distributed decision-making algorithms. The methodology improves transportation efficiency while minimizing the environmental impact of transportation systems in real-time. It involves: (1) Autonomous Distributed decision-making, with nodes equipped with decision-making algorithms that make autonomous decisions based on local data and feedback allowing the system to adapt to changing conditions in real-time. (2) Real-time data collection, to inform decision-making, including information on routes, schedules, capacities, and other factors that may impact transportation logistics. (3) Optimization algorithms. (4) Feedback mechanisms for nodes to provide/receive feedback and learn/improve based on their performance. To automatically run this math framework as required, we must embed all the models as a library of smart algorithms for the Optimization of the Intermodal Network, independently engaged in parallel but mathematically coordinated to achieve ARTDO across the full network. We will use the optimization platform to integrate the framework as a set of massive distributed although interconnected parallel routines. We must connect all the data models, and math models with data sources, to automatically generate (and maintain) master tables for the whole intermodal network. The system can incorporate real-time data on GHG emissions from transportation modes to identify the most efficient transportation modes and routes for minimizing GHG emissions, while meeting transportation needs, optimizing transportation modes and routes in RT, based on RT data on traffic congestion, weather conditions, and other factors. The system can be programmed to switch transportation modes/routes in response to changing conditions for GHG emissions or the economic cost of avoided carbon, while meeting efficiency needs (economic cost/freight ton-Km).

2.4 Designing the Decision Support Information System

The DSS is built in OPTEX (Velasquez-Bermudez, 2020), and it will group all math models, and predictive/prescriptive analytics for the system. The MMIS (Math Modeling information system) manages elements (objects, entities) i.e., tables, fields, indexes, sets, variables, parameters, constraints, equations, objectives, problems, models, DSS, and applications. MMIS standardizes the management of entities and relationships centered on its database algebraic language for linear/non-linear equations. These objects are critical to address large-scale problems by coordinating multi-problem models and the information flow. The output of one model is used as the input to others. Due to the complexity of the real system, the DSS consists of multiple math models integrated through the data stream, thereby generating the information required by the decision maker to address all levels (strategy/tactic/real-time). The different models share information stored on a common/coherent standardized database to allow for data integration along with the decision-making chain, so that this coordinated effort guarantees "optimization" of the entire system. The latter is practically impossible to obtain with a single model. From the platform we can generate math programs in high-level algebraic languages, like GUROBI or CPLEX. Optex (Fig. 3) is a generic meta-platform that works as interface for multiple technologies. The modular concept is fundamental to implement large-scale methodologies, based on partitioning and system decomposition.

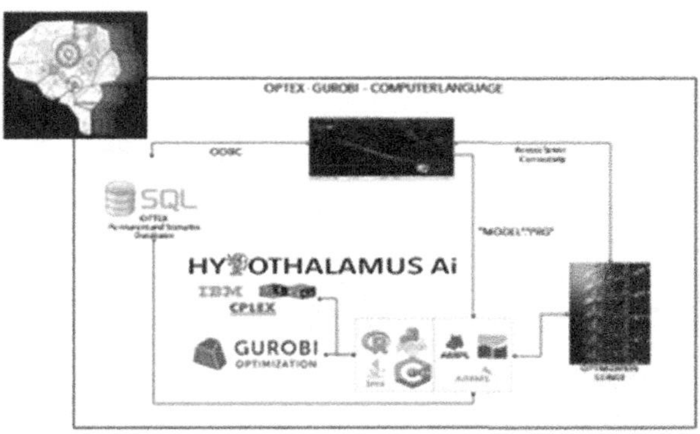

Fig. 3. The Optex meta-modeling system

The main large-scale concept in our system is Real-Time Distributed Optimization (RT-DO), where multiple agents coordinately keep the system on the optimality path (Velasquez-Bermudez et al., 2020). It follows a standard 7-step process:

- Step 1 – Algebraic Model Load: Fill the database to the MMIS and follow next steps.
- Step 2 – Model Data Load: Generated simultaneously with the loading of math models (table structures determined by the math model), by sets, parameters, variables, constraints.

- Step 3 – Generation of the visual user Interface: The system automatically generates a user interface. The shell windows are associated with main/secondary tables.
- Step 4 – Analysis and Review of the Algebraic Model Formulation: It involves coordinating two simultaneous activities: Review loaded algebraic formulation into MMIS, and results.
- Step 5 – Run the system and store the Algebraic Model results: Performed automatically.
- Step 6 – Set the Algebraic Model: Necessary changes to the MMIS and IDIS. This cyclic process ends when the implemented model produces the correct results, ready to be delivered.
- Step 7 – Data Access by the end-user: Finally, the end-user can access the model for use, based on the data stored in the IDIS and results generated by the models.

2.5 System's Artificial Intelligence

A decision support module will need to run in parallel to the AI process. As the AI optimizes, updates, or forecasts routes, the schedule will need to be updated to reflect these changes. Further, common routes and common alternate routes for each region optimized by the system or updated due to new routes (i.e., construction) need to be stored as the system generates them for efficient retrieval in the future. This will allow the system to retrieve optimal routes previously generated providing operators with options that are already optimized for CO2 emission reduction.

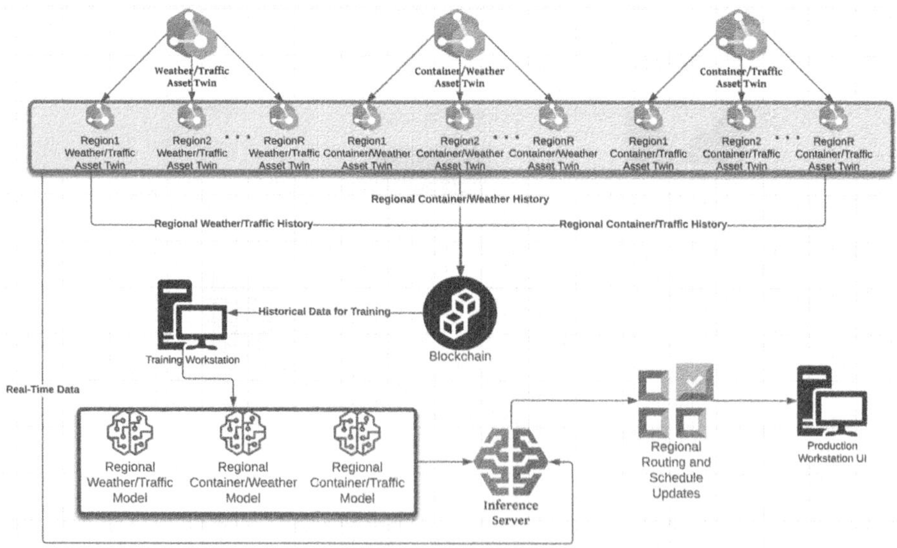

Fig. 4. High level view of the proposed AI process

The predictions from all three base models will be combined for the final regional inference of the best route the container should take based on the location, traffic conditions, and weather. The algorithms for the AI need to focus specifically on minimizing the CO_2 emissions overall based on the ton-mileage and minimizing the time-to-arrival when taking the route by avoiding any traffic. Since CO_2 emissions are based on ton-mileage, without exact emissions per hour data, the best the system can do is avoid idling in traffic to reduce those idling emissions by minimizing the time-to-arrival and ton-mileage for the route (Cammin et al., 2023; Paternina-Arboleda et al., 2023).

The AI system will continuously update this information as historical data continues to be generated and new optimized or updated routes are discovered. Figure 4 shows a high-level view of the AI Process from collecting regional historical data to generating decisions from inferences made by the system. In previous research articles, Paternina-Arboleda and Das (2001, 2005) demonstrate how artificial intelligence techniques, specifically Multi-Agent RL, can be used to address complex logistics problems. By leveraging the power of AI, logistics companies can optimize their operations, reduce costs, and improve efficiency and customer satisfaction.

3 Data Types and Structures

To successfully implement a digital twin infrastructure capable of real-time coordination and reduce carbon emissions for intermodal freight transportation systems, several sources of data and information will need to be integrated to form various component twins. There will need to be lots of data and information inputs needed to build out an AI-based model that will provide positive value to a transportation service business. The AI-based model portion of the system will be built out using the information and data inputs that are laid out below.

For this system to work and function as intended, there is a large amount of raw data that the system collects from various sources. These sources include the Global Positioning Systems (GPS), local cyber sensors at each fielded unit, historical transportation metrics, personnel information, real-time traffic, and weather data, vessel AIS data, among others. There will be more added as the project continues to grow in scope. The more data that can be cleaned, indexed, and inserted into the system, the more AI can learn and adapt to optimize the transportation routes. Dzemydienė et al. (2023) present a system architecture for monitoring and managing freight intermodal transportation using the IoT and WSNs.

Before any data or information is collected, there needs to be a shared data repository to collect the data. This data repository, also known as a data lake, will be primarily in the cloud with incremental, local hard drive backups. The repository will be internal to the company's private network and protected through various cybersecurity controls. After the shared data repository is established, data can start getting collected. The system will have a centralized data collection point at the Hub as well as local storage of data on the system data sensor. The sensor will also monitor data as it transits through the network and into the model to make sure the data is not compromised.

Historical transportation production data will be used to have a baseline of the historically best routes to take. The historical data should be gathered and broken up in a logical manner for ease of analysis. This includes recent data on the actual paths the truck, train or boat took to get from point A to point B. The inputted data can be broken up by month, year, season, quarters, and year over year changes. Different months and seasons have different weather patterns that must be kept in mind. Comparing yearly data could prove to show an abundance of statistical insights. By gathering this historical data, the AI model will have some data points and ability to make rudimentary decisions.

There is a variety of different information metrics that will assist in the training of the model. To start off, priority levels need to be set for each method of transportation, cost, schedule, weather, payload type and traffic patterns. These set priority levels will lead the model to make more accurate predictions. These priority levels will also be a large part of the COA selection list that the model outputs.

The mode of transportation and associated personnel are required to physically move the goods from point A to point B. Trucks are, and will continue to be, the primary method of travel. However, the transportation method could also be a boat or train and the associated personnel for each method. Driver information for each situation will have to be inputted into the system and protected. Driver will be used as a colloquial term in this paper to represent a truck driver, ship driver and train driver into one central category. This information varies from driver to driver and method to method. For example, a truck driver will need to have all their medical information, personal information such as social and next of kin, time on the road, consecutive days traveled, average speed, follow on trip and GPS positioning data.

The system will need to keep payload information with set priorities for different manifests. Each item or good will include the name, Radio Frequency ID (RFID), weight and priority level. Each item in the manifest will combine to bring the overall payload to a quantifiable level of priority. This will be inserted into the model for further course of action training of data.

For the data to reach the Hub and central data repository securely, a data transportation method needs to be established. The endpoint devices and users will be connected to the Hub via a private Virtual Private Network (VPN). A VPN is used to "mitigate the security risks inherent to providing remote network access by offering strong encryption to provide data security and strong authentication to limit access to applications based on defined security policies" (Loshin, 2019). Aggarwal, (2022), and Aggarwal (2023) define data encryption as a security tool that transforms plaintext data into encoded data called ciphertext that can only be read with a unique key that is given at the time of the encryption, which can be used for both in transit and at rest data. The two different types of VPN that the system can implement are TLS VPN or IPsec VPN in tunnel mode. Both modes reach the same conclusion of secure data traffic and communication through slightly different means. A TLS VPN lives in the application layer, layer 4. IPSec VPNs live in the network layer, layer 3. In other words, "The major difference between an IPsec VPN and an SSL VPN comes down to the network layers at which encryption and authentication are performed" (Loshin, 2019). Again, both VPNs provide a private, secure network for communication, data storage, data transmission and network operations. The project manager can implement whichever one his engineering team recommends.

The above criteria, data, and information can be combined for model use to output the Courses of Action (COAs). The model will use the data as inputs and produce COAs that show cost-reduction, environmental benefit, scheduling patterns, transportation method, destinations, and departure suggestions. These COAs will be the optimal transportation strategy and give management options to pursue.

3.1 Identifying and Structuring the Data

The goal of our system is to provide transportation efficiency through automation, costs-reducing methods, and increase sustainability of the transportation ecosystem. Artificial intelligence (AI) has the potential to improve the intermodal freight transportation system's efficiency by optimizing operations in real-time and self-evolving the models to make better/faster decisions. The system accomplishes this goal. For the system to give accurate predictive and reactive solutions, there needs to be data structure, software system, and hardware system requirements of the system. When implemented correctly, the system will output a corrective course of action that is an optimal solution.

Identifying and establishing a data structure is the beginnings of building out the system. The data structure needs to be set up in a way that optimizes the dashboard's utilities. The structure of the data will be in a data frame form. What this will do is allow for data to be structured cleanly and in a format that can be queried. A data frame is defined as "a data structure that organizes data into a 2-dimensional table of rows and columns, much like a spreadsheet" ("Data Frames," 2022). This allows for easy sorting and indexing of the raw data. The data structure will be set up very similarly to an excel spreadsheet with numbered rows and columns. Data frames are "one of the most common data structures used in modern data analytics because they are a flexible and intuitive way of storing and working with data" ("Data Frames," 2022). This ease of implementation and flexibility will pay dividends once queries, analysis and data start to flow through. As an AI-based model that will be learning from the data provided, the flexibility of data frames allows for results to be optimized.

The proposed decision support system follows as an extension of Port Community Systems (PCS), Freight optimization systems, and Freight brokering systems. A PCS is a platform that connects the various stakeholders in a port community, such as shipping companies, freight forwarders, port authorities, and customs officials, to facilitate communication, coordination, and collaboration. Data is a crucial component of a PCS, and various data types are involved in the system (Moros-Daza et al., 20167, 2018, 2020). Vehicle routing optimization (VRO) is the process of finding the most efficient routes for vehicles to transport goods or people. Data is a crucial component of VRO, and various data types are involved in the optimization process (De la Cruz et a., 2013, Amador et al., 2014, Palma et al., 2019). A freight brokering system is a platform that connects shippers with carriers to facilitate the movement of goods. Data is a crucial component of a freight brokering system, and various data types are involved in the system (Moros-Daza et al., 2019). Sarabia et al. (2006), present simulation-based decision support models as computer-based tools used to optimize river cargo transportation. These models simulate the river system and cargo flows to help decision-makers identify the most efficient transportation routes and schedules. Various data types are involved in SDSM for river cargo transportation. The typical data types that need to be consider in such systems follow (Table 1).

3.2 System Data Flow Model

This section focuses on the design of the data flow system that enables real-time synchromodal transportation optimization using digital twin technology and AI. The proposed system aims to provide a comprehensive view of the transportation network, including infrastructure, assets, and operations, to optimize the transportation flow and minimize carbon emissions. The system's design includes the integration of various data sources, such as real-time sensor data, historical transportation data, and external data sources, to enable the AI algorithms to make informed decisions in real-time. Figure 4 shows the context diagram for the system data flow.

The primary data input into the system at regular intervals will be the GPS technology tracking the containers. The GPS tracking will be used by the system to create the content twin of the containers as they are moved between modes of transport from starting point to destination. Supplemental information such as the current engine being used to move the container, current starting point, and destination will also need to be gathered each time the container changes mode of transport until the container reaches its destination. This information will allow the system to track CO2 emissions based on the engine being used for transport and calculate anticipated & actual CO2 emissions based on the starting point, destination, and actual miles traveled.

To create the content twins of weather and traffic conditions, real-time weather, and traffic data APIs such as Weather.gov, WeatherAPI.com and Google Traffic will be utilized to access the available data from the cloud. With this information collected, the system will be able to monitor the weather conditions and local traffic conditions where transport is taking place. Adjustments to routes will be made possible by analyzing the weather and traffic data allowing the system to make routing decisions in a timely and emission friendly manner. Figure 5 shows the context diagram of the system data flow.

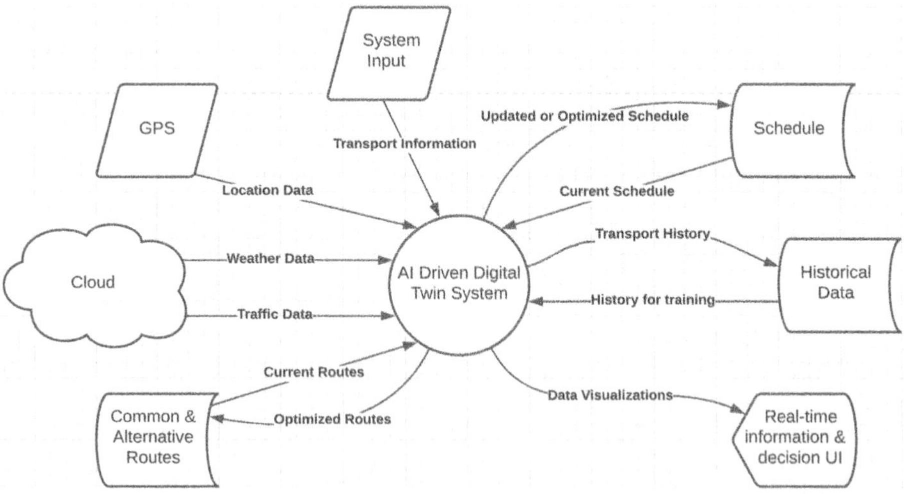

Fig. 5. Context Diagram of System Data Flow

The core component twins of the container, weather, and traffic will work together to form three distinct asset twins within the digital twin system. Container and weather component twins will form a single asset twin to study the interactions of the container routes and weather. Similarly, the container and traffic component twins will form a single asset twin to study the interactions between container routes and traffic.

Finally, the weather and traffic component twins will form a single asset twin to study the interactions between weather and traffic where intermodal transport occurs. The data collected from these three asset twins will be processed and analyzed by the system for optimization of routes, schedules, and CO2 emission reduction during intermodal container transport, forming the complete digital twin data structure (Fig. 6).

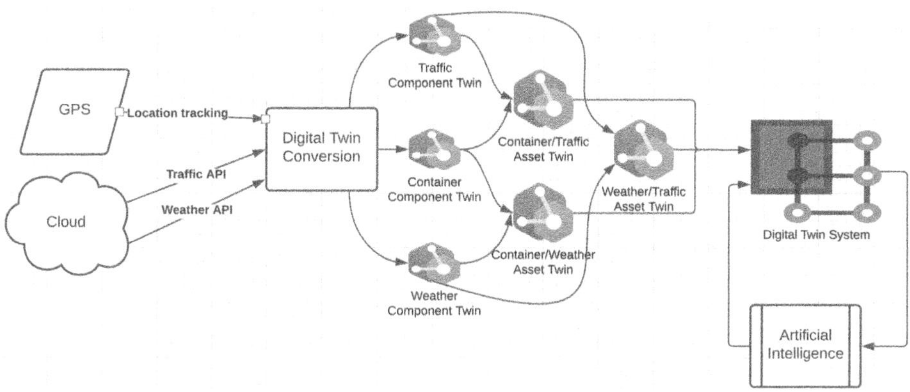

Fig. 6. High-Level Data Structure of the Digital twin system.

3.3 Dynamic Data Acquisition

Real-time data can be obtained from a variety of sources. Advanced analytics and ML algorithms can be used to process and analyze real-time data, providing insights and suggestions to stakeholders in real-time. Table 1 specifies the update frequency, latency, and spatial granularity of dynamic data. The goal is for system level optimizations to be computed within a day and dynamic adjustments in under 1 h. Real-time data can be critical for optimizing intermodal transportation networks by providing up-to-date information on infrastructure, traffic patterns, weather conditions, and other factors that can impact transportation operations. Some common types of RT data used in intermodal transportation optimization include Vessel AIS, GPS data, Rail freight traffic, road Traffic, Port traffic, Weather, Inventory and shipment data, and data from Customer Experience (CX) and Customer Relationship Management (CRM) platforms along with feedback channels (for which Natural Language Processing models are needed). All the above sources can provide RT or near-RT information. Effective use of RT data improves network optimization, leading to increased efficiency, reduced costs, and improved customer satisfaction.

Table 1. Sample Data Sources

Requirement	Historic data source	Dynamic data source: freq., latency, spatial dimension
Maritime freight traffic	Same as dynamic, 60 days active, 4+ years in cold store, Port of Los Angeles 5+ years Wharfinger, Spire	Customs and Border Protection, Manifest for the Port of Los Angeles This applies to the main ocean carriers except for COSCO, Wan Hai shipping lines
Rail freight traffic	Rail data provider such as Railinc	Rail data provider such as Railinc
Road freight traffic	5+ years in-gate/out-gate for POLA	POLA In/out-gate (Excludes Road traffic), GeoStamp
Maritime routes	Reports from ocean carriers' web	Dynamic routes accessible from carriers' websites
Rail routes	Class 1 and short lines, Wabtec	Class 1 and short lines, Wabtec
Inland Waterways routes	Inland waterways Carriers	Information on the river system, such as its topology, current, and water levels. This data is used to simulate the river system and the flow of cargo on it
Truck routes	Dray providers	Providers (area of focus). Data can be provided daily
Port traffic	2+ Y historical of Marine Exchange, Spire Global API, Live data for ALL vessels within USA EEZ	Marine Exchange, GeoStamp Vessel to Port ETA functionality. Ability to call on all historical data Spire has (back to 2011)
Security Data	Own source	Security threats, risk assessments, and incident reporting. This data is used to ensure the safety and security of the port community
Shipment Data	On demand Freight data	O/D, type of goods being transported, and desired delivery date. Used to match shippers with carriers to meet needs
Weather Data	Several sources	The latency and frequency of weather data can vary depending on the source and the type of data. Data collected from ground-based sensors may have lower latency and higher frequency than weather data collected from satellites. Similarly, certain types of weather data, such as temperature and precipitation, may be collected and updated more frequently than other types of weather data, such as cloud cover or wind speed

4 Cybersecurity Considerations

The CIA triad, which stands for Confidentiality, Integrity, and Availability, is a fundamental concept in cybersecurity that applies to various systems and technologies, including digital twins. Let's discuss the CIA triad in the context of ports, container, and shipping digital twin systems:

Confidentiality: Confidentiality in the context of digital twin systems for ports, containers, and shipping refers to protecting sensitive information from unauthorized access. It involves ensuring that only authorized individuals or entities can access and view the data related to the digital twin system. Confidentiality measures can include strong access controls, encryption of sensitive data, and secure communication channels to prevent eavesdropping or data interception. For example, in a shipping digital twin, confidential information may include cargo details, shipping schedules, or trade secrets of the involved parties. Safeguarding this information is critical to prevent unauthorized disclosure or exploitation by malicious actors.

Integrity: Integrity refers to the assurance that the data and information within the digital twin system remain accurate, unaltered, and trustworthy. It involves protecting the data from unauthorized modifications, ensuring that it reflects the true state of the physical system being represented. In the context of ports, containers, and shipping digital twins, maintaining data integrity is crucial to avoid manipulation or tampering that could result in incorrect decisions, compromised safety, or financial losses. Implementing integrity controls such as data validation, digital signatures, and audit trails can help ensure the reliability and authenticity of the digital twin's data.

Availability: Availability refers to ensuring that the digital twin system is accessible and operational whenever it is needed. It involves safeguarding the system against disruptions, outages, or denial-of-service attacks that could render it inaccessible or unusable. For ports, containers, and shipping digital twins, availability is vital for maintaining smooth operations and efficient logistics. Downtime or unavailability of the digital twin system can lead to delays, inefficiencies, and potential financial losses. Implementing robust backup and disaster recovery mechanisms, redundancy, and proactive monitoring can help ensure high availability of the digital twin system.

In brief, the CIA triad provides a comprehensive framework for addressing cybersecurity concerns in ports, container, and shipping digital twin systems. By prioritizing confidentiality, integrity, and availability, organizations can establish a strong security foundation to protect sensitive data, maintain the accuracy of information, and ensure the continuous and reliable operation of their digital twin systems.

4.1 System's Cybersecurity Factors

The proposed optimization system will have cyber-attack resiliency through addressing key security factors. These key security factors aim to address the confidentiality, integrity, and availability (CIA) cybersecurity triad. Although the following factors are not fully encompassing of all security measures, they are the foundational factors for basic cyber hygiene.

Access controls is the first step to ensure data confidentiality. Limiting access to the system data lakes in the cloud, locally on premises, or off premises is essential to denying cyber-attacks. Access controls also play the role of giving the system's end user the proper level of access needed to do their jobs. For example, a system administrator, security analyst and truck driver will all need different levels of access. The later needing access to their specific data that is relevant to their logistic routes. Along with access control, authentication measures that match users with their digital identity is critical. The foundational authentication measures include using FIDO-compliant technology, a PKI methodology, and asymmetric encryption methods. A more in-depth description on these authentication measures will be covered in the next section regarding protecting privacy of sensitive data. The system will need to establish an asset management program to track, monitor and update assets as needed to complete orders. By having a comprehensive list and inventory of assets allows the security team to manage the security requirements of each asset and their associated components. The system assets fall into four general categories that need to be managed. These categories are central hub assets, digital assets, transportation assets, and local driver assets. Each category will have their own asset inventory list with full detail of the assets themselves. Knowing what assets and data goes along with those assets is critical to being able to protect them from cyber-attacks and implement a change management program. The change management program is another key cybersecurity measure to consider when designing the system. The goal is to track and document all proposed engineering changes to individual subsystems and components. These changes will be analyzed with a wholistic view. This validates that the changes to each subsystem or component will not degrade or eliminate the functionality of the system.

Another key security factor is being able to protect the data and system in case of catastrophic loss through an attack. The cybersecurity measure of Backup and Restore (BAR) is vital to success. The copying of physical or virtual files or databases to a secondary location for preservation in case of equipment failure or catastrophe, and backups provide a way of restoring deleted files or recovering a file when it is accidentally overwritten or becomes corrupted or may support recovery from a cyber-incident. To ensure successful backup and restore functionality, a full periodic full backup of the digital twin will be required at the current baseline. A full backup is the most complete type of backup where you duplicate all the selected data of the digital twin's configuration. This includes files, folders, SaaS applications, hard drives and more; while a full backup requires minimal to restore data, it takes longer to backup compared to other types of backups and places a burden on required storage space. When you back up data, all the information on your disk is saved as a single file called an image. If your digital twin crashes or gets corrupted, you may lose some or all your data. You can use this file to restore your digital twin exactly back to how it was before data loss.

Security monitoring is an important measure to implement to mitigate potential security violations and cyber-attacks. The Security Orchestration, Automated Response (SOAR) method security alert subsystem will have to be implemented to respond to the security alerts and potential attacks. This automated response method, SOAR, builds off the previously mentioned SIEM (security information and event management) alerting structure. Although the Security Incident/Event Management Subsystem is sufficient to accomplish security monitoring, SOAR takes things one step further by automating an actual response to help mitigate the risk as quickly as possible. Although SOAR is a more recent method to accomplishing security alert system along with the follow-on response playbooks. This is a cost-saving and efficiency optimization measure. Security alerts responses will largely be automated except for egregious violations.

SOAR improves the security operations when the subsystem is allowed to "automate investigation path workflows can significantly cut down on the amount of time required to handle alerts. They also provide lessons about the security admin skill set required to complete an investigation path" (Froehlich, 2023). This analysis by former Cisco Enterprise-level IT security professional, Andrew, points out two key factors of SOAR that provide an added security layer of responses to security alerts.

To effectively protect an AI-driven real-time optimization information system for synchromodal freight operations, it is essential to utilize industry-standard cybersecurity frameworks and guidelines such as the Security Technical Implementation Guideline (STIG), ISO 27002, and NIST standards.

As with the Security Technical Implementation Guideline (STIG), these guidelines are specifically designed for the technology stack and components used in the AI-driven system. Regularly update and patch software and hardware components as per STIG guidelines to address vulnerabilities and protect against emerging threats. Conduct periodic STIG compliance assessments and audits to ensure ongoing adherence to the guidelines.

ISO 27002 could also be adopted as a comprehensive framework for establishing and maintaining an information security management system (ISMS). The IT managers could conduct a risk assessment to identify potential security risks and vulnerabilities in the AI-driven system. Develop and implement security policies, procedures, and controls based on ISO 27002 to mitigate identified risks. Regularly monitor, review, and update the security controls to align with evolving threats and organizational requirements. Ensure compliance with ISO 27002 through internal audits and periodic assessments.

Last, follow the NIST Cybersecurity Framework, which provides a flexible and customizable approach to managing and improving cybersecurity. Identify and categorize the AI-driven system's assets, assess risks, and develop risk mitigation strategies following NIST guidelines. Implement appropriate security controls, such as access controls, encryption, intrusion detection systems, and incident response plans, as recommended by NIST. Continuously monitor, detect, respond to, and recover from security incidents by aligning with NIST's incident response and recovery best practices.

By leveraging the Security Technical Implementation Guideline (STIG), ISO 27002, and NIST standards, organizations can establish a robust security posture for their AI-driven real-time optimization information systems in synchromodal freight operations. These frameworks provide comprehensive guidance and best practices to mitigate risks, protect sensitive data, and ensure the system's resilience against cyber threats.

4.2 System's Cybersecurity Risks

A digital twin-enabled, AI-driven optimization system for intermodal freight operations is a semi-autonomous system that leverages digital twins and Artificial Intelligence (AI) to optimize logistical operations. This is accomplished by collecting raw data from active operations, analyzing real-time goods movement data, and generating insights on how to improve the system.

The first cybersecurity risk that arises is faulty code that is at fault due to malicious actors. A large part of cybersecurity checks and evaluations has historically been solely at the end of the development process. This is dangerous for a variety of reasons and allows these malicious actors to start their cyber-attack early in the process and hide a trojan-type virus into the system's code. To field a testable digital twin that mimics systems in production, the code cannot have this potential vulnerability.

The first code type that logically should be secured is the source code. The source code that is used as a baseline configuration for all development could potentially be compromised and go undetected until deployment. This type of source code data poisoning and embedded viruses can hide if the malicious actor enters them smartly in the beginning of the development process. These data vulnerabilities can be part of the implementation process and deployed to production units without the developer's knowledge. Drivers and cyber operations dashboards would not be able to track security alerts and be utilized as they were intended. To mitigate this risk, a best practice known as "Shift-Left" can be implemented into the systems' security posture.

The Development, Security, Operations (DevSecOps) process incorporates security into the early stages of the software development life cycle. According to IBM, DevSecOps "integrates application and infrastructure security seamlessly into Agile and DevOps processes and tools. It addresses security issues as they emerge when they are easier, faster, and less expensive to fix. Additionally, DevSecOps makes application and infrastructure security a shared responsibility of development, security, and IT operations teams, rather than the sole responsibility of a security silo" ("DevSecOps," 2023). DevSecOps gives developers access to security tools throughout the process so that there are no integration problems at the end. The security vulnerabilities and flaws would be shifted left and found sooner rather than later.

"Shift left", promotes the integration of security measures into the early stages of the DevOps process ("DevSecOps", 2023). By moving security from the right (end) to the left (beginning) of the development cycle, software engineers are encouraged to prioritize security from the very beginning of the project. In a DevSecOps environment, cybersecurity architecture and development engineering is incorporated as part of the development team to guarantee that every phase has security measures. Furthermore, the configuration items in the stack are securely patched, configured, and documented. This will benefit change management and version control measures. By adopting a shift left approach, DevSecOps teams can detect security risks and vulnerabilities early and take immediate action to address them. This ensures that not only is the product being built efficiently, but that security is also being implemented simultaneously.

The next cybersecurity risk that will be relevant to the system is the risk of lateral movement, network device compromises and privilege escalation after bypassing the initial access controls and authentication stages. This risk is because of the increased attack surface of traditional cybersecurity measures that focus on this initial access barrier (North/South traffic) and allow freedom to move around within the network (East/West traffic). To mitigate this risk, using zero trust cybersecurity practices would be a sufficient mitigation path. Zero Trust Architecture (ZTA) takes an orthogonal view of cybersecurity by accounting for internal movement and east/west traffic within a network. This lets ZTA be viewed as "data-centered" rather than "user-centered". ZTA secures the data that flows all through the network while traditional measures attempted to secure the users in entering the network. The United States Government Accountability Office (GAO), states "Zero trust architecture (ZTA) is a cybersecurity approach that authenticates and authorizes every interaction between a network and a user or device" (Zero Trust Architecture, 2022). In a normal cybersecurity paradigm, a network user is allowed to roam freely east and west through the network once access is granted. An attack surface is much smaller using a zero-trust mindset because there are consistent authorization measures that are implemented into the system design. This will be implemented as Policy-as-Code and will be automated through firewall parameters, router rules and ACLs. ZTA will be very important for the system because of the data structure and hybrid-cloud environment. The GAO describes the importance of ZTA with some background. "Given the increasingly complex nature of IT networks, including cloud and hybrid environments, ZTA's goals are to reduce opportunities for attackers by restricting access and to detect attacks by monitoring user behavior and other network activity" (Zero Trust Architecture, 2022). Given the hybrid data storage and data movement paths through secure VPNS, this major reduction of attack surface will directly lower system's security risk.

The last major cybersecurity risks the system will be faced with is being in the dark about security threats and attacks. The system will need the ability to receive notifications of cyber security attacks. Whenever there is data out there that can be compromised, the system vulnerabilities will be attacked by cyber criminals. The criminals hope to gain some sort of gain. Whether that gain be a financial, competitive advantage, competitor insights or some sort of notoriety. When these cyber-attacks occur, the system will have a prompt, security alert and security management subsystem to alert security analysts of the breach. As mentioned, the Security Incident/Event Management (SIEM) subsystem is sufficient to mitigate this cybersecurity risk and accomplish security monitoring. This subsystem will be expanded on in the next section to automate the responses. However, to automate a response to a security breach, a type of SIEM subsystem is the foundation for mitigating security alerts that will arise. The SIEM tools are "a way to centrally collect pertinent log and event data from various security, network, server, application, and database sources. SIEMs then detect and alert on security events" (Froehlich, 2023). This allows security analysts to review the log data, identify the threat, isolate, and mitigate as appropriate. As mentioned, this will be automated by another subsystem in later phases. Another benefit of the SIEM subsystem is that "Aggregated data is analyzed by the SIEM in real time to spot potential security issues. Because multiple data sources are analyzed, the SIEM identifies threats by correlating information from more than one source" (Froehlich, 2023). The system will leverage this feature to collect and store data at each local host and aggregated host data at the hub. Additionally, "The SIEM then intelligently ranks the events in order of criticality" (Froehlich, 2023). The SIEM AI feature that stacks and ranks the security alerts will be very beneficial to cost savings and efficiency. Buckbee (2022) states some of the top SIEM tools used including Splunk, IBM QRadar, and Logrhythm.

Table 2 shows a summary of the cybersecurity considerations and the measures to counteract.

Table 2. Cybersecurity threats and measures for system design

Cybersecurity threat	Measures suggested for system design
Malware and Ransomware Attacks	Implement Strong Endpoint Protection, Patch and Update Software, Conduct Employee Awareness Training, Enable Email Filtering and Spam Detection, Implement Network Segmentation, Regularly Backup and Encrypt Data, Enforce Strong Password Policies, Maintain Incident Response and Recovery Plans, Monitor Network Traffic and Behavior, Regularly Test and Update Security Measures
Phishing and Social Engineering	Employee Education and Awareness, Implement Email Filtering and Spam Detection, Multi-Factor Authentication (MFA), Encourage Reporting of Suspicious Activities, Strong Password Policies, Incident Response and Mock Exercises, Implement Web Filtering
Insider Threats	User Access Control, User Behavior Monitoring, Employee Awareness and Training, Confidentiality Agreements and Policies, Regular Security Awareness Programs, Segregation of Duties, Employee Offboarding Processes, Cultivate a Positive Work Environment
Distributed Denial of Service (DDoS) Attacks	Network Monitoring and Traffic Analysis, DDoS Mitigation Services, ensure a Scalable Network Infrastructure, Traffic Filtering and Rate Limiting, Content Delivery Network (CDN) Services, Deploy Intrusion Detection and Prevention Systems (IDPS), Incident Response Planning, Deploy Redundancy and Failover Systems, Traffic Scrubbing and Blackholing, Regular Testing and Preparedness
Data Breaches and Unauthorized Access	Data Encryption, Access Controls and Authentication, Secure Network Infrastructure, Vulnerability Assessments and Penetration Testing, Employee Education and Awareness, Data Backup and Disaster Recovery (Business Continuity), Intrusion Detection and Monitoring, Incident Response Planning, Data Privacy and Compliance, Regular Security Audits and Compliance Assessments
Supply Chain Attacks	Vendor Risk Management, Secure Development Lifecycle, Continuous Monitoring, Multi-Factor Authentication (MFA), Secure Software and Firmware Updates, Secure Configuration Management, Incident Response and Recovery Planning, Threat Intelligence Sharing, Employee Awareness and Training, Supply Chain Resilience, Use secure protocols, such as HTTPS or SFTP, for transmitting origin/destination data over networks, Minimize the collection, storage, and retention of origin/destination data to reduce the potential impact of a data breach, Third-Party Risk Management
IoT and Operational Technology (OT) Vulnerabilities	Implement strong security controls for IoT and OT devices, Network Segmentation, Access Control and Privileged Access Management, Regular Patching and Updates, Secure Configuration Management, Network Monitoring and Intrusion Detection, Security Testing and Penetration Testing, Vendor Management and Supply Chain Security, Employee Training and Awareness, Incident Response and Business Continuity Planning

4.3 Preserving Security and Privacy of Sensitive Data

There is a large need for the system to have overarching security protections on sensitive data to protect customer, supplier, and employee information. Data Privacy rulesets are baked into the source code that the system uses. Both data at rest and data in transit should have cybersecurity measures built into the system design.

The primary method to store and secure the data will be in a cloud instance. This allows the cloud storage infrastructure to be managed at the Hub and treats the production units as Thin Clients. Thin clients are defined as "a virtual desktop computing model that runs on the resources stored on a central server instead of a computer's resources" (Gillis, 2021). Both cloud and hard drive based local backup methods have advantages and disadvantages. To take advantage of both and fully address any possible data loss, a hybrid backup strategy is recommended, where backups are created locally and in the cloud. The 3-2-1 backup rule industry standard describes that the data is kept in three places, across two media, with one backup stored offsite, such as in the cloud.

Local hard drive data storage will be utilized on an incremental, scheduled basis. This local, hard drive backup refers to the process of backing up the system, applications, and data to a device located internally or as a connected component, such as tape, disk, hard disk, flash drive, CD, external hard drive, or other media. This type of backup will be located and kept solely by data custodians located on site at the Hub. Due to the growing storage capacity restraints for the massive amounts of data that gets produced, this will not be a full data storage strategy. However, a very important data storage strategy if the cloud was ever compromised.

On-Prem means the data is stored on the Hub's premises but in a cloud storage location. Cloud based data storage on-premises backup refers to the process of backing up the system, applications, and data to a public or private cloud that is located on the Hub premises. The cloud will be configured as a secure database that collects the data and stores it into the centralized servers. These servers are located on site at the Hub. Off-premises backup refers to the process of backing up the system, applications, and data to a public or private cloud that is located off the premises. (i.e., on a production unit). This will be the primary method of collecting and storing data for the different transportation methods and personnel involved. Off Prem is when the data is not part of the centralized cloud storage infrastructure. Rather, a means to store local data of driver information and movement in a separate, secure cloud storage that acts as a thin client. Thin clients are very useful because it reduces the cyber-attack surface and protects the data that is generated by each unit. However, there is a drawback. This drawback being "Normally thin clients take the form of low-cost computing devices that heavily rely on a server for computation" (Gillis, 2021). This puts the computational power back onto the server side located at the Hub instead of the clients themselves on the truck, train, or boat.

Protecting data at rest within the Hub database and storage locations can be accomplished by enforcing three key security procedures of database encryption, access and authentication ("Protecting data at rest," 2023). Enforcing access controls and proper authentication using MFA points protects the core cybersecurity triad. Confidentiality, data integrity and availability are protected because there is no unauthorized access to the data being stored. All data that is meant to be seen by authorized personnel is available.

If there is unauthorized access, the database encryption is the fallback security measure that ensures the sensitive data is protected. The method to protect sensitive data in transit is to set up an enterprise level Virtual Private Network (VPN) and direct, secure connection between the Hub and fielded units. This method of protecting sensitive data in transit allows the system to mitigate security risks inherent to providing remote network access by offering strong encryption to provide data security and strong authentication, to limit access to applications based on security policies (Loshin, 2019).

Having the ability to hide the identity of information is another way to protect private data, as it would make it difficult to pinpoint whose data it is. QueryPie (2022) goes into detail about the difference between anonymization and pseudonymization, but how both can be beneficial to protecting personal data. Anonymization is the process of eliminating all identifiers from the data, whereas pseudonymization uses a pseudonym identifier takes place of the actual identifier of the data.

Cybersecurity and data privacy are prioritized steps to ensuring safe use of the proposed optimization system. To reach the appropriate level of security and privacy for the system, there are several legal and regulatory issues that must be addressed. Intellectual Property (IP) rights are one of the leading legal obstacles that must be considered when using AI-driven models and algorithms. Medeiros and Sanft (2018) state that IP is associated with inventions, brands, new technologies, source code, and artistic work that have patents, trademarks, and copyright ownership.

5 Key Challenges in Integrating Cybersecurity and Data Privacy Considerations into the Proposed Optimization System

There are many cybersecurity and data privacy concerns that will need to be addressed before design and implementation occurs. This section will address and dive into three key challenges that the system will face integrating cybersecurity and data privacy. After the key challenge is identified and defined, the follow-on framework to address the privacy concern will be laid out.

Key challenge 1 (KC1) touches on both cybersecurity and data privacy considerations of the system through policy implementation. This key challenge is a cybersecurity policy implementation measure while also striving to protect data privacy. The second key challenge, KC2, will be to keep the system up to date with security and vulnerability guidance on the system components and subsystems. This mainly addresses the cybersecurity consideration portion. The third key challenge, KC3, is a pure data privacy consideration that involves securing personal data. The framework for this key challenge builds off the FIDO-based security technology that includes a public key infrastructure (PKI) and asymmetric encryption.

The first key challenge that the system will be faced with is policy implementation and policy enforcement. Cybersecurity policies implementation and enforcement is important because these policies "defines which conditions must be met in order for a code to pass a security control and be deployed" (Carroll, 2023). The system will be leveraging the DevSecOps process with built in policy implementation that act as guardrails. If these policies are violated, the code is considered to be not secure and should be flagged as a security alert. To address this policy implementation challenge,

Policy-as-Code (PaC) will be embedded to automate the process. Policy-as-Code (PaC) is defined as "an approach to policy management in which policies are defined, updated, shared, and enforced using code. By leveraging code-based automation instead of relying on manual processes to manage policies, policy-as-code allows teams to move more quickly and reduce the potential for mistakes due to human error" (Carroll, 2023). PaC allows policy enforcement and implementation to be automated, cheaper to audit, and allows for more efficiencies throughout the system. Implementing the PaC framework to put up guardrails during initial design and fielding puts security in a better posture as well. PaC is set up to be a collaboration tool as well. The system can use "a policy-as-code approach to domains like security makes it possible to define and manage policies in ways that different types of stakeholders – such as developers and security engineers – can understand" (Carroll, 2023). This improves the developer and manager collaboration and project communication. Regardless of technical skill or policy expertise, the PaC explicitly outlines the policies and sets up enforcement guidelines at the same time.

The next key challenge to cybersecurity and data privacy is to address security technical implantation guidance (STIGs) updates and procedures. STIGs are used "for verifying that the product has been configured properly, and/or for identifying unauthorized configuration changes to the product" (Quinn et al., 2018). Historically, this was very much a manual process of reviewing the STIGs and finding out how they differ than what is currently fielded. STIGS can be automatically delta checked and implemented through an automated checklist program. The checklist will be designed like how the U.S. government uses the National Checklist Program (NCP). The NCP is "the U.S. government repository of publicly available security checklists (or benchmarks)" (National Checklist Program, 2023). These components and subsystems that will need constant security implementation include operating systems, AI-model, the SIEM subsystem, database, and cloud services (i.e., AWS), firewalls, routers, switches, network logging subsystem, vulnerability subsystem, audit collection subsystem and the virtual hosting environment. The NCP is beneficial because "Applying checklists to operating systems and applications can reduce the number of vulnerabilities that attackers can attempt to exploit and lessen the impact of successful attack" (Quinn et al., 2018). Essentially, the checklist is a proactive security process that shores up the system for known vulnerabilities. The NCP is a checklist "that provides detailed low-level guidance on setting the security configuration of operating systems and applications" (Quinn et al. 2018). NIST identifies the main security benefit of using the NCP is to "minimize the attack surface, reduce vulnerabilities, lessen the impact of successful attacks, and identify changes that might otherwise go undetected" (Quinn et al., 2018). Lower impact, reduced vulnerabilities and less attack surface leads to lower project cost, heightened security posture and faster project implementation.

The last key challenge that will be addressed that poses a risk to the system operations is data privacy and governance of a data privacy program. The governance portion really looks at the business operations and aligns the data privacy measures accordingly. Using the appropriate level of data privacy measures and establishing a framework for the system is how this key challenge can be addressed.

6 Managerial Insights

This article highlights the critical managerial insights for designing an AI-driven distributed optimization system with a strong focus on cybersecurity considerations. By adopting a cybersecurity-first approach, investing in robust cybersecurity measures, fostering awareness, collaborating with industry partners, conducting regular risk assessments, and planning for incident response and recovery, managers can enhance the security and resilience of the system, protecting valuable data and ensuring the successful implementation of container carbon emissions reduction in freight operations.

It highlights the importance of adopting a cybersecurity-first approach when designing an AI-driven distributed optimization system for container carbon emissions reduction in freight operations. Managers should prioritize cybersecurity considerations right from the system's design phase to mitigate potential risks and safeguard sensitive data.

It highlights the importance of investing in robust cybersecurity measures. Given the increasing connectivity and interdependence of systems in the freight industry, it is imperative to invest in robust cybersecurity measures. Managers should allocate resources for implementing encryption mechanisms, access controls, anomaly detection systems, and other cybersecurity solutions to protect the system against cyber-attacks and unauthorized access.

The article also highlights the importance of fostering a culture of cybersecurity awareness. It is essential to conduct regular risk assessments and audits to identify vulnerabilities, evaluate the effectiveness of implemented cybersecurity measures, and ensure compliance with relevant industry standards and guidelines. Managers should allocate resources for periodic assessments, penetration testing, and audits to detect and address any weaknesses or gaps in the system's security.

Last, the article shows the importance of planning for incident response and recovery. Despite preventive measures, it is important to have a well-defined incident response plan in place. Managers should establish protocols for detecting, responding to, and recovering from cybersecurity incidents. This includes defining roles and responsibilities, establishing communication channels, and regularly testing incident response plans through tabletop exercises and simulations.

7 Conclusions

The design of a digital twin-enabled AI-driven real-time distributed optimization system for synchromodal freight operations has the potential to significantly reduce carbon emissions and increase efficiency in the transportation industry. However, with the use of advanced technologies also comes the potential for cybersecurity risks.

This article highlights the key cybersecurity considerations that need to be addressed in the design of such a system. These include securing the data flow, ensuring the security of the digital twin models, preserving the privacy for all stakeholders, and protecting the system against cyber-attacks. The proposed solutions to these challenges include the use of encryption, access control, and anomaly detection systems, and mitigation strategies when an attack happens, among others.

The success of the proposed system depends on the implementation of these cybersecurity measures. The transportation industry must prioritize cybersecurity to ensure the safety and integrity of the transportation network and its stakeholders. By adopting a cybersecurity-first approach, the users of this system can mitigate risks and ensure that the benefits of the system are fully realized.

Future research should focus on further refining the proposed cybersecurity solutions and addressing new cybersecurity challenges that may arise as the system is deployed. One area that requires attention is the potential impact of emerging technologies, such as quantum computing, on the security of the system. Quantum computing has the potential to break the encryption algorithms currently used to secure data, and thus, there is a need to explore new encryption methods that are resistant to quantum attacks.

Another area of interest is the development of improved, more automated machine learning algorithms that can detect and prevent cyber-attacks in real-time. Traditional cybersecurity measures, such as firewalls and intrusion detection systems, may not be sufficient in detecting sophisticated cyber-attacks that can exploit system vulnerabilities. Machine learning algorithms can learn from past cyber-attacks and detect new and unknown cyber-attacks, leading to better and more effective cybersecurity measures.

Furthermore, future research should also explore the potential of blockchain technology in securing the system. Blockchain technology provides a decentralized and tamper-proof data storage and transaction control mechanism that can enhance data security and integrity, making it a promising technology for securing digital twin-enabled AI-driven real-time distributed optimization systems.

Overall, this paper describes certain topics as to how a cybersecurity-aware design approach can enable the successful implementation of a digital twin-enabled AI-driven real-time distributed optimization system for synchromodal freight operations, leading to significant benefits for the transportation industry and the environment.

References

Cost of a Data Breach Report 2022. IBM (2022). https://www.ibm.com/reports/data-breach?utm_medium=OSocial&utm_source=Blog&utm_content=SSSWW&utm_id=Security-Intelligence-Blog-Banners%20&_ga=2.169531361.1119445732.1681783239-1093745095.1681783239. Accessed 14 Apr 2023

What is DevSecOps? IBM (2023). https://www.ibm.com/topics/devsecops#Benefits%20of%20DevSecOps. Accessed 17 Apr 2023

Zero Trust Architecture. GAO (2022). https://www.gao.gov/products/gao-23-106065. Accessed 15 Apr 2023

Protecting data at rest. AWS Inc. (2023). https://docs.aws.amazon.com/wellarchitected/latest/security-pillar/protecting-data-at-rest.html. Accessed 17 Apr 2023

US Department of Commerce, National Oceanic and Atmospheric Administration: API web service (2023). https://www.weather.gov/documentation/services-web-api. Accessed 10 Apr 2023

NIST. Post-quantum cryptography: CSRC (2017). https://csrc.nist.gov/projects/post-quantum-cryptography. Accessed 18 Apr 2023

NIST. Round 3 submissions - post-quantum cryptography: Computer Security Resource Center (CSRC) (2023). https://csrc.nist.gov/Projects/post-quantum-cryptography/post-quantum-cryptography-standardization/round-3-submissions. Accessed 17 Apr 2023

NVIDIA. NVIDIA H100 Tensor Core GPU Datasheet. NVIDIA (2022). https://resources.nvidia.com/en-us-tensor-core/nvidia-tensor-core-gpu-datasheet. Accessed 13 Apr 2023

NVIDIA. Triton Inference Server. NVIDIA Developer (2023). https://developer.nvidia.com/nvidia-triton-inference-server#ecosystem. Accessed 14 Apr 2023

NVIDIA. Nvidia TENSORRT. NVIDIA Developer (2023). https://developer.nvidia.com/tensorrt. Accessed 14 Apr 2023

JSON and XML weather API and Geolocation Developer API. Free Weather API - WeatherAPI.com (n.d.). https://www.weatherapi.com/. Accessed 10 Apr 2023

Abril, D., Velasquez-Bermudez, J., Paternina-Arboleda, C.D., Cantillo, V.: Integrated tactical-operational event-driven real-time optimization framework for smart ports operations planning. Marit. Econ. Logist. (2023, Submitted)

Aggarwal, B.K., Gupta, A., Goyal, D., Gupta, P., Bansal, B., Barak, D.D.: A review on investigating the role of block-chain in cyber security. Mater. Today Proc. **56**(Part 6), 3312–3316 (2022). ISSN: 2214-7853. https://doi.org/10.1016/j.matpr.2021.10.124

Aggarwal, A., Dhurkari, R.K.: Association between stress and information security policy non-compliance behavior: a meta-analysis. Comput. Secur. **124**, 102991 (2023). ISSN: 0167-4048. https://doi.org/10.1016/j.cose.2022.102991

Amador-Fontalvo, J.A., Paternina-Arboleda, C.D., Montoya-Torres, J.R.: Solving the heterogeneous vehicle routing problem with time windows and multiple products via a bacterial meta-heuristic. Int. J. Adv. Oper. Manag. **6**(1), 81–100 (2014)

Auld, J., Hope, M., Ley, H., Sokolov, V., Xu, B., Zhang, K.: POLARIS: agent-based modeling framework development and implementation for integrated travel demand and network and operations simulations. Transp. Res. Part C Emerg. Technol. **64**, 101–116 (2016)

Beaumont, P.: Cybersecurity risks and automated maritime container terminals in the age of 4IR. In: Information and Cybersecurity in the Fourth Industrial Revolution. IGI Global (2018). https://doi.org/10.4018/978-1-5225-4763-1.ch017

Cammin, P., Yu, J., Voß, S.: Tiered prediction models for port vessel emissions inventories. Flex Serv. Manuf. J. **35**, 142–169 (2023). https://doi.org/10.1007/s10696-022-09468-5

Cobb, M.: What is the RSA algorithm? Definition from search security. Security (2021). https://www.techtarget.com/searchsecurity/definition/RSA. Accessed 17 Apr 2023

De la Cruz, J.J., Paternina-Arboleda, C.D., Cantillo, V., Montoya-Torres, J.R.: A two-pheromone trail ant colony system—tabu search approach for the heterogeneous vehicle routing problem with time windows and multiple products. J. Heuristics **19**, 233–252 (2013). https://doi.org/10.1007/s10732-011-9184-0

De la Peña-Zarzuelo, I., Soeane, M.J.F., Bermúdez, B.L.: Industry 4.0 in the port and maritime industry: a literature review. J. Ind. Inf. Integr. **20**, 100173 (2020). ISSN: 2452-414X. https://doi.org/10.1016/j.jii.2020.100173

Dzemydienė, D., Burinskienė, A., Čižiūnienė, K., Miliauskas, A.: Development of E-service provision system architecture based on IoT and WSNs for monitoring and management of freight intermodal transportation. Sensors **23**(5), 2831 (2023). https://doi.org/10.3390/s23052831

Froehlich, A.: SOAR vs. SIEM: What's the difference? Tech Target (2023). https://www.techtarget.com/searchsecurity/answer/SOAR-vs-SIEM-Whats-the-difference. Accessed 15 Apr 2023

Gillis, A.: Thin client (lean client). Tech Target (2021). https://www.techtarget.com/searchnetworking/definition/thin-client. Accessed 16 Apr 2023

Guo, X., He, J., Lan, M., Yu, H., Yan, W.: Modeling carbon emission estimation for hinterland-based container intermodal network. J. Clean. Prod. **378**, 134593 (2022). ISSN: 0959-6526. https://doi.org/10.1016/j.jclepro.2022.134593

Jubiz-Diaz, M.A., Saltarin-Molino, M.A., Arellana, J., Paternina-Arboleda, C.D., Yie-Pinedo, R.: Effect of infrastructure investment and freight accessibility on gross domestic product: a data-driven geographical approach. J. Adv. Transp. **2021** (2021). Article ID: 5530114. https://doi.org/10.1155/2021/5530114

Lipner, S.B., et al.: Security kernels. In: Proceedings of the May 6–10, 1974, National Computer Conference and Exposition on - AFIPS 1974, vol. 43, pp. 977–978 (1974). https://doi.org/10.1145/1500175.1500361

Loshin, P.: IPsec vs. SSL VPN: comparing speed, security risks and technology. Tech Target (2019). https://www.techtarget.com/searchsecurity/tip/IPSec-VPN-vs-SSL-VPN-Comparing-respective-VPN-security-risks

Moros-Daza, A., Solano, N.C., Amaya, R., Paternina, C.: A multivariate analysis for the creation of Port Community System approaches. Transp. Res. Procedia **30**, 127–136 (2018). ISSN: 2352-1465. https://doi.org/10.1016/j.trpro.2018.09.015

Moros-Daza, A., Hoz, D.-D., Jaller-Martelo, M., Paternina-Arboleda, C.D.: Using advanced information systems to improve freight efficiency: results from a pilot program in Colombia. In: Paternina-Arboleda, C., Voß, S. (eds.) ICCL 2019. LNCS, vol. 11756, pp. 22–38. Springer, Cham (2019). https://doi.org/10.1007/978-3-030-31140-7_2

Moros-Daza, A., Amaya-Mier, R., Paternina-Arboleda, C.: Port Community Systems: a structured literature review. Transp. Res. Part A Policy Pract. **133**, 27–46 (2020). ISSN: 0965-8564. https://doi.org/10.1016/j.tra.2019.12.021

Möller, M., Vuik, C.: On the impact of quantum computing technology on future developments in high-performance scientific computing. Ethics Inf. Technol. **19**(4), 253–269 (2017). https://doi.org/10.1007/s10676-017-9438-0

Nichols, B.: The Current State of DevSecOps Metrics. CMU (2021). https://insights.sei.cmu.edu/blog/the-current-state-of-devsecops-metrics/

Palma-Blanco, A., González, E.R., Paternina-Arboleda, C.D.: A two-pheromone trail ant colony system approach for the heterogeneous vehicle routing problem with time windows, multiple products and product incompatibility. In: Paternina-Arboleda, C., Voß, S. (eds.) ICCL 2019. LNCS, vol. 11756, pp. 248–264. Springer, Cham (2019). https://doi.org/10.1007/978-3-030-31140-7_16

Paternina-Arboleda, C.D., Das, T.K.: A multi-agent reinforcement learning approach to obtaining dynamic control policies for stochastic lot scheduling problem. Simul. Model. Pract. Theory **13**(5), 389–406 (2005)

Paternina-Arboleda, C.D., Das, T.K.: Intelligent dynamic control policies for serial production lines. IIE Trans. **33**(1), 65–77 (2001). https://doi.org/10.1023/A:1007641824604

Paternina-Arboleda, C.D., Montoya-Torres, J.R., Fabregas-Ariza, A.: Simulation-optimization using a reinforcement learning approach. In: 2008 Winter Simulation Conference, Miami, FL, USA, pp. 1376–1383 (2008). https://doi.org/10.1109/WSC2008.4736213

Paternina-Arboleda, C.D., Agudelo-Castañeda, D., Voß, S., Das, S.: Prediction of SO2 ports emissions inventories. Sustainability (2023, Submitted)

Rakos, D.: Understanding GPU caches. [web log] (2021). https://www.rastergrid.com/blog/gpu-tech/2021/01/understanding-gpu-caches/. Accessed 12 Apr 2023

Sarabia, Carolina, M., John, H., Rios-Griego, Carlos, D., Paternina-Arboleda: Simulation-based decision support models for river cargo transportation. In: 2006 IEEE Systems and Information Engineering Design Symposium, pp. 142–145 (2006)

Saxon, S., Stone, M.: Container shipping: the next 50 years. A McKinsey & Company report (2017)

Saxena, A.: What are AI accelerators and how does it work? BISinfotech (2022). https://www.bisinfotech.com/what-are-ai-accelerators-and-how-does-it-work/. Accessed 14 Apr 2023

Shankland, S.: Quantum computers could crack today's encrypted messages. That's a problem. CNET (2021). https://www.cnet.com/tech/computing/quantum-computers-could-crack-todays-encrypted-messages-thats-a-problem/. Accessed 17 Apr 2023

Song, D.: A literature review, container shipping supply chain: planning problems and research opportunities. Logistics **5**, 41 (2021). https://doi.org/10.3390/logistics5020041

Trucco, P., Petrenj, B.: Characterisation of resilience metrics in full-scale applications to interdependent infrastructure systems. Reliab. Eng. Syst. Saf. **235**, 109200 (2023). ISSN: 0951-8320. https://doi.org/10.1016/j.ress.2023.109200

Tsvetkova, A., Gustafsson, M., Wikström, K.: Digitalizing maritime transport: digital innovation as a catalyzer of sustainable transformation. In: Montero, J., Finger, M. (eds.) A Modern Guide to the Digitalization of Infrastructure. Elgar Modern Guides, pp. 123–148. Edward Elgar (2021)

Velasquez-Bermudez, J.M., Abril, D., Paternina-Arboleda, C.D.: Optimizing port operations to cope with shipping congestion in South American countries. OR/MS Today **49**(2) (2022)

Velásquez-Bermúdez, J.M., Khakifirooz, M., Fathi, M. (eds.): Large Scale Optimization in Supply Chains and Smart Manufacturing: Theory and Applications. Springer, Cham (2020). ISBN: 978-3-030-22790-6. https://doi.org/10.1007/978-3-030-22788-3

Wang, Z., Liu, X.: Cyber security of railway cyber-physical system (CPS) – a risk management methodology. Commun. Transp. Res. **2**, 100078 (2022). ISSN: 2772-4247. https://doi.org/10.1016/j.commtr.2022.100078

Woschank, M., Rauch, E., Zsifkovits, H.: A review of further directions for artificial intelligence, machine learning, and deep learning in smart logistics. Sustainability **12**, 3760 (2020). https://doi.org/10.3390/su12093760

Yang, Z., et al.: Indicator-based resilience assessment for critical infrastructures – a review. Saf. Sci. **160**, 106049 (2023). ISSN: 0925-7535. https://doi.org/10.1016/j.ssci.2022.106049

Zemp, B.: The Intersection Between AI and Blockchain Technology – Industries of Tomorrow. Forbes (2023). https://www.forbes.com/sites/forbesbooksauthors/2023/02/28/the-intersection-between-ai-and-blockchain-technology--industries-of-tomorrow/?sh=1731ee7d4de7. Accessed 14 Apr 2023

Zhang, W., Guhathakurta, S., Khalil, E.B.: The impact of private autonomous vehicles on vehicle ownership and unoccupied VMT generation. Transp. Res. Part C Emerg. Technol. **90**, 156–165 (2018)

Customer's Choice in the Context of Cross-Border E-Commerce: An Application of Structural Equation Modelling

Yijia Liu[1](✉) and Xiaoning Shi[2]

[1] Faculty of Mathematics, Informatics and Natural Sciences, University of Hamburg, Hamburg, Germany
yijia.liu@studium.uni-hamburg.de

[2] Institute of Transport Research, DLR (Deutsches Zentrum für Luft- und Raumfahrt, German Aerospace Center), Berlin, Germany
xiaoning.shi@dlr.de

Abstract. Emerging E-Commerce enables the purchasing and delivery activities during the pandemic. Along with the eased situation of the post-pandemic era, however, the E-Commerce business model is facing an increasing number of competitive service providers and demanding customers. One of the discriminating issues between service providers seems to relate to the Customer Repurchase Intention (CRI). Especially in the textile industry in the context of Cross-Border E-Commerce (CBEC), CRI might be influential. In this context, we investigate the customer's choice to provide commercial insights to E-Commerce service providers. To achieve this, we apply Structural Equation Modeling (SEM). More specifically, the combination of ESEM (Exploratory Structural Equation Modelling) and CFA (Confirmatory Factor Analysis) is used as an important SEM approach to explore which factors most significantly impact the CRI of textile products in the context of CBEC. The study is conducted based on the 187 feedback of distributed questionnaires. In our results, Satisfaction and MIS (Management Information System) Technical Factor have significant impacts on CRI.

Keywords: E-Commerce · Structural Equation Modeling (SEM) · Customer Repurchase Intention · Cross-Border E-Commerce

1 Introduction

In the post-pandemic era, all business models, i.e., traditional business models, E-Commerce and Cross-Border E-Commerce (CBEC) have some gradual developments. With the popularity of smart phones and other devices, the development of the Internet of Things (IoT) technologies, the establishment of 5G

Supported by the Project 'FuturePorts', DLR (Deutsches Zentrum für Luft- und Raumfahrt, German Aerospace Center).

© The Author(s), under exclusive license to Springer Nature Switzerland AG 2023
J. R. Daduna et al. (Eds.): ICCL 2023, LNCS 14239, pp. 85–102, 2023.
https://doi.org/10.1007/978-3-031-43612-3_5

stations, logistics industry services and the improvement of information security collectively provide the foundation for the prosperous development of CBEC. According to [43], the E-Commerce revenue of the fashion industry in Germany will rise to around 45.33 billion U.S. dollars in 2025. Some statistics in [42] explicates the T-shirt and hoodie as the two most purchased product categories. Additionally, from the perspective of the supply side of logistics services, e.g., rapid development of logistics network connectivity and Asia-Europe railway infrastructures and facilities, CBEC between Europe and Asia is making rapid progress. However, considering the demand side, a challenging economic situation in the post-pandemic era occurs. With a three-year observation on the freight rates of the containerized rail freight provided by Transfracht (TFG) [46], compared to 2022 and 2021 the freight rates in 2023 increase by approximately 12.94% and 24.63%, respectively.

No matter of the traditional business process or the E-Commerce model, merchants intend to increase the Return of Investment (ROI) through providing high quality goods or services. Merchants study consumer's behavior in order to build a long-term relationship with customers [22]. They often carry out a series of strategies to amplify a Customer Repurchase Intention (CRI) and to attract potential customers through improvement of service quality according to customer demand (Fig. 8). CRI is a customer decision behavior [16]; therefore, it is meaningful to analyze which factors can affect, trigger and amplify the repurchase intention. However, it is noted that there exists not only one factor affecting the CRI. Instead, there may be a series of unique factors, such as perceived benefits, perceived risk [38], and so on.

This paper aims to explore the causality among several factors and CRI of textile products in the context of CBEC. Although T-shirt and hoodie are the particularly most purchased products in the CBEC business [42], T-shirts seem to be more widely and commonly used. Hence, during the process of conducting this research we focus on the customer's choice of T-shirt products. At the outset, SPSS is utilized to determine the factor number based on rotated analysis. Following that, the ESEM+CFA[1] framework is to be constructed on Mplus for analyzing the significant impacts derived from different factors. The process of redefining factors is conducted based on the results of the factor analysis provided by Mplus. A questionnaire is designed and distributed digitally for the purpose of data collection. We employ SmartPLS 4 to evaluate the measurement model.[2] In case a company or platform plans to proactively increase its revenue within a limited budget, the outcome of our research would provide commercial insights as well as indicate some prioritized strategies.

Nevertheless, some challenges exist in this research. Firstly, ESEM+CFA are not yet widely applied in the CBEC field. The available references are therefore limited. Secondly, in empirical research, the sample size plays a crucial role. However, it is difficult to reach a large sample size by collecting huge

[1] ESEM+CFA is a combination of ESEM and CFA. It exhibits the similarity with ESEM within CFA, which is introduced in Mplus User's Guide [29].

[2] SmartPLS 4: the current Version is SmartPLS 4.0.9.4, https://www.smartpls.com/.

amounts of feedback within the limited time. Thirdly, instead of naming the factors in ESEM in advance, significant factors are to be redefined by running ESEM+CFA. Fourthly, in ESEM indicators have cross-loading, the assignment of indicators may differ from our original design. In other words, it is challenging for the process of factor redefinition. Moreover, while refining the model fit, the modification indices (MI) are not unified. Therefore, two distinctive processes are discussed and applied based on a better result. Lastly, some evaluation criteria of PLS-SEM are applied for assessing the measurement models with some concerns on their validity. The factor redefining process provided by this research is going to overcome the above-mentioned challenges.

2 Literature Review

CBEC is a business model based on Internet and E-Commerce websites or platform, where two parties involved in the transaction come from different countries or territories [15]. Hu and Luo [17] state that CBEC is efficient and low-cost, and it is an application of internet technology on the field of foreign trade. Different roles in CBEC are characterized by different functions and responsibilities (Fig. 1). For instance, customs is regulating and facilitating international trade [6] and the customs also aims to maintain a certain degree of fairness and transparency in global trade. It is vital for all parties involved in CBEC to know customs declarations and regulations. The customs releases declared items comprehensively, such as, the calculation of customs duties including over-size or over-weight products' duties and taxes. When the sellers launch their products, the CBEC platform should automatically inform them about the relevant regulations. Generally speaking, the owner of products and its representative are responsible to submit declarations [45]. For the purpose of reducing the operational time, such a declaration should be submitted with considerations of accuracy, authenticity and completeness. It is noted for cross-border trade that the payment of customs duties complies with Incoterms[3] such as Delivered Duty Paid (DDP), Delivered Duty Unpaid (DDU), etc., where DDP is relative widely used due to efficiency and safety concerns in E-Commerce [9].

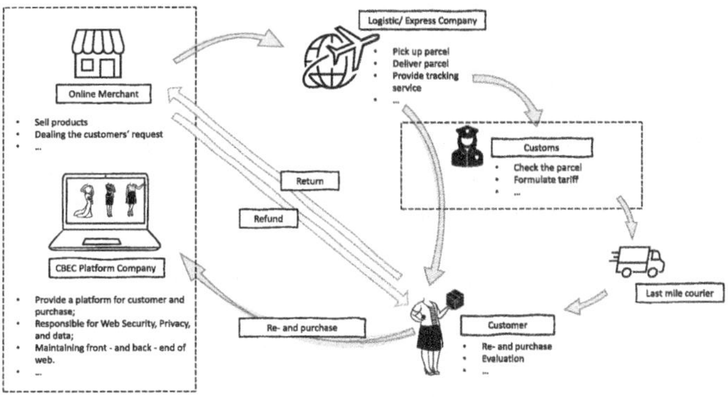

Fig. 1. Process of CBEC

[3] Incoterm: International Commercial Term.

Our research is empirical research based on quantitative methods such as surveys [7], though this type of approach might be criticized; see, e.g., [50] indicating the possible use of mystery shopping instead. It often lacks a theoretical foundation [11]. Kawa and Zdrenka [19] point out that the biggest barrier in CBEC is delivery-service-related cost with required time windows, which becomes an important factor affecting customer satisfaction. In [36] customer satisfaction, enjoyment and trust are found to exert positive impacts on repurchase intentions. Obviously, service and system quality have positive impacts on repurchase intentions [23]; see also [51]. Consumer's choice behavior is actually influenced by various values including functional, social, emotional, and other values [39]. Customer's repurchase intention is actually a judgement and decision behavior [16] affected by several factors. Repurchase behavior and repurchase intention can be regarded as consumer's choice influenced by various factors including satisfaction, trust, perceived value, etc.

In [3], the authors consider the perspectives of service quality and commercial and technical safety, and depict some keywords, namely, "privacy", "online payment security", "website design", "website speed", etc. Valdez-Juárez et al. [49] also consider "website security" in their study. The user interface (UI) including its usability and attractiveness affects the repurchase intention [26]. According to [31], customer's satisfaction is categorized as a level of fulfillment associated with a consumption perspective. However, perceived value is different from satisfaction [44]. Perceived value [24], online service quality, and logistics service [32] have been investigated in E-Commerce research in the past. Product variety has been regarded as an important factor for customer satisfaction [18]. Trust can be deemed as customer's confidence on the involved business partner [5,30]. Service is usually intangible, heterogeneous, inseparable and perishable [20]. In E-Commerce, service is often divided into online and offline categories. Online service usually refers to handling customer complaints through the platform, while offline service usually refers to the logistics service, product replacement and re-delivery [51]. Thus, these two categories of service are considered in our research, too. In addition, Mou et al. [28] explore the perceived risk of "customs clearance" in CBEC.

In our research, such as customs duties declaration, chat-bot service, etc. are also considered. Essentially, IT and Management Information Systems (MIS) are preconditions for business intelligence, digitization and digital transformation. A qualified MIS and infrastructure can facilitate the performance of E-Commerce. For instance, a well-designed E-Commerce website interface gains customer's curiosity. In fact, a tracking Application Programming Interface (API) is a very practical tool acknowledged by many. In a policy of Amazon, the Valid Tracking Rate (VTR) is analyzed as one key indicator to evaluate the performance of a seller [1]. Hence, the implementation of an API makes sense, and we deploy an API-based indicator. Besides, some technologies can be utilized for the identity authentication [33], which provides us insights to a technological perspective. CRI is deemed as a willingness leading a customer repeatedly towards purchasing goods or services from the same seller [51]. In CBEC, it also stands for repeated purchases on the same platform. A series of studies have explored the repurchase intention or behaviour with SEM.

Methodologies, principles, concepts, the criteria of metrics, and theories of SEM are listed in this section as prerequisite for the next sections. RMSEA (Root Mean Square Error of Approximation), CFI (Comparative Fit Index), TLI (Tucker Lewis Index), df (Degree of Freedom), and the probability of RMSEA $\leq$ 0.05 as criteria are comprehensively introduced in the references [21,37,41]. For evaluation of the measurement model in SEM, an Average Variance Extracted (AVE) ≥ 0.5 is acceptable [13]. However, Shrestha [41] states if composite reality > 0.6 but AVE < 0.5, the convergent validity remains acceptable. The theory of ESEM, guideline of Mplus, and examples of Mplus support our research [2, 27,29]. Modification benefits a better model fit. With regard to investigating the exploration of the ESEM framework, at the outset, a pair with highest modification index is modified [48]. Even though many articles have explored the CRI prior to the pandemic, it remains valuable to investigate it in the post pandemic era.

3 Methodology

3.1 Analysis Process

Model specification is conducted as the first step. Since EFA+CFA has both exploratory and confirmatory characteristics, ESEM+CFA is applied (EFA: Exploratory Factor Analysis). Following that, we design a questionnaire with 7 Likert scale for data collection. Our questionnaire covers 16 questions, and it is distributed through different software and platforms (Table 2). Next, data is implemented on SPSS for EFA and Mplus for ESEM+CFA, respectively. The factor numbers are to be determined based on the result of EFA in advance, so that we can use it in ESEM+CFA. After that, before the model is going to be evaluated according to the criteria. Modification based on different assumptions for refining model fit is conducted. Next, the model is extracted for analysis forward. We implement it on SmartPLS for assessing the measurement model. However, some criteria are derived from PLS-SEM. Hence, the p-value remains a crucial metric. After that, we attempt to discuss the experimental results based on different sample size, refined measurement model, and a different structural model. Besides, a comparison with related literature is also to be discussed in the final stage. Figure 2 displays the our analysis process.

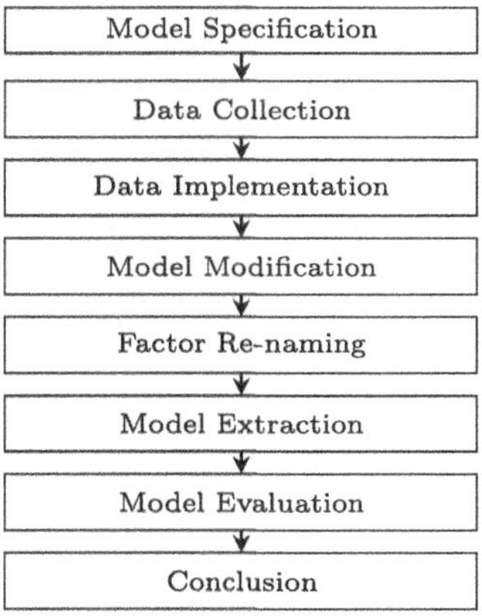

Fig. 2. Analysis Process

3.2 ESEM+CFA

In the early stage, EFA is applied to observe the extracted factor numbers, which will be utilized in ESEM+CFA. ESEM within CFA is introduced in Mplus User's Guide [29] and Mai and Wen's study [25]. Instead of ESEM within CFA, we prefer to call it ESEM+CFA, as we think that this model is constructed by two independent models. Hence, this model is an integration, not an inclusion. Accordingly, we suppose two different modification processes in Sect. 3.3.

Beyond their original structural models they also share the same structural model through connection with each other. Being different from typical SEM, the hypothesis is not to be established in advance. After estimation, the factors are named based on their indicators. In our view, the CFA or EFA is an analysis method for factor analysis. While factor analysis do not place emphasize on the analysis of factor relationship, SEM concentrates on it. ESEM is a SEM based on EFA, highlighting the analysis of significant relationships among factors. Such an exploratory process is not only for the relationship among factors, but also for indicators. The definition of ESEM also provides us a new understanding of SEM. For instance, how to understand the Confirmatory Structural Equation Modelling (CSEM). In other words, if researchers plan to verify an old model, whether this process can be called CSEM. Furthermore, there are two kinds of SEM, i.e., PLS-SEM (Partial Least Squares SEM) and CB-SEM (Covariance Based SEM). They can be distinguished by some differences including distinct criteria for model assessment. PLS-SEM is for the extension of a verified model, theory testing and comparison is a feature of CB-SEM [13,14]. To conduct an analysis of ESEM+CFA based on CB-SEM, Mplus is to be applied. ESEM, Bi-factor, ESEM+CFA are highlights of Mplus [29]. At present Mplus 8.9 is available [29], and in our study Mplus 8.3 is deployed for data implementation. To observe the measurement model, SmartPLS 4 is also applied. The applied criteria are succinctly depicted in Table 1, providing a overview.

Table 1. Criteria for Model Evaluation

Metrics	Cut-off value	Sources
RMSEA	$\leq$0.08	[8, 12, 13, 21, 29, 35, 37, 41, 48]
SRMR	$\leq$0.08	
CFI	$\geq$0.8	
TLI	$\geq$0.8	
Probability of RMSEA$\leq$0.05	$\geq$ 0.05	
Chi Square	–	
$\frac{Chi\ Square}{df}$	$\leq$3	
Cronbach's alpha	$\geq$0.6	
AVE	$\geq$0.5	
R Square	$\geq$0.5	
NFI (Normed Fit Index)	$\geq$0.9	
Indicators loading	$\geq$0.6	
Composite reliability	$\geq$0.6	
HTMT (Heterotrait-Monotrait Ratio)	$\leq$0.9	

3.3 Modification

As described, two different modification processes are applied according to two assumptions.

Assumption 1. Considering the restriction of model, modification is based on a priority principle. Firstly, crossing structural model is not to be allowed. The indicator are initially modified through deletion, as they are pointed to by some factors residing in different structure model. Secondly, the indicators are to be modified by correlation within a same structural model. Next, the indicators residing in different measurement model are going to be correlated in last steps.

Assumption 2. Despite structural limitations, the modification is started from the highest MI. The principle of "each step, one pair" are adhered to by both two assumptions. Additionally, uniform utilization of modification is guided by a better result of model fit.

3.4 Questionnaire

This research applies a questionnaire with a 1–7 Likert scale. Because of the exploratory nature of our research, we apply a questionnaire by self-defining for collecting feedback. A sample of 187 responses is collected. Respondents come from China (circa 64%), Germany (circa 25%), the USA (circa 4%), Canada (circa 2%) and other countries[4] (circa 5%). Additionally, around 103 respondents have purchased in Amazon before (Figure 3). 75.4% of the respondents are between 21 to 30 years old, while 43.9% are students. To filter the valid response, respondents are asked by a question, namely *"Have you ever purchased in one of CBEC before?"*. Then 162 valid data are implemented. 28 indicators are extracted and summarized from different perspectives, namely

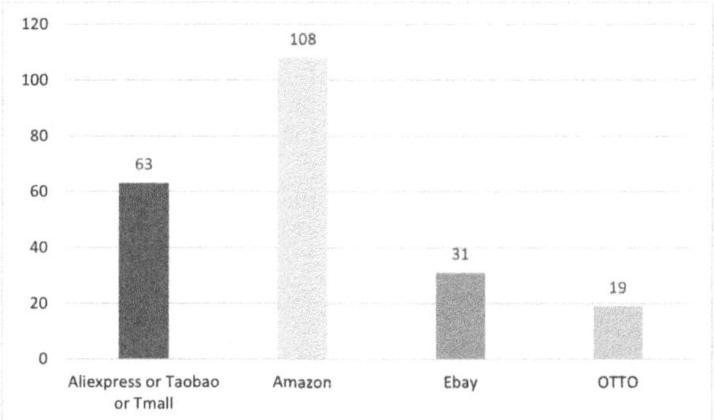

Fig. 3. The most visited CBEC website

Table 2. Questionnaire content

Questionnaires	Content
Collection Period	Feb 20. 2023 to March 17. 2023
Numbers of question	16
Total participants	187
Response Rate	around 36%
Languages	English, Chinese, German
Female, Male	46%, 54%
Spread medium	Linkedin, WeChat, Email and What'sApp, Survey Circle, SMS

[4] UK, Australia, Japan, Panama, Norway, Ireland, and Switzerland.

satisfaction, online service quality, offline service quality, trust, and technical factors. 28 indicators are analyzed using SPSS to study EFA. and six indicators from CRI are employed for CFA. Their indicators are defined from different literature. The keywords of indicators are succinctly described in Table 3.

Table 3. Keywords of indicators

Perspectives	Description of Items (Keywords)
Satisfaction (y1–y4)	1: service quality, 2: logistics service, 3: product quality, 4: product variety
Trust (y5–y10)	5: website privacy, 9: product description, 6 and 10: authenticity of evaluation, 7: website security, 8: payment method,
Offline service quality (y11–y16)	11: pick-up and delivery, 12: fee rate, 13: responsibility of logistics, 14: customs declaration and clearance, 15: customs duty, 16: go through Customs
Online service quality (y17–y22)	17: urgent service, 18: 24-hours service, 19: chat bot service, 20: return service, 21: problem resolving, 22: human service accessibility
Technical factor (y23–y28)	23: attractive UI, 24: shipping API, 25: multilingual UI, 26: promotion newsletter, 27: log-in authentication, 28: payment authentication
CRI (cri1–cri6)	1: repurchase other T-shirts in the same vendor 2: repurchase same products in the same vendor 3: repurchase other T-shirts in the same web 4: repurchase other products in the same web 5: preference for future shopping 6: recommend to friends and family

4 Results and Discussions

4.1 Results

(1) 28 indicators are estimated on SPSS with rotated Varimax under Maximum Likelihood. According to the estimation performed by SPSS, the KMO (Kaiser-Meyer-Olkin) is 0.878, and the p-value is approximate to 0. Hence, in accordance with [41] the result is acceptable. Therefore, 28 indicators are extracted into six factors to be applied for the subsequent steps.

(2) The integration of ESEM+CFA is implemented on the Mplus. Based on the first-round estimation, RMSEA is 0.076, CFI is 0.878, the probability of RMSEA is 0.000, and SRMR is 0.050. So the model does not fit. Afterwards, it is to be modified using the MI until no pair exceeds 10. According to the first modification method, 12 steps are carried out. After being modified by the second modification process, its model fit is also acceptable. Despite this, it does not outperform the first one (Table 4b).

(3) After being modified, 3 factors have significant impacts on the CRI. According to the result and their indicators, they are redefined as *Satisfaction (SA)*, *MIS Technical factor (MIS)*, and *Facilitation (FA)*, respectively (Fig. 5a).

Table 4. Result of ESEM+CFA

Criteria	Result	
RMSEA	0.051	Acceptable
CFI	0.950	Acceptable
TLI	0.925	Acceptable
SRMR	0.041	Acceptable
Probability of RMSEA ≤ 0.05	0.423	Acceptable

(a) With the first modification process

Criteria	Result	
RMSEA	0.056	Acceptable
CFI	0.938	Acceptable
TLI	0.907	Acceptable
SRMR	0.040	Acceptable
Probability of RMSEA ≤ 0.05	0.144	Acceptable

(b) With the second modification process

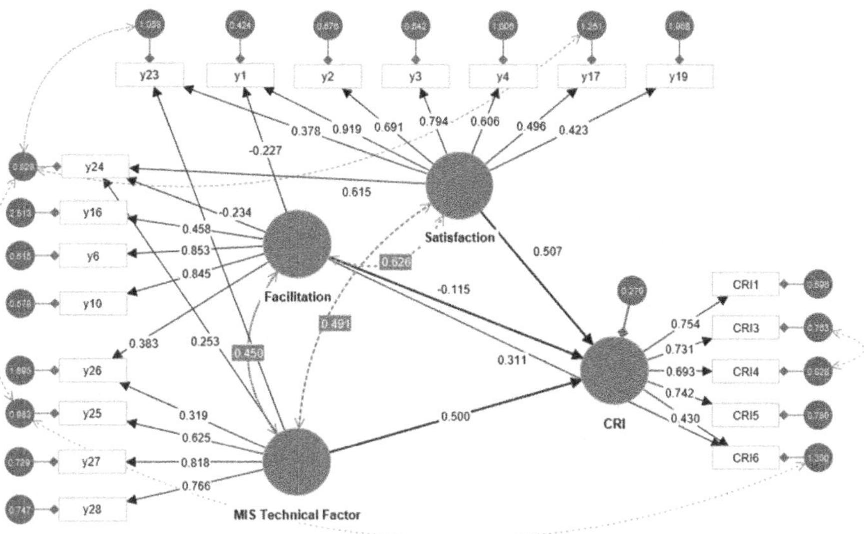

Fig. 4. Diagram on SmartPLS

Other 3 factors are not going to be defined any more. However, the coefficient of *Facilitation* is negative, i.e. −0.216, it is inconsistent with common sense. Following that, in order to proceed with further exploration these 3 factors with CRI are extracted for establishing a new model further (Fig. 5a).

(4) As estimated, *Facilitation* has no significant impact on CRI anymore. This provides a new vision which is different from current policies and common sense which is previously accepted [10,40,47]. In contrast to that, the impacts of *MIS Technical factor* and *Satisfaction* persist significantly. Figure 5a → Fig. 5b demonstrates the transformation of model. In the extracted model, correlations that cross structural model have existed, therefore, model-crossing is allowed. This step is implemented on Mplus. Following that, the further evaluation of measurement model and structural model are required.

Since the current SmartPLS 4 supports CB-SEM, we implement it on the SmartPLS 4 for measurement model analysis (Fig. 4). Table 6 displays the esti-

Table 5. Result on SmartPLS 4 and Mplus 8

Criteria	Result on SmartPLS 4	Result on Mplus 8	
p-value	0.001	0.000	Acceptable
RMSEA	0.051	0.050	Acceptable
CFI	0.953	0.955	Acceptable
TLI	0.942	0.943	Acceptable
SRMR	0.058	0.055	Acceptable
NFI	0.859	–	Inadequate
Probability of RMSEA ≤ 0.05	–	0.423	Acceptable
$\frac{Chi\ Square}{df}$	1.414	1.405	Acceptable
R^2	0.645	0.641	Acceptable

mation of reliable indicator loading based on SmartPLS. Firstly, there are 8 indicators' loading higher than 0.708. According to [8] and [12], in CB-SEM an AVE needs to be higher than 0.5, and an acceptable loading need to exceed 0.6. Thereof, 13 indicators are noted. Hence, although the model fits good, but convergent validity is insufficient. Cheung et al. [4] support this points too. However, it is uncertain to apply them for testing the validity in our ESEM+CFA model. Hence, we are going to use it to evaluate measurement model. In Table 6, the results of Cronbach's alpha are acceptable, while all composite reliability are greater than 0.6. Although results in AVE are less than 0.5, but the convergent validity remains adequate [41]. Discriminant validity is evaluated through HTMT (Heterotrait-Monotrait Ratio). If HTMT < 0.85, it indicates conceptually different factors (Table 7). Considering the result of measurement model is not very sufficient; therefore, the model is optimized for further refinement. According to [13], researchers can to enhance measurement model through indicator deletion. Furthermore, we still concentrate on p-value.

Table 6. Result of measurement model based on SmartPLS 4

Factors	Indicators	Coefficient	Cronbach's alpha (standardized)	Composite reliability (rho_c)	Convergent validity (AVE)
CRI	cri1	0.754	0.834	0.796	0.487
	cri3	0.731			
	cri4	0.693			
	cri5	0.742			
Facilitation	y6	0.853	0.745	0.632	0.314
	y10	0.845			
MIS TechnicalFactor	y25	0.625	0.788	0.722	0.310
	y27	0.818			
	y28	0.766			
Satisfaction	y1	0.919	0.829	0.826	0.412
	y2	0.691			
	y3	0.794			
	y4	0.606			
	y24	0.615			

The minimum path loading ω_{min} is inversely derived in accordance with our sample size and applied significance level 5% [13]. Based on observation, the path loading of Satisfaction and MIS Technical Factor exceed 0.167, but Facilitation not. Apart from that, it is discussed whether the factor loading needs to be higher than 0.4, 0.5 or 0.7 [4]. CRI is an endogenous variable in the model, its R Square on SmartPLS is 0.645, while on Mplus is 0.641. Therefore, the power of prediction of CRI is moderate [13]. Table 5 explicates the result of the extracted model estimated on Mplus and SmartPLS, but Mplus can output the probability of RMSEA ≤ 0.05 individually. Regardless of the differences of outputs, the results are almost the same. Hence, the structural model of the extracted model fits well.

With the result of the extracted model, a proactive business strategy journey is designed (Fig. 8). In terms of that, some items are hoped to applied for improvement. Even though not all of the indicators loading are acceptable. For the purpose of further observation and verification on this extracted model and those of criteria forward this diagram is derived from the valid p-value.

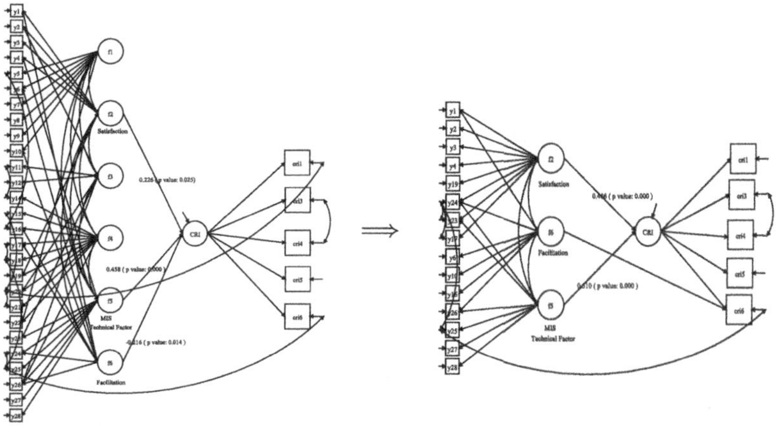

(a) ESEM+CFA (b) Extracted ESEM+CFA

Fig. 5. Model Extraction

4.2 Discussions

(1) The measurement models are going to be optimized by removing indicators, namely the indicator with lowest loading is deleted initially. In line with modification only one pair is deleted in each step. In Fig. 6, Facilitation remains insignificantly. There is no cross-loading among different measurement model. Additionally, all of 13 indicators are reliable theoretically. Table 8a and 8b depict the results of the variation in the measurement model and the model fit. All of the metrics are definitely improved, especially AVE. The results of convergent reliability of CRI, Facilitation and MIS Technical Factor meet the required criteria and are deemed as acceptable, and AVE of Satisfaction is approximate to 0.5.

Through this operation some metrics of model fit are enhanced. For instances, it increases CFI, TLI, RMSEA, SRMR, $\frac{Chi\ Square}{df}$, NFI, respectively, as well as HTMT. Moreover, the p-value of model is also increased to 0.005. In the beginning, for a better model fit performed on Mplus, we modify our model. Perhaps due to that, the measurement model in our ESEM+CFA is not so good. However, it lacks of rich evidence to be verified so far.

Table 7. Result on SmartPLS 4

	CRI	FA	MIS
FA	0.734	–	–
MIS	0.807	0.848	–
SA	0.776	0.841	0.761

Table 8. Result of refined model on SmartPLS 4

	Cronbach's alpha	**Composite reliability (rho_c)**	**AVE**
CRI	0.842	0.792	0.539
FA	0.845	0.856	0.744
MIS	0.771	0.769	0.632
SA	0.826	0.829	0.499

(a) Result of measurement model

Criteria	**Result**	
RMSEA	0.057	Acceptable
CFI	0.967	Acceptable
TLI	0.955	Acceptable
SRMR	0.050	Acceptable
NFI	0.912	Acceptable
$\frac{Chi\ Square}{df}$	1.535	Acceptable

(b) Result of model fit

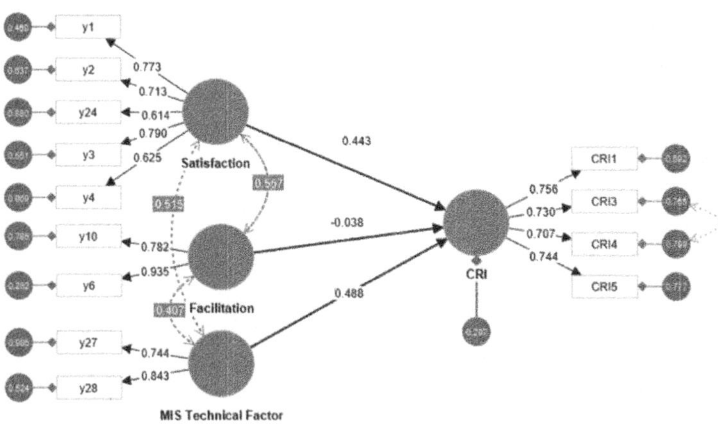

Fig. 6. Refined extracted model on SmartPLS 4

(2) Variation of the sample size within ESEM+CFA. To investigate the effect of the sample size, the different sample sizes are applied for additional comparison on Mplus; therefore, experiments with three different sample sizes are conducted. They are distinguished by the response time, namely the first week (75 available responses), the second week (124 available responses) and overall, respectively. The result of 75 sample sizes shows the model fit is not acceptable. After modification, almost all metrics dissatisfy with cut-off value. With the increased sample sizes the model fit is definitive improved. The Fig. 7 displays that the probability of RMSEA ≥ 0.05 is influenced by sample size most significantly. Beyond that, all of metrics are refined with the increased sample sizes. Accordingly, it is valuable to study on it with a larger sample size in the future.

(3) Comparison with previous research. On one hand, our experiment explicates the significant recursive relationship of "Satisfaction → CRI" and "MIS Technical → CRI". As described in literature, Satisfaction has significant impacts on CRI. Perhaps the definition of factors and the design of indicators jointly affect the result. On the other hand, the loading reliability of "as a preference for future shopping" in our case is regarded as acceptable. However, in [28], "as a preference for future shopping" and "recommend it to others" are both acceptable. Maybe the different research objectives, sample sizes, different backgrounds, different models or respondents (target groups) lead to the above-mentioned different results.

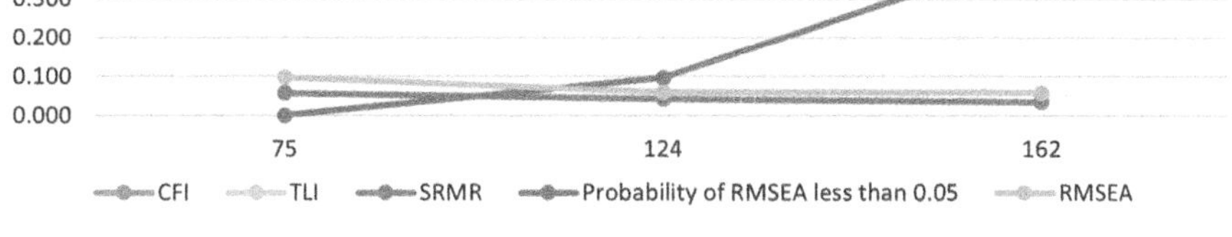

Fig. 7. Comparison of different sample sizes within ESEM+CFA

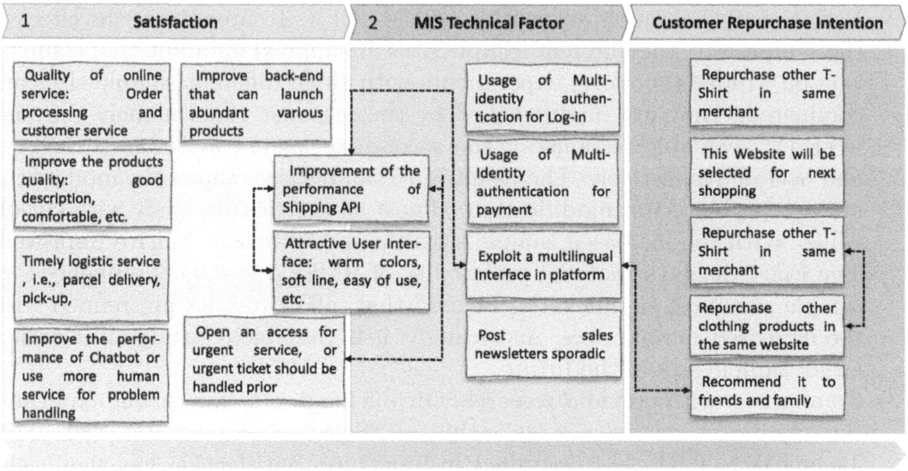

Fig. 8. Strategy journey with output of extracted model

5 Conclusions and Future Research

With an application of ESEM+CFA the CRI in the context of the CBEC is investigated and explored. In addition, 28 indicators are simulated within ESEM on Mplus, while six indicators are used for CRI to study CFA. Satisfaction, Facilitation, and MIS Technical Factor have significant impacts on CRI. After that, the model is extracted into a new independent cluster model to explore further. Facilitation has no significant impact on CRI any more. In fact, our result demonstrates a process from the model specification, generation, extraction, and improvement. In addition, we also analyze the measurement model and structural model with the new version of SmartPLS. We design a strategy journey based on the significant indicators and factors. In terms of that, with the increased sample size the model fit of ESEM+CFA is improved. But it cannot be concluded that, as long as the sample size is increased, the result can be improved constantly, because questionnaire's design plays a role in this regard. Besides, the process of refining model is performed by applying SmartPLS. The process ends when all metrics are beyond threshold.

In future research, some experiments focusing on the increased sample sizes will be considered initially, because 187 respondents is indeed insufficient for a conclusive result. In addition, some investigations on the changes and upgrades of current insignificant factors would be of value in the new norm of global trade. It is also of interest to conduct a Confirmatory Tetrad Analysis (CTA) and compare it with the formative measurement model [34]. The above-mentioned future directions would contribute and push forward modification processes. Some factors are going to be selected for observing moderation and mediation [13], such as perceived and individual factors in the questionnaire. In summary, there is still space to refine and leverage our understanding on the CBEC with focus on customer intention, choice and derived cargo volumes.

Acknowledgements. Special thanks go to the 187 respondents of the questionnaire, and the support of FuturePorts Project, DLR (Deutsches Zentrum für Luft- und Raumfahrt, German Aerospace Center). In addition, the constructive comments provided by the anonymous referees are greatly appreciated.

References

1. Amazon: Valid Tracking Rate (VTR) (2023). https://sellercentral.amazon.co.uk/help/hub/reference/external/G201817070?locale=en-GB. Accessed 11 Apr 2023
2. Asparouhov, T., Muthén, B.: Exploratory structural equation modeling. Struct. Equ. Model. **16**(3), 397–438 (2009). https://doi.org/10.1080/10705510903008204
3. Cao, X., Shen, B., Liu, Y., Wang, M.: Research on evaluation of B to C e-commerce website based on AHP and grey evaluation. In: Second International Symposium on Electronic Commerce and Security, vol. 2, pp. 405–408 (2009). https://doi.org/10.1109/ISECS.2009.242
4. Cheung, G., Cooper-Thomas, H., Lau, R., Wang, L.: Reporting reliability, convergent and discriminant validity with structural equation modeling: a review and best-practice recommendations. Asia Pac. J. Manage. (2023). https://doi.org/10.1007/s10490-023-09871-y
5. Corbitt, B.J., Thanasankit, T., Yi, H.: Trust and e-commerce: a study of consumer perceptions. Electron. Commer. Res. Appl. **2**(3), 203–215 (2003). https://doi.org/10.1016/S1567-4223(03)00024-3
6. Customs & Excise Division Dominica: Role of Customs (2022). http://www.customs.gov.dm/index.php/about-customs/role-of-customs. Accessed 20 Mar 2023
7. Dan, V.: Empirical and Nonempirical Methods, pp. 1–3. Wiley (2017). https://doi.org/10.1002/9781118901731.iecrm0083
8. Dash, G., Paul, J.: CB-SEM vs PLS-SEM methods for research in social sciences and technology forecasting. Technol. Forecast. Soc. Chang. **173**, 121092 (2021). https://doi.org/10.1016/j.techfore.2021.121092
9. Deutsche Post Group DHL: Customs, duties & taxes (2023). https://www.dhl.com/discover/en-my/e-commerce/e-commerce-advice/ddu-vs-ddp-for-ecommerce-business. Accessed 17 Mar 2023
10. Fang, L., Shi, X., Hu, H.: Analysis of influencing factors and location prediction of dry port based on logit model. J. Chongqing Jiaotong Univ. **5**, 31 (2012)
11. Gaskell, T.: The process of empirical research: a learning experience? Res. Post-Compulsory Educ. **5**(3), 349–360 (2000). https://doi.org/10.1080/13596740000200084
12. Hair, J., Black, W., Babin, B.: Multivariate Data Analysis: A Global Perspective. Global Edition, Pearson Education (2010)
13. Hair, J., Hult, G.T.M., Ringle, C., Sarstedt, M., Danks, N., Ray, S.: Partial Least Squares Structural Equation Modeling (PLS-SEM) Using R: AWorkbook. Springer, Heidelberg (2021). https://doi.org/10.1007/978-3-030-80519-7
14. Hair Jr., J.F., Matthews, L.M., Matthews, R.L., Sarstedt, M.: PLS-SEM or CB-SEM: updated guidelines on which method to use. Int. J. Multivariate Data Anal. **1**, 107–123 (2017). https://doi.org/10.1504/IJMDA.2017.087624

15. Hazarika, B.B., Mousavi, R.: Review of cross-border e-commerce and directions for future research. J. Glob. Inf. Manag. **30**(2), 1–18 (2021). https://doi.org/10.4018/JGIM.20220301.oa1
16. Hellier, P., Geursen, G., Carr, R., Rickard, J.: Customer repurchase intention: a general structural equation model. Eur. J. Mark. **37**, 1762–1800 (2003). https://doi.org/10.1108/03090560310495456
17. Hu, B., Luo, Q.: Cross-border e-commerce mode based on Internet +. In: IOP Conference Series: Materials Science and Engineering, vol. 394, no. 5, p. 052014 (2018). https://doi.org/10.1088/1757-899X/394/5/052014
18. Kaiser, U., Kesler, R., Reisinger, M.: The interplay between product variety and customer satisfaction: theory and evidence (2023). https://doi.org/10.2139/ssrn.4022124. Accessed 09 Apr 2023
19. Kawa, A., Zdrenka, W.: Conception of integrator in cross-border E-commerce. LogForum **12**, 63–73 (2016). https://doi.org/10.17270/J.LOG.2016.1.6
20. Khan, M.K., Nawaz, M., Ishaq, M.I., Tariq, M.I.: Product versus service: old myths versus new realities. J. Basic Appl. Sci. Res. **4**(1), 15–20 (2014)
21. Kline, R.: Principles and Practice of Structural Equation Modeling. Methodology in the Social Sciences, 4th edn. Guilford, London (2015)
22. Lei, F., Lei, S., Liu, J., Wu, L.: Studying customer behavior of shopping on e-commerce platforms from the perspective of college students. In: 2020 International Conference on E-Commerce and Internet Technology (ECIT), pp. 41–44 (2020). https://doi.org/10.1109/ECIT50008.2020.00017
23. Luo, H., Liang, Y., Wu, Z., Liu, Z., Shu, B., Luo, Y.: Research on the impact of cross-border e-commerce platform quality on customer cross-buying intention. In: 16th International Conference on Service Systems and Service Management (ICSSSM), pp. 1–6 (2019). https://doi.org/10.1109/ICSSSM.2019.8887725
24. Luo, H., Zhang, X., Huang, J., Su, F., Huang, W., Luo, Y.: An empirical study on customer repurchase willingness of fresh e-commerce products based on customer perceived value. In: 16th International Conference on Service Systems and Service Management (ICSSSM), pp. 1–6 (2019). https://doi.org/10.1109/ICSSSM.2019.8887610
25. Mai, Y., Wen, Z.: Exploratory structural equation modeling (ESEM): an integration of EFA and CFA. Adv. Psychol. Sci. **21**(5), 934 (2013). https://doi.org/10.3724/SP.J.1042.2013.00934
26. Matthew, D., Hellianto, G.R., Putra, N.S., Sundjaja, A.M.: The effect of monthly promotion, gamification, user interface usability & attractiveness on the marketplace repurchase intention. In: International Conference on Informatics, Multimedia, Cyber and Information System, pp. 193–199 (2021). https://doi.org/10.1109/ICIMCIS53775.2021.9699114
27. Morin, A.J.S., Marsh, H.W., Nagengas, B.: Supplementary materials for: Chapter 10. Exploratory structural equation modeling (2013). https://www.statmodel.com/download/Chapter%2010%20-%20ESEM-%20supplements%2020131.pdf. Accessed 11 Feb 2023
28. Mou, J., Cui, Y., Kurcz, K.: Trust, risk and alternative website quality in B-Buyer acceptance of cross-border e-commerce. J. Glob. Inf. Manag. **28**, 167–188 (2020). https://doi.org/10.4018/JGIM.2020010109
29. Muthén, L.K., Muthén, B.O.: MPlus version 8 user's guide. Muthén & Muthén (2017)
30. Nurdani, Y., Sandhyaduhita, P.I.: Impact of express delivery service quality towards repurchase intention by B2C and C2C: a case of Indonesia. In: Inter-

national Conference on Advanced Computer Science and Information Systems (ICACSIS), pp. 221–227 (2016). https://doi.org/10.1109/ICACSIS.2016.7872779
31. Oliver, R.: Satisfaction: A Behavioral Perspective on the Consumer. McGraw Hill (1997). https://doi.org/10.4324/9781315700892
32. Rachmawati, D.Z., Agus, A.A.: E-service and logistics service quality in e-commerce, study case: shopee Indonesia. In: 2020 3rd International Conference on Computer and Informatics Engineering (IC2IE), pp. 218–223 (2020). https://doi.org/10.1109/IC2IE50715.2020.9274597
33. Rajesh, H.M., Song, I.: E-commerce websites/blogs - hassles and predicaments. In: Proceedings of the 6th International Conference on Communication and Network Security, ICCNS 2016, pp. 56–61. Association for Computing Machinery, New York (2016). https://doi.org/10.1145/3017971.3017990
34. Ringle, C.M., Wende, S., Becker, J.M.: Confirmatory tetrad analysis in PLS (CTA-PLS) (2022). https://www.smartpls.com/documentation/algorithms-and-techniques/cta-pls/. Accessed 20 Mar 2023
35. Ringle, C.M., Wende, S., Becker, J.M.: SmartPLS 4 (2022). https://www.smartpls.com/documentation/algorithms-and-techniques/model-fit/. Accessed 20 Mar 2023
36. Rini, D.P., Josephat, E., Ririmasse, Y.R., Sundjaja, A.M.: The effect of trust, satisfaction and enjoyment toward repurchase intention in E-commerce. In: 2021 3rd International Conference on Cybernetics and Intelligent System (ICORIS), pp. 1–6 (2021). https://doi.org/10.1109/ICORIS52787.2021.9649504
37. Schumacker, R., Lomax, R.: A Beginner's Guide to Structural Equation Modeling, 4th edn. Taylor & Francis (2015). https://doi.org/10.4324/9780203851319
38. Shan, S., Hua, F., Zeng, Q.: B2C e-commerce consumer decision-making model based on perceived benefit and perceived risk. In: 2010 International Conference on E-Business and E-Government, pp. 2222–2225 (2010). https://doi.org/10.1109/ICEE.2010.561
39. Sheth, J.N., Newman, B.I., Gross, B.L.: Why we buy what we buy: a theory of consumption values. J. Bus. Res. **22**(2), 159–170 (1991). https://doi.org/10.1016/0148-2963(91)90050-8
40. Shi, X., Ma, L., Voß, S.: On designing a slot sharing E-platform for liner shipping services. In: Stephanidis, C., Marcus, A., Rosenzweig, E., Rau, P.-L.P., Moallem, A., Rauterberg, M. (eds.) HCII 2020. LNCS, vol. 12423, pp. 499–513. Springer, Cham (2020). https://doi.org/10.1007/978-3-030-60114-0_34
41. Shrestha, N.: Factor analysis as a tool for survey analysis. Am. J. Appl. Math. Stat. **9**, 4–11 (2021). https://doi.org/10.12691/ajams-9-1-2
42. Statista: What is your best selling streetwear product? (2019). https://www.statista.com/statistics/1092487/best-selling-products-among-streetwear-retailers-worldwide/?locale=en. Accessed 10 Jan 2023
43. Statista: E-commerce revenue forecast in Germany from 2017 to 2025, by segment. https://www.statista.com/forecasts/480260/e-commerce-revenue-in-germany-fashion-by-segments. Accessed 10 Apr 2023
44. Sweeney, J.C., Soutar, G.N.: Consumer perceived value: the development of a multiple item scale. J. Retail. **77**(2), 203–220 (2001). https://doi.org/10.1016/S0022-4359(01)00041-0
45. Taxation and Customs Union: Customs declaration (2021). https://taxation-customs.ec.europa.eu/customs-4/customs-procedures-import-and-export-0/customs-procedures/customs-declaration_en. Accessed 10 Apr 2023
46. TFG Transfracht GmbH: Transfracht (2023). https://www.transfracht.com/transfracht. Accessed 20 Mar 2023

47. Tousypanah, H., Shi, X., Viohl, B., Hoffmann, J.: Analysis of influencing factors and location prediction of dry port based on logit model. UNCTAD Transp. Newsl. **43**, 6–10 (2009)
48. Tóth-Király, I., Bõthe, B., Rigó, A., Orosz, G.: An illustration of the exploratory structural equation modeling (ESEM) framework on the passion scale. Front. Psychol. **8** (2017). https://doi.org/10.3389/fpsyg.2017.01968
49. Valdez-Juárez, L.E., Gallardo-Vázquez, D., Ramos-Escobar, E.A.: Online buyers and open innovation: security, experience, and satisfaction. J. Open Innov.: Technol. Mark. Complexity **7**(1), 37 (2021). https://doi.org/10.3390/joitmc7010037
50. Voß, S., Mejia, G., Voß, A.: Mystery shopping in public transport: the case of bus station design. In: Stephanidis, C., Marcus, A., Rosenzweig, E., Rau, P.-L.P., Moallem, A., Rauterberg, M. (eds.) HCII 2020. LNCS, vol. 12423, pp. 527–542. Springer, Cham (2020). https://doi.org/10.1007/978-3-030-60114-0_36
51. Yu, Y.W., Chiu, S.C., Chumpoothepa, S., Chen, J.K.: Factors influencing online repurchase intention: the case of clothing customers in Thailand. In: Proceedings of PICMET 2014 Conference: Portland International Center for Management of Engineering and Technology; Infrastructure and Service Integration, pp. 658–669 (2014)

Maritime Shipping

Towards a Deep Reinforcement Learning Model of Master Bay Stowage Planning

Jaike van Twiller(✉), Djordje Grbic, and Rune Møller Jensen

IT University of Copenhagen, Rued Langgaards Vej 7, 2300 Copenhagen, Denmark
{jaiv,djgr,rmj}@itu.dk

Abstract. Major liner shipping companies aim to solve the stowage planning problem by optimally allocating containers to vessel locations during a multi-port voyage. Due to a large variety of combinatorial aspects, a scalable algorithm to solve a representative problem is yet to be found. This paper will show that deep reinforcement learning can optimize a non-trivial master bay planning problem. Our experiments show that proximal policy optimization efficiently finds reasonable solutions, serving as preliminary evidence of the potential value of deep reinforcement learning in stowage planning. In future work, we will extend our architecture to address a full-featured master bay planning problem.

Keywords: Maritime logistics · Liner shipping · Stowage planning · Deep reinforcement learning · Markov decision processes

1 Introduction

In the past century, maritime transport has become the backbone of global trade and modern consumerism. Many transported goods are shipped by container vessels of liner shipping companies. To ensure timely arrivals and resource-efficient operations, these liner companies use stowage planning to allocate containers to vessel slots at each port of the voyage. The goal is to maximize vessel utilization and minimize operational costs by creating robust stowage plans. This is an NP-hard task due to (hatch-)overstowage [18,35], which is further complicated by the problem size (20,000 Twenty Foot Equivalent Unit (TEU) vessels visiting at least 10 ports) and combinatorial aspects as container dimensions, seaworthiness and stowage regulations, demand uncertainty and planning best practices.

Several contributions have been unable to directly solve their problem formulation (e.g., [8,23]). Consequently, it is suggested to hierarchically decompose the stowage problem into master bay and slot planning (e.g., [28,37]), which is further explained in Sect. 3. Even though plenty of contributions tried, a scalable algorithm for a representative decomposed problem is yet to be found.

This paper will provide a proof of concept for a novel application of deep reinforcement learning (DRL) to solve the master bay planning problem (MBPP)

This work is partially sponsored by the Danish Maritime Fund under grant 2021-069.

© The Author(s), under exclusive license to Springer Nature Switzerland AG 2023
J. R. Daduna et al. (Eds.): ICCL 2023, LNCS 14239, pp. 105–121, 2023.
https://doi.org/10.1007/978-3-031-43612-3_6

as a Markov decision process (MDP). To the best of our knowledge, the only stowage contributions involving reinforcement learning (RL) relax many of the complex combinatorial aspects [33,38]. Furthermore, DRL is used to solve optimization problems similar to MBPP [14,17,22,24]. Hence, we believe that DRL implementations can contribute to solving the stowage planning problem.

In our work, we model an episodic MDP that maximizes vessel utilization and minimizes hatch-overstowage for equal-sized cargo with two weight classes, while satisfying demand and location capacity, as well as ensuring longitudinal and vertical stability. We refer to Sect. 4 for details on the problem. This is not a full-featured MBPP, but rather a non-trivial problem to provide us with a proof of concept. Each episode generates a Gaussian equivalent to the Mixed instances by [4]. We have implemented a proximal policy optimization (PPO) architecture that learns an actor and critic network to find a policy that can efficiently solve the MDP. This architecture is compared against an equivalent mixed integer program (MIP) to evaluate performance.

Our experiments show that PPO can learn a policy that optimizes the objective function on a limited training budget. Subsequently, the policy can be generalized to efficiently find reasonable solutions for a non-trivial MBPP in a fraction of the MIP runtime on limited hardware. Thus, we have provided preliminary evidence for the potential of DRL in stowage planning.

The remainder of this paper is structured as follows: Sect. 2 introduces the domain of container vessel stowage planning. Section 3 outlines related work, and Sect. 4 defines the MBPP with a MIP formulation. In Sect. 5, some RL preliminaries are provided, while our MDP and PPO architecture are described in Sect. 6. Finally, Sect. 7 compares the results of our PPO architecture with a MIP solver, and Sect. 8 concludes the main findings of this study.

2 Domain of Container Vessel Stowage Planning

We will first give a brief introduction to container vessel stowage planning. For a comprehensive description of the domain, we refer to [18]. Liner shipping employs a fleet of container vessels to serve ports with fixed schedules on a closed-loop route. An intuitive analogy is a maritime bus line that transports cargo instead of people between ports. Visiting all ports once is referred to as a voyage.

To transport cargo efficiently, container vessels have a cellular design as shown in Fig. 1. The vessel is divided into *bays* (02–38) with *stacks* and *rows* that contain *cells* capable of holding one 40' container or two 20' containers. To secure the *below deck* stacks (02–12), the vessel incorporates *cell guides*. In addition, the below-deck hold is sealed with *hatch covers*. Any stacks *on deck* (82–92) either rest on hatch covers or the ship deck. *Twist locks* are used to bind stacked containers together, *lashing rods* connect container corners to the deck or lashing bridges that increase stability. Each stack has weight limits, while below-deck stacks also have height limits. Figure 1 shows cells (82–84) with power plugs for refrigerated containers (*reefers*) indicated by the symbol $*$.

The cargo is typically 20 ft., 40 ft. and 45 ft. long, 8 ft. wide, and 8 ft. 6 in. high for *dry cargo* or 9 ft. 6 in. high for *highcubes*. Container weight ranges between 4 and 30 tons, depending on the load. Note that empty containers also need to be redistributed from time to time. Any container has an origin named *port of load* (POL), and a destination called the *port of discharge* (POD). Furthermore, cargo types can also differ, as *Specials* include reefers, IMDG that carry dangerous goods, and OOG containers that deviate from the typical cargo dimensions. To ensure safety, IMDGs are often separated from other cargo types.

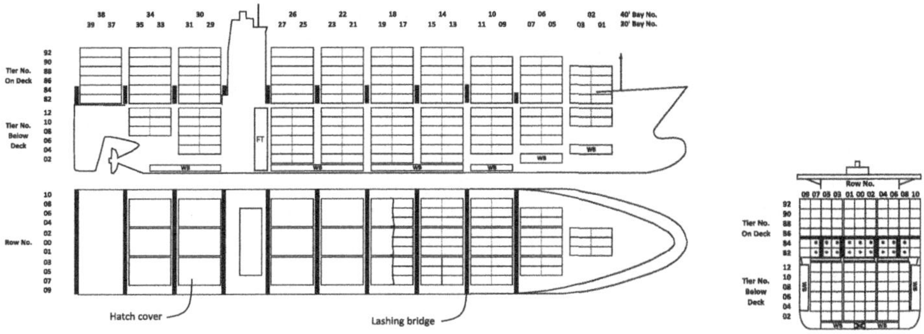

Fig. 1. Vessel side, top and front view [36].

Above and below-deck locations are separated by hatch covers, and thus the cover must be removed to reach below-deck cargo in any bay. If cargo destined for future ports is still placed on the cover, cranes must remove and reload (*restow*) the on-deck containers that overstow the below-deck cargo. This is referred to as *hatch overstowage*. Note that minimizing hatch overstowage is an NP-hard task, which prevents us from finding an optimal solution in polynomial time [35]. Equivalently, *stack overstowage* can also occur if stacks are not in ascending order of PODs from top to bottom. Furthermore, vessels must be seaworthy according to safety regulations. In general, the cargo must be distributed along the vessel to ensure acceptable levels of stability and stress forces [18].

3 Related Work

In essence, container vessel stowage planning is a multi-port problem, which aims to balance a myriad of combinatorial aspects [18]. The field can roughly be subdivided into single-port work to create light-weight operational stowage plans (e.g., [2,3,10,23]), and multi-port work to generate realistic stowage plans (e.g., [4,8,28,30,31,37]). As demonstrated by [8,23], an exact and optimal solution to the multi-port problem is yet to be found. Consequently, [37] suggested a hierarchical decomposition into master bay planning to allocate groups of containers to general locations on the vessel (e.g., [7,9,26]), and slot planning to subsequently allocate containers to slots in locations (e.g., [19,21,29]). For a comprehensive description of hierarchical decomposition, we refer to [18]. Recently, heuristic frameworks have also gained traction as an alternative to hierarchical decomposition (e.g., [23,27]).

Regardless, several solution methods have been proposed to solve different stowage planning problems, for instance, exact methods (e.g., [31,39]), greedy heuristics (e.g., [4,11]), population-based (e.g., [12,16]) or neighborhood-based metaheuristics (e.g., [2,27]), matheuristics (e.g., [21,30]), tree-based methods (e.g., [5]), or hybrid frameworks (e.g., [7,37]). To the best of our knowledge, the number of contributions related to RL in stowage planning is limited, which addressed single-port problems without key combinatorial aspects by deep Q-learning [33] and Monte Carlo tree search [38]. Despite this variety, we are yet to find scalable algorithms that solve representative stowage planning problems.

DRL has been rather successful for various combinatorial optimization problems (e.g., 0–1 knapsack [22], capacitated vehicle routing [14,17,22], and job shop scheduling [17]). Similar to stowage planning with the master bay subproblem, chip design is accelerated significantly by optimizing the chip floorplanning subproblem with DRL [24]. Furthermore, actor-critic methods can mitigate known drawbacks of learning from experience and policy gradients by combining both techniques [34]. In general, actor-critic methods are relatively sample-efficient with reliable performance, from which PPO performs best in several continuous control problems [32]. Thus, we believe that PPO merits further investigation.

4 Problem Formulation of Master Bay Planning Problem

Given the previous sections, we can introduce the MBPP. During a voyage, the MBPP assigns groups of containers on port loadlists to vessel locations. By doing so, we effectively abstract away individual containers and slots.

The unidirectional voyage is represented by an ordered set $P = \{1, 2, ...\}$ of port calls, of which a set of all possible transport pairs $T = \{\tau = (i, j) \in P^2 \mid i < j\}$ is constructed to specify the POL and POD of cargo. At the departure from an arbitrary port p, the onboard cargo can be characterized by the set $T^{OB}(p) = \{(i, j) \in P^2 \mid i \leq p, j > p\}$. At the next port, this onboard cargo is either discharged or remains on board (*ROB*) as defined by set $T^{ROB}(p) = \{(i, j) \in P^2 \mid i < p, j > p\}$. Each group of containers has the same POL and POD $(i, j) \in T$ as well as class $k \in K$ that defines the dimensions, weight, and type of the containers in the group. Each vessel location is defined by bay $b \in B$ and deck $d \in D = \{D^O, D^H\}$, where D^O represents on-deck locations and D^H represents below-deck locations in the hold.

The capacity expressed in TEU of a location in bay $b \in B$ and deck $d \in D$ is given by $c_{b,d}$. The weight in tons per container in a group with class $k \in K$ is given by w_k. Notice that our cargo is equal-sized and specials are not taken into account. The cargo demand in TEU from port i (POL) to port j (POD) of class k is given by $q_{\tau,k}$, where $\tau = (i, j)$. Different instances are generated by sampling $q_{\tau,k}$ from a Gaussian distribution for each class k and transport τ as shown in Eq. 1. The expected value μ is a single random instance of the Mixed instances by [4] and σ represents the standard deviation to introduce variability around μ. Hence, Gaussian equivalents of Mixed instances are generated.

$$q_{\tau,k} \sim Q_{\tau,k} = \mathcal{N}(\mu, \sigma) \; \forall \tau \in T, k \in K \tag{1}$$

The primary objective is to maximize vessel utilization by loading cargo that satisfies port demand, while the secondary goal is to minimize hatch overstowage and arises from efficiency best practices. To prevent safety hazards (e.g., capsizing or falling containers), vessels must have an even keel and sufficient transverse stability, measured by trim and metacentric height (GM). Which in turn are determined by longitudinal (LCG) and vertical centre of gravity (VCG) [18].

4.1 MIP Model of the MBPP

The following model of the MBPP is inspired by the MIP formulation of [28].

$$\max \sum_{p \in P} \left(\sum_{b \in B} \sum_{d \in D} \sum_{k \in K} \sum_{\tau \in T^{OB}(p)} f_1 x^{b,d}_{\tau,k} - \sum_{b \in B} f_2 y_{b,p} \right) \tag{2}$$

$$\text{s.t.} \sum_{b \in B} \sum_{d \in D} x^{b,d}_{\tau,k} \leq q_{\tau,k} \qquad \forall p \in P, \tau \in T^{OB}(p), k \in K \tag{3}$$

$$\sum_{k \in K} \sum_{\tau \in T^{OB}(p)} x^{b,d}_{\tau,k} \leq c_{b,d} \qquad \forall p \in P, b \in B, d \in D \tag{4}$$

$$\sum_{k \in K} \sum_{j \in P: j > p} x^{b,d}_{(p,j),k} \leq M z_{b,p} \qquad \forall p \in P, b \in B, d \in D^H \tag{5}$$

$$\sum_{k \in K} \sum_{i \in P: i < p} x^{b,d}_{(i,p),k} \leq M z_{b,p} \qquad \forall p \in P, b \in B, d \in D^H \tag{6}$$

$$\sum_{k \in K} \sum_{\tau \in T^{ROB}(p)} x^{b,d}_{\tau,k} - M(1 - z_{b,p}) \leq y_{b,p} \qquad \forall p \in P, b \in B, d \in D^O \tag{7}$$

$$LM(p) - TW(p) LCG^* \leq \upsilon \cdot TW(p) \qquad \forall p \in P \tag{8}$$

$$LM(p) - TW(p) LCG^* \leq -\upsilon \cdot TW(p) \qquad \forall p \in P \tag{9}$$

$$VM(p) - TW(p) VCG^* \leq \upsilon \cdot TW(p) \qquad \forall p \in P \tag{10}$$

$$VM(p) - TW(p) VCG^* \leq -\upsilon \cdot TW(p) \qquad \forall p \in P \tag{11}$$

$$TW(p) = \sum_{k \in K} w_k \sum_{\tau \in T^{OB}(p)} \sum_{d \in D} \sum_{b \in B} x^{b,d}_{\tau,k} \qquad \forall p \in P \tag{12}$$

$$LM(p) = \sum_{b \in B} LP_b \sum_{k \in K} w_k \sum_{\tau \in T^{OB}(p)} \sum_{d \in D} x^{b,d}_{\tau,k} \qquad \forall p \in P \tag{13}$$

$$VM(p) = \sum_{d \in D} VP_d \sum_{k \in K} w_k \sum_{\tau \in T^{OB}(p)} \sum_{b \in B} x^{b,d}_{\tau,k} \qquad \forall p \in P \tag{14}$$

The primary decision variable of our MIP model is $x^{b,d}_{(i,j),k} \in \mathbb{R}_{\geq 0}$, which is the number of TEU from port i to j of class k planned to be stowed in bay b and deck d. The secondary decision variable $y_{b,p} \in \mathbb{R}_{\geq 0}$ is the number of TEU that causes hatch overstowage in bay b at port p, while the last decision variable $z_{b,p} \in \{0, 1\}$ indicates whether the hatch is opened in bay b at port p. Equation 2 shows that the MIP aims to maximize vessel utilization and minimize hatch overstowage, where f_1 is the gain per loaded TEU and f_2 is the cost per hatch overstow in TEU. Equation 3 limits the total vessel utilization by demand $q_{\tau,k}$, while Eq. 4 limits the onboard cargo by the capacity volume $c_{b,d}$. Equation 5 and 6 connects stowed containers $x^{b,d}_{(i,j),k}$ to hatch moves $z_{b,p}$ using the big M notation, whereas Eq. 7 computes hatch restows based on whether the cargo is placed on the to-be-opened hatch. Let us define $LCG(p) = LM(p)/TW(p)$ and $VCG(p) = VM(p)/TW(p)$ at port p, and their optimal equivalents $LCG^* = \sum_b LP_b/|B|$ and $VCG^* = \sum_d VP_d/|D|$. Equations 8 and 9 limit the difference between the actual and optimal LCG with parameter υ. Similarly, Eqs. 10 and 11 limit the difference between the actual and optimal VCG with parameter υ. Note that Eqs. 8–11 are linear transformations of $|LCG(p) - LCG^*| < \upsilon$ and $|VCG(p) - VCG^*| < \upsilon$. Equations 12–14 define the total weight $TW(p)$, longitudinal moment $LM(p)$, and vertical moment $VM(p)$. Notice that LP_b and VP_d refer to the longitudinal and vertical position of locations respectively.

5 Preliminaries of Reinforcement Learning

RL is a set of algorithms inspired by neurological reward processes, where agents learn how to take sequential decisions in environments [34]. The idea might be inspired by trial-and-error learning, in which experiments indicated that animals tend to strengthen or weaken connections to situations based on positive or negative outcomes respectively [34]. Those environments are often modeled by MDPs. The agent's goal is to find an optimal policy π^* that maximizes discounted future rewards, thereby solving the MDP. Since RL is relatively unknown in stowage research, we will introduce some fundamentals and refer to additional citations.

We define an episodic MDP with tuple $(\mathcal{S}, \mathcal{A}, \mathcal{P}, \mathcal{R})$, where $\mathcal{S}$ is a set of states and $\mathcal{A}$ is a set of actions. The stochastic function $\mathcal{P}(s'|s,a)$ provides the likelihood of reaching state s' given state s and action a. If the probability function is deterministic as in our case, $\mathcal{T} : \mathcal{S} \times \mathcal{A} \rightarrow \mathcal{S}$ is used as a transition function. The reward function is defined as $\mathcal{R} : \mathcal{S} \times \mathcal{A} \rightarrow \mathbb{R}$. We also define our policy $\pi(a|s)$ as the probability that action a is executed in state s. In the deterministic case, we can define a policy function $\pi : \mathcal{S} \rightarrow \mathcal{A}$.

Let us assume a stochastic transition and policy function. An episode starts with the agent in the initial state s_0 and obtaining action a from policy $\pi(a|s)$. This is referred to as an on-policy agent. Subsequently, the environment obtains the next state s' from $\mathcal{P}(s'|s,a)$ but also reward r from reward function $\mathcal{R}(s,a)$, then the agent observes s' and r. This closed-loop interaction continues until a terminal state s^{term} is reached, which ends the episode and returns the sum of accumulated rewards. The next episode resets the agent to s_0 and continues until the total number of steps Ts is reached. The performance of a trajectory under π is defined as the expected return in Eq. 15, which is extended to Eqs. 16 and 17 as the expected returns dependent on state s_t (i.e., value function), and state-action pair (s_t, a_t) (i.e., Q-function) respectively. Note that $\gamma \in [0, 1)$ is a discount factor that enables asymptotic convergence.

$$J = \mathbb{E}_\pi \left[\sum_{t=0}^{Ts} \gamma^t r_t \right] \quad (15) \qquad V(s_t) = \mathbb{E}_\pi \left[\sum_{k=0}^{Ts-t} \gamma^k r_{t+k} | s = s_t \right] \quad (16)$$

$$Q(s_t, a_t) = \mathbb{E}_\pi \left[\sum_{k=0}^{Ts-t} \gamma^k r_{t+k} | s = s_t, a = a_t \right] \quad (17)$$

Solving MDPs is analogous to finding an optimal policy π^* that prescribes actions to maximize future discounted rewards, thereby causing J to converge. Several RL algorithms can be used to do so. For instance, dynamic programming (DP) consists of model-based methods using knowledge of $\mathcal{P}(s'|s, a)$ and $\mathcal{R}(s, a)$ to estimate solution $V(s)$ by planning ahead as shown in Eq. 18. Even though convergence to $\pi^*(a|s)$ is guaranteed, DP is intractable for large state and action spaces and assumes perfect information which is often unrealistic [34].

$$V(s) = \max_a \mathcal{R}(s, a) + \gamma \sum_{s'} \mathcal{P}(s'|s, a) V(s') \quad (18)$$

Instead, one could consider learning from experience using model-free methods, often suffering from bias. For example, Monte Carlo methods perform trial-and-error simulations, whereas temporal difference learning obtains approximate functions with bootstrapping [34]. Another way is through DRL, which approximates good solutions with parameterized functions in large state and action spaces (e.g., policy π_θ). The policy gradient theorem states that the derivative of the expected return is proportional to the terms in Eq. 19, where $\psi_\pi(s_t)$ is the on-policy probability of state s_t. Doing so, π_θ can be learned by updating θ with respect to expected return J [34]. Due to large policy updates, gradient-based methods can suffer from variance. Anybody unfamiliar with RL is suggested to read more on the topic in [34].

$$\nabla J(\theta) \propto \mathbb{E}_\pi \left[\sum_{s_t} \psi_\pi(s_t) \sum_{a_t} \ln \nabla \pi_\theta(a_t|s_t) Q_\pi(s_t, a_t) \right] \quad (19)$$

6 Solving MBPP with Reinforcement Learning

The state $s_t \in \mathcal{S}$ at time step t is defined with pair $s_t = (u(t), q)$ and is fully observable. It consists of the vessel utilization $u(t) \in \mathbb{R}^{|B| \times |D| \times |T| \times |K|}$ and a constant voyage demand quantity $q \in \mathbb{R}^{|T| \times |K|}$. As an example $u^{b,d}_{(i,j),k}(t) = 0.05$ means that 5% of the vessel capacity is cargo stowed in bay b at deck d with POL i, POD j and class k at step t. Similarly, $q_{(i,j),k} = 0.13$ means that there is a cargo demand of 13% of the vessel capacity with POL i, POD j and class k.

At port p, the agent takes an action $a_t \in \mathcal{A}$ for every $(i, j) \in T^{OB}(p) : i = p, j = j'$. Each action is a combination of port p and future port j' as shown in Fig. 2. The action is defined by a pair $a_t = (l(t), \tau_t)$, where $l(t) \in \mathbb{R}^{|B| \times |D| \times |K|}$ is the fraction of vessel capacity to load in bay b at deck d of class k on transport $\tau_t = (p, j')$. In Eq. 20, we define the transition function to step $t+1$ with an input of τ_t. If cargo remains on board, then $u_{\tau,k}^{b,d}(t)$ is unchanged. If cargo should be loaded (i.e., $\tau = \tau_t$), then the utilization will become $l_k^{b,d}(t)$. Otherwise, cargo that should not be on board will be set to zero.

$$u_{\tau,k}^{b,d}(t+1) = \begin{cases} u_{\tau,k}^{b,d}(t) & \text{if } \tau \in T^{OB}(p) \setminus \{\tau_t\} \\ l_k^{b,d}(t) & \text{if } \tau = \tau_t \\ 0 & \text{otherwise} \end{cases} \quad \forall b \in B, d \in D, \tau \in T, k \in K \tag{20}$$

Since agents struggle with sparsity [13], a constant reward signal is necessary for each action. Equation 21 defines the reward of satisfying demand with reward coefficient f_1 and input $\tau_t = (p, j')$ for current port p and future port j'. A penalty is incurred with coefficient f_3 if the agent ships more cargo than demanded. Note that $f_3 > f_1$ holds to enforce feasibility.

$$r_{\tau_t}^{DS} = \begin{cases} f_1 \sum_{b,d,k} \sum_{\tau \in T^{OB}(p)} u_{\tau,k}^{b,d}, & \text{if } \sum_{b,d} u_{\tau_t,k'}^{b,d} \leq q_{\tau_t,k'} \\ -f_3 \sum_{b,d,k} \sum_{\tau \in T^{OB}(p)} u_{\tau,k}^{b,d}, & \text{otherwise} \end{cases} \quad \forall k' \in K \tag{21}$$

In addition, the following terms are evaluated at $(p, j') \in T : j' = |P|$. Equations 22 and 23 enforce that the actual longitudinal or vertical centre of gravity (i.e., LCG_t or VCG_t) can at most deviate v from the optimal longitudinal or vertical centre of gravity (i.e., LCG^* or VCG^*) with infeasibility penalty. Given the definitions of Eqs. 12 until 14, let us substitute $x_{\tau,k}^{b,d}$ by $u_{\tau,k}^{b,d}$ and define $LCG_t = \frac{LM(p)}{TW(p)}$ and $VCG_t = \frac{VM(p)}{TW(p)}$. Equation 24 incurs an infeasibility penalty for violating capacity. While hatch overstowage is evaluated in Eq. 25, where we penalize hatch restows with coefficient f_2. The cost of restowing a container is lower than its revenue, and thus $f_1 > f_2$ holds.

$$r_{(p,j')}^{LS} = \begin{cases} -f_3|LCG_t - LCG^*|, & \text{if } j' = |P| \wedge |LCG_t - LCG^*| > v \\ 0, & \text{otherwise} \end{cases} \tag{22}$$

$$r_{(p,j')}^{VS} = \begin{cases} -f_3|VCG_t - VCG^*|, & \text{if } j' = |P| \wedge |VCG_t - VCG^*| > v \\ 0, & \text{otherwise} \end{cases} \tag{23}$$

$$r_{(p,j')}^{CS} = \begin{cases} -f_3 \sum\limits_{b,d,k} \sum\limits_{\tau \in T^{OB}(p)} u_{\tau,k}^{b,d}, & \text{if } j' = |P| \wedge \exists b' \in B, d' \in D. \\ & \quad \sum\limits_{k} \sum\limits_{\tau \in T^{OB}(p)} u_{\tau,k}^{b',d'} > c_{b',d'} \\ 0, & \text{otherwise} \end{cases} \tag{24}$$

$$r^{HO}_{(p,j')} = \begin{cases} -f_2 \sum_{b,k,d \in D^O} \sum_{\tau \in T^{ROB}(p)} u^{b,d}_{\tau,k}, & \text{if } j' = |P| \land \exists b' \in B, d' \in D^H. \\ & \sum_{k} \sum_{i \in P: i < p} u^{b',d'}_{i,p,k} > 0 \\ -f_2 \sum_{b,k,d \in D^O} \sum_{\tau \in T^{ROB}(p)} u^{b,d}_{\tau,k}, & \text{if } j' = |P| \land \exists b' \in B, d' \in D^H. \\ & \sum_{k} \sum_{j \in P: j > p} u^{b',d'}_{p,j,k} > 0 \\ 0, & \text{otherwise} \end{cases} \quad (25)$$

Equation 26 defines a reward function $\mathcal{R}(s_t, a_t)$ for each step t, where the above-mentioned terms are summed. However, a final term penalizes unsatisfied demand by including the upper bound of $r^{DS}_{\tau_t}$ with parameter f_1. Hence, we maximize a reward function with an upper bound of 0.

$$r(s_t, a_t) = r^{DS}_{\tau_t} + r^{LS}_{\tau_t} + r^{VS}_{\tau_t} + r^{CS}_{\tau_t} + r^{HO}_{\tau_t} - \sum_{k, \tau \in T^{OB}(p)} f_1 q_{\tau,k} \quad (26)$$

Figure 2 illustrates an example with 4 ports of our episodic MDP. Each episode consists of $|T| = (|P|^2 - |P|)/2$ actions during a unidirectional voyage, corresponding to the number of above-diagonal elements in a matrix P^2. An episode is initialized with an empty vessel in state s_0 (i.e., u_0 is set to 0), whereas a sample $q_{\tau,k}$ is drawn from the demand distribution $Q_{\tau,k}$. During the episode, the agent traverses all ports $p \in P$ and takes an action according to policy $\pi_\theta(a_t|s_t)$ for each $\tau_t = (p, j')$ with $j' \in P : j' > p$. Figure 2 differentiates between rewards for each transport pair r_{τ_t} and the last action of each port $r_{(p,|P|)}$. An episode is terminated at arbitrary step t that satisfies $\mod t/|T| = 0$ as all actions are performed. Finally, the episodic reward is provided as output.

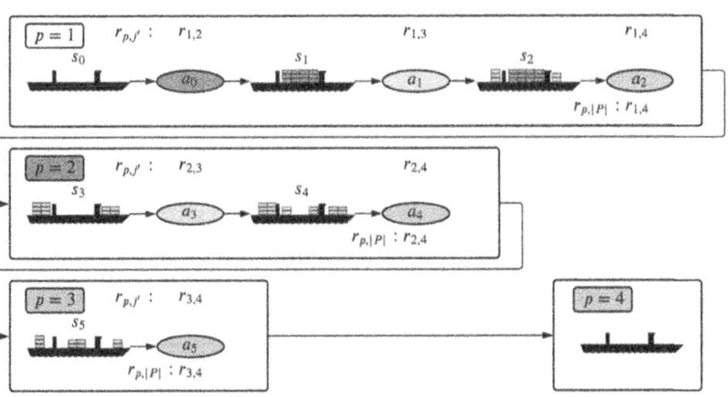

Fig. 2. Overview of master bay planning MDP with colours corresponding to PODs.

6.1 Proximal Policy Optimization Architecture

This on-policy architecture consists of an actor neural network with weights θ to create policy $\pi_\theta(a_t|s_t)$ and a critic neural network with weights ω to evaluate the performance of the policy by approximating the value function $V_\omega(s_t)$. The value function estimation $V_\omega(s_t)$ is used to express the relative advantage of taking an action. Equation 27 defines the general advantage estimate $\hat{A}_t$ of (s_t, a_t)-pair at step t, where λ is the exponential decay rate and δ_t is the temporal difference residual found by stepwise bootstrapping in Eq. 28. Both $\pi_\theta(a_t|s_t)$ and $V_\omega(s_t)$ are multilayer perceptrons that approximate non-linear functions by learning the mean and standard deviation of continuous Gaussian distributions.

$$\hat{A}_t = \sum_{l=0}^{H-(t+1)} (\gamma\lambda)^l \delta_{t+l} \quad (27) \qquad \delta_t = r(s_t, a_t) + \gamma V_\omega(s_{t+1}) - V_\omega(s_t) \quad (28)$$

Let us define the loss function with respect to ω as the mean squared error between the estimated value function and the sum of discounted rewards in Eq. 29. Given the estimated advantage $\hat{A}_t$, Eq. 30 defines a clipped loss function with respect to θ, where $p_t(\theta) = \frac{\pi_\theta(a_t|s_t)}{\pi_{\theta_{old}}(a_t|s_t)}$ is the importance sampling ratio between the current and previous policy distribution. The clipping limit ϵ prevents disruptive changes to θ. In Eq. 31, both functions are combined with entropy regularization, where cf_1 and cf_2 are coefficients and $S[\pi_\theta](s_t)$ is the entropy term that promotes exploration based on π_θ and s_t. Hence, Eq. 31 is maximized to update θ and thereby policy π_θ.

$$L^{VF}(\omega) = \hat{\mathbb{E}}_t \left[V_\omega(s_t) - \sum_{i=0}^{t} \gamma^t r(s_t, a_t) \right]^2 \quad (29)$$

$$L^{CLIP}(\theta) = \hat{\mathbb{E}}_t \left[\min(p_t(\theta)\hat{A}_t, \text{clip}(p_t(\theta), 1-\epsilon, 1+\epsilon)\hat{A}_t) \right] \quad (30)$$

$$L^{CLIP+VF}(\theta) = \hat{\mathbb{E}}_t \left[L^{CLIP}(\theta) - cf_1 L^{VF}(\omega) + cf_2 S[\pi_\theta](s_t) \right] \quad (31)$$

A description of PPO is shown in Algorithm 1. For each step t, let N parallel actors run policy $\pi_{\theta_{old}}$ based on parameter θ_{old} for a time horizon of H timesteps. The estimated advantage $\hat{A}_t$ is computed for every step $t \in \{1, ..., H\}$. Using a minibatch of M steps, we optimize the actor and critic loss w.r.t. θ and ω using the Adam solver [20] for E epochs. If θ and ω are trained for a sufficient number of steps, then we can obtain an actor with $\pi_\theta \approx \pi^*$ and a critic with $V_\omega \approx V^*$.

Algorithm 1: Proximal Policy Optimization

```
Initialize ω = ω_0, θ = θ_0;
for t = 1, 2, ..., Ts do
    for actor = 1, 2, ..., N do
        Run policy π_θold in environment for horizon with H timesteps;
        Compute general advantage estimates Â_1, ..., Â_H;
    Optimize L^VF(ω) w.r.t. ω with E epochs and minibatch M ≤ NH;
    Optimize L^CLIP+VF(θ) w.r.t. θ with E epochs and minibatch M ≤ NH;
    ω_old ← ω; θ_old ← θ;
return π_θ
```

6.2 Hyperparameter Tuning

There are many hyperparameters to be determined that impact the performance of PPO. We will, however, limit ourselves to the most impactful ones mentioned below. The time horizon with H steps is defined as the number of samples propagated through the network for each actor, while the number of epochs E is the number of passes through the experience buffer. The total buffer size amounts to NH and the minibatch size equals the buffer $M = NH$. The learning rate $\alpha \in (0, 1]$ defines the update size of network weights (i.e., θ, ω), which decreases over time to reduce the impact of updates. The actor and critic networks have the same number of hidden layers (depth) and neurons in each hidden layer (width). The layer activation function is ReLu to deal with vanishing gradients [15]. Both $\pi_\theta(a_t|s_t)$ and $V_\omega(s_t)$ are learned by their mean and log standard deviation that are initialized at 0 and init_log_std respectively.

We implement a tree-structured Parzen estimator using an optimization framework [1], which is a Bayesian method that can efficiently sample hyperparameters for various optimization use-cases [6]. The goal is to maximize the episodic return of trials in 10^6 steps based on samples. To improve efficiency, a median pruner stops trials if its best intermediate result is worse than the median of earlier trials at the same time step [1]. In total, we run 100 trials with different hyperparameters, of which 95 trials use the pruner.

The trials are run with the following MBPP parameters: ports $|P| = 4$, classes $|K| = 2$, bays $|B| = 4$, decks $|D| = 2$, location capacity in TEU $c_{b,d} = 50$, weight class $w_k = \{1, 2\}$, absolute centre of gravity tolerance $\upsilon = 0.05$, longitudinal position of bays $LP_b = \{0.25, 0.75, 1.25, 1.75\}$, vertical position of decks $VP_d = \{0.5, 1.5\}$, gain per loaded TEU $f_1 = 1$, cost per hatch overstowed TEU $f_2 = 1/3$, and penalty to violate constraints $f_3 = 3$. Given $N = 1$, the highest episodic return is obtained with $H = 512$, $E = 10$, $\alpha = 3\text{e}{-4}$, 3 hidden layers, 1024 neurons, and init_log_std $= 6.75$. Other hyperparameters are set as follows: $Ts = 4 \cdot 10^7$, $M = 512$, $\gamma = 0.99$, $\lambda = 0.95$, $cf_1 = 0.5$ and $cf_2 = 1\text{e}{-6}$.

7 Results

In Subsect. 6.2, the respective environment and PPO (hyper)parameters are defined. The usefulness of PPO is demonstrated by addressing a small-scale MBPP. Even though the MBPP is not representative of real-life stowage plans, it does capture fundamental combinatorial aspects to form a non-trivial problem. The results analyze whether the policy learns to optimize the objective, but also whether the policy generalizes to new test instances. To evaluate test performance, we compare the objective value and runtime of PPO with a MIP solver on two sets of instances. The first set of 100 instances Gaus-MBPP contains Gaussian equivalents to the Mixed instances of [4]. The second set of 100 instances Unif-MBPP consists of uniform versions of the Mixed instances. Due to reward shaping, the MIP objective and the reward function are proportional but not equal, and therefore we transform the objective before comparison.

The experiments are run on a Windows machine with an NVIDIA RTX A2000 Laptop GPU with 12.0 GB memory, and an Intel Core i7-11800H processor with 8 cores and 32.0 GB memory, running at 2.3/4.6 GHz. The work is implemented in Python 3.9 supported by libraries such as Gym 0.21 to model the environment, PyTorch 1.11 and Stable Baselines 1.6.2 to implement PPO, Optuna 3.0.3 to tune hyperparameters, and CPLEX 22.1 to solve the MIP model.

In Fig. 3, several training metrics are included to analyze training. Subfigure 3(a) plots the episodic return against episodes to evaluate the training performance of PPO on Gaus-MBPP. In general, the training curve seems to converge towards an increasingly stable return around 70,000 episodes. Due to the stochasticity of Gaus-MBPP, performance will vary over time. In early training, PPO learns to avoid large negative rewards associated with infeasible solutions, after which the episodic return follows an upward trend without converging definitely. In addition, Subfigure 3(b) shows the loss function optimized by the actor, which has yet to converge but starts to reduce in volatility. To evaluate the difference between distributions, one can use the approximate KL divergence [13]. Subfigure 3(c) shows that the approximate KL divergence between $\pi_\theta(a_t|s_t)$ and $\pi_{\theta old}(a_t|s_t)$ is stabilizing. Similarly, Subfigure 3(d) shows that the change to $p_t(\theta)$ is lower than the clipping range ϵ, indicating small actor changes. In Subfigure 3(e), we observe that log_std starts to converge, meaning that the variability of $\pi_\theta(a_t|s_t)$ reduces. Thus, we have found an increasingly stable policy with one actor on a limited training budget, suggesting there is room for improvement. Nonetheless, we have found a policy that optimizes the objective function.

In Table 1, we evaluate the performance of PPO and MIP on Gaus-MBPP and Unif-MBPP. Since the instance size is relatively small, the benchmark MIP will solve all instances. In comparison, PPO finds 98 feasible solutions with an average gap of 12.5% on Gaus-MBPP with low levels of variability. Even though the results are not near-optimal, a larger training budget is likely to improve performance as our policy approaches the global optimum [24,25]. Moreover, if MIP solvers become intractable for large-scale problems, the significantly shorter runtime of PPO will be advantageous. Hence, we find that PPO generalizes its policy to the Gaus-MBPP instances with reasonable performance.

Furthermore, the policy struggles to generalize to the Unif-MBPP instances, which is not the case for the MIP. Even if feasible solutions are found, then the average optimality gap is 81.3% with large variability in the objective value. Our function approximator struggles to accurately predict uniform instances with a different ratio than Gaus-MBPP. DRL methods generally learn to adapt to the underlying distribution, and thus it is likely that sampling outside of this distribution leads to performance loss. Though this is a clear drawback of PPO, it is our understanding that demand often follows predictable patterns. Therefore, it is important to accurately model demand based on real data.

Although we have found encouraging results, we realize that DRL demands considerably more computational power than provided by our machine appropriate for MIP optimization. Usually, laptop GPUs have fewer cores, less VRAM, and slower clock speeds than their desktop counterparts. This causes long train-

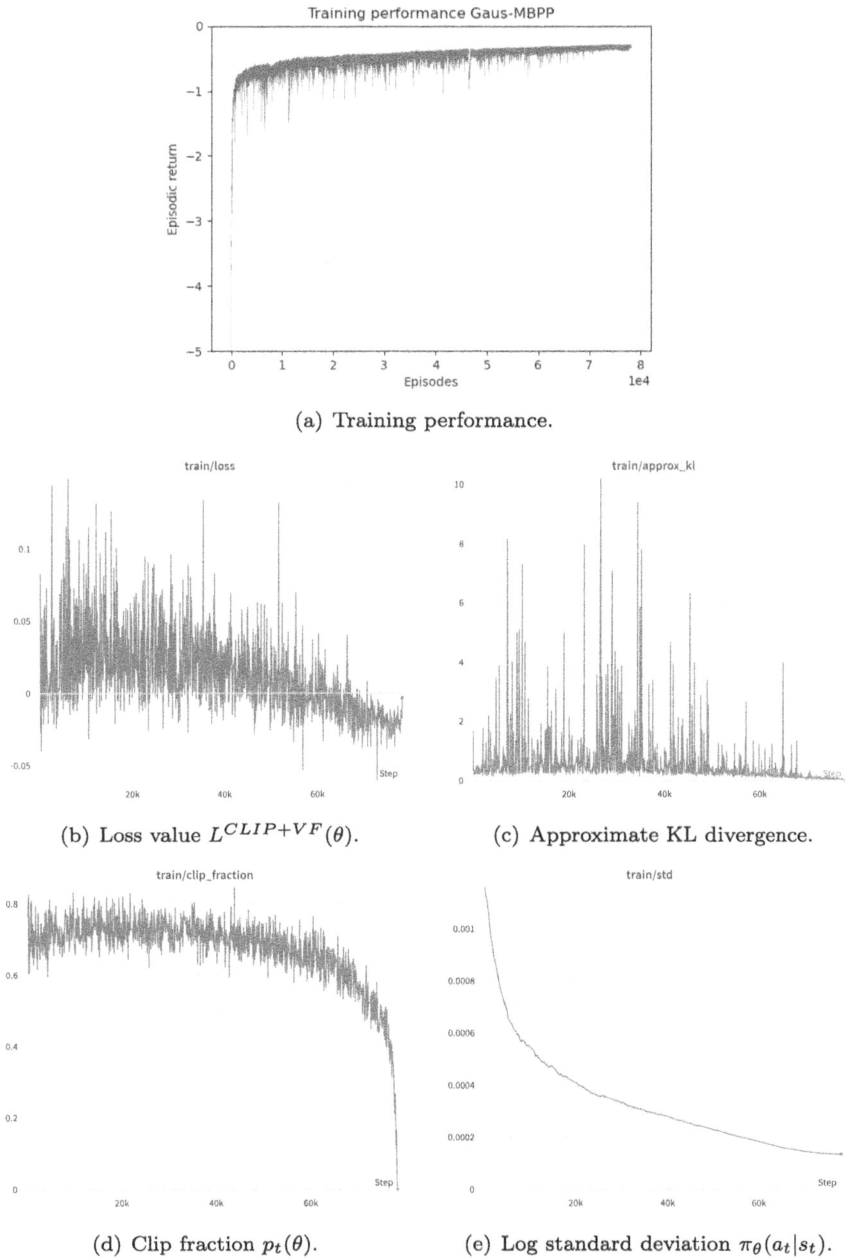

(a) Training performance.

(b) Loss value $L^{CLIP+VF}(\theta)$.

(c) Approximate KL divergence.

(d) Clip fraction $p_t(\theta)$.

(e) Log standard deviation $\pi_\theta(a_t|s_t)$.

Fig. 3. Training metrics on Gaus-MBPP instances.

Table 1. Evaluation of PPO and MIP on two sets of 100 test instances generated from Gaus-MBPP and Unif-MBPP. Results are expressed in the mean average and standard deviation metrics for the objective value (Obj.) and runtime in seconds (Time). The number of feasible solutions (#) is given without std. This also holds for the optimality gap (Gap) that is computed relative to the optimal MIP objective.

Methods	Metric	Gaus-MBPP				Unif-MBPP			
		#	Obj.	Gap	Time	#	Obj.	Gap	Time
PPO	Mean	98	2.092	12.5%	0.013	13	0.444	81.3%	0.006
PPO	Std		0.135		0.002		0.359		0.000
MIP	Mean	100	2.366	0.0%	0.058	100	1.930	0.0%	0.035
MIP	Std		0.261		0.022		0.387		0.016

ing times, sub-optimal convergence, and reduced test performance. To train a DRL model efficiently, it is therefore recommended to use specialized hardware such as high-end GPUs, TPUs, or cloud-based computing resources. Since this is not easily accessible, we will invest in comparable hardware to a workstation with 4x NVIDIA RTX A6000 with 48 GB memory and a Threadripper Pro 3955 WX with 16 cores and 256 GB memory, running at 3.9/4.3 GHz.

In conclusion, PPO can learn a policy that optimizes the objective function during training on Gaus-MBPP instances. Afterward, this policy can be generalized to efficiently achieve reasonable performance on unseen Gaus-MBPP test instances. When confronted with the Unif-MBPP instances, PPO mostly obtains infeasible or weak solutions. Using this proof of concept, we argue in favor of using PPO to solve the MBPP.

8 Conclusion

This paper presents a DRL approach towards solving the MBPP in container vessel stowage planning. In particular, we introduce a MDP equivalent to a MIP model with NP-hard combinatorial aspects, as well as suggest PPO to solve the MDP. These preliminary experiments show that PPO learns to optimize the objective value during training on limited hardware, after which its policy can be generalized to efficiently find reasonable solutions for test instances. Hence, we have provided a proof of concept for applying PPO to the MBPP.

In future work, we will extend the environment to become a full-featured MBPP with a representative demand simulator. The algorithm will also be improved to increase performance and deal with more complex problems. Since voyages are inherently sequential, we could implement temporal dynamic policies using recurrent neural networks (e.g., long short-term memory networks). Considering the cellular shape of container vessels, we might also leverage graph representation learning in our architecture.

References

1. Akiba, T., Sano, S., Yanase, T., Ohta, T., Koyama, M.: Optuna: a next-generation hyperparameter optimization framework (2019). http://arxiv.org/abs/1907.10902
2. Ambrosino, D., Anghinolfi, D., Paolucci, M., Sciomachen, A.: An experimental comparison of different heuristics for the master bay plan problem. In: Festa, P. (ed.) SEA 2010. LNCS, vol. 6049, pp. 314–325. Springer, Heidelberg (2010). https://doi.org/10.1007/978-3-642-13193-6_27
3. Ambrosino, D., Sciomachen, A., Tanfani, E.: Stowing a containership: the master bay plan problem. Transp. Res. Part A **38**(2), 81–99 (2004). https://doi.org/10.1016/j.tra.2003.09.002, http://linkinghub.elsevier.com/retrieve/pii/S0965856403000892, http://www.sciencedirect.com/science/article/pii/S0965856403000892
4. Avriel, M., Penn, M., Shpirer, N., Witteboon, S.: Stowage planning for container ships to reduce the number of shifts. Ann. Oper. Res. **76**(1-4), 55–71 (1998). http://search.ebscohost.com/login.aspx?direct=true&db=bth&AN=18925445&site=ehost-live, http://link.springer.com/article/10.1023/A:1018956823693
5. Azevedo, A., Cassilda Maria, R., de Sena, G.J., Chaves, A.A., Neto, L.L.S., Moretti, A.C.: Solving the 3D container ship loading planning problem by representation by rules and meta-heuristics. Int. J. Data Anal. Tech. Strategies **6**(3), 228–260 (2014). https://doi.org/10.1504/IJDATS.2014.063060
6. Bergstra, J., Bardenet, R., Bengio, Y., Kégl, B.: Algorithms for hyper-parameter optimization. In: NIPS 2011: Proceedings of the 24th International Conference on Neural Information Processing Systems, pp. 2546–2554 (2011). https://proceedings.neurips.cc/paper_files/paper/2011/file/86e8f7ab32cfd12577bc2619bc635690-Paper.pdf
7. Bilican, M.S., Evren, R., Karatas, M.: A mathematical model and two-stage heuristic for the container stowage planning problem with stability parameters. IEEE Access **8**, 113392–113413 (2020). https://doi.org/10.1109/ACCESS.2020.3003557
8. Botter, R., Brinati, M.: Stowage container planning: a model for getting an optimal solution. Comput. Appl. Autom. Shipyard Oper. Ship Design **VII**(C), 217–228 (1992)
9. Chao, S.L., Lin, P.H.: Minimizing overstowage in master bay plans of large container ships. Maritime Econ. Logist. **23**(1), 71–93 (2021). https://doi.org/10.1057/s41278-019-00126-6
10. Delgado, A., Jensen, R.M., Guilbert, N.: A placement heuristic for a commercial decision support system for container vessel stowage. In: 38th Latin America Conference on Informatics, CLEI 2012 - Conference Proceedings (2012). https://doi.org/10.1109/CLEI.2012.6427181
11. Ding, D., Chou, M.C.: Stowage planning for container ships: a heuristic algorithm to reduce the number of shifts. Eur. J. Oper. Res. (2015). https://doi.org/10.1016/j.ejor.2015.03.044, http://linkinghub.elsevier.com/retrieve/pii/S0377221715002660
12. Dubrovsky, O., Levitin, G., Penn, M.: A genetic algorithm with a compact solution encoding for the container ship stowage problem. J. Heuristics **8**(6), 585–599 (2002). https://doi.org/10.1023/A:1020373709350, http://link.springer.com/article/10.1023/A:1020373709350
13. Engstrom, L., et al.: Implementation matters in deep policy gradients: a case study on PPO and TRPO (2020). http://arxiv.org/abs/2005.12729
14. Foa, S., Coppola, C., Grani, G., Palagi, L.: Solving the vehicle routing problem with deep reinforcement learning (2022). http://arxiv.org/abs/2208.00202

15. Goodfellow, I., Bengio, Y., Courville, A.: Deep Learning. MIT Press (2016). http://www.deeplearningbook.org
16. Hamedi, M.: Containership load planning with crane operations. Ph.D. thesis, University of Maryland (2011)
17. Hottung, A., Kwon, Y.D., Tierney, K.: Efficient active search for combinatorial optimization problems. In: International Conference on Learning Representations 2022 (2021). http://arxiv.org/abs/2106.05126
18. Jensen, R.M., Pacino, D., Ajspur, M.L., Vesterdal, C.: Container vessel stowage planning. Weilbach (2018)
19. Kebedow, K.G., Oppen, J.: Including containers with dangerous goods in the slot planning problem. In: 2019 Proceedings of the International Conference on Industrial Engineering and Operations Management, pp. 225–232 (2019)
20. Kingma, D.P., Ba, J.: Adam: a method for stochastic optimization. In: 2015 International Conference on Learning Representations (2014). http://arxiv.org/abs/1412.6980
21. Korach, A., Brouer, B.D., Jensen, R.M.: Matheuristics for slot planning of container vessel bays. Eur. J. Oper. Res. **282**(3), 873–885 (2020). https://doi.org/10.1016/j.ejor.2019.09.042
22. Kwon, Y.D., Choo, J., Kim, B., Yoon, I., Gwon, Y., Min, S.: POMO: policy optimization with multiple optima for reinforcement learning (2020). https://doi.org/10.48550/ARXIV.2010.16011, https://arxiv.org/abs/2010.16011
23. Larsen, R., Pacino, D.: A heuristic and a benchmark for the stowage planning problem. Maritime Econ. Logist. **23**(1), 94–122 (2021). https://doi.org/10.1057/s41278-020-00172-5
24. Mirhoseini, A., et al.: A graph placement methodology for fast chip design. Nature **594**(7862), 207–212 (2021). https://doi.org/10.1038/s41586-021-03544-w
25. Mnih, V., et al.: Playing Atari with Deep Reinforcement Learning (2013)
26. Pacino, D.: An LNS approach for container stowage multi-port master planning. In: Computational Logistics, pp. 35–44 (2013). https://doi.org/10.1007/978-3-642-41019-2_3, http://link.springer.com/10.1007/978-3-642-41019-2_3
27. Pacino, D.: Crane intensity and block stowage strategies in stowage planning. In: Cerulli, R., Raiconi, A., Voß, S. (eds.) ICCL 2018. LNCS, vol. 11184, pp. 191–206. Springer, Cham (2018). https://doi.org/10.1007/978-3-030-00898-7_12
28. Pacino, D., Delgado, A., Jensen, R.M., Bebbington, T.: Fast generation of near-optimal plans for eco-efficient stowage of large container vessels. In: Böse, J.W., Hu, H., Jahn, C., Shi, X., Stahlbock, R., Voß, S. (eds.) ICCL 2011. LNCS, vol. 6971, pp. 286–301. Springer, Heidelberg (2011). https://doi.org/10.1007/978-3-642-24264-9_22
29. Pacino, D., Jensen, R.M.: A 3-phase randomized constraint based local search algorithm for stowing under deck locations of container vessel bays (2010). https://en.itu.dk/-/media/EN/Research/About-ITU-Research/Technical-Reports/2010/ITU-TR-2010-123-pdf
30. Parreño-Torres, C., Çalık, H., Alvarez-Valdes, R., Ruiz, R.: Solving the generalized multi-port container stowage planning problem by a matheuristic algorithm. Comput. Oper. Res. **133**, 105383 (2021). https://doi.org/10.1016/j.cor.2021.105383
31. Roberti, R., Pacino, D.: A decomposition method for finding optimal container stowage plans. Transp. Sci. **52**(6), 1444–1462 (2018). https://doi.org/10.1287/trsc.2017.0795
32. Schulman, J., Wolski, F., Dhariwal, P., Radford, A., Klimov, O.: Proximal policy optimization algorithms (2017). http://arxiv.org/abs/1707.06347

33. Shen, Y., Zhao, N., Xia, M., Du, X.: A deep Q-learning network for ship stowage planning problem. Pol. Maritime Res. **24**(S3), 102–109 (2017). https://doi.org/10.1515/pomr-2017-0111
34. Sutton, R.S., Barto, A.G.: Reinforcement Learning: An Introduction. MIT Press, Cambridge (2018)
35. Tierney, K., Pacino, D., Jensen, R.M.: On the complexity of container stowage planning problems. Discrete Appl. Math. **169**, 225–230 (2014). https://doi.org/10.1016/j.dam.2014.01.005, http://dx.doi.org/10.1016/j.dam.2014.01.005
36. van Twiller, J., Sivertsen, A., Pacino, D., Jensen, R.M.: Literature survey on the container stowage planning problem. Under review (2023)
37. Wilson, I.D., Roach, P.A.: Container stowage planning: a methodology for generating computerised solutions. J. Oper. Res. Soc. **51**(11), 1248–1255 (2000). https://doi.org/10.1057/palgrave.jors.2601022, https://www.tandfonline.com/doi/full/10.1057/palgrave.jors.2601022
38. Zhao, N., Guo, Y., Xiang, T., Xia, M., Shen, Y., Mi, C.: Container ship stowage based on Monte Carlo tree search. J. Coastal Res. **83**, 540–547 (2018). https://doi.org/10.2112/SI83-090.1
39. Zhu, H., Ji, M., Guo, W.: Integer linear programming models for the containership stowage problem. Math. Probl. Eng. **2020** (2020). https://doi.org/10.1155/2020/4382745

The Dynamic RORO Stowage Planning Problem

Alastair Ronald Main(✉), Filipe Rodrigues, and Dario Pacino

DTU Management, Technical University of Denmark,
Akademivej Building 358, 2800 Kgs. Lyngby, Denmark
{aroma,rodr,darpa}@dtu.dk
https://www.man.dtu.dk/

Abstract. Reducing emissions from the Roll-on/Roll-off (RORO) shipping industry has seen an increase in focus in the past years. Reducing the turnaround time in ports through stowage planning will increase slow-steaming use. Stowage planning assigns cargo to positions on board the vessel. This paper studies how the dynamic arrival of cargo affects stowage planning by considering revenue from shipping cargo vs. fuel costs incurred from time spent waiting and stowing cargo. A mixed-integer program formulation and a heuristic approach are presented to solve the problem. The computational study shows how the heuristic can find stowage plans for the dynamic arrival of cargo. A sensitivity analysis is conducted to investigate algorithm sensitivity in relation to revenue, fuel costs, and cargo handling time. The results indicate a high sensitivity in the number of units of cargo stowed when these parameters fluctuate.

Keywords: RORO shipping · Dynamic stowage planning · Heuristic

1 Introduction

The interest in reducing Green House Gas (GHG) emissions within the shipping sector has greatly increased over the past few years [17]. Governments and organizations are adopting new targets for reducing GHG emissions. The International Maritime Organization's (IMO) target is to reduce GHG emissions by 50% from shipping by 2050 compared to the GHG levels in 2008 [2]. The GHG emissions from shipping depend on various parameters, i.e., ship size, weight, hull shape, ballast water management, and sailing speed [17]. As the shipping industry is experiencing a general increase in demand, it is paramount to develop new strategies and technologies for the industry [2,6].

One of these shipping industries is Roll-on/Roll-off (RORO) shipping. RORO shipping focuses on the transportation of wheeled cargo such as semi-trailers, cars, buses, and farm equipment. RORO ships have the advantage of being able

This work is partly funded by the Innovation Fund Denmark (IFD) under File No. 0177-00022B.

© The Author(s), under exclusive license to Springer Nature Switzerland AG 2023
J. R. Daduna et al. (Eds.): ICCL 2023, LNCS 14239, pp. 122–138, 2023.
https://doi.org/10.1007/978-3-031-43612-3_7

to transport heterogeneous cargo with respect to weights, sizes, and shapes, allowing for more flexibility. RORO cargo is the fourth largest shipping type, only surpassed by liquid, dry bulk, and container shipping [11].

A known way to reduce GHG emissions of ships is through slow steaming. By reducing the sailing speed, the consumption of fuel is significantly reduced. To increase the time available to sail between port calls, the turnaround time in ports needs to be reduced. This can be done by optimizing the stowage planning. Stowage planning is the process of assigning cargo to specific locations on board the vessel. When assigning cargo on board the vessel, several constraints must be considered. The allocation must ensure vessel stability. Hazardous and refrigerated cargo requires special attention due to the need for electrical connections or safety distances [7,14]. Other cargo can have size and weight limitations. Since RORO vessels handle cargo approximately as a Fist-In-Last-Out (FILO) queue, great care must be taken when assigning cargo. Cargo for later ports can end up in front of cargo with an earlier discharge port. Such situations can result in unnecessary cargo moves, called "*shifts*", and increase the turnaround time for vessels at the port [4].

Prior research assumes that all the cargo is available for stowage when the ship arrives at the port. In real life, the dynamic arrival time of cargo creates a trade-off between waiting for cargo to arrive, resulting in a revenue increase, and incurring an increase in costs due to an increase in fuel consumption resulting from the necessary speed increase, to reach the next port on time.

The contributions of this paper are twofold. First, we propose the extension of the RORO stowage planning problem with dynamic arrival times and emission considerations (modeled in the objective function weighted against revenue gains). Second, we propose a novel mixed-integer programming formulation for the problem and present a heuristic approach to solve it.

The remainder of this paper is structured as follows. Section 2 presents the prior research regarding stowage planning for RORO shipping. Section 3 presents a mathematical model formulation and performance. Section 4 presents the heuristic framework for optimizing the stowage plan. Section 5 presents a computational study analysis of the heuristic performance along with a sensitivity analysis of the heuristic. We conclude on the findings and present future work in Sect. 6.

2 Related Work

Initial research regarding the optimization of stowage plans for RORO shipping utilized a lane layout. The deck would be divided into a set of strips; whereafter the cargo would be stowed in a FILO queue. A mathematical model was developed to maximize revenue gained by stowing cargo in FILO lanes. The model would define the lanes' length, width, and height and simultaneously ensure ship stability [12]. The mathematical model could not solve large instances, so a heuristic approach was applied to large real-life instances. The authors also studied optimizing the routing and scheduling of RORO vessels [13].

A different approach was later proposed, where the lane layout was replaced by a grid, which allowed for sideways movement of cargo. A mathematical model was proposed to assign positions of cargo on board. Several objectives were utilized for finding good positioning, including grouping constraints of cargo to minimize shifting. The solutions structure was evaluated by calculating the shortest path for cargo to exit the vessel. The complexity of the model, however, would limit its use in real-life instances [5]. Later a shortest path heuristic for evaluating the stowage plan was presented [3].

Following the grid layout's introduction, research focused on increasing the performance of using MIP formulations for stowage planning and maximizing revenue. The discretization of the vessel layout was optimized to reduce the need for a very fine grid representation. Furthermore, refrigerated cargo and hazardous cargo were considered during the stowage process. The need for shifting of cargo was removed by computing the shortest path from a position to an exit and utilizing inequality constraints to force a non-shift policy. The mathematical model also includes ship stability; however, the model was shown to solve medium-sized problems well but not large instances [14].

An Adaptive Large Neighborhood Search was presented to minimize the number of cargo shifts. The study introduced a mathematical model to optimize cargo assignment on board and showed that it was incapable of solving large instances. This method showed that a ship could be stowed efficiently for each deck by minimizing the number of shifts. The model utilizes Dijkstra's algorithm to evaluate how many shifts are generated by a given stowage plan [4].

The grid layout increases the computational complexity. A third approach to the deck layout is to use slots. The slots represent specific positions on the deck, and cargo can be assigned to these positions. To reduce the GHG emission by shipping cargo, the assignment of cargo could be used to minimize the amount of ballast water needed to stabilize the ship, thus reducing dead weight [8] and thereby fuel consumption. The authors also conducted studies to estimate cargo discharge times [9] and optimize the discharging process by dual cycling [10].

Drawing on the prior research within RORO stowage planning, the study of this paper focused on the interconnection between maximizing revenue and GHG emissions. A grid representation was utilized to describe the shifting and cargo movement better. Ballast tanks and stability constraints were not included. However, dynamic cargo arrival times were added to analyze the relationship between time spent stowing the vessel, fuel consumption, and revenue.

3 Mathematical Model Formulation

The following mathematical model is an extension of the work done by [3]. The original model has been modified to include the arrivals of each individual piece of cargo. Furthermore, the objective function has been modified to be a weighted function between fuel consumption and revenue. The weight α can be set to how important it is for shippers to reduce GHG emissions vs. transporting cargo. The function for fuel consumption is assumed to be non-linear with respect to sailing speed. The consumption of fuel has previously been described as cubic [15]. For the mathematical model, the function is linearized by discretizing it into W points, where $B(v)$ is the fuel consumption, v is the speed, v^* is the design speed, and $B(v^*)$ is the design consumption.

$$B(v) = \left(\frac{v}{v^*}\right)^3 B(v^*) \tag{1}$$

A predefined route for port calls is assumed to be available, resulting in a set of ports P. The ports are assumed to be separated into a loading region P^L and an unloading region P^U. Each piece of cargo can be picked up at its loading port P_c^L and unloaded at its unloading port P_c^U. In the original model, each piece of cargo $c \in C$ consisted of several vehicles of the same width, length, and weight. However, in the following model, each piece of cargo is assumed to have a single vehicle. This allows for a better description of the individual arrival times of each cargo. The inter-arrival times of the cargo were assumed to follow an exponential distribution.

The deck layout of the ship follows a grid representation of I rows and J columns resulting in (i, j) pairs of locations. Each piece of cargo is modeled as a rectangle. The positioning of a piece of cargo follows the cargo's lower left corner. Due to cargo width and height, a piece of cargo will span over several grid points. The grid layout contains restricted areas where, e.g., pillars, ramps, and walls are located.

If a piece of cargo is shifted, it is removed from the vessel and returned to its original position. The model guarantees that the ship makes it in time for the next port. The ship can, therefore, in order not to experience tardiness regulate sailing speed.

Table 1. Sets, Parameters, and Decision Variables for the mathematical model

Sets	
C	Set of cargoes
P	Set of ports
I	Set of rows
J	Set of columns
N	Set of squares where cargo can be placed $N \subseteq I \times J$
N_c	Set of squares where the lower left corner of cargo $c \in C$ can be placed, $N_c \subseteq N$
Q_{ijc}	The set of squares where placing cargo $c \in C$ would cover position (i, j)
D_{ijcd}	If cargo $d \in C$ is in position (i, j). The set contains all squares that would initiate a shift of cargo d if cargo $c \in C$ uses these squares

(*continued*)

Table 1. (*continued*)

Sets	
D^L_{ijcd}	Same as D_{ijcd}, however, specifically for when cargo is being loaded individually and sequentially
B_{ij}	Set of neighboring squares for position (i, j)
P^L	Set of loading ports, $P^L \subseteq P$
P^U	Set of unloading ports, $P^U \subseteq P$
P^L_c	Set of loading ports $p \in P^L$ for cargo $c \in C$
P^U_c	Set of unloading ports $p \in P^U$ for cargo $c \in C$
P^{LU}	Set of ports where shifting can occur $P^{LU} = P \backslash \{1, \lvert P \rvert\}$
P^{LU}_c	Set of ports where shifting can occur for cargo $c \in C, P^{LU} = P \backslash \{1, \lvert P \rvert\}$
C^R_p	Set of cargo to be loaded or unloaded at port $p \in P$
C^N_p	Set of cargo not to be loaded or unloaded at port $p \in P$
C^{RL}_p	Set of cargo to be loaded at port $p \in P$ including $p = 1$
W	Set of discrete points for nonlinear fuel consumption discretization
E^I, E^J	Set of exit squares for row and column pair (I, J).
Parameters	
α	Parameter for choosing the importance level between fuel consumption and revenue
M_{dp}	Big M
R_c	Number of vehicles in cargo $c \in C$
h_c	Handling time of cargo $c \in C$
A_{cp}	Arrival time of cargo $c \in C$ at port $p \in P$
T^{mean}_p	Average time to sail between ports $p, p+1 \in P$
T^{slow}_p	Time to sail between ports $p, p+1 \in P$ at the slowest vessel speed possible
T^{fast}_p	Time to sail between ports $p, p+1 \in P$ at the fastest vessel speed possible
C^{rev}	Revenue gain for transporting a piece of cargo
C^{fuel}	Fuel cost per ton
C^{con}_w	Coefficient of fuel consumption at discrete point $w \in W$
C^{time}_{pw}	Coefficient of time to sail at discrete point $w \in W$ at port $p \in P$

(*continued*)

Table 1. (*continued*)

Sets	
Decision Variables	
x_{ijc}	1 if the lower left corner of a vehicle from cargo $c \in C$ is placed in position (i, j), 0 otherwise
y_{cdp}	1 if cargo $c \in C$ is stowed before cargo $d \in C$ in port $p \in P^L$, 0 otherwise
δ_{ijcp}	1 if cargo c is shifted at position (i, j) in port p
d_{ijcp}	Supply or demand variable for cargo c at position (i, j) in port p. If $d_{ijcp} > 0$, then position (i, j) is a supply square. If $d_{ijcp} < 0$, it is a demand square. If $d_{ijcp} = 0$, it is a transit square
f_{ijklcp}	Flow of cargo c from position (i, j) to position (k, l) at port p.
B_p	Fuel consumption per time unit between port p and $p + 1$
ST_{cp}	Start time of loading of cargo $c \in C$ at port $p \in P_c^L$
TTS_p	Time to sail between port p and $p + 1$ ensuring $T_p^{fast} \leq TTS_p \leq T_p^{slow}$
λ_{wp}	Used to select the discrete point $w \in W$ of the nonlinear fuel consumption function between port p and $p + 1$
$Dept_p$	Departure time at port $p \in P$

The notation for the mathematical model is described in Table 1, and the formulation is as follows.

$$\min \quad \alpha \sum_{p \in P^{LU}} C^{fuel} B_p T_p^{mean} - (1 - \alpha) \sum_{c \in C} \sum_{(i,j) \in N_c} C^{rev} x_{ijc} \tag{2}$$

Subject to:

$$\sum_{(i,j) \in N_c} x_{ijc} \leq R_c \qquad \forall c \in C \tag{3}$$

$$\sum_{(i',j') \in Q_{ijc}} x_{i'j'c} \leq 1 \qquad \forall (i, j) \in N \tag{4}$$

$$\delta_{ijcp} \leq x_{ijc} \qquad \forall p \in P^{LU}, c \in C_p^N, (i, j) \in N_c \tag{5}$$

$$d_{E^I E^J cp} \leq R_c \qquad \forall c \in C, p \in P_c^L \tag{6}$$

$$d_{ijcp} = -x_{ijc} \qquad \forall c \in C, p \in P_c^L, (i, j) \in N_c \setminus \{E^I, E^J\} \tag{7}$$

$$d_{E^I E^J cp} \geq -R_c \qquad \forall c \in C, p \in P_c^U \tag{8}$$

$$d_{ijcp} = x_{ijc} \qquad \forall c \in C, p \in P_c^U, (i, j) \in N_c \setminus \{E^I, E^J\} \tag{9}$$

$$\sum_{(k,l) \in B_{ij}} f_{ijklcp} - \sum_{(k,l) \in B_{ij}} f_{klijcp} = d_{ijcp} \qquad \forall p \in P^{LU}, c \in C_p^R, (i, j) \in N_c \tag{10}$$

$$\sum_{c\in C_p^R}\sum_{(k',l')\in D_{klcd}}\sum_{(i,j)\in B_{k'j'}}(f_{ijk'l'cp}+f_{k'l'ijcp})\le M_{dp}(1-x_{kld}+\delta_{kldp}) \quad \forall p\in P^{LU}, d\in C_p^N, (k,l)\in N_d \tag{11}$$

$$ST_{cp}+h_c-(1-y_{cdp})M_{cdp}\le ST_{dp} \quad \forall p\in P^{LU}, c\in C_p^{RL}, d\in C_p^{RL}, c\neq d \tag{12}$$

$$y_{cdp}+y_{dcp}=1 \quad \forall p\in P^{LU}, c\in C^{RL}, d\in C^{RL}, c\neq d \tag{13}$$

$$ST_{cp}\ge A_{cp}-M_{cp}(1-x_{ijc}) \quad \forall c\in C, p\in P_c^L, (i,j)\in N_c \tag{14}$$

$$\sum_{(k'l')\in D_{klcd}^L}\sum_{(i,j)\in B_{k'j'}}(f_{ijk'l'cp}+f_{k'l'ijcp})\le M_{dp}(2-x_{kld}-y_{dcp}) \quad \forall p\in P^{LU}, c\in C_p^{RL}, d\in C_p^{RL}, (k,l)\in N_d, c\neq d \tag{15}$$

$$Dept_p\ge ST_{cp}+h_c \quad \forall c\in C, p\in P_c^L \tag{16}$$

$$B_p=\sum_{w\in W}C_w^{con}\lambda_{wp} \quad \forall p\in P^{LU} \tag{17}$$

$$TTS_p=\sum_{w\in W}C_{pw}^{time}\lambda_{wp} \quad \forall p\in P^{LU} \tag{18}$$

$$\sum_{w\in W}\lambda_{wp}=1 \quad \forall p\in P^{LU} \tag{19}$$

$$Dept_p=T_p^{slow}-TTS_p-\sum_{c\in C,(i,j)\in N_c}2\delta_{ijcp}h_c \quad \forall p\in P^{LU} \tag{20}$$

$$Dept_p\le T_p^{Fast} \quad \forall p\in P^{LU} \tag{21}$$

$$x_{ijc}\in\{0,1\} \quad \forall (i,j)\in N_c, c\in C \tag{22}$$

$$\delta_{ijcp}\in\{0,1\} \quad \forall p\in P^{LU}, (i,j)\in N_c, c\in C \tag{23}$$

$$d_{ijcp}\in\mathbb{R} \quad \forall p\in P_c^{LU}, c\in C, (i,j)\in N_c \tag{24}$$

$$d_{ijcp}\in[-1,1] \quad \forall p\in P_c^{LU}, c\in C, (i,j)\in N_c\backslash\{E^I,E^J\} \tag{25}$$

$$f_{ijklcp}\in\mathbb{R}^+ \quad \forall p\in P^{LU}, (i,j)\in N_c, (k,l)\in N_c, c\in C_p^R \tag{26}$$

$$ST_{cp}\in\mathbb{R}^+ \quad \forall p\in P_c^{LU}, c\in C \tag{27}$$

$$y_{cdp}\in\{0,1\} \quad \forall p\in P^{LU}, c\in C, d\in C \tag{28}$$

$$B_p, TTS_p, Dept_p\in\mathbb{R}^+ \quad \forall p\in P^{LU} \tag{29}$$

$$\lambda_{wp}\in\{0,1\} \quad \forall w\in W, p\in P^{LU} \tag{30}$$

The objective function (2) minimizes the weighted function between the cost of fuel consumption vs. the revenue from shipping cargo. Constraints (3) ensure that the cargo is stowed on board the vessel if chosen. Constraints (4) ensure that each square can only be covered by one piece of cargo. Constraints (5) ensure that cargo $c\in C$ may only be shifted from position $(i,j)\in I\times J$ in port $p\in P$ if it is indeed in position (i,j). Constraints (6) set the supply of cargo c equal to the vehicle numbers in c at the loading port. Constraints (7) set the demand for cargo in position (i, j), which is the chosen spot for cargo c. Constraints (8)–(9) state the demand and supply for cargo c in port p similar to (6)–(7). Constraints 10 ensure that the outflow minus the inflow must be equal to the demand/supply in the position (i, j) for each cargo c in port p. Constraint (11) ensure that if a piece of cargo that is being loaded or unloaded in port p uses a position (k, l) from a stationary piece of cargo d, it would result in the shifting of cargo d. Constraints (12) ensure that the start time plus handling time for stowing cargo c in port p is less than the starting time of cargo d if we stow cargo c before cargo d. Constraints (13) ensure a sequence of stowing one piece of cargo c after another d in port p. Constraints (14) ensure that the start time for stowing cargo c in port p must be greater than or equal to the arrival time of cargo c if at all chosen to be stowed. Constraints (15) ensure that if position (i, j) is chosen for cargo c, all other pieces of cargo stowed after cannot cross the covered positions by cargo c. Constraints (16) ensure that the departure time must be greater than the starting time of cargo c plus the handling time of cargo c. Constraints (17) calculate the fuel consumption for a given λ_{wp} value chosen. Constraints (18) calculate the time to sail between port p and $p + 1$ given a λ_{wp}-value chosen. Constraints 19 ensure only one point on the discretized non-linear fuel consumption curve can be picked. Constraints (20) calculate the time to sail between ports p and $p + 1$. The departure time is given to be between the time it takes to sail at the fastest and slowest speed. The departure time is penalized if shifting of cargo occurs. Constraints (21) ensure that the ship leaves at the latest time possible. The remaining constraints (22)–(30) are for variable declarations.

4 A Heuristic Approach

To represent the deck layout without having an over-representation of the spaces taken up by cargo, a grid size of 150×400 is needed [4]. Since the MIP formulation is not able to solve the problem even for toy-size instances, we present a heuristic approach. The heavy computations required to evaluate a single solution indicate the need to use strongly guided solution methods that do not require many iterations. We propose a heuristic procedure where a pool of candidate solutions is iteratively improved by a truncated local search.

The pseudo-code for the heuristic is presented in Algorithm 1. The algorithm encodes the solution as a sequence of cargo loads. A deterministic procedure then decodes the sequence by assigning specific positions to the cargo. The initial solution is constructed by a sequence where cargo is sorted in descending order with regard to their leg length (line 1). The cargo positions are generated by the deterministic decoding `heuristic_placement` (described later). An initial pool of solutions is created in line 2. For the first iteration of the heuristic, the pool only contains a single solution; however, later, it will represent the set of current solutions. Out of all the solutions in the pool of current solutions, only the best β solutions are selected for further processing (line 4). The next step of the algorithm is to generate a new pool of solutions (lines 13–15). For each of the best solutions (*sols*), η truncated local search procedures are executed. Each of the found solutions is added to the new pool of current solutions.

Algorithm 1: Heuristic for DRSPP

Input: Problem instance $\pi \in \Pi$, Time limit τ^1, Time limit τ^2, Number of nodes to expand β, Number of swaps κ, Layer limit ξ, Pertubation indicator ϵ, Number of expansions per node η

Output: Stowage plan $s \in S$ or $\emptyset$

$s \leftarrow$ heuristic_placement(init_sequence())
pool $\leftarrow \{s\}$
while *time limit* (τ^1) *is not reached* **do**
    sols $\leftarrow$ best_solutions(*pool*, β)
    if ξ *iterations or* τ^2 *seconds have passed* **then**
        Eval(*sols*)
        sols $\leftarrow$ best(*sols*)
        if *No improvement after* ϵ *iterations* **then**
            sols $\leftarrow$ double_bridge(*sols*)
        end
    end
    pool $\leftarrow \emptyset$
    for $r \in$ *sols* **do**
        pool $\leftarrow$ {LocalSearch(r, κ) $\forall\ i \in 1..\eta$}
    end
end
$s \leftarrow$best(Eval(*pool*))

The local search procedure performs κ swaps in the stowage sequence. From the heuristic placement, it is known which piece of cargo blocks most other cargo. The most blocking cargo is swapped to a new random position within the stowage sequence. Using the heuristic placement again, the new sequence is evaluated. If the solution is not better, the second worst piece of cargo is tried swapped. If the solution is better, a new, better stowage sequence has been discovered, and the most blocking cargoes have therefore changed. The local search continues until a total of κ swaps have been performed.

During the search, all solutions are evaluated using an approximation. Given a cargo stowage sequence, the placement heuristic assigns cargo to a specific position iteratively. For each piece of cargo, a set of available positions is calculated (starting from the top-right corner of the cargo). A position is not available if any of the grid positions, potentially occupied by the cargo, are already occupied. This is calculated for the entire leg the cargo will be on board. Figure 1 shows an example set of available positions in green. Notice how only positions in direct contact with the vessel structure or other placed cargo are available. Each available position is evaluated based on its potential impact on the objective function. Positions towards the bow and starboard are prioritized. Calculating shifting costs is computationally heavy; we approximate the evaluation considering cargo $c \in C$ blocking cargo $d \in C$ iff $P_d^L > P_c^L \vee P_d^U < P_c^U$ looking from cargo c towards the bow.

At each ξ iterations (or at intervals of τ^2 seconds), a full evaluation of the best solutions is performed. The full evaluation requires the calculation of all the shortest-paths between the cargo and the exit. This is done using an A* algorithm (line 6). Furthermore, should the best solutions not be improved after ϵ iterations, a double bridge move over the cargo sequence is performed as diversification (line 9). The search continues until a time limit τ^1 is reached (line 3). After termination, the best solution is returned (line 17).

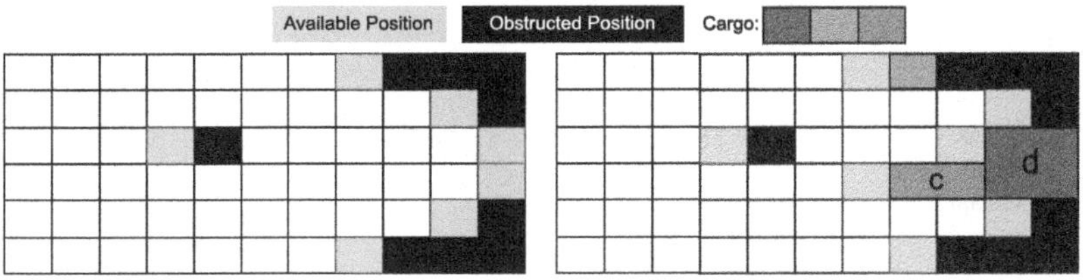

Fig. 1. Creation of available positions for the heuristic placement procedure

5 Computational Study

The instances were available online [4] and were changed to fit the new problem formulation in relation to cargo only containing a single vehicle and adding arrival times of cargo. The inter-arrival times of the cargo were assumed to follow an exponential distribution with $\mu = 60$, and it was assumed that 20% of cargo was available to stow immediately. The distances between ports were generated by selecting routes between ports within the European RORO market. The fuel costs were estimated through available bunker prices [16]. The revenue generated for a piece of cargo was selected by analyzing pricing for spot cargo in the RORO market. Due to a lack of better data, fuel consumption was estimated based on the smallest vessel from LinerLib [1]. The grid resolutions used range from 75×200 to 150×400 and are described as large instances. The number of port calls ranges from 6–10, and the number of cargo units is app. 200–300.

The study was conducted on an Intel® Xeon® Gold6226R processor. The mathematical model was solved for toy instances with a grid resolution of 10×10 up to 35×35. The number of cargoes was 77–193. The MIP was given 4 h to perform precomputation of needed sets and model generation and given 1 h to solve the problem. The problem was solved using Gurobi 9.1.0 and four processor cores. It was not possible to generate solutions for the instances within 1 h for grid resolutions as low as 10×10 and 77 pieces of cargo. The heuristic was tested on several large problem instances. For each of these problem instances, several different arrival patterns were generated. Furthermore, the algorithm was tested several times for each instance with different seeds to evaluate the algorithm's performance. The heuristic was implemented in Julia 1.6.1 and proved capable of generating stowage plans.

There are several parameters for the heuristic ($\eta = 2, \kappa = 5, \beta = 2, \xi = 15, \tau^2 = 20\,\mathrm{s}, \epsilon = 4$). These parameters were tuned manually to find a set that performed well for large instances. Initially, the algorithm was tested with baseline parameters to find the general behavior with respect to changes in α - values. The algorithm was given half an hour (τ^1) to optimize the stowage plan.

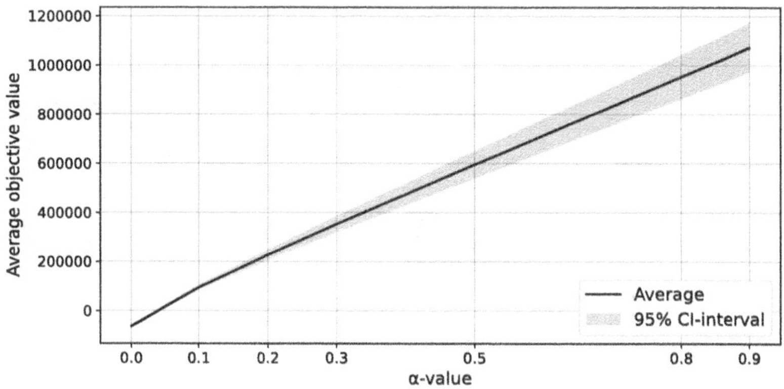

Fig. 2. The average objective function plotted for different α-values along with the 95% confidence interval.

The initial analysis showed that increasing the α-value will result in less cargo being stowed. This is intuitively supported by the nature of the objective function. Increasing the α-value will emphasize fuel consumption (and thereby GHG emissions) more than revenue. However, the variance increases as α goes to 1, as can be seen in Fig. 2. Instances generally differ regarding the number of port calls and the different port sequences. The timing becomes more pronounced as the cargo stowed does not dominate the objective function. If we look at the amount of cargo stowed in Fig. 3 and the number of shifts occurring in the stowage plan in Fig. 4, the number decreases with increasing α-values. This also holds true for the variance. However, this is expected as the variance must follow when less cargo is stowed.

We aimed to investigate how the heuristic behaved if the coefficients of the objective function changed. The objective function was affected by the cargo's revenue, the fuel cost, and indirectly by the handling time of the cargo. The handling time impacted the vessel's departure time and, thereby, fuel consumption. From the initial analysis, we can conclude that the algorithm is of most interest if $0.00 \leq \alpha \leq 0.30$. The most cargo was stowed in this interval, so a sensitivity analysis is conducted within this range.

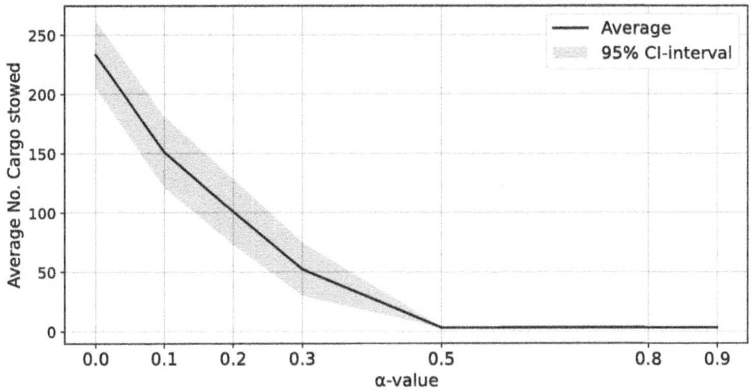

Fig. 3. The average number of stowed cargo plotted for different α-values along with the 95% confidence interval.

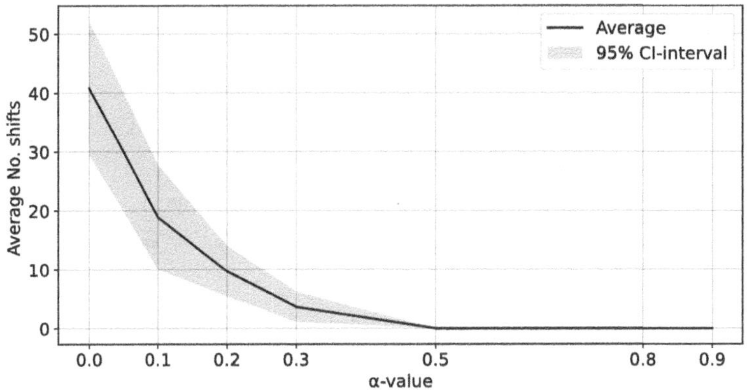

Fig. 4. The average number of shifts incurred in the stowage plan plotted for different α-values along with the 95% confidence interval.

An initial baseline was established for the sensitivity analysis. The problems were solved for a handling time of 2 min per cargo, a revenue of 270 euros per cargo, and a fuel consumption cost of 520 euros per ton. A baseline was generated for each α-value. For the baseline, the mean and standard deviation were calculated across the instances for how many units of cargo were stowed on board. The sensitivity analysis used the same setup as the one used for the computational study above. The first analysis was conducted where the handling time was kept fixed, whereafter the other parameters varied slightly. The percentage change in the number of cargo stowed changed significantly when revenue and fuel costs fluctuated, as shown in Fig. 5. For an α-value of 0.0, there is very little change in the amount of cargo stowed. However, as α increases, the variance becomes significantly more noticeable. Lowering the revenue results in a negative percentage change in the amount of cargo stowed, and an increase in fuel costs has the same effect.

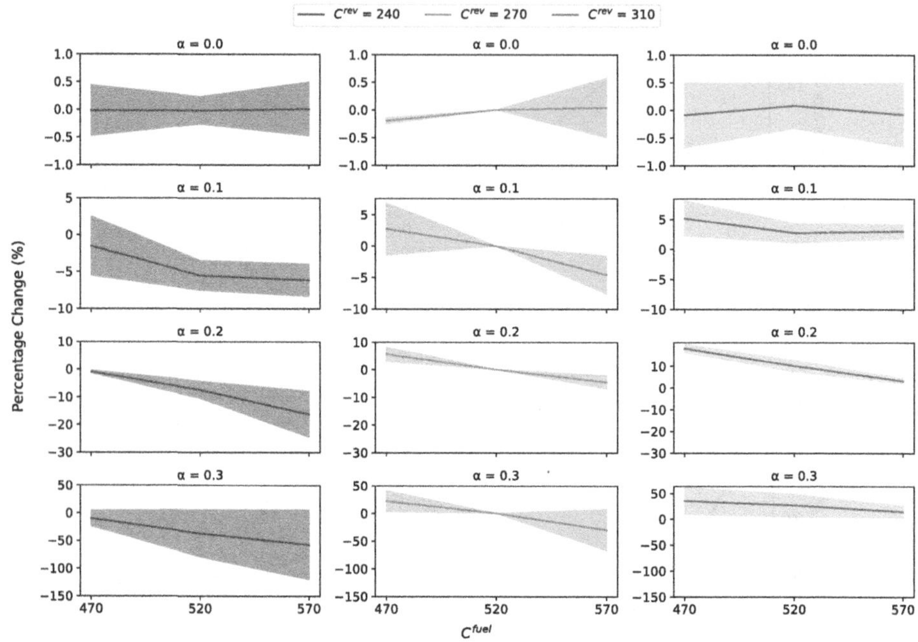

Fig. 5. The percentage change in the average number of cargoes stowed and the 95% confidence intervals for fixed handling time.

Fixing the fuel costs at the baseline level will allow the handling time to fluctuate. The heuristic was highly susceptible to increased handling time, as seen in Fig. 6. An increase in handling time of a single minute resulted in a significant drop in stowed cargo irrespective of the α-value compared to the baseline. The susceptibility of the algorithm is most likely connected to the stowage sequence and the number of cargoes stowed. If the stowage list is badly ordered in relation to cargo arrival, a lot of time will be spent waiting for cargo. This is only exacerbated by potential cargo shifts. The time penalty for each shift is double the handling time. This results in the algorithm being penalized heavily in relation to fuel consumption incurred. This also holds true for an α-value of 0.0. No direct cost is incurred at this alpha value; however, shifts result in time being spent not stowing cargo. Thereby less cargo could end up being stowed as the ship is forced to leave port.

Increasing fuel costs and handling time resulted in a significant decrease in the amount of cargo stowed. The algorithm was very sensitive to the handling time. In contrast, when fluctuating, the fuel costs changed very little, as can be seen in Fig. 7. The algorithm displayed a high sensitivity to an increase in α-values. Furthermore, when allowing handling time to fluctuate, the amount of cargo stowed decreases with respect to the baseline.

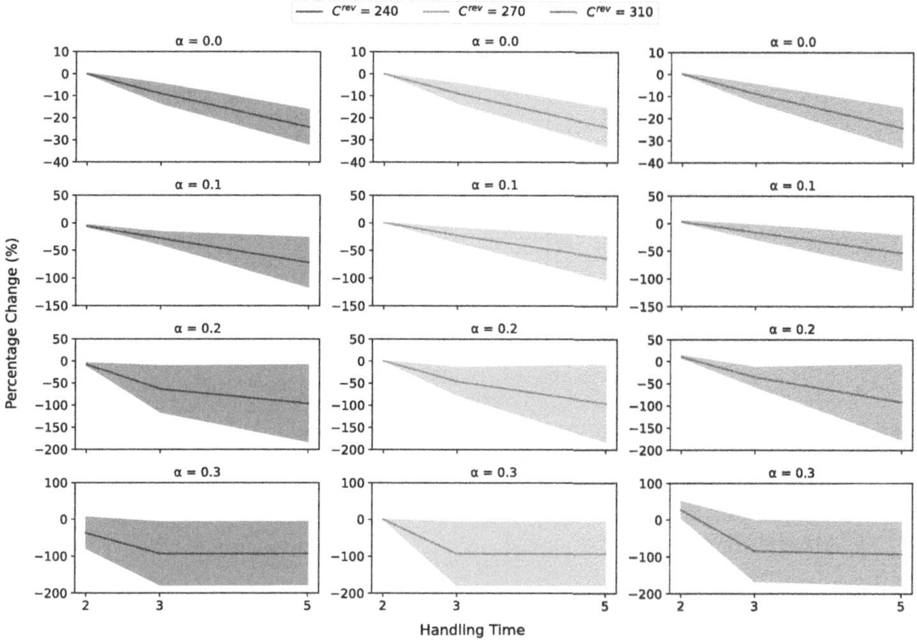

Fig. 6. The percentage change in the average number of cargoes stowed and the 95% confidence intervals for fixed fuel costs.

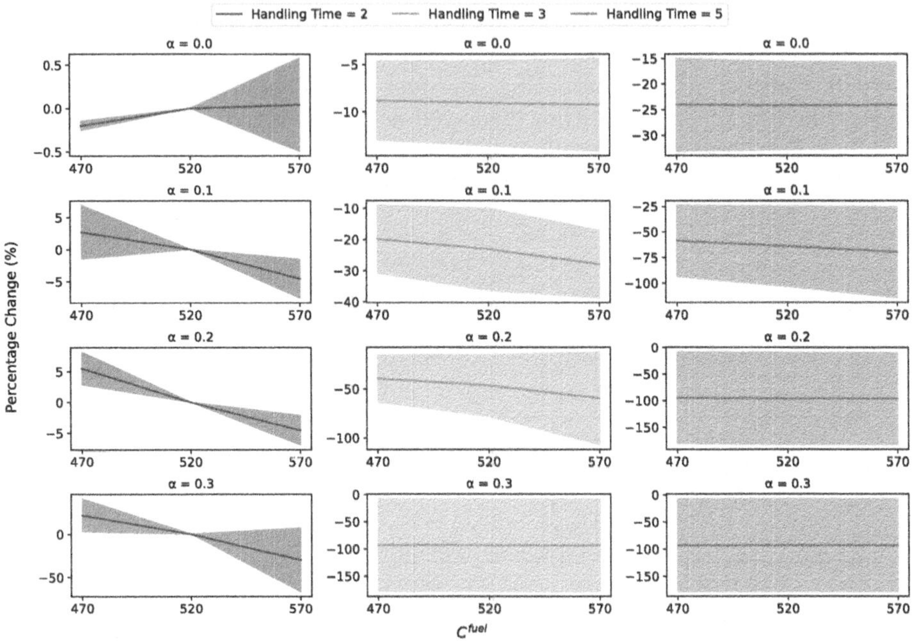

Fig. 7. The percentage change in the average number of cargoes stowed and the 95% confidence intervals for fixed revenue.

6 Conclusion

This study of the dynamic RORO stowage planning problem focused on cargo arriving at the port over time. The cargo had to be assigned a position on board the vessel. Sailing between ports, the stowage plan should consider the fuel consumption incurred from waiting for arriving cargo, and the vessel could leave early to reduce costs. Furthermore, the number of cargo re-handling could be minimized to reduce time spent stowing the ship. A MIP formulation was presented; however, it could not solve even toy-sized instances of the problem, so a heuristic was applied instead. The heuristic proved effective in generating feasible stowage plans. The heuristic showed a clear sensitivity to changes in coefficients for revenue and fuel consumption costs. However, the algorithm was highly sensitive to the handling time of each piece of cargo on board the vessel. Given how sensitive the solutions are to changes in the parameters, it might be advisable to study different cost structures and to perform a deeper analysis of alternative objectives as seen in [18]. Furthermore, an investigation into a different problem representation could prove advantageous in relation to the algorithm's performance.

References

1. Brouer, B.D., Alvarez, J.F., Plum, C.E.M., Pisinger, D., Sigurd, M.M.: A base integer programming model and benchmark suite for liner-shipping network design. Transp. Sci. **48**(2), 281–312 (2014). https://doi.org/10.1287/trsc.2013.0471
2. Faber, J., et al.: Fourth IMO GHG study 2020. Technical report, International Maritime Organization, London (2021)
3. Hansen, J.R., Fagerholt, K., Stålhane, M.: A shortest path heuristic for evaluating the quality of stowage plans in roll-on roll-off liner shipping. In: Bektaş, T., Coniglio, S., Martinez-Sykora, A., Voß, S. (eds.) ICCL 2017. LNCS, vol. 10572, pp. 351–365. Springer, Cham (2017). https://doi.org/10.1007/978-3-319-68496-3_24
4. Hansen, J.R., Fagerholt, K., Stålhane, M., Rakke, J.G.: An adaptive large neighborhood search heuristic for the planar storage location assignment problem: application to stowage planning for Roll-on Roll-off ships. J. Heuristics **26**(6), 885–912 (2020). https://doi.org/10.1007/s10732-020-09451-z
5. Hansen, J.R., Hukkelberg, I., Fagerholt, K., Stålhane, M., Rakke, J.G.: 2D-packing with an application to stowage in roll-on roll-off liner shipping. In: Paias, A., Ruthmair, M., Voß, S. (eds.) ICCL 2016. LNCS, vol. 9855, pp. 35–49. Springer, Cham (2016). https://doi.org/10.1007/978-3-319-44896-1_3
6. IEA: International Shipping. Technical report, International Energy Agency, Paris (2022). https://www.iea.org/reports/international-shipping. Accessed 29 Apr 2023
7. Jia, B., Fagerholt, K.: Step-wise stowage planning of roll-on roll-off ships transporting dangerous goods. Maritime Transp. Res. **2**(June), 100029 (2021). https://doi.org/10.1016/j.martra.2021.100029
8. Jia, B., Fagerholt, K., Reinhardt, L.B., Rytter, N.G.M.: Stowage planning with optimal ballast water. In: Lalla-Ruiz, E., Mes, M., Voß, S. (eds.) ICCL 2020. LNCS, vol. 12433, pp. 84–100. Springer, Cham (2020). https://doi.org/10.1007/978-3-030-59747-4_6
9. Jia, B., Rytter, N.G.M., Reinhardt, L.B., Haulot, G., Billesø, M.B.: Estimating discharge time of cargo units – a case of Ro-Ro shipping. In: Paternina-Arboleda, C., Voß, S. (eds.) ICCL 2019. LNCS, vol. 11756, pp. 122–135. Springer, Cham (2019). https://doi.org/10.1007/978-3-030-31140-7_8
10. Jia, B., Tierney, K., Reinhardt, L.B., Pahl, J.: Optimal dual cycling operations in roll-on roll-off terminals. Transp. Res. Part E: Logist. Transp. Rev. **159**(February), 102646 (2022). https://doi.org/10.1016/j.tre.2022.102646
11. Mattfield, D.C.: The Management of Transshipment Terminals, 1st edn. Springer, New York (2006). https://doi.org/10.1007/0-387-30854-7
12. Øvstebø, B.O., Hvattum, L.M., Fagerholt, K.: Optimization of stowage plans for RoRo ships. Comput. Oper. Res. **38**(10), 1425–1434 (2011). https://doi.org/10.1016/j.cor.2011.01.004
13. Øvstebø, B.O., Hvattum, L.M., Fagerholt, K.: Routing and scheduling of RoRo ships with stowage constraints. Transp. Res. Part C: Emerg. Technol. **19**(6), 1225–1242 (2011). https://doi.org/10.1016/j.trc.2011.02.001
14. Puisa, R.: Optimal stowage on Ro-Ro decks for efficiency and safety. J. Marine Eng. Technol. **20**(1), 17–33 (2018). https://doi.org/10.1080/20464177.2018.1516942
15. Reinhardt, L.B., Plum, C.E., Pisinger, D., Sigurd, M.M., Vial, G.T.: The liner shipping berth scheduling problem with transit times. Transp. Res. Part E: Logist. Transp. Rev. **86**, 116–128 (2016). https://doi.org/10.1016/j.tre.2015.12.006
16. Ship & Bunker: EMEA Average (2023). https://shipandbunker.com/prices/av/global/av-g20-global-20-ports-average#VLSFO. Accessed 29 Apr 2023

17. UNCTAD: REVIEW OF MARITIME TRANSPORT 2020. Technical report, UNCTAD, New York, NY (2020)
18. Voß, S., Schwarze, S.: A note on alternative objectives for the blocks relocation problem. In: Paternina-Arboleda, C., Voß, S. (eds.) ICCL 2019. LNCS, vol. 11756, pp. 101–121. Springer, Cham (2019). https://doi.org/10.1007/978-3-030-31140-7_7

Allocation of Shore Side Electricity: The Case of the Port of Hamburg

Jingjing Yu[1,2(✉)], Philip Cammin[1], and Stefan Voß[1]

[1] Institute of Information Systems, University of Hamburg, Von-Melle-Park 5, 20146 Hamburg, Germany
{philip.cammin,stefan.voss}@uni-hamburg.de

[2] State Key Laboratory of Coastal and Offshore Engineering, Faculty of Infrastructure Engineering, Dalian University of Technology, Dalian 116024, Liaoning, China
jingjing.yu@uni-hamburg.de

Abstract. This study addresses the problem of allocating shore side electricity (SSE) supply points. We consider a group of terminals, for which the overall environmental benefit is to be maximized. To this end, an optimization model is developed that yields the optimal SSE supply point allocation plan. The proposed model solves the berth allocation problem with port call data. The novelty of this model lies in the distinction of terminals, respecting the individual target terminal per vessel. This supports the application on a group of terminals, even spanning multiple ports. Previous models only support such a use case by requiring further analysis on the results of per-terminal applications. We examine the results for various generated scenarios based on historical port call data of one month for a container terminal group in the Port of Hamburg, Germany. The results show that the best found allocation plan in this study, enabling 2.54 GWh of SSE consumption, is slightly better than the allocation plan published by the Port of Hamburg.

Keywords: Shore side electricity · container terminal · berth allocation

1 Introduction

Shore side electricity (SSE) has been given great attention to significantly reduce at-berth emissions from vessels. For instance, as of 2023, the Port of Los Angeles invested in 79 SSE supply points and requires all container, cruise, and reefer vessels to use SSE or an approved emission control technology during berthing (POLA, 2023). By 2021, the average coverage rate of SSE at 11 major coastal ports in China is about 71.5%, and vessels that have berthing durations longer than three hours are required to use SSE (CAA, 2022). The European Commission aims at reducing net greenhouse gas emissions by at least 55% by 2030 compared to 1990 levels; for instance, vessels larger than 5,000 gross tonnages berthing at European ports for more than two hours would be required to use

© The Author(s), under exclusive license to Springer Nature Switzerland AG 2023
J. R. Daduna et al. (Eds.): ICCL 2023, LNCS 14239, pp. 139–153, 2023.
https://doi.org/10.1007/978-3-031-43612-3_8

SSE as of January 2030 (see the "Fit for 55" package (EP, 2023)). In 2021, the ports of Rotterdam, Hamburg, Bremen, Antwerp, and Haropa agreed to a memorandum of understanding (MOU) to provide SSE to ultra-large container vessels, 2028 at the latest (POA, 2021).

More specifically, the Port of Hamburg contribution manifests in the provision of eight SSE supply points for container vessels (HPA, 2022). From an economic perspective, Williamsson et al. (2022) note that one of the obstacles to the adoption of SSE is the huge initial investment in SSE supply points. For example, the cost of constructing one SSE supply point at the Port of Hamburg is about nine million EUR (HPM, 2019). The correct allocation of SSE supply points to terminals is crucial to maximize the SSE consumption, and thus, to maximize the environmental benefit with a limited investment. Consequently, allocation plans should be scrutinized by using suitable methods; however, we deem the existing methods having some drawbacks. Our literature review outlines that most methods are lacking consideration of the temporal overlap of arriving vessels (neglecting the berth allocation problem (BAP)); this potentially reduces the accuracy concerning past assessment periods. Moreover, existing methods do not consider terminal-assigned port calls for a terminal group with the shared objective to maximize the overall environmental benefit; this requires separate applications of methods for each port or terminal, as well as further analysis to find the best allocation that maximizes the overall environmental benefit.

Consequently, this paper integrates the shared investment and shared goal by terminals to maximize the overall environmental benefit by maximizing the SSE consumption. Different scenarios are explored, which concern a variable number of SSE supply points and SSE-enabled vessels. The objective of this paper is (1) to optimize the allocation of SSE supply points among container terminals under different scenarios with respect to an uncertain future, and (2) to provide the environmental benefit of this allocation. The aim of this paper is to adapt the methodological support for SSE adoption to fit a grouped terminal setting and to investigate the current plan for the Port of Hamburg. Toward this aim, an optimization model and a solution approach using a genetic algorithm (GA) are implemented and the obtained allocations are discussed. To the best of our knowledge, this paper is the first to focus on the shared investment and shared goal of a terminal group. The case study concerns the three container terminals operated by the Hamburger Hafen und Logistik AG (HHLA) at the Port of Hamburg.

The remainder of this paper is structured as follows. Section 2 presents a review of relevant studies. Section 3 then describes the optimization model. In Sect. 4, the developed optimization model is applied in a case study followed by a presentation of the results and discussions. At last, conclusions are summarized in Sect. 5.

2 Literature Review

Table 1 summarizes the most recent literature concerning the adoption of SSE in maritime ports. The first research branch, assessment, primarily estimates the environmental benefit of using SSE for ports for a certain time horizon. Herein, we present the building blocks that are changed for different future scenarios. For instance, Lathwal et al. (2021) estimate the environmental benefits of using SSE with varying electricity generation structures, such as reducing the share of coal generation and increasing the share of renewable generation in 2030 compared to 2017. This leads to different emission factors. Most works in this branch assume all vessels to be SSE-enabled and SSE-served. Contrary, Dai et al. (2019) experiment with the number of SSE supply points for ten consecutive years. The authors calculate the SSE consumption by multiplying the increasing adoption rate of SSE with the total energy consumption of vessels during berthing. The adoption rate is a simple fraction between the total number of berths and the number of SSE supply points. Nguyen et al. (2021) feature two scenarios based on two shipping routes, each of which has a different number of SSE-enabled vessels. Gore et al. (2023) consider different numbers of SSE-enabled vessels based on their calling frequency and make assumptions on the subsequently required number of SSE supply points. In summary, the building blocks that are changed for different future scenarios comprise varying emission factors, the number of SSE-enabled vessels, the number of SSE supply points, as well as the annual energy demand at berths.

The second branch, optimization, in a nutshell, yields the number of SSE supply points to be installed to abate air emissions. Unlike the works in the assessment branch, only the emission factors are subject to change to build different scenarios. Peng et al. (2019, 2021) optimize which specific berths of one terminal should be equipped with SSE supply points to minimize the cost and minimize the CO_2 emissions, providing a trade-off analysis. Similarly, Vaishnav et al. (2016) maximize inter alia the economic benefits. In contrast to the assessment works, Peng et al. (2019, 2021) do not change the number of SSE-enabled vessels for scenarios. To address the question of which berths should be equipped with SSE supply points, it is useful to know which berths are actually used the most. Insights to more detailed operational data may be helpful, such as those data obtained by solving the berth allocation problem for vessels. Berths with the longest utilization rate, and occupied by large vessels with a higher energy demand are to be preferred. The work by Peng et al. (2021) solves the BAP. The authors assume all vessels to be SSE-enabled, arrival times to be based on a probability distribution, their berthing durations to be based on averaged historical vessel size, and the berth utilization to be based on the case study port. The use of averaged historical data is commonly observed in strategic-oriented works as can be seen in Table 1, and applies to both the optimization and assessment branches. The takeaway is that the works in the optimization branch do not consider a varying number of SSE-enabled vessels for different scenarios. This cannot reflect current or near-future scenarios. Taken together, the references foci are either concerned only with a single terminal or a group of ports. We deem it necessary to address the rate of SSE-enabled vessels, as well as a new scope of application, i.e., a group of terminals. We justify this grouping with the case of the Port of Hamburg where HHLA operates three terminals whose berths

Table 1. Summary of literature regarding the investment of SSE supply points in ports

Reference	Objective	Input data	Scenario development
Winkel et al. (2016)	Assess the economic and environmental benefit of SSE for each port	Seven typical European seaports' one-year throughput	○ Annual energy demand at berths estimated for 2010 and 2020 • All vessels are SSE-enabled and SSE-served
Dai et al. (2019)	Assess the reduced CO_2 emission and economic benefit of using SSE for one port	Number and size of vessels calling at the Port of Shanghai in one year	○ Accumulated annual adoption rate of SSE supply points from 2018 to 2028 • Berthing duration based on vessel size • All vessels are SSE-enabled
Lathwal et al. (2021)	Assess environmental and economic benefit of SSE for each port	21,937 port calls by 5,732 vessels at 12 ports in India	○ Emission factors based on changes in electricity generation structure in local grid estimated for 2017 and 2030 • All vessels are SSE-enabled and SSE-served
Martínez-López et al. (2021)	Assess environmental benefit of SSE for each port	Port calls during one year of two vessels with specified sizes and types in three selected European shipping routes	• Berthing duration at ports based on vessel size and type • All vessels are SSE-enabled and SSE-served
Nguyen et al. (2021)	Assess environmental benefit of SSE for each port	1,122 port calls during one year at two container terminals at the Port of Kaohsiung	○ Number of SSE-enabled vessels based on shipping routes, e.g., only local vessels or international vessels are SSE-enabled • All vessels are SSE-enabled and SSE-served
Spengler and Tovar (2021)	Assess environmental benefit of SSE for each port	Port calls during one year of vessels to all ports in Spain	• External costs of emissions based on local city population • All vessels are SSE-enabled and SSE-served
Stolz et al. (2021)	Assess environmental benefit of SSE for each port	10,710 vessels at 714 European ports during one year	• Berthing duration and energy demand at berths based on vessel type • All vessels are SSE-enabled and SSE-served
Herrero et al. (2022)	Assess environmental benefit of SSE for each port	18,071 port calls during 11 years at the Port of Santander	○ Emission factor of CO_2 based on changes in electricity generation structure in local grids from 2011 to 2021 • Auxiliary engine powers based on vessel size and type • All vessels are SSE-enabled and SSE-served

(*continued*)

Table 1. (*continued*)

Reference	Objective	Input data	Scenario development
Gore et al. (2023)	Assess cost and environmental benefit of SSE for each port	4,664 port calls during one year by 21 passenger vessels at Dublin and Belfast ports	∘ Number of SSE-enabled vessels based on calling frequency, e.g., top 5 or top 10 vessel callers are SSE-enabled ∘ Number of SSE supply points based on average berthing duration of SSE-enabled vessels and the assumption of temporal overlaps among vessels
Vaishnav et al.(2016)	Optimize the number of SSE supply points at each port and SSE-enabled vessels' number to maximize the environmental and net benefits	46,000 port calls during 18 months by 3,300 vessels at 187 U.S. ports	∘ External cost of emissions based on two different emission impact assessment models • Berthing duration based on vessel size and average rate of utilization of berths of each port
Peng et al. (2019)	Optimize the allocation of SSE supply points for one terminal to minimize the cost and CO_2 emissions	Container terminal in China with five berths and its throughput, service level, quay crane working efficiency	• Time interval and daily number of arriving vessels based on empirical distribution • Berthing duration based on vessel size and average rate of utilization of berths in one terminal • All vessels are SSE-enabled
Peng et al. (2021)	Optimize the allocation of SSE supply points at berths and solve the BAP for one terminal to minimize costs and vessel emissions	Bulk terminal in China with 10 berths and its throughput and service level	∘ External cost of CO_2 based on environmental tax rate • Time interval and daily number of arriving vessels based on a probability distribution • Berthing duration based on vessel size and average rate of utilization of berths in one terminal • All vessels are SSE-enabled
This paper	Optimize the allocation of SSE supply points and solve the BAP for a group of terminals at one port	473 port calls during one month by 135 vessels at three container terminals at Hamburg port	∘ Number of SSE supply points based on budget ∘ Number of SSE-enabled vessels based on vessel size

Empty bullet points (∘) signal varying parameters leading to multiple scenarios, whereas filled bullet points (•) signal fixed parameters.

are planned to be equipped with SSE supply points. Moreover, the use of vessels' actual arrival times and berthing durations (port call data) is instrumental in increasing the accuracy of the results, at least for an a posteriori analysis. For future scenarios with uncertain port call data, an a priori analysis can be fed with adapted/generated port call data, e.g., increasing the number of port calls.

Based on the literature review, we consider the following aspects to build various scenarios: The number of SSE-enabled vessels and the number of SSE supply points. Furthermore, we solve a BAP using a varying number of SSE-enabled vessels together with the use of vessels' actual arrival times and berthing durations. The aim is to identify the number of berths that should be equipped with SSE supply points, i.e., to optimize the allocation of SSE supply points among the three terminals of HHLA in our case study.

3 Optimization Model

In this section, we develop an optimization model to allocate SSE supply points to different terminals, and to solve the BAP, with the objective to maximize the total SSE consumption of all vessels. Each vessel can only berth at its individually defined target terminal. The set of terminals can be appended, imaginably even spanning multiple ports. The BAP is simplified by using the historic berthing start and departure time as parameters. Let us introduce the assumptions, input sets and parameters, as well as the decision variables:

Assumptions

- There is no distinction between the characteristics of berths, such as capacity, length and depth.
- One berth can be equipped with exactly one SSE supply point providing power for SSE-enabled vessels at this berth.

Sets

$\mathbf{G}$ set of terminals, $\mathbf{G} = \{1, 2, ..., g, ..., G\}$
$\mathbf{B}_g$ set of berths at terminal g, $\mathbf{B}_g = \{1, 2, ..., i, ..., B_g\}$
$\mathbf{V}$ set of vessels, $\mathbf{V} = \{1, 2, ..., j, ..., V\}$
$\mathbf{V}_g$ set of vessels calling at target terminal g, $\mathbf{V}_g \subset \mathbf{V}$

Parameters

P_j^{aux} auxiliary engines' power of vessel j, kW
λ^{aux} auxiliary engines' load factor during berthing
s_j berthing start time of vessel j, h
d_j departure time of vessel j, h
W_j SSE consumption of vessel j during berthing, kWh
ϕ_{ig} 1 if berth i at terminal g is equipped with an SSE supply point, 0 otherwise
M a large positive number

Decision variables

y_{ijg} 1 if vessel j is served at berth i at terminal g, 0 otherwise

Objective function

$$max \quad C^{SSE} = \sum_{g \in \mathbf{G}} \sum_{i \in \mathbf{B}_g} \sum_{j \in \mathbf{V}_g} W_j \phi_{ig} y_{ijg} \tag{1}$$

Subject to

$$\sum_{i \in \mathbf{B}_g} y_{ijg} = 1 \qquad \forall j \in \mathbf{V}_g, \forall g \in \mathbf{G} \tag{2}$$

$$d_{j-1} y_{i(j-1)g} \leq s_j y_{ijg} + M\left(1 - y_{ijg}\right) \qquad \forall i \in \mathbf{B}_g, \forall j \in \mathbf{V}_g, \forall g \in \mathbf{G} \tag{3}$$

$$W_j = P_j^{aux} \lambda^{aux} \left(d_j - s_j\right) \qquad \forall j \in \mathbf{V} \tag{4}$$

The objective function (1) is to maximize the SSE consumption of SSE-enabled vessels, C^{SSE}. Constraints (2) ensure that each SSE-enabled vessel is served at exactly one berth at its target terminal. Constraints (3) are used to avoid the temporal overlap of two SSE-enabled vessels that are assigned to the same berth. Constraints (4) gauge the SSE consumption of each SSE-enabled vessel. Subsequently, based on the allocation of SSE supply points and the SSE consumption, the saved emissions and the total emissions of vessels are calculated by Eq. (5) and Eq. (6), where EF_k^{fuel} and EF_k^{SSE} are emission factors of emission type k by using fuel oil and SSE, $k \in \mathbf{K} = \{SO_x, NO_x, PM_{2.5}, PM_{10}, CO_2\}$.

$$SavedEmissions = C^{SSE}\left(EF_k^{fuel} - EF_k^{SSE}\right) \qquad \forall k \in \mathbf{K} \tag{5}$$

$$TotalEmissions = \sum_{j \in \mathbf{V}} W_j EF_k^{fuel} - SavedEmissions \qquad \forall k \in \mathbf{K} \tag{6}$$

4 Case Study

The case study is based on the container terminals operated by HHLA in the Port of Hamburg. Those terminals comprise the Container Terminal Altenwerder (CTA), the Container Terminal Burchardkai (CTB), and the Container Terminal Tollerort (CTT) with four, ten, and four berths, respectively. In the aforementioned MOU of five large ports in Europe (including the Port of Hamburg), it is stated that "[Article 2] The Parties agree that all berths at container terminals serving, on a regular basis, Ultra Large Container vessels (ULCV) with a length overall (LOA) above 366 m, will be subject to this MoU [...] OPS [onshore power supply] installations, as referred to in Article 2, must be operational by 1 January 2028 at the latest" (POA, 2021). The plan of the Port of Hamburg is to allocate five SSE supply points to HHLA's container terminals by 2024, i.e., CTA (1), CTB (3), and CTT (1) (HPA, 2022).

4.1 Input Data

The dataset includes the entire port calls made at those terminals during December 2021. Those accumulate to 473 port calls by 135 unique vessels. The dataset has been obtained on 27 January 2022 from HHLA (2020).

For each port call, the vessel name, vessel type (seagoing vessel, feeder), scheduled berthing start time, departure time, and target terminal are available. Based on the vessel name, the deadweight tonnage (DWT) and vessel length in meters are collected from vesselfinder.com. The power of a vessel's auxiliary engines is estimated as $P^{aux} = 0.22 \times P^{main}$, where P^{main} is the power of the main engines estimated by the DWT regression equation, i.e., $P^{main} = 2.4351 \times DWT^{0.8673}$ (Wan et al., 2020). Based on some collected sample data, we adjust the regression equation by multiplying a correction factor of $\frac{2}{3}$. The power of the auxiliary engines is used to estimate the energy consumption of the vessel during berthing by Eq. (4). The load factor, λ^{aux}, is highly correlated with the port and its determination would constitute a separate project (see, e.g., efforts by the Port of Los Angeles to express a nonlinear relationship between the load factor and capacity, where container vessels are binned by twenty-foot equivalent unit (TEU) (POLA, 2022)); here, we simplify and set λ^{aux} as 0.1. Emission factors are used to assess the environmental benefit of using SSE (UBA, 2022) compared to using auxiliary engines with low sulphur marine gas oil (LSMGO) (POLA, 2022) and are shown in Table 2.

Table 2. Emission factors

Factor	Unit	SO_x	NO_x	$PM_{2.5}$	PM_{10}	CO_2
Emission factors by LSMGO	g/kWh	0.42	2.0	0.17	0.19	696
Emission factors by SSE	g/kWh	0.178	0.355	0.001	0.008	375

4.2 Scenario Development

We use two aspects to develop a series of scenarios: the number of SSE supply points and the number of SSE-enabled vessels. Increasing the number of SSE supply points enables the exploration of the trade-offs between investments and environmental benefits. With a maximum of nine SSE supply points to be allocated among the three terminals, 150 allocations exist ($\phi_{ig} \geq \phi_{(i+1)g}, \forall i \in \mathbf{B}_g, \forall g \in \mathbf{G}$). This is sufficient to provide some solution space under and above the planned allocation of five SSE supply points by the Port of Hamburg.

The number of SSE-enabled vessels is uncertain and beyond the decision scope of the port. It is reasonable to suspect that larger container vessels are prioritized for being equipped with SSE in the initial build or for retrofitting. Hence, DWT classes are suitable to increase the number of SSE-enabled vessels for different scenarios. The inspection of the extended port call data shows that all vessels having a length larger than 366 m fall in the class of vessels ≥140,000 DWT. This class represents the type of vessels that the Port of Hamburg aims at providing SSE first. In total, three DWT classes are defined to provide some solution space for future developments, i.e., ≥200,000 DWT, ≥140,000 DWT, and ≥100,000 DWT. The vessels in the three DWT classes are subsequently treated as SSE-enabled vessels. Figure 1 provides the distribution of port calls at each terminal in three DWT-intervals: [100,000, 140,000) DWT, [140,000, 200,000) DWT, and [200,000, 250,000) DWT.

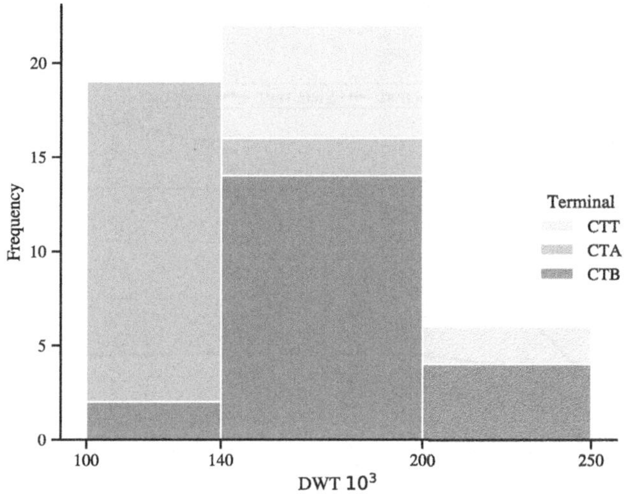

Fig. 1. Frequency of port call DWT-intervals by terminal

Table 3. Parameter settings of GA

Parameter	Values
Maximum number of generations	300
Population	100, 120
Crossover probability	0.8
Mutation probability	0.01
Crossover function	scattered, intermediate
Mutation function	adaptive feasible

4.3 Application

The presented optimization model, presented in Sect. 3, is solved using the MATLAB GA optimization toolbox. The performance of the GA is largely influenced by its parameters. The parameter settings of the GA are listed in Table 3, which are based on initial experiments with respect to the scenarios developed in Sect. 4.2.

Based on the 150 allocations and the three DWT classes (i.e., ≥200,000 DWT, ≥140,000 DWT, and ≥100,000 DWT) described in Sect. 4.2, two population values, two crossover functions, and three GA execution repetitions to increase the probability to find better solutions, there are 5,400 solutions obtained.

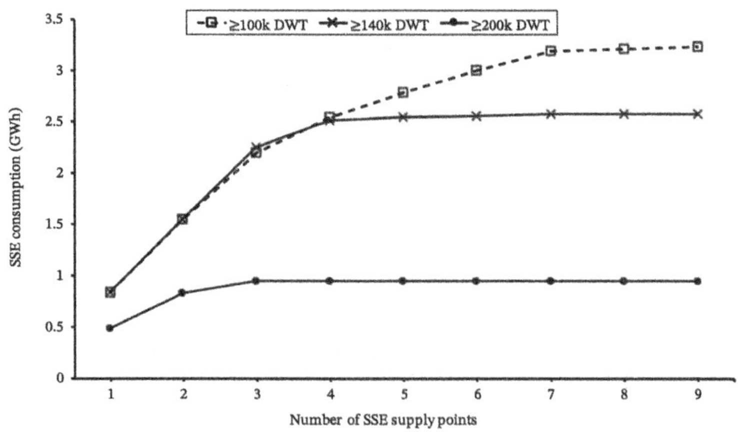

Fig. 2. SSE consumption of best solutions under different scenarios

4.4 Results and Discussion

For each scenario, the best solution is selected and shown in Fig. 2. The objective value represents the SSE consumption of SSE-enabled vessels. Table 4 presents the two best solutions for each scenario in more detail. Moreover, the best solution that adheres to the MOU-based constraint is shown. The MOU text provides some room for interpretation concerning when a berth *regularly* serves vessels in class ≥140,000 DWT: "The Parties agree that all berths at container terminals serving, on a regular basis, Ultra Large Container vessels (ULCV) with a length overall (LOA) above 366 m [140,000 DWT], will be subject to this MoU" (POA, 2021). The MOU could imply that each terminal should be allocated at least one SSE supply point (MOU-based constraint), to be able to serve vessels of class ≥140,000 DWT at all terminals.

For the class ≥200,000 DWT, three supply points are sufficient to meet the energy demand of all SSE-enabled vessels. The best solution is to allocate two

Table 4. Allocation of SSE supply points for different scenarios

Scenario		SSE allocation			SSE	SO_x (t)			NO_x (t)			$PM_{2.5}$ (t)			PM_{10} (t)			CO_2 (kt)		
Class	No.	CTA	CTB	CTT	(GWh)	T	S	%	T	S	%	T	S	%	T	S	%	T	S	%
≥0	0	0	0	0	n/a	1.97	n/a	n/a	9.39	n/a	n/a	0.80	n/a	n/a	0.90	n/a	n/a	3.27	n/a	n/a
≥200	1	0	1	0	0.50	1.85	0.12	6.13	8.57	0.82	8.74	0.72	0.08	10.50	0.81	0.09	10.13	3.11	0.16	4.90
≥200	1	0	0	1	0.33	1.89	0.08	4.11	8.84	0.55	5.86	0.75	0.06	7.05	0.83	0.06	6.80	3.16	0.11	3.29
≥200	2	0	1	1	0.83	1.77	0.20	10.24	8.02	1.37	14.60	0.66	0.14	17.55	0.74	0.15	16.92	3.00	0.27	8.19
≥200	2	0	2	0	0.62	1.82	0.15	7.65	8.36	1.02	10.91	0.70	0.11	13.12	0.78	0.11	12.65	3.07	0.20	6.12
≥200	3	0	2	1	0.96	1.74	0.23	11.76	7.81	1.57	16.77	0.64	0.16	20.16	0.72	0.17	19.44	2.96	0.31	9.41
≥200	3	0	1	2	0.83	1.77	0.20	10.24	8.02	1.37	14.60	0.66	0.14	17.55	0.74	0.15	16.92	3.00	0.27	8.19
≥200	3	1	1	1	0.83	1.77	0.20	10.24	8.02	1.37	14.60	0.66	0.14	17.55	0.74	0.15	16.92	3.00	0.27	8.19
≥140	1	0	1	0	0.85	1.76	0.21	10.42	7.99	1.39	14.85	0.66	0.14	17.85	0.74	0.15	17.21	2.99	0.27	8.33
≥140	1	0	0	1	0.71	1.80	0.17	8.75	8.21	1.17	12.48	0.68	0.12	15.00	0.77	0.13	14.47	3.04	0.23	7.00
≥140	2	0	1	1	1.56	1.59	0.38	19.17	6.82	2.57	27.33	0.54	0.26	32.86	0.61	0.28	31.68	2.77	0.50	15.32
≥140	2	0	2	0	1.54	1.60	0.37	18.89	6.86	2.53	26.93	0.54	0.26	32.38	0.62	0.28	31.22	2.77	0.49	15.10
≥140	3	0	2	1	2.26	1.42	0.55	27.77	5.67	3.72	39.60	0.42	0.38	47.60	0.48	0.41	45.90	2.54	0.73	22.20
≥140	3	0	3	0	1.74	1.55	0.42	21.38	6.52	2.86	30.49	0.51	0.29	36.65	0.58	0.32	35.34	2.71	0.56	17.09
≥140	3	1	1	1	1.58	1.59	0.38	19.37	6.79	2.59	27.61	0.54	0.27	33.20	0.61	0.29	32.01	2.76	0.51	15.48
≥140	4	0	3	1	2.52	1.36	0.61	30.94	5.25	4.14	44.11	0.38	0.43	53.03	0.44	0.46	51.13	2.46	0.81	24.73
≥140	4	0	2	2	2.28	1.42	0.55	27.99	5.64	3.75	39.91	0.42	0.38	47.98	0.48	0.41	46.26	2.54	0.73	22.38
≥140	4	1	2	1	2.28	1.42	0.55	27.97	5.64	3.74	39.88	0.42	0.38	47.94	0.48	0.41	46.23	2.54	0.73	22.36
≥140	5	0	4	1	2.54	1.35	0.61	31.24	5.21	4.18	44.54	0.37	0.43	53.55	0.43	0.46	51.63	2.45	0.82	24.97
≥140	5	1	3	1	2.53	1.36	0.61	31.11	5.22	4.16	44.36	0.37	0.43	53.33	0.44	0.46	51.42	2.45	0.81	24.87
≥140	6	0	4	2	2.56	1.35	0.62	31.46	5.18	4.21	44.85	0.37	0.43	53.92	0.43	0.47	51.99	2.44	0.82	25.15
≥140	6	1	4	1	2.56	1.35	0.62	31.44	5.18	4.21	44.82	0.37	0.43	53.89	0.43	0.47	51.96	2.45	0.82	25.13
≥140	7	1	4	2	2.58	1.35	0.62	31.65	5.15	4.24	45.13	0.37	0.44	54.26	0.43	0.47	52.32	2.44	0.83	25.31
≥140	7	0	4	3	2.56	1.35	0.62	31.46	5.18	4.21	44.85	0.37	0.43	53.92	0.43	0.47	51.99	2.44	0.82	25.15
≥100	1	0	1	0	0.85	1.76	0.21	10.48	7.98	1.40	14.94	0.66	0.14	17.96	0.74	0.16	17.32	2.99	0.27	8.38
≥100	1	0	0	1	0.71	1.80	0.17	8.75	8.21	1.17	12.48	0.68	0.12	15.00	0.77	0.13	14.47	3.04	0.23	7.00
≥100	2	0	1	1	1.56	1.59	0.38	19.17	6.82	2.57	27.33	0.54	0.26	32.86	0.61	0.28	31.68	2.77	0.50	15.32
≥100	2	0	2	0	1.55	1.59	0.37	19.02	6.84	2.55	27.12	0.54	0.26	32.60	0.61	0.28	31.43	2.77	0.50	15.21
≥100	3	0	2	1	2.20	1.44	0.53	27.03	5.77	3.62	38.54	0.43	0.37	46.33	0.50	0.40	44.68	2.56	0.71	21.61
≥100	3	1	2	0	1.85	1.52	0.45	22.78	6.34	3.05	32.49	0.49	0.31	39.05	0.56	0.34	37.65	2.67	0.59	18.21
≥100	4	0	3	1	2.55	1.35	0.62	31.33	5.19	4.19	44.68	0.37	0.43	53.71	0.43	0.46	51.79	2.45	0.82	25.05
≥100	4	1	2	1	2.37	1.39	0.57	29.14	5.49	3.90	41.56	0.40	0.40	49.96	0.46	0.43	48.17	2.51	0.76	23.30
≥100	5	1	3	1	2.78	1.30	0.67	34.22	4.81	4.58	48.79	0.33	0.47	58.65	0.39	0.51	56.55	2.37	0.89	27.36
≥100	5	2	2	1	2.66	1.32	0.64	32.74	5.00	4.38	46.69	0.35	0.45	56.12	0.41	0.48	54.11	2.41	0.86	26.18
≥100	6	2	3	1	3.00	1.24	0.73	36.91	4.45	4.94	52.64	0.29	0.51	63.28	0.35	0.55	61.01	2.30	0.96	29.51
≥100	6	1	4	1	2.90	1.27	0.70	35.59	4.62	4.76	50.75	0.31	0.49	61.01	0.37	0.53	58.83	2.34	0.93	28.46
≥100	7	3	3	1	3.20	1.20	0.77	39.28	4.13	5.26	56.01	0.26	0.54	67.33	0.31	0.58	64.93	2.24	1.03	31.41
≥100	7	2	4	1	3.13	1.21	0.76	38.52	4.23	5.15	54.92	0.27	0.53	66.03	0.33	0.57	63.66	2.26	1.01	30.80

• Total amount of emissions in the current scenario (T), i.e., emissions by all port calls ≥0k DWT. Saved emissions in the current scenario, absolute (S), percent (%) compared to the baseline scenario.
• The baseline scenario requires vessels to use LSMGO only (first row). • The SSE consumption is the objective value (SSE).

SSE supply points to CTB and one to CTT, i.e., CTA (0), CTB (2), CTT (1), leading to 0.96 GWh of SSE consumption. Generally, this allocation correlates to the distribution of port call DWT-classes at each terminal as shown in Fig. 1.

As mentioned before, the class ≥140,000 DWT covers the prioritized vessels based on the MOU. Based on Fig. 2, four supply points appear to be sufficient, and Table 4 confirms a marginal performance difference between the best allocations using four and five SSE supply points. The best allocation using four is CTA (0), CTB (3), CTT (1), 2.52 GWh, as well as CTA (0), CTB (4), CTT (1), 2.54 GWh, using five. This best allocation using five supply points is slightly better compared to the allocation planned by the Port of Hamburg, i.e., CTA (1), CTB (3), CTT (1) with 2.53 GWh of SSE consumption.

Concerning the class ≥100,000 DWT, up to seven SSE supply points can be exhausted, leading to 3.20 GWh of SSE consumption. Notably, in this class, the allocation CTA (1), CTB (3), CTT (1), leading to 2.78 GWh, as planned by the Port of Hamburg, is the best for allocating five supply points.

Negative implications for the MOU-based constraint are exhibited, only if less than five supply points are allocated. More concretely, for the class ≥200,000 DWT and allocating three supply points, the only feasible allocation is CTA (1), CTB (1), CTT (1) that decreases SSE consumption by 0.13 GWh compared to the best allocation, i.e., CTA (0), CTB (2), CTT (1). For the classes ≥140,000 DWT and ≥100,000 DWT, more significant implications are observed with three and four supply points. Regarding ≥140,000 DWT, for instance, the SSE consumption is reduced by 0.68 GWh and 0.24 GWh.

In summary, Fig. 2 shows SSE supply points and SSE-enabled vessels to correlate positively with the consumed SSE until the energy demand is fully met. The energy demand by port calls in class ≥140,000 DWT is almost satisfied by four supply points. Allocating more than four supply points yields a much lower cost-effectiveness, e.g., an increase from four to five supply points leads to only 0.02 GWh more SSE consumption, while an increase from three to four yields 0.26 GWh. However, in the advent that class ≥100,000 DWT vessels are SSE-enabled, further increasing the supply points to seven is beneficial.

Let us describe the limitations of this study. First, the results are limited by the data set of one month. Future studies could include annual data sets. Second, this study assumes vessels to use SSE during the entire berthing duration. However, only a partial consumption may take place with respect to time of usage energy pricing (Yu et al., 2022), or insufficient power supply due to energy production or infrastructure limitations. The third limitation is the heuristic approach that cannot guarantee to find the best solution for a BAP that could further increase the SSE consumption and therefore change the ranking of the presented allocation plans. Fourth, the BAP in this paper is simplified by using the historic scheduled berthing start and departure time of our case study terminals that have no SSE supply points yet. If the port had SSE supply points, the times might have been adjusted in favor of SSE consumption. Fifth, the auxiliary engines' power and load factor are based on simplified methods where obtaining precise values requires a case study per port. Moreover, the emission factors could be implemented to change over the assessed time period. At last, the potential use of scrubber and heavy fuel oil is neglected, leading to uncertainty of the presented SO_x emissions. At the end of 2020, about 14% of the container vessel world fleet had been equipped with scrubbers (ICCT, 2021). The SSE implementation performance depends on the SSE allocation plan and other factors such as the BAP plan, electricity pricing, incentives, and the number of SSE-enabled vessels. An emissions inventory, such as presented in Table 4, thus can only be regarded a composite index, a proxy measure for the SSE implementation performance. However, emissions inventory methodologies and key figures can be standardized (Cammin and Voß, 2021), and subsequently be utilized to establish sensible goals, i.e., specific, measurable, achievable, relevant, and time-bound (SMART) goals (Drucker, 1954). A component of a SMART goal could be the saved emissions relative to the baseline emissions, as presented in Table 4. So far, SMART goals incorporating such quantifications of emissions have not been declared in the MOU. Thus, rethinking the design of goals could benefit future evaluations of SSE implementations.

5 Conclusions

In this study, we addressed the SSE supply point allocation problem. More specifically, we implemented an optimization model for a terminal group with the shared objective to maximize the environmental benefit by using SSE while solving the BAP. We applied our model to a case study concerning the largest container terminal group in the Port of Hamburg under a series of scenarios with varying numbers of SSE supply points (from one to nine) and SSE-enabled vessels (classes ≥200,000 DWT, ≥140,000 DWT, and ≥100,000 DWT). Based on the results, we discussed the trade-offs between the environmental benefit and the allocation of SSE supply points. For instance, the energy demand of vessels in classes ≥200,000 DWT, ≥140,000 DWT, and ≥100,000 DWT are almost satisfied by three, four, and seven supply points, respectively. With a total number of five supply points, as planned by the Port of Hamburg, the best plan enables 0.96 GWh, 2.54 GWh, and 2.78 GWh of SSE consumption, for vessels in class ≥200,000 DWT, ≥140,000 DWT, and ≥100,000 DWT, respectively. We believe our work can spark discussions revolving the intelligent use of funds, concerning terminal groups, and future port cooperations. Future studies could extend this study by considering the entirety of terminals of the ports of Rotterdam, Hamburg, Bremen, Antwerp, and Haropa that are subject to the MOU to promote SSE, and to expose the implications to local air quality.

References

CAA. Evaluation of Air and Climate Synergies of Typical Chinese Ports. Clean Air Asia (2022). http://allaboutair.cn/uploads/soft/230308/1-23030Q34007.pdf. Accessed 15 Apr 2023

Cammin, P., Voß, S.: Towards smart maritime port emissions monitoring: a platform for enhanced transparency. In: Chandra Kruse, L., Seidel, S., Hausvik, G.I. (eds.) DESRIST 2021. LNCS, vol. 12807, pp. 71–76. Springer, Cham (2021). https://doi.org/10.1007/978-3-030-82405-1_9

Dai, L., Hao, H., Wang, Z., Shi, Y., Ding, W.: An environmental and techno-economic analysis of shore side electricity. Transp. Res. Part D: Transp. Environ. **75**, 223–235 (2019). https://doi.org/10.1016/j.trd.2019.09.002

Drucker, P.: The Practice of Management. Harper, New York (1954)

EP: Sustainable maritime fuels 'Fit for 55' package: the FuelEU Maritime proposal (2023). https://www.europarl.europa.eu/RegData/etudes/BRIE/2021/698808/EPRS_BRI(2021)698808_EN.pdf

Gore, K., Rigot-Müller, P., Coughlan, J.: Cost-benefit assessment of shore side electricity: an Irish perspective. J. Environ. Manage. **326**, 116755 (2023). https://doi.org/10.1016/j.jenvman.2022.116755

Herrero, A., Piris, A.O., Diaz-Ruiz-Navamuel, E., Gutierrez, M.A., Lopez-Diaz, A.-I.: Influence of the implantation of the onshore power supply (OPS) system in Spanish medium-sized ports on the reduction in CO_2 emissions: the case of the Port of Santander (Spain). J. Marine Sci. Eng. **10**(10), 1446 (2022). https://doi.org/10.3390/jmse10101446

HHLA. Report vessel operations: Sailing list. Hamburger Hafen und Logistik AG (2022). https://coast.hhla.de/report?id=Standard-Report-Segelliste. Accessed 10 Feb 2023

HPA. Plugging in to eliminate emissions. Hamburg Port Authority (2022). https://www.hafen-hamburg.de/en/port-of-hamburg-magazine/hafen-und-klima/stecker-rein-emissionen-aus/. Accessed 10 Feb 2023

HPM. Cleaner air and climate protection in Port of Hamburg - New shore-based power units for cruise liners and containerships. Hamburg Port Marketing (2019). https://www.hafen-hamburg.de/en/press/news/cleaner-air-and-climateprotection-in-port-of-hamburg-new-shore-based-power-units-for-cruiseliners-and-containerships-36499/. Accessed 10 Feb 2023

ICCT. Global scrubber washwater discharges under IMO's 2020 fuel sulfur limit. International Council on Clean Transportation (2021). https://theicct.org/sites/default/files/publications/scrubber-discharges-Apr2021.pdf. Accessed 10 Mar 2023

Lathwal, P., Vaishnav, P., Morgan, M.G.: Environmental and health consequences of shore power for vessels calling at major ports in India. Environ. Res. Lett. **16**(6), 064042 (2021). https://doi.org/10.1088/1748-9326/abfd5b

Martínez-López, A., Romero, A., Orosa, J.A.: Assessment of cold ironing and LNG as mitigation tools of short sea shipping emissions in port: a Spanish case study. Appl. Sci. **11**(5), 2050 (2021). https://doi.org/10.3390/app11052050

Nguyen, D.-H., et al.: Reduction of NOx and SO2 emissions by shore power adoption. Aerosol Air Qual. Res. **21**(7), 210100 (2021). https://doi.org/10.4209/aaqr.210100.

Peng, Y., Dong, M., Li, X., Liu, H., Wang, W.: Cooperative optimization of shore power allocation and berth allocation: a balance between cost and environmental benefit. J. Clean. Prod. **279**, 123816 (2021). https://doi.org/10.1016/j.jclepro.2020.123816

Peng, Y., Li, X., Wang, W., Wei, Z., Bing, X., Song, X.: A method for determining the allocation strategy of on-shore power supply from a green container terminal perspective. Ocean Coast. Manag. **167**, 158–175 (2019). https://doi.org/10.1016/j.ocecoaman.2018.10.007

POA. Memorandum of understanding onshore power ambitions for container terminals in port. Port of Antwerp, Port of Bremerhaven, Port of Hamburg, Haropa Port, Port of Rotterdam (2021). https://www.portofrotterdam.com/sites/default/files/2021-07/mou_ops_ports_of_antwerp-bremerhaven-hamburgharopa_port-rotterdam_-_final_20210618_003.pdf. Accessed 01 Mar 2023

POLA. Port of Los Angeles inventory of air emissions 2021. Port of Los Angeles (2022). https://kentico.portoflosangeles.org/getmedia/f26839cd-54cd-4da9-92b7-a34094ee75a8/2021_Air_Emissions_Inventory. Accessed 15 Feb 2023

POLA. Alternative maritime power (AMP). Port of Los Angeles (2023). https://www.portoflosangeles.org/environment/air-quality/alternative-maritimepower-(amp). Accessed 15 Apr 2023

Spengler, T., Tovar, B.: Potential of cold-ironing for the reduction of externalities from in-port shipping emissions: the state-owned Spanish port system case. J. Environ. Manage. **279**, 111807 (2021). https://doi.org/10.1016/j.jenvman.2020.111807

Stolz, B., Held, M., Georges, G., Boulouchos, K.: The CO2 reduction potential of shore-side electricity in Europe. Appl. Energy **285**, 116425 (2021). https://doi.org/10.1016/j.apenergy.2020.116425

UBA. Specific emission factors for electricity mix in Germany. Umweltbundesamt (2022). https://www.umweltbundesamt.de/themen/luft/emissionen-vonluftschadstoffen/spezifische-emissionsfaktoren-fuer-den-deutschen. Accessed 01 Mar 2023

Vaishnav, P., Fischbeck, P.S., Morgan, M.G., Corbett, J.J.: Shore power for vessels calling at U.S. ports: benefits and costs. Environ. Sci. Technol. **50**(3), 1102–1110 (2016). https://doi.org/10.1021/acs.est.5b04860.

Wan, Z., Ji, S., Liu, Y., Zhang, Q., Chen, J., Wang, Q.: Shipping emission inventories in china's Bohai bay, Yangtze river delta, and pearl river delta in 2018. Mar. Pollut. Bull. **151**, 110882 (2020). https://doi.org/10.1016/j.marpolbul.2019.110882

Williamsson, J., Costa, N., Santén, V., Rogerson, S.: Barriers and drivers to the implementation of onshore power supply–a literature review. Sustainability **14**(10), 6072 (2022). https://doi.org/10.3390/su14106072

Winkel, R., Weddige, U., Johnsen, D., Hoen, V., Papaefthimiou, S.: Shore side electricity in Europe: potential and environmental benefits. Energy Policy **88**, 584–593 (2016). https://doi.org/10.1016/j.enpol.2015.07.013

Yu, J., Voß, S., Song, X.: Multi-objective optimization of daily use of shore side electricity integrated with quayside operation. J. Clean. Prod. **351**, 131406 (2022). https://doi.org/10.1016/j.jclepro.2022.131406

Stockyard Storage Space Allocation in Dry Bulk Terminals Considering Mist Cannons and Energy Expenditure

Xinyu Tang(✉) and Frederik Schulte

Delft University of Technology, 2600AA Delft, The Netherlands
{X.Tang-3,F.Schulte}@tudelft.nl

Abstract. Storage space management in bulk terminals has become an important focus for research and practical operation due to the increasing demand for bulk cargo and limited storage space in stockyards. The study of storage space management in dry bulk terminals is less thorough and comprehensive, and the existing research investigates the storage space allocation problem with other operational problems like berth allocation problems, but little environmental consideration has been incorporated. We investigate the storage space allocation problem with the consideration of stacker-reclaimer assignment and mist cannon operation to deal with the dust generated during material stacking. A mixed integer programming model has been established with the aim of minimizing energy consumption to reflect the pursuit of the growing emphasis on climate-neutral operations and sustainability. We test the effectiveness of the model by conducting computational experiments. We use the commercial solver CPLEX to obtain the optimal solutions for most of the test instances. Useful managerial insights extracted from the computational results may serve as a reference for storage space management in dry bulk terminals.

Keywords: Storage space allocation · Dry bulk terminal · Mist cannon operations · Stacker-reclaimer operations · Energy consumption

1 Introduction

Stockyard in dry bulk terminal acts as a centralized storage area for bulk materials, and also functions as an essential buffer for differences between incoming and outgoing streams of bulk materials [16]. Under the influence of the increasing demand for bulk cargo and the trend towards larger vessels, storage space in the stockyard tends to become a scarce resource, leading terminal operators to focus on stockyard storage space management. Utilizing the storage space reasonably can help improve the operational efficiency of the cargo transport chain. Therefore, it is necessary to study the storage space allocation problem in dry bulk terminals.

© The Author(s), under exclusive license to Springer Nature Switzerland AG 2023
J. R. Daduna et al. (Eds.): ICCL 2023, LNCS 14239, pp. 154–169, 2023.
https://doi.org/10.1007/978-3-031-43612-3_9

Apart from the operation efficiency, the port now needs to take responsibility for environmental concerns driven by the growing emphasis on a cleaner environment, neutral climate, and sustainability. A large amount of dust is generated during the operation in the dry bulk stockyard, such as stacking materials into the empty fields of stock pads. Mist cannon (also known as dust cannon, or dust suppression cannon) is a widely used facility to control dust. The fogging process involves the action of fog nozzles which nebulize water into very small micro-droplets of water under pressure. The fog drives airborne dust particles to the ground and wets the surface to prevent fugitive dust particles. When water is combined with dust in the air, due to the adhesion of the surface of water molecules, it will be combined with the dust, and the effect of gravity will drop after condensing, to achieve the purpose of dust suppression. Materials are stacked into stock pads accompanied by the water spray of the mist cannon. We consider mist cannon operation in the space allocation process, which is rarely addressed in the existing literature.

The stockyard is a complex logistics system that consists of components of different operation machines like stacker-reclaimers and mist cannons. We study Storage Space Allocation Problem (SSAP) in the stockyard of dry bulk terminals, which together considers the assignment of stacker-reclaimers and mist cannons for incoming materials. In this study, we consider import dry bulk terminals in which cargo flows from the berth area to the stockyard area. We aim to determine the specific storage locations for incoming materials with the objective of minimizing energy consumption. The contributions of the paper include the following: (1) We first model the operations of mist cannons to control the dust and study the storage space allocation, stacker-reclaimer assignment and mist cannon assignment in an integrated manner. (2) We incorporate energy consumption into the optimisation objective, corresponding to the requirements of sustainable operations.

The rest of the paper is organized as follows. Section 2 reviews relevant papers in the literature. Section 3 describes the storage space allocation problem followed by mathematical formulation in Sect. 4. Section 5 shows the preliminary results from computational experiments to test the effectiveness of the mathematical model. Finally, conclusions are drawn in Sect. 6.

2 Literature Review

Storage space management in dry bulk terminal stockyards has received far less attention than that in container terminal yards. Storage space allocation problem (SSAP) is usually investigated with other operational problems (such as berth allocation problem (BAP), train scheduling, etc.) in an integrated manner. Table 1 lists the related work on the SSAP problem in dry bulk terminals.

Ouhaman et al. [13] studied the SSAP in an export dry bulk terminal. The authors formulated the problem as a mixed-integer linear programming (MILP) problem and proposed a heuristic method to solve large-scale data sets. They limited the problem to the material flow from the production plant to storage

Table 1. Related literature on storage space allocation problem in dry bulk terminals

Literature	Publication year	Problem studied	Solution
Ouhaman et al. [13]	2020	SSAP	heuristic method
Tang et al. [17]	2016	SSAP, BAP	Benders decomposition
Sun et al. [16]	2020	SSAP	logic-based Benders decomposition
Tang et al. [18]	2022	SSAP	genetic algorithm
Ago et al. [1]	2007	SSAP, conveyor belt routing	Lagrangian decomposition
Menezes et al. [12]	2017	scheduling and planning of product flows	branch and price
De Andrade et al. [3,4]	2021,2022	BAP, SSAP, scheduling and planning of product flows	column generation, diving heuristic
Boland et al. [7]	2012	SSAP, BAP	heuristic method
Robenek et al. [14]	2014	SSAP, BAP	branch and price
Al-Hammadi and Diabat [2]	2017	SSAP, BAP	branch and price
Babu et al. [5]	2015	SSAP, ship scheduling, train scheduling	logic-based Benders decomposition
Hu and Yao [9]	2012	SRSP	genetic algorithm
Belassiria et al. [6]	2019	SRSP	branch and bound method, tabu search algorithm
Hanoun et al. [8]	2013	operational scheduling of the continuous coal handling	bi-objective Optimization
van Vianen et al. [20]	2015	SRSP	simulation
Unsal and Oguz [19]	2019	SSAP, BAP, SRSP	logic-based Benders decomposition
Our work	2023	SSAP with environmental consideration	MIP

SSAP: Storage space allocation problem, BAP: Berth allocation problem, SRSP: Stacker-reclaimer scheduling problem, MIP: Mixed integer programming.

hangars. Tang et al. [17] addressed the integrated berth scheduling and SSAP in the context of bulk raw material ports of large iron and steel companies. They developed an integer programming model to minimize total costs and solved the model using a Benders decomposition-based approach. Sun et al. [16] followed up on the work of Tang et al. [17]. They first developed a mixed-integer programming (MIP) formulation that could avoid generating scattered small fields and schedule the unloading, stacking and reclaiming operations. A logic-based Benders approach was proposed to solve the problem optimally. SSAP in large iron ore terminal stockyards was studied in the work of Tang et al. [18]. They used continuous variables to describe the specific locations of the empty fields to highlight the continuous cargo flow characteristic of dry bulk stockyard operation. A MIP model was developed and a heuristic algorithm based on genetic algorithm was proposed to solve it. Ago et al. [1] considered both the SSAP and conveyor belt routing problems, using a Lagrangian decomposition algorithm.

Menezes et al. [12] studied a production planning and scheduling problem in bulk cargo terminals. The problem considered planning and scheduling the flow of products between supply, storage, and demand nodes and a branch and price algorithm was applied to solve it. De Andrade et al. [3,4] extended this problem by integrating berth allocation and yard assignment decisions.

Boland et al. [7] studied stockyard management in coal export terminals, considering the rail system transporting coal from mines to the terminal. The decisions in this study included berth allocation, stockpile location and the start times of stockpile assembly and reclaiming decisions. Robenek et al. [14] solved the integrated berth allocation and yard assignment problem in import and export bulk ports as a single large-scale optimization problem. They constructed a MIP model and applied an exact algorithm based on a branch and price framework. Al-Hammadi and Diabat [2] added constraints on the stacking space capacity to the model of Robenek et al. [14]. Babu et al. [5] minimized the delay of ships in bulk terminals by simultaneously considering ship scheduling, stockyard planning, and train scheduling.

As an important component in the stockyard, the stacker-reclaimer is also a factor that could influence the operation in the stockyard, which is considered in the decision-making of stockyard operation. Hu and Yao [9] discussed the stacker-reclaimer scheduling problem (SRSP) with the objective of minimizing the maximum completion time. The scheduling problem is formulated as a MIP model, and a genetic algorithm is developed to solve it. Belassiria et al. [6] also studied SRSP and developed two different heuristic methods, a branch and bound method, and a tabu search algorithm. Hanoun et al. [8] addressed the operational scheduling of the continuous coal handling problem. A model of stockyard operations within a coal mine was described and the problem was formulated as a Bi-Objective Optimization Problem (BOOP). In van Vianen et al.'s work [20], simulation was applied to reschedule the stacker-reclaimers operation to increase the dry bulk terminal's performance by reducing the waiting time of cargo trains being loaded at the terminal. Unsal and Oguz [19] integrated berth allocation, yard space allocation, and SRSP and modelled the master and subproblems with MIP and constraint programming, respectively, solving the problem with a logic-based Benders decomposition algorithm.

While the climate and environmental sustainability objectives are increasingly recognized in port (operations) research [10,11,15], the existing research related to the considered problem mostly focuses on the operation efficiency of the stockyard with little consideration of environmental aspects. Dust suppression in the stockyard is paid little attention to. Our study is an attempt to incorporate environmental protection considerations and neutral climate targets into stockyard space management.

3 Problem Description

The whole stockyard consists of some long stock pads, which may be pre-occupied by existing stockpiles, leaving empty fields available for incoming materials. Figure 1 shows the layout of a typical dry bulk terminal stockyard. One stacker-reclaimer (abbreviated as "SR" below) travels on a track between two pads, and the two pads are served by the same SR. Between two stock pads is a space interval. Three intervals can be found in Fig. 2, and we label them as Int 1, 2, and 3. Like SR, mist cannon (abbreviated as "MC" below) is also mobile. The difference is that MC can move among intervals instead of moving on a fixed track. They usually move from one interval to another through the end area of the stock pad. When an SR stacks materials into the stockyard, the MC sprays water mist to control the dust generated. There are two moving routes for the SR in Fig. 2. After completion of handling material 1, if the MC continues to serve material 2, it needs to move from Int 1 to Int 2, which brings vertical transport distance. Otherwise, if the MC continues to serve material 3 planned to be allocated in pad 2, it only needs to move horizontally.

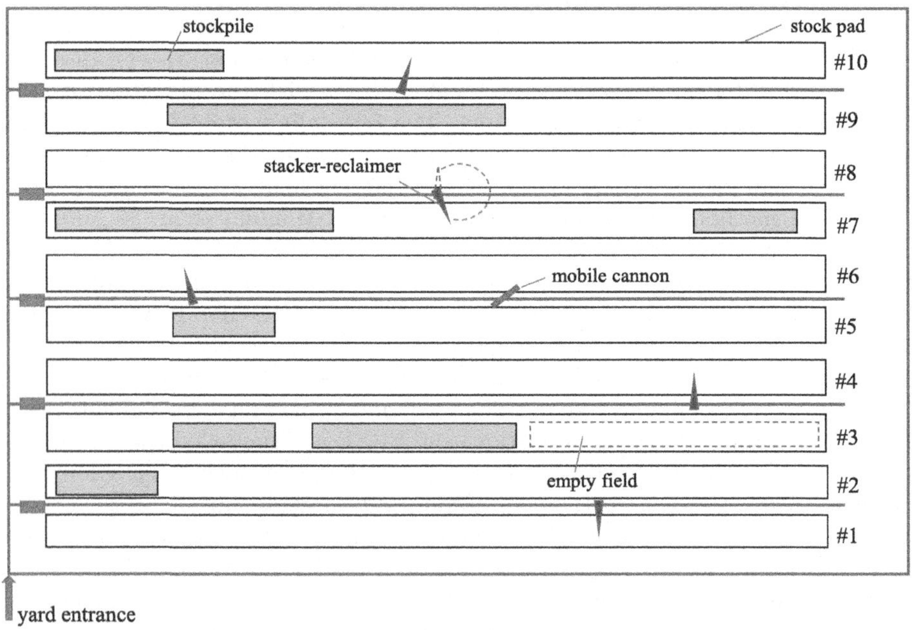

Fig. 1. Typical stockyard layout in dry bulk terminals.

We investigate the Stockyard Storage Space Allocation Problem with the MC operation to control the dust generated during stacking. We aim to find the

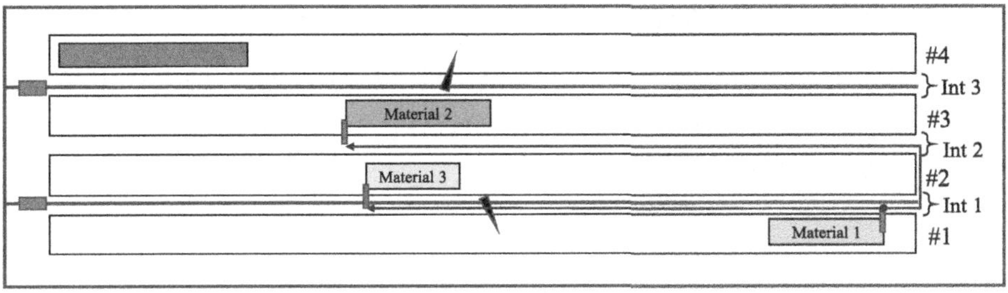

Fig. 2. Representation of mist cannon operation.

specific storage position for each incoming material with the objective of minimizing the energy consumption of operations in the stockyard. The main energy consumers in the stockyard are conveyor belts, SRs, and MCs. The energy consumption of SR and MC are further divided into two parts: energy consumption when handling materials and moving from the position of handled material to the position of material to be next served. To calculate energy consumption, we multiply the power of operating machines by the time consumed during handling or moving. Time can be obtained by dividing distance by moving speed.

When calculating the travel distance, we need to mark the position of each material and the working machine. We, therefore, introduce a virtual material 0 for each SR and MC (each SR and MC will at least serve material 0) and then set the position of the virtual material as the initial position of the machines. Hence, the moving distance can be normally calculated.

4 Mathematical Model

4.1 Assumptions

The following assumptions are made in this problem:

(1) There are plenty of empty fields to accommodate the incoming materials over the whole planning period, which means there is always enough space for stacking.
(2) One material can be stacked next to another material if a safe distance is maintained to avoid mixing. We consider a dedicated terminal for a particular cargo type. For example, in an iron ore terminal, the different types of iron ore are usually distinguished from each other by the size of the diameter of the particles and there is no strict restriction that they cannot be stacked next to each other, only that a safe distance is maintained to avoid mixing.
(3) Once the goods are stacked in the yard, the position will not change during the planning period, which is consistent with the situations in practice.
(4) The operating capability of machines in the stockyard is constant during the handling process.
(5) The moving distance is calculated from the end coordinate of the material that has just been completed handling to the start coordinate of the material to be next served.

4.2 Model Formulation

In this section, we present the mathematical model of the stockyard storage space allocation problem.

Sets and Parameters

P	set of stock pads
C	set of incoming materials
S	set of stacker-reclaimers
W	set of mist cannons
N	set of intervals
L	the horizontal length of a pad
dis	the distance between two intervals in stockyards
l_i	length of the space needed to stack the material i, $i \in C$
m_i	mass of the incoming material i, $i \in C$
ly_p	the vertical distance from the entrance of the stockyard to stock pad p, $p \in P$
α^{st}_{nw}	binary parameter which indicates whether MC w is in the interval n before planning starts, $n \in N$, $w \in W$; if $\alpha^{st}_{nw} = 1$, MC w is in the interval n
a_{sp}	binary parameter which indicates whether SR s can cover stock pad p, $s \in S$; if $a_s p = 1$, SR can cover stock pad p
b_{pn}	binary parameter which indicates whether pad p is adjacent to interval n, $n \in N$; if $b_{pn} = 1$, pad p is adjacent to interval n
xs_{s0}	the start position of SR s when the stacking operation starts
xs_{w0}	the start position of MC w when the stacking operation starts
cap_{srh}	handling capability of SR
cap_c	handling capability of conveyor belt
spe_{srm}	moving speed of SR
spe_{wcm}	moving speed of MC
spe_{cm}	moving speed of conveyor belt
P_{srh}	power of SR when handling materials
P_{srm}	power of SR when moving
P_{wch}	power of MC when spraying water mist
P_{wcm}	power of MC when moving
P_c	power of conveyor belt
sd	safe distance between two adjacent materials
M	a positive number that serves as infinity for the problem

Decision Variables

k_{ip}	0–1 variable, equal to 1 if and only if the material i is allocated to stock pad p
xs_i	start coordinate of material i
z_{ijp}	0–1 variable, equal to 1 if and only if material i and j are allocated to stock pad p and material i is allocated to the left of material j satisfying safe distance constraint
x_{is}	0–1 variable, equal to 1 if material i is handled by SR s
y_{iw}	0–1 variable, equal to 1 if material i is handled by MC w
α_{in}	0–1 variable, equal to 1 if the MC serving material i is located in the interval n
θ_{ijs}	0–1 variable, equal to 1 if and only if the material i and j are both handled by SR s, and material j is handled by SR s right after material i
μ_{ijw}	0–1 variable, equal to 1 if and only if the material i and j are both handled by MC w, and material j is handled by MC w right after material i
ρ_{ijw}	0–1 variable, equal to 1 if and only if MC w moves in the same interval when complete serving material i and then continues to serve material j
π_{ijw}	0–1 variable, equal to 1 if and only if MC w move from one interval to another when completing serving material i and then continues to serve material j
u_i, v_i	random number related to material i
δ, τ	0–1 variable

The mathematical model can be formulated as follows:

$$
\begin{aligned}
min \; & \sum_i P_{srh} \frac{m_i}{cap_{srh}} + \sum_i P_{wch} \frac{m_i}{cap_{srh}} + \sum_i P_c \frac{m_i}{cap_c} + \sum_i \frac{P_c \left(xs_i + \sum_p ly_p k_{ip} \right)}{spe_{cm}} \\
& + \sum_s \sum_j P_{srm} \frac{\theta_{0js} \left| xs_j - xs_{s0} \right|}{spe_{srm}} + \sum_s \sum_i \sum_j P_{srm} \frac{\theta_{ijs} \left| xs_j - xs_i - l_i \right|}{spe_{srm}} \\
& + \sum_w \sum_j P_{wcm} \frac{\mu_{0jw} dis \left| \sum_n n\alpha_{jn} - \sum_n n\alpha_{nw}^{st} \right|}{spe_{wcm}} \\
& + \sum_w \sum_i \sum_j P_{wcm} \frac{\mu_{ijw} dis \left| \sum_n n\alpha_{jn} - \sum_n n\alpha_{in} \right|}{spe_{wcm}} \\
& + \sum_w \sum_j P_{wcm} \frac{\rho_{0jw} \left| xs_j - xs_{w0} \right|}{spe_{wcm}} + \sum_w \sum_j P_{wcm} \frac{\pi_{0jw} (L - xs_{w0} + L - xs_j)}{spe_{wcm}} \\
& + \sum_w \sum_i \sum_j P_{wcm} \frac{\rho_{ijw} \left| xs_j - xs_i - l_i \right|}{spe_{wcm}} \\
& + \sum_w \sum_i \sum_j P_{wcm} \frac{\pi_{ijw} (L - xs_i - l_i + L - xs_j)}{spe_{wcm}}
\end{aligned}
\tag{1}
$$

s.t.

$$\sum_{p \in P} k_{ip} = 1, \quad \forall\, i \in C \setminus \{0\} \tag{2}$$

$$x_{0\,s} = 1, \quad \forall\, s \in S \tag{3}$$

$$\sum_{s \in S} x_{is} = 1, \quad \forall\, i \in C \setminus \{0\} \tag{4}$$

$$\sum_{\{p \in P | a_{sp}=1\}} k_{ip} \geq 1 + M\,(1 - x_{is})\,, \quad \forall\, i \in C \setminus \{0\}\,,\; s \in S \tag{5}$$

$$\sum_{\{p \in P | a_{sp}=1\}} k_{ip} \leq 1 - M\,(1 - x_{is})\,, \quad \forall\, i \in C \setminus \{0\}\,,\; s \in S \tag{6}$$

$$\sum_{i} \theta_{ijs} \leq 1 + M\,(1 - x_{js})\,, \quad \forall\, j \in C \setminus \{0\}\,,\; s \in S \tag{7}$$

$$\sum_{i} \theta_{ijs} \geq 1 - M\,(1 - x_{js})\,, \quad \forall\, j \in C \setminus \{0\}\,,\; s \in S \tag{8}$$

$$\sum_{j \in C \setminus \{0\}} \theta_{ijs} \leq 1 + M\,(1 - x_{is})\,, \quad \forall\, i \in C \setminus \{0\}\,,\; s \in S \tag{9}$$

$$\sum_{i} x_{is} > 1 - M\,(1 - \delta)\,, \quad \forall\, s \in S \tag{10}$$

$$\sum_{j \in C \setminus \{0\}} \theta_{0js} \geq 1 - M\,(1 - \delta)\,, \quad \forall\, s \in S \tag{11}$$

$$\sum_{j \in C \setminus \{0\}} \theta_{0js} \leq 1 + M\,(1 - \delta)\,, \quad \forall\, s \in S \tag{12}$$

$$v_i < v_j + M\,(1 - \theta_{ijs})\,, \quad \forall i, j \in C \setminus \{0\}\,, s \in S \tag{13}$$

$$\theta_{ijs} + \theta_{jis} \leq 1, \quad \forall\, i, j \in C,\; s \in S \tag{14}$$

$$\theta_{ijs} \leq x_{is}, \quad \forall i, j \in C,\; i \neq j,\; s \in S \tag{15}$$

$$\theta_{ijs} \leq x_{js}, \quad \forall\, i, j \in C,\; i \neq j,\; s \in S \tag{16}$$

$$xs_j - (xs_i + l_i) - sd > M\,(z_{ijp} - 1)\,, \quad \forall\, i, j \in C \setminus \{0\}\,,\; i \neq j,\; p \in P \tag{17}$$

$$xs_j - (xs_i + l_i) - sd \leq M z_{ijp}, \quad \forall\, i, j \in C \setminus \{0\}\,,\; i \neq j, p \in P \tag{18}$$

$$z_{ijp} + z_{jip} \geq 1 - M\,(2 - k_{ip} - k_{jp})\,, \quad \forall\, i, j \in C \setminus \{0\}\,,\; i \neq j, p \in P \tag{19}$$

$$z_{ijp} \leq\; k_{ip}, \quad \forall\, i, j \in C \setminus \{0\}\,, p \in P \tag{20}$$

$$z_{ijp} \leq\; k_{jp}, \quad \forall\, i, j \in C \setminus \{0\}\,, p \in P \tag{21}$$

$$\sum_{n \in N} \alpha_{in} = 1, \quad \forall\, i \in C \setminus \{0\} \tag{22}$$

$$\sum_{\{n \in N | b_{pn}=1\}} \alpha_{in} \geq 1 - M\,(1 - k_{ip})\,, \quad \forall i \in C \setminus \{0\}\,,\; p \in P \tag{23}$$

$$\sum_{\{n\in N|b_{pn}=1\}} \alpha_{in} \leq 1 + M\left(1 - k_{ip}\right), \quad \forall\, i \in C\setminus\{0\},\ p \in P \tag{24}$$

$$y_{0w} = 1, \quad \forall\, w \in W \tag{25}$$

$$\sum_{w} y_{iw} = 1, \quad \forall\, i \in C\setminus\{0\} \tag{26}$$

$$\sum_{i} \mu_{ijw} \leq 1 + M\left(1 - y_{jw}\right), \quad \forall\, j \in C\setminus\{0\},\ w \in W \tag{27}$$

$$\sum_{i} \mu_{ijw} \geq 1 - M\left(1 - y_{jw}\right), \quad \forall\, j \in C\setminus\{0\},\ w \in W \tag{28}$$

$$\sum_{j\in C\setminus\{0\}} \mu_{ijw} \leq 1 + M\left(1 - y_{iw}\right), \quad \forall\, i \in C\setminus\{0\},\ w \in W \tag{29}$$

$$\sum_{i} y_{iw} > 1 - M\left(1 - \tau\right), \quad \forall\, w \in W \tag{30}$$

$$\sum_{j\in C\setminus\{0\}} \mu_{0jw} \geq 1 - M\left(1 - \tau\right), \quad \forall\, w \in W \tag{31}$$

$$\sum_{j\in C\setminus\{0\}} \mu_{0jw} \leq 1 + M\left(1 - \tau\right), \quad \forall\, w \in W \tag{32}$$

$$u_i < u_j + M\left(1 - \mu_{ijw}\right), \quad \forall\, i,j \in C\setminus\{0\}, w \in W \tag{33}$$

$$\mu_{ijw} + \mu_{jiw} \leq 1, \quad \forall\, i,j \in C,\ w \in W \tag{34}$$

$$\mu_{ijw} \leq y_{iw}, \quad \forall\, i,j \in C,\ w \in W \tag{35}$$

$$\mu_{ijw} \leq y_{jw}, \quad \forall i,j \in C,\ w \in W \tag{36}$$

$$\sum_{n} n\alpha_{jn} \leq \sum_{n} n\alpha_{in} + M\left(1 - \rho_{ijw}\right), \quad \forall i,j \in C\setminus\{0\}, w \in W \tag{37}$$

$$\sum_{n} n\alpha_{jn} \geq \sum_{n} n\alpha_{in} - M\left(1 - \rho_{ijw}\right), \quad \forall\, i,j \in C\setminus\{0\}, w \in W \tag{38}$$

$$\sum_{n} n\alpha_{jn} \leq \sum_{n} n\alpha_{nw}^{st} + M\left(1 - \rho_{0jw}\right), \quad \forall\, j \in C\setminus\{0\}, w \in W \tag{39}$$

$$\sum_{n} n\alpha_{jn} \geq \sum_{n} n\alpha_{nw}^{st} - M\left(1 - \rho_{0jw}\right), \quad \forall\, j \in C\setminus\{0\}, w \in W \tag{40}$$

$$\rho_{ijw} \leq \mu_{ijw}, \quad \forall\, i,j \in C, w \in W \tag{41}$$

$$\pi_{ijw} \leq \mu_{ijw}, \quad \forall\, i,j \in C, w \in W \tag{42}$$

$$\rho_{ijw} + \pi_{ijw} \leq 1 + M\left(1 - \mu_{ijw}\right), \quad \forall\, i,j \in C, w \in W \tag{43}$$

$$\rho_{ijw} + \pi_{ijw} \geq 1 - M\left(1 - \mu_{ijw}\right), \quad \forall\, i,j \in C, w \in W \tag{44}$$

$$0 \leq xs_i \leq L, \quad \forall\, i \in C \tag{45}$$

$$0 \leq xs_i + l_i \leq L, \quad \forall\, i \in C \tag{46}$$

$$\begin{aligned} &k_{ip}, x_{is}, y_{iw}, \theta_{ijs}, \mu_{ijw}, z_{ijp}, \alpha_{in} \in \{0,1\}, \\ &\forall\ i,j \in C, p \in P,\ s \in S,\ w \in W,\ n \in N \end{aligned} \tag{47}$$

The objective (1) is to minimize the total energy consumption of operation in the stockyard. The first three terms are the energy consumption of SRs, MCs and conveyor belts, respectively of handling (SRs and MCs) and transporting (conveyor belts) materials. The fourth term is the energy consumption of the conveyor belt when moving from the stockyard entrance to the stacking position of materials in the stockyard. The next two terms represent the energy consumption of SRs when moving from the position of the material they have just handled to the position of the material they will next serve. The energy consumption of MC when moving from one material to the next one is calculated by the last six terms. The transport distance is calculated vertically and horizontally respectively. The terms with variable μ_{0jw}, ρ_{0jw}, π_{0jw} calculate the energy consumption when moving from the initial position of each MC to the position of material they first serve.

Constraint (2) guarantees that each material can be allocated to only one stock pad. Constraint (3) allocates a virtual starting material for each SR. Constraint (4) ensures that each material is served by only one SR. Constraint (5) and (6) define the relationship between variable x_{is} and k_{ip}. If material i is served by SR s, the material i will be allocated to the stock pad p which stacker-reclaimer s can cover. Constraints (7)–(13) ensure that for each SR, if it is assigned to serve material in the planning period, the served material number will form a sequence beginning with the number 0, with each number of served material appearing only once. Constraint (14) states that two materials served by one SR can not be handled simultaneously. Constraints (15) and (16) are the premise of the non-overlapping constraints in time for materials served by the same SR. Constrains (17), (18), and (19) are the non-overlapping restrictions for any two materials stacked in the same pad and they must satisfy the safe distance restriction. Constraints (20) and (21) are the premise of the non-overlapping restrictions in space.

Constraint (22) guarantees that the MC serving each material can be located to only one interval. Constraint (23) and (24) defines the relationship between variable α_{in} and k_{ip}. If material i is located in stock pad p, the MC serving material i must be located in the interval to which the stock pad p is adjacent to. Constraint (25) allocates a virtual starting material for each MC. Constraint (26) states that each material is served by only one MC. Constraints (27)–(33) ensure that for each MC, if it is assigned to serve material in the planning period, the served material number will form a sequence beginning with the number 0, with each number of served material appearing only once. Constraint (34) states that two materials served by one MC can not be handled simultaneously. Constraints (35) and (36) are the premise of the non-overlapping constraints in time for materials served by the same MC. The meaning of ρ_{ijw} is defined in constraints (37) and (38). If MC w remains in the same interval when moving from the position of material i to that of material j, the MC serving material i and j are in the same interval. Constraints (39) and (40) have the same meaning as the above two constraints, but they describe the situation of an MC moving from the initial position to its first serving material. Constraints (41) and (42) are the premise of variable ρ_{ijw} and π_{ijw}. Constraint (43) and (44) state that only one of the two variables ρ_{ijw} and π_{ijw} can be 1 if there is pair $i \to j$ in the material handling sequence of MC w. Constraint (45) and (46) show the value range of start and end coordinates. Lastly, constraint (47) determines the domains of 0–1 variables.

5 Computational Experiments

In this section, we conducted computational experiments to test the effectiveness of the proposed mathematical model using solver CPLEX 22.1 under C++ environment with a time limit of 3600 s.

5.1 Instance Generation and Computational Results

We generated 12 instances and divided them into 3 sets according to the number of stock pads, SRs, and MCs. We consider $|C|$ materials, $|P|$ stock pads, $|S|$ SRs and $|W|$ MCs in computational experiments. The configuration of each instance can be found in Table 1. Set 1 has 4 stock pads with 2 SRs and 1 MC. Set 2 has the same configuration as set 1, except for 2 MCs. Set 3 has 6 stock pads with 3 SRs and 3 MCs. Each set consists of computational instances with different material numbers. The material information (mass and length) in instances with the same material numbers is the same. (Instances 1, 5, and 9 have the same information, which is the same situation for instances 2, 6, and 10; instances 3, 7, and 11 and instances 4, 8, and 12.) The material information is generated randomly.

Table 2 shows the results obtained within the time limit. Since the first three terms in the objective (1) are fixed terms, we use "Objective value of variable parts" in the table to explicitly show the objective value dependent on decision variables, that is, the value of objective (1) excluding the first three terms. The "objective value" in the following text refers to the value of objective excluding the fixed terms. Optimal solutions can be found for 9 of the 12 instances. The increase in the number of stock pads, SRs, MCs and materials expands the scale of the model, thus making the computation time increase dramatically. It can be noticed that the results of instances 1, 5, and 9 are the same (Instances 2, 6, and 10 are in the same situation.), which means the change of some parameters like the number of stock pads, SRs and MCs have little influence on optimal solutions to some extent.

We compare the composition of objective value (of variable parts) of instance 5–8 in Fig. 3. The energy consumption of the conveyor belt moving to the specified stacking position for materials takes a larger proportion compared to the other two components (energy consumption of SR and MC) during moving. It is observed that there is a clear absolute variation of the energy consumption of the belt conveyor moving among different instances, while the change of energy

Table 2. Computational results for the test instances

Set	Ins No.	$\|C\|$	$\|P\|$	$\|S\|$	$\|W\|$	Objective value of variable parts(kW·h)	time(s)
1	1	5	4	2	1	15.25	4.64
	2	5	4	2	1	13.25	5.04
	3	6	4	2	1	19.76	68.61
	4	7	4	2	1	24.17	2480.27
2	5	5	4	2	2	15.25	9.91
	6	5	4	2	2	13.25	41.12
	7	6	4	2	2	19.76	104.54
	8	7	4	2	2	24.17	3600
3	9	5	6	3	3	15.25	226.45
	10	5	6	3	3	13.25	216.92
	11	6	6	3	3	19.76	3600
	12	7	6	3	3	23.36	3600

consumption of SR and MC moving is rather less obvious. The possible reason is that each SR and MC moves between two stock pads (in one interval), the transport distance of SR and MC is therefore relatively shorter than the distance the conveyor belt travels.

5.2 Managerial Insights

With the calculation results in Sect. 5.1, we can extract some managerial insights which may be helpful for storage space management in the stockyard.

(1) The number of stock pads open can be determined according to the number of incoming materials. Stockyards do not always need to open all the stock pads. We can find that the objective values of instances 1,5,9 are the same, which means the results obtained in the background of 4 stock pads and 6 stock pads are the same. Opening stock yards depending on the number of materials may help save operational costs of the stockyard.

(2) Materials are stacked into the adjacent stock pads which one stacker-reclaimer and mist cannon can cover, which could shorten the travel distance of SR and MC, thus saving the energy consumed. As shown in Fig. 4 and 5, all the materials are stacked in the adjacent pad 1 and 2.

(3) Materials tend to be stacked in the stock pads close to the stockyard entrance so that the conveyor belts do not need to move a long distance, which could reduce the energy consumption of the conveyor belt. Figure 4 and 5 show that materials are stacked in the pad 1 and 2 which are closest to the entrance of the stockyard.

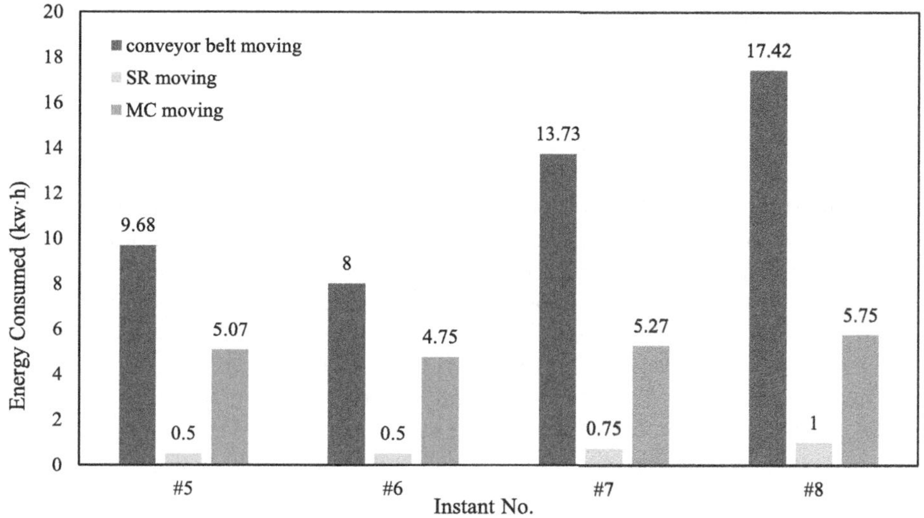

Fig. 3. Comparison of the objective value of instance 5–8.

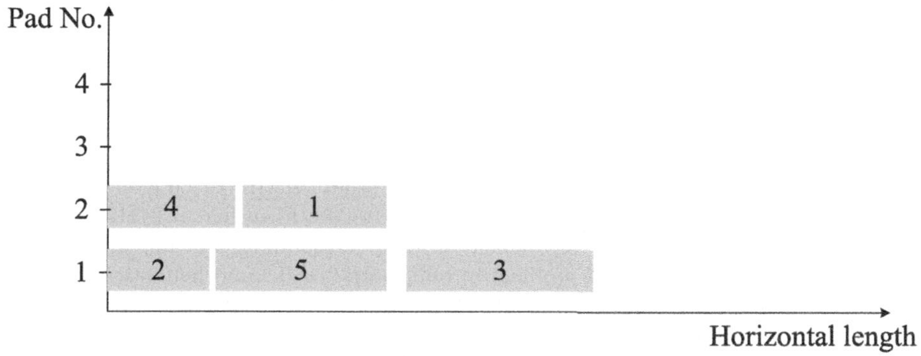

Fig. 4. Representation of solution for instance 5.

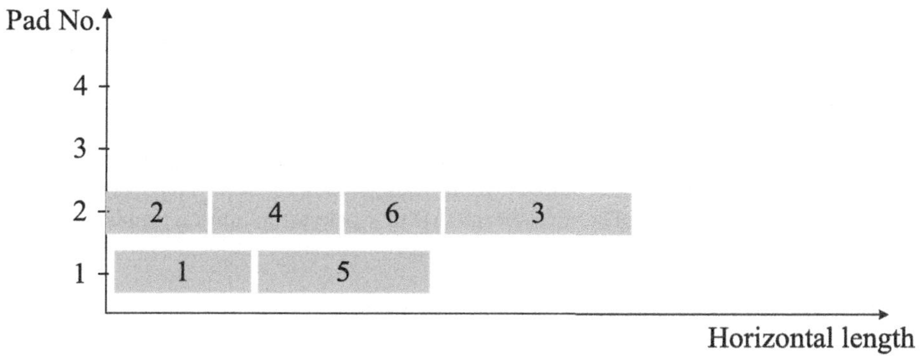

Fig. 5. Representation of solution for instance 7.

6 Conclusion

We study the Storage Space Allocation Problem with the consideration of operation machines in the stockyard. Existing studies investigate the storage space allocation problem with other operation problems such as berth allocation and stacker reclaimer scheduling. However, they pay little attention to environmental sustainability. We take the operation of mist cannon to control dust during stacking into consideration and aim to minimize the energy consumption during stacking operation. A mixed integer programming model is established, and we show the effectiveness of the proposed model by conducting computational experiments on some small-scale instances. Some managerial insights are extracted, which may help in storage space management as a reference.

Our future work will focus on the improvement of the formulation of the model and the development of an efficient algorithm to solve the model for large-scale instances. And we need to collect operational data from real-world practice as the input of computational experiments to validate the results considering practical implications.

References

1. Ago, M., Nishi, T., Konishi, M.: Simultaneous optimization of storage allocation and routing problems for belt-conveyor transportation. J. Adv. Mech. Design Syst. Manuf. **1**(2), 250–261 (2007)
2. Al-Hammadi, J., Diabat, A.: An integrated berth allocation and yard assignment problem for bulk ports: formulation and case study. RAIRO - Oper. Res. **51**(1), 267–284 (2017). https://doi.org/10.1051/ro/2015048. Identifier: ro151165
3. de Andrade, J.L.M., Menezes, G.C.: An integrated planning, scheduling, yard allocation and berth allocation problem in bulk ports: model and heuristics. In: Mes, M., Lalla-Ruiz, E., Voß, S. (eds.) ICCL 2021. LNCS, vol. 13004, pp. 3–20. Springer, Cham (2021). https://doi.org/10.1007/978-3-030-87672-2_1
4. de Andrade, J.L.M., Menezes, G.C.: A column generation-based heuristic to solve the integrated planning, scheduling, yard allocation and berth allocation problem in bulk ports. J. Heuristics **29**(1), 39–76 (2022). https://doi.org/10.1007/s10732-022-09506-3
5. Babu, S.A.K.I., et al.: Minimizing delay of ships in bulk terminals by simultaneous ship scheduling, stockyard planning and train scheduling. Maritime Econ. Logist. **17**(4), 464–492 (2015). https://doi.org/10.1057/mel.2014.20
6. Belassiria, I., Mazouzi, M., Elfezazi, S., Torbi, I.: A heuristic methods for stacker and reclaimer scheduling problem in coal storage area. In: 2019 International Colloquium on Logistics And Supply Chain Management (LOGISTIQUA) (2019)
7. Boland, N., Gulczynski, D., Savelsbergh, M.: A stockyard planning problem. EURO J. Transp. Logist. **1**(3), 197–236 (2012). https://doi.org/10.1007/s13676-012-0011-z
8. Hanoun, S., Khan, B., Johnstone, M., Nahavandi, S., Creighton, D.: An effective heuristic for stockyard planning and machinery scheduling at a coal handling facility. In: 2013 11th IEEE International Conference On Industrial Informatics (INDIN), pp. 206–211 (2013)

9. Hu, D., Yao, Z.: Stacker-reclaimer scheduling in a dry bulk terminal. Int. J. Comput. Integr. Manuf. **25**(11), 1047–1058 (2012)
10. Iris, Ç., Lam, J.S.L.: A review of energy efficiency in ports: operational strategies, technologies and energy management systems. Renew. Sustain. Energy Rev. **112**, 170–182 (2019)
11. Lam, J.S.L., Notteboom, T.: The greening of ports: a comparison of port management tools used by leading ports in Asia and Europe. Transp. Rev. **34**(2), 169–189 (2014)
12. Menezes, G.C., Mateus, G.R., Ravetti, M.G.: A branch and price algorithm to solve the integrated production planning and scheduling in bulk ports. Eur. J. Oper. Res. **258**(3), 926–937 (2017). https://doi.org/10.1016/j.ejor.2016.08.073
13. Ouhaman, A.A., Benjelloun, K., Kenne, J.P., Najid, N.: The storage space allocation problem in a dry bulk terminal: a heuristic solution. In: 21st IFAC World Congress on Automatic Control - Meeting Societal Challenges, vol. 53, pp. 10822–10827 (2020). https://doi.org/10.1016/j.ifacol.2020.12.2868
14. Robenek, T., Umang, N., Bierlaire, M., Ropke, S.: A branch-and-price algorithm to solve the integrated berth allocation and yard assignment problem in bulk ports. Eur. J. Oper. Res. **235**(2), 399–411 (2014). https://doi.org/10.1016/j.ejor.2013.08.015
15. Schulte, F., Voß, S., Ascencio, L.M., González-Ramírez, R.G.: Directions for sustainable ports in Latin America and the Caribbean. Int. J. Transp. Econ. **43**(3), 315–337 (2016)
16. Sun, D., Meng, Y., Tang, L., Liu, J., Huang, B., Yang, J.: Storage space allocation problem at inland bulk material stockyard. Transp. Res. Part E: Logist. Transp. Rev. **134** (2020). https://doi.org/10.1016/j.tre.2020.101856
17. Tang, L., Sun, D., Liu, J.: Integrated storage space allocation and ship scheduling problem in bulk cargo terminals. IIE Trans. **48**(5), 428–439 (2016). https://doi.org/10.1080/0740817x.2015.1063791
18. Tang, X., Jin, J.G., Shi, X.: Stockyard storage space allocation in large iron ore terminals. Comput. Industr. Eng. **164**, 107911 (2022). https://doi.org/10.1016/j.cie.2021.107911
19. Unsal, O., Oguz, C.: An exact algorithm for integrated planning of operations in dry bulk terminals. Transp. Res. Part E: Logist. Transp. Rev. **126**, 103–121 (2019). https://doi.org/10.1016/j.tre.2019.03.018
20. van Vianen, T., Ottjes, J., Lodewijks, G.: Simulation-based rescheduling of the stacker-reclaimer operation. J. Comput. Sci. **10**, 149–154 (2015). https://doi.org/10.1016/j.jocs.2014.06.004

Planning LNG Annual Delivery Programs with Speed Optimization and Multiple Loading Ports

Helle V. Haug[1], Sigrid H. Solum[1], Sanna B. Warholm[1], Kjetil Fagerholt[1(✉)], Mingyu Li[2], and Inge Norstad[2]

[1] Department of Industrial Economics and Technology, Norwegian University of Science and Technology, Trondheim, Norway
kjetil.fagerholt@ntnu.no
[2] Quorum Software, Houston, TX, USA
inge.norstad@quoromsoftware.com

Abstract. We study the planning problem of creating Annual Delivery Programs (ADPs) in the Liquefied Natural Gas Industry (LNG), in which an LNG producer must fulfill a series of long-term contracts for LNG deliveries with customers all over the world with a given fleet of LNG vessels. We expand existing models in the literature by also considering speed optimization and multiple loading ports. We denote this planning problem as the LNG-ADP with Speed Optimization and Multiple Load Ports (LNG-ADP-SO-MLP). We propose a novel and efficient mixed integer programming (MIP) model for the LNG-ADP-SO-MLP. The model is solved using a commercial MIP-solver on a number of realistic instances for two different LNG producers. It is shown that the solver obtains solutions with less than 1% optimality gaps within one hour for instances with a planning horizon of up to 180 days. This indicates that the model can efficiently be embedded within a rolling horizon heuristic to solve instances with longer planning horizons.

Keywords: Liquefied Natural Gas · Annual Delivery Program · Ship Routing · Inventory Management · Speed Optimization

1 Introduction

The earth contains enormous amounts of natural gas, which are often located far from where the gas is needed. For long distances the gas must be transported by sea. To make transportation volume-efficient and safe, the natural gas is cooled down and condensed to its liquid form, i.e., into Liquefied Natural Gas (LNG), at liquefaction plants, before being loaded onto specially designed LNG vessels for transportation to its destination where the LNG is boiled to natural gas at a regasification port.

The demand for LNG has steadily been increasing and today there are liquidation and regasification ports organized for shipping of LNG in large parts of

© The Author(s), under exclusive license to Springer Nature Switzerland AG 2023
J. R. Daduna et al. (Eds.): ICCL 2023, LNCS 14239, pp. 170–184, 2023.
https://doi.org/10.1007/978-3-031-43612-3_10

the world. Countries in some areas, especially the Middle East, USA, and Australia, are net exporters of LNG, while countries in areas including China, Japan, and Europe are net importers. Large geographical distances between suppliers and customers create a high demand for shipping LNG by sea.

The average charter rate (rental price) for a 160 000 cubic meter LNG vessel in 2021 was around 89 000 USD/day, up from around 59 300 USD/day in 2020 [4]. However, the spot charter rate reached as high as 400 000 USD/day during 2022, mainly due to political tensions related to Russia being at war and cutting off gas supplies to Europe, as well as the sabotage of two pipelines in the Baltic Sea [3]. Although this is an unusual situation, it highlights the current importance of optimizing LNG transportation to maximize the utilization of the vessel fleet.

In this paper, we study a special case of the maritime inventory routing problem for an LNG producer, which is the planning of so-called Annual Delivery Programs (ADPs). We denote this planning problem as the LNG-ADP, in which the producer must fulfill a series of long-term contracts with customers all over the world while also having the option to sell LNG in the spot market. The producer is in charge of the inventory of LNG at its liquefaction plant(s), the loading port with a limited number of berths, and the routing and scheduling of a heterogeneous fleet of LNG vessels. The LNG-ADP describes the customer deliveries of LNG cargoes for the next 12 months. In the LNG-ADP, the LNG producer aims at maximizing the profits, which consists of the revenue from the sales of LNG less the sailing and vessel chartering costs.

The LNG-ADP is, due to its importance, well studied. An important pioneering study was published by Rakke et al. [10], who proposed a Rolling Horizon Heuristic (RHH) for this planning problem. Later, Stålhane et al. [11] used a construction and improvement heuristic that makes a set of solutions with a greedy insertion procedure, improves them with a first-descent neighborhood search and/or branch-and-bound on a mathematical formulation. Al Haidous et al. [1] base their model on the same assumptions as [10], but consider the specific case of using a homogeneous fleet of LNG-delivery vessels, with the goal of minimizing fleet size. Andersson et al. [2] also model the LNG-ADP problem in the same way as [10], but add four families of valid inequalities to improve the lower bounds on the problem's optimal value.

The study by Mutlu et al. [8] stands out by including two extensions: 1) the production of LNG is a decision variable and not an input parameter, and 2) allowing split deliveries, where a vessel can unload partial cargoes in more than one unloading port. Li et al. [6] were the first to include transshipment in the LNG-ADP problem, motivated by the Yamal LNG case where a transshipment port helps the producer to avoid longer-than-necessary voyages with ice-breaking LNG vessels, as normal LNG vessels can take over the LNG and deliver it to the customers. Li et al. [6] introduce a continuous-time formulation for this problem, while Li et al. [5] later proposes a time-discrete model for the same problem. Both models are embedded into and solved with an RHH.

In this paper, we expand previous models of the LNG-ADP by including optimization of the vessels' sailing speeds. In contrast to currently existing models from the literature, our models also allows for multiple loading ports, which is becoming relevant for some producers as the industry develops. Hence, we refer to our version of the LNG-ADP with Speed Optimization and Multiple Loading Ports (LNG-ADP-SO-MLP). Speed optimization in ship routing has been widely studied, e.g., [9,12], although not in the context of LNG-ADP planning. We propose a novel Mixed Integer Programming (MIP) model for the LNG-ADP-SO-MLP. We generate a number of realistic instances based on data from two LNG producers and show that our MIP model can be efficiently solved with low optimality gaps for instances with a planning horizon of up to 180 days using a commercial MIP-solver. Furthermore, the results show that including speed optimization in the planning can improve the profits and make the planning more flexible.

The remaining of this paper is organized as follows. Section 2 gives a formal definition of the LNG-ADP-SO-MLP, while our MIP model for this problem is introduced in Sect. 3. The computational study is presented in Sect. 4, before we conclude in Sect. 5.

2 Problem Definition

The LNG-ADP-SO-MLP considers an LNG producer's planning of the supply of LNG to customers over a planning horizon with a given vessel fleet. The producer controls one or more loading (liquefaction) ports where the LNG is produced (liquefied). Each loading port has a given daily production, which may vary throughout the year. Furthermore, each loading port has a given set of berths from which the vessels load LNG. The number of available berths may also vary over time, e.g., due to maintenance. In addition, each loading port has storage tanks with a given maximum and minimum storage capacity.

There is a given set of customers, which either require LNG Delivered Ex-Ship (DES), where the LNG producer transports the cargo to the customer with its own vessels, or Free-On-Board (FOB), where the customers pick up the cargo at an agreed loading port with their own vessels. Each DES contract has an associated unloading port, where the vessels unload the LNG cargoes. Since the customer decides when it wants the LNG delivered, we assume there is always available inventory capacity and berth capacity at the unloading ports. Both DES and FOB customers define their demand in advance for specific subsets of the planning horizon, hereby referred to as *partitions*. A customer typically has annual, quarterly, and/or monthly partitions with an associated delivery requirement. The customers' required contract volumes are satisfied by one or more deliveries in each partition. For a DES customer, the minimum demand within each partition must be satisfied, and a revenue is associated with deliveries above this minimum up to a specified maximum demand within the partition. For FOB contracts, each delivery must be the size of the vessel picking it up. In addition to these contract deliveries, it is also possible to have optional one-time deliveries of spot cargoes with associated customer destinations and revenues. These have to be delivered either using the LNG producer's vessels (like DES) or by using the customer's own vessel (like FOB).

Each vessel in the LNG producer's fleet has a given fuel consumption depending (non-linearly) on the sailing speed, as well as a maximum and minimum sailing speed. The distances between ports are known in advance. If the LNG producer is short on vessels, additional vessels can be chartered at a given daily rate. Each vessel has a specific loading capacity and is always loaded up to capacity due to physical limitations. It is also required to unload the entire load at the unloading port, except for a minimum tank volume share that is needed to keep the tanks cool due to the *boil-off effect*, which means that a fraction of the LNG that is transported will evaporate during a voyage, typically at a rate of 0.10–0.12% per day [7]. The actual delivery volume of each delivery is therefore defined by the capacity of the vessel and the boil-off, which depends on the sailing distance. Each vessel has a given start position at the beginning of the planning horizon. A vessel becomes available for a new voyage when it returns to a loading port, and may therefore become available some days into the beginning of the planning horizon.

Some vessels might be scheduled for maintenance during the planning horizon. This must take place at a pre-defined maintenance port and start within a given time window. After maintenance, the vessel has to go through a purge and a cool-down procedure, which must be done at a loading port and is assumed to take a given amount of time. All vessels are assumed to have the same specified time associated with loading and unloading (i.e., one day).

The main decisions of the LNG-ADP-SO-MLP are where to send each vessel at what times and at what speeds, i.e., the vessel routes and schedules, while making sure that all customer delivery requirements are satisfied and that the inventory levels at the loading ports are kept within its limits at all times. Not all vessels can visit all ports, and some vessels cannot serve all customers due to their properties not being compatible with the customer's unloading port. Also, some vessels are restricted to serving specific customer contracts. Furthermore, no more vessels than there are available berths can load on a given day at a given production port. Additional decisions include how much spot cargo to sell within certain demand and revenue specifications.

The planning objective of the LNG-ADP-SO-MLP is to maximize the gross margin less the transportation costs (hereby referred to as the "profit"). The revenue comes from spot cargoes transported DES and FOB, from long-term contracted LNG deliveries (DES and FOB), and lastly from the value of the remaining LNG at the end of the planning period. The costs are the (speed-dependent) sailing costs for the producer's fleet of vessels, as well as the chartering costs. The resulting plan is an Annual Delivery Program, describing the routes and schedules for the vessels in the fleet over the given planning horizon.

3 Mathematical Model

In the following, we explain the modeling assumptions and generation of the underlying network in Sect. 3.1. We introduce the notation in Sect. 3.2, before the model is presented in Sect. 3.3.

3.1 Modeling Assumptions and Network Generation

The proposed MIP model is time-discrete where an arc represents a one-way sailing between two ports in a time-space network. Each time period is one day, which is a reasonable resolution for the LNG-ADP-SO-MLP. Before running the MIP model, an arc generation procedure generates feasible arcs, which are given as input to the MIP model. The arcs are generated so that we allow that the LNG vessels can wait at a port before loading/unloading for up to a specified number of days. This makes the model more flexible when it comes to handling both inventory constraints at the loading ports and contract delivery requirements for the customers.

A node in the time-space network is a combination of a port and a time period, denoted (i, t) or (j, t'), where i and j denote ports, and t and t' denote time periods. Each port represents one of five port types: 1) a loading port, where LNG is stored before being loaded onto the vessels before transportation; 2) an unloading (customer) port, where LNG is unloaded from the vessel and regasified; 3) a maintenance port, which the vessels that require maintenance must visit within the specified time winodws; 4) a spot unloading port, which is similar to an unloading port, except that only optional cargoes can be unloaded here; 5) the artificial initialization and destination ports for the vessels.

An arc in the network $((i, t), (j, t'))$ for a vessel links two nodes. The start time of an arc is defined by the point in time when the vessel starts sailing from the start port. The end time of an arc is the start time of the arc, plus the time it takes to complete four vessel activities: 1) sailing; 2) potential waiting; 3) potential purge and cool-down procedure; 4) the port operations, i.e., the time for loading/unloading. An example of an arc in the time-space network is shown in Fig. 1. The blue line represents the arc $((i, t), (j, t'))$, and the pink lines represent the actual processes included in the arc. Waiting is relevant when the sailing distance and times of an arc imply a speed lower than the minimum speed of the vessel. The vessel will then sail at its minimum speed and wait outside the port in order to fulfill the time requirement. The purge and cool-down process is only relevant when a vessel comes from a maintenance port.

As shown in Fig. 1, the arcs are defined so that the sailing precedes the other activities. This modeling choice is made to simplify the berth constraints at the loading port and to reduce symmetry. In the case of purge and cool-down, a vessel requires more time in the loading port after maintenance. An arc provides information about what type of node a vessel came from (the i in $((i, t), (j, t'))$). Therefore, we know if a purge-and-cool down is necessary, and thus how long a berth is busy before the next vessel can arrive.

Artificial nodes and their associated arcs are included for two purposes. First, this makes sure only one journey is started for each vessel. This is done by having only one electable arc from the artificial origin node to the time and location where the vessel first becomes available. The artificial origin node is located in $(i, t) = (0, 0)$. The arcs from the artificial origin node have 0 associated costs. Second, it easily allows for not using a vessel at all, represented by an arc going from the artificial origin node in $(i, t) = (0, 0)$ to the artificial destination node

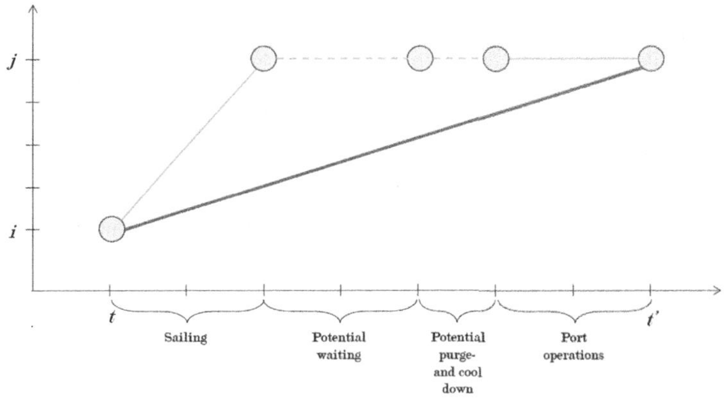

Fig. 1. Illustration of an arc $((i,t),(j,t'))$ *and the vessel activities it represents*

in $(i,t) = (0,|\mathcal{T}|+1)$, where $|\mathcal{T}|$ is the length of the planning horizon. These arcs also have 0 associated costs.

Since there is always an option to either shut down production or accept potential additional spot contracts for the LNG producer throughout the year, an assumption about defining an *artificial spot FOB contract* is made. This artificial spot FOB contract has zero revenue and allows surplus LNG to potentially be sold throughout the planning period. Each cargo loaded by the artificial spot FOB contract in the final ADP represents a possibility for the LNG producer to find a corresponding real-life spot contract for the given cargo's pick-up interval.

Following this, we generate the network that is used as input to the MIP model. Note that each arc has a calculated cost and also represents a given associated sailing speed, and hence fuel cost. As an example, consider the two arcs $((i,t),(j,t'))$ and $((i,t),(j,t'+1))$, the latter arc allows for spending an additional day than the former on the sailing between the ports i and j. This allows for sailing at a lower speed and sailing cost.

3.2 Notation

Sets

$\mathcal{V}$ Set of producer-operated vessels that are available during the planning horizon
$\mathcal{V}^M$ Set of vessels that require maintenance during the planning horizon, $\mathcal{V}^M \subset \mathcal{V}$
$\mathcal{V}_i$ Set of vessels that can serve node i, $\mathcal{V}_i \in \mathcal{V}$
$\mathcal{N}$ Set of ports
$\mathcal{N}^L$ Set of loading ports, $\mathcal{N}^L \subset \mathcal{N}$
$\mathcal{N}^U$ Set of unloading ports, $\mathcal{N}^U \subset \mathcal{N}$
$\mathcal{N}^S$ Set of spot unloading ports, $\mathcal{N}^S \subset \mathcal{N}$
$\mathcal{N}^M$ Set of maintenance ports, $\mathcal{N}^M \subset \mathcal{N}$

$\mathcal{A}_v$ Set of feasible arcs vessel v can sail
$\mathcal{A}_v^M$ Set of feasible maintenance arcs vessel v can sail to start maintenance, $\mathcal{A}_v^M \subset \mathcal{A}_v$
$\mathcal{A}_v^U$ Set of feasible arcs ship v can sail to deliver a DES long-term contracted cargo, $\mathcal{A}_v^U \subset \mathcal{A}_v$
$\mathcal{A}_v^S$ Set of feasible arcs ship v can sail to deliver a DES spot cargo, $\mathcal{A}_v^S \subset \mathcal{A}_v$
$\mathcal{F}_i$ Set of FOB cargoes of LNG that want to be picked up at loading port i
$\mathcal{F}_i^U$ Set of long-term contracted FOB cargoes of LNG that must be picked up at loading port i, $\mathcal{F}_i^U \subset \mathcal{F}_i$
$\mathcal{F}_i^S$ Set of Spot FOB cargoes who's load can be picked up by a FOB vessel at loading port i, also including the artificial FOB-pickup ($f = 1$), $\mathcal{F}_i^S \subset \mathcal{F}$
$\mathcal{P}_j$ Set of time partitions where customer j has DES delivery requirements
$\mathcal{T}$ Set of time periods (days) in the planning horizon
$\mathcal{T}^L$ Set of time periods in loading days, where the vessels can lift LNGÂ from a loading port, $\mathcal{T}^L \subset \mathcal{T}$
$\mathcal{T}^U$ Set of time periods in unloading days, where vessels can deliver LNGÂ to a customer, $\mathcal{T}^U \subset \mathcal{T}$
$\mathcal{T}_{jp}$ Set of time periods within partition p for customer j, $\mathcal{T}_{jp} \subset \mathcal{T}$
$\mathcal{T}_f^{FOB}$ Set of time periods where FOB cargo f can be picked up, $\mathcal{T}_f^{FOB} \subset \mathcal{T}$
$\mathcal{T}_v$ Set of time periods where vessel v is available to be scheduled, $\mathcal{T}_v \subset \mathcal{T}$
$\mathcal{T}_v^M$ The time period where maintenance of vessel v is scheduled to start, $\mathcal{T}_v^M \subset \mathcal{T}_v$

Parameters

$C_{vitjt'}^S$ Sailing cost of each feasible arc $((i,t),(j,t'))$ for vessel v
C_{itj}^C Costs of using a charter vessel to deliver a cargo at port j, loading the cargo at loading port i at time t
$\mathcal{N}_v^{START}$ Start port of vessel v
T_v^{START} First time period where vessel v is available to be scheduled
T_{vij}^O Operational time associated with sailing from port location i to port location j for vessel v
T_{ij}^C Sailing time for a charter vessel sailing from loading port i to unloading port j
T_{fi}^{OFOB} Operational time associated to port location j for FOB cargo f
L_v Capacity of vessel v
$\overline{L}^C$ Upper limit for capacity of a charter vessel
$\underline{L}^C$ Lower limit for capacity of a charter vessel
L_f^{FOB} Loading quantity of FOB cargo f
$\overline{D}_{jp}$ Maximum demand of unloading port j in partition p
$\underline{D}_{jp}$ Minimum demand of unloading port j in partition p
R_f^{SFOB} Revenue per volume unit of LNG loaded for FOB spot contract f
R_f^{UFOB} Revenue per volume unit of LNG loaded for long-term FOB contract f
$R_{jt'}^{DES}$ Revenue per volume unit of LNG for delivering DES contract to customer j at time t'
R_i^{END} Unit value of LNG left in storage tanks at loading port i at the end of the planning horizon
$B_{jt'}$ Berth capacity at port j at time t'
Q_{it}^P Produced quantity of LNG in loading port i in time period t

$\overline{S}_i$ Maximum storage level of LNG at loading port i
$\underline{S}_i$ Minimum storage level of LNG at loading port i
S_i Initial storage level of LNG at the start of the planning horizon at loading port i
E Boil-off rate in percent of total vessel capacity

Variables

$x_{vitjt'}$ 1 if vessel v sail arc $((i,t),(j,t'))$, and 0 otherwise

$z_{ft'}$ 1 if a cargo from FOB contract f is done loading in time period t', and 0 otherwise

w_{itj} 1 if a charter vessel starts sailing from loading port i at time t to deliver a cargo at j, and 0 otherwise

g_{itj} Amount loaded by a charter vessel in loading port i at time t to deliver in unloading port j

s_{it} Remaining storage at loading port i at the end of time period t

3.3 Mathematical Model

Objective Function. The Objective function (1) maximizes profit, which is represented by revenue less vessel sailing costs. The first seven terms represent 1) the revenue from the long-term DES contracts served by own vessels, 2) the long-term DES contract shipments shipped by charter vessels, 3) the DES spot contracts served by own vessels, 4) the DES spot contract served by charter vessels, 5) the long-term FOB contracts, 6) the revenue from the spot FOB contracts, and 7) the value of the remaining LNG at the end of the planning horizon, respectively. Note that the boil-off effect is accounted for by including the boil-off rate E in terms 1 to 4. The last two terms are the cost terms. The first cost term is the cost of sailing the producer-operated vessels, while the last term represents the cost of using charter vessels.

$$
\begin{aligned}
max z = & \sum_{v\in\mathcal{V}}\sum_{((i,t),(j,t'))\in\mathcal{A}_v^U} R_{jt'}^{DES} L_v(1-(t'-t)E)x_{vitjt'} \\
& + \sum_{i\in\mathcal{N}^L}\sum_{t\in\mathcal{T}^L}\sum_{j\in\mathcal{N}^U} R_{j,t+T_{ij}^C}^{DES}(1-T_{ij}^C E)g_{itj} + \sum_{v\in\mathcal{V}}\sum_{((i,t),(j,t'))\in\mathcal{A}_v^S} R_{jt'}^{DES} L_v(1-(t'-t)E)x_{vitjt'} \\
& + \sum_{i\in\mathcal{N}^L}\sum_{t\in\mathcal{T}^L}\sum_{j\in\mathcal{N}^S} R_{j,t+T_{ij}^C}^{DES}(1-T_{ij}^C E)g_{itj} + \sum_{i\in\mathcal{N}^L}\sum_{f\in\mathcal{F}_i^U}\sum_{t'\in\mathcal{T}} R_f^{UFOB} L_f^{FOB} z_{ft'} \\
& + \sum_{i\in\mathcal{N}^L}\sum_{f\in\mathcal{F}_i^S}\sum_{t'\in\mathcal{T}} R_f^{SFOB} L_f^{FOB} z_{ft'} + \sum_{i\in\mathcal{N}^L} R_i^{END} s_{i,|\mathcal{T}|} \\
& - \sum_{v\in\mathcal{V}}\sum_{((i,t),(j,t'))\in\mathcal{A}_v} C_{vitjt'}^S x_{vitjt'} - \sum_{i\in\mathcal{N}^L}\sum_{t\in\mathcal{T}}\sum_{j\in\mathcal{N}^U} C_{itj}^C w_{itj}
\end{aligned}
\tag{1}
$$

Inventory Constraints. Constraints (2) to (4) handle the inventory at the loading ports. Constraints (2) initialize the constraint for each loading node, while Constraints (3) make sure that the inventory requirement is fulfilled for each day afterwards. Constraints (4) ensure that the inventory level is always within its limits.

$$
\begin{aligned}
s_{i1} = S_i + Q_{i1}^P & - \sum_{j\in\mathcal{N}^U}\sum_{t'\in\mathcal{T}}\sum_{v\in\mathcal{V}_i} L_v x_{vi1jt'} - \sum_{j\in\mathcal{N}^U} g_{i1j} \\
& - \sum_{f\in\mathcal{F}_i}\sum_{t'\in\mathcal{T}_f^{FOB}} L_f^{FOB} z_{ft'}, \qquad i\in\mathcal{N}^L
\end{aligned}
\tag{2}
$$

$$s_{it} = s_{i,t-1} + Q_{it}^{P} - \sum_{j \in \mathcal{N}^U} \sum_{t' \in \mathcal{T}} \sum_{v \in \mathcal{V}_i} L_v x_{vitjt'} - \sum_{j \in \mathcal{N}^U} g_{itj} - \sum_{f \in \mathcal{F}_i} \sum_{t' \in \mathcal{T}_f^{FOB}} L_f^{FOB} z_{ft'}, \qquad i \in \mathcal{N}^L, t \in \mathcal{T}^L \setminus \{1\} \tag{3}$$

$$\underline{S_i} \leq s_{it} \leq \overline{S_i}, \qquad i \in \mathcal{N}^L, t \in \mathcal{T}^L \tag{4}$$

Maintenance and Vessel Flow Constraints. Constraints (5) state that the vessels in need of maintenance perform this exactly one time. Constraints (6) ensure that each vessel either starts at its start position at its first available day or is not used at all. Constraints (7) are vessel flow conservation constraints.

$$\sum_{((i,t),(j,t')) \in \mathcal{A}_v^M} x_{vitjt'} = 1, \qquad v \in \mathcal{V}^M \tag{5}$$

$$x_{v,0,0,N_v^{START},T_v^{START}} + x_{v,0,0,0,|\mathcal{T}|+1} = 1, \qquad v \in \mathcal{V} \tag{6}$$

$$\sum_{i \in \mathcal{N}} \sum_{t=0}^{t'-1} x_{vitjt'} = \sum_{i \in \mathcal{N}} \sum_{t=t'+1}^{|\mathcal{T}|} x_{vjt'it}, \qquad v \in \mathcal{V}, j \in \mathcal{N}, t' \in \mathcal{T} \tag{7}$$

Demand Constraints. Constraints (8) are demand constraints ensuring that demand is satisfied for each DES long-term contract in each time partition. The constraints account for the difference in loading and unloading volumes by subtracting the boil-off.

$$\underline{D}_{jp} \leq \sum_{v \in \mathcal{V}_i} \sum_{i \in \mathcal{N}^L} \sum_{t \in \mathcal{T}_v} \sum_{t' \in \mathcal{T}_{jp}} L_v(1 - (t' - t)E) x_{vitjt'} + \sum_{i \in \mathcal{N}^L} \sum_{t \in (\mathcal{T}_{jp} - T_{ij}^C)} g_{itj}(1 - T_{ij}^C E) \leq \overline{D}_{jp}, \quad j \in \mathcal{N}^U \cup \mathcal{N}^S, \quad p \in \mathcal{P}_j \tag{8}$$

Constraints (9) and (10) are the FOB contract constraints. Constraints (9) make sure that each long-term FOB cargo contract is fulfilled once within its time window, while Constraints (10) make sure each that spot FOB cargo contract is fulfilled at most once in the relevant time window, except for the artificial spot FOB contracts (contract 1), which can be fulfilled as many times as wanted.

$$\sum_{t' \in \mathcal{T}_f^{FOB}} z_{ft'} = 1, \qquad j \in \mathcal{N}^L, f \in \mathcal{F}_j^U \tag{9}$$

$$\sum_{t' \in \mathcal{T}_f^{FOB}} z_{ft'} \leq 1, \qquad j \in \mathcal{N}^L, f \in \mathcal{F}_j^S \setminus \{1\} \tag{10}$$

Berth and Charter Constraints. Constraints (11) are the berth capacity constraints. Constraints (12) ensure that if a charter vessel loads a cargo, the amount loaded is bounded within an upper and lower limit. This allows for some flexibility in the capacities of the charter vessels.

$$\sum_{v\in\mathcal{V}^P}\sum_{i\in\mathcal{N}}\sum_{t\in\mathcal{T}}\sum_{\tau=t'+1}^{t'+T^O_{vij}} x_{vitj\tau} + \sum_{j'\in\mathcal{N}^U} w_{jt'j'} + \sum_{f\in\mathcal{F}_j}\sum_{\tau=t'+1}^{t'+T^{OFOB}_{fj}} z_{f\tau} \le B_{jt'}, \quad j\in\mathcal{N}^L,\quad t'\in\mathcal{T}^U \tag{11}$$

$$\underline{L}^C w_{itj} \le g_{itj} \le \overline{L}^C w_{itj}, \quad i\in\mathcal{N}^L, t\in\mathcal{T}^L, j\in\mathcal{N}^U\cup N^S \tag{12}$$

Variable Domains. Constraints (13) to (17) specify the domains of our three binary variables $x_{vitjt'}$, $z_{ft'}$ and $w_{vitjt'}$ as well as the continuous variables g_{itj} and s_{it}. The binary variable $z_{ft'}$ is only defined for loading ports and the relevant time periods. The binary decision variable for using a charter vessel, variable w_{itj}, is only defined for arcs that go from a loading node to an unloading node.

$$x_{vitjt'} \in \{0,1\}, \quad v\in\mathcal{V}, ((i,t),(j,t'))\in\mathcal{A}_v \tag{13}$$

$$z_{ft'} \in \{0,1\}, \quad j\in\mathcal{N}^L, f\in\mathcal{F}_j, t'\in\mathcal{T}^{FOB}_f \tag{14}$$

$$w_{itj} \in \{0,1\}, \quad i\in\mathcal{N}^L, t\in\mathcal{T}^L, j\in\mathcal{N}^U\cup N^S \tag{15}$$

$$g_{itj} \ge 0, \quad i\in\mathcal{N}^L, t\in\mathcal{T}^L, j\in\mathcal{N}^U\cup N^S \tag{16}$$

$$s_{it} \ge 0, \quad i\in\mathcal{N}, t\in\mathcal{T}^L \tag{17}$$

4 Computational Study

The MIP model (including the network generation) was implemented in Python and solved by Gurobi (version 10.0.0) on a Dell Optiplex 7780 computer with an Intel Core i7-10700 @ 2.90 GHz. In the following, we describe the test instances used in Sect. 4.1, before we present the computational results in Sect. 4.2 and provide some managerial insights in Sect. 4.3.

4.1 Input Data and Test Instances

A number of realistic test instances are generated based on data for two different LNG producers, one with only one liquefaction (loading) port, and one with two. Table 1 presents the different configurations of test instances, varying in the number of loading- and unloading ports $|\mathcal{N}^L|$ and $|\mathcal{N}^U|$, long-term FOB contracts $|\mathcal{F}^U|$, vessels $|\mathcal{V}|$, and time periods $|\mathcal{T}|$. Three different test instances were generated for each configuration, slightly differing in the number of unloading ports (customer ports) and long-term FOB contracts.

The black horizontal line in Table 1 splits the configurations into two sets, where the upper set of configurations (with a prefix 'n') is based on data for the LNG producer with one loading port, while the set at the bottom (with a prefix 'a') is based on data from the producer with two loading ports. The leftmost column represents the configuration ID, where each of the numbers indicates the corresponding size of the set on the corresponding position in the instance ID. For example, configuration **n-2-6-12-11-60** has two loading ports, six unloading ports, 12 FOB long-term contracts, 11 vessels, and 60 time periods of one day.

4.2 Computational Results

A summary of the configurations' optimality gaps and objective function values are presented in Table 2 (averaged over the three instances for each configuration). Columns 2–4 show the optimality gaps after 300, 3600, and the maximum run time of 10 800 s, respectively. A gap of 0.0% means that a guaranteed optimal solution was found. The next column presents the instances' average objective function values after running the commercial solver to the maximum time limit of 10 800 s. The rightmost column, TTFFS, indicates how much time it takes for the solver to find the first feasible solution. Note that we were not able to find any feasible solution within the time limit for instance n-1-17-75-23-365.

We see from the results in Table 2 that once the solver finds a feasible solution to an instance, the corresponding optimality gap gets reasonably small after a relatively short amount of time. Furthermore, we see that the solver is able to find good feasible solutions with small optimality gaps to instances with planning horizons up to 180 days within minutes, which is very promising. To make some comparison, test instance B4 in [10] (16 vessels, 121 days) is close in size to instances in our configuration **n-1-7-27-23-120**. [10] obtains a gap of 10.63% for instance B4 after 24 h. It should be noted though that [10] minimizes the sum of costs minus revenues from the sale of spot, leading to a relatively lower objective value than our model for same-sized problems. The optimality gaps thereby seem larger measured in percent. Due to the time-varying LNG prices in our model, we were not able to remove revenues from long-term DES and FOB contracts in our objective function to better compare the gaps with ones in [10]. Furthermore, it is worth mentioning that the both MIP solvers and computers have improved over the last 12 years since [10], which also can explain some of the differences in gaps.

Table 1. Overview of the different test instances' problem sizes, differing in the number of loading ports $|\mathcal{N}^L|$, average number of unloading ports $|\mathcal{N}^U|$, average number of long-term FOB contracts $|\mathcal{F}^U|$, number of vessels $|\mathcal{V}|$ and number of time periods $|\mathcal{T}|$.

Configuration ID	$\|\mathcal{N}^L\|$	$\|\mathcal{N}^U\|$	$\|\mathcal{F}^U\|$	$\|\mathcal{V}\|$	$\|\mathcal{T}\|$
n-1-2-2-18-30	1	2	2	18	30
n-1-6-16-18-45	1	6	16	18	45
n-1-6-16-18-60	1	6	16	18	60
n-1-6-10-18-75	1	6	20	18	75
n-1-7-21-18-90	1	7	21	18	90
n-1-7-27-23-120	1	7	23	23	120
n-1-7-40-23-180	1	7	40	23	180
n-1-17-75-23-365	1	17	75	23	365
a-1-6-12-11-60	1	6	12	11	60
a-2-6-12-11-60	2	6	12	11	60
a-2-6-38-15-180	2	6	38	15	180

Table 2. Summary of the configurations' optimality gaps and objective function values averaged over three instances for each configuration.

Configuration ID	Optimality Gap [%]			Objective value	TTFFS
	300 s	3600 s	10 800 s	[mill. USD]	[s]
n-1-2-2-18-30	0.0	0.0	0.0	73.1	0
n-1-6-16-18-45	0.40	0.30	0.27	426.3	3
n-1-6-16-18-60	0.39	0.23	0.23	668.1	12
n-1-6-10-18-75	0.37	0.26	0.19	675.7	12
n-1-7-21-18-90	0.34	0.21	0.17	867.7	23
n-1-7-27-23-120	0.71	0.51	0.48	1 168	58
n-1-7-40-23-180	1.55	0.42	0.22	1 615	240
n-1-17-75-23-365	-	-	-	-	-
a-1-6-12-11-60	1.63	1.32	1.30	263.1	33
a-2-6-12-11-60	2.27	1.70	1.48	294.4	26
a-2-6-38-15-180	1.11	1.10	0.42	1 400	154

Even though one should be careful with comparisons like this, the low gaps from running our model indicates that our modeling approach is efficient and can be used to find good solutions for all practical purposes. It should be noted though that we were not able to find feasible solutions for the largest test instance with 365 days planning horizon. However, the results show that our model could be embedded in a rolling horizon heuristic, e.g., like in [5,10], for obtaining practical solutions also for instances with longer planning horizons.

4.3 Managerial Insights: Effect of Speed Optimization

To test the effect of speed optimization, we compare the solutions obtained when including speed optimization and when using only the vessels' service speeds. When running these tests, we noticed that the number of binary variables more than doubled when including speed optimization since it generates more arcs in the network. As a representative example, Table 3 shows the breakdown of the objective function for two cases of an instance from configuration **n-1-7-27-23-120**, i.e., without (1) and with (2) speed optimization. The objective function is broken down into six terms. Our objective function 1 has nine terms but since there were no spot contracts in this particular instance, three terms have been omitted from further study in this section.

Table 3. Objective function breakdown for an instance of configuration ***n-1-7-27-23-120*** (run time 1800 s, optimality gap 0.24% for case 1 and 0.19% for case 2).

Configuration ID	1: With default speed	2: With speed optimization	Change [%]
Revenue, DES long-term contracts, own vessels	747.7	815.8	+9.1
Revenue, DES long-term contracts, chartered	181.8	116.8	-35.7
Revenue, FOB long-term contracts	304.3	304.3	0
Revenue, tank left-over LNG	1.6	2.1	+23.1
Costs, own vessels	79.9	90.1	+12.9
Costs, chartering vessels	38.9	22.9	-41.2
Total profit	1 117	1 126	+0.83

We know that each of the two cases in Table 3 has the same lower demand limits and LNG prices regardless of speed configuration. Therefore, the increase in DES revenue comes from delivering amounts of LNG that are closer to the upper demand limits of the customers. Overall, the DES revenue (the first two terms) increase by 3.1 mill. USD compared to the configuration without speed optimization, which is an increase of 0.34%. This is possible including speed optimization allows for sailing at higher speeds so that the producer can deliver somewhat larger volumes of LNG to the customers. The higher sailing speeds also results in higher fuel costs for the own vessels (increase of 12.9%). Charter costs decrease by 35.7% in the case of speed optimization since the producer's own fleet is able to transport more due to the higher sailing speeds. This indicates that if the charter rates were to increase, speed optimization could turn out even more valuable than it does in the current test instances.

It should be noted that our test instances do not include spot contracts, nor does our model place a value on artificial FOB. The effect of speed optimization is expected to become even stronger if these elements are included since there would be more potential to exploit additional revenue sources. The additional cost that any extra revenue would imply is often relatively low, so exploiting more revenue opportunities is likely to be beneficial.

Figure 2 shows the distribution of the speeds of the vessels in the optimal solution of instance **n-1-7-27-23-120-a**. The left violin plot is the case with

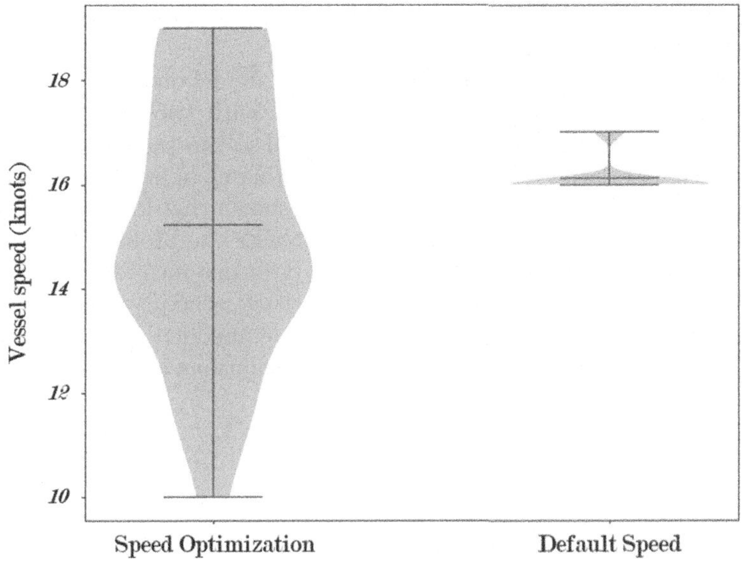

Fig. 2. Distribution of vessel speeds with- and without speed optimization for instance ***n-1-7-27-23-120-a***. The central horizontal line denotes the average speed of the vessels.

speed optimization, while the right plot is the case with default speeds. The plots show that the speed optimization model uses the whole spectrum of allowed vessel speeds, with a slight peak at around 14 and 15 knots. The average is slightly lower than the default service speeds, which are concentrated around 16 and 17 knots. This would imply a lower fuel cost per distance traveled on average.

5 Concluding Remarks

We have considered the planning Annual Delivery Programs (ADPs) in the Liquefied Natural Gas (LNG) industry, in which an LNG producer must fulfill a series of long-term contracts with customers all over the world with a given fleet of LNG vessels. We have expanded previous definitions and models for this problem by including speed optimization and the possibility of having multiple loading ports, which is becoming relevant for some producers as the industry develops. We denote this planning problem as the LNG-ADP with Speed Optimization and Multiple Load Ports (LNG-ADP-SO-MLP).

Our contribution to the literature is a rich formulation of the LNG-ADP planning problem, modeled as a mixed-integer programming (MIP) model. The model is designed to handle each leg of a voyage separately (because of the multiple loading ports), rather than a round trip (as in the previous models in the literature). This also allows for efficient modeling of vessel maintenance, as the vessel can sail directly to a maintenance port after unloading without returning to a loading port.

We used a commercial MIP-solver to test our model on a number of realistic instances for two different LNG producers (one with two loading ports). The computational study showed that the commercial solver was able to find feasible solutions with less than 1% optimality gaps within one hour for instances with a planning horizon of up to 180 days. It was also shown that including speed optimization brings some extra flexibility and increases the profit. The commercial solver did not find a feasible solution for the largest instance with a full planning horizon of a year. However, the promising results for the instances with shorter planning horizons show that our model can be embedded into a Rolling Horizon Heuristic (RHH) in order provide practical solutions also for instances with longer planning horizons.

References

1. Al-Haidous, S., Msakni, M.K., Haouari, M.: Optimal planning of liquefied natural gas deliveries. Transp. Res. Part C: Emerg. Technol. **69**, 79–90 (2016)
2. Andersson, H., Christiansen, M., Desaulniers, G., Rakke, J.G.: Creating annual delivery programs of liquefied natural gas. Optim. Eng. **18**(1), 299–316 (2017)
3. FreightWaves: LNG shipping rates 'shooting for the stars' at $500,000 per day. https://www.freightwaves.com/news/lng-shipping-rates-shooting-for-the-stars-at-500000-per-day
4. GIIGNL: GIIGNL Annual Report 2022. The International Group of Liquefed Natural Gas Importers, Neuilly-sur-Seine, France. https://giignl.org/resources2/ (2022)
5. Li, M., Fagerholt, K., Schütz, P.: Maritime inventory routing with transshipment: the case of Yamal LNG. Flex. Serv. Manuf. J. (2022). https://doi.org/10.1007/s10696-022-09476-5
6. Li, M., Schütz, P.: Planning annual LNG deliveries with transshipment. Energies **13**(6), 1490 (2020)
7. Msakni, M.K., Haouari, M.: Short-term planning of liquefied natural gas deliveries. Transp. Res. Part C: Emerg. Technol. **90**, 393–410 (2018)
8. Mutlu, F., Msakni, M.K., Yildiz, H., Sönmez, E., Pokharel, S.: A comprehensive annual delivery program for upstream liquefied natural gas supply chain. Eur. J. Oper. Res. **250**(1), 120–130 (2016)
9. Norstad, I., Fagerholt, K., Laporte, G.: Tramp ship routing and scheduling with speed optimization. Transp. Res. Part C: Emerg. Technol. **19**(5), 853–865 (2011)
10. Rakke, J., et al.: A rolling horizon heuristic for creating a liquefied natural gas annual delivery program. Transp. Res. Part C: Emerg. Technol. **19**(5), 896–911 (2011)
11. Stålhane, M., Rakke, J.G., Moe, C.R., Andersson, H., Christiansen, M., Fagerholt, K.: A construction and improvement heuristic for a liquefied natural gas inventory routing problem. Comput. Ind. Eng. **62**(1), 245–255 (2012)
12. Wen, M., Ropke, S., Petersen, H.L., Larsen, R., Madsen, O.B.G.: Full-shipload tramp ship routing and scheduling with variable speeds. Comput. Oper. Res. **70**, 1–8 (2016)

Tramp Ship Routing with Bunker Optimization and Flexible Cargo Quantities: Case from Dry Bulk Shipping

Simen Omholt-Jensen[1], Kjetil Fagerholt[1], and Frank Meisel[2](✉)

[1] Department of Industrial Economics and Technology, Norwegian University of Science and Technology, Trondheim, Norway
simen.omholt-jensen@ntnu.no, kjetil.fagerholt@ntnu.no
[2] Faculty of Business, Economics and Social Science, Kiel University, Kiel, Germany
meisel@bwl.uni-kiel.de

Abstract. We study the Tramp Ship Routing and Scheduling Problem with Bunker Optimization (TSRSPBO). The TSRSPBO includes, in addition to the routing and scheduling of the vessels in the given fleet, decisions about how much to bunker (refuel) in which ports. Furthermore, the cargo quantities to be transported are given in an interval, which means that determining the optimal transport quantities also becomes a decision. We propose an arc flow model and a solution method based on a reformulation into a path flow model that uses all feasible vessel routes (columns) as input. For each route, we determine the optimal bunker amounts and cargo quantities along the route. The path flow solution method is tested on a set of instances generated based on data from our case company. The computational results show that the path flow solution method outperforms the arc flow model solved by a commercial solver. We also present how chartering managers may use this as decision support in the negotiation of freight contracts and bunker prices.

Keywords: Ship routing and scheduling · Bunkering optimization · Dry bulk shipping

1 Introduction

Maritime transportation is the backbone of international trade, with more than 80% of the total volume traded internationally [12]. One important segment is dry bulk shipping, which concerns transporting raw materials shipped in bulk, such as iron ore, coal, and grain. In this paper, we study a real-life tramp ship routing and scheduling problem in which a dry bulk shipping operator is to deploy its vessel fleet to maximize the profit for the entire fleet. To do so, the operator has to select from sets of mandatory contracted cargoes and optional spot cargoes, potentially paying a cost for not servicing a contracted cargo. In dry bulk shipping, an operator can often choose the amount of cargo to transport

© The Author(s), under exclusive license to Springer Nature Switzerland AG 2023
J. R. Daduna et al. (Eds.): ICCL 2023, LNCS 14239, pp. 185–201, 2023.
https://doi.org/10.1007/978-3-031-43612-3_11

within a predetermined interval. Thus, the operator also needs to decide how much of each cargo to transport, which can be challenging given that the vessels may carry multiple cargoes simultaneously. Furthermore, as the ships eventually run out of bunker (fuel), the operator must choose where to bunker and the quantity of bunker to purchase. We denote this planning problem as the Tramp Ship Routing and Scheduling Problem with Bunker Optimization (TSRSPBO).

There have been significant contributions to the academic field of tramp ship routing and scheduling over recent years, summarized in the review papers [6,9,11]. The aspect of flexible cargo quantities in ship routing is considered by [2,7,8], while bunker optimization was included by [10,13]. However, none of the previous studies integrates these two important aspects. Furthermore, the latter two studies do only consider full shiploads, meaning that a vessel can have at most cargo on board at the same time, in contrast to the problem we consider in this paper. Hence, to our knowledge, the TSRSPBO studied here is the first to integrate both flexible cargo quantities and bunker optimization. Furthermore, by allowing vessels to detour to refuel bunker and the simultaneous service of multiple cargoes, the TSRSPBO realistically represents our case company Western Bulk's operational environment. We propose an arc flow model for the TSRSPBO, and to solve instances of larger sizes, we propose a solution method based on a path flow model with routes (columns) generated a priori. For each of these routes, we have to determine the optimal cargo and bunker quantities along the route, which we do by solving a linear programming model. By solving test instances based on real-life data, we show how our models and proposed solution method may act as an aid to chartering managers in dry bulk shipping companies.

The remaining of this paper is organized as follows. Section 2 provides a definition of the TSRSPBO, while Sect. 3 presents its arc flow model. Then, in Sect. 4, we propose the path flow solution method. The computational study is provided in Sect. 5, while concluding remarks are given in Sect. 6.

2 Problem Definition

This section formally defines the TSRSPBO, which is relevant to many shipping companies operators, e.g., in the dry bulk shipping industry. The TSRSPBO considers a ship operator controlling a given heterogeneous fleet of *vessels* with differing cargo and bunker carrying capacities, as well as initial positions and bunker levels. Each vessel has a given sailing speed and fuel consumption.

The vessel fleet is set up to transport a set of *cargoes* for the following planning horizon, e.g., the next two months. Each cargo is specified by its cargo type, pickup and delivery ports and time windows, and freight rate. A cargo can either be a contractual mandatory cargo or a spot cargo. A contractual cargo usually stems from a long term Contract of Affreightment (CoA), and is therefore denoted a *CoA* cargo. A *spot* cargo is an optional cargo for which the ship operator not yet has signed a contract. In dry bulk shipping it is common that the cargo contracts offer some flexibility to the ship operator regarding the quantities to be transported through a contractual term called More or Less (ship-)Owners Option (MoLOO). A MoLOO term states that the cargo quantity can be selected from within a given range. For example, the quantity range may be defined as 66,000 metric tonnes with 10% MoLOO. This means that the operator can choose to transport any quantity between 59,400 to 72,600 metric tonnes. The times spent in port for loading and unloading then depend on the chosen cargo quantity. A cargo's pickup (delivery) time windows define the earliest and latest time for when the loading (unloading) of the cargo can start in the pickup (delivery) port.

In addition to the ship operator's fleet, *spot ships* can be chartered on voyage charter contracts to service the CoA cargoes. In addition to the cargoes' pickup and delivery ports, there is a predefined set of available *bunker ports*, from which the ships in the fleet can bunker fuel. The bunker ports have different fuel prices, which are assumed to be known and constant over the planning horizon.

A vessel will start its route from a given initial position. A vessel route consists of a sequence of ports, which may be pickup, delivery, and bunker ports. Depending on the cargo quantities and vessel capacities, a vessel might have the possibility to transport multiple cargoes simultaneously. For each sailing leg between two ports, there is an associated vessel-dependent sailing time and cost. Ships traveling through a canal will have to pay an additional canal cost.

The main *decisions* of the TSRSPBO are the routes and schedules of each vessel in the operator's fleet. This implicitly incorporates the following additional decisions: 1) which spot cargoes to service, 2) which vessels should service which cargoes, 3) which CoA cargoes should be serviced by spot vessels, and 4) which port the vessels should stop for bunkering. Furthermore, we need to determine the quantity of each cargo along the vessels' routes (within its limits), as well as the bunker amounts. All these decisions impact each other and must be determined simultaneously.

All transported cargoes must be picked up within their pickup time windows and delivered within their delivery time windows. The cargo capacity limit of each vessel must be respected along its route, and its bunker level must be above a safety limit and not exceed the bunker capacity limit.

The overall *objective* of the TSRSPBO is to maximize the vessel fleet's profit over the planning period. Profit is the generated revenue of the transported cargoes less the sum of all variable costs. The variable costs consists of the fuel, port, and canal costs, as well as voyage chartering costs for spot vessels.

3 Arc Flow Model

This section presents the arc flow (AF) model for the TSRSPBO. We call this model an AF model because we here use arc flow variables specifying which arcs the vessels traverse within a network representation of the problem. Section 3.1 describes the modeling assumptions and notation, while Sect. 3.2 presents the AF model.

3.1 Modeling Assumptions and Notation

In Sect. 2, it was stated that there is a delivery time window for each cargo. In reality, it is often only a pickup time time window, while it is specified that delivery should occur at the "earliest convenience". Thus, to exclude the possibility of a vessel carrying a cargo for too long time, artificial delivery time windows are constructed by multiplying the direct sailing time between the cargo's pickup and delivery ports and port time with a factor, e.g., 1.5. This design choice allows detours to purchase bunker and pick up other cargoes while ensuring the delivery of all cargoes within a reasonable time.

Furthermore, we assume that the time it takes to load bunker is not dependent on the amount. This assumption is in line with [13]. A fixed bunker time is therefore added to the sailing time for trips arriving at a bunker port. At the beginning of the planning period, vessels might be in port or at sea as they operate 24/7. We assume that each vessel becomes available at a given port, represented by an origin node, corresponding to the discharge port of their ongoing voyage. After completing the last port call in the planning horizon, a vessel ends its route by traveling to an artificial destination node at zero cost and time. The vessel's bunker load at this destination node is considered a resource, so the difference in bunker load between the origin and destination node is priced at an average price for all the bunker ports. The value of this additional bunker is reflected in the model's objective.

The notation and formulation presented here is based on the arc flow formulation presented in [4,5,13]. Let the fleet of vessels be represented by the set $\mathcal{V}$. There are N cargoes available for transport in the following planning horizon, where the sets of pickup and delivery nodes are given by $\mathcal{N}^P = \{0, \ldots, N\}$ and $\mathcal{N}^D = \{N+1, \ldots, 2N\}$, respectively. These sets allow each cargo i to be represented by a pickup node $i \in \mathcal{N}^P$ and a delivery node $(N+i) \in \mathcal{N}^D$. As such, the set of all cargo-related nodes is represented as $\mathcal{N} = \mathcal{N}^P \cup \mathcal{N}^D$. The set of pickup nodes $\mathcal{N}^P$ is partitioned into $\mathcal{N}^P = \mathcal{N}^C \cup \mathcal{N}^O$, where $\mathcal{N}^C$ and $\mathcal{N}^O$ denote the mandatory contracted and optional spot cargoes, respectively. A vessel v has a node of origin $o(v)$, while it is assigned an artificial destination node $d(v)$. Due to cargo capacity, depth, and cargo handling equipment restrictions, some vessels in $\mathcal{V}$ and nodes in $\mathcal{N}$ may be incompatible. Thus, the set of nodes a vessel v may visit is represented as $\mathcal{N}_v \subseteq \mathcal{N} \cup \{o(v), d(v)\}$. $(\mathcal{N}_v, \mathcal{A}_v)$ defines a base network for each vessel v, where the set of arcs $\mathcal{A}_v \subseteq \{(i,j)|i \in \mathcal{N}_v, j \in \mathcal{N}_v\}$ represents all arcs traversable by vessel v with respect to time, capacity and bunker consumption. The pickup and delivery nodes compatible with vessel v are defined as $\mathcal{N}_v^P = \mathcal{N}^P \cap \mathcal{N}_v$ and $\mathcal{N}_v^D = \mathcal{N}^D \cap \mathcal{N}_v$.

The next step is extending the base network $(\mathcal{N}_v, \mathcal{A}_v)$ to allow vessel visits at bunker nodes (ports). Let $\mathcal{B}_v$ be the set of bunker nodes that vessel v may visit. The set of base nodes $\mathcal{N}_v$ for vessel v is extended to include the nodes in $\mathcal{B}_v$ such that $\hat{\mathcal{N}}_v = \mathcal{N}_v \cup \mathcal{B}_v$. Furthermore, the set of base arcs $\mathcal{A}_v$ is extended by adding all feasible arcs connecting nodes in $\mathcal{N}_v \backslash d(v)$ with nodes in $\mathcal{B}_v$. As such, the extended set of arcs is defined as $\hat{\mathcal{A}}_v = \mathcal{A}_v \cup \mathcal{A}_v^B$, where $\mathcal{A}_v^B$ is the set of arcs for vessel v connecting bunker option nodes $\mathcal{B}_v$ to the nodes in $\mathcal{N}_v$. The extended cargo-bunker network is thereby $(\hat{\mathcal{N}}_v, \hat{\mathcal{A}}_v)$.

Let T^S_{ijv} be the sailing time between nodes i and j for vessel v. If node j is a bunker node, a fixed time is added to T^S_{ijv}, signifying the time spent bunkering. The time required to load or discharge one unit of cargo i with vessel v is defined as T^Q_{iv}. The variable voyage cost C_{ijv} accounts for the costs of visiting node i and the sailing from node i to node j for vessel v. Note that the cost of the purchased bunker is not included in this parameter as the purchase of bunker is modeled separately. Instead, let P_i denote the cost of purchasing one unit of bunker available in bunker node i. The bonus bunker remaining at the destination node $d(v)$ is rewarded by P per unit (calculated as the mean of all available bunker node prices). The voyage charter cost of servicing a CoA cargo i by a spot ship is denoted C^S_i. Furthermore, the bunker consumption for vessel v traversing arc $(i,j) \in \hat{\mathcal{A}}_v$ is denoted B^S_{ijv}. The bunker consumed per time unit in port i by vessel v is given by B^P_{iv}.

The quantity of cargo that can be transported is flexible within interval $\left[\underline{Q}_i, \overline{Q}_i\right]$. There is a per unit revenue R_i for transporting cargo $i \in \mathcal{N}^P$ and a time window $\left[\underline{T}_{iv}, \overline{T}_{iv}\right]$ for when service must start at node i (strengthened for each vessel v). Additionally, the bunker level on board each vessel v must be within a lower limit $\underline{B}_v$ and an upper limit $\overline{B}_v$ to ensure realistic and safe operation. Finally, the cargo carrying capacity of vessel v is denoted K_v.

The binary arc flow variable x_{ijv} is assigned the value 1 if vessel v traverses arc $(i,j) \in \hat{\mathcal{A}}_v$, and 0 otherwise. The variable t_{iv} denotes the time vessel v begins service at node i. The quantity of cargo i transported by vessel v is represented by q_{iv}, and the quantity of bunker purchased by vessel v at bunker node i is given by the variable b_{iv}. The total cargo load on board a vessel v when it leaves node i is represented by the variable l^C_{iv}. Similarly, the variable l^B_{iv} represents the total bunker load on board vessel v just after completing service at node i. To represent whether a CoA cargo is serviced by a spot ship, the binary variable z_i is assigned the value 1, or 0 otherwise. Finally, the binary variable y_i is assigned a value of 1 if the optional spot cargo i is serviced, and 0 otherwise.

3.2 Arc Flow Formulation

Using the above notation, we can now formulate the AF model as follows.

Objective Function

$$
\begin{aligned}
\max \quad & \sum_{v \in \mathcal{V}} \sum_{i \in \mathcal{N}^P} R_i q_{iv} - \sum_{v \in \mathcal{V}} \sum_{(i,j) \in \hat{\mathcal{A}}_v} C_{ijv} x_{ijv} - \sum_{i \in \mathcal{N}^C} C^S_i z_i \\
& - \sum_{v \in \mathcal{V}} \sum_{i \in \mathcal{B}_v} P_i b_{iv} + \sum_{v \in \mathcal{V}} P \cdot (l^B_{d(v)v} - B^0_v)
\end{aligned} \tag{1}
$$

The objective function (1) maximizes the total profit. The first term specifies the revenue generated for both contracted and optional cargoes, while the second term specifies the variable voyage costs. The third term represents the voyage charter costs associated with servicing CoA cargoes with spot ships. The fourth term describes the cost associated with purchasing bunker, while the last term calculates the value of the bonus bunker remaining at the destination node. Note that if the bunker level at the destination is higher than at the origin, this term will be positive.

Network Flow Constraints

$$\sum_{v\in\mathcal{V}}\sum_{j\in\hat{\mathcal{N}}_v} x_{ijv} + z_i = 1 \qquad i \in \mathcal{N}^C \tag{2}$$

$$\sum_{v\in\mathcal{V}}\sum_{j\in\hat{\mathcal{N}}_v} x_{ijv} - y_i = 0 \qquad i \in \mathcal{N}^O \tag{3}$$

$$\sum_{j\in\hat{\mathcal{N}}_v} x_{o(v)jv} = 1 \qquad v \in \mathcal{V} \tag{4}$$

$$\sum_{j\in\hat{\mathcal{N}}_v} x_{ijv} - \sum_{j\in\hat{\mathcal{N}}_v} x_{jiv} = 0 \qquad v \in \mathcal{V}, i \in \hat{\mathcal{N}}_v \backslash \{o(v), d(v)\} \tag{5}$$

$$\sum_{i\in\hat{\mathcal{N}}_v} x_{id(v)v} = 1 \qquad v \in \mathcal{V} \tag{6}$$

$$\sum_{j\in\hat{\mathcal{N}}_v} x_{ijv} - \sum_{j\in\hat{\mathcal{N}}_v} x_{N+i,jv} = 0 \qquad v \in \mathcal{V}, i \in \mathcal{N}_v^P \tag{7}$$

Constraints (2) ensure that all mandatory CoA cargoes are transported by a vessel in the predefined fleet or by a spot ship. In contrast, Constraints (3) state that all spot cargoes may be transported. Constraints (4) ensure that all vessels begin their routes from their origin node and travel to a pickup node, a bunker option node, or directly to their destination node. Constraints (5) denote the flow conservation, while Constraints (6) force each vessel's route to end at its artificial destination node. Constraints (7) ensure that the same vessel services both the pickup and the cargo's corresponding delivery node.

Temporal Constraints

$$x_{ijv}\left(t_{iv} + T_{iv}^Q q_{iv} + T_{ijv}^S - t_{jv}\right) \leq 0 \qquad v \in \mathcal{V}, (i,j) \in \hat{\mathcal{A}}_v \,|\, i \in \mathcal{N}_v^P \tag{8}$$

$$x_{ijv}\left(t_{iv} + T_{iv}^Q q_{i-N,v} + T_{ijv}^S - t_{jv}\right) \leq 0 \qquad v \in \mathcal{V}, (i,j) \in \hat{\mathcal{A}}_v \,|\, i \in \mathcal{N}_v^D \tag{9}$$

$$x_{ijv}\left(t_{iv} + T_{ijv}^S - t_{jv}\right) \leq 0 \qquad v \in \mathcal{V}, (i,j) \in \hat{\mathcal{A}}_v \,|\, i \notin \mathcal{N}_v^P \wedge i \notin \mathcal{N}_v^D \tag{10}$$

$$t_{iv} + T_{iv}^Q q_{iv} + T_{i,N+i,v}^S - t_{N+i,v} \leq 0 \qquad v \in \mathcal{V}, i \in \mathcal{N}_v^P \tag{11}$$

$$\underline{T}_{iv} \leq t_{iv} \leq \overline{T}_{iv} \qquad v \in \mathcal{V}, i \in \hat{\mathcal{N}}_v \tag{12}$$

Constraints (8)–(9) specify the time progression for the pickup and delivery nodes, respectively. Note, however, that the cargo quantity variable q_{iv} is only defined for pickup nodes. Constraints (10) describe a similar time flow for origin, bunker, and destination nodes as there is no cargo loading or unloading at these nodes. Constraints (11) are precedence constraints forcing the pickup node to be serviced before its corresponding delivery node. Finally, Constraints (12) are the time window constraints.

Cargo Constraints

$$x_{ijv}\left(l_{iv}^C + q_{jv} - l_{jv}^C\right) = 0 \qquad v \in \mathcal{V}, (i,j) \in \hat{\mathcal{A}}_v \,|\, j \in \mathcal{N}_v^P \tag{13}$$

$$x_{i,N+j,v}\left(l_{iv}^C - q_{jv} - l_{N+j,v}^C\right) = 0 \qquad v \in \mathcal{V}, (i,N+j) \in \hat{\mathcal{A}}_v \,|\, j \in \mathcal{N}_v^P \tag{14}$$

$$x_{ijv}\left(l_{iv}^C - l_{jv}^C\right) = 0 \qquad v \in \mathcal{V}, (i,j) \in \hat{\mathcal{A}}_v \,|\, j \in \mathcal{B}_v \tag{15}$$

$$l_{o(v),v}^C = 0 \qquad v \in \mathcal{V} \tag{16}$$

$$q_{iv} \leq l_{iv}^C \leq \sum_{j \in \hat{\mathcal{N}}_v} K_v x_{ijv} \qquad v \in \mathcal{V}, i \in \mathcal{N}_v^P \tag{17}$$

$$0 \leq l_{N+i,v}^C \leq \sum_{j \in \hat{\mathcal{N}}_v} (K_v - q_{iv})\, x_{N+i,jv} \qquad v \in \mathcal{V}, i \in \mathcal{N}_v^P \tag{18}$$

$$\sum_{j \in \hat{\mathcal{N}}_v} \underline{Q}_i x_{ijv} \leq q_{iv} \leq \sum_{j \in \hat{\mathcal{N}}_v} \overline{Q}_i x_{ijv} \qquad v \in \mathcal{V}, i \in \mathcal{N}_v^P \tag{19}$$

Constraints (13)–(15) represent the cargo load balance constraints for pickup, delivery and bunker nodes, respectively. Constraints (16) initialize the cargo load on board the vessels to zero. Constraints (17) and (18) describe the cargo load capacity restrictions at pickup nodes and delivery nodes, respectively. Finally, Constraints (19) ensure that the cargo loaded at pickup port i is within the minimum and maximum cargo load limits. The summations in Constraints (17)–(19) are introduced to strengthen the formulation.

Bunker Constraints

$$x_{ijv}\left(l_{iv}^B - B_{ijv}^S - B_{jv}^P T_{jv}^Q q_{jv} - l_{jv}^B\right) = 0 \quad v \in \mathcal{V}, (i,j) \in \hat{\mathcal{A}}_v \,|\, j \in \mathcal{N}_v^P \tag{20}$$

$$x_{ijv}\left(l_{iv}^B - B_{ijv}^S - B_{iv}^P T_{jv}^Q q_{j-N,v} - l_{jv}^B\right) = 0 \quad v \in \mathcal{V}, (i,j) \in \hat{\mathcal{A}}_v \,|\, j \in \mathcal{N}_v^D \tag{21}$$

$$x_{ijv}\left(l_{iv}^{B}-B_{ijv}^{S}+b_{jv}-l_{jv}^{B}\right)=0 \quad v\in\mathcal{V},(i,j)\in\hat{\mathcal{A}}_v \,|\, j\in\mathcal{B}_v \tag{22}$$

$$x_{ijv}\left(l_{iv}^{B}-B_{ijv}^{S}-l_{jv}^{B}\right)=0 \quad v\in\mathcal{V},(i,j)\in\hat{\mathcal{A}}_v \,|\, j\in\{d(v)\} \tag{23}$$

$$l_{o(v)v}^{B}=B_v^0 \quad v\in\mathcal{V} \tag{24}$$

$$\sum_{j\in\hat{\mathcal{N}}_v}\left(\underline{B}_v+B_{ijv}^{S}+B_{jv}^{P}T_{jv}^{Q}q_{jv}\right)x_{ijv}\le l_{iv}^{B}\le\overline{B}_v\sum_{j\in\hat{\mathcal{N}}_v}x_{ijv} \quad v\in\mathcal{V},i\in\hat{\mathcal{N}}_v \tag{25}$$

$$b_{iv}\le\left(\overline{B}_v-\underline{B}_v\right)\sum_{j\in\hat{\mathcal{N}}_v}x_{ijv} \quad v\in\mathcal{V},i\in\mathcal{B}_v \tag{26}$$

Constraints (20)–(23) describe the bunker balance constraints for the pickup, delivery, bunker and destination nodes, respectively. Constraints (24) specify the bunker level on board vessel v at the beginning of the planning period. Constraints (25) make sure that the bunker loads on board the vessels are kept within its limits, while Constraints (26) ensure that the amount bunker purchased is feasible. The summations in (25) and (26) are again included to strengthen the formulation.

Variable Domains

$$x_{ijv}\in\{0,1\} \quad v\in\mathcal{V},(i,j)\in\hat{\mathcal{A}}_v \tag{27}$$

$$y_i\in\{0,1\} \quad i\in\mathcal{N}^O \tag{28}$$

$$z_i\in\{0,1\} \quad i\in\mathcal{N}^C \tag{29}$$

$$t_{iv},l_{iv}^{C},l_{iv}^{B}\in\mathbb{R}^+ \quad v\in\mathcal{V},i\in\hat{\mathcal{N}}_v \tag{30}$$

$$q_{iv}\in\mathbb{R}^+ \quad v\in\mathcal{V},i\in\mathcal{N}_v^P \tag{31}$$

$$b_{iv}\in\mathbb{R}^+ \quad v\in\mathcal{V},i\in\mathcal{B}_v \tag{32}$$

In the above arc flow model, the balance constraints for time, cargo, and bunker are non-linear. The same is the case for Constraints (18), handling the discharge load capacities of the vessels, as well as for Constraints (25), controlling the bunker load capacities of the vessels. These constraints are all linearized, using standard linearization techniques with big-M constraints (e.g., [4]), to make the model solvable by a commercial MIP-solver.

4 Path Flow Solution Method

Since a commercial MIP-solver can only solve very small instances of the arc flow model presented in Sect. 3.2, we propose a path flow solution method. By inspecting the arc flow model, it is clear that only Constraints (2) and (3) are fleet-specific, while the remaining constraints, as well as the objective function, are vessel-specific with no interaction among the vessels. As such, the structure of the problem lends itself to Dantzig-Wolfe decomposition, in which the vessel-specific constraints concerning the routing and scheduling can be handled separately in a subproblem for each vessel. The fleet-specific constraints can thus be placed in a path flow formulation (or a master problem) with a reduced number of constraints but with a large number of columns. Here, we propose a solution method based on such a path flow model, presented in Sect. 4.1, for which the columns and parameters are generated through an a priori generation of all feasible columns, i.e., vessel routes, as described in Sect. 4.2.

4.1 Path Flow Formulation

Let $\mathscr{R}_v$ be a *feasible route* for vessel v. In this setting, feasible means a route adhering to Constraints (4)–(26). $\mathcal{R}_v$ denotes the set of all such feasible routes for vessel v. For each feasible route $\mathscr{R}_v$ for vessel v, the optimal amounts of the cargoes to be transported and bunker to be purchased are found as later described in Sect. 4.2. We refer to such an *optimized* route as a *schedule* s since it also includes information on the timing of the activities along the route. Each such schedule is associated with an optimal vessel-specific profit, denoted P_{sv}. Let $\mathcal{S}_v$ be the set of all optimal schedules for vessel v. The new parameter, A_{isv}, is defined to be equal to 1 if vessel v carries cargo i in schedule s, and 0 otherwise. The binary variable x_{sv} takes the value of 1 if vessel v is chosen to sail schedule s, and 0 otherwise. Reusing some of the notation defined in Sect. 3.1, we can now define the path flow model as follows:

$$\max \sum_{v\in\mathcal{V}}\sum_{s\in\mathcal{S}_v} P_{sv}x_{sv} - \sum_{i\in\mathcal{N}^C} C_i^S z_i \tag{33}$$

$$\sum_{v\in\mathcal{V}}\sum_{s\in\mathcal{S}_v} A_{isv}x_{sv} + z_i = 1 \qquad i\in\mathcal{N}^C \tag{34}$$

$$\sum_{v\in\mathcal{V}}\sum_{s\in\mathcal{S}_v} A_{isv}x_{sv} - y_i = 0 \qquad i\in\mathcal{N}^O \tag{35}$$

$$\sum_{s\in\mathcal{S}_v} x_{sv} = 1 \qquad v\in\mathcal{V} \tag{36}$$

$$x_{sv}\in\{0,1\} \qquad v\in\mathcal{V}, s\in\mathcal{S}_v \tag{37}$$

Objective function (33), corresponding to objective function (1) in the arc flow model, maximizes the fleet profit, which consists of the vessel-specific profit of the selected schedules less the cost of hiring a spot ship to service a CoA cargo. Constraints (34) state that each contracted cargo is either transported by a vessel in the fleet or by a spot ship, similar to Constraints (2) in the arc flow model. Constraints (35) specify that optional cargoes may be serviced by a vessel in the fleet, similar to Constraints (3). Constraints (36) ensure that each vessel is assigned exactly one schedule. Finally, Constraints (37) define the domains of the binary schedule assignment variables.

4.2 A Priori Column Generation with Cargo and Bunker Optimization

First, all routes are generated using a depth-first search for each vessel. Here, we use the minimum cargo quantities $\underline{Q}_i$ to ensure that all feasible routes are generated, and we also make sure that they adhere to the vessel-specific constraints in the arc flow model. Given the set of all feasible routes, we solve a Vessel Scheduling Problem (VSP) to determine the optimal amounts of bunker and the cargo quantities along the route (together with timing of the activities).

It should be noted that, since the route is now given, the VSP does not have any binary variables and is a Linear Programming (LP) model, which is considerably easier to solve than the whole AF model. Solving the VSP for each feasible route for each vessel yields the set of optimal schedules $\mathcal{S}_v$ for each vessel v. The objective function value associated with each optimal schedule s is the vessel-specific optimal profit P_{sv} for route s used in the path flow formulation.

5 Computational Study

The arc flow and the path flow models were implemented in C++ and solved by Gurobi (version 10.0.0). All of the computational experiments were performed on a MacBook Pro with an Apple M1 Pro processor. In the following, we describe the test instances used in Sect. 5.1, before we present the computational results in Sect. 5.2 and provide some managerial insights in Sect. 5.3.

5.1 Input Data and Test Instances

This section explains how real-life cargo and voyage data from the industry partner, Western Bulk[1], was compiled into suitable test instances. In addition to Western Bulk's operational data, routing and port information were provided by Maritime Optima[2], a maritime data analytics company. The remaining input data needed to generate realistic test instances was either gathered or constructed from open sources, estimated from available data, or randomly sampled from reasonable uniform intervals.

We generated a set of test instances of different size classes, as summarized in Table 1. Within each class, we generated five instances. For each test instance,

[1] www.westernbulk.com.

[2] www.maritimeoptima.com.

Table 1. Classes of generated test instances

Name	Size	# Cargoes	# Vessels	# Bunker nodes
C6V2B4	Small	6	2	4
C9V2B4	Small	9	2	4
C9V3B4	Small	9	3	4
C15V5B10	Medium	15	5	10
C30V5B10	Medium	30	5	10
C30V10B10	Large	30	10	10
C45V10B10	Large	45	10	10

the number of spot cargoes was fixed to be twice the number of CoA cargoes. As such, for a test instance with 15 cargoes, there are five CoA cargoes and 10 spot cargoes. This is representative for Western Bulk's operational environment.

The cargoes' MoLOO limits were estimated by creating a ±10% interval from the actual quantities of historical transported cargoes. The origin ports of the vessels were randomly drawn from a set of the most frequent delivery ports visited by Western Bulk's vessels. A final group of parameters was randomly sampled from sensible intervals. These include the time when vessels first become available to transport cargoes, $\underline{T}_{o(v)v}$, the beginning of the time windows for pickup ports, $\underline{T}_{iv}, i \in \mathcal{N}_v^P$, and the initial bunker level on board the vessels, B_v^0. For pickup ports, the upper time windows were constructed by adding ten days to the start, which corresponds to what is typical in Western Bulk's operation.

5.2 Computational Results and Comparison of Solution Methods

The results for the arc flow model are summarized in Table 2. The column **Solved** shows the number of test instances within each class that were solved to optimality for the AF model within the maximum allowed running time, which is set to one hour. The **Time** column shows the average solution times in seconds. The **BestBound$_{\mathbf{AF}}$** column displays the best dual bound found when solving the AF model, averaged over the test instances in each class. Similarly, the **ObjVals$_{\mathbf{AF}}$** column states the best primal bounds, i.e., the average profit of the obtained solutions. The **Gap** column shows the average percentage difference between the best primal and dual bounds.

Table 2 shows that only the instances of the first two classes were solved to optimality within one hour. For the C9V3B4 class, two out of five test instances were solved to optimality. For the larger instances, the AF model could not provide an optimal solution within one hour, and the gaps are high. It should be noted that introducing bunker optimization to the tramp ship routing and scheduling problem significantly increases the problem complexity. To illustrate this, the arcs going to and from the bunker nodes constitute as much as 62.5% of the total number of arcs (on average across all test instances).

Table 2. Arc flow (AF) model results averaged over instances in each instance class

Instance Class	Size	Solved	Time (seconds)	$\text{BestBound}_{\text{AF}}$ (mill. USD)	$\text{ObjVal}_{\text{AF}}$ (mill. USD)	Gap (%)
C6V2B4	Small	5/5	86	3.76	3.76	0.00
C9V2B4	Small	5/5	153	5.22	5.22	0.00
C9V3B4	Small	2/5	2,890	9.24	6.75	34.26
C15V5B10	Medium	0/5	3,600	22.3	11.1	104.39
C30V5B10	Medium	0/5	3,600	44.3	12.8	250.77
C30V10B10	Large	0/5	3,600	49.9	27.6	81.56
C45V10B10	Large	0/5	3,600	69.9	26.2	169.93

The results of the path flow solution method are summarized in Table 3, where the **Solved** column shows the number of test instances within each class that were solved to optimality within one hour. The $\mathbf{N_R}$ column displays the average number of routes generated for instances within each class. The column **Time** shows the solution times in seconds, wheremost of the time is spent in the generation of the routes and solving the LPs to determine the optimal bunker amounts and cargo quantities. The $\mathbf{N_{SS}}$ and $\mathbf{N_{SC}}$ columns state the average number of spot ships used and the number of spot cargoes transported in the optimal solutions, respectively. Furthermore, the $\mathbf{ObjVal_{TOT}}$ column states the optimal objective values, i.e., the profit, averaged over the test instances in each class. Finally, the Δ column reports the average percentage improvements in the objective value found when solving the path flow model compared to the best objective value found when solving the AF model (after one hour).

Table 3. Path flow model results averaged over the instances in each instance class

Instance Class	Size	Solved	N_{R}	Time (secs)	N_{SS}	N_{SC}	$\text{ObjVal}_{\text{TOT}}$ (mill. USD)	Δ (%)
C6V2B4	Small	5/5	816	0.3	1	2	3.76	0.00
C9V2B4	Small	5/5	1370	0.6	1	2	5.22	0.00
C9V3B4	Small	5/5	1581	0.6	1	3	6.76	0.15
C15V5B10	Medium	5/5	90,194	56.3	1	6	12.6	13.51
C30V5B10	Medium	5/5	406,435	416	5	7	15.5	21.09
C30V10B10	Large	5/5	1,312,606	1,516	0	14	31.4	13.77
C45V10B10	Large	2/5	2,095,022	3,708	3	13	34.7	32.44

In general, the path flow solution method clearly outperforms the AF model, both with respect to solution time and quality. As we can see from Table 3, the path flow solution method is able to solve all except for three of the largest instances. Nevertheless, the run time grows quickly along with the number of feasible routes/columns when the instance size increases. Eventually, this also results in memory problems, and the largest instances solved here represent more or less the limit of the path flow solution method. For even larger test instances, either heuristics or more advanced exact methods will be needed.

5.3 Managerial Insights

Our model offers potential for a wide range of analyses that can help managers in making the addressed decisions. In this section, we concentrate on exploring how the negotiation of flexible cargo quantities and bunker purchase discounts may impact profits. There is surely a large range of further factors that could be analysed, such as fleet diversity, fleet age, or repositioning flexibility (see [1]) but we leave this to future research also as some of these issues may require extensions of our proposed model.

Impact of Flexible Cargo Quantities: The MoLOO limits are subject to negotiation between the ship operator and the shippers. As such, ship operators would benefit from understanding the impact of increased flexibility in cargo quantity flexibility. Figure 1 shows the effect on profit for different levels flexibility cargo quantities for a test instance in the `C15V5B10` class.

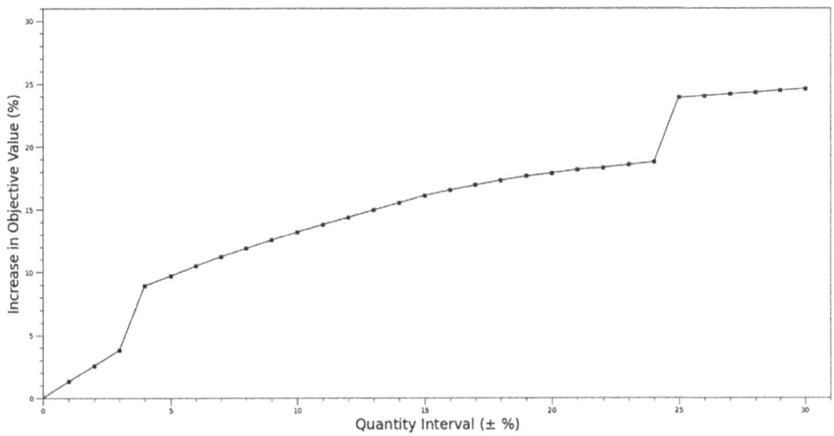

Fig. 1. The effect of utilizing flexible cargo quantities for a test instance in `C15V5B10`

For large parts of Fig. 1, there is a (close to) linear profit increase from increased flexibility. This comes simply from the possibility of transporting larger quantities of the same cargoes. However, when the MoLOO limits are increased from ±3% to ±4% and from ±24% to ±25%, we notice two jumps in the profit. This is because the additional flexibility makes it possible to reduce the quantities for some cargoes, and hence be able to transport additional spot cargoes. This shows that increased contract flexibility in cargo quantities may have a huge impact on profitability. These results are in accordance with [8].

Impact of Bunker Price Negotiations: The bunker prices used in these tests were retrieved from Maritime Optima's [3] interface. As such, the prices are considered market prices and available to anyone who might want to purchase bunker at a given port. In reality, shipping companies devote resources to acquire favorable bunker purchase deals ahead of time. For example, Western Bulk has an entire department responsible for negotiating bunker purchase deals with different ports. Here, we show how we can provide decision support in this process.

Figure 2 shows the bunker prices and the total number of visits to bunker ports over all test instances in class C15V5B10. It can be seen that the ports of Hong Kong, Busan, Lianyungang, Port Elizabeth, and Gladstone are never visited, even though some of them are offering bunker at very low prices. For Gladstone and Port Elizabeth this observation is explained by their positioning in Australia and South Africa, respectively, which is too far for vessels operating in the Indo-Pacific region as is the case in our instances. Furthermore, neither of these countries is a major oil producer, which explains their relatively high prices. However, the other mentioned ports are actually closer located to the operation areas of the ships, yet they do not play a role in bunkering either. For those ports, it is less clear what there disadvantages are. They are probably just marginally worse compared to those ports that are actually visited frequently, i.e., Al Fujayrah and Singapore.

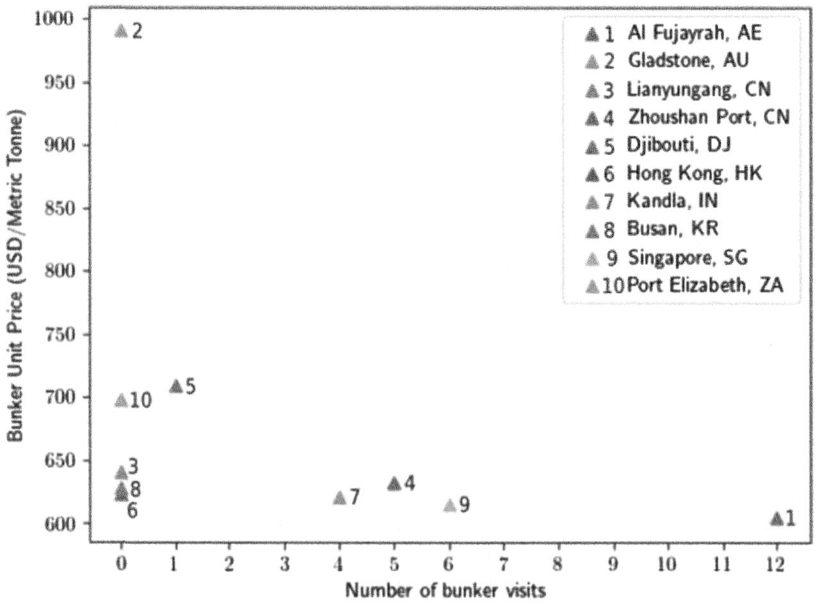

Fig. 2. Bunker prices and total number of bunker port visits in test instances C15V5B10

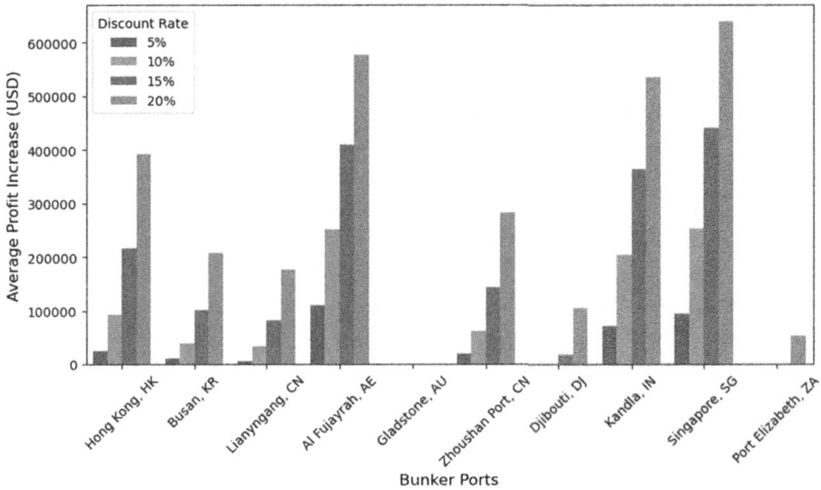

Fig. 3. Averaged effects of procuring discounted bunker for test instances C15V5B10

Figure 3 shows the increase in profit averaged over the five test instances in C15V5B10 at different bunker discount rates. The bunker discount rates are applied one at a time to each of the bunker ports. As expected, increasing the discount rate leads to increased profit. A bunker price discount at the ports of Singapore, Al Fujayrah and/or Kandia has the highest impact on the profits. Their impact on profits is in line with Fig. 2, as these ports are among the most frequently visited ports. As such, if Western Bulk has to choose which port they should focus their efforts on procuring a discounted bunker purchase contract, Fig. 3 suggests either one of these. For the previously discussed unattractive ports Gladstone and Port Elizabeth, even a bunker price discount of 20% has (almost) no impact on the solutions. Interestingly, Hong Kong, a port that was never visited in Fig. 2, displays a greater impact on the average profit for the test instances than Zhoushan Port, which was visited five times even without a bunker discount. The explanation is that Hong Kong is more centrally located in the Indo-Pacific region than Zhoushan Port. Whereas Zhoushan Port is located further north, closer to Shanghai, Hong Kong lies further south, closer to Singapore. As such, decreasing the price of bunker in Hong Kong can lead to more port visits than lowering the bunker price in Zhoushan. Bunker purchase managers in Western Bulk may therefore leverage the information provided in Fig. 3 during bunker purchase negotiations.

6 Concluding Remarks

We have considered a real rich ship routing problem arising in the dry bulk shipping segment, a problem we have denoted Tramp Ship Routing and Scheduling Problem with Bunker Optimization (TSRSPBO). The TSRSPBO includes, in addition to the routing and scheduling of the given vessels in the fleet, decisions about how much to bunker (refuel) in which ports. Furthermore, the cargo quantities to be transported in the TSRSPBO are given in an interval (i.e., MoLOO limits), which means that determining the optimal transport quantities also becomes a decision. We presented an arc flow model for the TSRSPBO, but the commercial MIP solver is only able to solve tiny instances of the problem, partly because the size of the network increases drastically with the inclusion of the bunker ports. Hence, we have proposed a path flow solution method based on a Dantzig-Wolfe decomposition of the problem. This solution method consists of a path flow model using all feasible vessel routes (columns) as input. For each such route, we determine the optimal amounts of both the bunker and cargoes along the route by solving an LP problem.

The solution method was tested on a set of realistic instances generated based on data from Western Bulk, a dry bulk shipping operator. The computational study suggests that the path flow solution method outperforms solving the arc flow model by a commercial solver and that it is able to consistently solve instances of up to 30 cargoes, 10 vessels, and 10 bunker ports within 30 min. Furthermore, additional tests show how different MoLOO limits and bunker discounts in different ports may affect the ship operator's profit. Hence, the ship operator may use these insights in the negotiation of freight contracts and to determine for which ports it is most beneficial to negotiate bunker price discounts.

References

1. Bai, X., Cheng, L., Çağatay, I.: Data-driven financial and operational risk management: empirical evidence from the global tramp shipping industry. Transp. Res. Part E: Logistics Transp. Rev. **158**, 102617 (2022). https://doi.org/10.1016/j.tre.2022.102617
2. Brønmo, G., Christiansen, M., Nygreen, B.: Ship routing and scheduling with flexible cargo sizes. J. Oper. Res. Soc. **58**(9), 1167–1177 (2007). https://doi.org/10.1057/palgrave.jors.2602263
3. BunkerEx: BunkerEx — Bunker Prices — Bunker Broker United Kingdom (2022). https://www.bunker-ex.com. (accessed 2022-11-11)
4. Christiansen, M., Fagerholt, K.: Chapter 13: ship routing and scheduling in industrial and tramp shipping. In: Toth, P., Vigo, D. (eds.) Vehicle Routing, pp. 381–408. Society for Industrial and Applied Mathematics, Philadelphia, PA (2014). https://doi.org/10.1137/1.9781611973594.ch13
5. Christiansen, M., Fagerholt, K., Nygreen, B., Ronen, D.: Chapter 4 maritime transportation. In: Barnhart, C., Laporte, G. (eds.) Handbooks in Operations Research and Management Science, Transportation, vol. 14, pp. 189–284. Elsevier (2007). https://doi.org/10.1016/S0927-0507(06)14004-9
6. Christiansen, M., Fagerholt, K., Nygreen, B., Ronen, D.: Ship routing and scheduling in the new millennium. Eur. J. Oper. Res. **228**(3), 467–483 (2013). https://doi.org/10.1016/j.ejor.2012.12.002
7. dos Santos, P.T.G., Kretschmann, E., Borenstein, D., Guedes, P.C.: Cargo routing and scheduling problem in deep-sea transportation: case study from a fertilizer

company. Comput. Oper. Res. **119**, 104934 (2020). https://doi.org/10.1016/j.cor.2020.104934
8. Korsvik, J.E., Fagerholt, K.: A tabu search heuristic for ship routing and scheduling with flexible cargo quantities. J. Heuristics **16**(2), 117–137 (2010). https://doi.org/10.1007/s10732-008-9092-0
9. Ksciuk, J., Kuhlemann, S., Tierney, K., Koberstein, A.: Uncertainty in maritime ship routing and scheduling: a Literature review. Eur. J. Oper. Res. **308**, 499–524 (2023). https://doi.org/10.1016/j.ejor.2022.08.006
10. Meng, Q., Wang, S., Lee, C.Y.: A tailored branch-and-price approach for a joint tramp ship routing and bunkering problem. Transp. Res. Part B: Methodol. **72**, 1–19 (2015). https://doi.org/10.1016/j.trb.2014.11.008
11. Pache, H., Kastner, M., Jahn, C.: Current state and trends in tramp ship routing and scheduling. In: Hamburg International Conference of Logistics (HICL), vol. 28, pp. 369–394. epubli GmbH (2019). https://doi.org/10.15480/882.2504
12. UNCTAD: Review of maritime transport 2021. United Nations, S.l. (2022). https://unctad.org/publication/review-maritime-transport-2021, Accessed 19 June 2023
13. Vilhelmsen, C., Lusby, R., Larsen, J.: Tramp ship routing and scheduling with integrated bunker optimization. EURO J. Transp. Logistics **3**(2), 143–175 (2013). https://doi.org/10.1007/s13676-013-0039-8

Digital Twins in Seaports: Current and Future Applications

Julian Neugebauer[(✉)], Leonard Heilig, and Stefan Voß

Institute of Information Systems, Universität Hamburg, Von-Melle-Park 5, 20146 Hamburg, Germany
julian.neugebauer@uni-hamburg.de
https://www.bwl.uni-hamburg.de/iwi.html

Abstract. Information systems in major seaports have evolved to digital hubs where state-of-the-art technologies are used to gather and analyze (near) real-time data from infrastructure and superstructure. Digital twins are seen as key enabler of Industry 4.0 applications and digital transformation in seaports. This paper presents case studies of digital twins in global seaports and investigates implementation layers and decision support. Based on a literature review and interviews with port stakeholders from different seaports, we identify potentials, challenges and requirements for integrating digital twins in seaports. Moreover, we present results and insights from a major project building a digital twin for the EUROGATE container terminal in Hamburg, Germany. As such, the paper provides an overview on the maturity of digital twin applications in the port sector and discusses important aspects to be considered during implementation.

Keywords: Digital Twins · Seaports · Container Terminals · Case Studies · Maritime Logistics

1 Introduction

Digital twins have evolved as one of the main drivers for digital transformation in major seaports and are seen as key technology of Industry 4.0 applications. In industry, digital twin technologies are recognized as one of the most important areas of investment for terminal operators in the coming years [27]. The main reason is that they can be implemented in various forms and support many use cases to enable automation and improve productivity, efficiency, resilience and sustainability in terminals and seaports.

According to Vanderhorn et al. [39] a digital twin is a "virtual representation of a physical system (and its associated environment and processes) that is updated through the exchange of information between the physical and virtual system." As such, it is comprised of a set of technologies to gather (near) real-time data from infrastructure and superstructure and its environment, associate it with related port processes, visualize and analyze it to make decisions having

© The Author(s), under exclusive license to Springer Nature Switzerland AG 2023
J. R. Daduna et al. (Eds.): ICCL 2023, LNCS 14239, pp. 202–218, 2023.
https://doi.org/10.1007/978-3-031-43612-3_12

an impact on port operations by controlling infrastructure and superstructure automatically. Moreover, they can be viewed as a tool for applying a variety of methods for enabling data-driven decision making, such as by using simulations, machine learning (ML) or advanced optimization algorithms utilizing the vast amounts of data being collected within a digital twin.

Different forms of digital twins have been discussed and established in research and practice in recent years [20]. As the term is used as another buzzword in industry, one has to be careful regarding applications being coined as digital twin. Using established definitions from literature, it is important to analyze present applications in research and practice to analyze the current state-of-the-art and to explore potentials and challenges in seaports. In this paper, we present case studies of major implementations of digital twins in maritime seaports and terminals. Based on a set of aspects and criteria, we provide an overview and lessons learned from different forms of implementation. In this context, we analyze which requirements or conditions must be met to successfully implement or integrate digital twins in seaports and how these affect the interaction or coordination between different port stakeholders. For that purpose, we analyze implementations on different layers and present insights from interviews with industry experts involved in digital twin projects. Finally, we showcase the implementation of an advanced digital twin being developed for the EUROGATE Container Terminal Hamburg (CTH) and provide insights about the key challenges and developments in the project.

The remainder of the paper is structured as follows. Section 2 describes related literature to get an overview on the current state of research in this area. In Sect. 3, we present a framework to categorize a case study for the identified digital twin applications in industry. Using this framework, we investigate the details of each case and carve out the specific features, challenges, shortcomings and potentials. This includes findings from interviews with various port experts being involved in the respective projects. We further analyze the application of advanced methods for decision support and explore a digital twin being realized in the Port of Hamburg in Sect. 4. The overall results and lessons learned from the case studies are discussed in Sect. 5. Finally, we provide some conclusions and an outlook to future research.

2 Related Literature

Each digital twin, as defined by Vanderhorn et al. [39], consists of a model of a physical system or operation with varying levels of complexity [11]. Complexity in this context refers to the level of detail, including the number of variables and equations used in a model. For a digital twin to be realized, it must be updated in (near) real time with changes in the underlying physical system or operation, and it must learn and adapt automatically. Seaports, facing high demand, are undergoing digital transformation [13], utilizing technologies such as the Internet of Things (IoT), big data, simulation, and ML applications. There are countless other technologies and concepts available, leading to numerous use cases.

One example is the implementation of renewable energy sources in Italian port areas, which involves modeling wind and solar energy production for decision making and then incorporating IoT monitoring [2]. Others are described by Pavlic Skender et al. [26], whether they are autonomous drones for emissions tracking used at the Port of Antwerp (Belgium), automated gates for dispatching in Kaohsiung (Taiwan), or the application of 5G for various other purposes as described by the Port Authority of Hamburg (Germany).

A more advanced utilization of digital twins in use cases is decision support. Hofmann and Branding [16] describe this for container terminal operations planning, discuss dispatching support and continuous monitoring and evaluation. This is made possible by full modeling of key container terminal processes and python-based simulation connected to IoT enabled devices. To do this, the collected data is used to give the digital twin a picture of the current state, which must be adjusted according to the information needed to meet the respective task [45]. If the goal is to create a more resilient port, for example, analyzing the implications of power supply shortages, different scenarios can be simulated using the O^2DES.Net open source framework for allocating power to different vehicles in a container terminal using automated guided vehicles (AGV) based on power and container terminal simulations [46]. The simulation as part of the digital twin allows decisions for future challenges to be analyzed in (near) real time and an optimal strategy for vehicles and the entire container terminal to be defined. Similar analyses are helpful for ongoing operations. These take over the automated storage yard scheduling and work in the form of simulation-based optimization [12].

To develop a digital twin with decision support in the domain of container terminals, the framework described by Wang et al. [40] can be applied. The development is in five steps starting with the "data aquisition" and creating a "georeferenced design" which is not only used for visualization but also for mapping data. Thirdly the integration of (near) real-time data to a model is described, followed by an implementation of some form of "simulation, analysis and optimization" for progressing the model and utilizing it to give new insights from the digitally twinned perspective. Last but not least, the sharing and delivery of insights is described to ensure that the potential lessons and outcomes of the digital twin are understood and executed. Yang et al. [43] describe and apply a similar framework at the Port of Qingdao (China), albeit focusing on the different layers of application. It is comparable to the framework described by Zheng et al. [45]. The following areas are categorized as part of the framework:

- Physical resource layer (system-wide resources and their description)
- Virtual resource layer (model of, and mapping to real components)
- Data connection layer (network, interfaces and data exchange)
- Twin data layer (providing data of analysis, simulation and virtual scenes)
- Application service layer (information for a dynamic knowledge base)

Redelinghuys et al. [28] present a digital twin system from a manufacturing perspective and use similar layers with an additional configuration layer that takes into account the self-adaptation and self-improvement of the digital twin system.

However, a suitable procedure and selection of the use cases to be implemented must be made according to the area of application and the application goals.

The large number of possible use cases, technologies that can be used, and ways to implement them effectively demonstrate the complexity of implementing a digital twin. In addition, suitable criteria are needed to describe use cases in a precise way so that a structured decision can be made in the selection process.

3 Digital Twin Enabled Use Cases

3.1 Digital Twins in Global Ports

To get an overview on current digital twin implementations, we categorize a number of digital twin applications in the port domain and analyze them from different angles. We classify them based on their application area, namely port infrastructure (PI), container terminal (CT), multi-purpose terminal (MPT), and bulk terminal (BT). For each digital twin, we identify the application purpose, data sources, data processing techniques, type of user interface, integration approach and a general level of detail based on a comparison. The latter gives a rough estimate for the amount and granularity of data being mapped in the respective digital twin, the general complexity of the implementation, and the capability to support decision making. The results are gathered from a case study and interviews with port experts involved in respective digital twin projects, as indicated in Table 1.[1] For further insights from the conducted interviews and additional references the reader is referred to the authors upcoming paper "Digital Twins in the Context of Seaports and Terminal Facilities" [23].

The results in Table 1 show that digital twins have diverse application areas in the port domain, ranging from infrastructure management to cargo handling. They are also used to monitor and manage port infrastructure, improve operational efficiency, predict maintenance, and improve the ecological footprint. While the applications have similarities regarding the use of information technology, they differ in terms of the utilization of data for advanced analytics and decision support. For port infrastructure, often managed by a port authority, the digital twin in the Port of Antwerp-Bruges, Belgium, can be seen as a good example. One of many use cases is the identification of pollution sources, mostly caused by ships in the ports or on the river sections between the ports. To enable proper identification of emission sources, a large number of sensors was installed in the ports, but for accurate localization, autonomous drones are also sent to the locations where emissions are measured outside the norm. These drones also take measurements, which are then sent in (near) real time to the digital twin and used as a basis for visualizing and simulating certain scenarios. The results provide decision support for the port authority and help lowering greenhouse gas (GHG) emissions. Another example is the Port of Hamburg, Germany, where sensor technologies and BIM are applied to visualize conditions of

[1] BIM: building information modeling; VR: virtual reality; AR: augmented reality; GNSS: global navigation satellite systems; TOS: terminal operating system.

Table 1. Categorization of Digital Twins in Global Seaports

Location of the Use Case	Application Area	Application Purpose	Data Sources	Data Processing	User Interface	Twin Integration	Level of Detail	Source
Antwerp-Bruges, Belgium	PI	General port and emissions management	IoT, BIM, cameras, power- and weather data, autonomous drones	Big data, simulation, ML	3D visualization, VR/AR	(Near) Real-time data integration and feedback loop	•••••	[26] Interview
Anzio, Italy	PI	Renewable energy utilization	IoT, BIM, geological data	Simulation	Dashboards	(Near) Real-time data	••	[1]
Bremen, Germany	BT	Position monitoring and move optimization	GNSS, IoT, cameras, weather data	Big data, simulation, ML	3D visualization, integrated into control units	(Near) Real-time data integration, automated decision making and (near) real-time control	••••••	Interview
Dalian, China	CT	Equipment and terminal management and overall optimization	IoT, BIM, cameras, GNSS, TOS	Big data, simulation, ML	3D visualization	(Near) Real-time data integration, automated decision making and (near) real-time control	••••••	[21] Interview
Genoa, Italy	Multiple	Renewable energy utilization and process monitoring	IoT, TOS	Simulation	Dashboards	Data integration and process model for predictions	•••	[4,9]
Gothenburg, Sweden	Multiple	Infrastructure and traffic management	IoT	Big data, ML	n.a.	n.a.	•••	[8]
Hamburg, Germany	PI	Infrastructure and traffic management	IoT, cameras, GNSS, weather data	Big data, simulation, ML	3D visualization, VR/AR, dashboards, integrated into traffic displays	(Near) Real-time data integration, automated decision making and (near) real-time control	•••••	[3,29,37] Interview
Livorno, Italy	PI, BT	Infrastructure and traffic management	IoT, cameras, GNSS, weather data	Big data, simulation, ML	3D visualization, VR/AR	(Near) Real-time data integration and feedback loop	•••••	[7,25,33] Interview
Mawan, China	BT, CT	Fleet and terminal management	IoT, cameras, GNSS, TOS	Big data, simulation, ML	3D visualization	(Near) Real-time data integration, automated decision making and (near) real-time control	•••••	[17]
Multiple, Thailand	BT, CT	Terminal management	IoT, TOS	Big data, simulation	Dashboards	Data integration and process model for predictions	••••	[26,41]
Oulu, Finland	MPT	General port and process management	IoT, BIM, cameras	Big data, simulation	3D visualization, dashboards	(Near) Real-time data integration and feedback loop	•••	[5]
Qingdao, China	CT	Equipment and terminal management and overall optimization	IoT, BIM, cameras, GNSS, TOS, weather data	Big data, simulation, ML	3D visualization	(Near) Real-time data integration, automated decision making and (near) real-time control	••••••	[6,42,43]
Rotterdam, Netherlands	PI	Infrastructure and traffic management	IoT, cameras, GNSS, weather data	Big data, simulation, ML •	n.a.	(Near) Real-time data integration, automated decision making and (near) real-time optimization	•••••	[15,24,26], [17,32,34]
Shanghai, China	CT	Process monitoring and general optimization	GNSS, cameras, BIM, TOS	Big data, simulation, ML	3D visualization	(Near) Real-time data integration, automated decision making, predictions and (near) real-time control	•••••	[10,19,26,44] Interview
Singapore, Singapore	CT, PI	Infrastructure and terminal management	n.a.	Simulation	3D visualization	Data integration and process model for predictions	••••	[17,18,21,26] Interview
Valencia, Spain	CT	Terminal management	IoT, GNSS, BIM, TOS	Big data, simulation, ML	3D visualization	(Near) Real-time data integration and feedback loop	••	[30,31] Interview

port infrastructure (e.g., streets, bridges, locks), which supports infrastructure planning. One example is the project smartBridge to optimize maintenance by monitoring (near) real-time conditions of the Köhlbrand Bridge connecting the port with a main highway.[2]

Applications in bulk terminals include the precise positioning of steel coils using various movement sensors attached to the forklifts, as done in Bremen, Germany. Such precise positioning of goods and vehicles avoids seek times and enables a better warehouse management in their enterprise resource planning (ERP) system. With accurate positioning and transparent start and end times for all handling operations, the bulk terminal is able to predict movement times and control the number of vehicles needed for a given workload. In the Port of Mawan, China, a similar system was implemented, but with the additional use

[2] See, e.g., https://www.homeport.hamburg/portfolio/smartbridge.

case of fleet management. In this case, the focus is on historical data, which serves as a basis for analyzing bottlenecks and technical problems in order to avoid them during planning [17]. Another example in this context can be found in the Port of Livorno, Italy, where advanced technologies, such as 3D LIDAR sensors and Wide Dynamic Range (WDR) cameras, are used for the localization of cargo boxes and forklifts. Based on the planned tasks, the forklift driver is guided within the terminal by wearing AR glasses.[3] An example of a digital twin in multi-purpose terminals is the Port of Oulu, Finland, where both vessel- and terminal related information are represented in a geographic information system (GIS) in order to increase situational awareness for improving the efficiency and safety in the terminals. The digital twin provides a number of tools enabling planning of port infrastructure elements, such as industrial lighting or cameras of the monitoring system [5].

Looking at the application area of container terminals, the digital twin at the Port of Qingdao realizes a wide variety of use cases. The status of vehicles along with respective processes are represented in a complex 3D visualization. Not only the positions and possible technical problems are displayed based on (near) real-time GNSS and IoT data, but also simulations and optimization methods for path planning and forecasts of the future handling rate based on ML are integrated. As required for digital twins, decisions of the digital twin are propagated to the control units of the AGVs [43]. Another focus is on various visualizations for the operating status or the system behavior, as well as the structured implementation [42]. Similar applications can be found in the Port of Shanghai and Dalian, China, where a very detailed digital twin supporting decision making for automated and semi-automated terminals has been developed [10,21]. Several digital twins apply big data technologies, such as Hadoop, to process various sources of data. In the Port of Valencia, for instance, key performance indicators are calculated based on operational data, AIS (automatic identification system), and weather data. Another advanced digital twin for a container terminal in the Port of Hamburg, Germany, is detailed in Sect. 4.

3.2 Maturity and Applied Layers

The analysis of the digital twins in Table 1 reveals that data sources, processing techniques, user interfaces and twin integration vary across the different application areas. For example, some applications rely solely on IoT data, while others use many data sources and establish advanced decision support. Similarly, some use cases require a high level of detail, while others can operate at a more abstract level. Although the described applications give a good idea of the use cases, the following section will take a generalized look at the different layers of implementations and their maturity. The following analysis focuses on the technical layers described in Sect. 2 which were developed by Yang et al. [43] and extended by a sixth layer of self-adaption in Redelinghuys et al. [28].

[3] See, e.g., https://www.ericsson.com/en/blog/2020/12/digital-twins-port-operations.

The physical resource layer is present in all digital twins listed in Table 1, albeit to very different degrees. In the Port of Anzio, Italy, only certain aspects regarding energy production and consumption are represented while the digital twin in Shanghai includes models of vehicles, infrastructure, weather and other factors influencing terminal operations. Interacting mechanisms as well as the current state of each object are taken into account and thus show the physical resources in more detail. Across the layer, it is important to note that the level of detail and the number of objects being represented are almost unlimited. The trade off between the complexity and utility of displaying detailed physical resources and the associated cost of implementing them must be considered. This layer describes only the resource and its general attributes, excluding more advanced process definitions or rules and more extensive environmental and business-related information.

To model additional aspects besides the physical objects, especially environmental aspects and business processes (as required by digital twins by Van Der Horn [39]), the virtual resource layer is used. Similar to the previous level, the more detailed and extensive the contextual information, the better and more accurate the digital twin. During the interviews, the person in charge at the ports of Antwerp-Bruges mentioned their goal to build the port's nervous system, including things like smell, which was an example for air quality sensors and sight for example, realized with cameras and various visualizations. Other environmental factors are derived from IoT and external data, which included, for example, infrastructure conditions and vessel tracking. Examples for combining physical objects with business processes in which they interact are given in the case study presented in Sect. 4.

Data connectivity as a layer of digital twins is described in detail in the Port of Qingdao. In order to use all the information and connect the representation of physical resources and their behavior as well as 3D models, the network, protocols, interfaces and general data exchange must be defined and managed. This is critical for establishing an integration and is the focus of many digital twin projects. For the Port of Singapore, for example, an open source framework was used to model the digital twin in order to ensure future ease of integration and extensibility, and all of the ports interviewed cited the specification of interfaces as one of the biggest challenges in development. The data connection layer is directly linked to the twin data layer, which includes the storage and processing of data, but also advanced data processing techniques such as big data analytics and other data mining techniques. For example, in the interview with the Port of Hamburg, it was mentioned that traffic information is combined with simulation data to be used in various applications. Another example is a BIM infrastructure model, used for the before-mentioned Köhlbrand bridge, which was then used in the application service layer to predict damage and schedule maintenance.

The application service layer includes decision support, using advanced methods, such as simulation modeling, optimization approaches and ML, but also monitoring and business intelligence dashboards for supporting human decision making. Examples from the digital twins include the actual traffic management service and its visualization implemented at the Port of Livorno but also the analysis and optimization of operations for the container terminal at the Port of Mawan. Note that although all projects listed in Table 1 incorporate this layer, albeit with varying degrees of detail, not all feed these insights back into the physical domain in an automated or semi-automated and (near) real-time manner.

The self-adaptation layer can be realized when data from the lower layers are considered on the application layer to adapt to certain situations and propagate decisions back to the physical resources so that they can adapt accordingly. If the self-adaptation layer is implemented in an architecture for cross-layer information and the various layers are implemented with a high level of detail, it is assumed that there is a huge potential for automation. In addition, a large number of use cases can then be supported. This is also the goal in the presented case study in the following section.

4 Digital Twin at the EUROGATE Container Terminal Hamburg

The research-industry project *TwinSim*, currently carried out by EUROGATE Holding, EUROGATE Technical Services, Akquinet port consulting and the Institute of Information Systems (IWI), University of Hamburg, is pursuing the development of a digital twin for the visualization and simulation-based optimization of terminal operations at the EUROGATE Container Terminal Hamburg (CTH). The research project has a project volume of 3.65 million Euros and is funded by the German Federal Ministry of Digital Affairs and Transport (BMDV) within the frame of the Innovative Port Technologies (IHATEC) program over a period of three years [38]. The scope is on container terminal processes and maintenance for straddle carrier (SC) and gantry crane operations in order to strengthen the efficiency, eco-awareness, and resilience of the terminal. In a comprehensive requirements analysis a multitude of use cases utilizing a digital twin were identified in several workshops (for details, the interested reader is referred to by Neugebauer [22]). The final result of the requirements analysis was a selection of 14 use cases to be implemented within the project and moreover serve to develop a best practice implementation of a digital twin for the application area of container terminals considering all levels discussed in Sect. 2.

Starting with the representation of the physical resources of the terminal, the digital twin firstly considers containers, infrastructure and superstructure involved in container transport and storage processes for both sea- and landside operations. The following list represents physical objects and potential dynamic attributes to be mapped:

- Container (position, reefer status)
- Straddle carrier (position, technical status, operational status)
- Gantry cranes (position, technical status, operational status)
- Special handling equipment (e.g., overheight frames) (position)
- Vessel (position, estimated time of arrival)
- Truck and trailers (position, operational status)
- Light (operational status)
- Reefer station (position, technical status)
- Yard (operational status)
- Truck gate (operational status)
- Buildings

These objects are modeled as 3D representations in a simulation model, which is later also used for (near) real-time visualizations. Buildings are included for reference purposes only, as they have no influence on the operation of the container terminal. The container yard, albeit represented with different roads as well as one-way driving restrictions, is also only modeled as a reference and provided with information on transshipment areas, hazardous materials and reefer storage locations, and other higher level information. Surface conditions, for example, are not included. A preview of the visualization can be seen in Fig. 1.

Fig. 1. 3D Visualization of CTH

However, only a part of the data comes directly from the physical devices. In the first phase, the project focuses on collecting data from SCs and gantry cranes. This is achieved by connecting the equipment's programmable logic controller (PLC), sensors, and GNSS though an edge processor to an on-premises message broker, which is communicating with a cloud message broker using the MQTT (Message Queuing Telemetry Transport) protocol, as shown in Fig. 2.

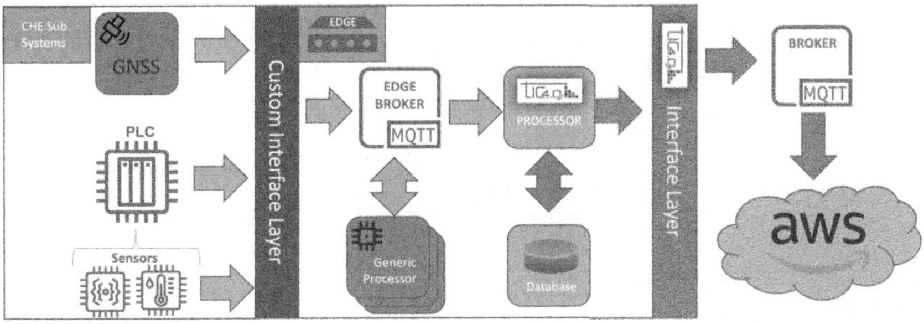

Fig. 2. IoT-Edge Architecture

The virtual resource layer focuses mainly on building cycles of SCs and gantry cranes. A cycle contains all equipment activities for moving a container from one position (e.g., in the yard) to another position (e.g., at the quay). In some situations also dual cycles need to be considered, meaning that two cycles are considered together, such as when loading and unloading a full container from a vessel in two subsequent moves. Note that one cycle can also contain more than one container move (e.g., twin moves). For building cycles, from the edge device containing PLC, GNSS and sensor data are combined with TOS data in order to relate the IoT data with the business process context. The contextual data is given by a job instruction from the TOS, representing all information to conduct the movement of a container, such as the start and end positions, container information, planned schedules, etc., resulting from the first planning phases (e.g., vessel planning). The combination enables situational awareness about the behavior and conditions of terminal equipment in relation to certain operations, time, and other environmental impacts, such as weather if provided. Moreover, it supports multiple use cases and has implications for all areas of operations since it allows to analyze operations in detail and use extracted insights to improve the planning and enhance the transparency for terminal operators and customers. Added to this is ecologically relevant information such as fuel consumption or tire wear, which can also be used later to monitor the total GHG emissions, not only in general, but also the consumption of individual containers during their lifetime at the terminal. In the project, the data from the equipment is further used to enable predictive maintenance. As shown in Fig. 3, the IoT and contextual data is shown when selecting physical objects in the digital twin. Note that this is an interim result; later, extensive data dashboards and predictions are included to better monitor conditions and key performance indicators.

Data connectivity, especially in a project of this size, with a multitude of stakeholders, with data sources from various types of equipment from different suppliers and different information systems (e.g., TOS, ERP) in numerous formats, becomes a complex task and thus requires standardized interfaces. Currently one major problem with respect to the equipment is that suppliers are not using the same definitions for measuring certain aspects, e.g., the operational time of a SC. In one case the engine-on time is used, in the other case, the

Fig. 3. Contextual information for SC

working hours of the driver are used. At the EUROGATE container terminals, SCs of different suppliers are in use, making it difficult to compare metrics.

The Terminal Industry Committee 4.0 (TIC 4.0) is working on data standards for container terminals and includes crane manufacturers, TOS suppliers and more (see [36]). A number of publications has been done for standardizing the syntax and semantics for different equipment data sources [35]. In the project, TIC 4.0 standards are used to assemble position data and technical information from SCs (e.g., tire pressure, oil temperature, etc.) and gantry cranes, send them in (near) real-time to message brokers and combine them with standardized job instructions filled with information from the TOS to build respective cycles. One major advantage of the proposed digital twins is that the standardization allows to connect information systems (e.g., TOS) and equipment from different suppliers/providers without changing the core implementation by talking or translating into the same language. Therefore, all higher level applications, including advanced decision support functionality, can read and write data in this predefined format and solutions can be developed without spending time on interface definition and in an agile manner. As equipment suppliers have just started with implementing TIC 4.0 compliant data for newer equipment, it is still necessary to transform the equipment data in TIC messages. As shown in Fig. 2, a special edge processor has been implemented in the project to transform all data records before forwarding them to the cloud. The (near) real-time data connectivity is enabled by a scalable message broker system that connects edge devices from physical objects in on-premises networks with the cloud-based streaming processors and the twin data layer.

The gathered data is processed in several data processing stages for multiple purposes in the twin data layer, which is build with AWS cloud services. This layer includes a cloud-based data lake and big data technologies to prepare the data for the higher level applications. At both the data connectivity and twin data layers, some data streams need to be processed in (near) real time (e.g., objects for (near) real-time visualization). This affected the cloud services and technologies chosen. A list of all applications realized for the digital twin at the CTH is almost impossible to compile and is also not the goal of this work. Rather, those that show the decision area of the digital twin are discussed. Currently the terminal planning is realized with rule-based approaches using the TOS. For dispatching the SCs, for example, a score for each container is calculated based on several weighted factors, such as the shortest distance from a theoretical position of an SC to its planned position. This is a rather greedy approach that does not consider the combination of different moves.

Therefore, the goal is to improve this planning with more advanced algorithms based on the vast availability of granular data, which will be discussed in future works. Starting from the integration of accurate positions based on GNSS data, the distance-based calculations can be replaced by those that include, for example, the estimated actual distances traveled by the SCs. In the project, a ML model for predicting travel times will be implemented. In order for these predictions to be as accurate as possible and thus represent the physical resources most accurately, weather information is collected by sensors on the container terminal. This provides information on precipitation, wind speed and direction, current visibility and much more. Weather conditions also have an impact on planned operations and maintenance activities, which may need to be postponed due to several weather conditions. Thus, weather predictions also serve for early warnings so that plannings can be adjusted accordingly. In addition, water levels and more as well as arrival time predictions of vessels from external sources are integrated.

As a second stage a simulation will provide a feedback loop for optimization methods and will allow for a more in-depth analysis of manual decisions. Through simulating past shifts with new conditions (e.g., more SCs being used) lessons learned can be taken for improving the current situation. By simulating the next shift, the future performance of the terminal can be evaluated without interrupting ongoing operations. In the final phase of realizing the described digital twin, a simulation-based optimization is implemented for the dispatching of SCs and container storage allocation, using all available information, integrating ML, and applying operations research methods to find an optimized plan and evaluate it through simulation. By taking into account granular data from the past, the simulation helps to validate the plan in a more accurate and complex representation of the container terminal. The results are subsequently reported to the TOS and passed on, e.g., to SC drivers, who then take an optimized route better utilizing available resources, avoiding unproductive moves, waiting times, and minimizing the environmental impact. Moreover, the solution can lead to a greater operational resilience as unforeseen events can be simulated and emergency plans or more resilient plans can be assessed in advance. Since this system controls for the movement of the vehicles, it is also easier to use automated equipment in the future.

5 Discussion and Conclusion

Digital twins offer many benefits and opportunities for seaports and container terminals, such as improving efficiency, safety, sustainability, and resilience. However, they also pose some challenges and limitations. From the analyzed cases, interviews, and from the on-going project, we could identify the following recurring challenges, which may require more research:

- Choosing and integrating suitable IoT devices and data processing technologies, also regarding implementation and operation costs
- Ensuring data quality, standardization, and security
- Scaling and adapting to changing needs
- Interacting with other systems and stakeholders (e.g., port community systems)
- Complying with ethical and legal regulations (e.g., the General Data Protection Regulation (GDPR) in Europe)
- Estimating and managing implementation costs and time
- Avoiding model bias and prejudice
- Expanding the scope to other parts of the supply chain
- Anticipating long-term impacts and dependencies on the digital twin

This paper has examined how digital twins can be used in seaports and container terminals to optimize and improve terminal planning and operations as well as maintenance. To this end, a review of existing publications on the topic was conducted and a number of port cases were discussed to assess the current state of research and practice. The interviewed experts expressed a need for more standardization, further collaboration, and more empirical evidence to support the adoption and evaluation of digital twins in this domain. Some possible solutions or recommendations to address the challenges and limitations of digital twins are:

- Developing standards and guidelines for data collection, processing, sharing, and protection
- Enhancing collaboration and communication among different stakeholders, such as port authorities, terminal operators, shipping companies, logistics providers, regulators, and researchers
- Conducting more empirical studies and evaluations to measure the impact and value of digital twins for seaports and container terminals

Regarding the latter aspect, we see that in industry the question whether digital twins are just costly toys or valuable support tools still arises.[4] In this context, this work has shown the possibilities of a digital twin on different levels and with different degrees of complexity. Furthermore, it has been shown that an in-depth requirements analysis in terms of valuable use cases for the individual port or terminal is decisive to gain value (as further discussed in [22]).

[4] See, e.g., http://www.bpoports.com/BPC/agenda-3.pdf.

As digital twins become more mature and widely adopted, we expect to see more benefits and opportunities for seaports and container terminals in two main areas. The first area is expanding the scope and impact of digital twins to other parts of the supply chain. Digital twins can enable a seamless integration and coordination of port operations with other actors and processes in the supply chain, such as shippers, carriers, logistics providers, customs authorities, and end customers. This can improve the visibility, resilience, and efficiency of the entire supply chain, as well as reduce costs, risks, and environmental impacts. Digital twins can also support the development of new supply chain concepts and solutions, such as synchromodality or the circular economy. The second area is creating new business models and value propositions for port services and products. Digital twins can enable ports and terminals to offer new services and products that leverage their data and insights to create value for their customers and partners. For example, ports and terminals may provide data-driven services such as (near) real-time monitoring, forecasting, optimization, or simulations of port operations and processes to their customers. They can also integrate data-enabled objects such as "smart" containers that can communicate and interact with the digital twin (see, e.g., [14]). These services and products can create new revenue streams and competitive advantages for worldwide ports and container terminals.

References

1. Agostinelli, S., Cumo, F., Nezhad, M.M., Orsini, G., Piras, G.: Renewable energy system controlled by open-source tools and digital twin model: zero energy port area in Italy. Energies **15**(5), 1817 (2022). https://doi.org/10.3390/en15051817
2. Agostinelli, S., Neshat, M., Majidi Nezhad, M., Piras, G., Astiaso Garcia, D.: Integrating renewable energy sources in Italian Port areas towards renewable energy communities. Sustainability **14**(21), 13720 (2022). https://doi.org/10.3390/su142113720
3. Ali-Tolppa, J., Kajo, M.: Mobility and QoS prediction for dynamic coverage optimization. In: Proceedings of the IEEE/IFIP Network Operations and Management Symposium (NOMS), pp. 1–2. IEEE, Budapest, Hungary (2020). https://doi.org/10.1109/NOMS47738.2020.9110396
4. Battilani, C., Galli, G., Arecco, S., Casarino, B., Granero, A., Lavagna, K., Varna, R., Ventura, M., Revetria, R., Damiani, L.: Business process re-engineering in public administration: the case study of Western Ligurian sea port authority. Sustain. Futures **4**, 100065 (2022). https://doi.org/10.1016/j.sftr.2022.100065
5. Blare.Tech: Increasing port operations efficiency and safety thanks to the full situational awareness through the use of digital twin (2023). https://www.blare.tech/project/port-of-oulu-digital-twin
6. Cai, J., Li, G., Zhang, L.: Study on the construction of digital twin-oriented operation ecosystem model of large-scale comprehensive port. In: Yang, M., Lanzinha, J.C., Samui, P., Bao, X., Hu, J. (eds.) Advances in Transdisciplinary Engineering, pp. 1280–1285. IOS Press (2022). https://doi.org/10.3233/ATDE220998
7. Cavalli, L., et al.: Addressing efficiency and sustainability in the port of the future with 5G: the experience of the Livorno port. A methodological insight to measure

innovation technologies' benefits on port operations. Sustainability **13**(21), 12146 (2021). https://doi.org/10.3390/su132112146
8. Dalaklis, D., Christodoulou, A., Ölcer, A., Ballini, F., Dalaklis, A., Lagdami, K.: The port of Gothenburg under the influence of the fourth stage of the industrial revolution: implementing a wide portfolio of digital tools to optimize the conduct of operations. Marit. Technol. Res. **4**(3), 1–18 (2021). https://doi.org/10.33175/mtr.2022.253844
9. Damiani, L., Revetria, R., Morra, E.: A digital twin for supporting energy management in complex maritime terminals. In: Proceedings of the International Maritime Transport and Logistics Conference, pp. 1–19. Rome, Italy (2019). https://marlog.aast.edu/attachments/cms/solid/0920ac36890175d746314dd28d79a004.pdf
10. Ding, Y., et al.: Real-time monitoring and optimal resource allocation for automated container terminals: a digital twin application at the Yangshan Port. J. Adv. Transp. **2023**, 6909801 (2023). https://doi.org/10.1155/2023/6909801
11. Fuller, A., Fan, Z., Day, C., Barlow, C.: Digital twin: enabling technologies, challenges and open research. IEEE Access **8**, 108952–108971 (2020). https://doi.org/10.1109/ACCESS.2020.2998358
12. Gao, Y., Chang, D., Chen, C.H., Xu, Z.: Design of digital twin applications in automated storage yard scheduling. Adv. Eng. Inform. **51**, 101477 (2022). https://doi.org/10.1016/j.aei.2021.101477
13. Heilig, L., Lalla-Ruiz, E., Voß, S.: Digital transformation in maritime ports: analysis and a game theoretic framework. Netnomics **18**, 227–254 (2017). https://doi.org/10.1007/s11066-017-9122-x
14. Heilig, L., Voß, S.: A cloud-based SOA for enhancing information exchange and decision support in ITT operations. In: González-Ramírez, R.G., Schulte, F., Voß, S., Ceroni Díaz, J.A. (eds.) ICCL 2014. LNCS, vol. 8760, pp. 112–131. Springer, Cham (2014). https://doi.org/10.1007/978-3-319-11421-7_8
15. Henríquez, R., Martínez de Osés, F.X., Martínez Marín, J.E.: Technological drivers of seaports' business model innovation: an exploratory case study on the port of Barcelona. Res. Transp. Busi. Manage. **43**, 100803 (2022). https://doi.org/10.1016/j.rtbm.2022.100803
16. Hofmann, W., Branding, F.: Implementation of an IoT- and cloud-based digital twin for real-time decision support in port operations. IFAC-PapersOnLine **52**(13), 2104–2109 (2019). https://doi.org/10.1016/j.ifacol.2019.11.516
17. Klar, R., Fredriksson, A., Angelakis, V.: Assessing the maturity of digital twinning solutions for ports (2022). https://doi.org/10.48550/ARXIV.2212.07722
18. Li, H., Cao, X., Sharma, P., Lee, L.H., Chew, E.P.: Framework of O^2 DES.NET: digital twins for next generation ports and warehouse solutions. In: Proceedings of the Winter Simulation Conference (WSC), pp. 3188–3199. IEEE, Orlando, USA (2020). https://doi.org/10.1109/WSC48552.2020.9384111
19. Li, Y., Chang, D., Gao, Y., Zou, Y., Bao, C.: Automated container terminal production operation and optimization via an AdaBoost-based digital twin framework. J. Adv. Transp. **2021**, 1–16 (2021). https://doi.org/10.1155/2021/1936764
20. Madusanka, N.S., Fan, Y., Yang, S., Xiang, X.: Digital twin in the maritime domain: a review and emerging trends. J. Mar. Sci. Eng. **11**(5), 1021 (2023). https://doi.org/10.3390/jmse11051021
21. Mi, W., Liu, Y.: Smart port and digital monitoring and diagnosis. In: Mi, W., Liu, Y. (eds.) Smart Ports, pp. 171–188. Springer, Singapore (2022). https://doi.org/10.1007/978-981-16-9889-7_10

22. Neugebauer, J., Heilig, L., Voß, S.: Anforderungsanalyse zur Umsetzung eines digitalen Zwillings im Containerterminal. HMD Praxis der Wirtschaftsinformatik **60**(1), 110–131 (2023). https://doi.org/10.1365/s40702-022-00941-1
23. Neugebauer, J., Heilig, L., Voß, S.: Digital twins in the context of seaports and terminal facilities. In: Flexibil Services and Manufacturing, pp. 1–57 (2023)
24. Özkanli, A., DeniZhan, B.: Digitalization roadmap for Turkish seaports. Eur. J. Sci. Technol. 358–363 (2020). https://doi.org/10.31590/ejosat.araconf46
25. Pagano, P., Antonelli, S., Tardo, A.: C-ports: a proposal for a comprehensive standardization and implementation plan of digital services offered by the "ort of the future" Comput. Ind. **134**, 103556 (2022). https://doi.org/10.48550/arXiv.2104.13175
26. Pavlić Skender, H., Ribarić, E., Jović, M.: An overview of modern technologies in leading global seaports. Pomorski Zbornik **59**(1), 35–49 (2020). https://doi.org/10.18048/2020.59.02. https://hrcak.srce.hr/249260
27. Port Technology: PSA highlights digital twin as biggest emerging technology trend (2021). https://www.porttechnology.org/news/psa-highlights-digital-twin-as-biggest-emerging-technology-trend/
28. Redelinghuys, A.J.H., Basson, A.H., Kruger, K.: A six-layer architecture for the digital twin: a manufacturing case study implementation. J. Intell. Manuf. **31**(6), 1383–1402 (2019). https://doi.org/10.1007/s10845-019-01516-6
29. Rost, P., et al.: Customized industrial networks: network slicing trial at Hamburg seaport. IEEE Wirel. Commun. **25**(5), 48–55 (2018). https://doi.org/10.1109/MWC.2018.1800045
30. Sarabia-Jacome, D., Lacalle, I., Palau, C.E., Esteve, M.: Enabling industrial data space architecture for seaport scenario. In: Proceedings of the IEEE 5th World Forum on Internet of Things (WF-IoT), p. 101–106. IEEE, Limerick, Ireland (2019). https://doi.org/10.1109/ACCESS.2019.2963283
31. Sarabia-Jacome, D., Palau, C.E., Esteve, M., Boronat, F.: Seaport data space for improving logistic maritime operations. IEEE Access **8**, 4372–4382 (2020). https://doi.org/10.1109/ACCESS.2019.2963283
32. Simoni, M., Schiavone, F., Risitano, M., Leone, D., Chen, J.: Group-specific business process improvements via a port community system: the case of Rotterdam. Prod. Plan. Control **33**(4), 371–385 (2022). https://doi.org/10.1080/09537287.2020.1824029
33. Tardo, A., Pagano, P., Antonelli, S., Rao, S.: Addressing digitalization though out a prototyping framework for agile smart services development: the case of Livorno Port. J. Phys: Conf. Ser. **2311**(1), 012007 (2022). https://doi.org/10.1088/1742-6596/2311/1/012007
34. Taylor, S.J.E., Johansson, B., Jeon, S., Lee, L.H., Lendermann, P., Shao, G.: Using simulation and digital twins to innovate: are we getting smarter? In: Proceedings of the Winter Simulation Conference (WSC), pp. 1–13. IEEE, Phoenix, USA (2021). https://doi.org/10.1109/WSC52266.2021.9715535
35. Terminal Industry Committee 4.0: Publications of the Terminal Industry Committee 4.0 (2023). https://tic40.org/publications/
36. Terminal Industry Committee 4.0: TIC4.0 Members (2023). https://tic40.org/tic4-0-members/
37. Tesse, J., Baldauf, U., Schirmer, I., Drews, P., Saxe, S.: Extending internet of things enterprise architectures by digital twins exemplified in the context of the Hamburg port authority. In: Proceedings of the 27th Americas Conference on Information Systems (AMCIS), pp. 1–11. Montreal, Canada (2021)

38. TÜV Rheinland: Verbundprojekt TwinSim zum 01.10.2021 gestartet IHATEC (2021). https://www.innovativehafentechnologien.de/verbundprojekt-twinsim-zum-01-10-2021-gestartet/
39. Van Der Horn, E., Mahadevan, S.: Digital twin: generalization, characterization and implementation. Decis. Support Syst. **145**, 113524 (2021). https://doi.org/10.1016/j.dss.2021.113524
40. Wang, K., Hu, Q., Zhou, M., Zun, Z., Qian, X.: Multi-aspect applications and development challenges of digital twin-driven management in global smart ports. Case Stud. Transp. Policy **9**(3), 1298–1312 (2021). https://doi.org/10.1016/j.cstp.2021.06.014
41. Wattanakul, S., Henry, S., Napaporn, R., Ouzrout, Y.: A port digital twin model for operational uncertainty management. J. Modern Project Manage. **9**(3), 154–167 (2022). https://hal.archives-ouvertes.fr/hal-03579344
42. Yang, A., Liu, Y., Xin, C., Chen, Q., Wang, L.: Towards intuitive visualisation goals for the operation optimisation of automated container terminal based on digital twin technology. Marit. Policy Manage. 1–22 (2023). https://doi.org/10.1080/03088839.2023.2166686
43. Yang, W., et al.: A digital twin framework for large comprehensive ports and a case study of Qingdao Port. Int. J. Adv. Manuf. Technol. (2022). https://doi.org/10.1007/s00170-022-10625-1
44. Yao, H., Wang, D., Su, M., Qi, Y.: Application of digital twins in port system. J. Phys. Conf. Ser. **1846**(1), 012008 (2021). https://doi.org/10.1088/1742-6596/1846/1/012008
45. Zheng, Yu., Yang, S., Cheng, H.: An application framework of digital twin and its case study. J. Ambient. Intell. Humaniz. Comput. **10**(3), 1141–1153 (2018). https://doi.org/10.1007/s12652-018-0911-3
46. Zhou, C., et al.: Analytics with digital-twinning: a decision support system for maintaining a resilient port. Decis. Support Syst. **143**, 113496 (2021). https://doi.org/10.1016/j.dss.2021.113496

A Neural Network Approach for ETA Prediction in Inland Waterway Transport

Peter Wenzel[1], Raka Jovanovic[2], and Frederik Schulte[1](✉)

[1] Technical University of Delft, Mekelweg 5, 2628 Delft, CD, Netherlands
{p.a.wenzel,f.schulte}@tudelft.nl
[2] Qatar Environment and Qatar Environment and Energy Research Institute, Hamad bin Khalifa University, PO Box 5825, Doha, Qatar
rjovanovic@hbku.edu.qa

Abstract. Ensuring the accuracy of the estimated time of arrival (ETA) information for ships approaching ports and inland terminals is increasingly critical today. Waterway transportation plays a vital role in freight transportation and has a significant ecological impact. Improving the accuracy of ETA predictions can enhance the reliability of inland waterway shipping, increasing the acceptance of this eco-friendly mode of transportation. This study compares the industry-standard approach for predicting the ETA based on average travel times with a neural network (NN) trained using real-world historical data. This study generates and trains two NN models using historical ship position data. These models are then assessed and contrasted with the conventional method of calculating average travel times for two specific areas in the Netherlands and Germany. The results indicate by using specific input features, the quality of ETA predictions can improve by an average of 20.6% for short trips, 4.8% for medium-length trips, and 13.4% for long-haul journeys when compared to the average calculation.

Keywords: Neural Networks · Machine Learning · Inland Waterway Transport · Estimated Time of Arrival Prediction

1 Introduction

In 2021, the total volume of goods transported on European inland waterways was 524 million tonnes, increasing by 3.9 % compared with the previous year. The complete transport reached 136 billion tonne-kilometres, up 3.3 % of the prior year [9]. Inland Waterway Transportation (IWT) is part of the critical infrastructure that provides essential services that are substantial to the safety and the economic and social welfare of society [20]. Therefore inland waterway infrastructure maintenance and management is critical but not ideal. In 2015, for example, around 85% of locks, 73% of weirs, and 87% of pumping stations were in an inadequate state of repair [20]. Navigation hazards and safety measures in inland waterways play an important role. For 2010, 2011, and 2013, the

© The Author(s), under exclusive license to Springer Nature Switzerland AG 2023
J. R. Daduna et al. (Eds.): ICCL 2023, LNCS 14239, pp. 219–232, 2023.
https://doi.org/10.1007/978-3-031-43612-3_13

most frequent accident was the collision with infrastructure and bridges. This type accounted for 38–40% of all accidents. The second most frequent type of accident was the collision between ships (18–19%). Due to increasing low water periods caused by climate change, low water levels will lead to smaller vessels and, therefore, an increase in transportation costs [13]. In order to make accurate predictions, it is critical to consider and account for exceptions in the inland waterway network.

Intermodal connectivity and transport efficiency in inland waterways are crucial to model cost competitiveness compared with other transportation modes such as road and rail [21]. Waterway transportation has an irreplaceable key position in the entire transportation development process. It is also one of the important modes of transportation to have a significant ecological impact [12].

The maritime operations in a port involve many parties, including pilots, tug boats, boatmen, agents, supervision agencies such as customs and police, stevedores and others. The arrival of a ship triggers activities at all these parties, who then determine the performance of the port as a whole by each contributing their specialist activity [19]. The need for reliable tools to verify and ensure the accuracy of the estimated time of arrival (ETA) information provided by ships as they approach ports has never been more critical than it is today [3, 6]. This paper establishes a groundwork for future research by demonstrating the advantages of using neural networks (NN) with simple input parameters for ETA prediction in inland waterway transportation. The development and testing of various NN architectures make it possible to consider external factors such as weather forecasts, river depth forecasts, and infrastructural factors when predicting ETA.

In Sect. 2, this paper presents the related research. The methodology used is delineated, and the process of data preparation is provided in Sect. 3. Moving on to Sect. 4, the training of our neural network model is detailed, along with the accompanying results. Finally, the conclusion of the paper offers the limitations and potential future research in Sect. 5.

2 Related Research

The utilisation of Automatic Identification System (AIS) data for ETA prediction in seagoing vessels is a widely researched topic. It has been shown in various research work [11,15,23] that data-driven algorithms achieve higher accuracy in terms of the time of ETA error. The main goal of this research work is to improve ETA time calculation to improve efficiencies in port operations. Valero [18] predicts ETA times to improve short sea shipping. El Mekkaoui [8] focuses more on the improvements of predictions for bulk ports, and Pani [16], and Yu [23] focus on container and transhipment terminals. The applied methods in overseas shipping research used vary from machine learning algorithms such as NNs [2,7], random forest [23], reinforcement learning [17], bayesian learning [15] and deep learning [8,11] to pathfinding algorithms [1].

There are significant differences in IWT when estimating the ETA for seagoing vessels. Water levels and weather conditions are crucial factors that can affect the vessel's speed and route. Also, ports are only sometimes fixed, and routes may need to be adjusted accordingly, making ETA prediction more complex. Limited research is carried out to address ETA predictions in the context of IWT specifically. Zhong et al. [25] proposed a deep learning method based on bi-directional long short-term memory recurrent neural networks (BLSTM-RNNs) for restoring AIS trajectory data and applied it to inland ship trajectory restoration. The paper focused on ETA prediction in IWT. Noman et al. [14] developed a data-driven approach for ETA prediction using gradient boosting decision trees (GBDT), multi-layer perceptron neural networks (MLP), and gated recurrent unit NNs (GRU) algorithms trained on past inland waterway AIS data. The approach was tested for both natural and artificial waterways, and the results showed that the GRU model outperformed the other models in accuracy and efficiency. Overall, both papers focused on ETA prediction in the context of IWT and proposed different machine-learning algorithms to address this problem. Zhong et al. [25] focused on restoring AIS trajectory data, while Noman et al. [14] focused on developing a data-driven approach for ETA prediction. Two closely related papers have been identified. The paper of Xie and Liu [22] proposed a deep learning model based on long short-term memory networks (LSTMs) for vessel traffic flow prediction in inland waterways. The model was designed to predict a wide range of traffic flow aspects, including short-term, long-term, and the influence of water level factors. Yu et al. [24] explored deep learning approaches for AIS data association in the context of maritime domain awareness. The paper presented two methods for inferring ship association probability. One predicts the ship's position before computing association probability, while the other compute association probability directly using only longitude, latitude, and time.

The literature review highlights the significance of accurate ETA predictions in facilitating port operations. Specifically, the research emphasises sea-going vessels, mainly in deep sea ports, with relatively less attention paid to inland waterway shipping. However, predicting precise ETA times in inland shipping for smaller terminals, river terminals, and transhipment terminals is crucial. Achieving reliable IWT, comparable to rail and road transportation, is vital to encourage a modal shift towards IWT.

Unlike a road network with numerous crossings and decision points, a river network is relatively straightforward. Derrow-Pinion [5] put forth a technique in their publication that involves dividing a road network into segments and transforming it into a graph. They subsequently employ a Graph Neural Network (GNN) to analyse the network. Our approach uses real-world AIS data to segment the river network data, thus simplifying the network. This simplification allows us to use a NN for travel time prediction.

In line with the works of Fancello [10] and Yu [24], a NN is employed for ETA time prediction. Yu [24] partitions the Baltic and North Seas close to Copenhagen into segments and utilises track projection and ETA prediction on the dataset. This work also creates segments for the inland waterway. Meanwhile, Xie [22] incorporates data from the Wuhan Yangtze River, including water levels that fluctuate during flood periods throughout the year. This model does not consider water levels. The author optimises the model instead of comparing the prediction outputs to average calculations.

3 Methodology

This work's objective is to predict the duration it takes for ships to travel from the initial location A to the final location B, with a route passing through several segments s. An A* algorithm is implemented to determine the segments travelled from A to B, followed by the typical industry practice of computing the average travel time. Afterwards, a NN is designed and trained to compare the model's predictions with the computed average. Our methodology and data preparation process are outlined in Sect. 3, while the training of our NN model and the corresponding results are presented in Sect. 4.

3.1 Data Description and Data Preparation

The maritime domain utilises the AIS to enhance ship traffic safety through real-time broadcasting of vessel information, including identity, speed, location, and course. For this study, prefiltered AIS data was downloaded from a cooperation partner via an API call. The received data contains the position data of the ships, including the following information, MMSI (Maritime Mobile Service Identities, the unique ship number), Status of the ship (underway, moored, etc.), speed over ground, course over ground, true heading, time of last update, ETA, destination (manual input from the skipper), data source, maximum draught of the ship, new streaming update and location (latitude and longitude). The data were filtered based on the "Moored" status and vessels, not in motion, requiring a speed over ground greater than zero.

Segments with a radius of 2.5 km are generated to cover the entire area. The position data, consisting of start latitude, longitude, and end latitude and longitude, is mapped to start node ID and end node ID. The position data is then looped through to eliminate multiple position data for each segment, keeping only the data closest to the midpoint of the segment. The resulting table is referred to as segment crossings. The crossing duration is computed from the start and end times of each segment crossing. For each segment, the number of ships crossing it is calculated. Segments with less than 50 appearances and trip durations below 50 s are excluded. From the resulting ship-crossing data, the stop time and destination were dropped from the dataset. The dataset was further enriched by adding this additional data, such as compass bearing. Any rows with missing values were removed to ensure data integrity and accuracy in the analysis. A NN model is created to predict the duration to travel from one segment to another.

To improve the reliability of predictions for IWT, it is advisable to make predictions for individual segments and obtain accurate predictions for complete ship trips that traverse multiple sections. Therefore, developing and incorporating trip-level prediction models in addition to segment-level models is recommended. Consequently, an algorithm was created to identify the travels of a ship and add a trip ID to the dataset. The code iterates over all segment's crossings and adds a new value, "trip id". For each row, it assigns a trip ID based on the MMSI (an identifier for a vessel), the start time, and the start and end nodes. If the MMSI changes or the time difference between consecutive rows is more than 1000 s seconds, or the start node of the current row is not the same as the end node of the previous row, then it increments the trip ID counter. The following Fig. 1 shows a sample trip in the dataset.

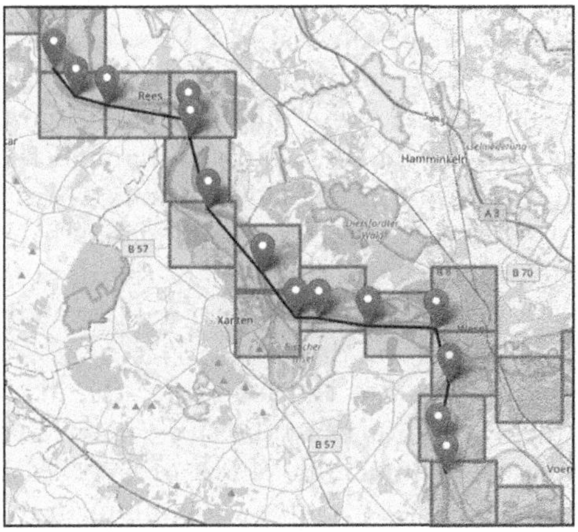

Fig. 1. River network with segment ids

3.2 Average Travel Time Calculation

Similar to Derrow-Pinion [5], the Average Travel Times (ATT) between each pair of cells are calculated based on the actual times d_s for a ship-crossing s. The ATT is calculated by the sum of the duration of the ship-crossing $\mathrm{d_s}$ of the number of start and end node pairs N and then divided by N.

$$ATT = \frac{\sum_{i=1}^{N} t_i}{N} \tag{1}$$

3.3 Neural Network

Transposing and describing train features in Python is an essential step in preparing the data for machine learning, as it ensures that the data is organised in a format suitable for training models and provides valuable information about the characteristics of the features. To ensure that the features are organised in the correct format for training the model, train features are transposed and described. Using z-score normalisation in the previous approach could have been more effective in producing accurate results. This paper utilised min-max normalisation to scale the data between 0 and 1, preserving the original range. The equation for min-max normalisation is as follows:

$$x' = \frac{x - min(x)}{max(x) - min(x)} \tag{2}$$

x is the original value of the data, $min(x)$ is the minimum value of the data, $max(x)$ is the maximum value of the data, and x' is the normalized value of x between 0 and 1. The numerator, $(x - min(x))$, subtracts the minimum value from the original value to measure the distance between the original value and the minimum value of the data. The denominator, $(max(x) - min(x))$, calculates the range of the data by subtracting the minimum value from the maximum value. By dividing the distance between the original value and the minimum value by the range of the data, the resulting value is normalised between 0 and 1.

A validation set that is not used for training but to evaluate the model's performance on unseen data is created. 80 % of the data are used for training, 20 % are used for validating the model. The actual travel duration was excluded from both the train and validation datasets.

The used input parameters are the following: the id of the start segment, the id of the end segment, the Status of the ship (underway, moored, reserved), Course over ground, True heading, Time of last update, ETA, Destination (manual input from the skipper), Data Source, Maximum draught of the ship, new streaming update, location (latitude and longitude), compass bearing and the actual travel time from origin segment to destination segment.

Several correlations can be observed among the provided input parameters. The course over ground and true heading is typically closely related, representing the direction of ship movement. The time of last update and the new streaming update are correlated, with the new streaming update expected to have a more recent timestamp. The maximum draught of the ship and moored status might be correlated, as the draught becomes less critical when the ship is stationary. Furthermore, a correlation exists between the specified destination and the estimated ETA, as the ETA reflects the projected time of reaching the destination.

The created model design is adapted from Chondrodima [4] using similar parameters for performance evaluation and hyper-parameter selection. This is a sequential NN model, an artificial deep-learning architecture. The sequential model is a linear stack of layers, where the output of one layer serves as the input for the next layer sequentially. The model has three layers, the first dense layer with 30 output units and 510 trainable parameters. The activation function is a ReLu function-the second dense layer (hidden layer) with 30 output units. The activation function is a ReLu function. The third and final dense layer, with one output unit, represents the model's output prediction. It has 31 trainable parameters. The activation function is a ReLu function. The model has 1,471 parameters, all of which are trainable. The parameters of the model are adaptively adjusted during training based on the patterns and information contained in the training data. This adaptive learning process allows the model to learn the appropriate representations and relationships in the data, enabling it to make better predictions on new, unseen dataThese parameters are adjusted during training to optimise the model's performance on the given task. The model has no non-trainable parameters, meaning all parameters are updated during training. Figure 2 shows the design of the NN.

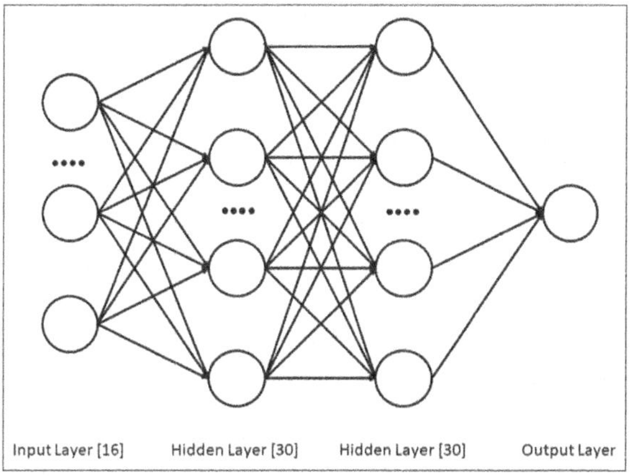

Fig. 2. NN with three layers, an input layer, two hidden layers and one output layer

Similar to the work of Xiu [22], the root two widely used criteria are adopted to measure the error of the predicted data, they are the Root Mean Squared Error (RMSE) and the Mean Relative Error (MRE). These criteria are commonly used to evaluate the accuracy of predictive models.

4 Results

A case study was conducted to demonstrate the higher accuracy of neural network-based ETA prediction for IWT. The code was implemented in Python within a Google Colab environment, utilising an Intel Xeon CPU @2.20 GHz, 25 GB RAM, a Tesla K80 accelerator, and 12 GB GDDR5 VRAM.

The following section provides an overview of the case study data and an evaluation of the model training results. Subsequently, the predictions are compared with the average results of the entire network and two specific areas.

4.1 Case Study Data

This study's position data covers January to April 2022 and encompasses a 50km radius around Rees. Figure 3 shows the segments.

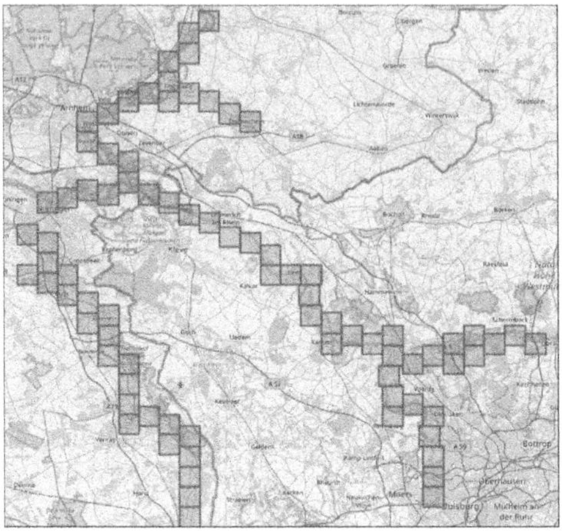

Fig. 3. Filtered river network segments with applied filters

The resulting area contains the busy area in Duisburg, a crossing close to Doornenburg, the border crossing in Bimmen, and a straight line without any stops between Emmerich and Wesel. After data preparation, 82 segments and 152,650 rows of ship-crossing data were obtained. Figure 3 illustrates the remaining segments post-data filtering.

4.2 Model Evaluation

For comparison, two different approaches were employed. The first approach, the Overall NN (ONN), involved using the entire network to train the model. The second approach Individual NN (INN), utilised individually trained models for each start and end node pair. The training and validation are made for the same in the dataset, allowing for a comprehensive assessment of the performance of each method.

The model was trained using data from January to March, and the training process involved 100 epochs. The history epoch loss graph shows the model's MAE change over successive epochs and is illustrated in the following Fig. 4.

Similarly, the validation loss graph shows the change in loss on a separate validation set during training. The validation graph provides insights into how well the model generalises to new data. Since the validation loss remains consistently low with the training loss, the model performs well on both the training and validation data. After the 20th epoch, the ONN model's learning rate is not improving significantly. For the different INN models, the learning drops at the 80th epoch.

Xie [22] conducted predictions on a more granular level. The evaluation metrics for the models are crucial, and the Root Mean Square Error (RMSE) for the ONN model is 5.8%, and the Mean Relative Error (MRE) is 12.32 %. For

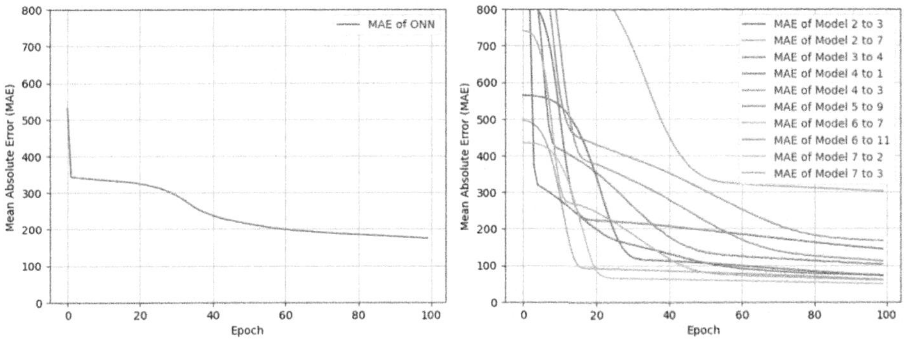

(a) Loss function for ONN (b) 10 sample loss functions for INNs

Fig. 4. Loss and Validation Loss Function shows the differences between ONN and INN

the INN model, the RMSE is 25%, and the MRE is 35.8%. However, the model trained in this study produced similar results for a one-day prediction.

4.3 Comparison of Averages to NN

NNs are commonly evaluated by randomly partitioning data into training, validation, and testing sets. However, this section uses historical data to predict future data. Although the predicted data is also historical, it represents the future concerning the training data used. A future dataset containing 59,000 entries of start and end segment information for April was obtained and preprocessed for analysis.

$$t = (s_1, s_2, \ldots, s_n) \tag{3}$$

A trip t contains multiple segment-crossings s_i, for $i = 1 \ldots n$. Using the structure of the trip t, the total duration is calculated using the following equation.

$$d_t = \sum_{s=1}^{N_s} d_s \tag{4}$$

In (4), N_s is defined as the number of segments per trip. Each segment-crossing has a duration of d_s. Therefore the sum of all segments crossing is the duration of the trip d_t.

$$ATT_t = \sum_{s=1}^{N_s} ATT_s \tag{5}$$

The averages ATT_t are calculated for all the segment-crossings s in trip t.

$$ATT = \frac{\sum_{t=1}^{N_t} ATT_s}{N_t} \tag{6}$$

For all trips N_t in the test dataset, the average ATT is calculated. The following Eq. 7 shows the prediction error PE for the Average Calculation (AC):

$$PE_{AC} = ATT - \sum_{t=1}^{N_t} d_t \tag{7}$$

PE_{AC} is calculated by substracting the sum of all trip durations d_t from the average travel times.

To create trip duration predictions from the NN, the algorithm iterates over each segment in the route and predicts the duration of the segment-crossings. The predicted duration is added to the current timestamp, which serves as an input to the NN, and this updated timestamp is used to make the next prediction for the next segment crossings. Predictions are made for ONN, and INN uses the same methodology. Both the ONN and INN models are employed to generate the predictions.

$$PNN_t = \sum_{i=1}^{N_s} PNN_i \tag{8}$$

The prediction duration of the trip for the NN (PNN) is the sum of all segment crossing predictions.

$$PNN = \frac{\sum_{i=1}^{N_t} PNN_i}{N_t} \tag{9}$$

For all trips N_t in the test dataset, the average of PNN is calculated.

$$PE_{NN} = PNN - \sum_{i=1}^{N_t} d_i \tag{10}$$

The prediction error for the NN is calculated by subtracting the sum of all trip durations from the PNN.

The dataset was analysed and segmented into short trips (3 segment crossings), medium trips (9 segment crossings), and long trips (18 segment crossings). To compare different trip lengths, long trips with more than 18 segment crossings were truncated to 18 segment crossings, ensuring that at least 100 trips were available for each trip length category.

The results of ETA prediction error using the three different models - AC, ONN, and INN - on different data sets with varying numbers of segments and durations. The first column in table 1 indicates the number of crossed segments N_s per trip t, while the second column represents the duration d_t in seconds. The following three columns show the average predictions made by each model for the respective data sets. Finally, the last three columns indicate the relative standard deviation in percentage for each model's predictions.

Table 1. Results of the comparison of prediction methods

N_s	d[s]	Prediction error			Relative. Std.[%]		
		AC	NN	INN	AC	NN	INN
18	6898	1743	820	1220	25.3	11.9	17.7
9	5944	358	343	539	12.8	5.8	9.1
3	3687	143	34	268	2.4	0.9	2.1

The results indicate that the NN methods have smaller prediction errors than the AC method for all three trip length sets. The relative standard deviation is the smallest for the ONN method for the 3-segment and 9-segment crossings, while the INN method has the lowest relative standard deviation for the 18-segment crossing. Overall, the results suggest that the ONN and INN method are slightly more accurate in predicting segment-crossing duration than the AC method.

Computational experiments have been performed on two selected regions to provide an additional comparison, as shown in Fig. 5.

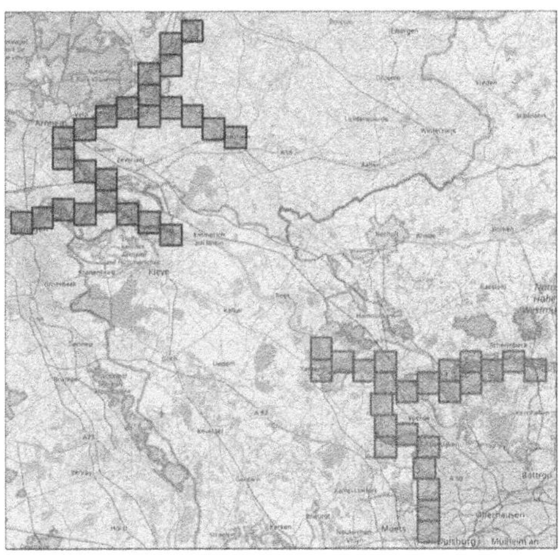

Fig. 5. Area of Kleve (green) and Duisburg (red) for comparison. (Color figure online)

The region surrounding Duisburg is assigned the abbreviation "DUI," while the red region near Kleve is designated as "KLE." Given the smaller geographical scope and absence of long-distance port journeys, emphasis is placed on trips with three and 9-segment crossings. After segmenting the data, 100 random samples were selected for each 3-segment and 9-segment crossing trip.

Similar to Table 1, the prediction errors are shown in Table 2 for the three methods: AC, NN and INN.

Table 2. Results of the comparison of prediction methods for DUI and KLE

N_s	d[s]	Prediction error			Relative. Std.[%]		
		AC	NN	INN	AC	NN	INN
9 (DUI)	5500	745	652	742	13.5	11.9	13.5
3 (DUI)	3105	102	38	130	3.2	1.2	4.1
9 (KLE)	6085	774	10	193	12.7	0.1	3.1
3 (KLE)	3578	704	37	111	19.7	1.0	3.1

Trip durations are, in general, a bit shorter in the DUI area. The largest inland port in Europe is located in Duisburg, so the dataset includes shorter trips that involve docking at specific locations within the port. In the case of the Klave region, noisy data may be attributed to crossing the border between Germany and the Netherlands.

5 Conclusion

Previous studies have emphasised the significance of enhancing ETA prediction accuracy for efficient terminal and inland port operations [3,6]. Xie [22] has showcased the effectiveness of using LSTM models for ETA prediction. However, related studies mainly focused on fine-tuning predictions for a single segment crossing rather than predicting entire trips.

The paper discusses the advantages of precise ETA prediction in IWT and uses real-world data to train a dedicated NN. The results demonstrate a considerable enhancement in ETA prediction compared to conventional travel time averages. Additionally, this work showcases how predictions can be utilised for complete ship trips crossing multiple segments using an A* path algorithm.

There are certain limitations that should be considered. Historical data's availability and representativeness could impact the predictions' generalizability. Additionally, the generalizability of the results may be limited if the experimentation is conducted only with specific segment sizes. Including additional input parameters such as weather data and river, depths could improve prediction accuracy. While effective in improving neural network model performance, hyperparameter selection techniques have certain limitations. These include computational complexity, sensitivity to initial conditions, and the need for careful consideration of the search space.

Future work should aim at enhancing the accuracy of results by downloading more historical data. In addition, further experimentation with smaller and larger segments will be conducted. More input parameters, including weather data and river depths, will be added to improve the accuracy of predictions. Future work will further incorporate infrastructural information, such as closed bridges and locks at certain timestamps, to provide more precise predictions. Finally, the results of this study will be compared across different river areas to validate the model's effectiveness. It is anticipated that Graph Neural Networks (GNNs) will be utilised for ETA prediction in IWT. The advantage of GNNs lies in their ability to learn from graph-structured data and model the dependencies among nodes in a graph. In the case of IWT, the river network can be represented as a graph where the nodes represent the various segments and the edges represent the waterways connecting them. By incorporating this graph structure into the GNN, the accuracy of ETA predictions is expected to be significantly improved.

References

1. Alessandrini, A., Mazzarella, F., Vespe, M.: Estimated time of arrival using historical vessel tracking data. IEEE Trans. Intell. Transp. Syst. **20**(1), 7–15 (2019). https://doi.org/10.3390/app11052429
2. Bautista-Sánchez, R., Barbosa-Santillan, L.I., Sánchez-Escobar, J.J.: Method for Select Best AIS Data in Prediction Vessel Movements and Route Estimation. Appl. Sci. **11**(5), 2429 (2021). https://doi.org/10.3390/app11052429
3. Bouchard, P., Moros-Daza, A., Voß, S.: Simulation of an AIS system for the port of Hamburg. In: Mes, M., Lalla-Ruiz, E., Voß, S. (eds.) ICCL 2021. LNCS, vol. 13004, pp. 21–35. Springer, Cham (2021). https://doi.org/10.1007/978-3-030-87672-2_2
4. Chondrodima, E., Georgiou, H., Pelekis, N., Theodoridis, Y.: Particle swarm optimization and RBF neural networks for public transport arrival time prediction using GTFS data. Int. J. Inf. Manage. Data Insights **2**(2), 100086 (2022). https://doi.org/10.1016/j.jjimei.2022.100086
5. Derrow-Pinion, A., et al.: ETA prediction with graph neural networks in google maps. In: Proceedings of the 30th ACM International Conference on Information & Knowledge Management, pp. 3767–3776 (2021). https://doi.org/10.1145/3459637.3481916
6. El Mekkaoui, S., Benabbou, L., Berrado, A.: Predicting ships estimated time of arrival based on AIS data. In: Proceedings of the 13th International Conference on Intelligent Systems: Theories and Applications, pp. 1–6 (2020)
7. El Mekkaoui, S., Benabbou, L., Berrado, A.: Machine learning models for efficient port terminal operations: case of vessels' arrival times prediction. IFAC-PapersOnLine **55**(10), 3172–3177 (2022)
8. El Mekkaoui, S., Benabbou, L., Caron, S., Berrado, A.: Deep learning-based ship speed prediction for intelligent maritime traffic management. J. Mar. Sci. Eng. **11**(1), 191 (2023). https://doi.org/10.3390/jmse11101019
9. Eurostat: eurostat Statistics explained. https://ec.europa.eu/eurostat/statistics-explained/index.php?title=Inland_waterway_transport_statistics#Eurostat#StatisticsExplained
10. Fancello, G., Pani, C., Pisano, M., Serra, P., Zuddas, P., Fadda, P.: Prediction of arrival times and human resources allocation for container terminal. Maritime Economics & Logistics **13**(2), 142–173 (2011). https://doi.org/10.1057/mel.2011.3
11. Huang, C., Huang, Y., Yu, Y., Xiao, B.: Predicting liner arrival time based on deep learning. In: 2021 IEEE 3rd International Conference on Civil Aviation Safety and Information Technology (ICCASIT), pp. 1127–1131. IEEE (2021)
12. Jing, M., Zheng, W.: Economic development advantages of low-carbon economy under waterway transportation. IOP Conf. Ser. Mater. Sci. Eng. **780**(6), 062029 (2020). https://doi.org/10.1088/1757-899X/780/6/062029

13. Jonkeren, O., Rietveld, P., van Ommeren, J., te Linde, A.: Climate change and economic consequences for inland waterway transport in Europe. Reg. Environ. Change **14**(3), 953–965 (2013). https://doi.org/10.1007/s10113-013-0441-7
14. Noman, A., Heuermann, A., Wiesner, S., Thoben, K.D.: Towards data-driven GRU based ETA prediction approach for vessels on both inland natural and artificial waterways. vol. 2021, pp. 2286–2291 (2021). https://doi.org/10.1109/ITSC48978.2021.956488
15. Ogura, T., Inoue, T., Uchihira, N.: Prediction of arrival time of vessels considering future weather conditions. Appl. Sci. **11**(10), 4410 (2021). https://doi.org/10.3390/app1110441
16. Pani, C., Fadda, P., Fancello, G., Frigau, L., Mola, F.: A data mining approach to forecast late arrivals in a transhipment container terminal. Transport **29**(2), 175–184 (2014). https://doi.org/10.3846/16484142.2014.930714
17. Park, K., Sim, S., Bae, H.: Vessel estimated time of arrival prediction system based on a path-finding algorithm. Marit. Transp. Res. **2**, 100012 (2021). https://doi.org/10.1016/j.martra.2021.100012
18. Valero, C.I., Martínez, n., Oltra-Badenes, R., Gil, H., Boronat, F., Palau, C.E.: Prediction of the estimated time of arrival of container ships on short-sea shipping: a pragmatical analysis. IEEE Latin Am. Trans. **20**(11), 2354–2362 (2022)
19. Veenstra, A., Harmelink, R.: On the quality of ship arrival predictions. Marit. Econ. Logistics **23**(4), 655–673 (2021). https://doi.org/10.1057/s41278-021-00187-6
20. Wehrle, R., Wiens, M., Schultmann, F.: A framework to evaluate systemic risks of inland waterway infrastructure. Prog. Disaster Sci. **16**, 100258 (2022). https://doi.org/10.1016/j.pdisas.2022.100258
21. Wiegmans, B., Konings, R.: Intermodal Inland waterway transport: modelling conditions influencing its cost competitiveness. Asian J. Shipping Logistics **31**(2), 273–294 (2015). https://doi.org/10.1016/j.ajsl.2015.06.006
22. Xie, Z., Liu, Q.: LSTM networks for vessel traffic flow prediction in inland waterway. In: 2018 IEEE International Conference on Big Data and Smart Computing (BigComp), pp. 418–425 (2018). https://doi.org/10.1109/BigComp.2018.00068
23. Yu, J., et al.: Ship arrival prediction and its value on daily container terminal operation. Ocean Eng. **157**, 73–86 (2018). https://doi.org/10.1016/j.oceaneng.2018.03.038
24. Yu, J.Y., Sghaier, M.O., Grabowiecka, Z.: Deep learning approaches for AIS data association in the context of maritime domain awareness. In: 2020 IEEE 23rd International Conference on Information Fusion (FUSION), pp. 1–8 (2020). https://doi.org/10.23919/FUSION45008.2020.9190283
25. Zhong, C., Jiang, Z., Chu, X., Liu, L.: Inland ship trajectory restoration by recurrent neural network. J. Navig. **72**(6), 1359–1377 (2019). https://doi.org/10.1017/S0373463319000316

Vehicle Routing

A Regret Policy for the Dynamic Vehicle Routing Problem with Time Windows

Peter Dieter(✉)

Paderborn University, Warburger Str. 100, 33098 Paderborn, Germany
peter.dieter@uni-paderborn.de

Abstract. In this work, we present a *regret* policy for the dynamic vehicle routing problem with time windows (DVRPTW) in which customer order arrivals are revealed over a day and which has been the considered problem in the *EURO Meets NeurIPS 2022 Vehicle Routing Competition.* The problem requires two types of decisions: Dispatching orders and planning the respective vehicle routes. The objective is to minimize the travel time while dispatching all orders over the day and adhering to the respective time windows. The *regret* policy we present in this paper focuses on the former decision, namely the dispatching of orders, as the routing can then be performed by a regular VRPTW solver. The basic idea of the policy is to calculate a regret value for each order which represents possible cost savings that we would miss when dispatching the order immediately. To attain this regret value, we make use of the customer distribution from which orders are sampled. If the value is below a predefined threshold, the order is dispatched and routes are planned with a state-of-the-art VRPTW solver. Otherwise, the order needs to be dispatched at a later stage. The proposed policy outperforms several benchmark policies and ranked 6th place among approximately 50 teams. Furthermore, the proposed *regret* policy has a high level of explainability, is simple to implement, and can be generalized to other problems in the domain of dynamic vehicle routing.

Keywords: Stochastic dynamic vehicle routing · Anticipatory vehicle routing · Vehicle dispatching

1 Introduction

The logistics industry is disrupted by customers' demand for services such as same-day delivery (SDD). For example, Amazon has introduced "Prime Now", a service that promises customers the delivery of goods in one hour [8]. According to a survey in the United States, more than half of the respondents say that they are interested in using same-day delivery but have a limited willingness to pay extra for this service [4]. Due to these developments, dynamic vehicle routing is becoming increasingly important [12] and efficient same-day delivery planning can give last-mile delivery companies a competitive edge. However,

© The Author(s), under exclusive license to Springer Nature Switzerland AG 2023
J. R. Daduna et al. (Eds.): ICCL 2023, LNCS 14239, pp. 235–247, 2023.
https://doi.org/10.1007/978-3-031-43612-3_14

efficient planning is difficult since customer orders arrive in the course of a day and before some decisions are already made and implemented. Next to planning vehicle tours, it is important to decide which customer orders to dispatch, especially when orders have time windows. Too early dispatching might lead to inefficiencies since it limits the possibility of consolidation. Too-late dispatching on the other hand might lead to limited flexibility in planning tours since time-windows need to be adhered to. This paper describes a *regret* policy for the dynamic vehicle routing problem with time windows (DVRPTW), which has been the posed problem in the *EURO Meets NeurIPS 2022 Vehicle Routing Competition* [9]. In the considered problem, orders are sampled from a known customer distribution over a day. Once an hour, it needs to be decided which orders need to be dispatched and which ones to postpone to consolidate with future requests that may arrive later. After it has been decided which orders are dispatched, feasible routes for these orders need to be created. Customer time windows are *hard* and an unlimited vehicle fleet is assumed. The overall goal is to minimize the time traveled during all decision epochs. The policy presented in this paper only focuses on the dispatching decision, as the routing task is then a standard VRPTW, for which there exists an abundance of literature [1]. This is done by calculating a regret value for each *undue* order, i.e., orders which can be postponed, considering the total set of customers from which orders are randomly sampled. Furthermore, we describe methods to extend the regret value with information on time windows and other undue orders. The resulting VRPTW instance is then solved by a state-of-the-art hybrid genetic search (HGS) algorithm developed by [10], which is an extension of the HGS solver which has been proven successful for other VRP variants [16,17]. We show that the proposed policy outperforms two benchmark policies. Due to its high level of explainability, easiness of implementation, and generalizability to other problem settings, we believe that the proposed policy can serve as a benchmark policy for other studies on dynamic vehicle routing, in which anticipating future customer orders is crucial. Furthermore, several possible policy extensions exist and could be considered in future work. The further structure of the paper is as follows: Sect. 2 includes related work. The problem is described in Sect. 3. In Sect. 4, we present the developed *regret* policy. In Sect. 5, we evaluate the policy by comparing it to the two benchmark policies. The paper concludes with a summary and an outlook in Sect. 6.

2 Related Work

The body of literature on dynamic vehicle routing is vast and covers different problem settings as well as various algorithmic contributions. For a general overview of stochastic dynamic vehicle routing, we refer to [13] and [5]. In this section, we first examine related work on the concept of *regret* in dynamic vehicle routing. Second, we present the winning approaches of the *EURO Meets NeurIPS 2022 Vehicle Routing Competition* challenge.

To the best of our knowledge, the study of [3] is the first one on dynamic vehicle routing that used the concept of *regret*. The authors consider a problem with the objective to maximize the number of orders served. The problem, therefore, involves deciding which orders to serve and which ones not to serve, considering time windows and a limited vehicle fleet. The authors suggest a multi-scenario approach in which scenarios are created by sampling potential future orders from a known customer distribution. A regret value for each order already in the system o is then calculated which is defined as the difference in objective value between the optimal solution considering all orders (i.e., already in the system or drawn in the scenario) and the best solution serving request o. This idea is further developed in [14].

[6] apply a multi-scenario approach for a problem in which the main objective is to maximize the number of orders served and is more similar to the problem considered in this paper, as orders can be postponed to later epochs. Rather than solving a problem for each scenario once and then choosing one of the solutions, they suggest a *branch-and-regret* heuristic which identifies structural decisions (e.g., postponing an order) for each scenario and branches on them until all scenario problems have solutions where all known orders are served according to the same plan. The concept of regret represents the possible improvement that might be gained from postponing an order to be dispatched in a later decision epoch. This is similar to our proposed *regret* policy. However, our suggested approach does not require sampling orders to create scenarios but directly uses the known customer distribution, which allows for faster computations. Furthermore, in contrast to [6], we consider a problem in which all orders need to be served and the total travel time over all decision epochs must be minimized.

The two most successful approaches to the challenge both applied machine learning to the problem. In the winning approach, [7] reformulated the problem into a prize-collecting VRPTW, i.e., a prize is assigned to each order during an epoch and this prize is collected if an order is visited in the respective epoch. The authors then apply imitation learning, by learning the prizes for each order based on solutions with complete information. Instead of learning from solutions with full information, [11] apply a reinforcement learning approach that learns how to modify the costs of traversing arcs to an order in a respective epoch. While the two approaches outperformed our proposed policy (by 4.95% and 2.4%, respectively), the regret policy is easier to implement and offers a higher degree of explainability.

3 Problem Description

The problem at hand can be defined as a multi-stage VRPTW. We consider a discrete-time horizon $H = \{1, ..., n\}$ such that each decision occurs at a discrete time (decision epoch) $h \in H$. Further, let $G_h = (V_h, A_h)$ be a complete graph, where $V_h = \{0, N_h\}$ is the set of nodes, N_h is a set of order nodes in epoch h and 0 identifies the depot. The set of arcs is denoted by $A_h = \{(i, j) : i, j \in V_h\}$. The time of traversing arc (i, j) is given by c_{ij}. Each order i possesses a time-window $\{e_i, l_i\}$ where e_i denotes the earliest arrival time and l_i the latest arrival time. Moreover, service times and demands for order i are given by s_i and q_i^d, respectively. A vehicle from an unlimited fleet is denoted by $k \in K_h$, where K_h is a set of vehicles in epoch h. The fleet is homogeneous and a vehicle possesses a capacity of q^v. In each decision stage h, a set of new orders O_h arrives. Orders which arrived before epoch h but have not been dispatched yet are denoted by F_h and the set of all available orders in epoch h is then given by $N_h = O_h \cup F_h$. Out of these orders, some might be *due* as dispatching them in a later epoch, would lead to non-adherence to its time window. We define the set of these due orders as $D_h \subseteq N_h$. In the last decision epoch n, all orders are due, so $N_n = D_n$. The decision variable x_{ijk} denotes if arc $(i, j) : i, j \in V_h$ is traversed by vehicle k and t_{ik} denotes the arrival time of vehicle k at order i. A decision vector in epoch h defined as $x_h = \{x_{ijk} : i, j \in V_h; k \in K_h\}$. As x_h indicates which orders are dispatched in h and which are not, the set of not dispatched orders at epoch $h+1$, F_{h+1}, is dependent on x_h. For example, if we would dispatch all orders in epoch h, F_{h+1} would be an empty set. The problem in epoch h can be formulated as follows:

$$\text{minimize} \sum_{i \in V_h} \sum_{j \in V_h} \sum_{k \in K} c_{ij} \cdot x_{ijk} + \mathbb{E}[Q(x_h)] \tag{1}$$

subject to

$$\sum_{\substack{j \in V_h \\ j \neq i}} \sum_{k \in K_h} x_{jik} = 1 \qquad \forall i \in D_h \tag{2}$$

$$\sum_{i \in V_h} x_{ijk} - \sum_{i \in V_h} x_{jik} = 0 \qquad \forall k \in K_h; j \in V_h \tag{3}$$

$$\sum_{j \in V_h} \sum_{i \in N_h} q_i^d \cdot x_{jik} \leq q^v \qquad \forall k \in K_h \tag{4}$$

$$t_{ik} + c_{ij} + s_i - M \cdot (1 - x_{ijk}) \leq t_{jk} \qquad \forall i \in V_h; j \in N_h; \forall k \in K_h \tag{5}$$

$$e_i \leq t_{ik} \leq l_i \qquad \forall i \in N_h; k \in K_h \tag{6}$$

$$t_{ik} \geq 0 \qquad \forall i \in N_h; k \in K_h \tag{7}$$

$$x_{ijk} \in \{0, 1\} \qquad \forall i, j \in V_h; k \in K_h \tag{8}$$

where $Q(x_h)$ is the future costs of implementing decision x_h in epoch h. The objective is to minimize the time the vehicle travels and waiting times are not considered. Constraint (2) assures that each due order is visited. Constraint (3) assures that if a vehicle visits a node it must also leave this node. Not exceeding the vehicle capacity is assured by Constraint 4. Constraints (5) and (6) assure that each order is visited in its time window and also serve as subtour elimination constraints, where M is a large enough number. Constraints (7) and (8) are non-negativity and binary constraints, respectively. The sets, parameters, and decision variables are summarized in Table 3 which is to be found in the Appendix. Further, we note that the problem is a sequential decision process and an alternative problem formulation would be to model it as a Markov

Decision Process (MDP). In such a formulation, a state would contain all orders revealed but not yet dispatched and the action space would contain all feasible vehicle tours. A transition between two decision epochs would occur by removing all dispatched orders from the state and adding all orders that newly entered the system. The objective is to find a policy that minimizes the expected cost of serving all orders. For a detailed problem formulation as an MDP, we refer to [2].

4 Regret Policy

In this section, we first describe the general algorithmic procedure of the *regret* policy. We then describe the regret function and explain two extensions of the basic regret function, namely the incorporation of information about time windows and undue orders. An open-source Python implementation of the policy is available on GitHub[1].

4.1 General Procedure

The general procedure of the algorithm is described in Algorithm 1. The procedure requires a set of due orders $D_h \subseteq N_h$, which are orders that need to be dispatched immediately in epoch h as postponement would lead to a time window violation. Moreover, the following is required as input: a set of undue orders $U_h \subseteq N_h$, a set of all customers from which orders are drawn, C, and a threshold value t which can further be tuned. To enter the while loop, we set the best (lowest) regret value r to t. While the best regret value is equal or below the threshold, we do the following: For each undue order $u \in U_h$ we calculate its regret value with the *GetRegret* function, which takes the order u, D_h, and C as input. This function is further explained in Subsect. 4.2. If the lowest regret value is below threshold value t, the respective order denoted by c (the one with the lowest regret value) is marked as dispatched, added to the set of due orders D_h, and removed from the set of undue orders U_h. This procedure is repeated until the regret values of all orders are above t, or U_h is an empty set. Therefore, the final set of D_h includes all orders which are dispatched, and consequently, feasible routes for these orders are determined by the HGS solver [10,15].

4.2 Regret Function

The motivation behind the proposed regret function is the following: If an undue order $u \in U_h$ is dispatched in epoch h, we can expect that u will be served consecutively before or after its closest order $d \in D_h$ which is marked as dispatched. Closest is here defined by the lowest average arc costs from u to d and vice versa. Let c_{ud} be the time (costs) needed to travel from the customer of order u to the customer of order d. We then approximate that dispatching order u will result

[1] https://github.com/PeterDieter/RegretPolicy_DVRPTW.

Algorithm 1. Regret policy procedure

Input: Set of due orders D_h, set of undue orders U_h, set of all customers C, threshold value t

$r \leftarrow t$
while $r \leq t$ **do**
    $R \leftarrow \{\}$
    for $u \in U_h$ **do**
        $R \leftarrow R \cup$ *GetRegret*(u, D_h, S)
    end for
    r, c $\leftarrow$ *min*(R), *argmin*(R)
    if $r \leq t$ **then**
        $D_h \leftarrow D_h \cup c$
        $U_h \leftarrow U_h \setminus c$
    end if
end while

Output: Set of orders to dispatch D_h

in additional costs of $\frac{c_{ud}+c_{du}}{2}$, assuming that c_{ud} does not deviate much from c_{du} and no further orders being dispatched. We note that this is only a simple approximation, as order u might be on the route to a dispatched order, which might result in lower costs. As order u is not due yet, better (closer) orders might arrive in the future. Let $B \subseteq C$ be those closer customers. The improvement of routing u consecutively after/before $i \in B$ compared to d is given by:

$$\frac{c_{ud}+c_{du}}{2} - \frac{c_{ui}+c_{iu}}{2} \tag{9}$$

These improvements can be seen as a *regret*, i.e., possible improvements which we would miss when dispatching u immediately. As the regret also depends on the probability that a *better* customer will be drawn until order u is due, we adjust the regret by this probability: Let n_o be the number of orders that are expected to be drawn until order u is due. The probability that a customer is drawn in a single draw is $\frac{1}{|C|}$ and its counter probability is, therefore, $1 - \frac{1}{|C|}$. The probability that a customer is not drawn in n_o drawings is then given by $(1-\frac{1}{|C|})^{n_o}$. The probability that a customer is drawn in n_o drawings is therefore, $1-(1-\frac{1}{|C|})^{n_o}$. The adjusted regret value R_u of order u is therefore given by:

$$R_u = \sum_{i \in C} \left(\frac{c_{ud}+c_{du}}{2} - \frac{c_{ui}+c_{iu}}{2}\left[\frac{c_{ui}+c_{iu}}{2} < \frac{c_{ud}+c_{du}}{2}\right]\right) \cdot \left(1-\left(1-\frac{1}{|C|}\right)^{n_o}\right) \tag{10}$$

where square brackets are *Iverson* brackets, i.e., its inner value is 1 if the condition $(\frac{c_{ui}+c_{iu}}{2} < \frac{c_{ud}+c_{du}}{2})$ holds and 0 otherwise.

To provide further explanation on the regret function, it is visualized in Fig. 1, where the regret value for order i is determined. There are two orders which are marked as due. The distance c_{id} is an approximation of the additional routing costs that would occur when order i is dispatched together with the two due orders. However, orders from two closer customers (1 and 2) might be drawn in the future and 99 orders are expected to be drawn until order i is due. If the calculated regret value of 1.2 is below the threshold, the order will be dispatched.

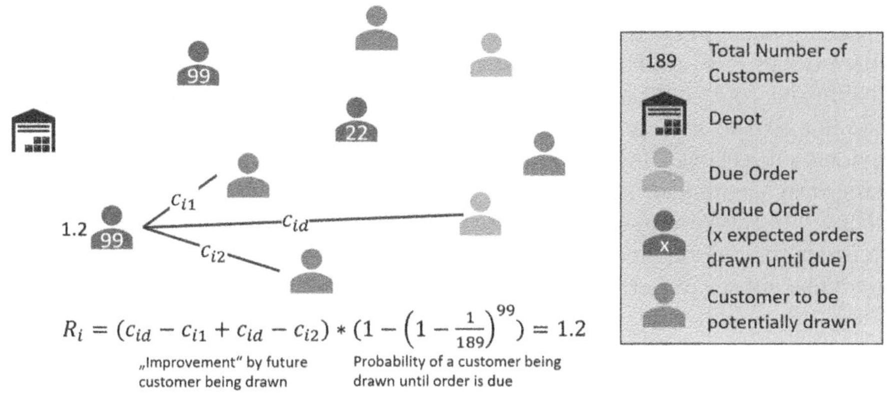

Fig. 1. Illustration of the regret function.

4.3 Incorporation of Time Windows

So far, the *regret* policy only takes time windows into account for determining when orders become *due*. However, neglecting time windows can lead to inefficient route plannings, in which vehicles need to wait before an order can be served. Therefore, we multiply the regret value with a term that penalizes the time a vehicle would need to wait if serving order u directly before/after order d. We note that also an additive term could be added, but pretests have shown that a multiplicative term leads to better solutions. Let $[e_d, l_d]$ be the time window of order d and $[e_u, l_u]$ of order u, respectively. The minimal waiting time for serving order u directly before order d is given by $w_{du} = max(0, e_u - l_d + c_{du})$ and respectively, w_{ud} is given by $max(0, e_d - l_u + c_{ud})$. The minimum waiting time of serving u directly before d or vice versa is then $min(w_{du}, w_{ud})$. Therefore, we update the regret value as follows:

$$R_u \leftarrow R_u \cdot (1 + min(w_{du}, w_{ud})) \cdot h_2 \tag{11}$$

where h_2 is a hyperparameter that determines how much waiting time is penalized. High values of h_2 lead to higher penalizations and its value should be carefully tuned.

4.4 Incorporation of Undue Orders

In the basic formulation of the regret function, other orders which are not due U_h are not taken into account. However, these known undue orders provide valuable information and should therefore be incorporated. Let us assume the following example: Two orders u and v are very close to each other and have compatible time windows. Moreover, u is due in one epoch while v is due in 5 epochs. Therefore, the regret value for v is likely to be high and the order might not be dispatched immediately. On the contrary, as order u is due soon, its regret value will likely be low and the order might be dispatched immediately. Orders u and v would therefore not be dispatched together, which might result in inefficient routes. The procedure of incorporating U_h into the regret function is similar to the incorporation of the set of all customers C described in the previous subsection. However, there are two important differences: Instead of taking into account all customers C, we now only consider customers of orders which are in the system and not dispatched yet. Let $d \in D_h$ be again the closest due order to u as defined by the lowest average arc costs from u to d and vice versa. The subset of better orders which are not due is then defined as $B \subseteq U_h$ where:

$$\frac{c_{uv} + c_{vu}}{2} < \frac{c_{ud} + c_{du}}{2} \quad \forall v \in U_h. \tag{12}$$

Furthermore, as orders B are already in the system, we do not correct the value with a probability term. Therefore, we update the regret value as follows:

$$R_u \leftarrow R_u + \sum_{i \in B} (\frac{c_{ud} + c_{du}}{2} - \frac{c_{ui} + c_{iu}}{2}) \cdot h_1 \tag{13}$$

where h_1 is a hyperparameter that determines the weight given to possible improvements by using the information of undue orders.

5 Experiments and Discussion

5.1 Experimental Setup

In this section, we evaluate the *regret* policy by comparing it to two benchmark policies. These benchmark policies are a greedy dispatching rule which dispatches orders as soon as possible and a lazy dispatching rule which dispatches only orders which are due. To tune hyperparameters for our proposed regret policy, we applied a grid search. Suitable ranges used in the grid search have been determined in pretests. The grid search ranges are presented in Table 1). This search resulted in the following best combination: $t = 0.08$, $h_1 = 0.01$, and $h_2 = 0.002$.

We test the policies on 50 randomly chosen instances which derive from real-world instances and are publicly available [9]. The problem instances derive from data of ORTEC, with an explicit duration matrix giving (non-euclidean) realistic road driving times between orders. The number of customers from which orders are sampled is between 200 and 1000. Further, 100 orders per epoch are randomly drawn from the given customer distribution and a typical instance has between 5 and 7 epochs. Moreover, we apply a random seed value of 1 (see [9] for further

Table 1. Grid search ranges

Parameter	Values
t	$\{0.04, 0.05, 0.06, 0.07, \mathbf{0.08}, 0.09, 0.10\}$
$h1$	$\{0.005, \mathbf{0.01}, 0.02, 0.03, 0.04\}$
$h2$	$\{0.01, \mathbf{0.004}, 0.002, 0.001, 0.0005\}$

information on the systems' environment). The time limit for the HGS solver is set to 10 s for all policies (regret and benchmark policies). Experiments are performed on an Intel Core i7 with 2.6GHz and 12 GB RAM.

5.2 Results

The results are summarized in Table 2, which shows the improvements of the policy in the row, compared to the policy in the column. Additionally, the percentage of instances in which one policy led to better results is shown in brackets. Detailed results over all tested instances can be found in the Appendix (Table 4). On average, the proposed policy leads to improvements of around 8.45% compared to the *greedy* benchmark and 40.88% compared to the *lazy* benchmark. Further, the *regret* policy always leads to better results in all cases compared to the greedy benchmark and in 47 out of 50 instances (94%) compared to the *greedy* policy. Moreover, we can deduce that a greedy policy performs better than a lazy policy (improvement of 35.14%).

5.3 Discussion

Firstly, we can see from the results that the *regret* policy outperforms the two benchmarks to a large extent. Further, we can see from the results that a greedy policy performs better than a lazy policy. Therefore, it might be better to attain some slack in the routing decision compared to trying to maximize the consolidation of orders by dispatching them as late as possible. The regret policy seems to achieve a better balance between those two extremes. In fact, our proposed method can be seen as a combination of these two benchmark policies. If the threshold value is 0, only due orders will be dispatched (lazy policy), if the threshold value is infinitely big, all orders will be dispatched (greedy policy). This perspective contributes to the explainability of the proposed method since the greediness/laziness of our method is determined by the threshold value and can be tuned accordingly. In terms of ease of implementation, the regret policy remains fairly simple compared to the two benchmarks, since standard operations can be used to calculate the regret. However, this simplicity also comes with a price, since it is difficult to capture all relevant information in a (simple) function. In the following Section (6), we mention how the regret function could be extended and further propose hybridizations of our proposed method with other methods.

Table 2. Policy Comparison

	Greedy benchmark	Regret policy
Lazy benchmark	35.14% (100%)	40.88% (100%)
Greedy benchmark	–	8.45% (94%)

6 Conclusion

In this paper, we present a *regret* policy for the dynamic vehicle routing problem with time windows (DVRPTW). In the studied problem, orders are sampled from a known customer distribution over a day. Once an hour, it needs to be decided which orders need to be dispatched and which ones to postpone. After it has been decided which orders are dispatched, feasible routes for these orders need to be created. The policy presented in this paper considers the first decision stage, i.e., determining which orders to dispatch, by anticipating orders that might arrive in the future.

We first introduce the general procedure of the policy and the basic regret function, which is applied to determine a regret value for each *undue* order, i.e., orders that can be postponed. This regret value represents possible improvements that might be gained by postponing the order and consolidating it with future orders. If the regret value is below a certain threshold, the order is dispatched. Furthermore, we present the methods applied to incorporate information about other *undue* orders and time windows in the regret function. The developed policy consistently outperforms benchmark policies such as a greedy dispatching rule which dispatches all orders as soon as possible or a lazy dispatching rule which dispatches only orders which are due. Due to its high level of explainability, ease of implementation, and generalizability to other variants of dynamic vehicle routing, the proposed *regret* policy can serve as a benchmark policy for other work on anticipatory vehicle routing. Moreover, multiple extensions of the proposed policy could be investigated. Currently, only the closest due order is regarded to determine the regret value. Future work could look for ways to incorporate the entire set of due (or already dispatched) orders to determine regret values. Furthermore, it could be tried to better account for time windows, e.g., by immediately constructing an initial route plan in the proposed policy. Another possible extension is the development of dynamic thresholds. Even though the time until an order is due is implicitly accounted for in the *regret* policy, dynamic thresholds could further improve the policy. For example, it might be beneficial to release orders more easily when the number of epochs the orders are in the system is low, as this results in wider time windows for the routing decision, and consequently, fewer vehicles could be used. Methods such as Value Function Approximation (VFA) could be used to determine these state-dependent thresholds. Another possible hybridization of methods would be to reformulate the problem as a price collection VRPTW and use the proposed regret function to determine prizes for undue orders.

Appendix

Table 3. Sets, Parameters and Decision Variables

Notation	Definition
Sets	
H	Set of decision epochs, $H := \{1, ..., n\}$
N_h	Set of all known orders in epoch h
O_h	Set of orders that arrived in epoch h
F_h	Set of orders that arrived before epoch h but have not been dispatched yet
D_h	Set of all orders that are due in epoch h, $D_h \subseteq N_h$
V_h	Set of all nodes in epoch h, where 0 is the Depot, $V_h := \{0\} \cup N_h$
K_h	Set of vehicles in epoch h
Parameters	
c_{ij}	Travel time from node $i \in V_h$ to node $j \in V_h$
q^v	Vehicle capacity (same for all vehicles)
q_i^d	Demand of order $i \in N_h$
s_i	Service time for serving order $i \in N_h$
$[e_i, l_i]$	Time window of order $i \in N_h$
Decision Variables	
x_{ijk}	$= 1$ if vehicle $k \in K_h$ travels from node $i \in V_h$ to node $j \in V_h$ (0 otherwise)
t_{ik}	arrival time of vehicle $k \in K_h$ at node $i \in V_h$

Table 4. Objective values over all tested instances.

Instance	Lazy benchmark	Greedy benchmark	Regret policy
n204-k12	708992	292545	**260257**
n206-k12	552684	350988	**326561**
n214-k12	443799	309934	**272562**
n214-k15	942720	**308814**	317443
n225-k14	606387	376851	**359847**
n225-k16	630183	442811	**418218**
n230-k15	1399494	728339	**717362**
n237-k16	509679	348427	**313138**
n237-k20	501440	327922	**303989**
n238-k30	583763	**276100**	281693
n241-k18	584001	452830	**373796**
n250-k15	654395	425656	**386436**
n254-k18	858338	328418	**312425**
n254-k20	555495	363851	**344465**
n270-k18	349255	255878	**226454**

(*continued*)

Table 4. (*continued*)

Instance	Lazy benchmark	Greedy benchmark	Regret policy
n290-k18	545620	**379116**	396671
n291-k16	641405	474666	**422344**
n299-k21	555080	331866	**292910**
n301-k16	821085	552070	**519155**
n302-k20	898116	435965	**376439**
n302-k25	753785	551246	**481033**
n308-k35	966468	468322	**436023**
n309-k19	605191	351529	**324527**
n311-k25	565430	357539	**341638**
n313-k20	531487	329314	**315648**
n316-k19	655239	437355	**380248**
n318-k20	366332	254295	**223473**
n319-k25	645225	483209	**454389**
n320-k20	833531	464472	**426446**
n321-k35	662557	536213	**472861**
n325-k20	394283	300151	**255569**
n326-k25	1032144	618376	**572630**
n327-k20	449911	283930	**255615**
n329-k25	696282	485038	**410575**
n332-k25	362024	254561	**233209**
n335-k22	624164	425939	**402006**
n338-k21	470721	371466	**344624**
n338-k24	704357	506885	**437091**
n339-k20	553098	402506	**368421**
n349-k30	601643	478866	**404215**
n353-k21	556843	368884	**335157**
n363-k22	631352	493885	**431556**
n413-k35	624703	390816	**358661**
n418-k28	989808	521679	**495567**
n420-k26	644202	462920	**397164**
n430-k35	628483	401273	**366917**
n455-k45	593949	372825	**341316**
n457-k30	597019	394398	**373642**
n491-k36	517331	431485	**374174**
n504-k38	636083	386395	**370372**

References

1. Baldacci, R., Mingozzi, A., Roberti, R.: Recent exact algorithms for solving the vehicle routing problem under capacity and time window constraints. Eur. J. Oper. Res. **218**(1), 1–6 (2012). https://doi.org/10.1016/j.ejor.2011.07.037, https://www.sciencedirect.com/science/article/pii/S0377221711006692
2. Baty, L., Jungel, K., Klein, P.S., Parmentier, A., Schiffer, M.: Combinatorial optimization enriched machine learning to solve the dynamic vehicle routing problem with time windows (2023)
3. Bent, R., Van Hentenryck, P.: Regrets only! Online stochastic optimization under time constraints. In: Proceedings of the 19th National Conference on Artifical Intelligence, pp. 501–506. AAAI'04, AAAI Press (2004)
4. Ecker, T., Hans, M., Neuhaus, F., Spielvogel, J.: Same-day delivery: ready for takeoff, January 2020. https://www.mckinsey.com/industries/retail/our-insights/same-day-delivery-ready-for-takeoff
5. Hildebrandt, F.D., Thomas, B.W., Ulmer, M.W.: Opportunities for reinforcement learning in stochastic dynamic vehicle routing. Comput. Oper. Res. **150**, 106071 (2023). https://doi.org/10.1016/j.cor.2022.106071
6. Hvattum, L.M., Løkketangen, A., Laporte, G.: A branch-and-regret heuristic for stochastic and dynamic vehicle routing problems. Networks **49**(4), 330–340 (2007). https://doi.org/10.1002/net.20182
7. Jungel, K., Baty, L., Klein, P.: Structured Learning for the EURO Meets NeurIPS 2022 Vehicle Routing Competition. Technical report (2022)
8. Klapp, M.A., Erera, A.L., Toriello, A.: The dynamic dispatch waves problem for same-day delivery. Eur. J. Oper. Res. **271**(2), 519–534 (2018). https://doi.org/10.1016/j.ejor.2018.05.032
9. Kool, W., et al.: EURO Meets NeurIPS 2022 Vehicle Routing Competition (2022). https://euro-neurips-vrp-2022.challenges.ortec.com/assets/pdf/euro-neurips-vrp-2022-rules-2-aug.pdf. Accessed 15 Nov 2022
10. Kool, W., et al.: Hybrid Genetic Search for the Vehicle Routing Problem with Time Windows: a High-Performance Implementation. Technical report, 12th DIMACS Challenge, April 2022
11. Kwon, Y.D., Choo, J., Bae, D., Kim, J., Hottung, A.: Cost Shaping via Reinforcement Learning for Vehicle Routing Problems. Technical report (2022)
12. Ulmer, M.W., Mattfeld, D.C., Köster, F.: Budgeting time for dynamic vehicle routing with stochastic customer requests. Transp. Sci. **52**(1), 20–37 (2018). https://doi.org/10.1287/trsc.2016.0719
13. Approximate Dynamic Programming for Dynamic Vehicle Routing. ORSIS, vol. 61. Springer, Cham (2017). https://doi.org/10.1007/978-3-319-55511-9
14. Van Hentenryck, P., Bent, R., Upfal, E.: Online stochastic optimization under time constraints. Ann. Oper. Res. **177**, 151–183 (2010). https://doi.org/10.1007/s10479-009-0605-5
15. Vidal, T.: Hybrid genetic search for the CVRP: open-source implementation and swap* neighborhood. Comput. Oper. Res. **140**, 105643 (2022). https://doi.org/10.1016/j.cor.2021.105643
16. Vidal, T., Crainic, T.G., Gendreau, M., Lahrichi, N., Rei, W.: A hybrid genetic algorithm for multidepot and periodic vehicle routing problems. Oper. Res. **60**(3), 611–624 (2012). https://doi.org/10.1287/opre.1120.1048
17. Vidal, T., Crainic, T.G., Gendreau, M., Prins, C.: A unified solution framework for multi-attribute vehicle routing problems. Eur. J. Oper. Res. **234**(3), 658–673 (2014). https://doi.org/10.1016/j.ejor.2013.09.045

A Tabu Search Algorithm for the Traveling Purchaser Problem with Transportation Time Limit

Ilker Kucukoglu[1(✉)], Pieter Vansteenwegen[2], and Dirk Cattrysse[2]

[1] Industrial Engineering Department, Bursa Uludag University, Bursa, Turkey
ikucukoglu@uludag.edu.tr

[2] KU Leuven, KU Leuven Institute for Mobility – CIB, Leuven, Belgium
{pieter.vansteenwegen,dirk.cattrysse}@kuleuven.be

Abstract. This study extends the well-known traveling purchaser problem (TPP) by considering a transportation time limit of perishable food in cold-chain logistics. The problem is called the traveling purchaser problem with transportation time limit (TPP-TTL). The objective of the TPP-TTL is to find a route and procurement plan for the purchaser to satisfy the demand of a number of product types with minimum cost. To satisfy the product demand, the purchaser visits a number of capacitated markets, in which the available amount of products is limited. Furthermore, since the travel times cause deterioration on the perishable products, a transportation time limit is taken into account in the TPP-TTL for each product type. The problem is formulated as a mixed-integer programming model and solved by using a tabu search (TS) algorithm. In the computational experiments, TS is carried out for a number of different-sized instances and the results are compared to the results obtained by GUROBI solver to determine the performance of the proposed algorithm. The results of the experiments show that the TS is capable to find many optimal results with less computational time than the GUROBI solver.

Keywords: Traveling Purchaser Problem · Combinatorial Optimization · Tabu Search Algorithm

1 Introduction

The traveling purchaser problem (TPP) is a well-known combinatorial optimization problem that was first introduced by Ramesh [17] in 1981. The TPP is a variant of the traveling salesperson problem (TSP), in which a set of product demands is satisfied from a number of markets. Distinct from the TSP, the TPP takes into account the decisions about the selection of the markets to be visited, the number of products purchased from each market, and the route of the purchaser. The aim of the problem is to satisfy product demand with minimum total traveling and procurement costs [13].

The original version of the TPP has been extended in many different ways in the literature. Boctor et al. [5] introduced the uncapacitated TPP, in which the amount of a product is sufficient to satisfy demand if it is available in a market. Almeida et al. [1]

© The Author(s), under exclusive license to Springer Nature Switzerland AG 2023
J. R. Daduna et al. (Eds.): ICCL 2023, LNCS 14239, pp. 248–259, 2023.
https://doi.org/10.1007/978-3-031-43612-3_15

proposed a bi-objective TPP by considering different goals in the objective function. A budget limit for the purchaser is taken into account by Choi and Lee [7], where the total cost of the procurement cannot exceed the specified budget limit. Batista-Galvan et al. [2] extended the TPP by considering the pick-up and delivery operations for multiple stacks. Bianchessi et al. [4] introduced a multi-vehicle TPP, in which a distance limit is defined for each vehicle. Gouveia et al. [11] limited the number of markets to be visited in the route for the purchaser. Cheaitou et al. [6] included the environmental effect of transportation in the TPP with variable speeds. Kucukoglu [12] extended the TPP with a duration time limit for the purchaser and a release time for each product at markets. Bianchessi et al. [3] introduced a capacitated multiple vehicles TPP for incompatible products, in which two incompatible products cannot be loaded into the same vehicle.

In almost all studies, the TPP has been extended by considering the route-based (i.e., pick-up and delivery, multiple-vehicle, vehicle speed), purchaser-based (i.e., budget limit, duration time limit, maximum market visit) or market-based (i.e., market capacity, the release time of products) limitations. However, the products to be purchased from the markets is another factor that may affect the route and procurement plan of the purchaser. In this context, perishable food procurement activity in cold chain logistics is a specific application of the TPP since maintaining the quality of perishable foods is critical to reduce the cost of quality loss due to the deterioration of products while they are in transportation. Therefore, in most real-life applications, the transportation time of perishable products is limited by product-specific service-level agreements. Hence, the time the products spend in the vehicle is an important factor in terms of product quality. Particularly, when traditional vehicles are used in logistics operations (instead of temperature-controlled vehicles), transportation of different types of foods having their own different storage requirements has to be well planned to ensure acceptable product quality [19].

Based on the aforementioned motivation, this paper introduces a new variant of the TPP based on the procurement of perishable food in cold chain logistics. Since the transportation time of the perishable products is limited to maintain product quality, the TPP is extended with a transportation time limit for each product type. The problem is called the traveling purchaser problem with transportation time limit (TPP-TTL). The aim of the problem is to minimize the total transportation and procurement cost of the purchaser while satisfying the market capacity and transportation time limit restrictions. In accordance with this purpose, a mixed-integer mathematical model formulation is introduced for the TPP-TTL. To solve the given model, a tabu search (TS) algorithm is proposed. Computational experiments are used to evaluate the performance of the TS on a number of different-sized TPP-TTL instances.

This study contributes to the literature in two ways: First, a new variant of the TPP is introduced regarding the procurement of perishable food in cold chain operations. To the best of our knowledge, the TPP has not been addressed in the literature with a transportation time limit for each product type. Distinct from the existing studies related to TPP, the mathematical model introduced for the TPP-TTL takes into account the real-life restrictions of cold chain activities by including the transportation time limits of perishable foods. The second contribution of this study is the proposed solution methodology, which employs an advanced local search procedure to explore the solution space.

The remainder of the paper is organized as follows. Section 2 introduces the details of the TPP-TTL and its mathematical formulation. The proposed TS is presented in Sect. 3. The computational results and performance analysis of the TS are given in Sect. 4. Finally, the conclusions are given in Sect. 5.

2 Problem Definition and Mathematical Model

The TPP-TTL is an extension of the well-known capacitated version of the TPP, in which the demand of a set of products is provided from a set of capacitated markets. In each market, the available quantity of a product can be less than the demand for that product. Therefore, the demand of a product type can be purchased from more than one market. In addition to the capacity restriction of the markets, the time each product can be transported is limited. The purchaser starts its route, visits a number of markets, and returns to the depot after all required products are purchased. The aim of the TPP-TTL is to minimize the total transportation and procurement cost of the purchaser. Based on the assumptions given above, the mathematical model of the TPP-TTL is formulated as follows.

Parameters

- K Set of products
- M Set of markets
- M_k Set of markets in which the product k is available ($M_k \subseteq M$), $k \in K$.
- $\{0\}$ Depot node
- V Set of markets and depot ($M \cup \{0\}$)
- d_k Demand amount of product k, $k \in K$.
- q_{ik} Available amount of product k at market i, $k \in K, i \in M_k$.
- p_{ik} Price of product k at market i, $k \in K, i \in M_k$.
- c_{ij} Traveling cost from node i to node j, $i, j \in V$.
- t_{ij} Traveling time from node i to node j, $i, j \in V$.
- h_i Unit service time to purchase any product at market i; $i \in M$.
- tl_k Maximum allowed transportation time for product k, $k \in K$.
- γ Large number.

Decision Variables

- x_{ij} Binary variable: 1 if the purchaser travels from node i to node j, otherwise 0; $i, j \in V$, $i \neq j$.
- y_i Binary variable: 1 if market i is visited by the purchaser, otherwise 0; $i \in M$.
- z_{ik} Amount of product k purchased from market i; $k \in K, i \in M_k$.
- o_{ik} Binary variable: 1 if product k is purchased at market i, otherwise 0; $k \in K, i \in M_k$.
- r_i Arrival time of purchaser to node i; $i \in V$.
- s_i Time spent at market i; $i \in M$.

Model

$$Min \sum_{i\in V}\sum_{j\in V} c_{ij}x_{ij} + \sum_{k\in K}\sum_{i\in M_k} p_{ik}z_{ik} \tag{1}$$

S.t.

$$\sum_{i\in M_k} z_{ik} = d_k \quad k \in K \tag{2}$$

$$z_{ik} \le q_{ik}y_i \quad k \in K, \quad i \in M_k \tag{3}$$

$$o_{ik} \le z_{ik} \le q_{ik}o_{ik} \quad k \in K, \quad i \in M_k \tag{4}$$

$$\sum_{\substack{j\in V\\ i\neq j}} x_{ij} = y_i \quad i \in M \tag{5}$$

$$\sum_{\substack{i\in V\\ i\neq j}} x_{ij} = y_j \quad j \in M \tag{6}$$

$$\sum_{i\in M} x_{i0} = 1 \tag{7}$$

$$\sum_{j\in M} x_{0j} = 1 \tag{8}$$

$$t_{0i} \le r_i + \gamma(1 - x_{0i}) \quad i \in M \tag{9}$$

$$t_{0i} \ge r_i - \gamma(1 - x_{0i}) \quad i \in M \tag{10}$$

$$r_i + s_i + t_{ij} \le r_j + \gamma\left(1 - x_{ij}\right) \quad i \in M, \quad j \in V, \quad i \neq j \tag{11}$$

$$r_i + s_i + t_{ij} \ge r_j - \gamma\left(1 - x_{ij}\right) \quad i \in M, \quad j \in V, \quad i \neq j \tag{12}$$

$$s_i = \sum_{k\in K} h_i z_{ik} \quad i \in M \tag{13}$$

$$r_0 - r_i - s_i \le tl_k + \gamma(1 - o_{ik}) \quad k \in K, \quad i \in M_k \tag{14}$$

$$x_{ij} \in \{0, 1\} \quad i, j \in V, \quad i \neq j \tag{15}$$

$$y_i \in \{0, 1\} \quad i \in M \tag{16}$$

$$o_{ik} \in \{0, 1\} \quad k \in K, \quad i \in M_k \tag{17}$$

$$z_{ik} \geq 0 \quad k \in K, \quad i \in M_k \tag{18}$$

$$r_i \geq 0 \quad i \in V \tag{19}$$

$$s_i \geq 0 \quad i \in M \tag{20}$$

Equation (1) in the proposed model describes the objective function to minimize the total transportation and procurement cost of the purchaser. Constraints (2) provide that each product demand is satisfied from the markets. Constraints (3) and (4) ensure that the purchased amount of a product type at a specific market cannot exceed the available stock. Constraints (5) and (6) guarantee that the purchaser enters and exits from a market if a procurement is made from the related market. Constraints (7) and (8) set the initial and last node of the route as the depot node. Constraints (9)–(12) determine the arrival time of the purchaser to the visited nodes considering the traveling time between the locations and service time at markets. These constraints also eliminate the sub-tours by tracking the arrival time between the visited nodes. Constraints (13) compute the service time at the visited markets. Constraints (14) guarantee that the travel time and service time of each product in the vehicle cannot exceed the corresponding time limit. Finally, constraints (15)–(20) identify the domain of the decision variables.

3 Solution Methodology

Tabu search, which was first introduced by Glover in 1986, is a well-known meta-heuristic to solve combinatorial optimization problems [9, 10]. The main feature of TS is the memory mechanism that prevents the search from cycling back to previously found solutions. The memory structure of TS, called tabu list, guides the search of the algorithm. The tabu list allows to find unexplored solutions by prohibiting the usage of recently utilized moves in the tabu list. With the help of this memory structure, TS has proved to be effective to solve various routing problems [8, 16, 18]. Moreover, TS is used in [20] to solve TPP, in which two dynamic tabu search strategies are operated. In this context, TS is employed in this study to find effective results for the TPP-TTL. Figure 1 presents the pseudo code of the proposed algorithm. The details of the main TS procedures are described in the following sub-sections.

3.1 Initial Solution

The proposed algorithm searches the solution space for a feasible solution considering the capacity of the markets and the transportation time limit of each product. Therefore, the initial solution generation procedure (Line 2 in Fig. 1) is designed to produce a feasible solution for the TPP-TTL. In this context, the procedure iteratively selects an unmet product that has the smallest transportation time limit and fulfills the demand of the product. First, the visited markets are taken into account to satisfy the demand. In

1: Set the algorithm parameters $Iter^{Max}$, L, $TL' = \emptyset$, $TL'' = \emptyset$
2: Generate an initial solution $\boldsymbol{X} = \boldsymbol{X_0}$
3: $\boldsymbol{X}^{Best} = \boldsymbol{X}$
4: **For** $Iter = 1$ **To** $Iter^{Max}$
5: Randomly select a procurement-based search and generate all possible neighbourhoods ($\{\boldsymbol{X}'_1, \boldsymbol{X}'_2, \boldsymbol{X}'_3, \ldots\}$) for $\boldsymbol{X}$
6: Select the best move ($\boldsymbol{X}'_*$) which is not in TL' or leads to a new best solution
7: Update the TL'
8: Randomly select a route-change-based search and generate all possible neighbourhoods ($\{\boldsymbol{X}''_1, \boldsymbol{X}''_2, \boldsymbol{X}''_3, \ldots\}$) for $\boldsymbol{X}'_*$
9: Select the best move ($\boldsymbol{X}''_*$) which is not in TL'' or leads to a new best solution
10: Update the TL''
11: $\boldsymbol{X} = \boldsymbol{X}''_*$
12: **If** $f(\boldsymbol{X}) < f(\boldsymbol{X}^{Best})$ **Then**
13: $\boldsymbol{X}^{Best} = \boldsymbol{X}$
14: **End If**
15: **Next**

Fig. 1. Pseudo code of the proposed TS

case the demand is not completely met from the visited markets, an unvisited market with minimum cost for the selected product is inserted into the first position in the route. This product selection and adding procedure repeats until all demand is satisfied. Although the capacity restriction of the markets can be completely satisfied by this procedure, the transportation time limit of any product may be violated while inserting another product into the solution. In such a case, a feasible solution is provided by randomly selecting a product that violates the time restriction and purchasing it from a proper market. Here, in addition to the visited markets, unvisited markets are also taken into account. Then, a market is randomly selected from the considered list of markets. If a proper market is not found, the initial solution generation procedure is restarted in the algorithm. Since the markets are randomly selected in this procedure, different results can be obtained at each restart. In this way, at the end of the procedure, a feasible initial solution (X_0) is generated to be improved in the main loop of the TS.

3.2 Neighborhood Generation

In each iteration of the TS, the algorithm employs two independent local search procedures to improve the existing solution$\boldsymbol{X}$. In the first local search procedure, a number of neighborhoods are generated by applying a procurement-based move operator (Lines 5–7 in Fig. 1). The procurement-based move operators are used to improve the existing solution by making changes in the procurement plan. To change the procurement plan, three moves are considered: unvisited market insertion, visited market removal, and product exchange between the visited markets. For each application of the procurement-based search, one of the move operators is randomly selected. Based on the selected operator, all feasible neighbor solutions are generated. Regarding the tabu list criteria of the TS, the best alternative solution $\boldsymbol{X}'_*$ is selected from a set of candidate neighborhoods $(\{\boldsymbol{X}'_1, \boldsymbol{X}'_2, \boldsymbol{X}'_3, \ldots\})$.

In the second local search procedure, a set of candidate solutions ($\{X''_1, X''_2, X''_3, \ldots\}$) are generated based on $X_{*'}$ by using a route-change-based move operator (Lines 8–10 in Fig. 1). Similar to the procurement-based search approach, four different move operators are used to generate neighborhoods. Four move operators are considered: market exchange, a market movement to a further position, a market movement to a backward position, and a sub-path reverse in the route. After all feasible candidate solutions are generated, the best solution X''_*, which is not tabu or leads to a new best solution, is selected to be assigned as the current solution X.

3.3 Tabu List Structure

The tabu list of the proposed algorithm includes the move information for both the procurement-based and route-change-based search procedures. In this context, two independent tabu lists (TL' and TL'') are employed in the algorithm, where TL' is used for the procurement-based search procedure while TL'' is used for the route-change-based search procedure. In each iteration of the TS, the information corresponding to the selected neighborhood in the applied move operator is added to the related tabu list. A capacitated tabu list strategy is taken into account with first-in-first-out logic, in which move information is kept in the tabu list for a specified number of iterations (L). A move, which is in the tabu list, is prohibited for L iterations. However, regarding the aspiration criterion, a move is accepted if it leads to a new best solution for the algorithm. At the end of each iteration of the TS, the oldest move information in the list is removed.

3.4 Termination Criterion

The main loop of the proposed algorithm consists of neighborhood generation, fitness evaluation, tabu list update, and best solution update procedures. The main loop of the TS is repeated until the termination criterion is met. For the termination criterion, a maximum iteration number ($Iter^{Max}$) is used in the algorithm.

4 Computational Results

In the computational studies, first, the difference between the TPP and TPP-TTL based on the total cost is analyzed by using the GUROBI solver. Following this analysis, the performance of the proposed TS is demonstrated by comparing the proposed algorithm with the GUROBI solver. For these studies, a well-known capacitated TPP benchmark problem set introduced by Laporte et al. [14] is used. The TPP instances are adapted to the TPP-TTL by randomly assigning a transportation time limit for each product type. To generate a random value for the transportation time limits, first, a reference duration time (RDT) for the problem is calculated regarding the transportation and service time of the purchaser. The transportation time of the purchaser is calculated by using the nearest neighborhood algorithm ignoring the transportation time limit of the products. On the other hand, the service time is determined regarding the lowest service time for each product type. After the RDT is obtained for the problem, a transportation time limit is randomly specified as $tl_k = 0.50 \times RDT + rnd() \times RDT$ where $rnd()$ is a uniformly distributed random number in the interval [0, 1]. In case the generated time limits leads an infeasible route for the purchaser, the procedure is restarted. Based on this procedure, 27 different-sized TPP-TTL instances are generated where the problem size is specified by the pair of two problem data: $\{|V|, |K|\}$ where the value of each parameter is specified as 10, 20, or 30 for TPP-TTL instance generation.

The proposed TS is implemented for each TPP-TTL instance by setting the $Iter^{Max} = 1000$ and $L = 50$. With these parameter settings, ten independent runs are carried out for each problem. The results of the TS are investigated through the total cost (f) and solution time (t) for both the best solution obtained in the runs and the average of the runs. Here, it should be noted that the f and t are used to represent the GUROBI results to indicate optimum solution and solution time, respectively. Each TS and GUROBI computation is carried out on a workstation with Intel® Xeon® CPU E5-2643 v3 CPU and 64 GB of memory.

To indicate the difference between the TPP and TPP-TTL results based on the total cost, the model formulation proposed for the TPP-TLL is simply adapted to the TPP by ignoring the constraints (9)–(14). However, the Miller-Tucker-Zemlin sub-tour elimination constraints [15] are included in the model to eliminate sub-tours. To find the optimal solution for TPP and TPP-TTL each instance, the GUROBI is executed without setting any time limit. Table 1 shows the results of the GUROBI for both the TPP and TPP-TTL instances, where the percentage gap between the two solutions is computed by using Eq. (21), where f_{TPP} and $f_{TPP-TTL}$ are the optimum solutions obtained for the TPP and TPP-TTL instances, respectively.

$$Gap^1\% = \frac{f_{TPP-TTL} - f_{TPP}}{f_{TPP}} \times 100\% \tag{21}$$

The $Gap^1\%$ values presented in Table 1 show that up to 15.02% increase on total cost is observed due to the transportation time limits of the products. Particularly, the gap between the solution is high when the number of product types is high (i.e., $\{|V|, |K|\} = \{(10, 30), (20, 30), (30, 30)\}$). On the other hand, the same results are obtained for four instances. In addition to the comparison based on the total cost, it should be seen from Table 1 that the solution time of GUROBI for the TPP-TLL is quite high according to the TPP model computation. Therefore, it should be stated that finding an optimal solution for the TPP-TTL requires more computational effort with respect to the TPP.

Table 1. GUROBI results for the TPP and TPP-TLL instances

Problem #	$\|V\|$	$\|K\|$	TPP		TPP-TTL		
			f	t	f	$Gap^1\%$	t
1	10	10	2652	0.42	2700	1.81	6.41
2	10	10	2608	0.62	2710	3.91	4.57
3	10	10	3292	0.39	3393	3.07	5.60
4	10	20	3432	0.48	3486	1.57	20.79
5	10	20	3499	0.42	3638	3.97	11.43
6	10	20	3818	0.44	3882	1.68	14.74
7	10	30	3895	0.42	4181	7.34	95.95
8	10	30	3885	0.39	4303	10.76	81.55
9	10	30	3521	0.44	4050	15.02	97.71
10	20	10	3048	2.03	3048	0.00	138.24
11	20	10	3530	3.34	3530	0.00	180.33
12	20	10	3983	2.21	3991	0.20	157.71
13	20	20	4074	0.97	4344	6.63	470.27
14	20	20	4109	1.36	4245	3.31	444.65
15	20	20	3688	4.65	3760	1.95	350.35
16	20	30	3975	1.05	4274	7.52	678.94
17	20	30	6483	1.06	6855	5.74	340.95
18	20	30	5120	2.20	5597	9.32	906.16
19	30	10	3467	8.52	3467	0.00	451.66
20	30	10	3684	8.02	3684	0.00	440.06
21	30	10	4865	5.82	4871	0.12	545.06
22	30	20	4748	8.70	4788	0.84	881.62
23	30	20	6938	10.11	7063	1.80	956.97
24	30	20	5836	7.74	5867	0.53	1118.01
25	30	30	5078	3.51	5250	3.39	955.05
26	30	30	6342	2.40	6572	3.63	884.27
27	30	30	7369	11.50	7507	1.87	858.87
Average			4331.1	3.30	4484	3.56	411.03

In addition to the comparison of TPP and TPP-TTL, the second part of the computational experiments is carried out to demonstrate the efficiency of the proposed TS. In this context, the TS results are compared to the optimal TPP-TTL solutions obtained by GUROBI. The results of GUROBI and TS, and the comparison are given in Table 2, in which $Gap^2\%$ indicates the percentage gap between the best/average result of the TS and GUROBI result. $Gap^2\%$ is calculated by using Eq. (22) where f_{TS} is the best/average result of the TS and f_{GUROBI} is the GUROBI result.

Table 2. TS and GUROBI comparison for the TPP-TTL instances

Problem #	GUROBI		TS					
			Best Solution			Average Solution		
	f	t	f	$Gap^2\%$	t	f	$Gap^2\%$	t
1	2700	6.41	2700	0.00	0.45	2700.0	0.00	0.53
2	2710	4.57	2710	0.00	0.94	2710.0	0.00	1.12
3	3393	5.60	3393	0.00	1.04	3393.0	0.00	1.32
4	3486	20.79	3486	0.00	0.79	3486.0	0.00	0.72
5	3638	11.43	3638	0.00	0.99	3638.0	0.00	0.92
6	3882	14.74	3882	0.00	0.73	3887.8	0.15	0.86
7	4181	95.95	4181	0.00	0.85	4181.0	0.00	0.93
8	4303	81.55	4303	0.00	1.06	4303.0	0.00	1.15
9	4050	97.71	4050	0.00	1.11	4052.6	0.06	1.09
10	3048	138.24	3048	0.00	1.15	3048.0	0.00	1.12
11	3530	180.33	3530	0.00	1.23	3530.0	0.00	1.29
12	3991	157.71	3991	0.00	1.32	3991.0	0.00	1.31
13	4344	470.27	4344	0.00	1.22	4348.9	0.11	1.19
14	4245	444.65	4245	0.00	1.41	4245.0	0.00	1.38
15	3760	350.35	3760	0.00	1.38	3771.3	0.30	1.41
16	4274	678.94	4274	0.00	1.44	4276.5	0.06	1.35
17	6855	340.95	6855	0.00	1.51	6855.0	0.00	1.49
18	5597	906.16	5597	0.00	1.47	5601.2	0.08	1.53
19	3467	451.66	3467	0.00	1.62	3467.0	0.00	1.55
20	3684	440.06	3684	0.00	1.58	3684.0	0.00	1.49
21	4871	545.06	4871	0.00	1.69	4872.1	0.02	1.71
22	4788	881.62	4788	0.00	1.55	4795.6	0.16	1.43
23	7063	956.97	7063	0.00	1.78	7077.9	0.21	1.74
24	5867	1118.01	5867	0.00	1.71	5869.7	0.05	1.73
25	5250	955.05	5250	0.00	1.83	5275.3	0.48	1.79
26	6572	884.27	6572	0.00	1.81	6593.3	0.32	1.83
27	7507	858.87	7507	0.00	1.93	7542.1	0.47	1.88
Average	4484	411.03	4484	0.00	1.32	4488.7	0.09	1.33

$$Gap^2\% = \frac{f_{TS} - f_{GUROBI}}{f_{GUROBI}} \times 100\% \tag{22}$$

Based on the best-found result of the TS given in Table 2, the optimal solution is provided for each instance by the proposed algorithm. Furthermore, the average result of the TS is the same with the optimal solution for 14 of 27 instances. For the remaining instances, the highest percentage gap is 0.48%. For the overall performance of the TS, the average percentage gap of the proposed algorithm is 0.09% with respect to the optimal solution. Furthermore, the average computational time of the TS is 1.33 s, while the average computational time of the GUROBI is 411.03 s. Regarding the solution quality and computational effort of the proposed algorithm, it can be stated that the TS is capable to find the optimal or near-optimal solution for the TPP-TTL in much less computational time.

5 Conclusions

In this study, the traveling purchaser problem with transportation time limit, which is an extension of the well-known traveling purchaser problem, is proposed by considering the transportation restrictions of perishable food in cold-chain logistics. The TPP-TTL extends the capacitated version of the TPP by including a transportation time limit for each product type in the vehicle. In this context, any product cannot be kept in the vehicle for more than a specified time limit. Regarding both the market capacity and product transportation restrictions, the TPP-TTL is formulated as a mixed-integer programming model, in which the objective is to minimize the total transportation and procurement cost of the purchaser. To solve the problem, a tabu search algorithm is introduced. The proposed algorithm employs a number of procurement-based and route-change-based local search moves to generate neighborhoods in each iteration. The performance of the proposed algorithm is tested on different-sized TPP-TTL problems generated by using a well-known TPP benchmark problem set. The TS is compared to the GUROBI solver to identify the solution quality of the proposed algorithm. Results of the computations show that the proposed TS outperforms the GUROBI solver by finding optimal results in much less computational time.

For future research, this study can be extended with considering different real-life restrictions of cold chain logistics. First, the deterioration cost of perishable products due to the traveling in a vehicle can be integrated. On the other hand, the procurement plan can consider multiple trips by the purchaser, where each trip can be done with a different type of vehicle (i.e., temperature controlled vehicle, traditional vehicle). With this assumption, the quality level of some products that are more sensitive to temperature change may be transported with a temperature-controlled vehicles with additional cooling cost. Another practical assumption for the TPP-TTL may be the proportional transportation time limit for the product at different markets. This assumption may be valid when a product is produced in different time periods in different markets. Considering the quality of a product at each market depends on the production date, the purchaser may need to include this assumption for its procurement and route plan.

Acknowledgement. This work is supported by the Commission of Scientific Research Projects of Bursa Uludag University, Project Number FUİ-2022-1042.

References

1. Almeida, C.P., Gonçalves, R.A., Goldbarg, E.F., Goldbarg, M.C., Delgado, M.R.: An experimental analysis of evolutionary heuristics for the biobjective traveling purchaser problem. Ann. Oper. Res. **199**(1), 305–341 (2012)
2. Batista-Galvan, M., Riera-Ledesma, J., Salazar-Gonzalez, J.J.: The traveling purchaser problem, with multiple stacks and deliveries: a branch-and-cut approach. Comput. Oper. Res. **40**, 2103–2115 (2013)
3. Bianchessi, N., Irnich, S., Tilk, C.: A branch-price-and-cut algorithm for the capacitated multiple vehicle traveling purchaser problem with unitary demand. Discret. Appl. Math. **288**, 152–170 (2021)
4. Bianchessi, N., Mansini, R., Speranza, M.G.: The distance constrained multiple vehicle traveling purchaser problem. Eur. J. Oper. Res. **235**, 73–87 (2014)
5. Boctor, F.F., Laporte, G., Renaud, J.: Heuristics for the traveling purchaser problem. Comput. Oper. Res. **30**(4), 491–504 (2003)
6. Cheaitou, A., Hamdan, S., Larbi, R., Alsyouf, I.: Sustainable traveling purchaser problem with speed optimization. Int. J. Sustain. Transp. **15**(8), 621–640 (2021)
7. Choi, M.J., Lee, S.H.: The multiple traveling purchaser problem for maximizing system's reliability with budget constraints. Expert Syst. Appl. **38**(8), 9848–9853 (2011)
8. Gendreau, M., Hertz, A., Laporte, G.: A Tabu search heuristic for the vehicle routing problem. Manag. Sci. **40**(10), 1276–1290 (1994)
9. Glover, F.: Tabu search – Part I. ORSA J. Comput. **1**(3), 190–206 (1989)
10. Glover, F.: Tabu search – Part II. ORSA J. Comput. **2**(1), 4–32 (1990)
11. Gouveia, L., Paias, A., Voß, S.: Models for a traveling purchaser problem with additional side-constraints. Comput. Oper. Res. **38**, 550–558 (2011)
12. Kucukoglu, I.: The traveling purchaser problem with fast service option. Comput. Oper. Res. **141**, 105700 (2022)
13. Manerba, M., Mansini, R., Riera-Ledesma, J.: The traveling purchaser problem and its variants. Eur. J. Oper. Res. **259**(1), 1–18 (2017)
14. Laporte, G., Riera-Ledesma, J., Salazar-González, J.-J.: A branch-and-cut algorithm for the undirected traveling purchaser problem. Oper. Res. **51**(6), 940–951 (2003)
15. Miller, C.E., Tucker, A.W., Zemlin, R.A.: Integer programming formulation of traveling salesman problems. J. ACM **7**(4), 326–329 (1960)
16. Qiu, M., Zhuo, F., Eglese, R., Qiong, T.: A Tabu search algorithm for the vehicle routing problem with discrete split deliveries and pickups. Comput. Oper. Res. **100**, 102–116 (2018)
17. Ramesh, T.: Traveling purchaser problem. Opsearch **18**(1–3), 78–91 (1981)
18. Taillard, E., Badeau, P., Gendreau, M., Guertin, F., Potvin, J.-Y.: A Tabu search heuristic for the vehicle routing problem with soft time windows. Transp. Sci. **31**(2), 170–186 (1997)
19. Tsang, Y.P., Choy, K.L., Wu, C.H., Ho, G.T.S., Lam, H.Y., Tang, V.: An intelligent model for assuring food quality in managing a multi-temperature food distribution centre. Food Control **90**, 81–97 (2018)
20. Voß, S.: Dynamic tabu search strategies for the traveling purchaser problem. Ann. Oper. Res. **63**, 253–275 (1996)

GRASP Solution Approach for the E-Waste Collection Problem

Aldy Gunawan[1](✉), Dang Viet Anh Nguyen[1], Pham Kien Minh Nguyen[2], and Pieter Vansteenwegen[3]

[1] School of Computing and Information Systems, Singapore Management University, 80 Stamford Road, Singapore 178902, Singapore
{aldygunawan,dvanguyen}@smu.edu.sg

[2] Department of Industrial Management, National Taiwan University of Science and Technology, No. 43, Keelung Rd., Taipei 106335, Taiwan
d10901807@gapps.ntust.edu.tw

[3] KU Leuven Institute for Mobility - CIB, University of Leuven, Celestijnenlaan 300, Leuven 3001, Belgium
pieter.vansteenwegen@kuleuven.be

Abstract. The digital economy has brought significant advancements in electronic devices, increasing convenience and comfort in people's lives. However, this progress has also led to a shorter life cycle for these devices due to rapid advancements in hardware and software technology. As a result, e-waste collection and recycling have become vital for protecting the environment and people's health. From the operations research perspective, the e-waste collection problem can be modeled as the Heterogeneous Vehicle Routing Problem with Multiple Time Windows (HVRP-MTW). This study proposes a metaheuristic based on the Greedy Randomized Adaptive Search Procedure complemented by Path Relinking (GRASP-PR) to solve the HVRP-MTW problem. The experiment demonstrates that the proposed algorithm can efficiently handle HVRP-MTW instances, even of large-scale. Moreover, the comparison with CPLEX indicates that our approach can achieve optimal solutions for small instances and outperform the commercial solver in large-scale instances.

Keywords: E-waste · Vehicle routing problem · time windows · GRASP · Path-relinking

1 Introduction

With the rapid advancement of technology and the continuous development of production and industrial design, electronic and electrical devices have become ubiquitous in lives, providing convenience and comfort on a daily basis. However, this progress has also resulted in a significant drawback-the ever-shortening life cycle of electrical and electronic devices. Consequently, there has been a marked increase in the annual amount of e-waste - discarded electrical and electronic

© The Author(s), under exclusive license to Springer Nature Switzerland AG 2023
J. R. Daduna et al. (Eds.): ICCL 2023, LNCS 14239, pp. 260–275, 2023.
https://doi.org/10.1007/978-3-031-43612-3_16

devices and their components which are not reused. According to UNITAR, in 2019, the world generated a staggering 53.6 Megatons of e-waste, of which only 17.35% was properly managed in an environmentally sound manner, while the fate of the remaining e-waste was unknown [1]. The collection of e-waste plays a pivotal role in its overall management and treatment cycle, typically involving the use of heavy vehicles and differing from conventional waste management practices. If not adequately planned, the e-waste collection process can create numerous challenges for urban areas, such as straining the urban transport system, contributing to increased air pollution, and burdening the e-waste management companies. Unfortunately, the literature on optimizing the e-waste collection process remains relatively limited. In the field of operations research, the e-waste collection problem can be effectively modeled as a variant of the Vehicle Routing Problem (VRP), which is extensively studied and widely applied in the realm of logistics and supply chain management. To gain a comprehensive understanding of the development of VRP models, methods, and applications, interested readers are encouraged to refer to the work by Braekers et al. [2].

We provide a summary and highlight relevant literature on various algorithms proposed to address different variants of the VRP in the context of e-waste management. Yao et al. [13] focused on two subproblems: optimizing the location of Waste of Electric and Electronic Equipment (WEEE) transit sites and the VRP. They proposed an exact method using the quadratic optimization and an ant colony algorithm to solve instances in the context of Shanghai (China). Mar-Ortiz et al. [11] formulated the WEEE collection problem as the VRP with Split Loads and Time Windows and proposed a Greedy Randomized Adaptive Searching Procedure (GRASP) metaheuristic to solve a large dataset in the context of Galicia (Spain). Król et al. [10] presented a model for e-waste collection at both doorsteps and collection points within a single day. The problem is formulated as the VRP with intermediate facilities, considering heterogeneous vehicles, breaks between shifts, and regional cost differences. A multiple neighborhood search algorithm was proposed to tackle this problem. Pourhejazy et al. [12] formulated the actual waste-collecting scheme as a Capacitated General Routing Problem with Time Windows and adopted Tabu Search to handle it. They considered population density to separate requests from on-call customers and also accounted for a scheme of heterogeneous vehicles.

To the best of our knowledge, none addresses the waste collecting with distinct periods within distinct days in the schedule. In the most recent research [7], a Heterogeneous VRP with Multiple Time Windows (HVRP-MTW) model is introduced to optimize e-waste collection vehicle routing. CPLEX is employed to solve the Mixed Integer Linear Programming formulation of the problem. However, CPLEX is inefficient in solving practical-scale instances due to a significant amount of time to handle the problem. In this work, we propose an efficient approach based on the GRASP metaheuristic to obtain solutions for larger instances within reasonable computational times. The remainder of this article is organized as follows. Section 2 provides details of the problem description and the proposed algorithm. In Sect. 3, we discuss our experimental setup, benchmark instances, and the computational results. Finally, we conclude this article and provide potential research directions in Sect. 4.

2 Methodology

2.1 Problem Description

The problem addressed arises from the e-waste collection process in the context of Singapore, which was modeled as a Mixed Integer Linear Program (MILP) in [7]. E-waste public drop-off bins (e-bins) have been set up across Singapore. Unlike conventional waste, which is collected daily, the e-bins only require collection when the amount of e-waste reaches a specified level. Every day, the system updates information about the e-bins that need to be collected, allowing staff to carry out the collection task. Additionally, companies also cater to on-demand e-waste collection requests from households and businesses. For each on-demand request, customers are charged a fee. Moreover, the on-demand collection requests need to be completed within a specific time frame specified by the customer when making the request through a mobile application, creating time windows.

Each customer's request includes the preferred collection days and time windows, resulting in a multiple time window problem. If the vehicle arrives before the lower bound of the time window, an idle cost will be incurred. Conversely, a penalty cost will be imposed if the vehicle arrives after the upper bound of the time window, with the penalty cost typically being greater than the idle cost due to its impact on the customer satisfaction. The company typically employs a heterogeneous fleet of vehicles with two different types. These vehicles have varying capacities and operating costs per unit of time. Different collection points have different amounts of e-waste that need to be collected and require a certain amount of time for processing. Figure 1 illustrates a solution of the described HVRP-MTW. The problem involves planning the routes for the existing vehicles within a specific collection period, with the objective of maximizing profits from the e-waste collection process.

2.2 Proposed Algorithm

GRASP is a multi-start and memoryless metaheuristic that has been successfully applied to solve various combinatorial optimization problems [4]. The original GRASP metaheuristic consists of two main phases: construction and improvement. In each iteration, an initial solution is constructed by a greedy randomized heuristic, and local search procedures are applied to improve the initial solution. The pseudocode for the basic GRASP algorithm for maximization problems is presented in Algorithm 1 with S and S^* representing the initial solution and the best-found solution so far, respectively. A two-phase construction heuristic is proposed to generate an initial solution. The first phase focuses on addressing the vehicle capacity constraint and heterogeneous fleet characteristics, while the second phase aims to ensure the feasibility of the collection period constraint.

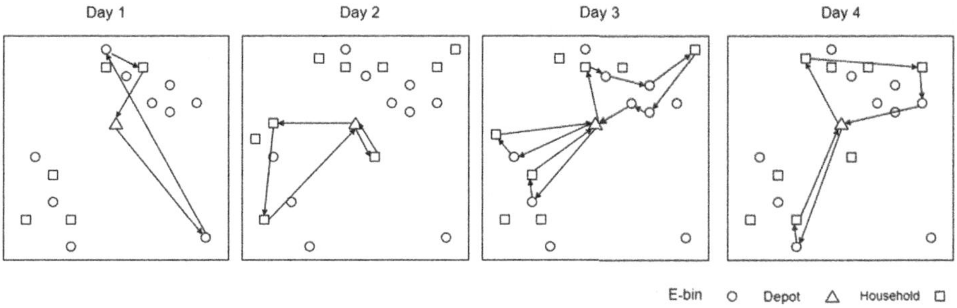

Fig. 1. A solution of the HVRP-MTW with four collection days

Algorithm 1. GRASP general structure for maximization problem

Input: Number of iterations i_{max}
$f(S^*) \leftarrow -\infty$; //Set the objective function of S^* to a negative infinite value
for $i \leftarrow 1$ to i_{max} **do**
    $S \leftarrow$ `ConstructionHeuristic()`; //Build the initial solution
    $S \leftarrow$ `LocalSearch(`S`)`;//Implement the local search
    if $f(S) > f(S^*)$ **then**
        $f(S^*) \leftarrow f(S)$;
        $S^* \leftarrow S$;
    end if
end for
Return: S^*

To establish initial routes that satisfy the capacity constraint, the Clarke and Wright savings heuristic is utilized [3]. However, the traditional Clarke and Wright procedure is ineffective when dealing with a heterogeneous vehicle fleet. In the merge step, the heuristic tends to combine all subtours until the total demand reaches the capacity of the largest vehicle in the fleet. However, relying solely on the use of large vehicles is not an optimal approach for solving the heterogeneous fleet problem. To address this issue, we have adopted the Realistic Opportunity Savings - γ ($ROS - \gamma$) [6] to calculate the savings of the Clarke and Wright heuristic in our solution construction phase: $s''_{ij} = s'_{ij} + (1 - \gamma)t_{ij}$. Where γ is a route-shape parameter with the value varying from 0.0 to 3.0 [6]. By varying the value of γ, the composition of the mixed fleet can be altered. For instance, when $\gamma = 0$, the solution tends to favor larger vehicles, while increasing γ to 2.5 results in the utilization of more small vehicles in the initial solution. Therefore, γ serves as a diversification factor in creating a mixed fleet initial solution. s'_{ij} are the savings calculated in Realistic Opportunity Savings (ROS): $s'_{ij} = \bar{s_{ij}} + \delta(\theta)F'(P(z_i + z_j) - z_i - z_j)$. The parameter $\delta(\theta)$ is a binary indicator of whether the vehicle threshold θ has been exceeded. This threshold is calculated by the formula $\theta = P(z_i + z_j) - P(\max(z_i, z_j))$, where $P(z)$ denotes the capacity of the smallest vehicle that can serve a demand of z. If the vehicle threshold is not exceeded, then $\delta(\theta)$ is set to 0. Conversely, when $\theta > 0$, indicating that the threshold has been exceeded, $\delta(\theta)$ is set to 1. $F'(z)$ in our study is the operation cost rate of the largest vehicle that has a capacity less than or equal to z. $\bar{s_{ij}}$ are savings computed in a Combined Savings (CS) approach: $\bar{s_{ij}} = s_{ij} + F(z_i) + F(z_j) - F(z_i + z_j)$. Here, $F(z)$ stand for the operation cost of the smallest vehicle that can service a demand of z. The maximum vehicle capacity in Clarke and Wright with the ROS-γ approach is set as the capacity of the largest vehicle minus 50 to relax the repair procedure.

Algorithm 2. Clarke and Wright savings heuristic with $ROS - \gamma$

```
1: Input: Set of nodes 𝒩
2: Initialize individual route for each node in 𝒩
3: Calculate the savings based on the ROS − γ approach, s'' for each pair of nodes
4: Sort the savings list in descending order
5: while the savings list is not exhausted do
6:     Select pair of nodes (i, j)|i ∈ v_i, j ∈ v_j with highest savings s''_ij
7:     if two distinct routes v_i and v_j are possible to merge then
8:         Merge two routes v_i and v_j to a single route v_m
9:         Remove pair (i, j) from the savings list
10:    end if
11: end while
12: Return: Merged routes
```

Algorithm 2 presents the Clarke and Wright savings heuristic with the $ROS - \gamma$ approach. First, the algorithm creates individual routes for each node (e-bins and households) (Line 2). Then, it calculates the savings for each pair of nodes using the $ROS - \gamma$ approach and sorts the savings list in the descending order (Lines 3–4). Starting with the top of the sorted savings list, the algorithm examines the savings s''_{ij} for two distinct routes, v_i and v_j. If it is possible to merge these two routes (i.e., i and j are endpoints of their respective subtours, and the merged subtour containing both i and j has a total demand not greater than the capacity of the largest vehicle), the algorithm combines both by removing the arcs $(i, 0)$ and $(j, 0)$ and adding a new arc (i, j). The merging process continues until no further pairs of routes is feasible to merge, and the merged routes are returned at the end of the algorithm (Lines 5–12).

Repair Procedure. The initial solution generated by ROS-γ satisfies the vehicle capacity constraint but it does not take the collection period into account. To address this issue, Algorithm 3 proposes a repair procedure. It is initiated with an initial solution, denoted as S. To ensure that all routes in S comply with the collection period constraint, the algorithm checks the routes violating the collection day and stores them in the infeasible routes set, denoted as Ω (Line 2). To identify the violated nodes in each infeasible route, we select a collection day for this route and then remove the nodes which are not available in the selected collection day. This step is done by the following procedures. The algorithm chooses the day with the highest customer availability as collection day k_ω of an infeasible route ω. If there are more than one day with same number of highest customer availability, we choose collection day k_ω randomly from these days K_ω (Lines 3 - 12).

The repair procedure then examines each node j in the infeasible route ω to determine its availability on day k_ω. Nodes that are unavailable on day k_ω are recorded in a set, denoted as $\pi_W \in \Pi$, where Π is the set that stores all nodes that violate the collection day of all infeasible routes. To repair the infeasible routes in S, the algorithm employs five repair operators (Lines 13–29). The repair operators have a primary focus on enhancing the solution feasibility while minimizing modifications to the initial solution's route structure. Additionally, these operators are designed to address varying levels of complexity in handling infeasible solutions. Ideally, the repair procedure aims to rectify an infeasible solution using a single swap operator, thus reducing the algorithm's time complexity. Below, we provide a breakdown of the five repair operators and their respective details:

- **R1**: This operator is implemented by swapping a violated node i from the set of violated nodes π_ω in route ω with another violated node j from the set of violated nodes π'_ω in another infeasible route $\omega' \in \Omega$. However, for this operator to be applied, it is necessary for the collection day k_ω of the infeasible route ω to be compatible with the available period H_j of node j. If the node j does not exist, meaning that R1 can only deal with several violated nodes, the operator will return *False*, and we need to employ additional repair operators to resolve the remaining violated nodes in ω (Line 15).
- **R2**: The R2 operator is implemented by selecting a violated node i from the set of violated nodes π_ω in an infeasible route ω and swapping it with another node $j \notin \pi'_\omega$ of another infeasible route ω'. Similar to R1, the R2 operator requires the available period H_j of node j to be compatible with the collection day k_ω of infeasible route ω. If the node j does not exist, the operator returns *False*, indicating that additional repair operators are required to address the remaining violated nodes (Line 17).
- **R3**: This operator operates on the same principles as R1 and R2, but instead of selecting a swap node j from an infeasible route ω', it selects j from a feasible route $v \notin \Omega$. Once j has been selected, R3 swaps the violated node $i \in \pi_\omega$ with j, provided that the available period H_j is compatible with the collection day k_ω of route ω. If there is no node j in any feasible route v available on k_ω, the operator returns *False*, indicating that additional repair operators are required to address the remaining violated nodes (Line 19).
- **R4**: The R4 operator inserts the violated node $i \in \pi_\omega$ into a feasible route $v \notin \Omega$, provided that there is at least one day where the available day of node i, H_i, matches the collection period K_v of feasible route v. If there is no feasible route v with a suitable collection period to insert the violated node i, the operator returns *False* (Line 21).
- **R5**: The R5 operator repairs the current infeasible solution by creating a new single trip with the violated node $i \in \pi_\omega$ and then deleting i from the current infeasible route ω (Line 23).

The initial solution then satisfies both capacity and collection period constraints. To diversify the initial solution, we randomly select a collection day in feasible collection day for each route. Moreover, to determine the departure time

d_v of the vehicle at each route v, we use the equation $d_v = \max(D_1^v, \ldots, D_{|D|}^v)$. Here, $D_i^v = \max(l_i - a_i, 0)$ is the idle time if the vehicle arrival time a_i is earlier than the lower bound l_i of the collection time window at node i. To determine the cost and revenue of a solution, we first assign vehicles in the fleet to their respective routes. The assignment process follows this principle: if the total demand of the considered route is less than the capacity of a small vehicle, we assign a small vehicle to that route. On the other hand, if the demand exceeds the capacity of a small vehicle or if no small vehicles are available in the fleet, we assign a large vehicle to the route.

Algorithm 3. Repair procedure

```
Input: An initial solution S
Ω ← infeasible routes in S;
for each route ω in Ω do
    K_ω ← period with highest number of available nodes;
    Select a random day k_ω ∈ K_ω as the collection period for infeasible route ω;
    for each node j in w do
        H_j ← available period of node j;
        if k_ω not in H_j then
            set of nodes violating period constraint in route ω, π_ω ← j;
        end if
    end for
end for
while Ω ≠ ∅ do
    while π_w ≠ ∅ do
        ω ← R1(ω)
        if R1(ω) returned False then
            ω ← R2(ω)
            if R2(ω) returned False then
                ω ← R3(ω)
                if R3(ω) returned False then
                    ω ← R4(ω)
                    if R4(ω) returned False then
                        ω ← R5(ω)
                    end if
                end if
            end if
        end if
    end while
end while
Return: S;
```

Local Search. Once the initial solution has been obtained, the following local search operators are applied to intensify the search for the optimal solution:

- **N1 - Intra-relocation:** The N1 operator explores the neighborhood solution by removing customer i from route v_i and then reinserting i at another position in the same route v_i.
- **N2 - Inter-relocation:** The N2 operator removes customer i from its current route v_i and reinserts i to a new route v_j provided that there is at least one day in the available period of i that coincides with the collection day of v_j. Additionally, the total capacity of v_j after the reinsertion must not exceed the capacity of the largest vehicle used.

- **N3 - Intra-swap:** The N3 operator selects node i in route v_i and swaps it with another node j in the same route.
- **N4 - Inter-swap:** The N4 operator selects node i from route v_i and another node j from a different route v_j. The selected nodes are swapped provided that their available periods are compatible with their target routes' v_i and v_j collection day. Furthermore, the total demand of the two routes v_i and v_j after swapping must not exceed the maximum capacity of the largest vehicle in the fleet.
- **N5- 2-opt (intra-route):** The N5 operator creates a new solution from an initial solution S by removing two consecutive arcs $E(i, i+1)$ and $E(j, j+1)$ from route v_i. Then, two other arcs $E(i, j)$ and $E(i+1, j+1)$ are added to reconnect the selected routes. Additionally, the subpath excluding the depot between nodes $i+1$ and j is inverted.
- **N6 - 2-opt* (inter-route):** The principle of generating a new solution using the N6 operator is similar to that of the N5 operator. However, the N6 operator selects and removes two arcs $E(i, i+1)$ and $E(j, j+1)$ from two distinct routes v_i and v_j, respectively. Two new arcs are then added to reconnect the selected routes, and both the inverted and non-inverted subpath versions of the new routes are considered. The N6 operator selects the higher-profit neighborhood between the two versions of new solutions. The condition of this operator is that two selected routes v_i and v_j have the same collection day and the two new routes after reconnecting have to satisfy the capacity constraint.
- **N7 - or-opt (inter-route):** The solution in the or-opt neighborhood is defined by relocating a subpath $(i+1, \ldots, j)$ from route v_i to another route v_j. The conditions for applying the N7 operator are the same as those for the N6 operator, which require that two selected routes v_i and v_j have the same collection day and the total demand of the route v_j after inserting the subpath is less than the capacity of the largest vehicle in the fleet.
- **N8 - 3-opt (intra-route):** The N8 operator deletes three arcs $E(i, i+1)$, $E(j, j+1)$, and $E(l, l+1)$ in a route v_i. It then considers all ways to reconnect these subpaths, including both inverted and non-inverted versions. In total, eight neighborhoods are explored, and the operator selects the one with the highest profit.
- **N9 - new route:** The N9 operator randomly selects a node i from route v_i and removes it. Then, it creates a new single tour v_i' from node i. The collection day k_v for tour v_i' is selected by comparing the profits of solution if route v_i' carries out in different days within the collection period K_v. Then the solution with highest profit is selected.
- **N10 - split to single:** The N10 operator deletes two randomly selected nodes i and j from two distinct routes v_i and v_j, respectively. It then creates a new tour by connecting the two nodes. There are two neighborhood created by N10 and the one with higher profit is created. The condition for this move is that the two selected nodes i and j must have at least one available day in common.

- **N11 - combine tours:** The N11 operator selects two random tours v_i and v_j that have a combined total capacity that is less than the maximum capacity of the largest vehicle in the fleet. It then combines these tours to create a new tour. Two neighborhoods are created by the N11 operator, and the one with the higher profit is selected.

All local search operators are applied in the first-improving strategy, as shown in Algorithm 4.

Algorithm 4. First-improving local search procedure

```
Input: A feasible solution, S
improvement ← TRUE
while improvement = TRUE do
    improvement ← FALSE
    for S' ∈ N(S) do
        if f(S') > f(S) then
            S ← S'
            improvement ← TRUE
        end if
    end for
end while
Return: S
```

Algorithm 5. Path-relinking

```
Input: S_i, S_g
S ← S_i;
f(S*) ← max{f(S_i), f(S_g)};
S* ← arg max{f(S_i), f(S_g)};
Symmetric difference, Δ(S, S_g) ← i : S[i] ≠ S_g[i];
while Δ(S, S_g) ≠ ∅ do
    An index t ∈ Δ(S, S_g) where S[t] ≠ S_g[t];
    Select a node i = S[t] and j = S[S_g[t]];
    S' ←Swap two selected nodes, swap(S_i, i, j);
    if valid(S') = True then
        if f(S') > f(S*) then
            S* ← S';
            f(S*) ← f(S');
        end if
    end if
end while
Return: S*, f(S*);
```

Path-Relinking (PR). PR is an intensification search strategy [5] to create a series of restricted neighborhood solutions by exploring the trajectory that connects two elite solutions from the solution pool. In our study, PR is employed to find the solution that can effectively deal with the penalty and idle time caused by the time windows soft constraint, as shown in Algorithm 5. Firstly, the PR procedure takes two solutions S_i and S_g and sets the solution with higher profit as the current best solution S^* (Lines 3–4). Then, Line 5 computes the symmetric difference Δ between two solutions S and S_g, which stores the index where nodes in S differ from S_g. The procedure performs the swap operator to relink the solution S to S_g (Lines 6–9). An example for a solution with eight nodes is illustrated in Fig. 2. If the explored solution S' in the relinking process has a higher profit than the current best solution S^*, it becomes the best solution in the following relinking path. There is a validity step in this procedure to avoid partial solutions created in the relinking process (Line 10). The procedure terminates when S reaches S_g (i.e., $\Delta(S, S_g) = \emptyset$), and it returns the best solution in the relinking process S^*.

Input:

Initial solution	S^I	[0, 3, 5, 6, 0], [0, 1, 7, 4, 0], [0, 8, 2, 0]
Guiding solution	S^g	[0, 1, 3, 7, 0], [0, 6, 2, 0], [0, 5, 8, 4, 0]

Path-relinking:

Initial solution	S^I	[0, 3, 5, 6, 0], [0, 1, 7, 4, 0], [0, 8, 2, 0]	$\Delta(S^I,S^g) = 8$	Swap (3, 1)
Intermediate solution 1	S^1	[0, 1, 5, 6, 0], [0, 3, 7, 4, 0], [0, 8, 2, 0]	$\Delta(S^1,S^g) = 7$	Swap (5, 3)
Intermediate solution 2	S^2	[0, 1, 3, 6, 0], [0, 5, 7, 4, 0], [0, 8, 2, 0]	$\Delta(S^2,S^g) = 6$	Swap (6, 7)
Intermediate solution 3	S^3	[0, 1, 3, 7, 0], [0, 5, 6, 4, 0], [0, 8, 2, 0]	$\Delta(S^3,S^g) = 5$	Swap (5, 6)
Intermediate solution 4	S^4	[0, 1, 3, 7, 0], [0, 6, 5, 4, 0], [0, 8, 2, 0]	$\Delta(S^4,S^g) = 4$	Swap (5, 2)
Intermediate solution 5	S^5	[0, 1, 3, 7, 0], [0, 6, 2, 4, 0], [0, 8, 5, 0]	$\Delta(S^5,S^g) = 3$	Swap (4, 0)
Reject partial solution 6	S^6	[0, 1, 3, 7, 0], [0, 6, 2, 0, 4], [0, 8, 5, 0]	$\Delta(S^6,S^g) = 2$	Swap (4, 0)
Intermediate solution 7	S^7	[0, 1, 3, 7, 0], [0, 6, 2, 0], [0, 4, 8, 5, 0]	$\Delta(S^7,S^g) = 1$	Swap (4, 5)
Guiding solution	S^g	[0, 1, 3, 7, 0], [0, 6, 2, 0], [0, 5, 8, 4, 0]	$\Delta(S^7,S^g) = 0$	S^g is reached

Fig. 2. The path-relinking process for solutions with eight nodes

Integration of PR in GRASP. Algorithm 6 presents the main procedure of GRASP complemented by PR. The original GRASP comprises two phases, executed from Lines 4 to 12. In each iteration, GRASP starts by creating an initial solution using the construction heuristic, followed by applying the repair operator to ensure feasibility with the available period constraint (Lines 5–6). Next, the collection day k of each tour in the initial solution S is randomly selected within the available period of that tour K (Line 8). Eleven local search operators are then applied to improve the quality of the initial solution S (Lines 10–12). If the local optimal solution S satisfies the condition $f(S) > (1-\mu)f(S^*)$, where μ is the diversification coefficient and S has not already been added to pool P, it is added to P (Line 13). If the pool is full, S replaces the oldest elite solution in the pool. If there is at least one elite solution in P, the algorithm stores the elite solution $p \in P$ having the same number of routes with current solution S to a set P'. After that, a random elite solution $S' \in P'$ is selected, and forward and backward PR are performed between the current solution S and elite solution S' (Lines 21–22). The better solution achieved from forward and backward PR becomes the current solution S, and if it is not in P, it is added to the pool (Lines 23–30). Next, the current solution S is compared with the best solution S^*. If S is better than S^*, it becomes the best solution S^* for the following iteration (Lines 32–34). After i_{max} iterations, the algorithm returns the best found solution S^* (Line 37).

Algorithm 6. GRASP reinforced by path-relinking

```
1: Input: Set of nodes, 𝒩
2: Number of iteration, i_max
3: Initial best profit f(S*) ← −∞
4: for i = 1 to i_max do
5:     S ← ConstructionHeuristic(𝒩)
6:     S ←RepairProcedure(S)
7:     for each route s in S do
8:         Randomly select a collection day k in available period K
9:     end for
10:    for each operator N ∈ {N6, N7, N8, N5, N1, N2, N4, N9, N10, N11, N3} do
11:        S ← N(S)
12:    end for
13:    if f(S) > (1 − μ)f(S*) then
14:        if S ∉ P then
15:            Add S to P
16:        end if
17:    end if
18:    if |P| > 0 then
19:        Set of elite solution which have the same number of routes with S, P'
20:        Randomly select an elite solution S' ∈ P'
21:        S^f ← PathRelinking(S, S')
22:        S^b ← PathRelinking(S', S)
23:        if f(S^f) > f(S^b) then
24:            S ← S^f
25:        else
26:            S ← S^b
27:        end if
28:        if S ∉ P then
29:            Add S to P
30:        end if
31:    end if
32:    if f(S) > f(S*) then
33:        f(S*) ← f(S)
34:        S* ← S
35:    end if
36: end for
37: Return: S*
```

3 Computational Results

We proposed a new set of instances based on the well-known Gehring & Homberger instances [7], by adding various attributes, as summarized in Table 1. N_1 and N_2 denote the number of households and e-bins, while V_1 and V_2 represent the numbers of vehicle types I and II, respectively. For vehicle type I, the instance specifications include a capacity of 500, an operating cost of 2, a penalty cost of 7, and an idle cost of 3. On the other hand, for vehicle type II, the corresponding values are 100, 1, 2, and 5, respectively. It is important to note that all instances consider a 4-day delivery period. Instances in Group C feature clustered customers, whereas instances in group R have customer locations generated randomly over a square.

Table 1. Summary of benchmark instances

No	Name	N_1	N_2	V_1	V_2	No	Name	N_1	N_2	V_1	V_2
1	C1_6_1_01	4	4	4	4	19	R1_6_1_01	15	15	8	8
2	C1_6_1_02	4	8	6	6	20	R1_6_1_02	20	20	10	10
3	C1_6_1_03	4	12	8	8	21	R1_6_1_03	25	25	13	13
4	C1_6_1_04	8	4	3	3	22	R1_6_1_04	30	30	15	15
5	C1_6_1_05	12	4	4	4	23	R1_6_1_05	35	35	18	18
6	C1_6_1_06	6	6	3	3	24	R1_6_1_06	40	40	20	20
7	C1_6_1_07	8	8	4	4	25	R1_6_1_07	45	45	23	23
8	C1_6_1_08	10	10	5	5	26	R1_6_1_08	50	50	25	25
9	C1_6_1_09	12	12	6	6	27	R1_6_1_09	55	55	28	28
10	C2_6_1_01	4	4	2	2	28	R2_6_1_01	15	15	8	8
11	C2_6_1_02	4	8	3	3	29	R2_6_1_02	20	20	10	10
12	C2_6_1_03	4	12	4	4	30	R2_6_1_03	25	25	13	13
13	C2_6_1_04	8	4	3	3	31	R2_6_1_04	30	30	15	15
14	C2_6_1_05	12	4	4	4	32	R2_6_1_05	35	35	18	18
15	C2_6_1_06	6	6	3	3	33	R2_6_1_06	40	40	20	20
16	C2_6_1_07	8	8	4	4	34	R2_6_1_07	45	45	23	23
17	C2_6_1_08	10	10	5	5	35	R2_6_1_08	50	50	25	25
18	C2_6_1_09	12	12	6	6	36	R2_6_1_09	55	55	28	28

The exact solutions are obtained by IBM ILOG CPLEX Optimization Studio - Academic version 12.10.0.0 using branch and bound methods on a personal computer with Intel Core i7-12700 2.10 GHz, 16 GB RAM, 1000 GB HDD + 500 GB SSD, Windows 10 Education version 22H2 64-bit. The time limits are set to 4 h per instance with the mathematical model adopted from [7]. Following a series of tuning experiments, we have determined the maximum number of iterations to $i_{max} = 5000$. For the PR procedure, we set a pool size of $\lambda = 20$ and a diversification coefficient of $\mu = 0.007$. The GRASP-PR algorithm was implemented by using Python 3.11.

Table 2 provides the results obtained by both GRASP-PR and CPLEX in terms of solution quality and computational time. The bold numbers are optimal solutions obtained by CPLEX, only 4 out of 36 instances. The remaining ones are the best found so far or unsolved. Even for small instances like C1_6_1_01 and C2_6_1_01, CPLEX requires 1200 and 2160 s seconds, respectively, to obtain results. On the other hand, GRASP-PR can generate solutions within significantly shorter computational times. For example, GRASP-PR can achieve an optimal solution for instance C1_6_1_01 in 0.54 s. The maximum computa-

Table 2. Comparison performance between MILP and GRASP-PR

No	Instance	CPLEX		GRASP-PR			No	Instance	CPLEX		GRASP-PR		
		Obj	CPU(s)	Best	Avg. 10	CPU (s)			Obj	CPU(s)	Best	Avg. 10	CPU (s)
1	C1_6_1_01	**377**	1200	377	377	0.54	19	R1_6_1_01	–	14400	867	323.3	185.36
2	C1_6_1_02	**−222**	14400	−222	−222	51.17	20	R1_6_1_02	–	14400	546	244.2	290.29
3	C1_6_1_03	−1059	14400	−749	−823.7	83.3	21	R1_6_1_03	–	14400	284	−278.1	388.25
4	C1_6_1_04	1161	14400	1191	1190.5	47.97	22	R1_6_1_04	–	14400	−796	−1201	442.99
5	C1_6_1_05	1997	14400	1884	1815.7	77.84	23	R1_6_1_05	–	14400	−619	−1464.9	578.9
6	C1_6_1_06	−77	14400	−77	−102.7	52.17	24	R1_6_1_06	–	14400	−1386	−2171	721.2
7	C1_6_1_07	730	14400	799	629.1	79.53	25	R1_6_1_07	–	14400	−1676	−3391.6	761.32
8	C1_6_1_08	572	14400	614	528	115.76	26	R1_6_1_08	–	14400	−3420	−5128.4	877.44
9	C1_6_1_09	–	14400	1963	1790.4	147.68	27	R1_6_1_09	–	14400	−3994	−6677.4	982.15
10	C2_6_1_01	**−306**	2160	−306	−306	29.64	28	R2_6_1_01	−1574	14400	−380	−901.4	184.09
11	C2_6_1_02	**−595**	14400	−595	−595	40.25	29	R2_6_1_02	–	14400	−1597	−2768.8	254.2
12	C2_6_1_03	−931	14400	−939	−1020.5	68.36	30	R2_6_1_03	–	14400	−3278	−5106	308.97
13	C2_6_1_04	639	14400	670	646.9	59	31	R2_6_1_04	–	14400	−9532	−13630.8	308.81
14	C2_6_1_05	852	14400	861	415.6	103.51	32	R2_6_1_05	–	14400	−6070	−11593.8	429.289
15	C2_6_1_06	346	14400	246	181.5	41.52	33	R2_6_1_06	–	14400	−15829	−20584.9	496.659
16	C2_6_1_07	494	14400	428	281.3	97.14	34	R2_6_1_07	–	14400	−23385	−37733.6	563.798
17	C2_6_1_08	320	14400	60	−163.4	111.4	35	R2_6_1_08	–	14400	−19285	−30553.5	730.22
18	C2_6_1_09	–	14400	371	93.9	146.04	36	R2_6_1_09	–	14400	−29888	−50331.5	819.195

tional time required by GRASP-PR for all instances is 982.15 s, with an average running time of 296.55 s per instance.

In terms of solution quality, unlike CPLEX, GRASP-PR can successfully solve all test instances and reach optimal solutions for instances solved by CPLEX optimally. Moreover, for the remaining instances where CPLEX fails to achieve optimality, the best found solution by GRASP-PR in 10 runs outperforms CPLEX in 7 out of 13 instances. For instance C1_6_1_03, the solution found by GRASP-PR can improve the profit in CPLEX's solution by 29.27%, while for a larger instance R2_6_1_01 with 30 customers, the improvement is as high as 75.85%. However, GRASP-PR shows limitations in its ability to scale up to larger problem instances. The solutions obtained by GRASP-PR for the same instances in different runs become inconsistent when the size of the problem increases. Specifically, for the two largest instances in our test set, R2_6_1_08 and R2_6_1_09, with 100 and 110 customers, respectively, the average objective value of ten runs is almost 1.5 times worse than the objective value of the best-found solution.

We also compare the 2-opt and 3-opt local search operators in terms of solution quality. We created two alternative scenarios: (i) the GRASP-PR metaheuristic without the 2-opt operator, and (ii) the GRASP-PR metaheuristic without the 3-opt operator. Results are summarized in Table 3, together with those of the original algorithm in terms of solution quality and computational times.

We observe that both scenarios produce worse solutions than those of the original GRASP-PR metaheuristic. This outcome is expected since the HVRP-MTW represents a tightly constrained problem, and reducing the local search operator leads to a decrease in the search space, thereby making it more chal-

Table 3. Comparing the impact of 2-opt and 3-opt on algorithm performance

No	Instance	GRASP-PR			i			ii		
		Best	Avg. 10	CPU (s)	Best	Avg. 10	CPU (s)	Best	Avg. 10	CPU (s)
1	C1_6_1_01	377	377	0.54	377	373.3	0.54	377	377	0.49
2	C1_6_1_02	-222	-222	51.17	-222	-228.4	51.65	-222	-222	48.35
3	C1_6_1_03	-749	-823.7	83.30	-1045	-1086.9	83.40	-1052	-1101.2	74.60
4	C1_6_1_04	1191	1190.5	47.97	1191	1187.9	49.41	1191	1187.8	42.77
5	C1_6_1_05	1884	1815.7	77.84	1850	1786.6	73.53	1884	1776.9	60.26
6	C1_6_1_06	-77	-102.7	52.17	-77	-104.1	49.84	-77	-99.8	45.63
7	C1_6_1_07	799	629.1	79.53	799	669.3	80.41	751	648.5	67.08
8	C1_6_1_08	614	528	115.77	596	507.5	118.63	592	513.6	101.48
9	C1_6_1_09	1963	1790.4	147.68	1932	1732.9	141.90	1863	1690.2	125.71
10	C2_6_1_01	-306	-306	29.64	-306	-306	30.71	-306	-306	25.65
11	C2_6_1_02	-595	-595	40.25	-595	-595	42.10	-595	-595	32.43
12	C2_6_1_03	-939	-1020.5	68.36	-957	-1034.5	65.50	-1019	-1083.1	55.09
13	C2_6_1_04	670	646.9	59.00	669	630.9	59.26	670	592.6	54.39
14	C2_6_1_05	861	415.6	103.51	516	367.4	104.50	595	377.5	86.38
15	C2_6_1_06	246	181.5	41.52	189	161.9	41.05	258	152.8	35.58
16	C2_6_1_07	428	281.3	97.14	303	229.7	93.32	363	286.8	82.50
17	C2_6_1_08	60	-163.4	111.40	5	-190.8	105.90	-24	-269.9	91.48
18	C2_6_1_09	371	93.9	146.04	328	44.6	141.26	196	22.2	119.51

lenging to achieve better solutions. Comparing both scenarios, alternative (i) exhibited better performance in most instances, confirming that the 3-opt operator outperforms the 2-opt operator in terms of solution quality. The reason for this disparity lies in the fact that the 3-opt operator enables the algorithm to explore much larger neighborhoods compared to the 2-opt operator. The better solution quality by the original algorithm, in comparison to the two scenarios, suggests that the 2-opt and 3-opt operators lead to different local optima. Consequently, combining both the 2-opt and 3-opt operators can enhance the algorithm's performance.

Regarding the computational time, the reduction in the 2-opt operator had a negligible impact, approximately 1%. Conversely, the GRASP-PR without the 3-opt operator exhibited an average acceleration of approximately 15%. This discrepancy can be attributed to the time complexity of the 3-opt operator being $O(n^3)$, whereas the 2-opt operator has a time complexity of $O(n^2)$.

4 Conclusions

In this study, we propose a GRASP with Path-Relinking to address the e-waste collection route planning problem modelled as Heterogeneous Vehicle Routing Problem with Multiple Time Windows (HVRP-MTW). To evaluate the proposed algorithm, named GRASP-PR, we conducted comparative experiments against a commercial solver. The results show that GRASP-PR can effectively handle HVRP-MTW instances with up to 110 customers within reasonable computational times. The comparison revealed that GRASP-PR outperforms the commercial solver in large-scale instances and can generate optimal solutions for small instances. However, the metaheuristic approach of GRASP-PR has its limitation in convergence when the problem size increases. For future research, the integration of advanced extensions with a learning process such as fixed set search [8,9] is considered to enhance the convergence and performance of the current metaheuristic.

Acknowledgement. This research was supported by the Singapore Ministry of Education (MOE) Academic Research Fund (AcRF) Tier 1 grant.

References

1. Baldé, C., D'Angelo, E., Deubzer, V.L.O., Kuehr, R.: Global transboundary e-waste flows monitor - 2022, United Nations Institute for Training and Research (UNITAR), December 2022. https://ewastemonitor.info/gtf-2022/. Accessed 26 June 2023
2. Braekers, K., Ramaekers, K., Van Nieuwenhuyse, I.: The vehicle routing problem: state of the art classification and review. Comput. Ind. Eng. **99**, 300–313 (2016)
3. Clarke, G., Wright, J.W.: Scheduling of vehicles from a central depot to a number of delivery points. Oper. Res. **12**(4), 568–581 (1964)
4. Feo, T.A., Resende, M.G.: A probabilistic heuristic for a computationally difficult set covering problem. Oper. Res. Lett. **8**(2), 67–71 (1989)
5. Glover, F.: Tabu search and adaptive memory programming-advances, applications and challenges. In: Barr, R.S., Helgason, R.V., Kennington, J.L. (eds.) Interfaces in Computer Science and Operations Research. Operations Research/Computer Science Interfaces Series, vol. 7, pp. 1–75. Springer, Boston, MA (1997). https://doi.org/10.1007/978-1-4615-4102-8_1
6. Golden, B., Assad, A., Levy, L., Gheysens, F.: The fleet size and mix vehicle routing problem. Comput. Oper. Res. **11**(1), 49–66 (1984)
7. Gunawan, A., Nguyen, M.P.K., F. Yu, V., Nguyen, D.V.A.: The heterogeneous vehicle routing problem with multiple time windows for the e-waste collection problem. In: submitted to IEEE CASE 2023 (accepted) (2023)
8. Jovanovic, R., Sanfilippo, A.P., Voß, S.: Fixed set search applied to the clique partitioning problem. Eur. J. Oper. Res. **309**(1), 65–81 (2023)
9. Jovanovic, R., Tuba, M., Voß, S.: Fixed set search applied to the traveling salesman problem. In: Blesa Aguilera, M.J., Blum, C., Gambini Santos, H., Pinacho-Davidson, P., Godoy del Campo, J. (eds.) HM 2019. LNCS, vol. 11299, pp. 63–77. Springer, Cham (2019). https://doi.org/10.1007/978-3-030-05983-5_5
10. Król, A., Nowakowski, P., Mrówczyńska, B.: How to improve WEEE management? Novel approach in mobile collection with application of artificial intelligence. Waste Manag. **50**, 222–233 (2016)
11. Mar-Ortiz, J., González-Velarde, J.L., Adenso-Díaz, B.: Designing routes for WEEE collection: the vehicle routing problem with split loads and date windows. J. Heuristics **19**, 103–127 (2013)

12. Pourhejazy, P., Zhang, D., Zhu, Q., Wei, F., Song, S.: Integrated e-waste transportation using capacitated general routing problem with time-window. Transp. Res. Part E Logist. Transp. Rev. **145**, 102169 (2021)
13. Yao, L., He, W., Li, G., Huang, J.: The integrated design and optimization of a WEEE collection network in Shanghai, China. Waste Manag. Res. **31**(9), 910–919 (2013)

The Heterogeneous Fleet Risk-Constrained Vehicle Routing Problem in Humanitarian Logistics

Robert M van Steenbergen(✉), Eduardo Lalla-Ruiz, Wouter van Heeswijk, and Martijn Mes

Department of High-Tech Business and Entrepreneurship, University of Twente, Enschede, The Netherlands
r.m.vansteenbergen@utwente.nl

Abstract. While distributing essential supplies in volatile environments, humanitarian transport is often exposed to threats such as attacks. To mitigate the negative consequences of attacks, we introduce the heterogeneous fleet risk-constrained vehicle routing problem (HFRCVRP), in which we aim to minimize transportation costs and the expected loss of getting robbed. An Adaptive Large Neighborhood Search (ALNS) heuristic is presented to solve the problem. The trade-off between transportation costs and expected loss of attacks is analyzed with a real-world case in South Sudan. Results show that the trade-off is especially relevant in the heterogeneous variant, in which Unmanned Aerial Vehicles (UAVs) can effectively mitigate risks of truck transport, providing a 7.1% improvement of the objective value compared to the same instance with only trucks. Risks can be completely eliminated by increasing transportation costs by a factor of five. Additionally, the risk variant decreases the objective value by 14.8% compared to considering only transportation costs and ignoring risks.

Keywords: Risk-constrained Routing · Humanitarian Logistics · UAVs · Heterogeneous Fleet · Metaheuristic

1 Introduction

During crises and disasters, humanitarian assistance is essential for alleviating the suffering of those in need. This involves transporting goods such as food, medicine, and in increasing numbers cash-based interventions [9]. However, these movements are not without risks. People may resort to violent behavior in desperate times with a lack of resources such as food, water, or medication. For instance, one week after the 2023 Turkey-Syria earthquake, multiple incidents of violence and armed looting were reported. Furthermore, in conflict zones, rebellious groups can also be interested in relief goods. Facing the attacks in multiple cities in Sudan in the spring of 2023, with explosions, gunfire, and looting in the streets, the World Food Programme had to suspend one of its largest food distribution missions. Moreover, during the civil war in South Sudan (2013–2020),

© The Author(s), under exclusive license to Springer Nature Switzerland AG 2023
J. R. Daduna et al. (Eds.): ICCL 2023, LNCS 14239, pp. 276–291, 2023.
https://doi.org/10.1007/978-3-031-43612-3_17

combined with hunger and malnutrition in the country, dozens of incidents were reported each month, including murders of aid workers. To avoid risks on the roads, costly airlifts by helicopters and aircraft are often performed, which are mainly suitable for large shipments. Unmanned Aerial Vehicles (UAVs) can provide a flexible and efficient alternative for smaller-scale distributions of aid organizations. Humanitarian cargo UAVs are not necessarily bound to fly between airports, have the ability to deliver supplies to numerous locations spread over an area, and can visit hard-to-reach places quickly [17].

Literature offers various secure routing approaches for high-value goods, often referred to as cash-in-transit (CIT) problems. The transportation of valuable relief goods in disaster areas can face comparable risks as cash transport. In most CIT problems, the risk of vehicle attacks is mitigated by diversifying routing plans through time inconsistency or path inconsistency [7]. However, randomization of routing plans is less suitable for humanitarian operations, as these often deal with urgent, variable or one-off demands, sparse road networks, and opponents that tend to operate opportunistically. An alternative approach is the risk-constrained vehicle routing problem (RCVRP) introduced by Talarico et al. [22], which limits the risk exposure in routes. Despite these approaches in CIT literature, security issues are seldom considered in humanitarian research, yet being a top concern for humanitarian organizations [3].

This paper investigates the problem of transporting high-value goods with a heterogeneous fleet (i.e., trucks and UAVs) in high-risk disaster environments. The following contributions are made in this paper. (i) We formulate the heterogeneous fleet risk-constrained vehicle routing problem (HFRCVRP) including indirect losses of an attack. (ii) We propose an adaptive large neighborhood search (ALNS) algorithm with specific operators to solve the HFRCVRP in a reasonable time, as the HFRCVRP may need to be solved daily or suddenly after a disaster. (iii) The methods are tested and results are analyzed using real-world data from South Sudan.

The remainder of this paper is organized as follows. Related literature on the HFRCVRP is reviewed in Sect. 2. In Sect. 3, we describe the problem and formulate the model. Section 4 introduces our ALNS heuristic. Section 5 describes the real-world case study of South Sudan, the experimental design, and the results. Finally, the conclusions and future research directions are stated in Sect. 6.

2 Related Work

In this section, we first describe the risk-constrained vehicle routing problem (RCVRP) and then review literature on variants of the RCVRP that are proposed in recent years. Talarico et al. [22] formally introduce the RCVRP. The expected loss along edge (i, j) is the product of the probability of being robbed p_{ij} (i.e., risk probability) and the loss D_i of valuables transported from node i. In the case of collecting cash, D_i will increase every stop, in the case of deliveries, D_i will decrease at a stop. As the probability of being robbed along an edge is low, Talarico et al. [22] simplify the expected loss associated with route r by taking the sum of expected losses of robbery on each arc (i, j):

$$\sum_{(i,j)\in r} p_{ij} \cdot D_i^r \tag{1}$$

The authors assume the probability of an attack (p_{ij}) is proportional to the length of the edge traversed. They aim to minimize the total length of the routes while constraining the expected loss in each route. As the RCVRP is more complex than the traditional VRP, which is already known to be NP-hard, the authors propose four construction heuristics in a greedy randomized adaptive search procedure (GRASP) and an iterative local search (ILS) to solve the problem in reasonable time. Talarico et al. [24] develop a combination in which ant colony optimization is used for generating an initial solution that is later improved by a large neighborhood search. Moreover, for the same problem, a fuzzy GRASP with path relinking is presented by Radojičić et al. [16]. Their method proves to be more effective and further improves the results of solving the RCVRP regarding solution objectives and computation times.

In recent years, several variants of the RCVRP have been proposed. The multi-objective variant of the RCVRP is proposed by Talarico et al. [23] and evaluated on real-world instances with capacity constraints. They minimize (i) the transportation costs and (ii) the maximum risk in a trip, instead of including risk as a routing constraint. A weighted sum of the objective is proposed to adjust the two terms according to the decision-maker's preference. A progressive multi-objective optimization with ILS is suggested to solve the problem. Ghannadpour & Zandiyeh [8] build upon the multi-objective variant and define a zero-sum game with two players (the vehicle and the robber) to periodically update the risk probabilities p_{ij}. For generating route plans each period and minimizing travel distance and risk, a multi-objective hybrid genetic algorithm is developed and its efficiency and effectiveness are examined through several instances. Soeanu et al. [21] introduce a multi-depot variant to minimize routing costs, vehicle breakdowns (i.e., risk based on vehicle value), and delivery failure costs (i.e., risk based on transported goods). A learning-based heuristic technique is proposed, combining a guided stochastic cost-insertion gradient descent technique with iterative solution improvement, and evaluated in a comparative study. Mazdarani et al. [15] analyze a multi-objective RCVRP problem with overlapping links (i.e., arcs) to minimize total costs and expected loss. The authors consider an increased risk when routes overlap and develop a hybrid genetic algorithm to solve the problem. Tikani et al. [25] extend the RCVRP with time-dependent travel times, where increasing travel times (e.g., due to traffic jams) increase the exposure to danger. A hybrid method based on dynamic programming and genetic algorithms is proposed and the results of this heuristic approximate the values of optimal solutions. Allahyari et al. [2] combine the time-dependent travel times and multi-objective RCVRP with pickup and delivery operations and time windows. An efficient approach combining GRASP and ILS, including a robust objective, is developed to minimize travel costs and a specific risk index. In this index, they are not only considering the probability and loss of a robbery (risk exposure) but also minimizing the use of overlapping arcs and the spread arrival times (i.e., route predictability). Allahyari et al. [1] apply the same risk index in a secure pickup and delivery problem with time windows and include facility location decisions as well. To solve realistic instances, they propose an adaptive large neighborhood search (ALNS) algorithm, which outperforms an exact method considering a computational time limit, and minimizes the risk index, depot costs, vehicle costs, and travel costs. A two-echelon variant of the RCVRP is presented by Fallahtafti et al. [6], which includes facility location decisions for multiple depots. A multi-objective simulated annealing approach provides the most promising results in a computational study to minimize depot costs, transportation costs, and risk exposure. Kian et al. [11] consider an RCVRP for cash-based interventions in the Syrian refugee crisis. They extend the works on facility location decisions and multi-echelon problems by introducing temporary facilities and mobile depots. The goal is to maximize the number of reached beneficiaries within a limited time period while minimizing logistics costs. A hierarchical metaheuristic is developed to obtain efficient solutions. An overview of all the works and their characteristics is presented in Table 1.

Table 1. Overview of literature regarding the RCVRP. (MO = multi-objective, MD = multi-depot, ME = multi-echelon, LR = location-routing, TD = time-dependent risk, PD = pickup and delivery, TW = time windows, OL = overlapping links, MP = multi-period, HF = heterogeneous fleet)

Work	Problem feature										Solution approach	Instances
	MO	MD	ME	LR	TD	PD	TW	OL	MP	HF		
Talarico et al. (2015) [22]											GRASP/ILS	Stylized
Talarico et al. (2017a) [23]	✓										PMOO-ILS	Stylized
Talarico et al. (2017b) [24]											ACO/LNS	Stylized
Radojičić et al. (2018) [16]											Fuzzy GRASP	Stylized
Ghannadpour & Zandiyeh (2020) [8]	✓								✓		Hybrid GA	Case study
Soeanu et al. (2020) [21]	✓	✓									SGD-ILS	Stylized
Fallahtafti et al. (2021) [6]	✓	✓	✓	✓							Archived SA	Case study
Tikani et al. (2021) [25]					✓						Hybrid DP-GA	Case study
Allahyari et al. (2021a) [1]	✓			✓		✓	✓				ALNS	Case study
Allahyari et al. (2021b) [2]	✓				✓	✓	✓				GRASP × ILS	Stylized
Kian et al. (2022) [11]	✓	✓	✓	✓					✓		Hierarchical LS	Case study
Mazdarani et al. (2023) [15]	✓							✓			Hybrid GA	Case study
This paper	✓									✓	**ALNS**	**Case study**

The trend of the RCVRP has shifted towards multi-objective problems, which minimize (weighted) risks and transportation costs. This creates a trade-off between the two often conflicting objectives, which can be adapted to the decision maker's preferences. Variants such as multi-depot, multi-echelon, time windows, and location-routing problems have been proposed. The heterogeneous fleet variant, where certain vehicle types may be exposed to different risks, has not received much attention. A mixed fleet of vehicles could benefit from risk mitigation compared to single-vehicle solutions. The application of the RCVRP to a humanitarian setting is limited as of yet (only [11]), despite daily threats of violence and the increasing importance of cash-based assistance [10]. Indirect or unforeseeable losses from attacks, such as human injury, vehicle damage, and road damage, are often ignored in the literature. These losses are considered to not be under the control of the transportation company [6,22]. Nonetheless, they can significantly impact operations and could still be mitigated by adapting decisions (e.g., avoiding them by using UAVs). The risk of vehicle failure is considered by [21], showing similarities with indirect losses, as vehicle failure is also unrelated to the amount of cargo. We address this gap in literature by including indirect losses by estimating the value of the indirect costs of an attack. Furthermore, we formulate the heterogeneous fleet RCVRP, propose an adaptive large neighborhood search heuristic with specific operators to solve the problem, and analyze the problem in a humanitarian context in South Sudan.

3 Heterogeneous Fleet Risk-Constrained Vehicle Routing Problem

In this work, we address the heterogeneous fleet risk-constrained vehicle routing problem (HFRCVRP), a new variant of the RCVRP. Following the research trend in this area, we propose a bi-objective variant, in which the objective is to minimize both the expected loss (risk exposure) and the transportation costs. The HFRCVRP is defined on a directed graph $G = (V, A)$, where $V = \{0\} \cup N = \{0, 1, ..., n\}$ corresponds to the depot (vertex 0) and the customers $N = \{1, ..., n\}$. Each customer $i \in N$ has a demand d_i. The set of arcs is defined as $A = \{(i, j) \in V \times V, i \neq j\}$. The transportation costs c_{ijk} and probability of being robbed p_{ijk} are associated with each arc $(i, j) \in A$ and vehicle type $k \in K$. Each vehicle type $k \in K$ has an associated vehicle capacity Q_k and multiple routes r can be planned for each type $k \in K$. Determining the number of routes for each vehicle type is part of the optimization problem, and is at most equal to the number of customers n in a solution in which one vehicle type visits each customer in a separate route. Hence, we define route index r on customer set N. The decision variables are as follows:

- x_{ijkr}, is equal to 1 if arc $(i, j) \in A$ is traversed along route $r \in N$ of vehicle type $k \in K$ and 0 otherwise.
- D_{ijkr} is the loss in case a robbery happens on arc $(i, j) \in A$ along route $r \in N$ of vehicle type $k \in K$.

Besides the direct consequences of a robbery (i.e., the loss of valuable goods), indirect losses may also occur, such as required vehicle repairs due to damages, emotional/physical abuse of employees, or administrative work (e.g., insurance). We include these indirect losses that occur irrespective of the amount of lost valuables in D_{ijr}. The objective function of the HFRCVRP is to find routes that minimize the total transportation costs and the total expected loss:

$$\min \sum_{k \in K} \sum_{r \in N} \sum_{(i,j) \in A} (c_{ijk} x_{ijkr} + p_{ijk} D_{ijkr}) \tag{2}$$

In the HFRCVRP, the following constraints are considered:

- The demand of each customer has to be fully fulfilled.
- All vehicle routes start and end at the depot.
- The sum of deliveries between depot visits cannot exceed the vehicle capacity.
- The loss in case of a robbery is determined by the value of the goods on the vehicle and a fixed amount of indirect losses. The number of goods on a vehicle is determined by the sum of planned deliveries before returning to the depot.

The RCVRP is an extension of the traveling salesman problem, both known as NP-hard. Hence, the HFRCVRP as an extension of the RCVRP is also NP-hard and even more challenging to solve. In the next section, we propose a heuristic approach to solve realistic-sized instances quickly.

4 Adaptive Large Neighborhood Search for the HFRCVRP

In this section, we adapt the adaptive large neighborhood search (ALNS) meta-heuristic, introduced by Ropke and Pisinger [18], to solve the HFRCVRP. The ALNS framework can be modified to various problems and has been successfully applied to many different VRP variants in the past, including heterogeneous fleet VRPs (e.g., [14,26]), VRPs with drones (e.g., [13,19]), and the RCVRP [1]. ALNS progressively improves an initial solution by repeatedly destroying and repairing the current solution. According to their performance achieved during the search process, the destroy- and repair operators are randomly selected following an adaptive mechanism. A new solution is accepted according to a pre-determined criterion. We subsequently describe the construction of the initial solution, the destroy and repair operators, the adaptive selection of operators, and the acceptance and stopping criteria.

4.1 Initial Solution

We develop a modified cheapest insertion heuristic with randomized selection. We define a route as a sequence of nodes, starting and ending at the depot (e.g., route $(0, 5, 3, 0)$). The construction heuristic starts with empty routes (only including the depot) and then determines for each customer the increase in the objective value when including it into a route of each vehicle type $k \in K$. The combination of customer and vehicle type that results in the lowest increase of the objective function (i.e., the cheapest insertion) is added to the (empty) route of the associated vehicle type. For each following iteration, the heuristic considers all possible insertion positions in existing and empty routes of each vehicle type and determines for each customer the insertion costs in these positions. The customer and insertion position with the cheapest insertion is included in this insertion position at the respective route of the associated vehicle type. Before the insertion, it is checked if the sum of deliveries in the route does not exceed the vehicle capacity. To diversify the constructive heuristic, the insertion costs are multiplied by a random number before selecting the cheapest insertion. The process is repeated until all customers are allocated.

4.2 Destroy Operators

We design five destroy operators that each remove q locations from the solution, where q is a random variable determined by the parameter settings. The removed locations are added to the removal list Φ.

- **Random removal.** Randomly selects q locations that are removed from the routes and added to Φ.
- **Distance removal.** Selects a random location and removes it together with its $q-1$ nearest neighbors based on Euclidean distance.
- **String removal.** This operator proposed in [4] removes adjacent sequences of locations (i.e., strings) in the routes. First, a seed location is selected, followed by the removal of a string that encompasses the seed location. Thereafter, a string is removed from another route that contains a location adjacent to the seed location.
- **Route removal.** Randomly selects an existing route of one vehicle type and completely destroys it. Specifically useful for heterogeneous fleets, as this allows to mix up the locations of one specific vehicle type.
- **Worst (cost/risk) removal.** These operators remove the location that results in the largest decrease in the objective value. To include some randomness in the worst removal, e.g., to avoid the same location removed multiple times and to avoid local optima, the removal value is randomized, by multiplying the value by a random number. This process is repeated until q locations are removed. Two additional variants are developed for the HFR-CVRP; the *worst cost removal* only considers the transportation costs and the *worst risk removal* only considers the expected loss of the objective value.

4.3 Repair Operators

Once we have partially destroyed the solution by removing locations, we have to repair the solution by inserting the locations until the removal list Φ is empty. We have defined four repair operators, related to, e.g., [1,18].

- **(Random) greedy repair.** The greedy repair operators insert the removed locations iteratively. In each iteration, the location with the smallest increase of the objective is inserted in the best possible position, which is either in an existing route or in a new route. For the random variant, the greedy repair is randomized by multiplying the insertion value with a random number, aiming to overcome the myopic behavior of the greedy repair [18].
- **(Random) regret repair.** The regret repair operators insert locations with the highest regret. Regret is the difference in the insertion value between inserting the location at its best position and at another position. When the other position is the second-best position, it is denoted as 2-regret. In each iteration of the regret operator, the location with the highest 2-regret is inserted at its best position. Hence, we insert the location that we would most regret if it later could not be inserted at its best position. For the random variant, the regret is multiplied by a random number.

4.4 Operator Selection and Adaptive Weight Adjustment

The choice of destroy and repair operators in each iteration of ALNS is based on the roulette-wheel selection principle (e.g., [12,18]). To select the different operators, each operator k has a weight $w_i, i \in \{1, 2, .., k\}$ and we select the operator j with probability:

$$\frac{w_j}{\sum_{i=1}^{k} w_i} \tag{3}$$

The weights of the operators are all initialized with a weight of 1 and updated throughout the search. The entire search is divided into a number of segments. Throughout each segment, we keep track of the performance of the operators by assigning scores σ_1, σ_2, and σ_3. At the start of each segment, the score is set to zero for each operator. If the operators find a new best solution, the score is increased by σ_1. If operators find a solution that is better than the current solution, the score is increased by σ_2. If the solution is worse than the current solution but is accepted, the score is increased by σ_3. The latter is included to encourage operators that diversify the search and explore new sections of the solution space [18]. At the end of a segment, weights are updated according to their scores. Let w_{ij} be the weight of operator i in segment j, π_i be the score of operator i, and θ_i be the number of times heuristic i is used in segment j. A reaction factor γ controls the weight update:

$$w_{i,j+1} = w_{ij}(1 - \gamma) + \gamma \frac{\pi_i}{\theta_i} \tag{4}$$

4.5 Acceptance and Stopping Criteria

The acceptance criterion we apply is the Record-to-Record Travel (RRT), proposed by [5], and according to a comparative study of [20], the preferred acceptance criterion for ALNS. When minimizing, this algorithm accepts a new solution s' if the gap between the value of the new solution $f(s')$ and the value of the best-known solution f^* is smaller than the positive parameter T. The threshold parameter T decreases every iteration moving towards its end value, such that near the end of the search process, only higher-quality solutions are accepted [20]. We incorporate a linear decay of T: T^{start}/I, where I is the number of iterations.

5 Case and Numerical Experiments

In this section, we describe the case, the instances, and the experimental settings which we use to solve the HFRCVRP, and clarify the tuning of the parameters of the ALNS.

5.1 South Sudan Case

A civil war, a widespread scarcity of food, and multiple floods have plagued South Sudan for years, especially in 2017. According to the humanitarian snapshots of the United Nations Office for the Coordination of Humanitarian Affairs (OCHA) in 2017, Unity was the state with severe food scarcity, the most internally displaced people, and the highest violence rate in South Sudan. Incidents in Unity included violence against humanitarian personnel (also murders), ambushes and looting, active hostilities, violence against humanitarian assets, and operational interference and restrictions of movement. In 2017, the OCHA reported 182 incidents in Unity, with 6 murders of aid workers among them. Tonnes of nutritional supplies, essential medicines, and utilities were stolen and in November 2017 food assistance was suspended in the south of Unity due to ongoing fights in November 2017. In this study, we focus on this southern part, containing the districts of Koch, Leer, and Mayiendit. Based on assessments from the International Organization of Migration (IOM), we obtain a set of 125 locations where internally displaced people rely on food assistance or health support (see Fig. 1). The depot is situated in the village of Leer, where a humanitarian hub and an airstrip are located. The locations contain between 19 and 2,579 individuals, with a total number of 42,654 individuals in the area.

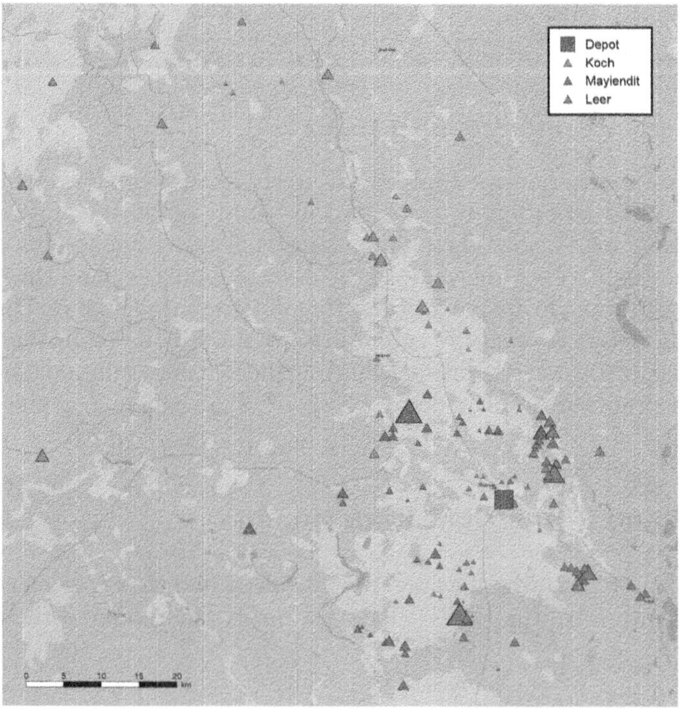

Fig. 1. Map of the operating area; the colors give a sense of the three districts and the size of the locations scales according to the number of individuals.

5.2 Experimental Design and Instances

To provide a safer alternative for trucks to distribute goods in the area, we compare trucks with the deployment of unmanned aerial vehicles (UAVs). Cargo UAVs can fly over high-risk environments, deliver goods without requiring an airstrip by means of airdrop or horizontal landing, and are generally cheaper than manned aircraft when transporting relatively small amounts of goods. The UAV specifications are based on the humanitarian MiniFreighter from Wings For Aid, and comparable to the conceptual Nuuva V300 from Pipistrel. We determine the UAV travel time by using the Euclidean distance between locations and a cruising speed of 120km/h. To obtain realistic estimates for truck driving times between all locations, we use ArcGIS 10.7 to obtain the rural driving times. To obtain the cost parameters c_{ijk} between node i and j for vehicle type k, we multiply the obtained travel times by hourly vehicle costs. Risk probabilities p_{ijk} can depend on various factors, such as the road type, travel time, time of the day, vehicle type, surroundings, and other information (e.g., insights that rebel soldiers are located near a specific road). As this detailed information on attacks is not available, we assume, for trucks, that the probability of an attack is proportional to the travel time of an arc. The travel times are weighted by a fixed risk factor to obtain the risk probabilities for trucks (p_{ij0}). In our experiments, we use a risk factor of 0.01, based on the information found on the Unity state in the humanitarian snapshots of the OCHA and the monthly figures of the Logistics Cluster in 2017. The value of indirect losses of a robbery, irrespective of the value of goods on the truck, is estimated to be 10,000 euro. For the UAVs, we omit the risk of a robbery, as they will fly over the risky environment, so the risk probability of being robbed $p_{ij1} = 0$ between each node i and node j for UAVs. The vehicle specifications are summarized in Table 2.

Table 2. Vehicle specifications used in the experiments.

	Speed (km/h)	Costs (€/h)	Capacity Q_k	Indirect loss (€)	Risk factor
Truck	37.5[a]	70	6,000	10,000	0.01
UAV	120	250	200	0	0.00

[a] On average, based on the obtained distances and travel times from ArcGIS

To evaluate the ALNS framework for the HFRCVRP, we perform experiments on seven subsets of the case instance. These subsets are summarized in Table 3 and are based on the three districts in the south of the Unity state: Koch, Mayiendit, and Leer. We solve the RCVRP with only trucks and we solve the HFRCVRP with trucks and UAVs. In the experiments, we sum the transportation costs and the expected loss to a single objective. Furthermore, we solve the instance with a focus on only costs, ignoring the expected loss in the objective. Lastly, as the results are dependent on the level of risk in an area, we perform a sensitivity analysis with the largest instance where we adapt the weights of the transportation costs and expected loss (risk exposure) in the objective function.

For all experiments, we consider that each individual requires 0.5kg of goods, with a value of 2 euro per kg.

Table 3. Instances with combinations of the three districts.

Subset	District	#locations	#individuals
1	Koch	31	9,756
2	Mayiendit	40	13,642
3	Leer	54	19,256
4	Koch-Mayiendit	71	23,398
5	Koch-Leer	85	29,012
6	Mayiendit-Leer	94	32,898
7	All	125	42,654

5.3 ALNS Parameter Tuning

The ALNS framework contains several parameters that can be tuned according to the problem setting, but once they are tuned on one instance, results tend to be robust for a wide range of instances [18]. We tune our parameters on instance 7, the largest and most complex instance. To find suitable parameters, we varied the parameters and chose the setting that showed the best performance. The number of locations to remove each iteration q (i.e., the degree of destruction) is picked from the uniform interval $[0.1n, 0.2n]$, where n is the total number of locations. The level of randomization of the costs for the initial construction, the worst removal operators, and the randomized repair operators is set to $[0.9, 1.1]$. Regarding the scoring and weight updating of the operators, we divide the search into segments of 50 iterations. In each iteration, weights get a score based on their performance and the scores σ_1, σ_2, and σ_3, which are set to 30, 10, and 5, respectively. The reaction factor γ for weight updating is set to 0.1. The acceptance threshold T of RRT is a function of the best solution f^*, with initial threshold $T^{start} = 0.05f^*$. The threshold decays linearly throughout the search until $T = 0$.

5.4 Experimental Results

The results obtained by the ALNS heuristic for all variants on the instances are presented in Table 4, and were obtained within minutes on a 4-core 1.90 GHz computer with 16GB RAM. Without considering risks, UAVs are only applied in three subsets and allocated to a total of five locations. About 1.1% in transportation costs is saved in these instances compared to truck-only scenarios. When including the expected loss in the objective, UAVs are deployed in all instances visiting on average 19% of the locations, improving the objective of transportation costs and expected loss by 7.1% on average compared to only trucks. Additionally, transportation costs per location decrease by 30% on average for trucks when UAVs are deployed, showing that UAVs visit locations further away from the depot. These relatively remote locations are also those that result in a high exposure to risk for trucks, due to their longer travel times.

When comparing the bi-objective results with the results of the single cost objective, we observe that for the truck-only instances, the transportation costs increase by 11.9% and the expected loss decreases by 13.4% on average. For the heterogeneous fleet instances, the effect is about four times as large, with an average increase of 53.0% in costs, and a 47.7% average decrease of expected loss, resulting in an overall decrease of 14.8% in the objective value.

Table 4. Results for all experiments, where each instance stands for the case subset (1–7), truck-only (T) or heterogeneous fleet with trucks and UAVs (HF), and a single objective based on costs (C) or bi-objective based on costs and risks (CR). The lowest total costs and expected losses per subset are marked in bold.

Instance	Truck costs	UAV costs	Expected loss	Total	# truck locations	# UAV locations
1-T-C	1824.2	0	4198.1	6022.2	31	0
1-T-CR	1850.8	0	3168.2	5019.0	31	0
1-HF-C	1824.2	0	4198.1	6022.2	31	0
1-HF-CR	622.9	2927.4	1076.8	**4627.2**	20	11
2-T-C	413.2	0	722.2	1135.4	54	0
2-T-CR	417.6	0	706.6	1124.2	54	0
2-HF-C	343.9	67.7	648.4	1059.9	51	3
2-HF-CR	269.9	204.8	484.7	**959.4**	42	12
3-T-C	837.1	0	1523.3	2360.4	40	0
3-T-CR	843.9	0	1453.2	2297.2	40	0
3-HF-C	762.7	54.9	1678.8	2496.5	39	1
3-HF-CR	445.7	946.2	733.8	**2125.8**	32	8
4-T-C	2186.7	0	4440.9	6627.6	85	0
4-T-CR	2224.2	0	3832.8	6057.0	85	0
4-HF-C	2186.7	0	4440.9	6627.6	85	0
4-HF-CR	896.8	3109.0	1591.3	**5597.0**	65	20
5-T-C	2283.9	0	4403.7	6687.6	71	0
5-T-CR	2294.9	0	3933.1	6228.0	71	0
5-HF-C	2214.1	54.9	4220.1	6489.1	70	1
5-HF-CR	1315.0	2078.8	2402.3	**5796.2**	63	8
6-T-C	1052.8	0	2474.0	3526.8	94	0
6-T-CR	1064.3	0	1910.1	2974.4	94	0
6-HF-C	1052.8	0	2474.4	3527.2	94	0
6-HF-CR	1034.5	72.4	1848.3	**2955.2**	92	2
7-T-C	2481.7	0	5194.7	7676.4	125	0
7-T-CR	2524.1	0	4398.7	6922.8	125	0
7-HF-C	2481.7	0	5194.7	7676.4	125	0
7-HF-CR	1481.3	2311.2	2831.8	**6624.3**	105	20

For the largest instance with all districts, we perform a sensitivity analysis to compare the separate objectives of transportation costs and the expected loss with different weights, see Fig. 2. We weigh the transportation costs by ξ and the expected loss by $1-\xi$ in the objective, with different values of $\xi \in [0,1]$. When the transportation costs weigh 0.6 or higher, UAVs are not deployed, and transportation costs and expected loss only slightly change. When risk becomes more important, UAVs are increasingly deployed. Expected loss can be eliminated by increasing transportation costs by a factor of five (i.e., from $\epsilon = 0.6$ for the case without UAVs to $\epsilon = 0.1$ where UAVs fully diminish the risk exposure). The changes in truck routes are minimal when risk becomes more important, which can be explained by the indirect loss. Multiple shorter routes that decrease the expected direct loss causes not only higher transportation costs but also increase the expected indirect loss due to more time on the road. This allows for fewer possibilities in reducing risks with only trucks.

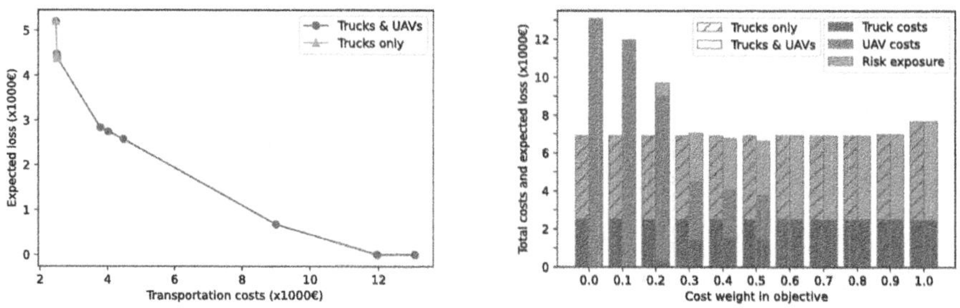

(a) Pareto chart

(b) Division of transportation costs and risk

Fig. 2. Results for case subset 7 for both trucks only and trucks & UAVs scenarios with different weights for transportation costs and expected loss.

6 Conclusions

Risks in disaster areas can have a significant impact on the operations of humanitarian organizations. In this work, we presented a heterogeneous fleet RCVRP with the consideration of indirect losses (loss irrespective of the amount of load carried, such as material- or emotional damage) to mitigate these impacts. We developed an ALNS metaheuristic with specific destroy and repair operators to solve this problem variant effectively. We tested this method on real-world instances from high-risk areas in South Sudan.

The results show that both the minimization of expected losses and the use of UAVs increase transportation costs, but simultaneously decrease the exposure to risks significantly. This enables safer operations for aid workers of humanitarian organizations. Hence, UAVs provide a valuable alternative in high-risk environments, with an average decrease of the objective value of 7.1% in the case of equal consideration of transportation costs and expected loss. UAVs are especially valuable in situations in which locations are scattered and relatively far away from humanitarian hubs. These locations cause long travel times and high exposure to risks for road transport. Hence, UAVs can take over the most challenging locations. In the largest instance, 16% of the locations were visited by UAVs.

The inclusion of indirect losses for a more accurate consideration of risks resulted in less flexibility in mitigating risks with trucks. Only minimal changes in routes and objective value were found for different weights of the transportation costs and the expected loss. For the heterogeneous fleet variant, risks could be eliminated entirely in the most extreme variants by increasing transportation costs by a factor of five. However, when the focus was mainly on transportation costs, UAVs were not deployed.

In future work, we aim to test the ALNS framework on benchmark instances and compare it with exact approaches to evaluate the performance of each method. Furthermore, we suggest introducing prioritization based on the vulnerabilities of specific beneficiaries, as the delivery of goods to certain groups might be more important than to others. This could be done by explicitly considering deprivation costs that can occur when beneficiaries have to wait when deliveries cannot be performed due to attacks. Facility location decisions could also be included, including setup costs for an operating base of UAVs.

References

1. Allahyari, S., Yaghoubi, S., Van Woensel, T.: A novel risk perspective on location-routing planning: an application in cash transportation. Transp. Res. Part E Logist. Transp. Rev. **150**, 102356 (2021). https://doi.org/10.1016/j.tre.2021.102356
2. Allahyari, S., Yaghoubi, S., Van Woensel, T.: The secure time-dependent vehicle routing problem with uncertain demands. Comput. Oper. Res. **131**, 105253 (2021). https://doi.org/10.1016/j.cor.2021.105253
3. Besiou, M., Van Wassenhove, L.N.: Humanitarian operations: a world of opportunity for relevant and impactful research. Manuf. Serv. Oper. Manag. **22**(1), 135–145 (2020). https://doi.org/10.1287/msom.2019.0799
4. Christiaens, J., Vanden Berghe, G.: Slack induction by string removals for vehicle routing problems. Transp. Sci. **54**(2), 417–433 (2020). https://doi.org/10.1287/trsc.2019.0914
5. Dueck, G.: New optimization heuristics: the great deluge algorithm and the record-to-record travel. J. Comput. Phys. **104**(1), 86–92 (1993). https://doi.org/10.1006/jcph.1993.1010
6. Fallahtafti, A., Ardjmand, E., Young Ii, W.A., Weckman, G.R.: A multi-objective two-echelon location-routing problem for cash logistics: a metaheuristic approach. Appl. Soft Comput. **111**, 107685 (2021). https://doi.org/10.1016/j.asoc.2021.107685
7. Fröhlich, G.E., Gansterer, M., Doerner, K.F.: Safe and secure vehicle routing: a survey on minimization of risk exposure. Int. Trans. Oper. Res. (2022). https://doi.org/10.1111/itor.13130

8. Ghannadpour, S.F., Zandiyeh, F.: A new game-theoretical multi-objective evolutionary approach for cash-in-transit vehicle routing problem with time windows (a real life case). Appl. Soft Comput. **93**, 106378 (2020). https://doi.org/10.1016/j.asoc.2020.106378
9. Hagen-Zanker, J., Ulrichs, M., Holmes, R.: What are the effects of cash transfers for refugees in the context of protracted displacement? findings from Jordan. Int. Soc. Secur. Rev. **71**(2), 57–77 (2018). https://doi.org/10.1111/issr.12166
10. Holm-Nielsen, P.V., Raju, E., Furu, P.: The transformative effect of cash and voucher assistance experienced by humanitarian organizations. Int. J. Disaster Risk Reduct. **80**, 103238 (2022). https://doi.org/10.1016/j.ijdrr.2022.103238
11. Kian, R., et al.: Logistics planning of cash transfer to Syrian refugees in Turkey. Eur. J. Oper. Res. **296**(3), 1007–1024 (2022). https://doi.org/10.1016/j.ejor.2021.04.054
12. Laporte, G., Musmanno, R., Vocaturo, F.: An adaptive large neighbourhood search heuristic for the capacitated arc-routing problem with stochastic demands. Transp. Sci. **44**(1), 125–135 (2010). https://doi.org/10.1287/trsc.1090.0290
13. Li, H., Wang, H., Chen, J., Bai, M.: Two-echelon vehicle routing problem with time windows and mobile satellites. Transp. Res. Part B Methodol. **138**, 179–201 (2020). https://doi.org/10.1016/j.trb.2020.05.010
14. Mancini, S.: A real-life multi depot multi period vehicle routing problem with a heterogeneous fleet: formulation and adaptive large neighborhood search based matheuristic. Transp. Res. Part C Emerg. Technol. **70**, 100–112 (2016). https://doi.org/10.1016/j.trc.2015.06.016
15. Mazdarani, F., Ghannadpour, S.F., Zandieh, F.: Bi-objective overlapped links vehicle routing problem for risk minimizing valuables transportation. Comput. Oper. Res. 106177 (2023). https://doi.org/10.1016/j.cor.2023.106177
16. Radojičić, N., Djenić, A., Marić, M.: Fuzzy grasp with path relinking for the risk-constrained cash-in-transit vehicle routing problem. Appl. Soft Comput. **72**, 486–497 (2018). https://doi.org/10.1016/j.asoc.2018.05.022
17. Rejeb, A., Rejeb, K., Simske, S., Treiblmaier, H.: Humanitarian drones: a review and research agenda. Internet Things **16**, 100434 (2021). https://doi.org/10.1016/j.iot.2021.100434
18. Ropke, S., Pisinger, D.: An adaptive large neighborhood search heuristic for the pickup and delivery problem with time windows. Transp. Sci. **40**(4), 455–472 (2006). https://doi.org/10.1287/trsc.1050.0135
19. Sacramento, D., Pisinger, D., Ropke, S.: An adaptive large neighborhood search metaheuristic for the vehicle routing problem with drones. Transp. Res. Part C Emerg. Technol. **102**, 289–315 (2019). https://doi.org/10.1016/j.trc.2019.02.018
20. Santini, A., Ropke, S., Hvattum, L.M.: A comparison of acceptance criteria for the adaptive large neighbourhood search metaheuristic. J. Heuristics **24**(5), 783–815 (2018). https://doi.org/10.1007/s10732-018-9377-x
21. Soeanu, A., Ray, S., Berger, J., Boukhtouta, A., Debbabi, M.: Multi-depot vehicle routing problem with risk mitigation: model and solution algorithm. Expert Syst. Appl. **145**, 113099 (2020). https://doi.org/10.1016/j.eswa.2019.113099
22. Talarico, L., Sörensen, K., Springael, J.: Metaheuristics for the risk-constrained cash-in-transit vehicle routing problem. Eur. J. Oper. Res. **244**(2), 457–470 (2015). https://doi.org/10.1016/j.ejor.2015.01.040
23. Talarico, L., Sörensen, K., Springael, J.: A biobjective decision model to increase security and reduce travel costs in the cash-in-transit sector. Int. Trans. Oper. Res. **24**(1–2), 59–76 (2017). https://doi.org/10.1111/itor.12214

24. Talarico, L., Springael, J., Sörensen, K., Talarico, F.: A large neighbourhood metaheuristic for the risk-constrained cash-in-transit vehicle routing problem. Comput. Oper. Res. **78**, 547–556 (2017). https://doi.org/10.1016/j.cor.2016.04.003
25. Tikani, H., Setak, M., Demir, E.: A risk-constrained time-dependent cash-in-transit routing problem in multigraph under uncertainty. Eur. J. Oper. Res. **293**(2), 703–730 (2021). https://doi.org/10.1016/j.ejor.2020.12.020
26. Vincent, F.Y., Jewpanya, P., Redi, A.P., Tsao, Y.C.: Adaptive neighborhood simulated annealing for the heterogeneous fleet vehicle routing problem with multiple cross-docks. Comput. Oper. Res. **129**, 105205 (2021). https://doi.org/10.1016/j.cor.2020.105205

The Snow Grooming Routing Problem

Henrik Andersson[1(✉)], Sondre Høyland[1], Jesper Anker Krogstad[1], Truls Flatberg[2], and Anders N. Gullhav[1]

[1] Department of Industrial Economics and Technology Management, Norwegian University of Science and Technology, Alfred Getz veg 3, Trondheim, Norway
henrik.andersson@ntnu.no

[2] SINTEF Industry/Sustainable Energy Technology, P.O. Box 4760, Torgarden, 7465 Trondheim, Norway

Abstract. There are more than 30,000 km of cross-country skiing tracks in Norway, and to maintain these track networks municipalities and local ski clubs spend more than 250 million NOK every year. The primary cost driver is the daily grooming operations which are manually planned based on the experience of the snowcat operators. Large networks with many vehicles starting at different depots complicate the problem of finding effective routes. The result is unnecessary high costs due to suboptimal route choices, yielding a benefit of solving the route planning problem.

Employees of the municipal enterprise responsible for the cross-country facilities in Trondheim, Trondheim Bydrift, explain that today's planning of grooming activities is based on experience and old habits. As Trondheim is an area known for unstable weather conditions, long-term planning lacks robustness. Meetings are therefore conducted every morning to handle the variations. The multifaceted Snow Grooming Routing Problem (SGRP) is an arc routing problem with profits that involves multiple depots, time windows, a heterogeneous fleet of vehicles and track segments having numerous attributes.

We formally define the SGRP and present a mathematical formulation of the problem. The formulation is then tested on a number of different networks taken from Bymarka, the largest cross-country area around Trondheim, Norway.

Keywords: Snow Grooming · Arc routing

1 Introduction

There are 5360 km of cross-country skiing tracks in Norway's top ten most popular ski facilities. Municipalities, ski clubs and commercial actors in these areas spend more than 50 million NOK in total each season to maintain their track networks [3].

According to Statistics Norway [13], 34266 km of tracks were planned to be groomed in 2022. Extrapolating the costs from the popular facilities results in a

© The Author(s), under exclusive license to Springer Nature Switzerland AG 2023
J. R. Daduna et al. (Eds.): ICCL 2023, LNCS 14239, pp. 292–306, 2023.
https://doi.org/10.1007/978-3-031-43612-3_18

rough estimate of 300 million NOK spent every year grooming Norwegian track networks. These networks are complex, consisting of wide and narrow track segments for the different styles of cross-country skiing. Popular routes must be prioritized and groomed more often than peripheral segments solely used by enthusiasts to maintain a certain standard across the whole network. Grooming requests from local ski clubs, winter sport events and competitions must be handled and included in the planning of the operations. These events often set high standards for the snow grooming, requiring the grooming to be done within specific time windows. Requests vary from being weekly requests known from the start of the season to urgent short-term requests. The fact that requested segments are mandatory complicates the planning.

In 2023, there were more than 700 snowcats grooming track networks and alpine slopes in Norway [12]. Popular areas have fleets of snowcats grooming simultaneously to meet demand. Statistics Norway show an increase in cabins and holiday homes in Norway, where an expected consequence is an increase in demand for cross-country tracks [14]. Current track networks will therefore probably meet an increase in skier traffic, requiring additional networks or expansion of the current ones to be practical. This will further increase the complexity of the grooming operations. New technology with GPS tracking of snowcats and websites like *skisporet.no* has made it easier for skiers to find freshly groomed tracks, but for the facilitators of the networks, helpful tools for planning grooming operations is hard to find.

The problem of planning the grooming operations, the Snow Grooming Routing Problem (SGRP) is a rich arc routing problem with profits, see for example [1,6] and [2] for recent surveys and a book on many aspects of arc routing problems. The SGRP has multiple depots and a heterogeneous fleet. The track network consists of wide and narrow segments, which are either requested, prioritized, or regular. A wide segment can be groomed by one large snowcat or two small snowcats. Requested segments have to be served within a given time window while the others can be groomed without regard to time. The optional segments are diversified by priority based on popularity for skiers but are groomed without precedence to ensure an efficient route through the network. Arc routing problems for snow plowing and road gritting have similar attributes, see for example [7–11], and [5] but this constitutes the first known attempt of solving the Snow Grooming Routing Problem.

This paper aims to give a formal description of the Snow Grooming Routing Problem (SGRP), formulate the problem as a mathematical model, and use the model to optimize the snow grooming operations on a set of test instances based on real-life data. First, we give some background to snow grooming and different aspects of planning snow grooming operations in Sect. 2. The problem description follows in Sect. 3 before the mathematical formulation in Sect. 4. Results from testing the model on five instance are presented in Sect. 5. We conclude the paper with a short discussion in Sect. 6.

2 Background

Networks of ski tracks vary in size and complexity from place to place. Some areas have huge and intricate networks, while others have only a couple of closed loops of tracks. The complexity comes from different track widths, the combination of prioritized and requested track segments, track crossings, bridges, lakes, swamps and road crossings. Small networks are usually groomed by a single snowcat, while large networks have a larger fleet and potentially multiple depots. Norway has hundreds of track networks, and Fig. 1 shows an overview of these in southern Norway. Figure 2 is a more detailed map of the track network in Bymarka, Trondheim. This is the main network in the Trondheim area and is the basis for the problem description and the test instances. The network is operated by Trondheim Bydrift and consists of more than 100 km of tracks. Three snowcats in two depots are used to groom the tracks.

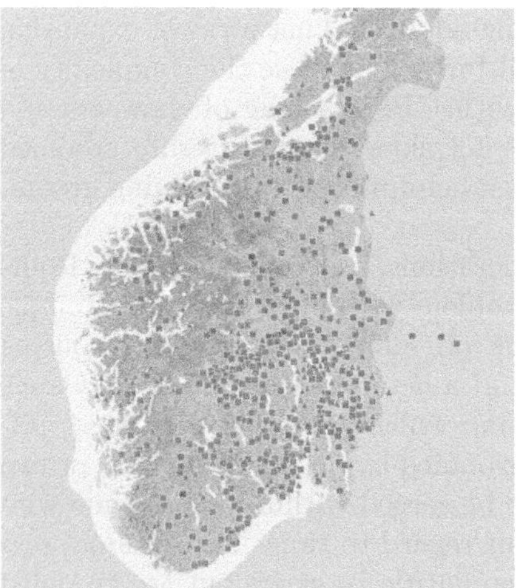

Fig. 1. Overview of track networks in southern Norway

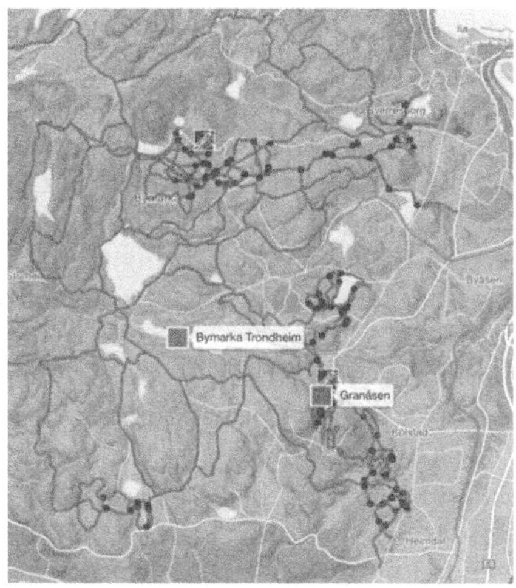

Fig. 2. The track network in Bymarka, Trondheim

Track networks with stadiums and tracks meant for competitions are often very dense, which means that they have many intersections and relatively short distances between them. Competition tracks are mostly loops stretching 3, 5 or 10 km, and should be groomed in a single route so that skiers can use them at once. The grooming of dense networks is often more challenging to plan because of the numerous possibilities, while scattered networks with fewer segments between intersections and longer track segments pose fewer options.

There are many stakeholders with different agendas regarding the snow grooming operation, the track network and the surrounding nature. The general public is the largest stakeholder, visiting popular cabins serving food as well as the outskirts of the track network. They are to some extent interested in quantity over quality when it comes to grooming, and that the track networks are large enough. The second largest stakeholder is the ski clubs and high-schools for athletes. They normally have a set of routes that they regularly use for organized training activities, and are mostly interested in top quality for these specific routes. They also hand in grooming requests for special events such as competitions. The municipalities want to facilitate for an active population, while at the same time preserve the regional nature and minimize local pollution in the area.

Decisions about which segments of the network to prioritize early in the season are made in collaboration with the stakeholders. On a daily basis, it is up to the snowcat operators to determine which tracks to groom and when to groom them. Planning longer time-spans is difficult and not robust enough, due to aspects like weather changes and short-term grooming requests.

During periods of consistent whether a weekly schedule for the network can be followed, but with an occurrence of precipitation or a change in temperature, the schedule is of little use. A snowfall resets the problem and all previously groomed segments will have to be groomed again. Since consistent weather is the exception for most of the season, the operators experience much overtime.

In some municipalities, the grooming of the tracks can be requested in advance by stakeholders, either as a repetitive request throughout the season or as a one-time request on an occasional basis. These requested tracks *must* be of a certain standard at a given time of day. To meet the quality requirements, the requested tracks must be groomed within a given time window. The time window is set based on weather forecasts and projected traffic of skiers in the network, a rule of thumb is that the grooming is finished an hour before the start of the event. The total duration of the time window depends on the length of the requested route. The possibility of requesting the grooming of certain tracks results in a further complication of the route planning.

There are some segments that are prioritized, typically popular roundtrips or routes leading to serviced cabins. Other segments are used less, but still they have to be groomed regularly because of snowfalls. The goal is, therefore, to ensure top track quality for the most popular tracks, while at the same time not neglecting the other segments, substantiating the importance of planning. Track networks with multiple depots are faced with a more complicated planning problem. Coordination of routes to minimize overlapping and non-groomed track segments is obtainable, but hard to plan since the route selection of the operators is often done in a myopic way with incomplete information of the plans of the other operators.

With different sizes of snowcats and different widths of tracks, comes the problem of assigning the right snowcat to the right track segment. Large snowcats are typically too wide to traverse narrow tracks with only classic skiing, meaning they can only be used on wide tracks (for both classic and skate). The small snowcats are used for the narrow tracks, but can also be delegated to grooming wide tracks. For a small snowcat to groom a wide track, it must traverse it twice.

3 Problem Description

The Snow Grooming Routing Problem (SGRP) is an extension of the arc routing problem with profits. The problem arises in cross-country skiing facilities around the world when scheduling the grooming of the track networks. The network is a set of tracks (edges) and intersections (nodes) between them. Each edge has a given length and topography and is classified according to width and priority. The width is either wide or narrow. An edge can be without priority, prioritized or requested. A requested edge must be groomed and there is a time window specifying when the edge can be groomed. The characteristics of a track segment can only change at the intersections. In general, the network is non-directional, meaning that it does not matter in which direction a snowcat traverses an edge. A network of ski tracks generally contains many intersections and relatively few track segments between every pair of intersections.

On narrow tracks, a small snowcat can choose to groom two classic sections or a combination of classic and skate. This is a dynamic setting that the operator can set with negligible setup time and cost. For wide track segments, a small snowcat will have to traverse the segment twice to be able to groom the whole width. The solution is often to acquire a larger snowcat for networks with many wide segments, which only have to traverse these segments once. These large snowcats cannot traverse the narrower segments. Every intersection poses the possibility of a change in track type, complicating the route planning and choice of snowcat type for the route. Different snowcats have similar attributes, apart from width and range. They operate at identical speeds under the same weather conditions. Within each snowcat size, there are no significant differences. Therefore, all track segments of the same type can be groomed by the same snowcats.

Figure 3 is a snippet of the larger track network in Bymarka, Trondheim (left), which is presented in the form of a graph (right). Each segment is represented by an edge in the graph.

When a track segment is groomed, there is no added benefit by grooming it over again, and it may even be undesirable for the skiing conditions during periods of consistent weather conditions. The problem aims to determine how the track network should be groomed. That is, which snowcats should groom which track segments, and at what time. The purpose is to ensure the effective use of the available resources.

4 Mathematical Formulations

Before presenting the notation and the mathematical model, we state some important assumptions:

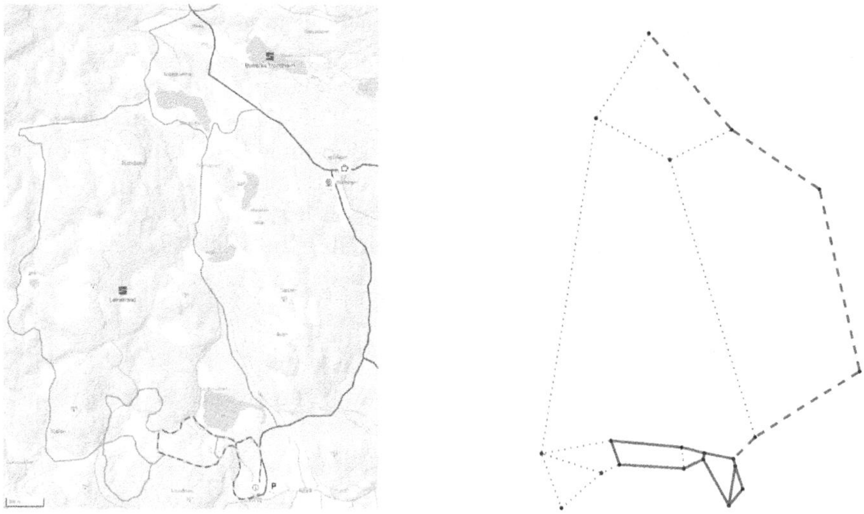

Fig. 3. Small part of the track network in Bymarka, Trondheim (left) and the corresponding graph (right). Nodes are intersections and edges are segments. The priorities are shown: dotted (no priority), dashed (prioritized), and solid (requested). Wide segments are marked with thick lines.

- Costs of grooming operations are not included in the model. Describing the problem for daily operations, long-term overhead costs like inventory and wages are considered sunk.
- The problem considers a single day. The weather conditions are known and consistent during the day.
- The working hours are fixed, imposed as an upper bound with no possibility of overtime.

We denote the track segments as *edges* and the intersections as *nodes*. The problem is formulated over a graph $G = (\mathcal{N}, \mathcal{E})$ where $\mathcal{N}$ is the set of nodes and $\mathcal{E}$ the set of edges. We also introduce $\mathcal{A}$ as the set of arcs to track directions, each edge corresponds to two arcs. A subset $\mathcal{E}^W \subseteq \mathcal{E}$ of the edges are wide edges, another subset $\mathcal{E}^P \subseteq \mathcal{E}$ of the edges are prioritized edges, and a third subset $\mathcal{E}^R \subseteq \mathcal{E}$ of the edges are requested edges that must be groomed within a given time window. We also define $\mathcal{K}$ to be the set of snowcats, and denote the set of small and large snowcats as $\mathcal{K}^S$ and $\mathcal{K}^L$, respectively.

We use (ij) to denote the edge connecting node i and j, with $i < j$. When the direction the edge is traversed matter, we use ij to denote the arc starting in node i and ending in node j. The time used to traverse edge (ij) is $T_{(ij)}$ and its length is $L_{(ij)}$. We use $[\underline{T}_{(ij)}, \overline{T}_{(ij)}]$ to denote the time window defined for the requested edge (ij). The time available for snowcat k is T_k^K and the node where it must start and end its route is denote $i(k)$. We introduce a reward $R_{(ij)}$ for grooming edge (ij) and a cost C per length unit groomed to penalize unnecessary grooming.

We use a leg-based formulation and introduce the index set $\mathcal{L} = \{0, \ldots, L+1\}$ for the set of legs where L is an upper bound on the number of arcs in the route of a snowcat. The binary variable x_{kijl} is 1 if snowcat k grooms arc ij on leg l, and 0 otherwise. The binary variable $v_{(ij)}$ is 1 if edge (ij) is groomed, and 0 otherwise, and $w_{k(ij)l}$ is 1 if edge $(ij) \in \mathcal{E}^R$ is groomed by snowcat k on leg l. The time variable t_{kl} is the time snowcat k starts leg l and $\tau_{k(ij)l}$ is the time when edge $(ij) \in \mathcal{E}^R$ is groomed by snowcat k on leg l.

With this notation, the SGRP can be formulated as follows:

$$\max z = \sum_{(ij)\in\mathcal{E}} R_{(ij)} v_{(ij)} - C \sum_{k\in\mathcal{K}} \sum_{(ij)\in\mathcal{E}} \sum_{l\in\mathcal{L}} L_{(ij)} \left(x_{kijl} + x_{kijl}\right) \tag{1}$$

The objective function (1) maximizes the reward from groomed edges and penalizes the traversal of an edge more than once.

$$x_{k0i(k)0} = 1 \qquad k \in \mathcal{K} \tag{2}$$

$$\sum_{ij\in\mathcal{A}} x_{kijl} = \sum_{ji\in\mathcal{A}} x_{kji,l+1} \qquad k \in \mathcal{K}, j \in \mathcal{N} \setminus \{0\}, l \in \mathcal{L} \mid l \leq L \tag{3}$$

$$\sum_{l\in\mathcal{L}} x_{ki(k)0l} = 1 \qquad k \in \mathcal{K} \tag{4}$$

Constraints (2) and (4) state that snowcat k must start and end its route in its depot $i(k)$. Node 0 is an artificial starting node with $T_{(0i(k))} = L_{(0i(k))} = 0$. Constraints (3) ensure the flow of snowcats through the nodes. They state that if snowcat k enters node j, it must exit the same node on its next leg.

$$v_{(ij)} \leq \sum_{k\in\mathcal{K}^S} \sum_{l\in\mathcal{L}} (x_{kijl} + x_{kjil}) \qquad (ij) \in \mathcal{E} \setminus \mathcal{E}^W \tag{5}$$

$$v_{(ij)} \leq \sum_{k\in\mathcal{K}^L} \sum_{l\in\mathcal{L}} (x_{kijl} + x_{kjil}) + \frac{1}{2} \sum_{k\in\mathcal{K}^S} \sum_{l\in\mathcal{L}} (x_{kijl} + x_{kjil}) \qquad (ij) \in \mathcal{E}^W \tag{6}$$

Constraints (5) and (6) keep track of if an edge (ij) is groomed or not. The right side of the constraints contains both arc ij and arc ji, so the model becomes non-directional. Constraints (6) also state that for wide edges, a small snowcat must groom the edge twice, while large snowcats only need one traversal. Constraints (5) ensure that only small snowcats can groom narrow edges.

$$w_{k(ij)l} - x_{kijl} - x_{kjil} \leq 0 \qquad k \in \mathcal{K}, (ij) \in \mathcal{E}^R, l \in \mathcal{L} \tag{7}$$

$$2 \sum_{k\in\mathcal{K}^L} \sum_{l\in\mathcal{L}} w_{k(ij)l} + \sum_{k\in\mathcal{K}^S} \sum_{l\in\mathcal{L}} w_{k(ij)l} = 2 \qquad (ij) \in \mathcal{E}^R \cap \mathcal{E}^W \tag{8}$$

$$\sum_{k\in\mathcal{K}^S} \sum_{l\in\mathcal{L}} w_{k(ij)l} = 1 \qquad (ij) \in \mathcal{E}^R \cap (\mathcal{E} \setminus \mathcal{E}^W) \tag{9}$$

Constraints (7) link the x-variable with the w-variable, so that a requested edge is considered groomed independent of which direction it is traversed. Constraints

(8) state that the prioritized track segments must be groomed, either once by a large snowcat or twice by a small snowcat. Constraints (9) state that narrow requested edges must be groomed by a small snowcat.

$$t_{k,l+1} \geq t_{kl} + \sum_{ij \in \mathcal{E}} T_{(ij)} \left(x_{kijl} + x_{kijl}\right) \qquad k \in \mathcal{K}, l \in \mathcal{L} \tag{10}$$

Constraints (10) update the starting time for snowcat k on leg $l+1$ by connecting it with the starting time on leg l.

$$\tau_{k(ij)l} \geq t_{kl} - M(1 - w_{k(ij)l}) \qquad k \in \mathcal{K}, (ij) \in \mathcal{E}^R, l \in \mathcal{L} \tag{11}$$

$$\tau_{k(ij)l} \leq t_{kl} + M(1 - w_{k(ij)l}) \qquad k \in \mathcal{K}, (ij) \in \mathcal{E}^R, l \in \mathcal{L} \tag{12}$$

$$\underline{T}_{(ij)} \leq \tau_{k(ij)l} \leq \overline{T}_{(ij)} \qquad k \in \mathcal{K}, (ij) \in \mathcal{E}^R, l \in \mathcal{L} \tag{13}$$

Constraints (11) and (12) link the τ-variable and the t-variable. Constraints (13) make sure that the requested edges are groomed within their time window.

$$x_{kijl} \in \{0, 1\} \qquad k \in \mathcal{K},\ ij \in \mathcal{A},\ l \in \mathcal{L} \tag{14}$$

$$w_{k(ij)l} \in \{0, 1\} \qquad k \in \mathcal{K},\ (ij) \in \mathcal{E}^R,\ l \in \mathcal{L} \tag{15}$$

$$v_{(ij)} \in \{0, 1\} \qquad (ij) \in \mathcal{E} \tag{16}$$

$$0 \leq t_{kl} \leq T_k^K \qquad k \in \mathcal{K}, l \in \mathcal{L} \tag{17}$$

$$\tau_{k(ij)l} \geq 0 \qquad k \in \mathcal{K},\ (ij) \in \mathcal{E}^R, l \in \mathcal{L} \tag{18}$$

Constraints (14)–(16) are binary restrictions, while constraints (17) set the bound on the time used. Constraints (18) ensure non-negativity. Variables x_{kijl} and $w_{k(ij)l}$ for large snowcats are not generated for narrow edges.

Reducing the Number of Variables Generated

We can reduce the number of variables generated for each snowcat. This strengthens the formulation and makes it easier to solve. For each snowcat k, we solve a shortest path problem from $i(k)$ to all other nodes where the length of each edge is 1. This gives the least number of edges snowcat k must traverse to reach each node. Let D_{ki} denote the minimum number of edges snowcat k must traverse to reach node i. This means that no x_{kjil} with $l < D_{ki}$ and no x_{kijl} with $l \leq L - D_{ki}$ are generated. If neither x_{kjil} nor x_{kijl} are generated, then $w_{k(ij)l}$ is not generated either.

Similarly, if we solve the shortest path problem with the traversal time as the length of each segment, we can calculate the earliest arrival T_{ki} in node i for snowcat k. If $T_{ki} > \overline{T}_{(ij)}$, then neither $\tau_{k(ijl)}$ nor $w_{k(ij)l}$ are generated. If $T_{ki} + T_{ij} + T_{kj} > T_k^K$, then x_{kijl} is not generated.

5 Results

We have collected data for Bymarka, Trondheim and created 5 instances. Relevant statistics for each instance are presented in Table 1. The table shows the name of the instance, the total length of the network in km, the number of nodes, the number of edges, the number of wide edges, the number of prioritized edges, the number of requested edges and the number of small and large snowcats respectively. The solution time is set to 7200 s for all instances. The optimization model is implemented in the programming language Mosel [4] and the models are solved using Xpress-Optimizer Version 9.0. All software is run on Lenovo ThinkSystem SD530 computers with the following specifications.

CPU: 2x 3.6 GHz Intel Xeon Gold 6244 CPU - 8 core
RAM: 384 Gb
Disk: 250 Gb SATA SSD

Table 1. Statistics over the test instances

Name	Length	$\lvert\mathcal{N}\rvert$	$\lvert\mathcal{E}\rvert$	$\lvert\mathcal{E}^W\rvert$	$\lvert\mathcal{E}^P\rvert$	$\lvert\mathcal{E}^R\rvert$	$\lvert\mathcal{K}^S\rvert$	$\lvert\mathcal{K}^L\rvert$
Leinstrand	20.8	20	28	17	5	12	1	0
SkistuaV	15.5	24	32	17	11	0	1	0
SkistuaO	22.1	44	64	47	4	28	1	0
Nilsbyen	22.8	40	55	21	15	19	1	1
N&L	44.1	57	82	37	18	31	1	1

Since each network is connected and there are positive revenues for all edges, we can assume that each network will be completely groomed given enough time. Our first test is therefore to run the model on each network without considering the time windows and the available time for different values on the number of legs L. A lower bound on the number of legs needed can be calculated as $\lvert\mathcal{E}\rvert + \lvert\mathcal{E}^W\rvert$ for the instances with one small snowcat. The results are presented in Table 2. The table shows the name of the instance, the maximum number of legs for each snowcat, the objective value of the best feasible solution, the dual bound, the number of edges groomed, and the number of edges traversed.

A first observation when studying the results in Table 2 is that the problem is very complex and most instances are not solved to proven optimality. Still, the gaps are low in all cases and we believe that valid concussions can be drawn based on the results.

If we analyze Leinstrand, the lower bound is 42 and we see that $L = 40$ is clearly not enough to groom all edges. Even though $L = 50$ is higher than the lower bound, we are still not able to groom all edges. The solutions for $L = 60$ and $L = 70$ show that 53 edges (excluding the artificial edges to and from node 0) must be traversed to groom the full network.

The results are the same for the other cases with one small snowcat. The lower bound on SkistuaV is 45 and 57 edges are needed to completely groom

Table 2. Results for different values on L

Name	L	$\underline{z}$	$\overline{z}$	$\sum v$	$\sum x$
Leinstrand	40	32570	33330	20	40
Leinstrand	50	36160	36644.86	26	49
Leinstrand	60	36410	36550	28	53
Leinstrand	70	36410	36604	28	53
SkistuaV	40	20720	20720	20	40
SkistuaV	50	22850	23120	28	50
SkistuaV	60	23090	23392.9	32	58
SkistuaV	70	23090	23375	32	57
SkistuaO	110	19510	21500	55	102
SkistuaO	120	20680	21540	60	116
SkistuaO	130	20630	21540	60	124
SkistuaO	140	21120	21540	64	127
Nilsbyen	40	58480	58560	47	66
Nilsbyen	50	59820	60132.63	55	75
Nilsbyen	60	59810	60153.57	55	77
Nilsbyen	70	59780	60126.17	55	80
N&L	70	87441.7	90408.84	75	113
N&L	80	87730	90418.64	76	115
N&L	90	88620	90451.2	80	126
N&L	100	88290	90501.09	79	120

the network and the lower bound for SkistuaO is 111 and the number of edges needed is 127. On the instances with more than one snowcat, the lower bound on the number of edges is $|\mathcal{E}|$, the small snowcat grooms all narrow edges and the large snowcat all wide edges, but how to set L based on this is an open question. The results in Table 2 show that $L = 50$ is enough for Nilsbyen. For N&L, $L = 90$ gives the best results.

Since restricting L causes changes to the solution that do not have to do with the planning problem in itself, we continue the computational study with L large enough to not affect the optimal solution of the problem. Still, since the number of variables and constraints depends on L, keeping it low is preferable.

Next, we analyse the effect of the available time and time windows. We test this on the Leinstrand instance where the snowcat spends 164.8 min to groom the complete network. We set the available time to 120 min and test without time windows. In the solution from Table 2 we note that about half of the requested edges are groom in the beginning of the route and the rest at the end of the route. We therefore also test with three different time windows; $[0, 60]$, $[30, 90]$, and $[60, 120]$. The results of these tests are presented in Table 3. The table shows the name of the instance, the maximum number of legs for the snowcat, the

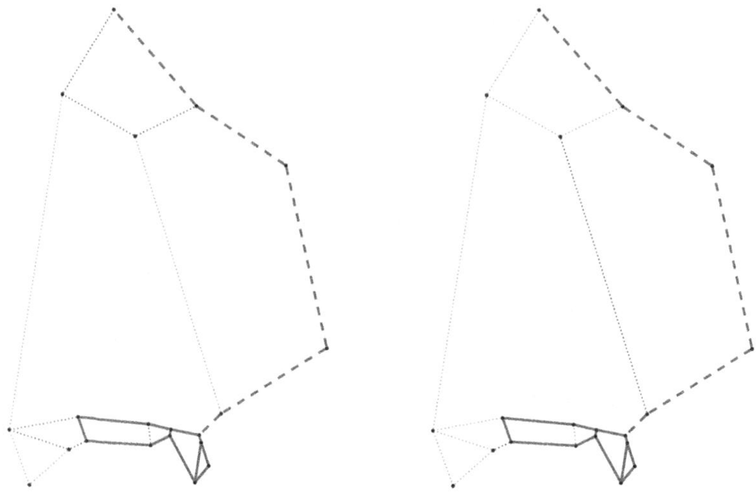

Fig. 4. Two examples of time constrained solutions for the Leinstrand instance. Without time windows (left) and with time windows [30, 90] (right). The edges that are not groomed are shown in orange. The priorities are shown: dotted (no priority), dashed (prioritized), and solid (requested). Wide segments are marked with thick lines. (Color figure online)

available time for the snowcat, the time windows $[\underline{T}_{(ij)}, \underline{T}_{(ij)}]$, which are the same for all requested edges, the objective value of the best feasible solution, the dual bound, the number of edges groomed, the number of edges traversed, and the time the snowcat uses to groom.

It is clear that the number of edges that are groomed decreases. In Fig. 4, the edges that are not groomed are marked in orange. The broad, prioritized edges are all groomed. The difference between the solutions without time windows and with early or late time windows is small. In the solution without time windows, almost all requested arcs are groomed in the first hour, and due to symmetry it is likely that there is an alternative solution where the remaining edges can also be groomed within the first hour. Since there are only edges, a route can be traversed in opposite direction without changing the cost. This means that a feasible route for the case with time windows [0, 60] can become a feasible route for the case with time windows [60, 120] by traversing it in the opposite direction. The solution for the time windows [30, 90] is worse. The snowcat cannot start grooming the requested edges and must return to do this later. This gives a situation where the farthest edges cannot be groomed. Not only is the number of edges lower, but the length of the edges not groomed is also longer. In the time restricted case without time windows, 8.2 km of the network is not groomed, while the corresponding number of the case with the time windows [30, 90] is 10.1 km.

In the last analysis, we study the effect of coordination on the two snowcats instances Nilsbyen and N&L. The variable restrictions (17) set an upper bound

Table 3. Results with restricted time and time windows

Name	L	T_k^K	TW	$\underline{z}$	$\overline{z}$	$\sum v$	$\sum x$	$t_{1,L+1}$
Leinstrand	60	∞	–	36410	36550	28	53	164.8
Leinstrand	60	120	[0,120]	29110	30510	24	44	118.9
Leinstrand	60	120	[0,60]	28080	30400.6	23	48	115.8
Leinstrand	60	120	[30,90]	27240	29327.65	19	44	117.4
Leinstrand	60	120	[60,120]	29100	29990	24	48	119.8

T_k^K on the available time for snowcat k. This models the case when one driver per snowcat grooms the track. Another interesting situation is when there is one driver that operates both snowcats and has an upper bound T^K on the total available time. To model this, we introduce the constraint

$$\sum_{k \in \mathcal{K}} t_{k,L+1} \leq T^K \tag{19}$$

To test coordination together with time windows, we introduce the binary variable o, which is 1 if the small snowcat is operated first and 0 otherwise. The sequencing of the snowcats is modeled by the following constraints

$$t_{k^S,L+1} - t_{k^L,1} \leq T_{k^S}^K (1 - o) \tag{20}$$

$$t_{k^L,L+1} - t_{k^S,1} \leq T_{k^L}^K o \tag{21}$$

$$o \in \{0, 1\} \tag{22}$$

where k^S and k^L are the indices for the small and large snowcat respectively. If the fleet of snowcats is larger, a more complex formulation of the sequencing is needed. Here, we limit the time using the variable bounds

$$t_{k,L+1} \leq T^K \qquad k \in \mathcal{K} \tag{23}$$

We run Nilsbyen and N&L with less available time than the time used in the solution from Table 2. We then take the same total available time, but let the model decide on how to divide the time between the snowcats. We also test with even less available time to see if coordination can compensate for less time. The results from these tests are given in Table 4. The table shows the name of the instance, the maximum number of legs for the snowcat, the available time for each snowcat when there is no coordination, the total available time when there is coordination, the time windows $[\underline{T}_{(ij)}, \overline{T}_{(ij)}]$, which are the same for all requested edges, the objective value of the best feasible solution, the dual bound, the number of edges groomed, the number of edges traversed, and the time spent by the small and large snowcat respectively.

Analyzing Nilsbyen, we see that the reduction to 60 min per snowcat does not affect the solution much. We also see that even though the number of groomed edges is less when the total time can distributed, the objective function value is higher. Comparing the 60 + 60 case and the 120 case, i.e. rows 2 and 3 in Table 4, we see that in the 60 + 60 case, 3.5 km of wide edges and 1.4 km of narrow edges are not groomed, while the corresponding numbers for the 120 case is 2 km and 2.1 km respectively. In both cases, all prioritized edges are groomed.

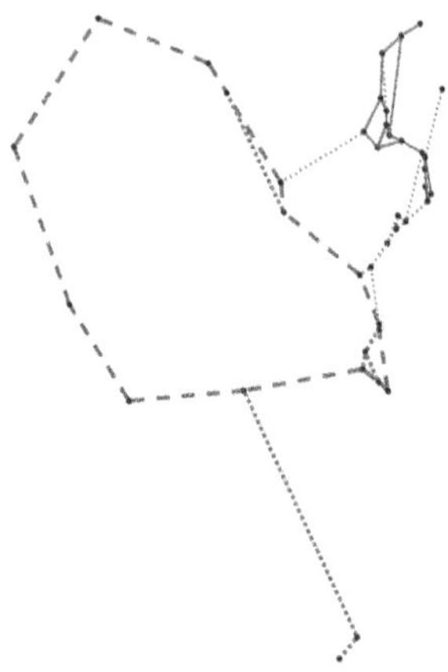

Fig. 5. The Nilsbyen instance

When the available time is restricted even more, we get to a point when it is no longer possible to groom the requested edges and the problem becomes infeasible without coordination. Table 4 shows that 30 min is not enough for the small snowcat to groom the requested narrow edges, while when 60 min in total is available a feasible solution is found. An interesting observation is that the large snowcat is not very much used when the time is very restricted, even though a wide prioritized edge can be groomed in one traversal. An explanation for this is the structure of the network together with the time restriction. The prioritized route shown in Fig. 5 takes too long to traverse and the large snowcat can only traverse a short part of

Table 4. Results with and without coordination

Name	L	T_k^K	T^K	TW	$\underline{z}$	$\overline{z}$	$\sum v$	$\sum x$	$t_{k^S,L+1}$	$t_{k^L,L+1}$
Nilsbyen	60	1200	–	–	59810	60153.57	55	77	80.5	76.7
Nilsbyen	60	60	–	–	55840	58524.43	51	68	55.9	53.9
Nilsbyen	60	–	120		56530	58330.12	48	63	48.1	66.7
Nilsbyen	60	–	120	[0,60]	56270	58297.65	48	63	46.1	66.7
Nilsbyen	60	–	120	[60,120]	56560	58526.26	49	64	49.3	69.1
Nilsbyen	60	45	–	–	14860	49110.03	35	58	44.8	23
Nilsbyen	60	–	90	–	26950	51431.11	37	56	88.1	0
Nilsbyen	60	30	–	–	–	–	–	–	–	–
Nilsbyen	60	–	60	–	11150	26317.42	39	53	51.6	6.2
N&L	90	1200	–	–	88620	90451.2	80	126	188.9	147.7
N&L	90	120	–	–	76830	89030.64	69	98	84.7	113.6
N&L	90	–	240	–	78050	89444.73	70	100	70.3	147.2
N&L	90	90	–	–	43420	81561.08	57	76	58.3	78.3
N&L	90	–	180	–	73690	81552.46	63	84	53.3	110.6

it before it has to return to the depot. When going back and forth on the same edges, the advantage of the large snowcat is lost.

The results are similar for the N&L instance, the case with a total available time is better than the case with individual available times. This is especially true for the 90 + 90 case compared with the 180 case. Figure 6 illustrates this case. When the total time can be distributed, more time can be given to the large snowcat so that it can groom all prioritized edges.

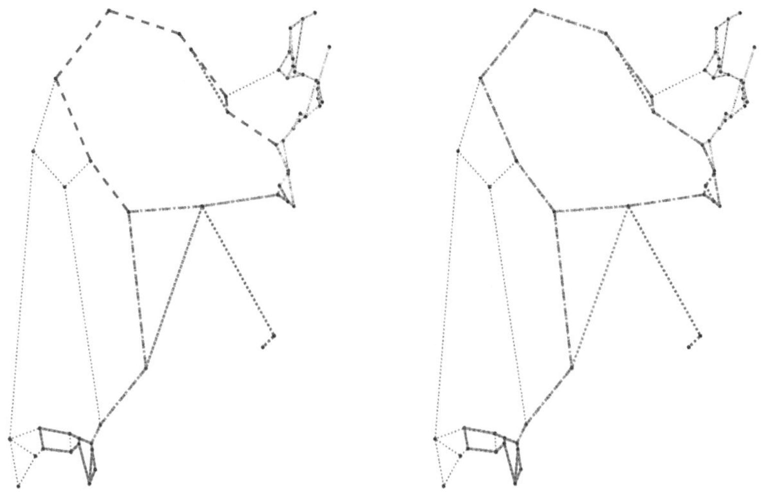

Fig. 6. A comparison between solutions without and with coordination for the N&L instance. In the left figure, each snowcat has 90 min available, in the right figure the total available time is 180 min. The route of the small snowcat is marked in orange and the route of the large snowcat is marked in green. The priorities are shown: dotted (no priority), dashed (prioritized), and solid (requested). Wide segments are marked with thick lines. (Color figure online)

6 Conclusion

We have introduced a new problem to the arc routing society, the Snow Grooming Routing Problem (SGRP). The SGRP is a rich arc routing problem with profits including multiple depots, heterogeneous vehicles, time windows, and edges that can be serviced in different ways. A mixed-integer linear formulation of the problem is given and tested on five different instances based on real-life data. The computational study highlights interesting findings regarding the effect of restricted time and time windows, and coordination. The problem is complex and hard to solve and developing both efficient heuristics and other exact solution methods are interesting avenues for future research. The SGRP studied here is a static version of the problem, extending it to a dynamic problem where both the initial condition of the tracks and the weather are included, which is an interesting topic for future research.

References

1. Corberán, A., Eglese, R., Hasle, G., Plana, I., Sanchis, J.M.: Arc routing problems: a review of the past, present, and future. Networks **77**(1), 88–115 (2021)
2. Corberán, A., Laporte, G.: Arc Routing. Society for Industrial and Applied Mathematics, Philadelphia (2015)
3. Dagens Næringsliv: Norges beste langrennsløyper (2013). https://www.dn.no/trening/norges-beste-langrennsomrader/1-1-5010947. Accessed 13 Apr 2023
4. Fair Isaac Corporation: FICO®Xpress Optimization Help (2023). https://www.fico.com/fico-xpress-optimization/docs/latest/overview.html. Accessed 02 Feb 2023
5. Gundersen, A.H., Johansen, M., Kjær, B.S., Andersson, H., Stålhane, M.: Arc routing with precedence constraints: an application to snow plowing operations. In: ICCL 2017. LNCS, vol. 10572, pp. 174–188. Springer, Cham (2017). https://doi.org/10.1007/978-3-319-68496-3_12
6. Mourão, M.C., Pinto, L.S.: An updated annotated bibliography on arc routing problems. Networks **70**(3), 144–194 (2017)
7. Perrier, N., Langevin, A., Amaya, C.A.: Vehicle routing for urban snow plowing operations. Transp. Sci. **42**(1), 44–56 (2008)
8. Perrier, N., Langevin, A., Campbell, J.F.: A survey of models and algorithms for winter road maintenance. Part I: system design for spreading and plowing. Comput. Oper. Res. **33**(1), 209–238 (2006)
9. Perrier, N., Langevin, A., Campbell, J.F.: A survey of models and algorithms for winter road maintenance. Part II: system design for snow disposal. Comput. Oper. Res. **33**(1), 239–262 (2006)
10. Perrier, N., Langevin, A., Campbell, J.F.: A survey of models and algorithms for winter road maintenance. Part III: vehicle routing and depot location for spreading. Comput. Oper. Res. **34**(1), 211–257 (2007)
11. Perrier, N., Langevin, A., Campbell, J.F.: A survey of models and algorithms for winter road maintenance. Part IV: vehicle routing and fleet sizing for plowing and snow disposal. Comput. Oper. Res. **34**(1), 258–294 (2007)
12. Skisporet: Skisporet - om oss (2023). https://www.skisporet.no/about. Accessed 13 Apr 2023
13. Statistisk Sentralbyrå: Tabell 12593: Tilrettelegging for friluftsliv (2022). https://www.ssb.no/statbank/table/12593/. Accessed 13 Apr 2023
14. Statistisk Sentralbyrå: Bygningsmassen (2023). https://www.ssb.no/bygningsmasse. Accessed 13 Apr 2023

A Constraint Programming Model for the Vehicle Routing Problem with Multiple Time Windows

Florian Linß(✉)

Faculty of Business and Economics, TUD Dresden University of Technology, 01069 Dresden, Germany
Florian.linss@tu-dresden.de

Abstract. In this paper, we address the vehicle routing problem with multiple time windows (VRPMTW), which extends the classic vehicle routing problem to allow customers to be visited only within one or more time windows. We propose a constraint programming (CP) model for the VRPMTW and apply model-strengthening techniques such as fixing variables and adding interval variables to improve the model's performance. The model's effectiveness is demonstrated by comparing its performance against an existing mixed-integer programming model. The study also analyzes the differences in solver performance and evaluates the impact of instance characteristics on the solvability of the problem instances. Our study demonstrates the benefits of using a CP model with model-strengthening techniques for solving medium-sized instances of the VRPMTW.

Keywords: vehicle routing · multiple time windows · constraint programming

1 Introduction

As e-commerce continues to grow and home parcel delivery volumes increase, logistics service providers place great importance on flexibility in delivery. One way to improve flexibility is by offering delivery in multiple time windows. From a decision support perspective, this can be described as the vehicle routing problem with multiple time windows (VRPMTW)—an extension of the vehicle routing problem with time windows (VRPTW). The VRPMTW aims to determine the minimum cost vehicle routes that serve each customer in one of the specified time windows while meeting vehicle capacity constraints.

The first mathematical formulation for the VRPMTW was introduced by [6]. Since then, heuristics have been widely used as solution methods. Among these heuristics, [2] proposed a variable neighborhood search (VNS) combined with tabu search, using new benchmark instances derived from the well-known

© The Author(s), under exclusive license to Springer Nature Switzerland AG 2023
J. R. Daduna et al. (Eds.): ICCL 2023, LNCS 14239, pp. 307–321, 2023.
https://doi.org/10.1007/978-3-031-43612-3_19

Solomon instances [14]. These benchmark instances have since served as a standard for evaluating future work for the VRPMTW. Other state-of-the-art heuristics include the adaptive large neighborhood search (ALNS) proposed by [8], the genetic VNS introduced by [3], the adaptive variable neighborhood search suggested by [5], and the ALNS presented by [13]. More recently, [15] extended the VRPMTW to the vehicle routing problem (VRP) with availability profiles, where successful delivery to customers depends on the probability of delivery within specific time windows. The proposed ALNS heuristic was also evaluated for the VRPMTW and produced new best-known solutions.

Regarding exact methods, different mixed integer programming (MIP) formulations exist in the related literature. Still, these are mainly problem definitions and have rarely been evaluated as exact approaches for the VRPMTW. [2] introduced a three-index (vehicle flow) formulation where each vehicle's flow is formulated separately. However, since the vehicles are homogeneous, differentiation between vehicles is not necessary. Thus, the formulation can be strengthened to a two-index formulation introduced by [13], where the flow is formulated aggregated for all vehicles. The authors implemented both MIP formulations using a standard solver and showed that the latter formulation performed significantly better. Nevertheless, there were already instances with only 15 customers that could not be solved optimally. In addition to the comprehensive MIP formulations, [4] presented a column generation approach and a post-optimization VNS heuristic. For this approach, the pricing problem - which involves the determination of an elementary shortest path with multiple time windows and capacity constraints - is solved using a standard solver. The authors were able to optimally solve instances with up to 17 customers. The rarity of exact approaches for the VRPMTW contrasts with the adoption of exact approaches for the VRPTW. As pointed out by [1], many exact methods are available for the latter. In recent research, [10] suggested that constraint programming (CP) is a viable alternative to more traditional MIP models and solvers in scheduling problems. This finding is relevant to the VRP context, as considering time windows and service times shares similarities to scheduling. [11] previously demonstrated the suitability, who applied CP to solve the traveling salesman problem with multiple time windows. Additionally, [12] employed a column generation approach for the VRPTW and integrated CP for solving the pricing problem.

This paper is the first approach that applies a CP formulation in the context of the VRPMTW. In addition, we show that fixing variables and additional interval variables improve the performance of the CP model. The CP model outperforms a comparable MIP formulation regarding the number of instances optimally solved, the time required to prove optimality, and remaining gap after a given runtime. We achieve proven optimality for almost all instances with 20 customers and for more than half of the instances with 25 customers. The work is structured as follows. In Sect. 2, the CP formulation is presented. Computation tests are discussed in Sect. 3. Finally, a conclusion is presented in Sect. 4.

2 Constraint Programming Formulation for the VRPMTW

2.1 Base Model

The VRPMTW involves the delivery to a set of customers using multiple homogeneous vehicles from a single depot. Each customer has a set of multiple time windows, and the service must begin within one of these time windows. To ensure that the routes are feasible, the capacity of the vehicles and the maximum length of the routes must not be exceeded. Similar to [8], we make two simplifying assumptions in the formulation based on the data provided in the benchmark instances. Firstly, the depot is assigned only a single time window, representing the planning horizon. Secondly, the maximum route length is modeled so each vehicle must return to the depot within this time window. The CP formulation is specifically designed for modeling with the SAT solver provided by Google OR-tools, but it can be easily adapted to other CP solvers[1].

Table 1 summarizes the necessary parameter and set definitions. We define $G = (\mathcal{V}, \mathcal{A})$ as a digraph with a set of vertices $\mathcal{V}$ and a set of arcs $\mathcal{A}$. The vertex set $\mathcal{V}$ consists of a depot vertex 0 and n customer vertices (denoted by set $\mathcal{C}$). Each vertex $i \in \mathcal{V}$ has an associated demand μ_i, a service time σ_i, and θ_i disjoint time windows. It follows that each vertex $i \in \mathcal{V}$ has a respective set of time windows $\mathcal{T}_i = \{\{\alpha_i^1, \beta_i^1\}, \ldots, \{\alpha_i^{\theta_i}, \beta_i^{\theta_i}\}\}$ in which the service can start. As described above, the depot has a single time window, i.e., $\theta_0 = 1$, and the end of this time window equals the planning horizon $T = \beta_0^1$.

Table 1. Parameter and set definitions for the CP model

Parameter	Description	Domain
σ_i	service time at customer $i \in \mathcal{C}$	integer
μ_i	demand at customer $i \in \mathcal{C}$	integer
θ_i	number of time windows at vertex $i \in \mathcal{V}$	integer
α_i^p, β_i^p	start and end of time window p at $i \in \mathcal{V}$	integer
τ_{ij}, γ_{ij}	time and cost related to the arc $(i,j) \in \mathcal{A}$	integer
κ	vehicle freight capacity	integer
γ^f	costs per vehicle used	integer
γ^w	costs per unit waiting time	integer
Set		
$\mathcal{V}$	set of vertices	$\{0, 1, \ldots, n\}$
$\mathcal{A}$	set of arcs	$\{(i,j) \vert i,j \in \mathcal{V}\}$
$\mathcal{C}$	set of customers	$\{1, 2, \ldots, n\}$
$\mathcal{K}$	set of vehicles	$\{1, 2, \ldots, K\}$
$\mathcal{T}_i$	set of time windows of vertex $i \in \mathcal{V}$	$\{\{\alpha_i^1, \beta_i^1\}, \ldots, \{\alpha_i^{\theta_i}, \beta_i^{\theta_i}\}\}$

[1] https://github.com/google/or-tools.

The arc set is defined as $\mathcal{A} = \{(i,j) | i \neq j, i,j \in \mathcal{V}\}$. Each arc $(i,j) \in \mathcal{A}$ is associated with a non-negative travel time τ_{ij} and travel costs γ_{ij}. All time windows ending before the earliest possible start of service and starting after the latest possible end of service can be removed from $\mathcal{T}_i$ of customer i. The earliest possible start of service is defined as $\alpha_0^1 + \tau_{0i}$ and the latest possible end can be calculated by $T - \sigma_i - \tau_{i0}$. We modify the new first and last time windows as follows: $\alpha_i^1 = \max\{\alpha_i^1, \tau_{0i}\}$ and $\beta_i^{\theta_i} = \min\{\beta_i^{\theta_i}, T - \sigma_i - \tau_{i0}\}$.

The vehicle set $\mathcal{K}$ denotes a homogeneous fleet of K vehicles with a freight capacity of κ and fixed vehicle costs γ^f. Following the definition in [13], the VRPMTW is considered in two variants, which differ in their objective function. The first variant aims to minimize vehicle and travel costs. In contrast, the second variant additionally considers waiting times in case a vehicle arrives at a customer when there is no time window open. The costs for waiting time are described by γ^w per time unit. To distinguish between both variants, the parameter B is used to differentiate between them: $B = 1$ indicates waiting times are considered, and $B = 0$ means they are not.

Table 2. Decision variables for the CP model

Variable	Description	Domain
x_{ij}	true, if arc (i,j) is used, 0 otherwise	boolean
y_{ik}	true, if customer $i \in \mathcal{C}$ is served by vehicle $k \in \mathcal{K}$	boolean
v_i	vehicle index for customer $i \in \mathcal{C}$	$\{1, 2, \ldots, K\}$
r	number of vehicles used	$\{1, 2, \ldots, K\}$
s_i	start time of service at vertex $i \in \mathcal{V}$	$\mathcal{T}_i$
w_i	waiting time at customer $i \in \mathcal{C}$	$\{0, 1, \ldots, T\}$

Table 2 summarizes the definition of the decision variables. The vehicle flow in the graph is described by the boolean variable x_{ij} indicating whether an arc $(i,j) \in \mathcal{A}$ is used or not. Additionally, the boolean variable y_{ik} defines the assignment of customer i to a vehicle k. For convenience and efficient determination of the number of vehicles, the variable v_i defines the vehicle index for each customer i, and the variable r denotes the number of vehicles used. The variable s_i describes the start time of a service at a vertex i. The time windows for each vertex are expressed by specifying multiple disjoint domains in the variable definition. With this notation, we state a CP model for the VRPMTW:

$$\min \gamma^f r + \sum_{(i,j) \in \mathcal{A}} \gamma_{ij} x_{ij} + B \sum_{j \in \mathcal{C}} \gamma^w w_i \tag{1}$$

$$\text{s.t. } \texttt{MultipleCircuit}\,(\mathcal{A}) \tag{2}$$

$$\texttt{ExactlyOne}\,(\{y_{ik} | k \in \mathcal{K}\}) \qquad \forall i \in \mathcal{C} \tag{3}$$

$$\max_{i \in \mathcal{C}}(v_i) = r \tag{4}$$

$$\sum_{j \in \mathcal{C}} x_{0j} = r \tag{5}$$

$$\sum_{i \in \mathcal{C}} \mu_i \cdot y_{ik} \leq \kappa \qquad k \in \mathcal{K} \tag{6}$$

$$y_{ik} \Rightarrow v_i = k \qquad \forall i \in \mathcal{C}, k \in \mathcal{K} \tag{7}$$

$$x_{ij} \Rightarrow v_i = v_j \qquad \forall i, j \in \mathcal{C} : i \neq j \tag{8}$$

$$x_{ij} \Rightarrow s_j = s_i + \sigma_i + \tau_{ij} + w_j \qquad (i, j) \in \mathcal{A} : i, j \neq 0 \tag{9}$$

The objective function (1) minimizes total costs consisting of total fixed vehicle costs, total travel costs, and total waiting costs in case of $B = 1$. The vehicle flow is modeled in constraint (2) using the global function `MultipleCircuit` implemented in Google OR-tools. The constraint ensures that every customer vertex has exactly one incoming and one outgoing arc. Additionally, vertex 0 has the same number of incoming and outgoing arcs, and cycles not including the depot are prohibited. The global functions `ExactlyOne` in constraints (3) ensure that exactly one variable of a set of boolean variables must be true. This relation ensures that only one vehicle is assigned to each customer.

Constraint (4) connects the number of vehicles used with the maximum vehicle index. Constraint (5) guarantees that the number of vehicles used corresponds to the sum of outgoing arcs from the depot. Constraints (6) ensure that each vehicle's capacity is respected. Constraints (7) set vehicle index variables v_i based on binary variables y_{ik}. Constraints (8) enforce that the head and tail of a traveled arc connecting customers have the same vehicle index. The scheduling of services is respected in constraints (9). If an arc x_{ij} is used, the service at its tail j must start at the arrival time $s_i + \sigma_i + \tau_{ij}$ plus a potential waiting time w_j.

2.2 Model Strengthening

We can strengthen the formulation of the base model by additionally fixing variables and adding optional interval variables.

Fixing of Variables

$$x_{0i} \wedge x_{0j} \Rightarrow v_i \neq v_j \qquad \forall i, j \in \mathcal{C} : i \neq j \tag{10}$$

$$\neg y_{ik} \Rightarrow v_i \neq k \qquad \forall i \in \mathcal{C}, k \in \mathcal{K} \tag{11}$$

$$v_1 = 1 \tag{12}$$

Constraints (10) defines that if two customers are assigned to two different routes, i.e., $x_{0i} \wedge x_{0j}$, their vehicle indices must differ, too. Similarly, we specify the vehicle index of a customer cannot be k if the customer is not assigned to vehicle k, see constraints (11). Since all vehicles are homogeneous, the first customer is assigned to the first vehicle by the symmetry breaking condition (12).

Optional Interval Variables. Optional interval variables are increasingly common in CP-based approaches [7,9]. These variables are introduced to determine whether a set of customers can be served by one vehicle. In addition to considering the service time as a fixed component, the travel time to the next vertex can be added to the interval variables as a variable component. Thus, the schedule can be modeled more accurately. Since the length of the interval depends on the next vertex, each interval variable, denoted as `IntervalVar([Start,Length, End))`, requires three variables to model its start, length, and end. Interval variables are defined as always present. In contrast, the presence of optional interval variables, denoted as `optIntervalVar(Boolean, [Start,Length,End))` is indicated by a boolean variable.

Table 3. Additional decision variables for defining variable service intervals

Variable	Description	Domain
s_k^0	start time of vehicle $k \in \mathcal{K}$ at the depot	$\mathcal{T}_0$
t_k^0	travel time of vehicle $k \in \mathcal{K}$ to the first customer	$\{\min_{j \in \mathcal{C}}(\tau_{0j}), \max_{j \in \mathcal{C}}(\tau_{0j})\}$
a_k^0	arrival time of vehicle k at the first customer	$\mathcal{T}_0$
a_i	arrival time at the next vertex after customer i	$\mathcal{T}_0$
t_i	travel time from customer $i \in \mathcal{C}$ to the next vertex	$\{\min_{j \in \mathcal{V}}(\tau_{ij}), \max_{j \in \mathcal{V}}(\tau_{ij})\}$
S_{0k}	$\texttt{IntervalVar}\left(\left[s_k^0, t_k^0, a_k^0\right)\right)$ for $k \in \mathcal{K}$	
S_{ik}	$\texttt{optIntervalVar}\left(y_{ik}, \left[s_i, \sigma_i + t_i, a_i\right)\right)$ for $k \in \mathcal{K}$, $i \in \mathcal{C}$	

Table 3 summarizes the definition of the additional variables. Since each vehicle starts at the depot, separate interval variables are defined for each vehicle. More precisely, the integer variable s_k^0 is introduced to define the start time of a vehicle k at the depot. With integer variables t_k^0 and a_k^0 denoting the travel time to and arrival time at the first customer, S_{0k} is defined as $\texttt{IntervalVar}\left(\left[s_k^0, t_k^0, a_k^0\right)\right)$. Since each customer is visited by one vehicle, exactly one interval variable is present per customer. Therefore, optional interval variables are introduced for each vehicle and customer. Their presence depends on the assignment of customers to vehicles. The variables t_i and a_i are introduced as travel to and arrival time at the next vertex for each customer i. Depending on whether a customer is assigned to a vehicle, the interval variable $\texttt{optIntervalVar}\left(y_{ik}, \left[s_i, \sigma_i + t_i, a_i\right)\right)$ is only present for vehicle k if y_{ik} is true.

In Fig. 1, the definitions above are illustrated by the interval variables of an example route, see Fig. 1b. The gantt chart in Fig. 1a shows each vertex's service time and travel time to the next vertex. Since the start times are only defined within the time windows, only an overlap of the intervals has to be prevented for a feasible schedule. This can be enforced efficiently with global constraints like `NoOverlap`. The corresponding constraints are listed below.

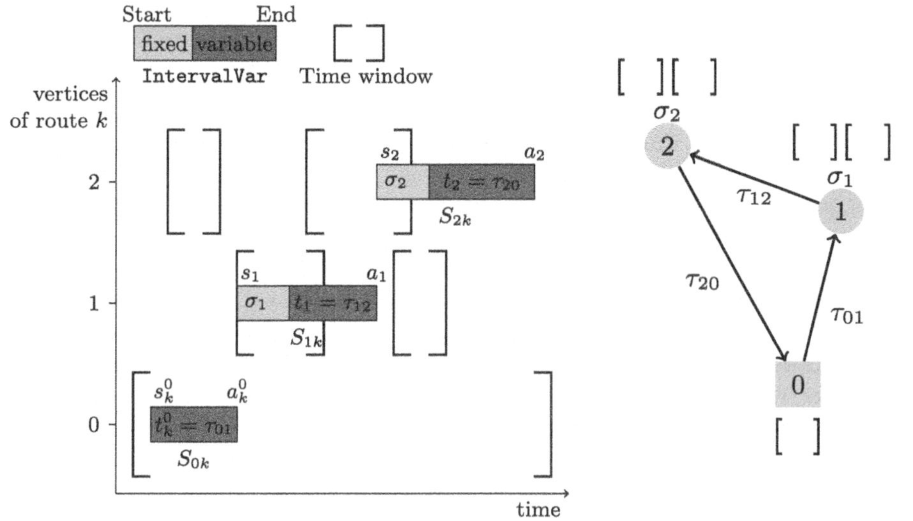

(a) Route schedule presented by an Gantt chart that includes the time windows and service intervals (S_{ik}). The service intervals have a fixed service time (σ_i) and a variable travel time to the next vertex (τ_{ij}).

(b) Example route starting at the depot (square) and visiting two customers (cycle).

Fig. 1. The schedule of an example route illustrates the definition of interval variables.

$$x_{ij} \Rightarrow t_i = \tau_{ij} \qquad (i,j) \in \mathcal{A} : i \neq 0 \tag{13}$$

$$x_{ij} \Rightarrow a_i \leq s_j \qquad (i,j) \in \mathcal{A} : i,j \neq 0 \tag{14}$$

$$x_{0j} \wedge y_{jk} \Rightarrow t_k^0 = \tau_{0j} \qquad j \in \mathcal{C}, k \in \mathcal{K} \tag{15}$$

$$x_{0j} \wedge y_{jk} \Rightarrow a_k^0 = s_j \qquad j \in \mathcal{C}, k \in \mathcal{K} \tag{16}$$

$$\texttt{NoOverlap}\left(\{S_{ik} | i \in \mathcal{V}\}\right) \qquad k \in \mathcal{K} \tag{17}$$

The length and the end of the optional interval variables of the customers are defined with the constraints (13) and (14). If j is visited after i, t_i is equal to the travel time τ_{ij} and the service start s_j at j must be after a_i. Similarly, the length and the end of the interval variable at the depot are described by constraints (15) and (16). If j is the first customer visited by vehicle k, t_k^0 must be equal to the travel time τ_{0j}. Since each vehicle can start every time within the planning horizon, the first customer's service start s_j equals a_k^0, and no waiting times occur. Finally, overlapping of the intervals can be prevented for each vehicle with the global constraint `NoOverlap`, see constraint (17).

3 Computational Tests

3.1 Experimental Design

We apply the MIP formulation introduced in [13] to validate and assess the CP model. We use the CP-SAT solver of Google OR-Tools (9.4) to solve the CP model and Gurobi (10.0.0) to solve the MIP formulation. Both approaches are implemented in C++ using MSVC v143. All tests were run with a limit of 8 parallel threads on an AMD EPYC 7513 with 2.6 GHz clock speed and 64 GB RAM. Each instance is run three times with different seed values to account for the variability in solver performance. Apart from that, both solvers were run with their default parameters. The runtime is limited to 3,600 s for each run.

We use the small to medium-sized instances provided by [13] in our experiments. These instances were derived from the instances presented in [2]. Specifically, the first 10, 15, 20, 25, and 50 customers from the instances cm101, cm105, cm201, cm205, rm101, rm105, rm201, rm205, rcm101, rcm105, rcm201, and rcm205 were selected to create a total of 60 instances. The instances are classified according to three metrics for the customers' location: clustered (cm), random (rm), and random clustered (rcm). Additionally, the first digit of the instance name indicates whether the vertices have short (1) or long (2) time windows. Since the CP model is only defined for integer domains, all parameter values were scaled with 10^4 and rounded.

3.2 Results

First, we investigate the impact of the model-strengthening methods and compare the formulations. Next, we examine different lower bounds for the number of required vehicles, which shed light on the varying performance of the solvers. After that, we evaluate how solvability is affected by the characteristics of the instance.

Model Comparison. To evaluate the impact of fixing the variables and adding interval variables, we solve all instances using the base formulation without model strengthening (CP^{Base}) and with model strengthening (CP^{Full}). In preliminary tests, we observed that CP^{Full} had difficulties finding a feasible solution for large instances. Therefore, CP^{Base} was solved for maximal 60 s as a starting solution and passed to CP^{Full}.

The results are shown in Table 4. The average values are grouped by their instance size, i.e., the number of customers. Apart from the count of optimally solved runs out of the 36 runs (12 instances $\times$ 3 runs per instance), the remaining gaps and runtime are computed considering the average of all runs. Analyzing the optimal objective function values shows the validity of the CP model compared to the MIP model. We were able to prove optimality for the first time in a total of 18 instances. For this, we refer to Table 6 in the Appendix for more detailed results for all instances.

Table 4. Performance evaluation of MIP, basic CP (CP^{Base}), and CP with variable fixing and interval variables (CP^{Full}); comparison of the number of optimally solved runs (#O), the average remaining gap (G) in [%] after 3,600 s, and the average runtimes (T) in [s] per instance size (12 instances × 3 runs). For CP^{Full}, T^S indicates the start solution time in [s].

$\|C\|$	MIP			CP^{Base}			CP^{Full}			
	#O	G	T	#O	G	T	#O	G	T	T^S
$B = 0$										
10	36	0.0	299.9	36	0.0	0.8	36	0.0	0.2	1.2
15	32	1.7	408.3	36	0.0	50.9	36	0.0	3.0	5.5
20	18	15.7	1,804.0	18	14.0	1,800.5	33	0.6	468.4	30.2
25	17	13.8	1,907.6	18	13.6	1,800.9	24	3.7	1,215.8	30.5
50	6	31.1	3,152.8	6	29.6	3,040.2	6	25.0	3,105.4	59.9
Total	21.8	12.5	1,514.5	22.8	11.4	1,338.7	27.0	5.8	958.6	25.5
$B = 1$										
10	36	0.0	202.0	36	0.0	10.7	36	0.0	0.6	8.1
15	33	1.8	339.6	33	2.1	304.6	36	0.0	16.2	11.4
20	18	16.0	1,837.6	18	14.4	1,804.9	33	0.6	607.3	34.6
25	12	14.7	2,484.4	15	14.5	2,138.3	21	7.5	1,654.2	42.3
50	3	31.0	3,344.6	3	30.9	3,357.9	3	25.8	3,425.9	59.9
Total	20.4	12.7	1,641.6	21.0	12.4	1,523.3	25.8	6.8	1,140.9	31.3

Although all models can optimally solve the small instances with 10 customers, a comparison between MIP and CP^{Base} reveals that the latter performs better regarding average gap and runtime over all instances. More considerable differences can be seen for CP^{Full}. For example, instances with up to 15 customers are solved within a few seconds, and, unlike other formulations, all but one of the 20 customer instances can be solved optimally. However, as the number of customers exceeds 25, the increasing complexity of the problem becomes apparent in CP^{Full}. This is reflected by higher runtimes and decreased instances for which optimality can be proven. Despite these challenges, CP^{Full} is still the most effective formulation for larger instances.

Comparing the two objective functions shows that including waiting costs makes the optimality proof more difficult since the runtimes are more extensive as only minimizing vehicle and travel costs. In summary, the CP model is clearly better than the MIP formulation due to the use of variable interval variables. Therefore, we will refer to the CP^{Full} model as the CP model in the following.

Impact of the Lower Bound for the Number of Required Vehicles. As an example, Fig. 2 shows the detailed solution of instance rm101 with 10 customers. The figure demonstrates that the volume utilization is no more than one–third of the vehicle capacity for both routes in the optimal solution. The fixed costs in the benchmark instances are very high. Therefore, a solution with fewer vehicles leads to lower costs [2]. However, the time windows of the depot and the customers do not permit a feasible sequence with only one vehicle, even though the volume capacity is sufficient to visit all customers using one vehicle.

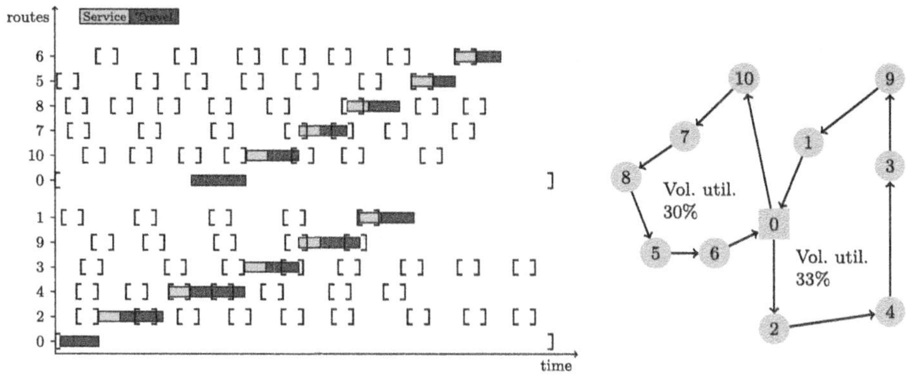

(a) Schedules are represented by a Gantt chart, including time windows and intervals (consisting of service and travel times) for each vertex.

(b) Routes starting at the depot (square) and visiting the customers (cycles).

Fig. 2. Optimal solution of instance rm101 with 10 customers presented by the schedules and the volume utilization of the routes.

The minimum number of vehicles required can be determined easily using the volume approximation, see Eq. (18).

$$\mathrm{LB}^{\mathrm{Vol}} = \left\lceil \frac{\sum_{i \in C} \mu_i}{\kappa} \right\rceil \tag{18}$$

To incorporate the time windows into determining the minimum number of vehicles required, the CP model was rerun using a modified objective function. Setting $B = \gamma_{ij} = 0$ and $\gamma^f = 1$ equals the minimization of vehicles required. The results of these additional runs with limited runtime of 60 s show that, for 16 out of the 60 instances, the lower bound determined by the CP model ($\mathrm{LB}^{\mathrm{CP}}$) was higher than the lower bound of the volume approximation ($\mathrm{LB}^{\mathrm{Vol}}$). This result was used to divide the instances into two sets with $\mathrm{LB}^{\mathrm{Vol}} = \mathrm{LB}^{\mathrm{CP}}$ and $\mathrm{LB}^{\mathrm{Vol}} < \mathrm{LB}^{\mathrm{CP}}$. Figure 3 shows these subsets' average gaps and runtimes for the MIP and the CP model.

For instances with the same vehicle lower bound, the gap values and runtimes of the CP model are slightly better than those of the MIP model. However, the differences are greater when the CP model quickly determines that more than $\mathrm{LB}^{\mathrm{Vol}}$ vehicles are necessary to serve all customers. The gap values of the CP model are only a quarter of the values of the MIP model, and the runtimes could

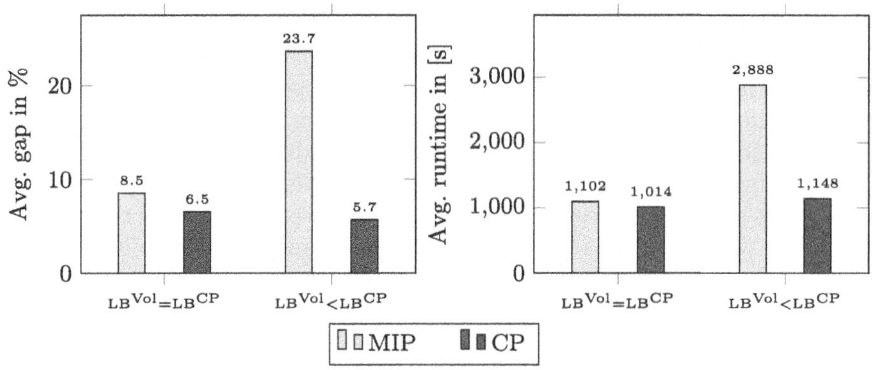

Fig. 3. Comparison of MIP and CP solver according to the average gap and runtime. The instances are divided into a set of 44 instances, where the lower bound for the number of required vehicles calculated by volume approximation (LB^{Vol}) equals the lower bound calculated by the CP solver (LB^{CP}) and a set of 16 instances, where $LB^{Vol} < LB^{CP}$.

also be halved. It becomes evident that the CP model can determine the LB for the number of vehicles much better than the MIP. As a result, the CP model leads to better solutions overall because the number of vehicles greatly influences the objective function due to high fixed costs.

Impact of Instance Characteristics. We observed varying difficulties in solving the instances. Therefore, in Table 5, we grouped the instances according to their metrics and the length of the time windows for both problem variants and then averaged the gap values and runtimes.

Table 5. Average remaining gap G in [%] after 3.600 s, average runtimes (T) in [s], and the average number of vehicles used (V) grouped by problem variant and time window lengths per instance metric (20 instances × 3 runs) are displayed.

Metric	$B = 0$						$B = 1$					
	short TW			long TW			short TW			long TW		
	G	T	V	G	T	V	G	T	V	G	T	V
cm	5.9	1,638.1	3.3	7.4	1,457.2	1.7	8.9	1,941.2	3.3	10.5	1,333.0	1.8
rcm	0.0	109.5	3.0	8.6	720.3	1.2	0.2	493.6	3.0	9.0	1,096.0	1.2
rm	6.3	1,086.6	3.5	6.9	720.5	1.2	6.3	1,121.6	3.4	5.8	835.0	1.1
Total	4.1	944.7	3.3	7.6	966.0	1.4	5.1	1,185.5	3.3	8.4	1,088.0	1.4

Interestingly, for both problem variants, the random clustered instance with short time windows can be solved easier than solving the remaining instances.

Due to the spatial structure of several randomly arranged customer clusters, infeasible customer combinations between these clusters can be excluded more effectively. This effect is weakened somewhat with long time windows since routes can also be formed here that visit multiple clusters. The increased complexity resulting from longer time windows is also reflected in other metrics. Since the problem is more weakly constrained, more customers can be combined on the routes. This is apparent from the number of the vehicle used in the solutions. Specifically, while the instances with short time windows involve an average of 3.3 vehicles, only 1.4 vehicles are used for those with long time windows.

4 Conclusion

This paper studies the vehicle routing problem with multiple time windows (VRPMTW). The goal is to visit all customers with multiple time windows and start and end within the depot time window. Two variants of the VRPMTW are considered with different objective functions: the first variant aims to minimize vehicle and travel costs. In contrast, the second variant considers waiting times in case a vehicle arrives at a customer when there is no time window open, in addition to vehicle and travel costs. We developed a constraint programming (CP) model with additional model strengthening by fixing variables and variable interval variables to address this problem. Experimental tests on benchmark instances reveal that model strengthening improves the performance of the CP model. As a result, the CP model performs considerably better than a comparable mixed–integer programming (MIP) model. In total, we solved 18 instances optimally for the first time. We achieve proven optimality for almost all instances with 20 customers and more than half with 25 customers. When reaching the time limit, the gap values are halved compared to the MIP model. In addition, we performed a more detailed analysis to better explain the difference in performance between the two models and to account for the influence of instance characteristics on the CP model's solution performance. The feasibility of the routes is defined by two factors: the respect to the vehicle capacity and the feasible sequence so that each customer is visited one of the time windows. The CP model is particularly well suited for instances where customer time windows constrain the number of required routes in addition to the vehicles' capacity. This way, solutions with too few vehicles can be excluded more quickly. Nevertheless, instances with longer time windows and, thus, more possible combinations of customers are challenging to solve.

Observations reveal that in instances with 50 customers, there are large differences in the solutions found by the CP solver between different runs on the same instance. To improve the upper bound in such instances, embedding other solution methods, such as heuristics, is a promising approach. Another extension involves the integration of the CP model into a sophisticated solution approach. The results regarding the lower bound of the required vehicles motivate using the CP model to solve the traveling salesman problem with multiple time windows as a feasibility problem on subsets of customers. Efficient feasibility checks through the CP model can determine that these customers must be served by at least two vehicles if their combination is infeasible. This information can be used to create cutting planes, e. g. cover inequalities in a branch-and-cut approach.

Appendix

Table 6. Detailed results of the best runs of MIP and CP for both problem variants according to objective value (λ), remaining gap (G) in [%] after the time limit 3,600 s (TL), and runtime (T) in [s].

Inst.	C	$B = 0$						$B = 1$					
		MIP			CP			MIP			CP		
		λ	G	T	λ	G	T	λ	G	T	λ	G	T
cm101	10	485.3	0.0	3174	485.3	0.0	**9.9**	490.8	0.0	1662	490.8	0.0	**62**
cm105	10	486.0	0.0	58	486.0	0.0	**0.7**	488.5	0.0	38	488.5	0.0	**4.8**
cm201	10	833.1	0.0	0.5	833.1	0.0	**0.3**	834.9	0.0	**0.4**	834.9	0.0	0.5
cm205	10	834.9	0.0	0.5	834.9	0.0	**0.3**	835.3	0.0	**0.3**	835.3	0.0	0.8
rcm101	10	566.0	0.0	0.4	566.0	0.0	**0.3**	566.0	0.0	**0.2**	566.0	0.0	0.4
rcm105	10	566.8	0.0	1.2	566.8	0.0	**0.3**	569.5	0.0	**0.2**	569.5	0.0	0.8
rcm201	10	1137.8	0.0	1.0	1137.8	0.0	**0.2**	1137.8	0.0	**0.2**	1137.8	0.0	0.3
rcm205	10	1137.8	0.0	0.4	1137.8	0.0	**0.2**	1137.8	0.0	**0.1**	1137.8	0.0	0.3
rm101	10	598.2	0.0	54	598.2	0.0	**0.5**	606.7	0.0	30	606.7	0.0	**3.5**
rm105	10	595.4	0.0	125	595.4	0.0	**1.9**	595.4	0.0	40	595.4	0.0	**27**
rm201	10	1173.0	0.0	**0.1**	1173.0	0.0	0.2	1189.1	0.0	1.3	1189.1	0.0	**0.9**
rm205	10	1173.0	0.0	**0.1**	1173.0	0.0	0.2	1173.0	0.0	**0.1**	1173.0	0.0	0.3
Mean	10	799.0	0.0	285	799.0	0.0	**0.2**	802.1	0.0	148	802.1	0.0	**0.5**
cm101	15	537.8	0.0	9.6	537.8	0.0	**3.9**	555.3	0.0	263	555.3	0.0	**148**
cm105	15	538.1	0.0	4.1	538.1	0.0	**1.6**	538.1	0.0	**4.2**	538.1	0.0	6.0
cm201	15	870.6	0.0	3.3	870.6	0.0	**1.1**	873.7	0.0	**4.6**	873.7	0.0	5.9
cm205	15	883.2	0.0	10	883.2	0.0	**4.1**	883.2	0.0	**4.8**	883.2	0.0	7.8
rcm101	15	586.9	0.0	2.3	586.9	0.0	**0.7**	589.3	0.0	**1.0**	589.3	0.0	2.0
rcm105	15	588.5	0.0	3.2	588.5	0.0	**1.1**	594.5	0.0	**1.2**	594.5	0.0	4.6
rcm201	15	1153.6	0.0	3.9	1153.6	0.0	**0.4**	1153.6	0.0	**0.5**	1153.6	0.0	0.8
rcm205	15	1153.6	0.0	28	1153.6	0.0	**0.4**	1156.2	0.0	**0.9**	1156.2	0.0	2.4
rm101	15	878.2	19.8	TL	878.2	**0.0***	86	883.8	21.3	TL	883.8	**0.0***	86
rm105	15	661.5	0.0	2.9	661.5	0.0	**1.3**	664.9	0.0	**1.1**	664.9	0.0	4.2
rm201	15	1229.2	0.0	**0.3**	1229.2	0.0	0.3	1237.2	0.0	**1.4**	1237.2	0.0	1.6
rm205	15	1229.2	0.0	**0.4**	1229.2	0.0	0.6	1229.2	0.0	**0.2**	1229.2	0.0	0.6
Mean	15	859.2	1.7	306	859.2	**0.0**	2.9	863.2	1.8	324	863.2	**0.0**	11
cm101	20	801.7	27.7	TL	801.7	**0.0***	1236	839.0	29.1	TL	832.0	**7.2**	TL
cm105	20	801.1	28.0	TL	801.1	**0.0***	558	802.6	28.5	TL	802.6	**0.0***	798
cm201	20	1599.0	44.3	TL	1599.0	**0.0***	65	1599.0	44.3	TL	1599.0	**0.0***	68
cm205	20	1607.2	44.5	TL	948.7	**6.7**	TL	1608.7	44.4	TL	948.7	**0.0***	2059
rcm101	20	883.7	0.0	6.4	883.7	0.0	**1.7**	887.3	0.0	**1.7**	887.3	0.0	4.5
rcm105	20	885.2	0.0	4.2	885.2	0.0	**2.4**	895.8	0.0	**6.3**	895.8	0.0	9.4
rcm201	20	1219.4	0.0	6.2	1219.4	0.0	**0.8**	1219.4	0.0	**0.9**	1219.4	0.0	1.2

(continued)

Table 6. (*continued*)

Inst.	C	B = 0						B = 1					
		MIP			CP			MIP			CP		
		λ	G	T	λ	G	T	λ	G	T	λ	G	T
rcm205	20	1219.4	0.0	6.3	1219.4	0.0	**0.7**	1229.6	0.0	194	1229.6	0.0	**111**
rm101	20	922.4	21.5	TL	922.4	**0.0***	76	938.1	22.8	TL	938.1	**0.0***	103
rm105	20	906.2	21.2	TL	906.2	**0.0***	76	906.2	21.5	TL	906.2	**0.0***	74
rm201	20	1262.3	0.0	0.7	1262.3	0.0	**0.7**	1280.4	0.0	98	1280.4	0.0	**17**
rm205	20	1262.3	0.0	**0.5**	1262.3	0.0	1.0	1262.3	0.0	**0.7**	1262.3	0.0	1.6
Mean	20	1114.2	15.6	1802	1059.3	**0.6**	443	1122.4	15.9	1825	1066.8	**0.6**	543
cm101	25	847.2	**5.5**	TL	825.2	6.3	TL	888.8	**8.1**	TL	876.3	11.7	TL
cm105	25	823.6	**2.0**	TL	823.6	5.8	TL	825.2	**2.3**	TL	825.2	6.0	TL
cm201	25	1629.8	44.6	TL	1626.9	**0.0***	195	1629.9	44.7	TL	1628.7	**0.0***	378
cm205	25	1619.7	44.2	TL	1023.3	**11.7**	TL	1624.8	**44.3**	TL	1624.8	44.5	TL
rcm101	25	895.0	0.0	5.6	895.0	0.0	**3.3**	898.6	0.0	**4.8**	898.6	0.0	5.4
rcm105	25	898.3	0.0	**5.5**	898.3	0.0	6.3	912.4	0.0	**35**	912.4	0.0	50
rcm201	25	1226.1	0.0	20	1226.1	0.0	**1.2**	1235.7	0.0	546	1235.7	0.0	**23**
rcm205	25	1226.1	0.0	24	1226.1	0.0	**1.2**	1255.2	**1.7**	TL	1255.2	2.3	TL
rm101	25	1185.8	35.7	TL	1185.8	**19.8**	TL	1209.3	36.8	TL	1209.3	**21.5**	TL
rm105	25	960.1	21.2	TL	960.1	**0.0***	66	976.2	22.8	TL	976.2	**0.0***	231
rm201	25	1316.9	0.0	13	1316.9	0.0	**2.3**	1342.0	0.8	TL	1342.0	**0.0***	243
rm205	25	1313.3	0.0	**1.6**	1313.3	0.0	1.6	1315.7	0.0	**1.4**	1315.7	0.0	5.3
Mean	25	1161.8	12.8	1806	1110.1	**3.6**	1213	1176.2	13.5	2449	1175.0	**7.2**	1562
cm101	50	1868.3	27.8	TL	1683.7	**21.5**	TL	1833.1	**25.4**	TL	1913.7	31.0	TL
cm105	50	1657.5	**18.4**	TL	1650.0	19.7	TL	1658.1	**17.5**	TL	1687.1	21.4	TL
cm201	50	3234.6	46.8	TL	3230.0	**23.9**	TL	3263.6	46.5	TL	3247.4	**24.3**	TL
cm205	50	2567.5	32.3	TL	2524.5	**30.9**	TL	2559.3	31.7	TL	2530.7	**31.1**	TL
rcm101	50	1525.8	0.0	261	1525.8	0.0	**232**	1537.3	0.0	**440**	1537.3	0.0*	980
rcm105	50	1548.5	0.0	1363	1548.5	0.0	**557**	1566.0	**1.1**	TL	1568.2	2.1	TL
rcm201	50	2398.4	43.3	TL	2398.4	**42.9**	TL	2448.2	44.0	TL	2423.0	**43.5**	TL
rcm205	50	2398.4	43.4	TL	2398.4	**42.9**	TL	2430.5	**43.5**	TL	2431.1	43.7	TL
rm101	50	1885.5	29.6	TL	2063.6	**26.7**	TL	2109.7	36.8	TL	1922.5	**21.4**	TL
rm105	50	1797.0	26.4	TL	1794.2	**15.8**	TL	1793.7	25.9	TL	1806.2	**16.4**	TL
rm201	50	2488.6	42.3	TL	2485.7	**41.2**	TL	2664.3	45.1	TL	2540.5	**42.5**	TL
rm205	50	2478.1	41.7	TL	1486.7	**1.7**	TL	2479.7	41.0	TL	1487.0	**1.7**	TL
Mean	50	2154.0	29.3	3136	2065.8	**22.3**	3068	2195.3	29.9	3337	2091.2	**23.2**	3390

Note. Start solution time is excluded for CP. Bold indicates the minimum gap per instance and variant. If both methods prove optimality, bold indicates minimum runtime. * denotes instances that the CP model solved optimally for the first time.

References

1. Baldacci, R., Mingozzi, A., Roberti, R.: Recent exact algorithms for solving the vehicle routing problem under capacity and time window constraints. Eur. J. Oper. Res. **218**(1), 1–6 (2012). https://doi.org/10.1016/j.ejor.2011.07.037
2. Belhaiza, S., Hansen, P., Laporte, G.: A hybrid variable neighborhood tabu search heuristic for the vehicle routing problem with multiple time windows. Comput. Oper. Res. **52**, 269–281 (2014). https://doi.org/10.1016/j.cor.2013.08.010
3. Belhaiza, S., M'Hallah, R., Brahim, G.B.: A new hybrid genetic variable neighborhood search heuristic for the vehicle routing problem with multiple time windows. In: 2017 IEEE Congress on Evolutionary Computation (CEC). IEEE (2017). https://doi.org/10.1109/cec.2017.7969457

4. Bogue, E.T., Ferreira, H.S., Noronha, T.F., Prins, C.: A column generation and a post optimization VNS heuristic for the vehicle routing problem with multiple time windows. Optim. Lett. **16**(1), 79–95 (2020). https://doi.org/10.1007/s11590-019-01530-w
5. Hoogeboom, M., Dullaert, W., Lai, D., Vigo, D.: Efficient neighborhood evaluations for the vehicle routing problem with multiple time windows. Transp. Sci. **54**(2), 400–416 (2020). https://doi.org/10.1287/trsc.2019.0912
6. de Jong, C., Kant, G., Van Vlient, A.: On finding minimal route duration in the vehicle routing problem with multiple time windows. Manuscript, Department of Computer Science, Utrecht University, Holland (1996)
7. Laborie, P., Rogerie, J., Shaw, P., Vilím, P.: Reasoning with conditional time-intervals. Part II: an algebraical model for resources. In: FLAIRS Conference, pp. 201–206 (2009)
8. Larsen, R., Pacino, D.: Fast delta evaluation for the vehicle routing problem with multiple time windows (2019). https://doi.org/10.48550/ARXIV.1905.04114
9. Liu, C., Aleman, D.M., Beck, J.C.: Modelling and solving the senior transportation problem. In: van Hoeve, W.-J. (ed.) CPAIOR 2018. LNCS, vol. 10848, pp. 412–428. Springer, Cham (2018). https://doi.org/10.1007/978-3-319-93031-2_30
10. Naderi, B., Ruiz, R., Roshanaei, V.: Mixed-integer programming vs. constraint programming for shop scheduling problems: new results and outlook. INFORMS J. Comput. (2023). https://doi.org/10.1287/ijoc.2023.1287
11. Pesant, G., Gendreau, M., Potvin, J.Y., Rousseau, J.M.: On the flexibility of constraint programming models: from single to multiple time windows for the traveling salesman problem. Eur. J. Oper. Res. **117**(2), 253–263 (1999). https://doi.org/10.1016/s0377-2217(98)00248-3
12. Rousseau, L.M., Gendreau, M., Pesant, G., Focacci, F.: Solving VRPTWs with constraint programming based column generation. Ann. Oper. Res. **130**(1–4), 199–216 (2004). https://doi.org/10.1023/b:anor.0000032576.73681.29
13. Schaap, H., Schiffer, M., Schneider, M., Walther, G.: A large neighborhood search for the vehicle routing problem with multiple time windows. Transp. Sci. **56**(5), 1369–1392 (2022). https://doi.org/10.1287/trsc.2021.1120
14. Solomon, M.M.: Algorithms for the vehicle routing and scheduling problems with time window constraints. Oper. Res. **35**(2), 254–265 (1987). https://doi.org/10.1287/opre.35.2.254
15. Voigt, S., Frank, M., Fontaine, P., Kuhn, H.: The vehicle routing problem with availability profiles. Transp. Sci. (2022). https://doi.org/10.1287/trsc.2022.1182

A Variable Neighborhood Search Algorithm for the Truck-Drone Routing Problem

Batool Madani(✉) and Malick Ndiaye

American University of Sharjah, Sharjah, United Arab Emirates
{g00050500,mndiaye}@aus.edu

Abstract. The rise in e-commerce sales has increased the demand for logistics companies to handle the problem of last-mile delivery, which is complex and incurs large operational expenses. The use of drones in the development of modern distribution networks opens new avenues for improving existing delivery systems. The integration of drones with traditional delivery trucks that form the truck-drone systems are being proposed by logistics firms for use in delivery procedures. In this paper, we consider a single truck and drone delivery system and address the associated routing problem. As a result, a variable neighborhood search algorithm is developed and tested on small and medium instances. The algorithm shows its potential ability to handle instances in a short time. Finally, the introduced truck-drone delivery system with multiple visits per drone dispatch generates cost-savings in comparison with the case of a single visit per delivery trip.

Keywords: Routing · truck-drone delivery · variable neighborhood search

1 Introduction

The rapid evolution of e-commerce has intensified the need for logisticians to resolve the problem of conveying goods from transportation hubs to their final destinations, known as the Last-Mile Delivery problem (LMD) (Boyer et al. 2009). It is the last leg of a product's journey, nevertheless the most challenging, with the highest transportation cost across all distribution networks (Gevaers et al. 2009). The inclusion of new technologies such as drones may help in overcoming these challenges.

Drones are now widely used in a variety of applications, including logistics, healthcare, and precision agriculture (Scott and Scott 2017; Mogili and Deepak 2018; Murray and Chu 2015). In this context, major drone manufacturers such as Zipline, Wing, Prime Air, Flirtey, and others have expressed interest in incorporating drone technologies into their operations (Wood 2019). For instance, Prime Air, developed by Amazon, can satisfy customers' orders within a 16 km radius of a fulfillment center by navigating using the onboard global positioning system (Lavars 2013). Similarly, Zipline drones have made over 13,000 deliveries across Rwanda, demonstrating their humanitarian capabilities by transporting blood for transfusions (Dragolea 2019).

Although drones have shown potential in improving delivery operations, they are limited by their technical characteristics such as payload capacity and flying range. As a

© The Author(s), under exclusive license to Springer Nature Switzerland AG 2023
J. R. Daduna et al. (Eds.): ICCL 2023, LNCS 14239, pp. 322–334, 2023.
https://doi.org/10.1007/978-3-031-43612-3_20

result, drones and delivery trucks can work in tandem to provide a more flexible delivery system, resulting in a truck-drone delivery system.

Truck-drone routing problems are viewed as extended versions of the classical Vehicle Routing Problems (VRP), which calls for the development of efficient solution methods to address the NP-hard nature of the related routing problem. Therefore, this study considers a specific setting of the truck-drone delivery system and proposes a solution method based on the variable neighborhood search (VNS) algorithm to solve the routing considerations. The main contribution of this work is as follows.

1. Developing an efficient VNS algorithm for a truck-drone delivery system where the drone is able to perform multiple visits per dispatch.
2. Conducting computational experiments to assess the algorithm's performance using small and medium instances.

The remainder of the paper is structured as follows. Section 2 presents a review of the truck-drone routing problems-related literature. Section 3 provides the proposed model description while Sect. 4 demonstrates the solution approach. The computational analysis is given in Sect. 5 and finally, Sect. 6 concludes and provides future research prospects.

2 Related Literature

The exploration of truck-drone systems is definitely appealing to academics and practitioners. According to UPS, truck-drone systems might save up to $50 million per year by reducing every driver's route by one mile every day (UPS 2017). Amazon has also been granted a patent for a truck-drone system in which the truck functions as a mobile facility for operating and repairing the drone (Wohlsen 2014).

The truck-drone problems-related literature has gained significant attention due to the various complexities associated with modeling and solving optimization problems. Interested readers may refer to (Madani and Ndiaye 2022; Chung et al. 2020; Boysen et al. 2021) reviews, among others, to understand the current state-of-the-art of truck-drone routing problems.

Researchers' efforts are devoted to studying the logistical uses of drones in enhancing the delivery processes and tackling the LMD challenges. These studies take into consideration the operational limitations of a drone and the routing optimization of a combined truck-drone system. In this context, Murray and Chu (2015) are among the first to investigate the flying side-kick traveling salesman problem (FSTSP), which considers a set of customers to be served once by either a truck or a drone, with the truck only fulfilling customer deliveries that the drone cannot serve. The FSTSP has been extended and solved in different ways by (Jeong et al. 2019; Windras Mara et al. 2022; Liu et al. 2022; Boccia et al. 2021; de Freitas and Penna 2018; Dell'Amico et al. 2019; Murray and Raj 2020), among others. For instance, Dell'Amico et al. (2019) proposed a new formulation for the FSTSP that uses two and three-indexed formulations and strengthened it by a set of valid inequalities and finally solved using branch-and-cut. This approach yielded solutions in a relatively shorter time frame. Murray and Raj (2020) considered a fleet of heterogeneous drones, each of which varies in terms of weight, volume capacity, and endurance.

Murray and Chu (2015) suggested the parallel drone scheduling traveling salesman problem (PDTSP) as another form of the truck-drone delivery problem. In particular, a truck and one or more drones perform delivery services independently, departing and returning to the depot simultaneously. The objective is to reduce the time required to service all customers and allow all vehicles to return to the depot, which was solved using exact solution methods and a saving heuristic. Lei and Chen (2022) designed an improved VNS algorithm that is based on reduced VNS for solving the PDSTP. The algorithm includes 9 neighborhood structures covering operators such as *relocate, 1-1 exchange, 2-2 exchange*, and other operators tailored to the specific problem.

In a different approach, Agatz et al. (2018) introduced the traveling salesman problem with a drone (TSP-D), in which the drone must follow the truck's road network and may be launched and returned to the same location, which is not allowed in the FSTSP. The objective of the TSP-D is to minimize the time required to serve all customers or minimize the arrival time to the depot. The VRP with a drone (VRP-D) considers the shared delivery operations between multiple trucks and multiple drones visiting a single customer location per dispatch. Wang et al. (2017) introduced the VRP-D which deals with multiple trucks and drones with the goal of minimizing the completion time, in which the drones can be dispatched from and picked up only at the depot and customers' nodes. The analysis was conducted on several worst-case scenarios, from which they propose bounds on the best possible savings in terms of completion time when using trucks and drones instead of trucks only in delivering parcels to customers. Further development of this research was studied by Poikonen et al. (2017), where they extended the worst-case bounds to more generic distance/cost metrics. Also, they explicitly consider the limitation of battery life and cost objectives. Sacramento et al. (2019) investigated the VRP-D with each truck equipped with a single drone and developed an adaptive large neighborhood search algorithm (ALNS). Kuo et al. (2022) studied a similar problem as Sacramento et al. (2019) but considered the time-window aspect and developed a VNS solution.

In the above studies, trucks and drones share the responsibility of fulfilling customer deliveries, while permitting the launching/collecting of drones to take place at the customer nodes visited by the truck.

Another truck-drone configuration is to limit the delivery role to the drone while the truck acts as a moving warehouse for launching, collecting, and refilling with the drone. In such cases, the drone's launching and collection operations occur at non-customer nodes such as drone stations/hubs, nodes along the truck route, and others. This system configuration can maximize the potential use of drones as they are not restricted to being launched from customer nodes which may not have all the proper facilities for launching/collecting the drone. It is also important to stress that few studies limited the launching/collection to non-customer nodes (Karak and Abdelghany 2019; Poikonen and Golden 2020a, b; Marinelli et al. 2018; Carlsson and Song 2018; Wang and Sheu 2019). In addition, the majority of the literature considers a single drone capacity while it would be interesting to investigate the case of allowing the drone to perform multiple visits per dispatch.

Therefore, this study considers the second configuration of the truck-drone delivery system while considering drone characteristics such as payload capacity and flying endurance.

3 Model Description

Given a single truck equipped with a single drone, the task is to deliver packages to a given set of customers. Each customer must be visited exactly once by the drone operating in conjunction with the truck while the truck acts as a platform for refilling, launching, and collecting the drone. The truck with its drone must depart and return to a single depot. The launching and collecting operations can take place at a set of potential locations. The objective is to determine the sequencing of the deliveries by drone while minimizing the total traveling cost of the delivery system. Several assumptions are taken into account and are described below.

- Drones can handle multiple deliveries per dispatch, according to their maximum payload capacity Q and flying endurance E.
- Customer demands are based on the weight of the packages.
- Trucks are assumed to have a large enough capacity to transport both parcels and drones during the whole operation.
- The drone may be launched/collected from the depot or at any of the launching/collecting potential locations.
- The drone can be collected at the same location from where it was launched or at any other location.
- The truck must precede the drone at the collection location for safety purposes. In other words, the arrival time of the truck at the collection location must be before that of the drone.

Figure 1 demonstrates the delivery operation performed by the truck and the drone.

4 Proposed Variable Neighborhood Search Algorithm

Truck-drone routing problems are regarded as extended variants of traditional VRPs. When considering a single truck stop and a single drone with a single delivery path, the truck-drone routing problem reduces to a traveling salesman problem, which is known to be NP-hard (Madani and Ndiaye 2019). As a result, the truck-drone problem is NP-hard, and the computing time necessary to reach optimality using exact solutions may increase exponentially as the problem size increases (Madani and Ndiaye 2019). This highlights the importance of developing efficient metaheuristic algorithms capable of providing acceptable solutions for large-scale instances (Salhi 2017). Therefore, an approximate solution method such as the VNS is developed.

The VNS, developed by Mladenović and Hansen (1997), works on a systematic neighborhood transformation in which a local search is included in the search. Add to that, it has the benefit of being simple and straightforward to apply, as it only requires the definition of neighborhoods (Salhi 2017).

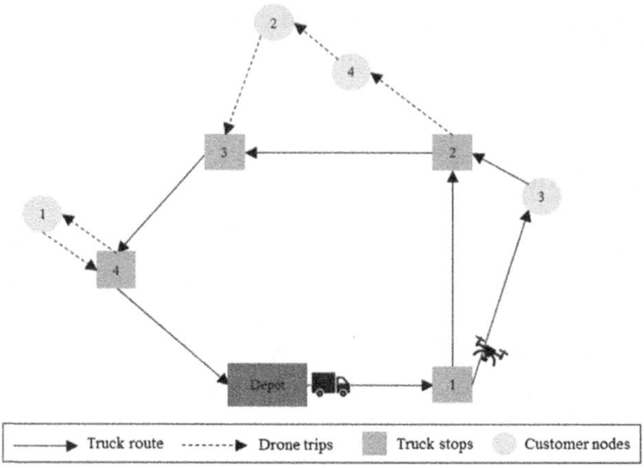

Fig. 1. Truck-drone delivery model configuration

The first step in developing the VNS algorithm is to examine the VNS literature in the context of truck-drone routing models. Table 1 summarizes the literature on VNS for solving the routing considerations of truck-drone systems. It can be clearly observed that only a few research have adopted the VNS algorithm. This necessitates the use of VNS in such problems to investigate its capabilities in the context of truck drone problems. In a study conducted by Kuo et al. (2022), the VNS proves its ability in providing quality solutions for problems related to truck-drone routing compared to other metaheuristics such as the ALNS. Therefore, it is worth exploring the adoption of VNS in this study.

Table 1. VNS-related literature in the context of truck-drone routing problems

Reference	VNS variant	No. neighborhoods	Size of instance
Schermer et al. (2019)	Basic VNS	3	Up to 50 nodes
de Freitas and Penna (2018)	RVND	5	Up to 100 nodes
de Freitas and Penna (2020)	General VNS	7	Up to 250 nodes
Salama and Srinivas (2022)	Basic VNS	6	Up to 50 nodes
Kuo et al. (2022)	Basic VNS	8	Up to 50 nodes
Gu et al. (2022)	VND	6	Up to 200 nodes
Luo et al. (2022)	VND	6	Up to 80 nodes
Lei and Chen (2022)	Reduced VNS	9	Up to 100 nodes

The structure of the VNS algorithm is divided into three elements, namely, the initial solution, neighborhood structures, and finally local search strategy. Next, each of the three elements is presented in detail.

4.1 Initial Solution

The initial solution procedure is based on selecting the launching and collecting nodes of each drone trip according to the drone's characteristics (payload capacity and flying endurance). The approach of the initial solution chooses the depot as the launching node of the first drone's delivery trip and assigns a customer node. If no customer node exists within the flight endurance of the drone from the depot, the next potential location is chosen, and so on. Following the selection of the launching point, and assuming that the payload limit has not been exceeded, a customer node can be added to the drone's delivery trip, or the current drone trip is terminated. After that, the collecting location of the drone is selected according to the drone's flying endurance limit. A new drone delivery trip can be initiated, and the same steps are repeated until all customers are served by the drone.

4.2 Neighborhood Structures

In this algorithm, eight neighborhood structures ($K_{max} = 8$), which are a combination of traditional neighborhoods and problem-specific neighborhoods, are used. It is worth noting that some of these neighborhoods correspond to the well-known VRP local search operators. The list of neighborhoods is presented below.

- N_1: Select a random customer node from two drone delivery trips and swap them. This neighborhood is similar to *1-1 exchange* operators where the positions of a pair of nodes are swapped.
- N_2: Select a random drone trip and split it into two delivery trips. In particular, a random trip is chosen, and a new stopping location is added at random between the initial launching and collecting nodes, splitting the initial trip.
- N_3: Select two random drone delivery trips and combine them into a single delivery trip.
- N_4: Remove a random customer node from a drone delivery trip and insert it in another drone trip. This move is related to *relocate* operator in that a node is injected from its original position and relocated to another.
- N_5: Select two random drone delivery trips and swap their order in the list of drone trips.
- N_6: Select a random drone trip and swap the launching and collecting locations. If they are similar, this neighborhood is neglected.
- N_7: Select a random drone trip and swap two customer nodes. This is comparable to the *1-1 exchange* operator, except it occurs within the same route (exchange intra-route).
- N_8: Select a random drone trip where the launching and collecting nodes are different and make the launching location similar to the collecting one.

4.3 Local Search

The local search, which is based on the exploration of a neighborhood structure, is an improvement procedure used within the VNS algorithm.

In the proposed algorithm, the solution generated in the shaking procedure $N_k(X)$ of neighborhood N_k is exhaustively examined. In specific, all the possible swaps between two customers within a drone delivery trip are performed and the solution with the best improvement is selected.

As there is a restriction on the drone's payload capacity, flying endurance, and arrival time at the collection site, the feasibility testing of the solution is obtained during the construction of the initial solution and shaking procedures. In other words, the solution is ignored if a movement results in violating the aforementioned constraints.

The structure of the VNS algorithm is summarized in Algorithm 1. The stopping criterion is based on the maximum number of iterations.

Algorithm (1): VNS framework

1 $X \leftarrow Initial\ Solution$
2 **while** $iteration < maximum\ iteration$ **do**
3   set $k \leftarrow 1$
4   generate X' at random from shaking X using the neighborhood $N_k(X)$
5    $X'' \leftarrow Local\ Seacrh(X')$
6   **if** $f(X'') < f(X)$ **then**
7     $X \leftarrow X''$ and repeat step 3
8   **end**
9   **else**
10   **if** $k = K_{max}$ **then**
11       $iteration = iteration + 1$ and repeat step 2
12   **else**
13       $k \leftarrow k + 1$ and repeat step 4
14 **end**
15 **return** X^*

5 Computational Experiments

In this section, the performance of the proposed VNS algorithm is assessed using instances derived from Sacramento et al. (2019). We first present the description of instances and the inputs used in the algorithm followed by the performance evaluation and additional analysis.

The algorithm is coded using the C++ programming language; all the runs and experiments were performed on a 64-bit operating system with an x64-based processor that is Intel(R) Core™ i7-8565U CPU @1.80 GHz and 8 GB memory.

5.1 Parameters and Datasets

The parameters used in the algorithm solution are as follows. Drone traveling cost is assumed to be 30% of the truck traveling cost (Campbell et al. 2017). The traveling distance of both vehicles is assumed to be Euclidean. Also, the drone is assumed to have a maximum payload capacity Q of 5 kg ($\sim$10 lbs) and a flying range E of 30 min, which are the typical characteristics of a drone. Finally, the drone's speed is set to 50 mph (Sacramento et al. 2019).

The instances used in the VNS performance evaluation are based on Sacramento et al. (2019) instances, which are formed on a grid size of $2d \times 2d$ where d is 5, 10, 20, 30, or 40 and follow a uniform distribution. Finally, customer packages are set to weigh less than 5 kg and follow a uniform distribution.

Given that Sacramento et al. (2019) presented the VRP-D where the launching/collecting nodes are customer nodes, we added additional nodes representing the potential launching/collecting location to each instance. We followed the p-median approach to generate the potential locations used as possible launching/collecting nodes. The number of potential locations is selected based on the number of customer nodes in each instance size. In this analysis, we chose 30 instances of size 6, 10, 12, 20, and 50 customer nodes to apply the modification on. The modified instances are named S[no. potential locations (including depot)].[no. customer nodes].[grid dimension].[instance number].

5.2 Performance Evaluation

To assess the performance of the VNS algorithm, we use modified instances and obtain the solution for each. Each instance is computed 10 times (10 runs) and the average C^{Avg} and best C^{best} solutions are recorded. In addition, the average computational time is documented t^{Avg} in seconds. Finally, the maximum number of iterations (*maximumiteration*) is fixed to 100 for all instances. Table 2 summarizes the results of the 30 modified instances.

The results show that the VNS generates solutions for instances with up to 50 customer nodes in less than 1 s. Add to that, the algorithm provides relatively consistent results given the difference between C^{best} and C^{Avg} in each instance. In terms of computational time, the suggested approach outperforms the previous VNS algorithms found in truck-drone literature (Lei and Chen 2022; de Freitas and Penna 2018 2020; Schermer et al. 2019; Kuo et al. 2022). Nevertheless, comparing to other heuristics based on computational time is insufficient and requires evaluation based on solution quality. Indeed, the suggested algorithm must be benchmarked against other algorithms or exact solution methods to assess its solution quality, which will be part of our future work.

5.3 Drone Capacity Impact: Single vs. Multiple Visits per Drone Dispatch

The ability of the drone to perform multiple visits may have a significant impact on the delivery cost.

According to Meng et al. (2023), allowing the drone to visit several customers in one route can bring cost savings.

In this part, we analyze the impact of the drone's payload capacity by preventing the drone from visiting more than a single customer per dispatch. The analysis is performed on S(3.6.5.1), S(5.10.5.1), S(6.12.5.1), S(8.20.5.1), and S(10.50.10.3) instances. Table 3 compares the objective function value for both cases using the above-mentioned

Table 2. Performance evaluation of the VNS algorithm

Instance	C^{best}	C^{Avg}	t^{Avg}
S(3.6.5.1)	4.23	4.40	0.0165
S(3.6.5.2)	4.12	4.32	0.0171
S(3.6.10.1)	8.66	9.07	0.0156
S(3.6.10.2)	9.07	9.19	0.0158
S(3.6.20.1)	14.80	15.16	0.0154
S(3.6.20.2)	14.65	16.45	0.0151
S(5.10.5.1)	5.20	6.07	0.1248
S(5.10.5.2)	5.24	6.32	0.1282
S(5.10.10.1)	13.49	15.64	0.1069
S(5.10.10.2)	10.50	11.42	0.1217
S(5.10.20.1)	20.54	23.92	0.1064
S(5.10.20.2)	24.80	33.04	0.1055
S(6.12.5.1)	6.40	7.78	0.2385
S(6.12.5.2)	6.04	8.05	0.2693
S(6.12.10.1)	12.66	14.38	0.3100
S(6.12.10.2)	12.65	15.40	0.3579
S(6.12.20.1)	30.78	36.85	0.3083
S(6.12.20.2)	33.15	43.42	0.2872
S(8.20.5.1)	12.03	12.88	0.3701
S(8.20.5.2)	12.51	13.94	0.3218
S(8.20.10.1)	20.76	23.46	0.3254
S(8.20.10.2)	29.23	31.61	0.3204
S(8.20.20.1)	51.57	61.80	0.3200
S(8.20.20.2)	53.91	59.59	0.3900
S(10.50.10.3)	65.69	73.40	0.6400
S(10.50.10.4)	65.61	68.05	0.6582
S(10.50.20.3)	140.48	153.71	0.6281
S(10.50.20.4)	134.76	147.08	0.6295
S(10.50.30.3)	148.23	171.89	0.6208
S(10.50.30.4)	180.38	198.22	0.6212

instances. The findings indicate that enabling the drone to service multiple customers can better leverage the drone's flying endurance, resulting in a shorter distance traveled by the truck to retrieve the drone, and thus generating cost-savings.

Table 3. Performance evaluation of the VNS algorithm based on the drone's payload capacity

Instance	Single visit C^{Avg}	Multiple visits C^{Avg}
S(3.6.5.1)	7.50	4.40
S(5.10.5.1)	11.83	6.07
S(6.12.5.1)	16.35	7.78
S(8.20.5.1)	23.97	12.88
S(10.50.10.3)	129.78	73.40

5.4 Drone Flying Range Impact

Using the above instances in Subsect. 5.3, the impact of the drone's flying range is evaluated, where E is set to 15, 20, 30, and 40 min. Table 4 summarizes the results of this experimental analysis based on C^{Avg}. As can be observed, reducing the flying range increases the traveling cost because the drone must make additional delivery trips to satisfy the needs of the customer. On the other hand, increasing it will reduce travel costs to an extent as the drone's performance is limited by other features such as its flying capacity.

Table 4. Performance evaluation of the VNS algorithm based on the drone's flying range

Instance	Flying range E			
	15 min	20 min	30 min	40 min
S(3.6.5.1)	5.18	4.61	4.40	4.23
S(5.10.5.1)	7.79	7.19	6.07	5.56
S(6.12.5.1)	9.78	8.44	7.78	6.43
S(8.20.5.1)	17.90	13.28	12.88	11.47
S(10.50.10.3)	81.31	79.92	73.40	69.35

6 Conclusion and Future Work

This paper proposed a VNS algorithm to solve the routing considerations of a truck-drone delivery system. In particular, a single truck functioning as a moving hub is in charge of operating the drone from potential truck locations while the drone is responsible for serving multiple customers per dispatch. The suggested approach has demonstrated its ability to solve small to medium instances in a short time.

This research can be further explored in a variety of ways. To begin, the truck-drone delivery system could look into using multiple trucks in tandem with multiple drones to service customers. Second, other aspects of the problem, such as time window and energy consumption, may be examined. Third, a mathematical formula for the given problem description may be presented. Fourth, the suggested algorithm must be compared to other solutions generated by exact solution methods and/or metaheuristic solutions to better assess its quality. Finally, extensive computational analysis of a large number of instances of various sizes may be performed.

References

Agatz, N., Bouman, P., Schmidt, M.: Optimization approaches for the traveling salesman problem with drone. Transp. Sci. **52**, 965–981 (2018). https://doi.org/10.1287/trsc.2017.0791

Boccia, M., Masone, A., Sforza, A., Sterle, C.: A column-and-row generation approach for the flying sidekick travelling salesman problem. Transp. Res. Part C **124** (2021). https://doi.org/10.1016/j.trc.2020.102913

Boyer, K.K., Prud'homme, A.M., Chung, W.: The last mile challenge: evaluating the effects of customer density and delivery window patterns. J. Bus. Logist. **30**(1), 185–201 (2009). https://doi.org/10.1002/j.2158-1592.2009.tb00104.x

Boysen, N., Fedtke, S., Schwerdfeger, S.: Last-mile delivery concepts: a survey from an operational research perspective. OR Spectr. **43**(1), 1–58 (2021). https://doi.org/10.1007/s00291-020-00607-8

Campbell, J.F., Sweeney, D., Zhang, J.: Strategic design for delivery with trucks and drones. Technical report (2017)

Carlsson, J.G., Song, S.: Coordinated logistics with a truck and a drone. Manag. Sci. **64**, 4052–4069 (2018). https://doi.org/10.1287/mnsc.2017.2824

Chung, S.H., Sah, B., Lee, J.: Optimization for drone and drone-truck combined operations: a review of the state of the art and future directions. Comput. Oper. Res. **123** (2020). https://doi.org/10.1016/j.cor.2020.105004

de Freitas, J.C., Penna, P.H.V.: A randomized variable neighborhood descent heuristic to solve the flying sidekick traveling salesman problem. Electron. Notes Discret. Math. **66**, 95–102 (2018). https://doi.org/10.1016/j.endm.2018.03.013

de Freitas, J.C., Penna, P.H.V.: A variable neighborhood search for flying sidekick traveling salesman problem. Int. Trans. Oper. Res. **27**(1), 267–290 (2020). https://doi.org/10.1111/itor.12671

Dell'Amico, M., Montemanni, R., Novellani, S.: Drone-assisted deliveries: new formulations for the flying sidekick traveling salesman problem. Optim. Lett. (2019). https://doi.org/10.1007/s11590-019-01492-z

Dragolea, N.: 9 Drones that will revolutionize Healthcare (2019). http://www.doctorpreneurs.com/9-drones-that-will-revolutionise-healthcare/. Accessed 26 Feb 2021

Gevaers, R., Van de Voorde, E., Vanelslander, T.: Characteristics of innovations in last-mile logistics-using best practices, case studies and making the link with green and sustainable logistics. Association for European Transport and Contributors (2009)

Gu, R., Poon, M., Luo, Z., Liu, Y., Liu, Z.: A hierarchical solution evaluation method and a hybrid algorithm for the vehicle routing problem with drones and multiple visits. Transp. Res. Part C **141** (2022). https://doi.org/10.1016/j.trc.2022.103733

Jeong, H.Y., Song, B.D., Lee, S.: Truck-drone hybrid delivery routing: payload-energy dependency and No-Fly zones. Int. J. Prod. Econ. **214**, 220–233 (2019). https://doi.org/10.1016/j.ijpe.2019.01.010

Karak, A., Abdelghany, K.: The hybrid vehicle-drone routing problem for pick-up and delivery services. Transp. Res. Part C **102**, 427–449 (2019). https://doi.org/10.1016/j.trc.2019.03.021

Kuo, R.J., Lu, S.-H., Lai, P.-Y., Mara, S.T.W.: Vehicle routing problem with drones considering time windows. Expert Syst. Appl. **191** (2022). https://doi.org/10.1016/j.eswa.2021.116264

Lavars, N.: Amazon reveals Prime Air drone capable of 30 minute deliveries (2013). https://newatlas.com/amazon-prime-air-delivery-drone/29982/. Accessed 20 Feb 2021

Liu, Z., Li, X., Khojandi, A.: The flying sidekick traveling salesman problem with stochastic travel time: a reinforcement learning approach. Transp. Res. Part E: Logist. Transp. Rev. **164** (2022). https://doi.org/10.1016/j.tre.2022.102816

Lei, D., Chen, X.: An improved variable neighborhood search for parallel drone scheduling traveling salesman problem. Appl. Soft Comput. **127** (2022). https://doi.org/10.1016/j.asoc.2022.109416

Madani, B., Ndiaye, M.: Autonomous vehicles delivery systems classification: introducing a tsp with a moving depot. In: 2019 8th International Conference on Modeling Simulation and Applied Optimization (2019). https://doi.org/10.1109/ICMSAO.2019.8880379

Luo, Q., Wu, G., Mao, Ni., Shi, J.: Hybridization of variable neighborhood search and simulated annealing for the collaborative truck-drone routing problem. In: Wu, M., Niu, Y., Gu, M., Cheng, J. (eds.) ICAUS 2021. LNEE, vol. 861, pp. 1505–1515. Springer, Singapore (2022). https://doi.org/10.1007/978-981-16-9492-9_149

Madani, B., Ndiaye, M.: Hybrid truck-drone delivery systems: a systematic literature review. IEEE Access **10**, 92854–92878 (2022). https://doi.org/10.1109/ACCESS.2022.3202895

Marinelli, M., Caggiani, L., Ottomanelli, M., Dell'Orco, M.: En route truck-drone parcel delivery for optimal vehicle routing strategies. IET Intell. Transp. Syst. **12**(4), 253–261 (2018). https://doi.org/10.1049/iet-its.2017.0227

Meng, S., Guo, X., Li, D., Liu, G.: The multi-visit drone routing problem for pickup and delivery services. Transp. Res. Part E: Logist. Transp. Rev. **169**, 102990 (2023). https://doi.org/10.1016/j.tre.2022.102990

Mladenović, N., Hansen, P.: Variable neighborhood search. Comput. Oper. Res. **24**(11), 1097–1100 (1997). https://doi.org/10.1016/S0305-0548(97)00031-2

Mogili, U.M.R., Deepak, B.B.V.L.: Review on application of drone systems in precision agriculture. Procedia Comput. Sci. **133**, 502–509 (2018). https://doi.org/10.1016/j.procs.2018.07.063

Murray, C.C., Chu, A.G.: The flying sidekick traveling salesman problem: optimization of drone-assisted parcel delivery. Transp. Res. Part C **54**, 86–109 (2015). https://doi.org/10.1016/j.trc.2015.03.005

Murray, C.C., Raj, R.: The multiple flying sidekicks traveling salesman problem: parcel delivery with multiple drones. Transp. Res. Part C **110**, 368–398 (2020). https://doi.org/10.1016/j.trc.2019.11.003

Poikonen, S., Golden, B.: Multi-visit drone routing problem. Comput. Oper. Res. **113** (2020a). https://doi.org/10.1016/j.cor.2019.104802

Poikonen, S., Golden, B.: The mothership and drone routing problem. INFORMS J. Comput. **32**, 249–262 (2020b). https://doi.org/10.1287/ijoc.2018.0879

Poikonen, S., Wang, X., Golden, B.: The vehicle routing problem with drones: Extended models and connections. Networks **70**(1), 34–43 (2017). https://doi.org/10.1002/net.21746

Sacramento, D., Pisinger, D., Ropke, S.: An adaptive large neighborhood search metaheuristic for the vehicle routing problem with drones. Transp. Res. Part C **102**, 289–315 (2019). https://doi.org/10.1016/j.trc.2019.02.018

Salama, M.R., Srinivas, S.: Collaborative truck multi-drone routing and scheduling problem: package delivery with flexible launch and recovery sites. Transp. Res. Part E **164** (2022). https://doi.org/10.1016/j.tre.2022.102788

Salhi, S.: Heuristic Search: The Emerging Science of Problem Solving. Springer, Heidelberg (2017)

Schermer, D., Moeini, M., Wendt, O.: A hybrid VNS/Tabu search algorithm for solving the vehicle routing problem with drones and en route operations. Comput. Oper. Res. **109** (2019). https://doi.org/10.1016/j.cor.2019.04.021

Scott, J., Scott, C.: Drone delivery models for healthcare. In: Proceedings of the 50th Hawaii International Conference on System Sciences (2017)

UPS tests drone delivery system. http://www.businessinsider.com/ups-tests-drone-delivery-system-2017-2. Accessed 15 Mar 2021

Wang, X., Poikonen, S., Golden, B.: The vehicle routing problem with drones: several worst-case results. Optim. Lett. **11**(4), 679–697 (2017). https://doi.org/10.1007/s11590-016-1035-3

Wang, Z., Sheu, J.-B.: Vehicle routing problem with drones. Transp. Res. Part B **122**, 350–364 (2019). https://doi.org/10.1016/j.trb.2019.03.005

Windras Mara, S.T., Rifai, A.P., Sopha, B.M.: An adaptive large neighborhood search heuristic for the flying sidekick traveling salesman problem with multiple drops. Expert Syst. Appl. **205** (2022). https://doi.org/10.1016/j.eswa.2022.117647

Wohlsen, M.: The next big thing you missed: amazon's delivery drones could work—they just need trucks. https://www.wired.com/2014/06/the-next-big-thing-you-missed-delivery-drones-launched-from-trucks-are-the-future-of-shipping/. Accessed 10 Mar 2021

Wood, L.: $91.5 Billion Autonomous Last Mile Delivery Market, 2030. https://www.prnewswire.com/news-releases/91-5-billion-autonomous-last-mile-delivery-market-2030--300895603.html. Accessed 10 Mar 2021

Traffic and Transport

Prediction and Analysis of Transit Ferries Travel Time: An Open Data-Based Case Study

Malek Sarhani[1(✉)], Mohammed El Amrani[2], and Abdelhak El Achhab[1]

[1] School of Business Administration, Al Akhawayn University in Ifrane, Ifrane, Morocco
m.sarhani@aui.ma
[2] Faculty of Sciences, Mohammed V University in Rabat, Rabat, Morocco

Abstract. The prediction of transit travel time using machine learning is an area of growing interest. Unlike previous research that focused on buses and rail transit systems, our work is focused on ferry transit. Specifically, the first contribution of this research is to compare machine learning techniques for predicting travel time in ferry transit. We then analyze the impact of various factors using different techniques. Our results indicate that weather significantly impacts travel time, in addition to the trip starting time and date.

Keywords: Public transport · Machine learning · Ferry transit · Travel time prediction · Open data

1 Introduction

Public transportation plays an increasingly important role in modern transportation systems and has emerged as one of the most crucial modes of transportation due to its positive environmental and cost impacts. One of the topics that have attracted considerable attention in recent years is travel time (TT) prediction, which refers to the estimation of the time required to traverse a road segment or a route under current or future traffic conditions. TT prediction is essential for various applications in intelligent transportation systems, such as route scheduling [5] and hence can lead to provide a better service to the passengers.

Public transport modes can be divided into buses (including trolleybuses), rail (including metros and trams), and ferries. While most of the research on delay and travel time predictions for transit focuses on buses and rail services (as evidenced by the fact that all papers included in [8] are about these modes), it is important to note that ferry transit is also a significant mode of transportation. For instance, the Sydney Ferry network in Australia carries an estimated 1.25 million passengers each month, and the Hamburg ferry system in Germany serves approximately nine million passengers annually. Therefore, providing accurate estimates of travel time for ferries should also be given importance, just like buses and rail transit systems.

© The Author(s), under exclusive license to Springer Nature Switzerland AG 2023
J. R. Daduna et al. (Eds.): ICCL 2023, LNCS 14239, pp. 337–349, 2023.
https://doi.org/10.1007/978-3-031-43612-3_21

Analyzing and predicting the travel time of a ferry is a challenging task due to several factors that can affect it. That is, ferries are ships, watercraft, or amphibious vehicles that transport passengers, and as such, their travel time can be influenced by a range of factors. Nevertheless, despite the difficulties in predicting ship travel times, there have been significant advances in this area in recent years. Indeed, accurate prediction of ship travel time is crucial for the maritime industry as it helps in obtaining more precise estimations of the estimated time of arrivals. The latter has a crucial impact on overall planning, as indicated in [20].

In particular, the use of machine learning (ML) in the transportation sector and maritime industry has gained considerable momentum due to the large amount of data generated by this transportation mode, and recent advancements in ML algorithms have made it possible to effectively analyze and make real-time predictions based on this data [4]. Indeed, ML algorithms such as support vector machines (SVM), random forests (RF), gradient boosting (GB), and neural networks (NN) are examples of ML algorithms that can be used to predict vessel arrival times and address the challenges in this area. These predictions take into account factors such as voyage information, vessel performance data, and weather conditions. This information enables organizations to make more informed decisions and reduces uncertainty about the travel time of ships. Additionally, there have been recent developments in ML, such as the analysis of feature importance, which aim to improve model interpretability and understand the impact of different features.

In this paper, our goal is to compare different ML algorithms to determine the most accurate model for estimating and predicting the travel time of ferry transit using various data sources. We will also evaluate the impact of different features and highlight the most important ones. These factors can have significant impacts on transit service quality, reliability, efficiency, and customer satisfaction.

The remainder of this paper is structured as follows: In the next section, we provide a brief literature review of the topic. Section 3 describes the data used and the various features employed in addition to the prediction approach. The experiments are presented in Sect. 4. Finally, we conclude with a discussion of the results and provide future research directions.

2 Literature Review

At the beginning of this section, we would like to note that we have not found any previous work that focuses on predicting ferry delays or TT, or analyzing the impact of different factors on these outcomes. To our knowledge, the main work that focuses on ferries, proposed by [1], is interested in the observed waiting time for ferry passengers. More information about the waiting time optimization problem can be found in [6]. [1]'s results indicate a positive relationship between waiting time and headway. The related literature review to our paper has primarily focused on ship TT prediction and understanding the factors that impact it. In this brief literature review, we highlight the different factors affecting transit or ship TT and delays and discuss some prediction methods.

First, as indicated above, predicting TT is a complex and dynamic problem that involves various factors, such as traffic demand, supply, incidents, weather, and human behavior. Moreover, reliable and timely data from multiple sources, such as GPS, sensors, cameras, and social media, are required for effective TT prediction. Disturbances are one of the main factors affecting transit delays, and many factors can be included in this category [9]. The COVID-19 pandemic, which greatly impacted public transport ridership and service provision worldwide, has been the main disturbance over the past few years [10]. However, there are other disturbances as indicated below. In our case, the other significant factor is the dwell time, which is the time spent by a transit vehicle at a stop or station for boarding and alighting passengers. Dwell time can increase travel time variability and reduce service regularity [12].

There are several studies that examine the factors affecting ship delays and transit time (TT). Delays are a major concern for shipping operators and port authorities, and studying TT is crucial to early detect and mitigate them. Ship delays can have significant economic and environmental consequences. For an overview of the importance of detecting delays in real-time and predicting vessel movement patterns until arrival, we refer to [11]. Therefore, it is essential to understand the causes of delays and find ways to minimize them.

Marine weather is one of the primary factors that affect ship delays and TT. It can impact vessel speed and route, as well as the availability and safety of berths in the port. [7] examines ship traffic and weather data from various sources and found that ship speed is significantly linked to weather variables such as wind direction, as well as ship characteristics. He developes a linear regression model that can estimate ship speed based on these variables, which may be beneficial for predicting arrival times. However, their model did not consider other factors such as weather, time and route information, which is why we use more advanced ML techniques in this paper. In fact, there is a need for more data collection and analysis to determine the impacts of ship delays on costs, efficiency, the environment, and customer satisfaction. Hence, further research is necessary to investigate these concerns and propose solutions to minimize ship delays and improve shipping reliability. Several ML algorithms, including a NN variant, RF, SVM, and a decision tree method, were utilized in [20] to establish a vessel arrival time prediction model. The results indicated that RF performed the best.

In terms of TT prediction, various methods and models have been proposed to overcome the challenges discussed earlier. These include traditional statistical and machine learning approaches as well as advanced deep learning and data fusion techniques. A recent survey by [19] provides an overview of the latest approaches for predicting ship arrival. From the survey, it is evident that ML methods hold great promise in addressing these challenges. It is worth noting that similar or closely related problems, such as ship speed prediction [2] and trajectory prediction, are also being studied. These problems share the same goal of real-time ship tracking. For instance, [21] employ a NN method to examine the trajectories of moving maritime vessels and classified them into three categories using Automatic Identification System data. In addition, [21] utilized another

NN variant to detect and track multiple vessels based on radar/laser tracking data.

To summarize, this literature review has examined several factors that contribute to ship delays, including marine weather and dwell time-related information. However, further data analysis is necessary to quantify the factors that influence TT and delay reasons. ML algorithms show great potential, and their effectiveness varies depending on the case study. In this study, our objective is to compare various ML algorithms for ferry prediction and assess the impact of different factors on TT.

It is important to note that when constructing features for predicting ferries' TT, we must take into account not only ship-related features such as weather and dwell time but also features related to transit service such as trips and routes. In the following section, we will demonstrate how we have integrated these various features.

3 The Proposed Approach

The purpose of this section is to outline the various data used for predicting transit delay. Firstly, we will describe how the data was collected, followed by a description of the different features. Finally, we will illustrate our prediction approach.

3.1 Data Acquisition

In this paper, we take the public transport ferry network serving the city of Sydney in Australia. Figure 1 shows a graphical overview of the line transit.[1] In this study, different data sources are adopted in order to study the possible delay patterns of the transit and to extract the different factors affecting its delay. More specifically, we adopt the NSW Open Data Portal (the data is available at https://opendata.transport.nsw.gov.au/search/type/dataset) which contain both GTFS static and GTFS real-time. In particular, for GTFS real-time, we used the free API provided by the website to extract the real-time information. For each observation, we provide a matching of the real-time information to the corresponding static information and the weather information about the correspond day. Weather information can be extracted from Wunderground. Table 1 illustrates the different features used in the study. (We note that the features used for merging, are available in two categories, e.g, GTFS static and GTFS real-time, we describe these features in the GTFS real-time category). We note that the dwell time, mentioned above, is not directly incorporated. However, related factors such as weekdays are included, as the dwell time is dependent on the number of passengers, which, in turn, is influenced by weekdays and specific time periods (in our case, specified by the hour of the day). We note that as no precipitation was recorded in the studied period, it has not been included in the study.

[1] More information on the network is available in https://transportnsw.info/travel-info/ways-to-get-around/ferry#/.

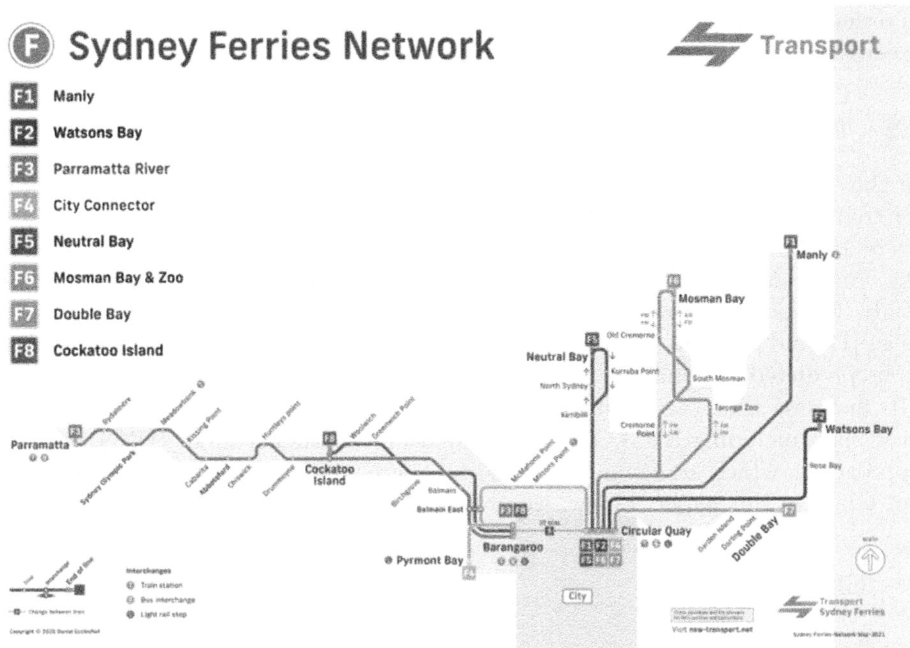

Fig. 1. Map of the Sydney Ferry System

Table 1. Description of the Features Used in the Study

	Feature	Description
GTFS static	Trip ID	A specific trip identification
	Route ID	A route is a group of trips that are displayed to riders as a single service
	Service ID	Identifies a set of dates when service is available for one or more routes
	Shape ID	Identifies a geospatial shape that describes the vehicle travel path for a trip
	Trip headsign	Text that appears on signage identifying the trip's destination to riders
	Direction ID	Indicates the direction of travel for a trip
	Route direction	Planned arrival time at a specific stop for a specific trip
GTFS real-time	Vehicle ID	Internal identification for the vehicle
	Vehicle Route ID	Route of the vehicle (used for merging GTFS real-time with GTFS static)
	Vehicle Trip ID	Trip of the vehicle (used for merging GTFS real-time with GTFS static)
	Vehicle Trip Start Time	Start time of the trip of the vehicle (used for merging GTFS real-time with GTFS static)
	Vehicle Trip Start Date	Start date of the trip of the vehicle (used for merging GTFS real-time with weather and GTFS static)
	Weekday	Weekday of the trip (extracted from the previous feature)
	Latitude	Latitude for the vehicle position
	Longitude	Longitude for the vehicle position
	Bearing	Bearing for the vehicle position
Weather	Temperature	Average temperature of the day
	Dew Point	the temperature the air needs to be cooled to in order to achieve a relative humidity
	Humidity	Average humidity of the day
	Wind Speed	Average wind speed of the day
	Pressure	Average pressure of the day

The data used in this study covered the period from March 5, 2023, to April 7, 2023. Specifically, the data encompasses the time between March 5 and March 7, as well as April 4 to April 7. We made an effort to include all possible data during these days, considering various weekdays and different weather conditions, in order to obtain a more comprehensive assessment of these factors. After preprocessing, the dataset consists of 8,264 instances.

3.2 The Prediction Process

In this part, we briefly describe the predicted output and the algorithms used for that. First, the travel time is based on the information sent by every vehicle every 10 s, which results in a huge stockpile of data. These information include the Timestamp and the other GTFS real-time are depicted in Table 1. in this study, we decided to normalize the travel time value as in several similar cases (e.g., [17] and [16]). So, the normalized travel time is chosen as the target variable to be predicted. Second, to predict the normalized travel time, we adopt Several ML methods that can produce satisfactory results for regression (continuous) problems, including SVM, RF, GB and deep neural networks (DNN). These approaches, which are commonly used for regression problems, are the focus of our study in this paper. Below, we provide the setting of the algorithms.

4 Experiment

In this section, we define the experimental setup of our case study, then present and discuss the results.

4.1 Experimentation Setup and Pre-processing

First, to implement the different algorithms, we adopt the Scikit-learn library [15]. In particular, for DNN, we use Keras 2.2.5 with TensorFlow as the back-end for its implementation. The DNN model is trained using the Adam optimizer, and mean absolute error is used as the loss function. The number of epochs is fixed at 100. For SVM, the parameter γ (kernel coefficient) is automatically trained while the values of C (regularization factor) and ϵ are set, respectively, to 10 and 0.01. We have chosen these values to enable a balance between overfitting and underfitting. For the other algorithms, we adopt the default values provided by the Scikit-learn. That is, for both RF and GB models, the following hyperparameters were used: Number of trees in the forest is set to 100, subsample is set to 1, minimum samples required for a split is 2, and minimum samples required to be at a leaf is 1. Additionally, for the GB model, the learning rate is set to 0.1.

Second, in order to have a fair assessment of the ML prediction, the data must be divided into a training set and a test set. In our experiment, 80% of the data is used for training, and the remaining 20% is used as test data. To ensure a better assessment, we perform the division five times using 5-fold cross-validation, and we report the average of the results.

All the experiments are carried out on a computer equipped with an Intel i7-9750H and 16 GB of RAM. The measures adopted in this paper are: R^2 (coefficient of determination), the mean absolute error (MAE), the mean square error (MSE) and the root mean square error (RMSE) and, in addition, the mean absolute percentage error (MAPE).

We will begin by displaying the correlation plot, as depicted in Fig. 2

Based on Fig. 2, we can observe that most features exhibit a moderate or low correlation (between -0.8 and 0.8), with the exception of weather-related features such as dew point and precipitation. We will discuss this later.

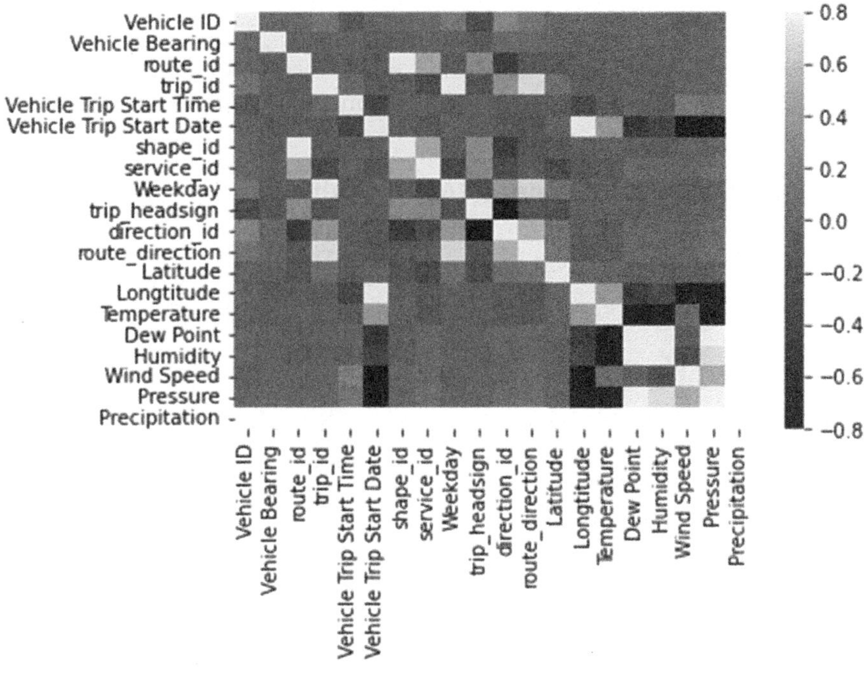

Fig. 2. Correlation Plot

4.2 Comparison of ML Predictions for the Transit Travel Time Prediction

First, for the different algorithms, we display in Table 2 a comparison of their prediction capabilities in the test set. In other words, we show in Table 2 the R^2, MAE, RMSE and MAPE values obtained by comparing the algorithm predictions with the real values in the test set.

Table 2. Comparison of ML Predictions for the Ferry Travel Time Prediction

	GB	RF	DNN	SVM
R^2	**0.9334**	0.9428	0.6924	0.1664
MAE	**0.0061**	0.0102	0.092	0.429
RMSE	**0.008**	0.0132	0.163	0.508
MAPE	**0.0989**	0.106	0.418	0.760

Moreover, to have a better readability of the results, we depict in Fig. 3 the same values of MAE, RMSE and MAPE obtained by the different algorithms.

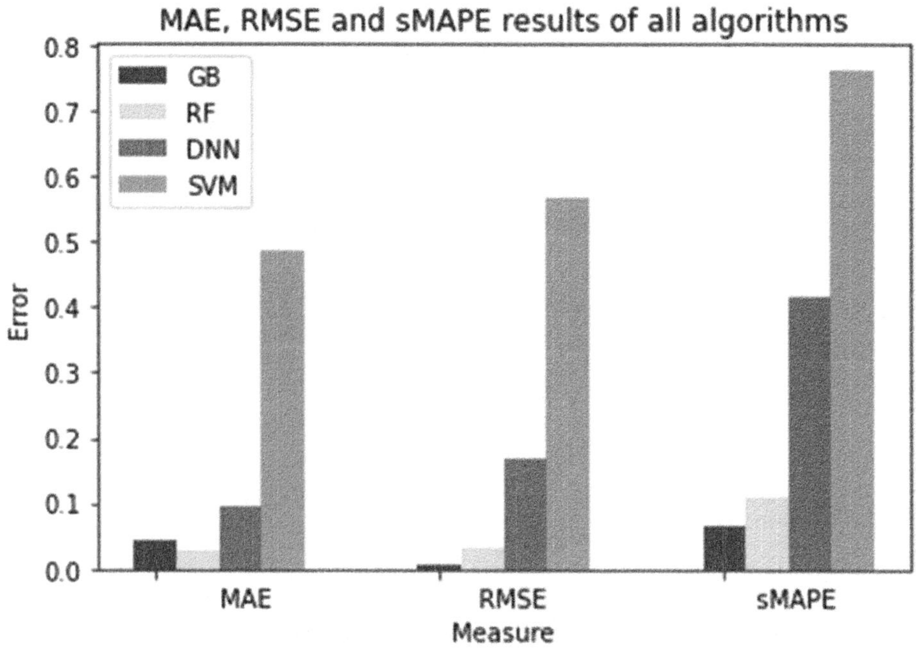

Fig. 3. Results for the Different Approaches

We can draw a preliminary conclusion from Table 2 that the predictive ability of ML algorithms varies significantly. The best results are obtained using GB, which is slightly better than RF. Their performance is superior to that of SVM and DNN. It should be noted that these results are specific to the given case study and the chosen dataset. However, we can conclude that RF and GB are effective approaches for this case. These methods have also been adopted to assess the feature importance, as shown below.

4.3 Analysis of the Factors Importance

The aim of this section is to analyze the importance of different features and to identify the most important ones for the prediction process.

First, we present Table 3, which displays the importance of the features obtained for different algorithms. Since there are multiple ways to measure feature importance, and it can be algorithm-specific, we have employed three techniques. The first two correspond to Gradient Boosting (GB) and Random Forest (RF), in addition to a permutation-based feature importance approach. We have chosen these two algorithms (GB and RF) as they yielded the best results. Further information on these techniques can be found in [3]. We have adopted these techniques to provide an overview of the impact of the various features.

Specifically, Table 3 shows the corresponding relative value for each feature. We have separated GTFS and weather features with a line in this table.

Table 3. Feature Importance

Feature	RF	GB	Permutation
Vehicle ID	0.00001	0.00001	0.00061
Vehicle Bearing	0.00003	0.00004	0.000105
Trip ID	0.02048	0.01582	0.025763
Trip Start Time	0.21010	0.21140	0.173025
Trip Start Date	0.20701	0.22431	0.18900
Route ID	0.00563	0.00437	0.069827
service ID	0.00000	0.00000	0.00000
shape ID	0.00000	0.00000	0.00000
Trip_headsign	0.00000	0.00000	0.00000
Direction_id	0.00000	0.00000	0.00000
Route_direction	0.00000	0.00000	0.00000
Weekday	0.03302	0.04368	0.04900
Hour	0.04004	0.04769	0.03529
Latitude	0.11721	0.13140	0.11521
Longitude	0.03560	0.04310	0.00000
Temperature	0.06835	0.03690	0.07
Dew Point	0.05735	0.05067	0.06456359
Humidity	0.0813	0.05098	0.0685
Wind Speed	0.18709	0.16185	0.1734
Pressure	0.06582	0.06377	0.06456359

Furthermore, Fig. 4 displays a bar plot of the Shapley values [14] for the 12 most significant features (which correspond to two of the third used features). Shapley values have gained popularity for this purpose [18]. They represent the average marginal contribution of a feature value across all possible combinations of features. Figure 4 illustrates the mean absolute value of each feature, indicating their importance under different feature combinations.

Table 3 and Fig. 4 indicate that most of the GTFS static features do not have a significant impact. Specifically, features such as shape ID, route direction, and trip headsign Type have little to no impact. This also holds true for certain GTFS real-time information, such as vehicle ID (though this only applies to the adopted case study). The most important GTFS real-time features are the trip start time and trip start date. Additionally, some weather features have demonstrated a significant impact except precipitation. Wind speed is the most important weather-related feature in this case study. This is expected as it is known to affect the travel time of ships and vessels. Other important weather features include temperature, dew point, humidity, and pressure. We should note that as shown in Fig. 2, dew point feature is highly correlated to other weather features. These are the primary findings, and further research should focus on utilizing this information to gain a better understanding of the factors that influence travel time.

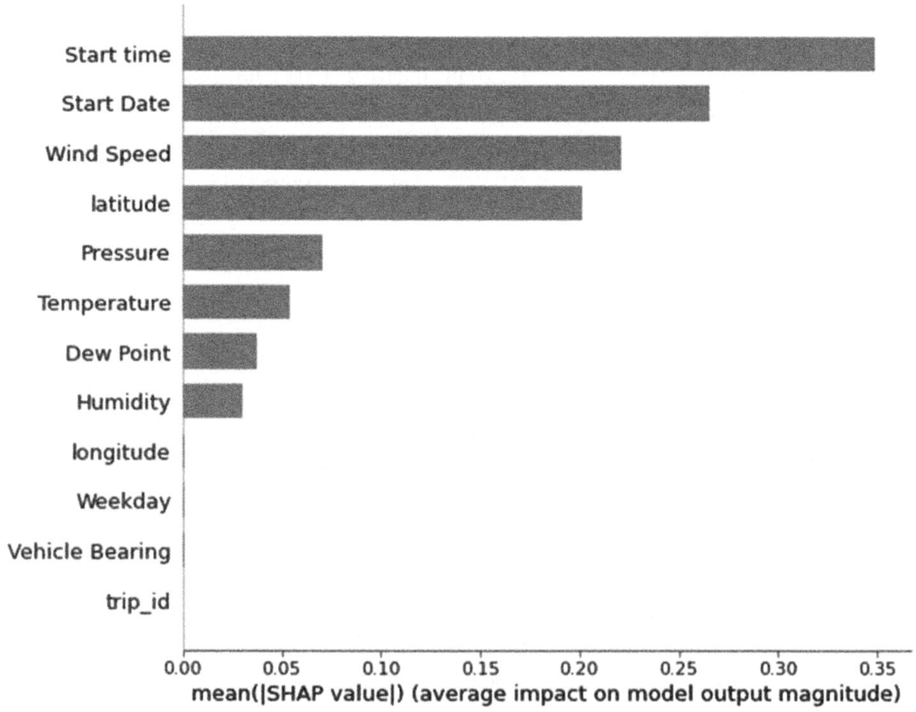

Fig. 4. Bar plot of the Shapley values

5 Conclusion

Travel time prediction for transit has recently become a recurring topic in the intelligent transportation literature. Transit travel time is influenced by several factors. This study proposes a systematic approach to predicting ferry transit travel time using publicly available timetables, real-time transit service feed data in the GTFS format, and weather data. In this paper, we merged different data sources to estimate travel time and showed how open data can be used to enhance the information provided to passengers. We compared various machine learning techniques for prediction and found that gradient boosting and random forest are the most suitable methods for the provided case study. Regarding the factors affecting travel time, the trip time and date were shown to be the most important features. Additionally, weather features such as wind speed have a significant impact.

Our proposed approach based on machine learning integrates heterogeneous data sources and can therefore be useful for a wide range of agencies worldwide. Thanks to the increasingly standardized data, it can be easily adopted by many cities.

The findings and accurate travel time predictions can be used for early detection of delays as in [13]. For this purpose, more information about the planned travel times is needed. In our data, we relied solely on actual travel times, but incorporating both actual and planned travel times is necessary for delay analysis. Additionally, travel time prediction can be used to obtain a better estimation of arrival travel time and improve service, as mentioned earlier [11]. The same methodology and features can be utilized for predicting both delays and estimated travel times. These topics are gaining increasing interest due to their importance in improving transit service, and acquiring more data is essential for addressing them effectively.

Future research should prioritize the acquisition of additional datasets and the exploration of alternative case studies. In fact, the availability of open data for ferry services is still limited compared to other transit services. To yield more comprehensive results, it is advisable to employ longer data periods for a more thorough evaluation of various factors (e.g., precipitation as no rain was recorded at that period). Additionally, beyond the findings presented in Fig. 2, it is essential to gain a deeper understanding of the relationships between different factors (e.g., whether wind speed has a positive or negative effect on travel time and to what extent it is linked to the date of the trip). For assessment, other measures such as adjusted R^2 can be used to detect the best combination of features for the prediction. The goal of this study is to lay the groundwork for further research in this crucial field.

References

1. Andersen, S.N., Tørset, T.: Waiting time for ferry services: empirical evidence from Norway. Case Stud. Transp. Policy **7**(3), 667–676 (2019). https://doi.org/10.1016/j.cstp.2019.04.006
2. Bauer, D., Tulic, M.: Travel time predictions: should one model speeds or travel times? Eur. Transp. Res. Rev. **10**, 1–12 (2018). https://doi.org/10.1186/s12544-018-0315-7
3. Brownlee, J.: https://machinelearningmastery.com/calculate-feature-importance-with-python/. Accessed 27 Feb 2022
4. Cammin, P., Sarhani, M., Heilig, L., Voß, S.: Applications of real-time data to reduce air emissions in maritime ports. In: Marcus, A., Rosenzweig, E. (eds.) HCII 2020. LNCS, vol. 12202, pp. 31–48. Springer, Cham (2020). https://doi.org/10.1007/978-3-030-49757-6_3
5. Daduna, J.R., Trépanier, M., Voß, S.: From computer-aided transit scheduling to systems and surveys in public transport. Public Transp. **14**(1), 1–3 (2022). https://doi.org/10.1007/s12469-022-00302-7
6. Daduna, J., Voß, S.: Practical experiences in schedule synchronization. In: Daduna, J.R., Branco, I., Paixão, J.M.P. (eds.) Computer-Aided Transit Scheduling. LNE, vol. 430, pp. 39–55. Springer, Heidelberg (1995). https://doi.org/10.1007/978-3-642-57762-8_4
7. Filtz, E., de la Cerda, E.S., Weber, M., Zirkovits, D.: Factors affecting ocean-going cargo ship speed and arrival time. In: Persson, A., Stirna, J. (eds.) CAiSE 2015. LNBIP, vol. 215, pp. 305–316. Springer, Cham (2015). https://doi.org/10.1007/978-3-319-19243-7_29
8. Ge, L., Sarhani, M., Voß, S., Xie, L.: Review of transit data sources: potentials, challenges and complementarity. Sustainability **13**(20), 11450 (2021). https://doi.org/10.3390/su132011450
9. Ge, L., Voß, S., Xie, L.: Robustness and disturbances in public transport. Public Transp. **14**(1), 191–261 (2022). https://doi.org/10.1007/s12469-022-00301-8
10. Gkiotsalitis, K., Cats, O.: Public transport planning adaption under the COVID-19 pandemic crisis: literature review of research needs and directions. Transp. Rev. **41**(3), 374–392 (2020). https://doi.org/10.1080/01441647.2020.1857886
11. Heilig, L., Stahlbock, R., Voß, S.: From digitalization to data-driven decision making in container terminals. In: Böse, J.W. (ed.) Handbook of Terminal Planning. ORSIS, pp. 125–154. Springer, Cham (2020). https://doi.org/10.1007/978-3-030-39990-0_6
12. Hörcher, D., Graham, D.J., Anderson, R.J.: Crowding cost estimation with large scale smart card and vehicle location data. Transp. Res. Part B: Methodol. **95**, 105–125 (2017). https://doi.org/10.1016/j.trb.2016.10.015
13. Kim, S., Kim, H., Park, Y.: Early detection of vessel delays using combined historical and real-time information. J. Oper. Res. Soc. **68**(2), 182–191 (2017). https://doi.org/10.1057/s41274-016-0104-4
14. Marcílio-Jr, W.E., Eler, D.M.: Explaining dimensionality reduction results using Shapley values. Expert Syst. Appl. **178**, 115020 (2021). https://doi.org/10.1016/j.eswa.2021.115020
15. Pedregosa, F., et al.: Scikit-learn: machine learning in Python. J. Mach. Learn. Res. **12**, 2825–2830 (2011)
16. Petersen, N.C., Rodrigues, F., Pereira, F.C.: Multi-output bus travel time prediction with convolutional LSTM neural network. Expert Syst. Appl. **120**, 426–435 (2019). https://doi.org/10.1016/j.eswa.2018.11.028

17. Taghipour, H., Parsa, A.B., Mohammadian, A.K.: A dynamic approach to predict travel time in real time using data driven techniques and comprehensive data sources. Transp. Eng. **2**, 100025 (2020). https://doi.org/10.1016/j.treng.2020.100025
18. Wagner, F., et al.: Using explainable machine learning to understand how urban form shapes sustainable mobility. Transp. Res. Part D: Transp. Environ. **111**, 103442 (2022). https://doi.org/10.1016/j.trd.2022.103442
19. Yan, R., Wang, S., Zhen, L., Laporte, G.: Emerging approaches applied to maritime transport research: past and future. Commun. Transp. Res. **1**, 100011 (2021). https://doi.org/10.1016/j.commtr.2021.100011
20. Yu, J., Voß, S.: Towards just-in-time arrival for container ships by the integration of prediction models. In: 56th Hawaii International Conference on System Sciences (2023). https://hdl.handle.net/10125/102778
21. Zissis, D., Xidias, E.K., Lekkas, D.: Real-time vessel behavior prediction. Evolving Syst. **7**, 29–40 (2016). https://doi.org/10.1007/s12530-015-9133-5

A Bi-Objective Column Generation Approach for Real-World Rolling Stock Circulation Planning Problems

Paul Päprer(✉), Janis S. Neufeld, and Udo Buscher

Faculty of Business and Economics, TUD Dresden University of Technology, 01069 Dresden, Germany
{paul.paeprer,janis_sebastian.neufeld,udo.buscher}@tu-dresden.de
https://tu-dresden.de/bu/wirtschaft/bwl/lim

Abstract. To make the planning in rail transport more efficient, this work deals with a real-world Rolling Stock Circulation Problem. In this study, sequences of trips and empty runs are formed for each traction unit to cover all scheduled trips. Practical restrictions for station-wise balanced planning are integrated into a Set Covering Problem formulation which is solved with a column generation approach. The decision makers give two objectives, the number of traction units and empty run kilometers. They have different priorities at different planning stages, and it is hard for the decision makers to quantify the cost of one traction unit or one empty run kilometer. A bi-objective column generation approach is built by integrating the epsilon constraint method, which is recognized as a classical method to handle multi-objective optimization problems. To evaluate the relation between both criteria, the algorithm is tested using real-world use cases. The generated circulation plans are presented in solution fronts, illustrating the targets' mutual influence. The identified trade-off between fewer traction units or fewer empty run kilometers can serve as decision support for planners in railway systems.

Keywords: Railways · Column Generation · Bi-objective

1 Introduction

In railway systems, the Rolling Stock Circulation Problem (RSCP) is a crucial step of the sequential planning cascade. It takes place after line planning, train timetabling and train platforming and is followed by train unit shunting, crew scheduling and crew rostering. Consequently, it not only allocates the most expensive resources of railway companies but also has a significant influence on further planning stages [9]. In the RSCP, the type and number of railway vehicles for every scheduled trip are defined. Therefore, the outcome of this task is given by circulations, i.e., sequences of trips and empty runs, for all railway vehicles used [3].

© The Author(s), under exclusive license to Springer Nature Switzerland AG 2023
J. R. Daduna et al. (Eds.): ICCL 2023, LNCS 14239, pp. 350–364, 2023.
https://doi.org/10.1007/978-3-031-43612-3_22

In real-world situations, decision makers often aim to minimize both the use of traction units and empty run kilometers, as they are major cost drivers. However, it is generally difficult to assign specific cost values to both aspects, which are necessary when integrating them into one objective function. This is due to the fact that they have different priorities at different planning stages. The contribution of this work is the development of a bi-objective column generation approach for the RSCP, whose solution front allows an evaluation of the relation between the two objectives and enables the decision makers to choose the currently most suitable circulation plan.

The remainder of this paper is organized as follows. Section 2 provides a brief literature review focusing on different models and approaches for RSCPs. Section 3 describes the real-world problem and its particularities verbally and mathematically. The bi-objective column generation approach is introduced in Sect. 4, and the results for real-world use cases are presented in Sect. 5. Finally, Sect. 6 concludes this work and gives a summary and possibilities for future research.

2 Literature Review

Many authors presented publications on the topic of RSCPs. First, the articles can be distinguished by the transport mode in rail passenger transport, e.g., [2], and rail freight transport, e.g., [13]. The next possible differentiation is based on which kind of railway vehicle the particular authors study. [13] deal with the assignment of locomotives to scheduled trips, [2] consider railcars, and [7] examine the routing of carriages.

An RSCP is usually formulated as a mixed integer problem. Most publications provide an arc-flow formulation in a time-space graph, e.g., [2]. Another option for modeling an RSCP is a Set Covering Problem (SCP) formulation as in [10]. The third formulation can be referred to as hyperarc-flow formulation in a hypergraph [11]. The difference from regular graphs is that in hypergraphs, an edge can join any number of nodes, not only two.

In order to generate optimal circulations for railway vehicles, appropriate evaluation criteria for the solutions must be established in advance. Most objective functions target the efficiency of the formed plans as in [2]. For example, the total costs incurred from allocating the vehicles, the driven kilometers, or the number of necessary railway vehicles are minimized. Other frequently used objectives can be combined into the quality of service, e.g., [7]. An example of this is the minimization of kilometers with seat shortages. The third group of criteria is intended to ensure highly robust solutions. For example, [12] interactively use optimization and simulation to focus on robustness. The criteria considered in this paper are the number of traction units and the number of empty run kilometers. Both are evaluated in [6] with the difference that costs are given to the criteria to combine them in one objective function. However, in practice this is often impossible since the decision makers can hardly quantify those values and thus want different solutions with various ratios between both objectives. This relationship has not been extensively studied in the literature so far.

Because there is an enormous diversity in the practical requirements of the particular use case, the applied methods to obtain reasonable solutions differ strongly. As a result, they can be distinguished into integer programming methods [5], heuristics [2], and column generation [1].

3 Problem Description

3.1 Real-World Rolling Stock Circulation Planning

The studied problem is based on a practical RSCP from the Austrian Federal Railways (ÖBB). The first sub-task of rolling stock circulation planning, i.e., the rolling stock assignment, is already given. This means that the traction unit type for every trip is known. Only the second sub-task, the train routing, needs to be solved here. Consequently, circulations must be created for a homogeneous set of vehicles to cover all scheduled trips requiring this type. The focus lies hereby on traction units, so carriages are not considered.

The railway network and a train schedule for a specific planning horizon are given and form the basis for the modeling. Every trip from the schedule has an origin station, a destination station, a start time, and an end time. The traction units are allowed to perform empty runs. These are unproductive trips that do not appear in the timetable and only serve to transfer a traction unit between two locations. To calculate the duration and distance for possible empty runs, the duration and distance between specific network points are used. Based on these fundamentals, a verbal formulation of the real-world circulation problem is given below, showing the objective function and relevant constraints.

There are two objectives when performing the circulation planning for the ÖBB. Besides the number of used traction units, minimizing empty run kilometers is important. Since the traction units are the most expensive resources of a railway company, purchasing new vehicles represents considerable acquisition costs. Therefore, circulation plans should strive for maximum efficiency in using the existing traction units, with the aim of minimizing the total number of units required. As the second part of the objective function, a small number of empty run kilometers is desired. Because traction unit drivers are an expensive resource, too, the ÖBB aims their drivers to perform as many productive, i.e., planned, trips as possible. Empty runs only cost money but do not generate any profit, so they should be avoided whenever possible.

There are several practical requirements in the real-world circulation problem. First, all trips from the previously planned timetable must be covered by at least one traction unit. Second, the planners aim at a round or cyclic planning solution. This means, in every station, the number of traction units at the beginning must equal the number of traction units at the end. Such a station-wise balanced circulation plan automatically puts the whole system back in its initial state. It is possible to perform the same circulation plan again in the next period. A third restriction limits the available traction units. Finally, all circulations must be spatially and temporally feasible. This means that after covering one trip, the next trip has to start later than the arrival of the previous one. Moreover, if the next trip has a different origin station, the time between both trips must be greater than the empty run needed to come to this station.

3.2 Mathematical Formulation

As shown in Sect. 2, an RSCP can be formulated as an SCP. The model constructed here is developed following existing approaches like in [10] and adapted to the specific real-world problem. The notation is given in Table 1.

Table 1. Notation for mathematical formulation

Type	Symbol	Description
Sets	P	set of possible circulations p
	T	set of scheduled trips t
	S	set of stations s
Parameters	c_p	cost of circulation p
	$a_{p,t}$	1 if circulation p covers trip t; 0 otherwise
	$b_{p,s}$	1 if station s is used by circulation p as origin station; -1 if used as destination; 0 if used as both or otherwise
	n	number of available traction units
Variables	x_p	binary variable; 1 if circulation p is used; 0 otherwise

The basic idea of the depicted SCP formulation is to have a set T of the trips to be covered and another set P of feasible circulations. The aim is now to identify the smallest or cost-minimal sub-collection of the circulation set to cover all elements of the trip set.

$$\min \sum_{p \in P} c_p \cdot x_p \tag{1}$$

$$\text{subject to} \quad \sum_{p \in P} a_{p,t} \cdot x_p \geq 1 \qquad \forall t \in T \tag{2}$$

$$\sum_{p \in P} b_{p,s} \cdot x_p = 0 \qquad \forall s \in S \tag{3}$$

$$\sum_{p \in P} x_p \leq n \tag{4}$$

$$x_p \in \{0, 1\} \qquad \forall p \in P \tag{5}$$

Equation (1) is the objective function of the model formulation and minimizes the total cost. This happens by summing up the cost of all used circulations.

Note that the term *cost* can represent both objectives and is defined explicitly in Sect. 4. Constraints (2) use the parameter $a_{p,t}$ to guarantee that every trip is assigned to at least one circulation. At this point, the character of the problem in the sense of an SCP formulation becomes clear because there is the possibility of over-covering. The constraints (3) ensure a station-wise balanced rolling stock circulation planning. These restrictions count the circulations which start (+1) and/or end (−1) at the specific station and provide a balanced overall plan (balance = 0). The methodology employed in this paper for modeling station-wise balanced plans draws from [1]. Constraint (4) ensures that the number of used traction units does not exceed the number of available ones. Finally, the decision variables have a binary character, as modeled in Eqs. (5). With this 0–1 integer linear programming model, the problem can be solved optimally when the set of all feasible circulations is built before. Since this is inefficient for large instances, a column generation procedure is applied.

4 Solution Approach

4.1 General Procedure

To solve the RSCP, column generation is used. The basic procedure of this solution method is described in [4]. It consists of a constructive heuristic, a Master Problem (MP), a Pricing Problem (PP), and an integrality step. The general process of the particular algorithm is depicted in Fig. 1. The picture shows the interaction of the four critical components in the algorithm.

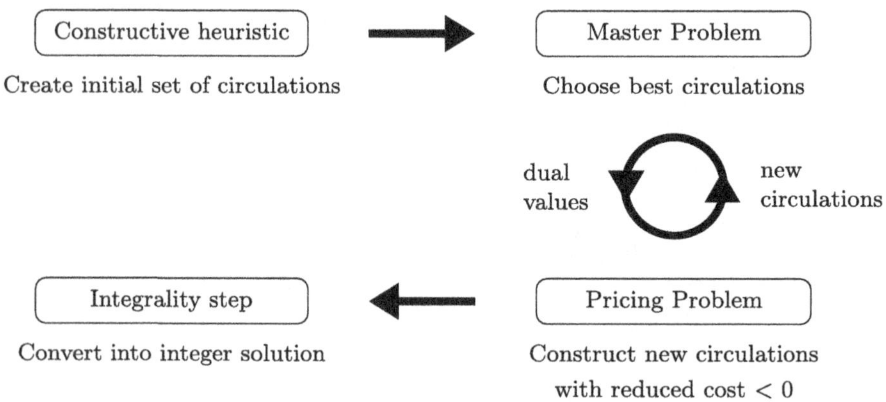

Fig. 1. Procedure of the applied column generation

The MP selects the most efficient combinations of columns, i.e., circulations, from a given circulation pool. For this purpose, it is necessary to have an initial pool of circulations that can lead to a feasible solution. Therefore, a constructive heuristic is presented, which builds an initial solution. After choosing the best circulations from the current circulation pool in the MP, the PP tries to construct new improving columns, i.e., circulations.

The applied column generation terminates if one of the following conditions is met: the best-found circulation in the PP has non-negative reduced cost, or the total number of 200 iterations is reached, or the objective value of the MP is improved less than 0.1 % in 20 consecutive iterations. Since the MP works with continuous variables, it is necessary to convert the found solution into an integer one after that.

4.2 Constructive Heuristic

The first step of the process of generating a starting solution is that all trips are sorted by their start times in ascending order, resulting in a list $T^{ordered}$. In addition, for each station s a sorted list $T_s^{ordered}$ is created in the same way, only considering the trips departing at s. Afterward, the construction of circulations can begin. For this purpose, the first trip t of $T^{ordered}$ is placed at the beginning of a new circulation p and removed from all trip lists. Now, the algorithm attempts to fill the current circulation with as many trips as possible. To search for suitable trips, the algorithm looks at the list of trips starting from the destination station of the current trip t. The first found trip u here, whose start time is greater than or equal to the current trip t's end time, is added to p. This procedure ensures that the resulting circulations are feasible in time and space. As explained above, every newly added trip is removed from the overall trip list and the ordered trip list of its origin station. If no additional trip can be added to the current circulation p, it is closed and added to the circulation plan P. After that, the algorithm starts with a new iteration, putting the first trip from the remaining ones in $T^{ordered}$ at the beginning of a new circulation. If $T^{ordered}$ is empty, the algorithm terminates, and the solution is given by the overall circulation plan P, consisting of all built circulations.

4.3 Master Problem

The mathematical formulation for the MP is an adjusted version of the SCP formulation discussed Sect. 3.2 and is depicted below. First, the equality constraint is split into two inequality constraints, (8) and (9), being more efficient and suited for column generation. Second, the solution of the constructive heuristic will always cover all trips but may not balance all stations or keep the available number of traction units. To have a feasible solution, balancing and capacity constraints (8)-(10) get auxiliary variables u_s, u_v, and w, converting them from hard to soft constraints. Exceeding these constraints is tolerated but punished in the objective function (6) by multiplying the auxiliary variables with a penalty cost parameter c^{punish}. A comparatively high-cost parameter will make the column generation seek true feasibility before optimizing the solution. In addition to these structural changes, two variable adoptions must be done. First, the Restricted Master Problem (RMP) is defined with the set of columns being a subset P' of all possible columns, i.e., circulations. The second step is to build the linear relaxation. Therefore, the integrality constraints for x_p, u_s, v_s, and w are removed. They can be positive real numbers, yielding the following relaxed Restricted Master Problem (rRMP). To obtain the necessary integer solution in the end, the variables can be set to integer (u_s, v_s, w) and binary (x_p) before solving the RMP model.

$$\min \quad \sum_{p \in P'} c_p \cdot x_p + \left(\sum_{s \in S} (u_s + v_s) + w \right) \cdot c^{punish} \tag{6}$$

$$\text{subject to} \quad \sum_{p \in P'} a_{p,t} \cdot x_p \geq 1 \qquad \forall t \in T \tag{7}$$

$$\sum_{p \in P'} b_{p,s} \cdot x_p \leq 0 + u_s \qquad \forall s \in S \tag{8}$$

$$\sum_{p \in P'} b_{p,s} \cdot x_p \geq 0 - v_s \qquad \forall s \in S \tag{9}$$

$$\sum_{p \in P'} x_p \leq n + w \tag{10}$$

$$x_p \in \mathbb{R}_0^+ \qquad \forall p \in P' \tag{11}$$

$$u_s, v_s \in \mathbb{R}_0^+ \qquad \forall s \in S \tag{12}$$

$$w \in \mathbb{R}_0^+ \tag{13}$$

4.4 Pricing Problem

After choosing the best circulations from the current circulation pool in the MP, the PP tries to construct new improving columns, i.e., circulations. The reduced cost of new variables evaluates their potential to improve the objective value. Therefore, dual values are required, which arise during the solution of the rRMP. Table 2 presents the dual values and to which restriction they belong.

Table 2. Dual values and their associated restrictions

Dual values	Associated constraints	Equation
π_t	covering constraints	(7)
σ_s^l	less-than-or-equal station balancing constraints	(8)
σ_s^g	greater-than-or-equal station balancing constraints	(9)
λ	capacity of traction units	(10)

Given this information, the equation for the reduced cost of a variable can be derived. The formula always starts with the cost of a new variable. Besides this term, every restriction of the rRMP appears in the equation by its calculated dual value and the decision variable coefficient. Note that parameters $a_{p,t}$ and

$b_{p,s}$ from the MP are now variables. Now, the PP aims to find the variable with the lowest reduced cost. Consequently, the equation for the reduced cost has to be formulated as follows.

$$\overline{c_p} = c_p - \sum_{t \in T} \pi_t \cdot a_{p,t} - \sum_{s \in S} \sigma_s^l \cdot b_{p,s} - \sum_{s \in S} \sigma_s^g \cdot b_{p,s} - \lambda \tag{14}$$

For constructing new circulations, we aim to build an exact subproblem. Thus, a new program with new constraints must be set up. The basis for this exact PP model formulation is a directed graph, i.e., digraph $G = (V, E)$. The set of nodes V is given by all scheduled trips T merged with an artificial start (i) and end (j) node. When building the set of edges E for the digraph, two trips are connected if one of the following two conditions is fulfilled:

1. Two trips can be connected without an empty run if the first's destination station is equal to the second's origin station and the second's start time is greater or equal to the first trip's end time.
2. Two trips with unequal destination station of the first and origin station of the second can be connected by an empty run. Therefore, the difference between the first trip's end time and the second trip's start time has to be greater than or equal to the duration of an empty run between these stations.

This setting allows empty runs between two trips. However, to meet the balancing constraints, it can be necessary to insert empty runs at the beginning or end of the circulation, too. For this purpose, two empty run nodes are created for all possible connections between two stations. One can be used right after the source node and one right before the sink node. Consequently, a set of empty run nodes R is added to the set of nodes V.

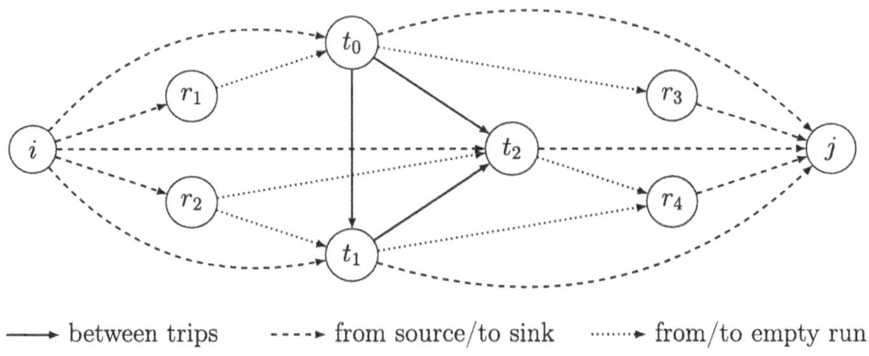

Fig. 2. Example of a representation of trips in a network

The connection between an empty run start node and a trip node is only possible when the empty run's destination station is the same as the trip's origin station. Analogously, a trip can only be followed by an empty run end node when the trip's destination station equals the empty run's origin station. Furthermore, the trip's start and end times must be considered when connecting empty run nodes and trips. Sometimes a trip starts right after the beginning of the planning period. In this case, inserting an empty run before the trip is impossible. The network representation resulting from this process is depicted in Fig. 2.

Now, the PP can be formulated as a shortest path problem [10], where the goal is to find a path from source i to sink j that generates the lowest reduced cost. For this purpose, a variable $x_{t,t'}$ indicates whether node t is followed by node t'. This variable is created for every directed edge of the network. Additionally, some other sets of nodes are needed. V^s is the subset of the node's successors in the network, and V^p is the subset of the node's predecessors. W combines the scheduled trips T and the empty runs R. The following constraints of the respective shortest path problem can find the cost-minimal circulation, i.e., the circulation with the lowest reduced cost.

$$\min \quad \overline{c_p} \tag{15}$$

$$\text{subject to} \quad \sum_{t' \in V^s} x_{t,t'} - \sum_{t' \in V^p} x_{t',t} = \begin{cases} 1 & \text{if } t = i \\ 0 & \text{if } t \in W \\ -1 & \text{if } t = j \end{cases} \qquad \forall t \in V \tag{16}$$

$$\sum_{t' \in V^s} x_{t,t'} = a_{p,t} \qquad \forall t \in T \tag{17}$$

$$\sum_{t \in W_s^{ori}} x_{i,t} - \sum_{t \in W_s^{des}} x_{t,j} = b_{p,s} \qquad \forall s \in S \tag{18}$$

$$x_{t,t'} \in \{0,1\} \qquad \forall (t,t') \in E \tag{19}$$

$$a_{p,t} \in \{0,1\} \qquad \forall t \in T \tag{20}$$

$$b_{p,s} \in \{-1,0,1\} \qquad \forall s \in S \tag{21}$$

The first group of constraints (16) are the typical flow conservation constraints of the shortest path problem. Only one outgoing arc is allowed for the source, and there will be exactly one ingoing arc for the sink. All other nodes must have an equal number of ingoing and outgoing arcs. The next two constraints (17) and (18) are the linking constraints between the variables $x_{t,t'}$, $a_{p,t}$, and $b_{p,s}$. If an arc is used, the respective trip is part of the circulation, and hence, $a_{p,t}$ needs to be 1 (17). For defining the $b_{p,s}$ variable, it is crucial to determine whether a station is used as an origin and/or destination station. For this purpose, a set of all trips or empty runs starting at the particular station (W_s^{ori}) and ending there (W_s^{des}) is formed. With the help of these two sets, the balance for every station can be calculated, which is then equal to the $b_{p,s}$ variable of the station s (18). The corresponding circulation is added to the circulation pool if the minimum reduced cost is negative.

4.5 Bi-Objective Column Generation

Because two objective criteria are considered for the circulation plans, two column generation variants are created, each focusing on a different objective.

- Column generation CG-TU: minimize **t**raction **u**nits
- Column generation CG-ER: minimize **e**mpty **r**un kilometers

They differ in formulating the objective function of the MP and the formulation of the reduced cost for the PP. We apply the ε-constraint method to the column generation approach to provide a front of different solutions. The general procedure of that method can be found in [8]. The developed method is depicted

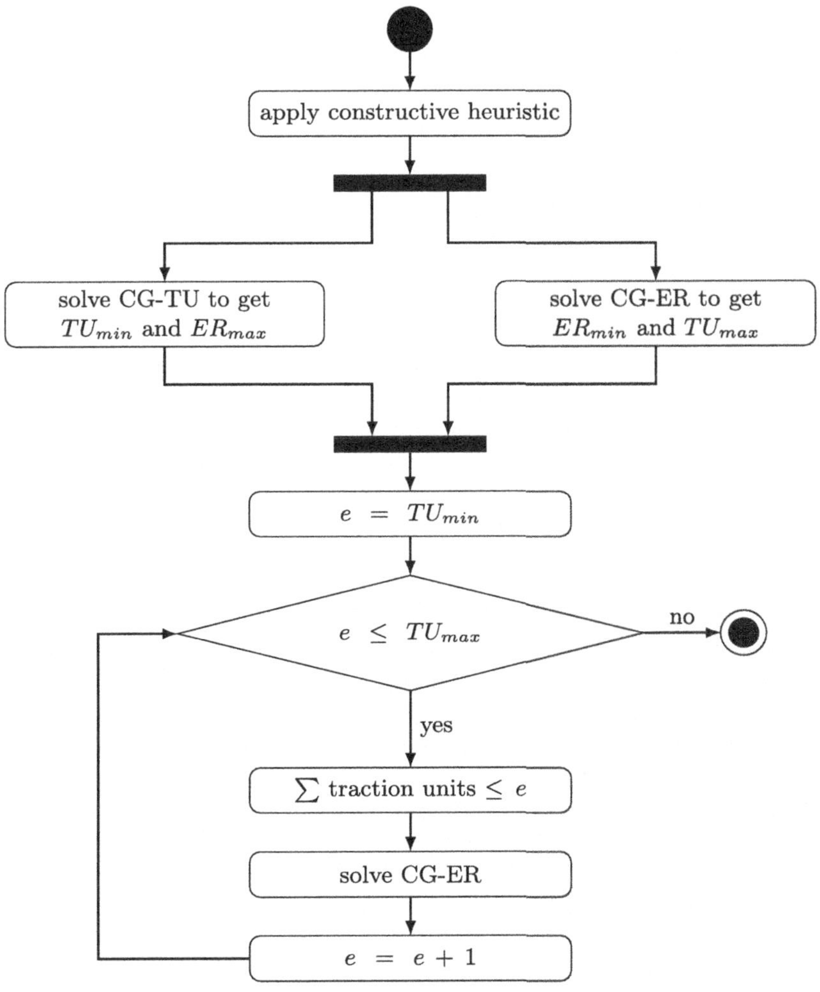

Fig. 3. Bi-objective column generation

in Fig. 3. It starts with two independent runs of both column generation variants. CG-TU will minimize the number of traction units TU_{min} leading to an upper bound of empty run kilometers ER_{max} because of neglecting this target. In contrast, CG-ER minimizes the number of empty run kilometers ER_{min}, providing an upper bound for the used traction units TU_{max}. Between those two extreme points, other solutions are calculated. Given two objective functions, one has to be chosen as the single objective making the other a constraint. Solving the column generation variant CG-TU is much more time-consuming because many solutions have the same objective value, i.e., number of traction units. For this reason, the second, more runtime-efficient column generation variant, CG-ER, is taken. The other objective of minimizing the number of traction units becomes a constraint, which is already part of the model as constraint (10). Starting from the CG-TU solution, CG-ER is run. The right-hand side of the capacity constraint starts with the minimal number of traction units TU_{min} and is increased step by step until the highest number of traction units, i.e., the one of the independent CG-ER run TU_{max}, is reached. This means, the algorithm can use more traction units, gradually reducing the number of empty run kilometers.

5 Computational Results

To test the column generation, it is applied to two real-world use cases given by the ÖBB (see Table 3). Some descriptive parameters are observed there to get an overview of the use cases. Furthermore, the graph in the bottom row visualizes the use case, where every node belongs to one station. The edges represent the scheduled trips in the style of an undirected graph. The thicker the line, the more often a trip occurs over the planning horizon. For this purpose, the trips are sorted into five classes whose borders are set by quantiles of the absolute frequencies.

The linear and integer programming formulations of the RSCP are implemented with Gurobi 10.0.1 using its C# API. C# is also used for the implementation of the proposed constructive heuristic and the column generation framework. All tests are run on an AMD EPYC^{TM} 7513 32-Core Processor using up to 24 physical cores and 128 GB RAM. The relevant parameters for the column generation algorithm are set to the following values: c^{punish} is 100,000, and n is 500.

To evaluate the proposed column generation approach, a distinction is made between the results of the constructive heuristic, CG-TU, and CG-ER. For all three solution types as well as both use cases, Table 4 shows the number of traction units, the empty run kilometers, the best rRMP value, and the runtime in seconds. The number of infeasibilities for the constructive heuristic only refers to the station balancing constraints and the capacity of traction units. An overused traction unit is one infeasibility. In addition, whenever there is a difference between departing and ending traction units for a station, this difference is added to the number of infeasibilities. The best rRMP value represents the best real solution before setting all variables to binary or integer. Consequently,

Table 3. Structure of the given use cases

Use case A	Use case B
freight transport	passenger transport
200 trips	1318 trips
38 stations	61 stations
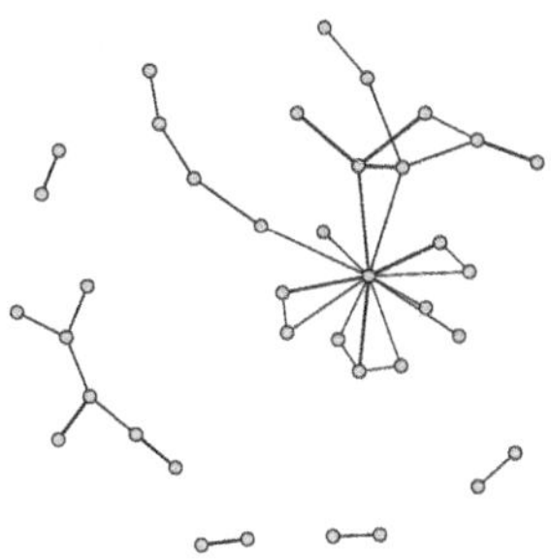	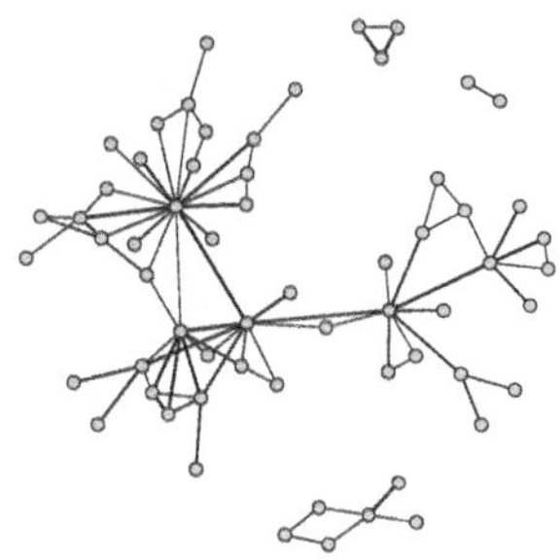

it refers to the traction unit number in CG-TU and empty run kilometers in CG-ER.

Table 4. Results of column generation for both use cases

		Use case A	Use case B
Constructive heuristic	Traction units	89	72
	Empty run kilometers	0	0
	Infeasibilities	156	54
	Runtime [s]	0.01	0.01
CG-TU	Traction units	25	76
	Empty run kilometers	77,306	91,018
	rRMP objective value	15.06	53.16
	Runtime [s]	307.23	6,952.91
CG-ER	Traction units	52	84
	Empty run kilometers	8,372	1,096
	rRMP objective value	6,678.04	661.87
	Runtime [s]	130.12	3,375.97

As explained in Subsect. 4.5, the ε-constraint method is adjusted and applied to column generation. This well-known multi-objective optimization procedure will create solutions that are efficient with respect to both objectives of the real-world problem, the number of traction units and the number of empty run kilometers. This means no weights are given to the objectives to obtain one single best solution but a set of non-dominated solutions are determined. Thereby, a solution S_1 dominates another solution S_2 if it is not worse than S_2 in both objectives and better in at least one objective [14]. Figure 4 visualizes the ten non-dominated solutions obtained by our method for use case A. It can be seen that a hyperbolic solution front is created. In the top left corner is a solution with a small number of traction units but many empty run kilometers. The opposite can be found in the bottom right corner, a solution with very low empty run kilometers and many traction units.

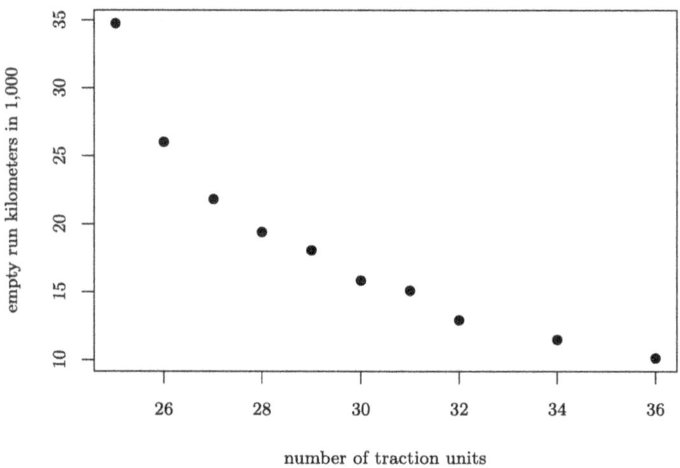

Fig. 4. Solution front of use case A

The assumption that the two objective criteria influence each other can be strengthened. The improvement of one criterion leads, ceteris paribus, to a deterioration of the other criterion. If up to 44 % more traction units are gradually deployed, the number of empty kilometers can be progressively reduced to 29 %. Now, it is up to the decision maker to decide which solution he/she chooses.

The same procedure of multi-objective column generation is applied to the large use case B. The resulting front of the solutions is shown in Fig. 5. Interestingly, allowing more traction units substantially decreases empty run kilometers between 73 and 79 traction units. The decision maker should consider using more traction units here to take the sizeable empty run advantages. Using more than 79 traction units also improves the empty run kilometers. However, the improvements are significantly smaller compared to the initial savings.

The figures illustrate the benefits of the approach presented. It helps to create solution fronts and allows an analysis of the relationship between the two objectives. This is very important for decision makers: they can focus on one direction or the other at different planning stages.

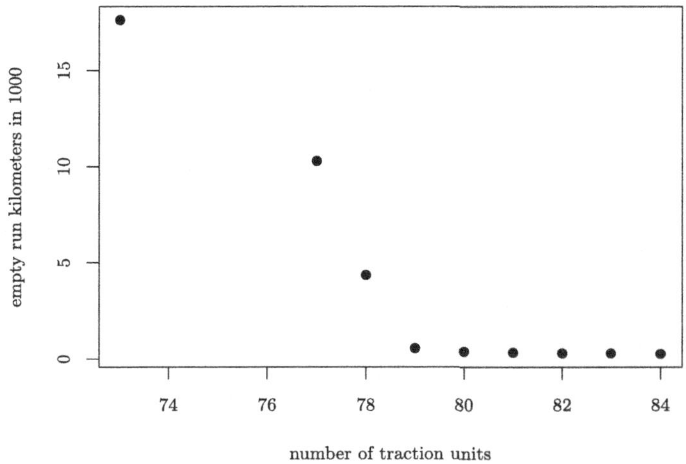

Fig. 5. Solution front of use case B

6 Conclusion and Future Research

This work presents a bi-objective column generation method to solve a real-world Rolling Stock Circulation Problem. The formulation is obtained by integrating a station balancing constraint in the classical Set Covering formulation for this problem. The ε-constraint method is applied to column generation to provide solutions with different quality regarding both objective criteria. The analysis reinforces the assumption that the two targets compete with each other. Hyperbolic solution fronts support this relationship.

Possible developments would be in the field of accelerating the solution process. It is necessary to find ways to solve significantly larger instances in a reasonable time, e.g., by solving the Pricing Problem heuristically or applying a fixing heuristic to reach the integer solution. In addition, the bi-objective column generation approach could also be an interesting approach to identify and examine other conflicting goals in rail transport or completely different fields.

Acknowledgements. This work was funded in the course of the project VIPES (FFG project number 893963) by the Federal Ministry for Climate Protection, Environment, Energy, Mobility, Innovation and Technology (BMK) as part of the call for proposals Mobilität der Zukunft. FFG is the central national funding organization and strengthens Austria's innovative power. We also want to thank Matthias Wastian, Senior Data Scientist at dwh GmbH, for providing all the necessary information to formulate the model and use cases to run the algorithm.

References

1. Bach, L., Gendreau, M., Wøhlk, S.: Freight railway operator timetabling and engine scheduling. Eur. J. Oper. Res. **241**(2), 309–319 (2015). https://doi.org/10.1016/j.ejor.2014.08.036

2. Cacchiani, V., Caprara, A., Toth, P.: An effective peak period heuristic for railway rolling stock planning. Transp. Sci. **53**(3), 746–762 (2019). https://doi.org/10.1287/trsc.2018.0858
3. Caprara, A., Kroon, L., Monaci, M., Peeters, M., Toth, P.: Passenger railway optimization. In: Handbooks in Operations Research and Management Science. vol. 14, pp. 129–187 (2007). https://doi.org/10.1016/S0927-0507(06)14003-7
4. Desrosiers, J., Lübbecke, M.E.: A primer in column generation. In: Desaulniers, G., Desrosiers, J., Solomon, M.M. (eds.) Column Generation, pp. 1–32. Springer, Boston (2005). https://doi.org/10.1007/0-387-25486-2_1
5. Fioole, P.J., Kroon, L., Maróti, G., Schrijver, A.: A rolling stock circulation model for combining and splitting of passenger trains. Eur. J. Oper. Res. **174**(2), 1281–1297 (2006). https://doi.org/10.1016/j.ejor.2005.03.032
6. Frisch, S., Hungerländer, P., Jellen, A., Primas, B., Steininger, S., Weinberger, D.: Solving a real-world locomotive scheduling problem with maintenance constraints. Transp. Res. Part B: Methodological **150**, 386–409 (2021). https://doi.org/10.1016/j.trb.2021.06.017
7. Lingaya, N., Cordeau, J.F., Desaulniers, G., Desrosiers, J., Soumis, F.: Operational car assignment at via rail Canada. Transp. Res. Part B: Methodological **36**(9), 755–778 (2002). https://doi.org/10.1016/S0191-2615(01)00027-3
8. Mavrotas, G.: Effective implementation of the ε-constraint method in multi-objective mathematical programming problems. Appl. Math. Comput. **213**(2), 455–465 (2009). https://doi.org/10.1016/j.amc.2009.03.037
9. Neufeld, J.S., Scheffler, M., Tamke, F., Hoffmann, K., Buscher, U.: An efficient column generation approach for practical railway crew scheduling with attendance rates. Eur. J. Oper. Res. **293**(3), 1113–1130 (2021). https://doi.org/10.1016/j.ejor.2020.12.058
10. Nishi, T., Ohno, A., Inuiguchi, M., Takahashi, S., Ueda, K.: A combined column generation and heuristics for railway short-term rolling stock planning with regular inspection constraints. Comput. Oper. Res. **81**, 14–25 (2017). https://doi.org/10.1016/j.cor.2016.11.025
11. Reuther, M., Schlechte, T.: Optimization of rolling stock rotations. In: Borndörfer, R., Klug, T., Lamorgese, L., Mannino, C., Reuther, M., Schlechte, T. (eds.) Handbook of Optimization in the Railway Industry. ISORMS, vol. 268, pp. 213–241. Springer, Cham (2018). https://doi.org/10.1007/978-3-319-72153-8_10
12. Rößler, M., et al.: Simulation and optimization of traction unit circulations. In: 2020 Winter Simulation Conference (WSC), pp. 90–101. IEEE (2020). https://doi.org/10.1109/WSC48552.2020.9383926
13. Scheffler, M., Neufeld, J.S., Hölscher, M.: An MIP-based heuristic solution approach for the locomotive assignment problem focussing on (dis-) connecting processes. Transp. Res. Part B: Methodological **139**, 64–80 (2020). https://doi.org/10.1016/j.trb.2020.05.020
14. Zitzler, E., Thiele, L., Laumanns, M., Fonseca, C.M., Da Fonseca, V.G.: Performance assessment of multiobjective optimizers: an analysis and review. IEEE Trans. Evol. Comput. **7**(2), 117–132 (2003). https://doi.org/10.1109/TEVC.2003.810758

An Effective Matheuristic Approach for Robust Bus Driver Rostering with Uncertain Daily Working Hours

Abtin Nourmohammadzadeh(✉) and Stefan Voß

Institute of Information Systems, University of Hamburg, Hamburg, Germany
{abtin.nourmohammadzadeh,stefan.voss}@uni-hamburg.de

Abstract. The bus driver rostering problem (BDRP) is a significant problem in public transportation that aims at assigning drivers to bus routes over a given time period while reducing system costs as well as inconveniences. In this work, a mixed-integer linear mathematical model is presented for the problem with the objective of minimizing the total assignment and driver dissatisfaction costs. Uncertainty is considered for the maximum daily working hours of drivers, which appears on the right-hand side of a block of constraints. A set of scenarios regarding the uncertain parameters and robust optimization are considered. A matheuristic approach is proposed consisting of a hybridization of particle swarm optimization (PSO), simulated annealing (SA) and mathematical programming of sub-problems based on the concept of partial optimization metaheuristic under special intensification conditions (POPMUSIC). It is shown that the proposed matheuristic is an effective approach for solving the BDRP by examining its performance on a set of benchmark instances.

Keywords: Bus driver rostering · Matheuristics · Partial optimization metaheuristic under special intensification conditions (POPMUSIC) · Particle swarm optimization (PSO)

1 Introduction

The driver rostering problem (DRP) is a critical problem in the transportation industry, particularly for bus companies that must efficiently create schedules for their drivers. The problem involves assigning drivers to shifts or duties over a specific period, such as a week or a month, while satisfying various constraints, including the availability of drivers, work regulations, and customer service requirements. The DRP is a complex and challenging optimization problem that has received significant attention from researchers in the fields of operations research, computer science, and transportation.

In recent years, researchers have developed various approaches to solve the DRP, including exact methods, heuristics, and metaheuristics. Exact methods are designed to solve the DRP to optimality but are computationally expensive

© The Author(s), under exclusive license to Springer Nature Switzerland AG 2023
J. R. Daduna et al. (Eds.): ICCL 2023, LNCS 14239, pp. 365–380, 2023.
https://doi.org/10.1007/978-3-031-43612-3_23

and may not be practical for large-scale problems. Heuristics are fast and efficient but do not guarantee optimal solutions. Metaheuristics are a compromise between exact methods and heuristics, offering the ability to find near-optimal solutions in a reasonable amount of time. Metaheuristics are particularly useful for solving large-scale problems with complex constraints. Besides these methods, combining elements of mathematical programming techniques with heuristics or metaheuristics has shown promise under the acronym matheuristics [15,16].

Matheuristics are able to find high-quality solutions in a relatively short amount of time, making them a popular choice for real-world applications where time and computational resources are limited. They are particularly effective when traditional optimization algorithms fail to find a solution or when a solution is required within a tight time frame. These methods are also highly adaptable and can be tailored to specific problem structures, making them a flexible tool for a wide range of optimization problems.

There are several related works which investigate the bus driver rostering problem (BDRP) with different assumptions and objectives. [21] presents a case study on the driver rostering problem for a Finnish bus transportation company. The authors use a mathematical programming model to create an initial solution, and then applied a local search heuristic to improve the solution. The results show that the proposed approach significantly improves the quality of the rosters compared to the manual process used by the company. [20] proposes a bi-objective evolutionary heuristic to the problem. The proposed method considers two objectives: minimizing the number of drivers needed and minimizing the number of working hours. The authors tested their approach on real-world data from a Portuguese bus company and demonstrated that their approach could provide high-quality solutions in reasonable computation times. [14] used a genetic algorithm to solve the balanced bus crew rostering problem, which is a variant of the BDRP where each bus trip requires two drivers to work together. The authors showed that their approach could generate high-quality solutions and outperformed other approaches from the literature.

[3] proposes a column generation metaheuristic for the DRP. The authors use a decomposition approach that allows for the creation of a large number of rosters in a short time while still maintaining quality. [9] propose an integrated and sequential solution method for the cyclic BDRP. The authors use a combination of column generation and branch-and-price. Their test instances are from a Canadian bus company.

[17] describes a heuristic method for solving the problem, which involves assigning drivers to shifts while taking into account their preferred days off. The proposed method uses multi-commodity flow models to decompose the problem into smaller subproblems, and then, uses a fixing process to optimize the solutions. [24] presents a mathematical model for solving the integrated driver rostering problem in public bus transport. The paper proposes a duty-block network approach that divides the scheduling process into two stages: duty assignment and block construction. The proposed model is compared with a traditional linear programming model, and the results show that the duty-block network

approach is more efficient and has better performance in terms of computational time and quality of the solution.

In [25], the authors propose an integrated approach that considers both the scheduling of drivers and the assignment of vehicles to routes, taking into account factors such as driver preferences, vehicle types, and passenger demand. The paper presents a mathematical model for the problem and describes a heuristic algorithm for solving it. The approach is tested on real-world data from a bus company in Germany, and the results show that the integrated approach can lead to significant improvements in efficiency and cost-effectiveness compared to traditional methods of driver scheduling.

There are two types of crew rostering, namely cyclic and non-cyclic. Cyclic rostering involves repeating patterns of shifts within a defined cycle, providing predictability and equal distribution of shifts. Non-cyclic rostering, on the other hand, offers stability and consistency with fixed shifts over a longer duration. While both methods have their advantages, our focus in this work is on non-cyclic rostering to provide employees with a stable and predictable schedule that promotes work-life balance and consistency.

[27] addresses the cyclic and non-cyclic crew rostering problems in public bus transit. The authors propose a mathematical model to describe these problems and present an exact algorithm to solve them. The paper also includes a case study based on real-world data from a German public transportation company to indicate the effectiveness of the proposed algorithm.

[26] presents a metaheuristic approach to solve a personalised crew rostering problem in public bus transit. The authors propose a hybrid metaheuristic that uses ant colony optimization, simulated annealing, and tabu search to generate high-quality solutions to this problem. The results show that the proposed algorithm outperforms the other methods in terms of both solution quality and computational efficiency.

In our current BDRP, we present a model for the problem which seeks to minimize the total assignment costs and the total number of undesired duties assigned to drivers. The aim of the latter is to increase the satisfaction of drivers. Since the maximum working hours of each driver on each day are usually not deterministic in the real applications and drivers can be unavailable during some periods because of health problems or personal engagements, we consider this parameter to be uncertain. Therefore, drivers cannot be assigned to duties which must be done during their unavailability periods. On the other hand, maybe the drivers are able to compensate these missing hours on some other days. This forms a model where the uncertainty emerges at the right-hand side of a constraint. To the best of our knowledge, this special characteristic has not yet been sufficiently investigated.

Short-term staff shortages, particularly among train and bus drivers, have become a common issue in the transportation sector. Several sources, such as [1] and [2], highlight the prevalence of this problem. The International Road Transport Union (IRU) conducted a survey revealing that in 2021, 7% of bus and coach driver positions in Europe were unfilled, with an expected increase to

8% in 2022. Furthermore, the survey noted a lack of young drivers, with only 3% of bus and coach drivers under the age of 25, contributing to a demographic crisis in the industry. Additionally, gender diversity in the profession is limited, as less than 3% of truck drivers and only 12% of bus and coach drivers in Europe are women. The primary cause of driver shortages, as reported by road transport operators, is a scarcity of skilled drivers in various regions.

Some previous attempts in right-hand side uncertainties are for example: [22], which discusses the bi-level knapsack problem with stochastic right-hand sides, exploring the optimal solution to this problem using mathematical modeling techniques, and [13], which addresses the maximization problem of monotone submodular functions under an uncertain knapsack capacity. [18] explores the complexity of 2-stage robust linear programming with right-hand side uncertainty and its applications. The paper provides useful insights for researchers and practitioners dealing with uncertainty in linear programming problems. The same author researches into the complexity of two-stage robust linear programming problems with right-hand side uncertainty in [19]. It is proven that the problem becomes NP-hard when the uncertainty set is defined as an ellipsoid, which is a more general set than the polyhedral set considered in the previous paper. The paper provides a detailed proof of the complexity result and discusses its implications for practical applications. Closely related to our paper are also issues to solve integrated vehicle and crew scheduling problems with simple uncertainty measures in [10,11] regarding the number of vehicles.

A robust optimization approach is chosen to deal with right-hand side uncertainties in our work. The concept of robustness is essential to address uncertainties inherent in the system. The motivation behind employing robust optimization techniques is to ensure that the proposed solutions remain of high quality and effective even when faced with various input variations or scenarios. By considering the uncertainties in the inputs, the objective is to develop strategies or models that can withstand these uncertainties and still perform optimally. Robustness measurement is a way to quantify the ability of a solution or approach to maintain its effectiveness and quality under different conditions or uncertainties. It allows for a more comprehensive evaluation and comparison of different strategies, taking into account their performance across a range of possible scenarios.

Due to the complexity of this problem, a matheuristic approach comprising the particle swarm optimization (PSO) [12] and partial optimization metaheuristic under special intensification conditions (POPMUSIC) [23] using consecutive mathematical optimization of sub-models of the problem, is devised. A set of benchmark instances and a peer algorithm from the literature are chosen to test the ability of our solution methodology.

The remainder of this paper is organized as follows. In Sect. 2, the problem is described and its mathematical model is presented. Section 3 explains our solution methodologies. The computational experiments are covered in Sect. 4. Finally, Sect. 5 is dedicated to the conclusions and directions to extend the work.

2 Problem Description

In the BDRP, there is a set of duties which have to be performed with a set of drivers within a planning horizon. Each duty has a duration and each driver has a set of desired duties. For the assignment of each duty to each driver, a specific cost incurs. There is also a cost corresponding to the assignment of a duty which is not included in the set of desired duties of the driver. The objective of this version of the BDRP is to minimize a weighted sum of the assignment costs and drivers' dissatisfaction. A big challenge is that the maximum time of the availability of each driver is not certain during each day. In other words, drivers can be unavailable in some periods but may make up the missing hours on other days. Therefore, the daily working time of drivers may become smaller or larger than the considered standard 8 h. Drivers do not usually work for more than a maximum number of consecutive days without taking any day off in between. This is regarded as another major restriction in rostering.

In the context of the BDRP, an additional restriction has been introduced to ensure efficient scheduling of duties while considering driver preferences. This constraint, referred to as the "no early duty after late duty" constraint, is designed to avoid assigning an early duty to a driver who has done a late duty on the previous day. The early duties are those which are done before 11:00 while the late duties start after 18:00. By incorporating the "no early duty after late duty" constraint into the BDRP, the scheduling algorithm can optimize the assignment of duties while respecting the drivers' preferences and promoting their well-being by acknowledging the need for appropriate rest and recovery periods. This constraint enhances the fairness and efficiency of the rostering process, contributing to improved driver satisfaction and overall operational performance.

The rostering constraints are respecting the maximum daily working hours of drivers as well as the maximum number of consecutive working days, which is here assumed to be 5. The notations used in the model are given in Table 1.

The mathematical formulation of our BDRP is as follows:

$$Min\ w_1 \sum_{d} \sum_{u \in U} c_{d,u} + w_2 \sum_{d} \sum_{u \notin P_d} x_{d,u} \tag{1}$$

$$\sum_{d} x_{d,u} = 1 \qquad u \in U \tag{2}$$

$$\sum_{u \in U_t} x_{d,u} H_u \leq MDWH_{d,t} \qquad d \in D, t \in T \tag{3}$$

$$\sum_{u \in U_l \cap U_t} x_{d,u} \leq 1 - \sum_{u \in U_e \cap U_{t+1}} x_{d,u} \qquad d \in D, t \in T \tag{4}$$

$$a_{d,t}|T| \geq \sum_{u \in U_t} x_{d,u} \qquad d \in D, t \in T \tag{5}$$

$$\sum_{t}^{t+5} a_{d,t} \leq 5 \qquad d \in D, 1 \leq t \leq |T| - 5 \tag{6}$$

$$x_{d,u}, a_{d,t} \in \{0, 1\} \qquad d \in D, u \in U_t, t \in T \tag{7}$$

Table 1. Notations used in the mathematical model

Parameters	Explanation
T	The set of days of the planning horizon; $t \in T$
D	The set of drivers; $d \in D$
U	The set of all duties; $u \in U$
U_t	The set of duties to be assigned to the drivers on day t; $u \in U_t$
U_e	The set of early duties; $u \in U_e$
U_l	The set of late duties; $u \in U_l$
H_u	The duration of duty u in hours
$MDWH_{d,t}$	The maximum daily working hours of driver d on day t (an uncertain parameter)
P_d	The duties which driver d desires to do
w_1	The weight of the total assignment cost for the bus company
w_2	The weight related to the importance of driver satisfaction for the company
$c_{d,u}$	The assignment cost of duty u to driver d
Variables	**Explanation**
$x_{d,u}$	Binary, =1, if driver d is assigned to duty u
$a_{d,t}$	Binary, =1, if driver d is active on day t

In the objective function (1), we calculate the weighted sum of the assignment costs and the number of undesired duties assigned to the drivers. Constraint (2) enforces each duty to be assigned to only one driver. Respecting the maximum working days of each driver is implied by Constraint (3). Constraint 4 prevents the assignment of an early duty to a driver if they were assigned a late duty on the previous day. This is an important constraint in our model because $MDWH_{d,t}$ are uncertain parameters and appear on the right-hand side. Constraint (5) activates variable $a_{d,t}$ if driver d works on day t. Constraint (6) avoids exceeding the maximum consecutive working days of each driver. The variable domains are expressed by (7).

3 Solution Methodology

Our solution methodology consists of a particle swarm optimization (PSO) framework hybridized with simulated annealing (SA). A random population of solutions are generated and regarded as particles. These particles are interactively moved according to the classical PSO rules as follows

$$v_i(t+1) = wv_i(t) + c_1 r_1 (pbest_i - x_i) + c_2 r_2 (gbest - x_i) \tag{8}$$

where $v_i(t)$ is the current velocity of particle i, $pbest_i$ is the personal best position of the particle, and $gbest$ is the best position of all particles in the swarm. The values r_1 and r_2 are random numbers between 0 and 1, and w is the inertia weight that controls the balance between exploration and exploitation.

Then, the positions are updated by:

$$po_i(t+1) = po_i(t) + v_i(t+1) \tag{9}$$

where po_i is the current position of particle i.

A proportion (RSA) of the particles are chosen based on their fitness by the roulette wheel method (see [6]) to be improved by SA. In SA, a number of neighboring solutions (NBS) of the chosen solution is evaluated in each iteration and we move to a neighboring solution if it has a better objective value; otherwise this movement happens with the probability:

$$P_{SA} = e^{\frac{-(f(s)-f(s'))}{T}} \tag{10}$$

where$f(s)$ and $f(s')$ are the objective values of the current and the neighboring solution, respectively. T is the current temperature. We begin from an initial temperature T_0 and reduce it after each iteration by dividing it by CT. When we move to a new solution, searching the remaining neighboring solutions of the iteration is continued around it. The termination condition of the SA is passing a number ($MISA$) of consecutive iterations without observing any improvement in the objective value.

Following the algorithms' procedure, a proportion of the best particles (PMB) and a proportion of other particles (PMO) are also improved according to the POPMUSIC framework. The latter group is selected again by the roulette wheel method. In the POPMUSIC, solutions are divided into K parts; then, each time, one of these parts (called s_{seed}) is selected at random and an area including it and the D adjacent parts to it called altogether A is processed by solving the mathematical model of the problem. So, we solve each time a sub-model of the problem by fixing all variables except for those existing in A at their values in the incumbent solution. The Gurobi solver is used to solve the sub-models. The POPMUSIC process on a solution stops when no more improvement can be done by choosing any part as s_{seed}.

The whole matheuristic terminates if the number of consecutive stagnant PSO iterations, which are iterations without any improvement in the objective, exceeds a limit ($MCUI$). This algorithm has several hyper-parameters, which have to be tuned properly in the beginning with an appropriate method. The pseudocode of this matheuristic algorithm is presented in Algorithm 1.

The solutions are encoded as strings. Each cell of the string belongs to a duty and is filled with the label of one driver. However, as PSO works usually with continuous domains, the cell contents are real numbers in the interval $[0,|D|]$. To convert the real numbers to the driver labels, assuming that cc is the cell content, we calculate $\lfloor cc \rfloor + 1$. Figure 1 shows the encoding of a simple BDRP with 5 drivers and 10 duties.

Algorithm 1: The proposed matheuristic

```
Data: Problem inputs
Result: A feasible solution expected to be of good quality
Set the parameters of the algorithm
Generate nPop random candidate solutions as the initial particles.
Evaluate the population.
It = 0.
Initialize a variable called BO, which keeps the best objective value found so far.
while It ≤ MCUI do
    Move the particles based on their new speed.
    Evaluate the particles.
    Choose ⌈PSA × nPop⌉ candidates from the population by the roulette
    wheel selection.
    Improve the selected candidates by neighborhood searches based on SA.
    Evaluate the SA results, and then, merge them with the previous
    population.
    Sort the total population based on the objective values.
    Choose ⌈PMB × nPop⌉ from the best solutions and ⌈PMO × nPop⌉ based
    on the roulette wheel selection from other solutions and input them in a set
    called PSET.
    for Each solution spm ∈ PSET do
        Decompose spm in K parts, i.e., the set of parts is
        H = {part_1, ..., part_K}
        Set P = ∅
        while P ≠ {part_1, ..., part_K} do
            Select a seed part s_seed ∈ H and s_seed ≠ P at random
            Build a sub-problem R composed of s_seed and its nearest D parts
            (corresponding to area A)
            Optimize R through solving the mathematical formulation by the
            Gurobi solver
            if R has been improved then
                Update solution S
                P ← ∅
            end
            else
                Include s_seed in P
            end
        end
    end
    Merge the POPMUSIC results with the population.
    Sort the population based on the objective value and choose the first nPop
    best of them as the new population.
    Set BO = Objective value of the first solution of the population.
    if BO is improved in comparison to its previous value then
        It = 0
    end
    else
        It = It + 1
    end
end
Report BO.
```

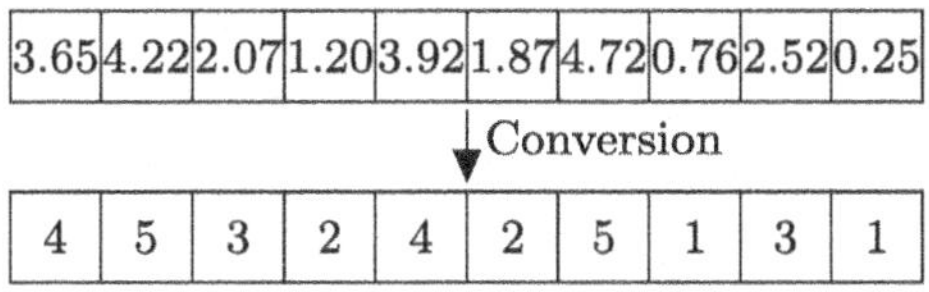

Fig. 1. Solution encoding

In the implementation of PSO, whenever the content of any cells violates the allowable domain, it is reflected back into the feasible area. In the SA, a neighboring solution is defined as one which differs from the current solution in the content of one cell. Therefore, to build a neighboring solution, a cell is chosen randomly and its content is changed to another random value.

For the implementation of the POPMUSIC, each cell is considered as a part. So, each time a cell is selected as s_{seed}, and area A is build by it and its nearest D cells located on both of its sides, i.e., one cell is selected from the right, and then, one from the left and this continues until D parts are completed. Whenever the beginning or end of the string is reached, the remaining parts are picked from the opposite side. The variables corresponding to these cells constitute the sub-model to be solved by mathematical programming. A simple example for the application of POPMUSIC on an encoded BDRP solution is illustrated in Fig. 2. s_{seed} is shown in dark grey, D is equal to 5, so the last part (cell) is picked from the right. The D-nearest genes to s_{seed} are shown in grey. It means that the variables related to the assignment of the third to sixth duties are reset and the drivers of these duties are optimally determined by solving the corresponding mathematical sub-model.

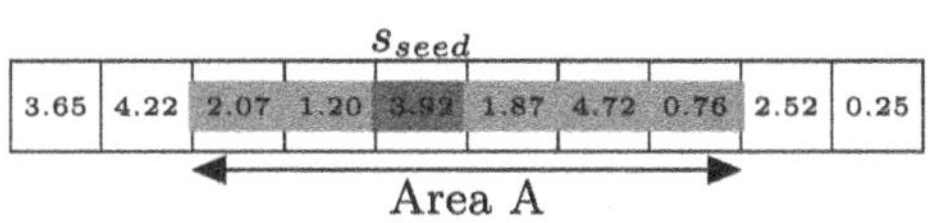

Fig. 2. Applying POPMUSIC to a chromosome

The constraints of the model are handled by generating the variables' values in their feasible interval. For this sake, the variables are filled with a feasible value one by one in the ascending order of the duties. When a variable is filled, its value is entered in the corresponding constraints and determines the feasible intervals for the next variables.

As the right-hand side of Constraint 3 is uncertain, the problem is solved once based on each combination of $MDWH_{d,t}$ values. Hence, we have one solution and objective value for each scenario. The solution corresponding to the worst objective value is considered as the robust solution because no scenario can lead to any objective value worse than that. This is in accordance with the definition of robustness presented in [4].

4 Computational Experiments

In this section, firstly, the used test instances, and then, the computational settings are explained. The important step of parameterization of the algorithm is declared next. Finally, the obtained results are presented and analyzed.

4.1 Test Instances

To test our proposed solution methodology, we use the 12 real-word benchmark instances given in [27] and also tackled in [26]. The number of drivers is considered to be $\lceil \frac{|U|}{50} \rceil$. The default maximum daily working hours of each driver is 8 h. The uncertainties are generated by choosing between 20% to 30% of the drivers and changing their working hours on 10% to 20% of the days by reducing them by 1 to 4 h, and subsequently, adding the same amount of time to the maximum working hours of another day chosen randomly. For each chosen driver, 5 different scenarios are build. For each unavailability scenario, the affected parameters and variables are set in the model. Regarding the assignment variables, some of them must be fixed at zero before starting the solution process because the driver is not available at the time of the corresponding duty. In the objective function (1), the cost of each undesired assignment is assumed to be five units, so we have $w_1 = 1$ and $w_2 = 5$.

The characteristics of these instances are shown in Table 2.

Table 2. Characteristics of instances

Instance	Nb. of duties	Nb. of drivers
48-75-6	1313	27
52-73-6	1288	26
52-75-6	1321	27
393-45-37	5420	109
392-45-37	5815	117
397-40-37	4917	99
96-70-8	3200	64
87-70-8	3273	66
89-70-8	3260	66
221-45-30	4214	85
211-45-34	4003	81
214-45-34	3966	80

4.2 Computational Settings

The mathematical model of the BDRP is programmed in Python and Gurobi is called. The considered time limit for the solver is 12 h. To examine the capabilities of our algorithm in comparison to other alternative methods, the pure mathematical programming (MP), the pure hybrid metaheuristic of PSO-SA (MH), i.e. our algorithm without the POPMUSIC, a counterpart algorithm from [26] called MMASPara (S), which is an ant-colony-based method with parallelization, and finally, our matheuristic, are applied to each instance. Since S is used for a different version of the BDRP, we re-implemented it for our case. Except MP, other methods are run five times for each instance and the average objective value and execution time are referred due to the possibility of a different result after each run. These algorithms are also coded in Python. All the computational experiments of this paper are executed in a Computer with an Intel Core i7-4790 3.60 GHz processor and 8 GB of RAM.

4.3 Parameterization of the Algorithm

Parameter setting is an important phase in the implementation of (meta/mat)-heuristics algorithms because their abilities are extremely affected by the values of their hyper-parameters. In this work, we use the response surface method (RSM) [7], which works based of design of experiments (DOE). In the RSM, an initial interval is considered for each parameter in which we are likely to find the best value for that parameter. Then, experiments based on different combinations of parameters are done and according to their results, the RSM chooses a value for each parameter. We implement the RSM in R language. The empirically considered initial values for the parameters of our algorithm are as follows. In PSO, w : $[0, 1]$, $nPop$: $[100, 500]$, c_1 : $[0, 1]$, c_2 : $[0, 1]$, in SA, RSA : $[0.1, 0.5]$ T_0 : $[1000, 100000]$, CT : $[1.5, 10]$, NBS : $[50, 200]$, $MISA = [10, 50]$, in POPMUSIC: $D = [10, 30]$, $PMB = [0.1, 0.5]$, $PMO = [0.1, 0.5]$, and for the whole algorithm $MCUI = [10, 50]$. The parameter tuning phase is executed for each instance separately and the required time is included in the total execution times of the algorithms for each instance, which are presented later. However, on average about 75% of the execution times belongs to the parameterization phase. The values of the algorithm's parameters set for each instance are shown in Table 3.

The RSM is similarly used for the parameter setting of any other algorithm used in this work.

4.4 Results and Comparisons

The results of the tested algorithms are summarized in Table 4. For each method, we have the (average) objective value and elapsed time to reach it. The objective value is shown as the (average) objective value found by the corresponding method divided by the best objective value found among all runs of all methods. These best objective values are shown as BVF in the last column.

Table 3. Parameter tuning of our algorithm

Instance	w	$nPop$	c_1	c_2	RSA	T_0	CT	NBS	$MISA$	D	PMB	PMO	$MCUI$
48-75-6	0.47	173	0.58	0.40	0.24	65547	5.02	128	22	16	0.31	0.20	29
52-73-6	0.52	119	0.55	0.57	0.26	77873	4.02	98	22	16	0.23	0.21	26
52-75-6	0.56	116	0.56	0.51	0.26	38120	5.41	103	26	15	0.23	0.30	20
393-45-37	0.47	262	0.58	0.45	0.26	84825	3.14	121	21	24	0.27	0.28	22
392-45-37	0.40	304	0.44	0.62	0.28	21263	3.11	105	28	26	0.33	0.35	31
397-40-37	0.58	341	0.66	0.60	0.32	31823	3.72	184	37	22	0.34	0.32	36
96-70-8	0.51	331	0.51	0.52	0.31	21264	2.58	150	42	22	0.28	0.30	43
87-70-8	0.47	340	0.59	0.47	0.32	23183	3.57	86	42	21	0.31	0.34	41
89-70-8	0.48	464	0.62	0.68	0.33	47419	2.51	124	45	17	0.38	0.36	40
221-45-30	0.53	411	0.54	0.64	0.32	86611	4.20	153	49	23	0.36	0.35	33
211-45-34	0.45	409	0.42	0.63	0.31	95091	2.53	188	40	25	0.34	0.35	32
214-45-34	0.57	201	0.42	0.65	0.29	94764	4.86	154	47	18	0.23	0.30	31

Table 4. Results of the examined methods (MP: mathematical programming, MH: hybrid metaheuristic of PSO-SA, S: state-of-the-art method, MMASPara of [26]), OA: our proposed matheuristic algorithm, BVF: best objective value found, Obj: $\frac{\textit{(average) objective value}}{\textit{Best objective value found (BVF)}}$, Time: (average) execution time in seconds

Instance	MP		MH		S		OA		BVF
	Obj	Time	Obj	Time	Obj	Time	Obj	Time	
48-75-6	1.00	12154.21	1.32	42.10	1.17	45.20	1.04	62.19	8.86×10^8
52-73-6	1.00	10534.53	1.26	37.15	1.06	48.62	1.02	66.73	8.92×10^8
52-75-6	1.00	11543.14	1.28	40.21	1.11	46.71	1.03	65.21	6.32×10^8
393-45-37	1.00	11397.19	1.31	41.64	1.33	182.27	1.07	63.31	4.19×10^8
392-45-37	1.00	13249.95	1.33	44.11	1.13	178.42	1.03	71.09	0.63×10^9
397-40-37	1.00	11864.44	1.25	39.45	1.33	202.82	1.08	68.91	4.07×10^8
96-70-8	1.00	10764.16	1.23	35.20	1.29	188.90	1.07	64.15	2.33×10^8
87-70-8	1.00	14177.99	1.29	41.72	4.10	219.62	1.18	72.63	2.08×10^7
89-70-8	2.65	43200	1.20	34.39	1.41	295.83	1.09	59.87	8.16×10^8
221-45-30	3.33	43200	1.23	36.58	1.23	478.62	1.05	62.42	1.42×10^{11}
211-45-34	1.00	15692.70	1.35	45.82	2.16	296.08	1.21	70.10	6.84×10^{10}
214-45-34	1.00	16480.40	1.24	43.17	2.25	352.52	1.19	67.06	6.21×10^{10}

It is observed that mathematical programming can find the optimal values in long computational times for the first 8 instances. However, the solver cannot find the optimal solutions within the considered time limit for instances 89-70-80 and 221-45-30. So, the time limit (43200 s or 12 h) and the best (last) proportional objective value of the solver are tabulated. It can be deduced that the gaps from the best known results are extremely large in terms of these two instances. The two final instances can be solved to optimality in longer execution times compared to the first 8 ones.

The PSO-SA (MH) and MMASPara (S) can find solutions slightly distant from the bests but in much shorter execution times compared to MP. On the other hand, our matheuristic spends a little more time than MH but achieves solutions of considerably better quality. It is also perceived that the POPMUSIC plays an important role in the success of our matheuristic since the solution quality significantly drops when we exclude it and use only PSO-SA (MH).

The proportional objective values of all runs are illustrated for the four examined algorithms as well as the model without uncertainties solved by our matheuristic (non-robust: shown as NR) as box plots in Fig. 3. It is evident that the four quartiles related to our approach are lower or better than the three first and this indicates its satisfactory performance and efficiency. In addition, we see that the costs of solving the robust model are not high because the box plot of NR does not considerably differ from OA.

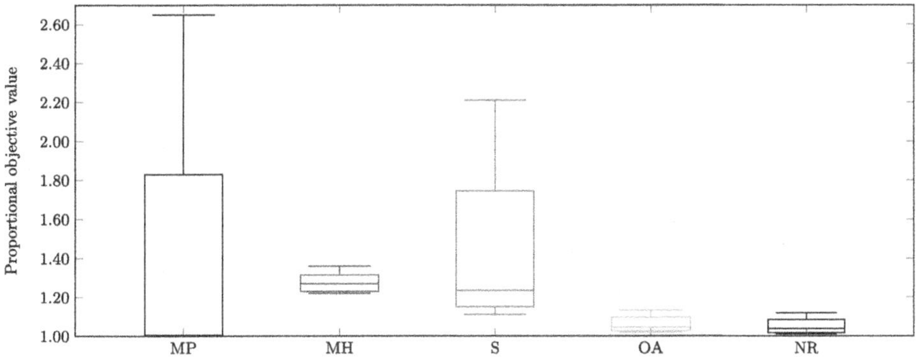

Fig. 3. Box plots of proportional objective values based on all runs of all instances

In the next step, we aim to conduct a statistical test to determine if the difference of the average objective values in any pair of the used algorithms are statistically significant. For this sake, a non-parametric test called Friedman with Bergman-Hommel post-hoc procedure ([5]) is used. [8] shows that this test is very appropriate to compare more than two methods in pairs. The obtained p-values are given in Table 5.

Table 5. P-values of the pairwise comparisons of the methods

	MP	MH	S	OA
MP	–	1.58×10^{-4}	2.61×10^{-4}	2.71×10^{-4}
MH	1.58×10^{-4}	–	3.73×10^{-5}	3.12×10^{-5}
S	2.61×10^{-4}	3.73×10^{-5}	–	4.90×10^{-3}
OA	2.71×10^{-4}	3.12×10^{-5}	4.90×10^{-3}	–

According to the very low p-values, we can reject the null hypothesis claiming the equality of averages for all pairs in the significance level of 0.01.

Generally, it can be deduced that this robust optimization with regard to the existence of uncertainties on the right-hand side of the model can be properly handled by the proposed matheuristic. So, we are able to provide driver rosters that remain effective even when the daily working hours of drivers change, which is very likely to happen over the course of the planning horizon.

5 Conclusions

In this work, we addressed the important problem of driver rostering of bus companies with the consideration of uncertain daily working hours of drivers. Concerning the fact that it is an uncertainty in right-hand side parameters of the corresponding mathematical model, a robust optimization problem which is less focused in the literature was surveyed. A matheuristic algorithm is proposed consisting of proper exploration and exploitation with PSO, SA and POPMUSIC. The results indicate that the combination of metaheuristics and mathematical programming techniques can provide a strong optimization power in a short time, which cannot be found in pure approaches of these types.

For extending this research, we can recommend applying the proposed method to other similar assignment problems. Another direction is to enhance the performance of the method by adding extra effective operators to it or to try other concepts of embedding mathematical optimization in metaheuristics. Investigation into fast and efficient parameter tuning can also be of great value.

Acknowledgements. This research is funded by dtec.bw - Digitalization and Technology Research Center of the Bundeswehr. dtec.bw is funded by the European Union - NextGenerationEU.

The helpful comments of two reviewers are gratefully acknowledged.

References

1. Current traffic situation. https://www.der-metronom.de/fahrplan/aktuelle-verkehrslage/. Accessed 20 June 2023
2. New survey reveals shocking shortage of bus drivers. https://www.unitetheunion.org/news-events/news/2021/november/new-survey-reveals-shocking-shortage-of-bus-drivers/. Accessed 20 June 2023
3. Barbosa, V., Alvelos, F., Respício, A.: Bus driver rostering by column generation metaheuristics. In: Fonseca, R.J., Weber, G.-W., Telhada, J. (eds.) Computational Management Science. LNEMS, vol. 682, pp. 225–231. Springer, Cham (2016). https://doi.org/10.1007/978-3-319-20430-7_29
4. Ben-Tal, A., Nemirovski, A.: Robust solutions of uncertain linear programs. Oper. Res. Lett. **25**(1), 1–13 (1999). https://doi.org/10.1016/s0167-6377(99)00016-4
5. Bergmann, B., Hommel, G.: Improvements of general multiple test procedures for redundant systems of hypotheses. In: Bauer, P., Hommel, G., Sonnemann, E. (eds.) Multiple Hypothesenprüfung / Multiple Hypotheses Testing, vol. 70, pp. 100–115. Springer, Heidelberg (1988). https://doi.org/10.1007/978-3-642-52307-6_8

6. Blickle, T., Thiele, L.: A comparison of selection schemes used in evolutionary algorithms. Evol. Comput. **4**(4), 361–394 (1996). https://doi.org/10.1162/evco.1996.4.4.361
7. Box, G.E.P., Draper, N.R.: Response Surfaces, Mixtures, and Ridge Analyses, 2nd edn. Wiley, Hoboken (2007)
8. Derrac, J., García, S., Molina, D., Herrera, F.: A practical tutorial on the use of nonparametric statistical tests as a methodology for comparing evolutionary and swarm intelligence algorithms. Swarm Evol. Comput. **1**(1), 3–18 (2011). https://doi.org/10.1016/j.swevo.2011.02.002
9. Er-Rbib, S., Desaulniers, G., Elhallaoui, I., Munroe, P.: Preference-based and cyclic bus driver rostering problem with fixed days off. Public Transp. **13**(2), 251–286 (2021). https://doi.org/10.1007/s12469-021-00268-y
10. Ge, L., Kliewer, N., Nourmohammadzadeh, A., Voß, S., Xie, L.: Revisiting the richness of integrated vehicle and crew scheduling. Public Transp. (2022). https://doi.org/10.1007/s12469-022-00292-6
11. Ge, L., Nourmohammadzadeh, A., Voß, S., Xie, L.: Robust optimization for integrated vehicle and crew scheduling based on uncertainty in the main inputs. In: The Fifth Data Science Meets Optimisation Workshop at IJCAI-22. Vienna (2022). https://sites.google.com/view/ijcai2022dso/. Accessed 30 Apr 2023
12. Kennedy, J., Eberhart, R.: Particle swarm optimization. In: Proceedings of ICNN'95 - International Conference on Neural Networks, vol. 4, pp. 1942–1948 (1995). https://doi.org/10.1109/ICNN.1995.488968
13. Kawase, Y., Sumita, H., Fukunaga, T.: Submodular maximization with uncertain knapsack capacity. arxiv (2018). https://arxiv.org/pdf/1803.02565
14. Ma, J.H., Liu, T., Guan, W.: Solving balanced bus crew rostering problem with genetic algorithm. Appl. Mech. Mater. **361–363**, 2070–2074 (2013). https://doi.org/10.4028/www.scientific.net/AMM.361-363.2070
15. Maniezzo, V., Boschetti, M.A., Stützle, T.: Automatic design for matheuristics. In: Matheuristics. EURO Advanced Tutorials on Operational Research, pp. 35–57. Springer, Cham (2021). https://doi.org/10.1007/978-3-030-70277-9_2
16. Maniezzo, V., Stützle, T., Voß, S. (eds.): Matheuristics: Hybridizing Metaheuristics and Mathematical Programming. Springer, New York (2010). https://doi.org/10.1007/978-1-4419-1306-7
17. Mesquita, M., Moz, M., Paias, A., Pato, M.: A decompose-and-fix heuristic based on multi-commodity flow models for driver rostering with days-off pattern. Eur. J. Oper. Res. **245**(2), 423–437 (2015). https://doi.org/10.1016/j.ejor.2015.03.030
18. Minoux, M.: On 2-stage robust LP with RHS uncertainty: complexity results and applications. J. Global Optim. **49**(3), 521–537 (2011). https://doi.org/10.1007/s10898-010-9645-2
19. Minoux, M.: Two-stage robust LP with ellipsoidal right-hand side uncertainty is NP-hard. Optim. Lett. **6**(7), 1463–1475 (2012). https://doi.org/10.1007/s11590-011-0341-z
20. Moz, M., Respício, A., Pato, M.V.: Bi-objective evolutionary heuristics for bus driver rostering. Public Transp. **1**(3), 189–210 (2009). https://doi.org/10.1007/s12469-009-0013-x
21. Nurmi, K., Kyngäs, J., Post, G.: Driver rostering for a Finnish bus transportation company. In: IAENG Transactions on Engineering Technologies, vol. 7, pp. 15–35. World Scientific, Singapore and Hackensack NJ (2012). https://doi.org/10.1142/9789814390019_0002

22. Özaltın, O.Y., Prokopyev, O.A., Schaefer, A.J.: The bilevel knapsack problem with stochastic right-hand sides. Oper. Res. Lett. **38**(4), 328–333 (2010). https://doi.org/10.1016/j.orl.2010.04.005
23. Taillard, É.D., Voß, S.: POPMUSIC – partial optimization metaheuristic under special intensification conditions. In: Ribeiro, C., Hansen, P. (eds.) Essays and Surveys in Metaheuristics, vol. 15, pp. 613–629. Springer, Boston (2002). https://doi.org/10.1007/978-1-4615-1507-4_27
24. Xie, L., Suhl, L.: A duty-block network approach for an integrated driver rostering problem in public bus transport. In: Longhurst, J., Brebbia, C.A. (eds.) Urban Transport XVIII, pp. 295–306. WIT Transactions on The Built Environment, WIT Press Southampton, UK (2012). https://doi.org/10.2495/UT120261
25. Xie, L., Kliewer, N., Suhl, L.: Integrated driver rostering problem in public bus transit. Procedia. Soc. Behav. Sci. **54**, 656–665 (2012)
26. Xie, L., Merschformann, M., Kliewer, N., Suhl, L.: Metaheuristics approach for solving personalized crew rostering problem in public bus transit. J. Heuristics **23**(5), 321–347 (2017). https://doi.org/10.1007/s10732-017-9348-7
27. Xie, L., Suhl, L.: Cyclic and non-cyclic crew rostering problems in public bus transit. OR Spectrum **37**(1), 99–136 (2015). https://doi.org/10.1007/s00291-014-0364-9

Beyond Cargo Hitching: Combined People and Freight Transport Using Dynamically Configurable Autonomous Vehicles

Joris J. A. Kortekaas[2], Breno A. Beirigo[1], and Frederik Schulte[2(✉)]

[1] Department of High-tech Business and Entrepreneurship, University of Twente, Hallenweg 17, 7522 NH Enschede, The Netherlands
b.alvesbeirigo@utwente.nl

[2] Department of Maritime and Transport Technology, Delft University of Technology, Mekelweg 2, 2628 CD Delft, The Netherlands
j.j.a.kortekaas@student.tudelft.nl, f.schulte@tudelft.nl

Abstract. A *Dynamically Configurable Autonomous Vehicle* (DCAV) is a new class of autonomous vehicle concept using a separable design of lower and upper parts—carriers and modules—to allow more flexible operation. A fleet of DCAVs consists of a set of carriers and a set of compatible modules. Different, possibly crowd-sourced, modules can increase the number of use-cases for DCAVs, possibly leading to disruptive changes in the transport sector. This study investigates the use of DCAV system operating on an *Autonomous Mobility-on-Demand* (AMoD) scenario, combining passenger and freight transport flows. The novel problem is denoted as the *Dynamically Configurable Autonomous Vehicle Pickup and Delivery Problem* (DCAVPDP). We propose a *mixed-integer linear programming* (MILP) model aiming to minimize DCAV-fleet size and distance traveled. We compare the performance of a DCAV fleet to the performance of a typical single-purpose fleet (consisting of dedicated passenger and freight vehicles). The numerical study, with 360 instances for each fleet type, considering four people-and-freight demand distribution scenarios, the inclusion of ridesharing, module-and-carrier (de)coupling locations, and different simulation horizon lengths, shows that the proposed modular DCAV system can fulfill a mixed people-and-freight demand using, on average, 18.77% fewer carriers than a regular AMoD system comprised of single-purpose vehicles while increasing on-duty fleet utilization by 4.82%.

Keywords: Dynamically Configurable Autonomous Vehicles · Shared Autonomous Vehicles · Cargo Hitching · Combined Passenger and Freight Transport · Ridesharing

1 Introduction

Dynamically Configurable Autonomous Vehicles (DCAVs) are a new class of autonomous vehicles using a separable design concept consisting of drive and transport units. The drive unit (also called the carrier, driveboard, or chassis)

© The Author(s), under exclusive license to Springer Nature Switzerland AG 2023
J. R. Daduna et al. (Eds.): ICCL 2023, LNCS 14239, pp. 381–395, 2023.
https://doi.org/10.1007/978-3-031-43612-3_24

is a standardized platform housing self-driving equipment (e.g., sensors, motors, battery). The transport unit (also referred to as module, capsule, pod, or body) is a switchable add-on part that can be dynamically and autonomously outfitted onto drive units to accommodate any commodity type (see Fig. 1). Such a modular nature of DCAVs increases operational flexibility, enabling various use-cases: transport providers can assign diverse modules to carriers to fulfill different demands.

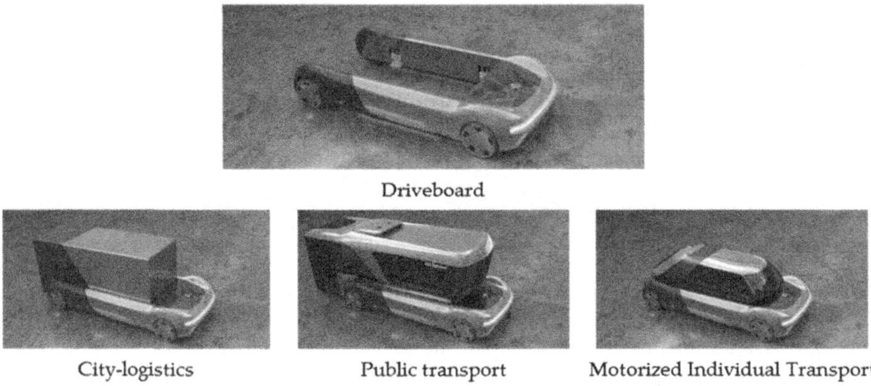

Fig. 1. Example of a Dynamically Configurable Autonomous Vehicle (DCAV) system [15]. The drive unit (carrier) can autonomously outfit diverse transport units (modules) on the fly to service heterogeneous demands such as freight and mobility.

By separating drive and transport units, providers can increase the utilization of self-driving carriers (presumably, the most expensive assets) while increasing profits, adapting to changing demand profiles such as people and freight on the operational level. Typically, vehicle acquisition is a long-term investment, which makes deciding on adequate fleet size and mix a complex strategical decision [2,7]. Therefore, relying on a DCAV fleet may also mitigate losses due to drastic demand shifts. For example, the COVID outbreak led to a surge in delivery services while social distancing decreased mobility, exposing the fragility of transportation systems based on single-purpose vehicles [12]. Ultimately, investing in additional freight modules to accommodate a higher freight demand is expected to be considerably cheaper than investing in entirely new freight vehicles.

Combined people and freight transportation systems have been gaining attention in the literature [3,9]. For example, solution approaches have been designed for settings where people and parcel share rides on taxis (see, e.g., [8]) and compartmentalized autonomous vehicles (see e.g., [1,13]). However, there is no study on optimizing the operations of a DCAV-based transportation system that dynamically switches transport units to fulfill heterogeneous demand. Only concept designs have been evaluated (see, e.g., [10,11,15]) and presented by companies such as the Continental BEE [4], the Mercedes Benz Vision Urbanetic [5] and the Toyota e-palette [14].

This study presents a *mixed-integer linear programming* (MILP) formulation for the *Dynamically Configurable Autonomous Vehicle Pickup and Delivery Problem* (DCAVPDP) arising on a transport system that services both passenger and freight demands. Our formulation extends the formulation by [6] for the *vehicle routing problem with trailers and transshipments* (VRPTT) by adding service level constraints as formulated in *dial-a-ride problems* (DARPs). Additionally, we consider the integration of passenger and freight transport, the use of parking locations, and allowing multiple trips and ridesharing. The model seeks to find an optimal routing solution that minimizes vehicle utilization in terms of linear combination of the distance traveled by carriers and modules.

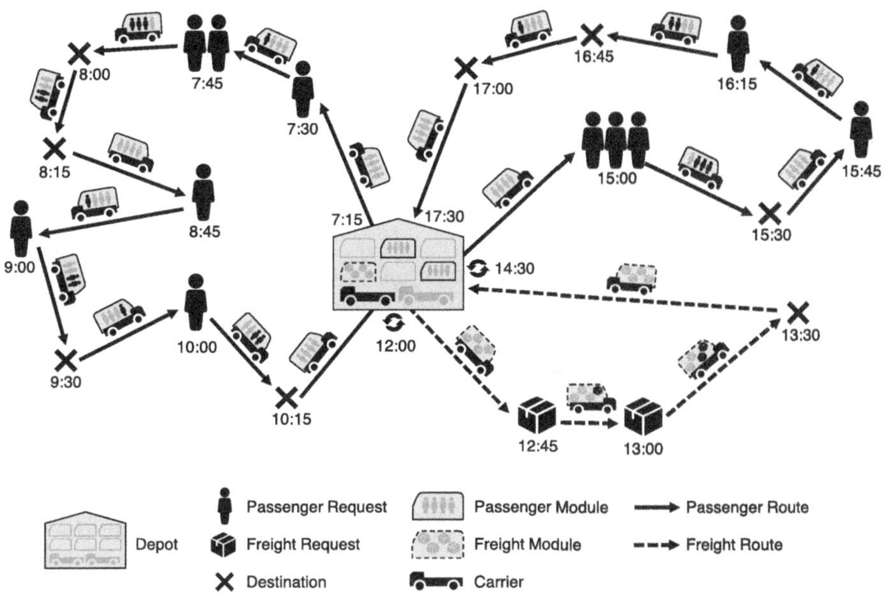

Fig. 2. Example of a DCAV fleet operation throughout a typical day.

Figure 2 shows an operational example of a DCAV fleet using different modules throughout the day to fulfill passenger and freight requests. The carrier starts at 7:15 at the depot and couples a passenger module to transport passengers during the morning rush hour. As long as the vehicle capacity is not exceeded, the vehicle is allowed to make multiple pickups and have passengers share the ride. When the latest passenger of the first trip is dropped off at 10:15 the vehicle gets called back to the depot. Next, the carrier switches its passenger module for a freight module and starts servicing freight requests as demand for passenger transport is low at the time. After picking up several packages the vehicle returns to the depot once more at 14:30 to switch over to a passenger module to transport passengers for the remainder of the afternoon. To meet demand the carrier has made three separate trips to and from the depot, changing modules for each trip. Even though demand fluctuates throughout the day, the carrier is being used to serve requests for either passengers or parcels, resulting in high carrier utilization.

We benchmark the performance of the DCAV fleet (consisting of carriers and passenger and freight modules) with a typical single-purpose fleet (consisting of dedicated passenger and freight vehicles). We consider carriers and dedicated vehicles of modular and single-purpose fleets have to start and end their route at a central depot. Vehicles are not allowed to arrive early and wait at a pickup location since requests are made on-demand, and there is little room for parking in city centers. However, parking locations are available for vehicles to wait until a pickup is requested; these locations can also be used for modular vehicles to switch modules. In contrast, modules do not have to start or end their route at the depot. They can also start and end their route from a parking location and do not have to return to the same location as where they originated from. We assume there is no limit to the number of times a module can be switched, except occupied modules, which are not allowed to be switched.

2 Problem Description

This study considers a *Dynamically Configurable Autonomous Vehicle Pickup and Delivery Problem* (DCAVPDP), which focuses on the daily operations of an on-demand transportation provider that uses a DCAV fleet to pick up and deliver requests of both passengers and parcels. We assume carriers are required to start and end their route at a central depot and are not allowed to arrive early and wait at a request location—there is little room for parking in an urban city environment. However, parking locations are available for vehicles to wait until a pickup is requested. These locations can also be used for modular vehicles to switch modules. Modules do not have to start or end their route at the depot and can be repeatedly switched when empty. Ridesharing is allowed between requests of the same commodity, with detours limited by maximum extra ride times.

Figure 3 highlights the difference between a modular and a single-purpose fleet when servicing one passenger and one freight request. The single-purpose fleet uses two dedicated vehicles traveling direct routes from the depot to the pickup and delivery. In contrast, the DCAV fleet uses available parking locations to gather modules closer to request locations and uses a single carrier to service both requests. The carrier leaves the depot and travels to a parking location where it couples a freight module to service the freight request. After reaching the destination of the freight request, it drives to another parking location to decouple the freight module and travel to the final available parking location to couple a passenger module. The passenger module is used to service the passenger request and returns together with the carrier to the depot.

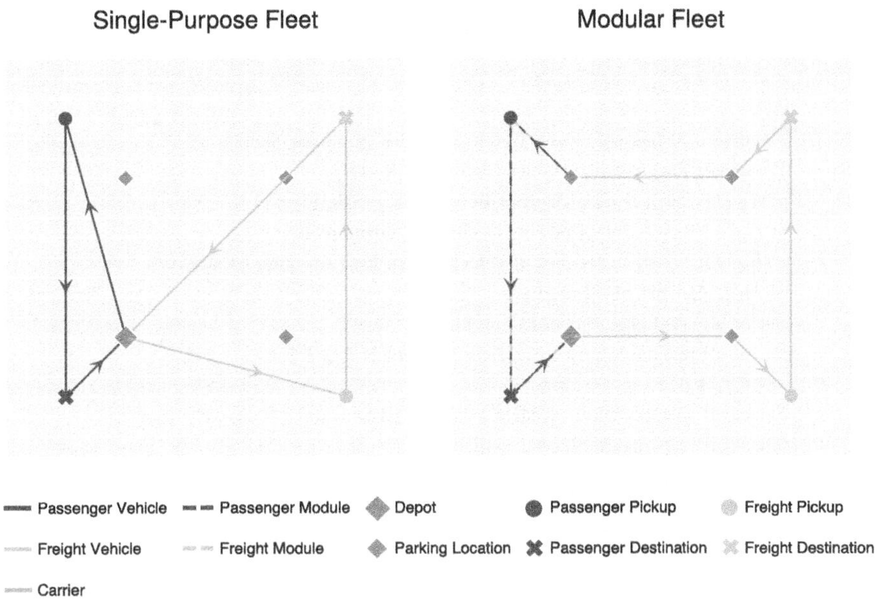

Fig. 3. Difference between single-purpose and modular DCAV fleets when servicing the same passenger and freight request set.

3 Problem Formulation

The DCAVPDP is defined on a directed graph $G = (V, A)$, consisting of vertices V and arcs A, and requires synchronisation in time and space of the movement of carriers and modules. We consider a grid service area where a total number of n_r requests is generated. The set of all vehicles is indicated by F, which is a collection of all vehicles that are available to the model. The set of all vehicles is further separated in the sets F_{a}, F_{q}, and F_{m}. All motorized vehicles in the model are indicated by F_{a}, which is a combination of all passenger and freight vehicles and the carriers. F_{q} is the set of all vehicles that have load-carrying capability, which consists of the passenger and freight vehicles and the passenger and freight modules. The final set regarding vehicles is F_{m}, which is a set of all modules in the model. Where V^k are all reachable vertices for vehicle k, V_{P}^k is a set of all reachable pickup vertices for vehicle $k \in F$.

The set of traversable arcs A^k is further specified in the following sets: A_{C}^m, A_{PD}^k, and A_{W}^k. The set A_{C}^m describes all traversable arcs module $m \in F_{\mathrm{m}}$ can travel along when being coupled to carrier $c \in C$, since modules are not capable of traveling between real-world locations without the assistance of a carrier. However, modules are allowed to travel to couple vertices on their own to allow for the distribution of modules across all parking locations. The number of parking locations in the model is specified by n_{p} and f and 0 correspond to the start and final vertex respectively. This ensures a module can be coupled at all available parking locations on the grid after being decoupled from a carrier. A_{PD}^k

Table 1. Sets, parameters, and variables of the DCAVPDP and dedicated people and freight integrated problem.

Sets	
$C, M_{\mathrm{p}}, M_{\mathrm{f}}$	Carriers and passenger and freight modules (modular fleet)
$K_{\mathrm{p}}, K_{\mathrm{f}}$	Passenger and freight vehicles (dedicated fleet)
F	$= K_{\mathrm{p}} \cup K_{\mathrm{f}} \cup C \cup M_{\mathrm{p}} \cup M_{\mathrm{f}}$. Set of all vehicles (fleet)
F_{a}	$= K_{\mathrm{p}} \cup K_{\mathrm{f}} \cup C$. Set of powered vehicles (autonomous)
F_{q}	$= K_{\mathrm{p}} \cup K_{\mathrm{f}} \cup M_{\mathrm{p}} \cup M_{\mathrm{f}}$. Set of vehicles with load carrying capability
F_{m}	$= M_{\mathrm{p}} \cup M_{\mathrm{f}}$. Set of all modules
V^k	Set of all reachable vertices for vehicle $k \in F$
V_{P}^k	Set of all reachable pickup vertices for vehicle $k \in F$
V_{P}	$= \bigcup_{k \in F} V_p^k$
V_{park}^k	Set of all vertices where vehicle k is allowed to wait
A^k	Set of all traversable arcs for vehicle $k \in F$
A_{C}^m	Set of arcs module $m \in F_{\mathrm{m}}$ can only traverse while spatially synchronised with a compatible carrier $c \in C$
A_{PD}^k	Set of traversable arcs between request pairs for vehicle $k \in F$
A_{W}^k	Set of arcs for vehicle $k \in F$ where waiting is not allowed at the arrival vertex
Parameters	
Vehicles	
n_{k}	Number of available vehicles with load carrying capability
n_{c}	Number of available carriers
Q^k	Capacity of vehicle $k \in F$
v^k	Speed of vehicle $k \in F$
Requests	
n_{r}	Number of requests
q_i	Demand of request at vertex $i \in V_{\mathrm{P}}$
e_i	Earliest pick up time of request at vertex $i \in V_{\mathrm{P}}$
δ_i	Maximum waiting time of request at vertex $i \in V_{\mathrm{P}}$
Δ_i	Maximum extra ride time of request at vertex $i \in V_{\mathrm{P}}$
Model	
0	Start vertex for all vehicles
f	Final vertex for all vehicles
n_{p}	Number of parking locations
s_i	Service time at vertex $i \in V$
$d_{i,j}$	Travel distance from vertex i to vertex j
$t_{i,j}$	Travel time from vertex i to vertex j
w_m	Weight of module travel distances
$w_{rejection}$	Requests rejection penalty
S	Simulation start time
H	Simulation horizon
Variables	
$x_{i,j}^k$	(Binary) 1 if vehicle k traverses arc (i, j), 0 otherwise
τ_i^k	Arrival time of vehicle k at vertex i
ω_i^k	Load of vehicle k after vertex i
r_i^k	Ride time of request i on vehicle k

is a set of traversable arcs for vehicle $k \in F$ that are composed of a pickup and delivery pair. Finally, A_{W}^{k} is a set of traversable arcs for vehicle $k \in F$ on which arriving early is not allowed since vehicles are not allowed to wait at request locations.

The total number of requests in the model is specified by n_{r}. Each request has a pickup vertex $i \in V_{\mathrm{P}}$, which has a demand size of q_i. The corresponding delivery vertex has a demand size of $-q_i$, effectively emptying the vehicle again. The pickup time window of request i is determined by the earliest pickup time e_i of the request and its maximum waiting time δ_i. The earliest pickup times of requests are being generated during simulation horizon H, starting from simulation start time S. Requests do not have a set delivery time window, instead, each request has a maximum extra ride time Δ_i. The destination of a request has to be reached within the sum of the travel time and the maximum extra ride time. Additionally each vertex $i \in V$ has a service duration of s_i seconds. n_{k} specifies the number of available vehicles in the model that have a load-carrying capability (passenger and freight vehicles as well as passenger and freight modules), while n_{c} specifies the number of carriers available to the model. All vehicles have a set capacity of Q^k and an average speed of v^k. Table 1 shows an overview of all sets and parameters used in the mixed-integer linear programming model.

The formulation of the MILP is as follows:

Minimize:

$$\sum_{k \in F_{\mathrm{a}}} \sum_{(i,j) \in A^k} x_{i,j}^k d_{i,j} + w_m \sum_{k \in F_{\mathrm{m}}} \sum_{(i,j) \in A^k} x_{i,j}^k d_{i,j} - \sum_{k \in F_{\mathrm{a}}} x_{0,f}^k + \sum_{i \in V_{\mathrm{P}}} (1 - \sum_{k \in F_{\mathrm{q}}} \sum_{(i,j) \in A^k} x_{i,j}^k) * w_{rejection} \tag{1}$$

Subject to:

$$\sum_{k \in F_{\mathrm{q}}} \sum_{(i,j) \in A^k} x_{i,j}^k \leq 1 \qquad \forall i \in V_{\mathrm{P}} \tag{2}$$

$$\sum_{(i,h) \in A^k} x_{i,h}^k - \sum_{(h,j) \in A^k} x_{h,j}^k = 0 \qquad \forall (i,j) \in A_{\mathrm{PD}}^k,\ \forall k \in F_{\mathrm{q}} \tag{3}$$

$$\sum_{0,j \in A^k} x_{0,j}^k = 1 \qquad \forall k \in F \tag{4}$$

$$\sum_{i,\mathrm{f} \in A^k} x_{i,\mathrm{f}}^k = 1 \qquad \forall k \in F \tag{5}$$

$$\sum_{(h,i) \in A^k} x_{h,i}^k - \sum_{(i,j) \in A^k} x_{i,j}^k = 0 \qquad \forall i \in V^k \backslash \{0, \mathrm{f}\},\ \forall k \in F \tag{6}$$

$$x_{i,j}^m - \sum_{k \in C} x_{i,j}^k = 0 \qquad \forall (i,j) \in A_{\mathrm{C}}^m,\ \forall m \in F_{\mathrm{m}} \tag{7}$$

$$x_{i,j}^k = 1 \Rightarrow \tau_j^m \leq \tau_j^k \quad \forall (i,j) \in A_{\mathrm{C}}^m,\ \forall k \in C,\ \forall m \in F_{\mathrm{m}} \tag{8}$$

$$x_{i,j}^m = 1 \Rightarrow \tau_j^k \leq \tau_j^m \quad \forall (i,j) \in A_{\mathrm{C}}^m,\ \forall k \in C,\ \forall m \in F_{\mathrm{m}} \tag{9}$$

$$\tau_j^k \geq (\tau_i^k + s_i + t_{i,j}) x_{i,j}^k \quad \forall (i,j) \in A^k,\ \forall k \in F \tag{10}$$

$$e_i \leq \tau_i^k \leq e_i + \delta_i \quad \forall i \in V_{\mathrm{P}}^k,\ \forall k \in F \tag{11}$$

$$\tau_j^k \geq \tau_i^k \quad \forall (i,j) \in A_{\mathrm{PD}}^k,\ \forall k \in F_{\mathrm{q}} \tag{12}$$

$$x_{i,j}^k = 1 \Rightarrow \tau_j^k - \tau_i^k \leq t_{i,j} + s_i \quad \forall (i,j) \in A_{\mathrm{W}}^k,\ \forall k \in F \tag{13}$$

$$r_i^k \geq \tau_j^k - \tau_i^k \quad \forall (i,j) \in A_{\mathrm{PD}}^k,\ \forall k \in F_{\mathrm{q}} \tag{14}$$

$$t_{i,j} \leq r_i^k \leq t_{i,j} + \Delta_i \quad \forall (i,j) \in A_{\mathrm{PD}}^k,\ \forall k \in F_{\mathrm{q}} \tag{15}$$

$$\omega_j^k \geq \omega_i^k + q_i x_{i,j}^k \quad \forall (i,j) \in A^k,\ \forall k \in F_{\mathrm{q}} \tag{16}$$

$$max(0, q_i) \leq \omega_i^k \leq Q_k \quad \forall i \in V^k,\ \forall k \in F_{\mathrm{q}} \tag{17}$$

$$\omega_i^k \leq 0 \quad \forall i \in V_{\mathrm{park}}^k,\ k \in F \tag{18}$$

$$x_{i,j}^k \in \{0,1\} \quad \forall i,j \in A^k,\ \forall k \in F \tag{19}$$

$$\tau_i^k \in \mathbb{N} \quad \forall i \in V^k \tag{20}$$

$$\omega_i^k \in \mathbb{N} \quad \forall i \in V^k \tag{21}$$

$$r_i^k \in \mathbb{N} \quad \forall i \in V_{\mathrm{P}} \tag{22}$$

The objective function (1) aims to minimize the travel distance of all motorized vehicles, as well as the total number of motorized vehicles used to find an optimal solution. Secondly, the travel distance of modules is also minimized, however, it is deemed less important and is offset by a factor of w_m. To allow the model to reject requests a penalty of $w_{rejection}$ is added if a pickup vertex is not visited. Constraints (2) to (6) are the general routing constraints, and (7) to (9) are spatial and temporal synchronisation constraints to couple the movement of carriers and modules. The time window constraints are described by constraints (10) to (13) and subsequently constraints (14) and (15) are the ride time constraints. Finally, constraints (16) to (18) are the vehicle load constraints. Equations (19) to (22) describe the decision variables in the model. Constraint (2) ensures that every request's pickup vertex is visited by at most one vehicle, however, every vertex does not need to be visited. A vehicle that has visited the pickup vertex of a request must also travel to the request's destination vertex, which is ensured by (3). Constraints (4) and (5) guarantee that every vehicle starts it's route at the start vertex and ends at the final vertex respectively. To preserve flow conservation, constraint (6) enforces every vehicle to leave the same vertex it has entered. Constraint (7) is a spatial synchronisation constraint to ensure modules are only able to traverse arcs between two different real-world locations (A_{C}^m) while being coupled with a carrier. Constraints (8) and (9) are temporal synchronisation constraints that impose identical arrival times of coupled carriers and modules. The arrival time of vehicles is defined by constraint (10). Constraint (11) ensures that a request is picked up after their earliest pick-up time and within their maximum waiting time. A vehicle should arrive at the destination vertex of a request pair after the pickup vertex has been visited, which is guaranteed by (12). Vehicles are not allowed to arrive early and wait at request pickup locations, constraint (13) ensures that for the set of arcs on which waiting is not allowed (A^k_W) vehicles won't arrive before the earliest pickup time. Constraint (14) defines the ride time of a request, and (15) makes sure the maximum extra ride time of a request is not exceeded. Constraint (16) defines the vehicle load and (17) enforces the load of a vehicle not to exceed the maximum capacity of the vehicle. Constraint (18) guarantees that vehicles are empty when arriving at parking or decoupling vertices, to ensure no occupied vehicles or modules are parked or decoupled. Finally, constraints (19) to (22) define the model's decision variables, which are the traversed arcs, arrival time, vehicle load and ride time variables respectively.

4 Numerical Study

In this section, the configuration of the MILP for the different instances will be discussed, as well as the generation of the passenger and freight request data. Next, the general parameters of the model will be given, followed by a discussion of key performance indicators of the transport systems.

4.1 Instance Design

We test the model on two fleet configurations (viz., single-purpose and DCAV fleets) using the same request data. We consider four different demand scenarios throughout the simulation horizon H:

- **Balanced scenario (BLS)**: Both request types are uniformly distributed over the horizon.
- **Passenger peak scenario (PPS)**: Passenger requests are generated during the first half of the horizon, while freight requests are uniformly distributed throughout the whole horizon.
- **Freight peak scenario (FPS)**: Freight requests appear only during the second half of the simulation horizon, while passenger requests are uniformly distributed.
- **Complementary scenario (COS)**: Passenger requests appear during the first half of the horizon and freight requests during the second half.

Besides, we test the effect of allowing **ridesharing** (same commodity requests can share a ride) and vary the **number of parking locations** n_p (0, 1, or 3), where carriers can park and switch modules during their route. We also determine 15 value combinations for **simulation horizon** $H \in \{1, 8\}$, the **total fleet size** $n_\mathrm{k} \in \{2, 4, 6\}$, and the **number of requests** $n_\mathrm{r} \in \{4, 8, 12, 16, 24\}$.

Values n_{k} and n_{r} are divided equally between passenger and freight vehicles and requests, respectively. Additionally, for each module in the model, there is a carrier available to be used, thus, the number of carriers n_{c} is equal to the number of vehicles n_{k}. In the worst-case scenario, the DCAV fleet could behave similarly to the single-purpose fleet by assigning a module to each carrier and having the same routes as the single-purpose vehicles. The parameter groups $(H, n_{\mathrm{k}}, n_{\mathrm{n}})$ are as follows: $(1,2,4)$, $(1,2,8)$, $(1,2,12)$, $(1,4,4)$, $(1,4,8)$, $(1,4,12)$, $(1,6,4)$, $(1,6,8)$, $(1,6,12)$, $(8,2,12)$, $(8,2,16)$, $(8,2,24)$, $(8,4,12)$, $(8,4,16)$, $(8,4,24)$.

An overview of the 720 instances generated can be found in Fig. 4.

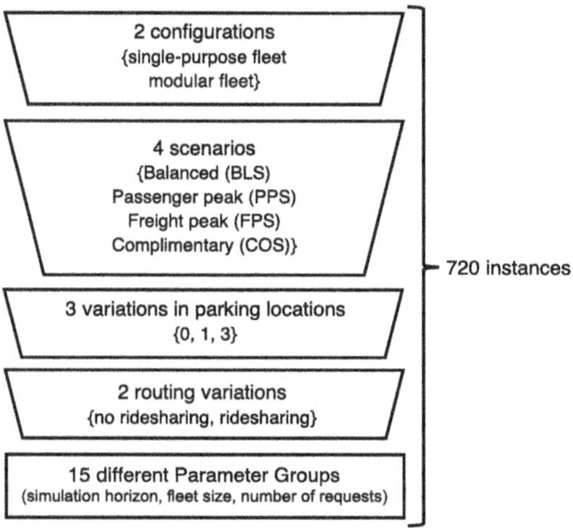

Fig. 4. Instances for the DCAVPDP and the benchmark single-purpose problem (dedicated vehicles for each commodity).

4.2 Model Parameters

The values of general parameters are shared by all instances. The grid on which the requests are being generated is $2,000$ by $2,000$ meters, with a distance between nodes of 100 m. The depot is located at (600 m, 600 m), and the three available parking locations are located at (600 m, 1400 m), (1400 m, 600 m), and (1400 m, 1400 m). When only one parking location is accessible for the fleet, it is located at (1400 m, 1400 m).

The locations of all request pickup and delivery locations are uniformly distributed over the rest of the nodes of the grid. Each request demands the transportation of one passenger or parcel (i.e., request size $q_i = 1$). Passenger and freight requests have different values for maximum waiting time δ_i, extra ride time Δ_i, and service duration s_i. All distances are calculated using the Manhattan distance formula and travel times are calculated using an average vehicle speed $v^k = 5$ m/s. To ensure vehicles will be able to reach the first request on time, we set the simulation start time $S = 900$ s since the longest possible travel time between opposing corners of the grid is 800 s. Passenger and freight vehicles and modules have a capacity $Q^k = 2$ for both the single-purpose and the DCAV fleet, respectively. Typically, passengers are more sensitive to waiting times and extra ride times, this is reflected in the model by giving more strict values to passenger requests. The maximum waiting time δ_i for passenger requests is 300 s and the maximum extra ride time Δ_i is 900 s. For freight requests, $\delta_i = 900$ s and $\Delta_i = 1800$ s. Regarding the service duration s_i, we assume a vehicle has to wait 120 s when servicing passengers and 300 s when picking up a parcel. Besides, we consider the modular DCAV fleet has an additional service duration $s_i = 120$ s to switch (i.e., couple or decouple) modules. Finally, rejecting requests incurs a penalty $w_{penalty} = 10^5$ and the traveling of modules is weighted down using $w_m = 10^{-3}$.

4.3 Performance Metrics

Our numerical study aims to assess whether a fleet of DCAVs improves vehicle utilization and occupancy while maintaining an equivalent service quality compared to a traditional single-purpose fleet. In order to highlight the differences between these two fleets, we consider the following fleet management performance metrics:

- **Utilization rate (on-duty)**: The time a vehicle is being actively used to service requests (i.e., traveling to pick up and deliver, service times at request locations), divided by the total simulation run time.
- **Utilization rate (total)**: Total time vehicles spent traveling divided by the total simulation run time. For the DCAV fleet, this time includes trips to parking locations to (de)couple modules and module replacement times.
- **Occupancy rate**: The fraction of the utilization time that vehicles are traveling loaded, taking into account their occupation ratio.
- **Service quality**: The service rate, the average pickup time of requests, and the average ride time of requests.
- **Fleet size**: Total number of autonomous vehicles (dedicated AVs or carriers).
- **Fleet capacity**: Total number of people-and-freight transportation upper parts. In the dedicated fleet, fleet capacity equals fleet size.
- **Distance traveled**: Total distance traveled by the whole fleet.

4.4 Computational Settings

The numerical study has been performed on an AMD Ryzen 5 3600 4Ghz CPU with access to 32GB of RAM. Python version 3.8.8 and commercial solver Gurobi Optimizer 9.1.2 were used to implement the DCAVPDP. All instances were run to optimality.

5 Results and Discussion

Table 2 shows the relative performance of the DCAV fleet compared to the single-purpose fleet. The first column features key fleet management performance indicators and the subsequent column "Avg. Diff." shows the overall average performance difference for all instances for both fleets. The columns "BLS", "PPS", "FPS", and "COS" show the performance difference for the corresponding scenarios. The last column shows the number of instances in which better results were achieved using the DCAV fleet. The on-duty utilization rate shows an increase of 4.82% for all scenarios with 241 instances resulting in better values for the DCAV fleet. Most of the performance gain is made in the complementary scenario (COS), where carriers can service both demand types consecutively. The occupancy rate of vehicles is slightly lower for all scenarios, which can be attributed to the increased use of modules and the difference in extra ride times and travel distance when compared to the single-purpose fleet. In 329 instances the percentage of requests served is similar or better than the single-purpose fleet. This difference might be caused by the coupling and decoupling delays of the DCAV fleet, costing additional time and resulting in time windows of requests not being met. Serving fewer requests can also contribute to the −1.30% average decrease in vehicle occupancy. The DCAV fleet show a decrease in the average waiting times of requests, except for the complimentary scenario. The latter can again be attributed to the couple and decouple times of the DCAV fleet, having to switch modules when the generated requests change from passenger to freight requests. Lower waiting times for the other scenarios can be explained by the 7.58% increased use of load-carrying vehicles by the DCAV fleet. When time windows allow, the DCAV fleet uses more modules to be able to handle requests of a similar type more quicker. The complementary scenario (COS) therefore shows a much smaller increase in the number of load-carrying vehicles. The DCAV average fleet size is 18.77% lower, with the complementary scenario (COS) featuring the largest drop—42.60% DCAV are needed. This lower total fleet size is reflected in the total vehicle utilization: the active carriers are used 23.75% more than the active single-purpose AVs.

The average fleet size and total travel distance across scenarios can be seen in Fig. 5. Comparing the number of vehicles shown in the first graph we see that the modular fleet uses more modules of each type while using fewer carriers on average. Due to the coupling and decoupling time, the number of modules might be higher than the equivalent single-purpose vehicles, however, the difference is mostly caused by an increase in the use of passenger modules. Another explanation could be that the modular fleet enables the use of more passenger modules when carriers are available to more quickly serve passenger requests since the model is not minimizing the number of modules used. The difference in total modules used and the number of carriers used does show that the modular system makes use of its flexibility. The lower average travel distance of the modules can be explained by the use of parking locations since modules are being coupled closer to request locations.

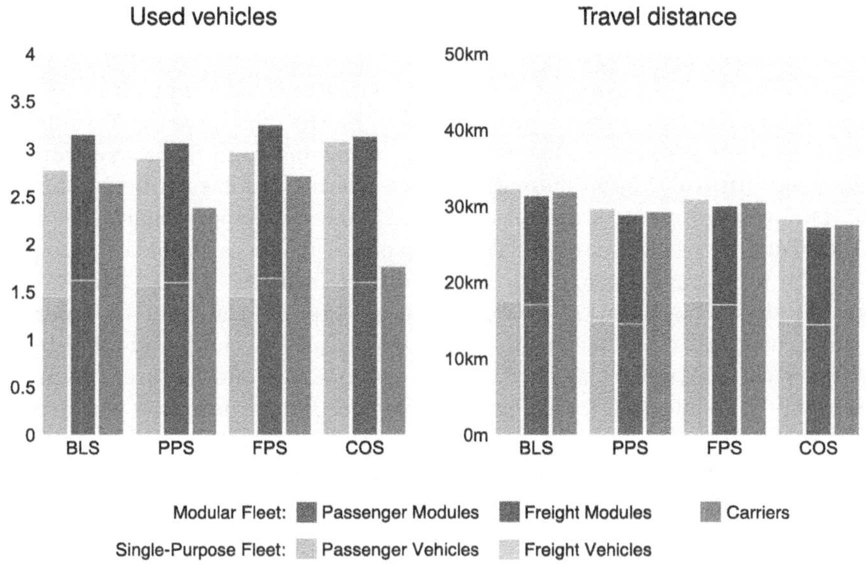

Fig. 5. Average fleet size and distance traveled for all fleet types across the four demand distribution scenarios.

Table 2. Performance difference of the modular DCAV fleet compared to the single-purpose fleet. The final column shows the number of ran instances that show better performance for the DCAV fleet.

Performance Indicator	Avg. Diff	BLS	PPS	FPS	COS	#DCAV best
Utilization rate (on-duty)	4.82%	−4.80%	3.82%	−1.14%	24.36%	241/360
Utilization rate (total)	23.75%	2.90%	16.82%	7.78%	74.71%	326/360
Occupancy rate	−1.30%	−1.49%	−0.47%	−2.35%	−0.97%	240/360
Service rate	−0.08%	−0.15%	0.00%	−0.15%	0.00%	329/360
Avg. pickup time	−9.70%	−22.23%	−10.27%	−8.17%	3.28%	219/360
Avg. ride times	−4.57%	−9.73%	−1.72%	−8.15%	−1.51%	330/360
Fleet capacity	7.58%	13.6%	5.75%	9.74%	1.81%	266/360
Fleet size	−18.77%	−4.80%	−17.62%	−8.24%	−42.60%	346/360
Distance traveled	−1.52%	−1.27%	−1.32%	−1.21%	−2.38%	218/360

6 Conclusion

This study has presented a MILP formulation for the *Dynamically Configurable Autonomous Vehicle Pickup and Delivery Problem* (DCAVPDP). The model provides the first quantitative method investigating the benefits of a DCAV-based transport system, which leverages automation and a novel automotive modular design concept to service multiple demand types by dynamically configuring vehicle upper compartments. We compare the performance of a single-purpose fleet consisting of dedicated passenger and freight vehicles and a DCAV fleet consisting of motorized autonomous carriers and switchable passenger- and freight-tailored compartments to service a mixed pickup and delivery heterogeneous demand comprised of passenger and freight requests considering various scenarios. Since autonomous carriers are expected to be the most expensive component of a DCAVPDP system, we have aimed at achieving high utilization rates for these assets. In total, 360 different instances were run for each fleet configuration. The average performance of all tested mixed-demand scenarios shows an improvement in average modular fleet utilization (carriers coupled to modules) in relation to average single-purpose mixed fleet utilization up to 24.36% when there is a distinct separation between demand types throughout the operation horizon (complementary scenario). The proposed model can be adapted to support more compartment types with varying capacities and features, giving rise to a highly customizable transportation service. Future research will focus on developing a dynamic problem formulation, the adoption of crowd-sourced heterogeneous lower and upper parts, and the repositioning of carriers and modules throughout parking locations anticipating future demand.

References

1. Beirigo, B.A., Schulte, F., Negenborn, R.R.: Integrating people and freight transportation using shared autonomous vehicles with compartments. IFAC-PapersOnLine **51**, 392–397 (2018). https://doi.org/10.1016/j.ifacol.2018.07.064
2. Beirigo, B.A., Schulte, F., Negenborn, R.R.: A learning-based optimization approach for autonomous ridesharing platforms with service-level contracts and on-demand hiring of idle vehicles. Transp. Sci. **56**(3), 677–703 (2022). https://doi.org/10.1287/trsc.2021.1069
3. Cheng, R., Jiang, Y., Nielsen, O.A.: Integrated people-and-goods transportation systems: from a literature review to a general framework for future research, pp. 1–24 (2023). https://doi.org/10.1080/01441647.2023.2189322
4. Continental: Continental launches bee in the urban world of the future (2017). https://www.continental.com/en/press/press-releases/bee-96328. Accessed 28 June 2023
5. Daimler: Vision urbanetic (2019). https://media.mercedes-benz.com/article/c518445b-9050-42ec-9be1-3446e1bf3973. Accessed 28 June 2023
6. Drexl, M.: On some generalized routing problems. Ph.D. thesis, Faculty of Business and Economics, RWTH Aachen (2007). http://publications.rwth-aachen.de/record/62536
7. Hörl, S., Ruch, C., Becker, F., Frazzoli, E., Axhausen, K.: Fleet operational policies for automated mobility: a simulation assessment for Zurich. Transp. Res. Part C: Emerg. Technol. **102**, 20–31 (2019). https://doi.org/10.1016/j.trc.2019.02.020
8. Li, B., Krushinsky, D., Reijers, H.A., Van Woensel, T.: The share-a-ride problem: people and parcels sharing taxis. Eur. J. Oper. Res. **238**(1), 31–40 (2014). https://doi.org/10.1016/j.ejor.2014.03.003
9. Mourad, A., Puchinger, J., Chu, C.: A survey of models and algorithms for optimizing shared mobility. Transp. Res. Part B: Methodol. **123**, 323–346 (2019). https://doi.org/10.1016/j.trb.2019.02.003
10. Münster, M., et al.: U-shift vehicle concept: modular on the road. In: Bargende, M., Reuss, H.-C., Wagner, A. (eds.) 21. Internationales Stuttgarter Symposium.

P, pp. 333–346. Springer, Wiesbaden (2021). https://doi.org/10.1007/978-3-658-33466-6_23
11. Şahin, T., Raulf, C., Kızgın, V., Huth, T., Vietor, T.: A cross-domain system architecture model of dynamically configurable autonomous vehicles. In: Bargende, M., Reuss, H.-C., Wagner, A. (eds.) 21. Internationales Stuttgarter Symposium, pp. 13–31. Springer, Wiesbaden (2021). https://doi.org/10.1007/978-3-658-33521-2_2
12. Sun, S., Wong, Y.D., Liu, X., Rau, A.: Exploration of an integrated automated public transportation system. Transp. Res. Interdisc. Perspect. **8**, 100275 (2020). https://doi.org/10.1016/j.trip.2020.100275
13. van der Tholen, M., Beirigo, B.A., Jovanova, J., Schulte, F.: The share-a-ride problem with integrated routing and design decisions: the case of mixed-purpose shared autonomous vehicles. In: Mes, M., Lalla-Ruiz, E., Voß, S. (eds.) ICCL 2021. LNCS, vol. 13004, pp. 347–361. Springer, Cham (2021). https://doi.org/10.1007/978-3-030-87672-2_23
14. Toyota: E-Pallete (2023). https://www.toyota-europe.com/startyourimpossible/e-palette. Accessed 28 June 2023
15. Ulrich, C., Friedrich, H.E., Weimer, J., Schmid, S.A.: New operating strategies for an on-the-road modular, electric and autonomous vehicle concept in urban transportation. World Electr. Veh. J. **10**(4), 91 (2019). https://doi.org/10.3390/wevj10040091

Impact of Public Transport Development on Health Care Services in Rural Areas

Joachim R. Daduna and Daniel Philipp(✉)

Berlin School of Economics and Law, Badensche Straße 52, 10825 Berlin, Germany
{daduna,Daniel.Philipp}@hwr-berlin.de

Abstract. In the context of cohesion policy, one of the main points is the divergent development between urban and rural areas. One critical problem is the undersupply of rural areas due to low demand potential. In addition, there are inadequate public transport services for many residents who, for various reasons, do not have access to private motorized transport. With technical advances in the field of road transport vehicles and comprehensive digitization, autonomous driving has opened up opportunities in recent years for development of new (flexible) forms of service based on quasi-individual mobility. The technical foundations required in this regard as well as the organizational and legal framework conditions are highlighted and critically analyzed. Using the example of health care in rural areas, a mobility concept is outlined that offers a suitable solution in conjunction with a hierarchically centralized location structure of medical care facilities. This approach is also suitable for reducing further structural deficits and supporting the creation of equal living conditions on a broader level, also with a view to broad participation in social and community life in rural areas.

Keywords: Autonomous Driving · Health Care · Rural Areas

1 Introduction

With the Second Industrial Revolution [17, 96], profound changes began (especially in the central European regions and North America) in the settlement and economic structures that had until then been largely dominated by agriculture and handicraft businesses The starting point for industrial developments was, in addition to new technologies, especially innovations in the transport sector. Thus, with the emergence of rail transport ([99] 74–86; [103] 565–573; [54] 234–244) for the first time an efficient transport mode was available for freight and passenger transport, the network design and operation of which were largely independent of geographical, topographical and weather-related influences. Very quickly, the (technical) performance capabilities as well as cost reductions of about 90% became apparent in comparison to the previously existing modes of land and water transport ([102] 95–96).

This was associated with the emergence of industrial areas and later also of service centers with a constantly increasing demand for labor, which had to be met mainly from rural residents or by immigration. This led to an extreme population growth in urban

© The Author(s), under exclusive license to Springer Nature Switzerland AG 2023
J. R. Daduna et al. (Eds.): ICCL 2023, LNCS 14239, pp. 396–415, 2023.
https://doi.org/10.1007/978-3-031-43612-3_25

regions ([54] 135–136), which inevitably brought about changes in social, economic and work structures. An essential prerequisite, however, was a fundamental change in agriculture ([46] 635–654). Significant increases in production with a lower demand for labor due to efficiency improvements on the agricultural estates and the transition from subsistence farms, which were widespread at the time, to commercial farming ([54] 141–157) or, through corresponding imports, to ensure the food basis in urban regions.

These developments have led to a divergence of living conditions between urban and rural areas over many years, which has resulted in considerable inequalities in social participation [68] and economic structures. This situation has been and can still be observed worldwide, with varying degrees of intensity. However, it is politically undesired, especially because of the inherent potential for social conflict, so that suitable concepts and approaches have been discussed for some time with the objective of eliminating structural disproportions and enabling equal living conditions. Thus, one of the priority objectives in the *European Union* (EU) is the implementation of a cohesion policy [27], increasingly also in the context of national measures of a regional policy [19]. For Germany, this has been written down in a legally binding way in Sect. 1 of the *Regional Planning Act* (ROG) for several years. One of the measures in this regard is to ensure that mobility for residents living in rural areas meets their needs, which is currently inadequate, ([6] 29–32). The emerging transition to autonomous driving in road traffic [79] and the possibility of a quasi-individualization of mobility in public transport (see Sect. 3) is a development step to enable profound changes.

In this paper, we show the extent to which new forms of mobility can be used in rural areas, to sustainably improve existing structural problems in health care, since these are of major importance for the population there. First, some aspects of spatial planning, in rural areas are considered. Subsequently, the operational and technical design options for improving mobility through the expansion of local and regional public transport will be addressed, with a focus on autonomous driving vehicles. In the following, it will be analyzed to what extent these measures can guarantee demand-oriented access to health care services for all population groups in rural areas. A key point here is the extent to which decentralized structures are desirable and feasible on the one hand, and centralization is necessary on the other, also from an economic and technological point of view. Finally, expectations and further development are discussed.

2 Spatial Planning and the Theory of Central Places

Due to political and also economic considerations, at the end of the 1960s [30] the development objectives for rural areas were already aligned with the hierarchically oriented centrality principle as described by Christaller ([16], 63–85) (see Fig. 1). According to § 2 para. 2, no. 2 ROG, this principle has also been a legally mandatory regulation in spatial planning in Germany since 2008. The underlying idea is the centralization of supply options and services ([39, 70], 223–241), taking into account existing settlement and demand structures and the associated holding costs, also with a view to the provision of public services, as well as the realization of a politically desired cohesion [23]. The provision of services to the inhabitants in this concept refers not only to the central places themselves, but also to their surrounding area, which is assigned to the respective hierarchical level. It is not unproblematic here that access to services at higher levels can be associated with increasing distances for parts of the inhabitants, depending on the location of the respective higher-level locations. With regard to accessibility, the availability of sufficient mobility, not only in the local area, is therefore absolutely mandatory.

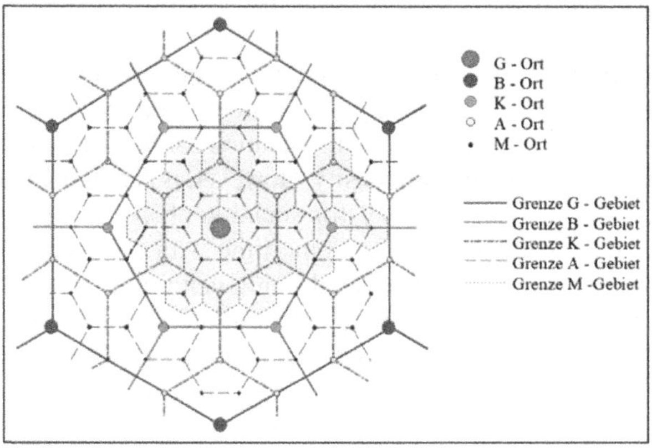

Fig. 1. Basic structure of the Christaller model

The problem of service provision in rural areas is clearly shown by the structural allocation of areas at the European level, starting from the NUTS classification (Level 3: Small regions for specific diagnoses) ([87] 13). This shows that densely populated as well as rural regions with aggregation approaches clearly dominate the European settlement structures. However, there is a certain problem with this (relatively rough) classification, which does not reflect the significant regional specific differentiation. In addition, there are also a number of different classification concepts, also for Germany.

Moreover, it must be taken into account that the framework conditions in the respective counties differ greatly in some cases, depending on demographic developments as well as on local labor market situation and economic framework conditions ([6] 30–33). In addition, there are regional location factors, especially with regard to dominant forms of economic use. An additional influencing factor is the spatial closeness of a county to (industrial) agglomerations or densification spaces, which can have inducing centrality effects. In order to ensure an adequate service structure for the population in rural areas, the availability of sufficient mobility is absolutely necessary. However, there are considerable deficits in this regard. One major reason for this is the technical developments in the field of individual mobility since the mid-1950s ([59, 97] 30–32). The steadily growing availability of private cars has led to reductions in public transport, as demand for it has become increasingly low. In 2017, the modal split in rural areas with small town and village structures was only 5%, compared to 70% for private motorized transport ([75], 40). Also, more than one third of all families here own at least two cars (30% have two cars, 6% three and more) ([75], 35).

This shows that a not inconsiderable share of the population in rural areas has no or only limited access to mobility [58]. Essentially, these are people without a driver's license (especially young people), people who cannot drive a vehicle due to their health situation or age, and people who do not own a car for financial reasons [68, 90] An expansion of the actually only rudimentary public transport service is not economically feasible due to the subsidies required for this [35]. This means that ultimately there is no sufficient mobility available and thus the framework conditions are not at all in place to be able to guarantee even approximately equivalent living conditions.

For some years now, developments toward autonomous driving have been achieved in the motor vehicle sector, also in conjunction with significant advances in digitization. Based on the current status, this technology will be fully ready for the market before the end of this decade, as shown by the ongoing research work worldwide as well as many test projects and initial implementations [67]. On this basis, there is the possibility of significantly and sustainably improving public transport in rural areas with new services and thus coming more closely to the goal of equal living conditions.

3 Impact of Autonomous Driving on Public Transport in Rural Areas

The known public transport services with minibuses and standard buses cannot be an adequate solution for operating in rural areas, both in terms of suitable structures and, in particular, for financial reasons. In their current structures, they cannot ensure sufficient quality of service ([6, 78] 29–32). For this reason, there have already been attempts several decades ago to develop better alternatives based on demand-oriented services for rural areas [9, 21, 66], but also in the suburban transition zones [86, 100]. A number of concepts have been developed, not only in Germany, and have also been tested in some cases, but often not implemented in regular operations.

The main reasons for this were the complexity of operational monitoring and control as well as the inadequate communication capabilities between provider and customer. In addition, there were labor law restrictions regarding to the driving personnel, which led to limitations in the operational planning of vehicle and duty schedules and also to considerable costs [66]. The necessary political support from local authorities was not always available due to the introduction of competing services for the already economically weakened public transport companies owned by the municipalities. In addition, there was resistance from the trade unions due to the flexible working time models associated with the modified forms of service [66].

For a number of years, therefore, considerable effort has been made to develop on-demand services with autonomous driving vehicles [67]. This also applies to broad research projects in the field of general public road traffic, such as the Niedersachsen Test Field project [3]. Standard legal framework conditions as a basis for the certification and operation of such vehicles have now been laid down in the *Road Traffic Act* and in the *Autonomous Vehicles Approval and Operation Regulation* of June 24, 2022.

Significant advantages for a service design based on such innovative operating concepts in public transport are the elimination of costs for the driving personnel as well as the partly (time-related) very restrictive labor law limitations. Added to this are far-reaching developments in vehicle technology, widespread digitization in operational monitoring and control as well as regarding information management. On this basis, more and more projects have been initiated worldwide [1, 42], where autonomous driving plays a significant role. One project in Germany is the public transport service with minibuses in the area of Bad Birnbach [7]. In the following, the development of autonomous driving is outlined first and then the design options are discussed.

3.1 State of Development of Autonomous Driving

The most important basis for the definition of autonomous driving is a classification based on the J 3016 standard of *SAE International* [88]. This includes six levels from SAE Level 0 to SAE Level 5, which define the different functions between the driver and the automated system (0: No form of automation, 1: Use of *automated driver assistance systems* (ADAS), 2: Partial automation, 3: Conditional automation, 4: High automation, 5: Full automation (autonomous driving). The final objective is to bring vehicles with level 5 into service [52] that means, all vehicle movements are controlled and monitored by automats. The essential aspect, which is to be seen as the basis of a quasi-individual mobility, is that point-to-point connections are possible, in which a vehicle can drive directly to a customer depending on demand.

The main foundations have been laid in recent years as part of the development of ADAS components [1, 4], that are already being used in practice. These include supporting functions such as the automatic speed adaptation, lane departure warning, adaptive cruise control, blind spot information system, collision avoidance, moving object detection, intelligent speed adoption and traffic sign recognition. In addition, there are ad hoc communication networks such as *vehicle-to-vehicle* (V2V) or *vehicle-to-infrastructure* (V2I) networks for a more efficient and environmentally oriented traffic flow management and to increase traffic safety [8, 107].

Automated detection systems installed at specific positions on the vehicle are used to continuously record the surrounding data. These include optical systems (cameras), radar-based sensors, and lightwave-based 3D techniques (e.g., 3D laser systems and LiDAR systems) [1, 47, 108]. The destination positioning as well as the routing are based on data from (digital) *Geographic Information Systems* (GIS) [48, 50] in connection with *Global Navigation Satellite Systems* (GNSS), such as the US American *Differential Global Positioning System* (DGPS) or the system *Galileo* developed in the EU [45, 48, 50]. Applications of autonomous driving in open area are also already possible at a contemporary time [80]. Based on the current state of development and the first steps toward realization, it can be assumed that the essential prerequisites for autonomous driving are in place in view of the technical developments. Deficits exist primarily in some necessary adjustments to the legal framework and also in the not always existing social acceptance, in spite of all the significant advantages.

3.2 Design Options in Public Transport

On the basis of autonomously driving vehicles, completely new design options arise for public transport, especially for services in rural areas [15, 71, 94]. In addition to the available technical bases, it is the replacement of the driver by intelligent automats that enables the independence from, in particular, labor law restrictions and drastically reduces the previously incurred personnel costs. The essential step here is a demand-oriented 24/7 service, through which quasi-individual mobility can be provided in rural areas. However, some legal issues need to be clarified regarding the integration of these services into the legal framework of the *Passenger Transportation Act* (PBefG) [83].

In the foreground are four basic types of services that can be applied here, point-to-point connections, on-demand based line and line band services as well as area services. For point-to-point connections, services can also be provided by robotaxis [43, 55] and in the framework of free-floating carsharing services [49] while in the other cases the focus will be on the use of minibuses and midibuses [7, 74]. In addition, ridesharing concepts [33, 64] can also be integrated, especially with regard to local feeder transport. However, the introduction of these services cannot imply that the existing ones are replaced, as it has been formulated, for example, by [31] with the convergence theory. In fact, they are a necessary supplement for a service in the area, but not a substitution of the existing regional bus services and of services in the regional rail passenger transport, which will continue to be absolutely necessary within the framework of commuter services due to the demand structures. However, exceptions exist [91] if demand on certain lines or line sections does not allow for economic operation and cannot be expected to do so in the future.

This means that in order to strengthen public transport in rural areas, it is absolutely necessary to combine the existing scheduled with possible on-demand services in order to be able to guarantee an adequately efficient public transport there. The main objective must be an extension of the service, especially in regions where it has not been feasible so far due to the existing framework conditions. With the new forms of service, suitably adapted organizational and operational structures are also required. The essential aspects in this context are outlined in a rough framework in the following section.

3.3 Necessary Framework Conditions for an Implementation of Changed Structures in Public Passenger Transport

In order to successfully implement the presented concept for improving public transport in rural areas, the necessary framework conditions must be provided. This concerns the legal framework [1, 56] as a mandatory prerequisite for the start of operations in the changed structures, insurance and liability aspects [63, 93, 95], cybersecurity, and also the legal question regarding the use of the recorded data [2, 38, 53]. However, the sometimes highly specified technical content, which requires continual adaptation due to further developments, is problematic. In addition, the necessary organizational structures and a suitable legal basis for cross-modal cooperation must be developed [13, 29, 104]. Linked to this are also the questions of financing and tariff structure design [35, 57], especially with regard to the economic conditions. Finally, the operational structures as well as the control and monitoring of the operational processes [20] must be designed and a case-specific (internal and external) information management [20] must be developed.

Only if appropriate framework conditions can be developed and established as well as stable structures can also be ensured in the long term it will be possible to implement attractive public transport services in rural areas. The resulting advantages are multilayered because in addition to the broad services of a quasi-individual mobility for residents without own access to private car use, a change is offered for many previous non-users of public transport. This leads to a reduction in car ownership and mileage, as well as a reduction in environmental impact when using vehicles with e-traction. Positive financial effects also result for households in rural areas, where the previously necessary multiple ownership of private cars (see the data in [75], 35) can be reduced.

3.4 Acceptance of Autonomous Driving and Ethical Discussions

In addition, the question of acceptance by potential users also plays a decisive role with regard to successful market penetration in the future. A certain skepticism is evident in (mostly hypothetical) surveys [5, 11, 60, 77]. Focus here is on the one hand on potential benefits, but on the other hand risks are also stated, although it must be considered that the discussions are being held in a far-reaching changing in social, technical and economic environment. Furthermore, from a psychological point of view, the importance of private vehicle ownership as a decades-old symbol of individual freedom must also be seen, which will be lost in a sharing economy. In the context of surveys accompanying projects [10], however the result of the surveys looks somewhat different, possibly due to direct contact with the new form of (quasi-individual) mobility. In addition, it must also be taken into account whether there is a sufficient supply of public transport or whether, as is the case for a not negligible proportion of the population in rural areas, use is largely restricted and there is a significant improvement in the situation from the point of view of those affected.

Recurring claims regarding an increased safety risk due to autonomous driving also do not meet reality. Looking at the current situation, the introduction of autonomous driving is more likely to have the opposite effect. Evaluations of accidents show, among other things also worldwide, that with more than 90%, the overwhelming share of accident causes lies in human error [72]. For Germany, in 2021, for police recorded accidents involving personal injury, the share was 90.7%, with 88.0% caused by vehicle drivers and 2.7% caused by pedestrians ([26] 49).

The probability of such accidents occurring in autonomous driving vehicles is marginal, since they are based on clearly defined (AI-based) reaction patterns that are designed on the basis of risk-averse control processes. This is based on high-performance technical components of ADAS [1, 4], which are clearly over human information taking and processing in critical situations. As a result, there is the possibility of significant damage limitation with considerable reductions in accident-related costs as well as costs to society as a whole in the health and social sectors, which amount to billions of euros. However, complete accident prevention will not be possible since human error of traffic participants can in principle not be completely avoided.

However, the situation is problematic in the case of automated decision-making in conflict situations [62, 85], which are repeatedly mentioned from an ethical perspective as an argument against the introduction of autonomous driving [37, 44, 92]. However, this overlooks the fact that dilemmatic ad hoc decisions are not a problem inherent of autonomous driving [61]. They occur in manual driving too, although it can be assumed that the responsiveness of automats is significantly better, that means, the extent of damage will be much smaller. In principle, no criminal law relevance can be assumed in connection with the programming of automats, as the remarks in [18] show. With regard to autonomous driving, however, there is also a mandatory need for clear political decisions and the resulting legal regulations and measures. Objections from an ethical (and also ideological) point of view may not play a role in this context, because philosophical brain games cannot ultimately replace decisions and their implementation, nor can they cause damage.

4 Opportunities for Structural Changes in the Design of Health Care in Rural Areas

The general practitioner as a country doctor continues to play a central role in rural health care, although it has not yet been possible to achieve the desired level of care despite funding programs. In *Mecklenburg-Vorpommern* (MV), a proportion of medical university seats is allocated as an advance quota to applicants who undertake to work for at least ten years in general practitioner care in under-served or potentially future underserved regions, as well as regions with a special local demand for care, after completing their studies and subsequent further training as a specialist.

In addition, the increasing ageing of the population has to be seen, which poses further challenges to the comprehensive health care system. Technically possible innovations in telemedicine, such as the use of virtual consultation hours, can be seen as support for general health care, but do not replace personal doctor contact ([32], 141–142). It should be noted, however, that the acceptance of this form of medical care has increased among both the population and physicians, essentially due to the contact restrictions during the COVID 19 pandemic. In 2017 less than 2% of doctors in MV offered video consultations, whereas in May 2020 this proportion had risen to around 50% ([32], 103). Whether the use of virtual consultation hours will continue to the same extent, however, remains to be seen. An essential point here is to what extent and when the mobility offers outlined above will be available to visit a physician's office. In order to achieve a continuation and possibly also an expansion of telemedical services after the pandemic, a comprehensive digital infrastructure is mandatory and the existing technical deficits have to be solved. In addition, there is the problem of insufficient knowledge in handling of technical devices, especially of older people. To further improve acceptance and feasibility, it must be ensured that recorded data and images can be transmitted in sufficient quality. Nevertheless, examinations and treatments which, due to their specificity, require comprehensive specialist experience and possibly also technical equipment that is associated with higher costs, are in need of other structures. Besides the already more centralized structures in the area of inpatient care, additional outpatient forms must be developed and established.

The outlined problem will be explained in the following using three examples, the organization of dialysis, the use of imaging techniques such as *Magnetic Resonance Imaging* (MRI) and *Computer Tomography* (CT) and *AI-based skin cancer screening*. With regard to the care structures in rural areas, the focus is on the conflict between a high level of service expected by the population, sufficient services as well as economic efficiency of this provision.

4.1 Cost-Intensive Treatments and the Tendency Towards Centralization

In order to implement the postulate of equal living conditions, the necessary infrastructure facilities (hospitals and other forms of medical services) must also be accessible to patients in rural areas at a reasonable cost. In order to ensure nationwide coverage in Germany, planners have long sought to decentralize hospital operations and distribute smaller care units over large areas [73]. This led to the German hospital landscape being characterized by a high number of small and less specialized hospitals by international standards, many beds (approx. 50% more than the EU average [36], many inpatient cases (also approx. 50% more than the EU average [13] and correspondingly high staff requirements. However, such a structure can no longer be effective in view of the growing disparity in the population structure be-tween rural and urban regions and increasing costs due to improved treatment methods. This has been recognized in recent years, and more recent reform efforts are again aiming at merging and centralizing essential care services [89]. The population development influences not merely the supply in health care system, since sufficient availability of specialized personnel within decentralized structures is not given, but also the demand, since expected medical expenditure increases quantitatively and qualitatively with patient age [34].

Organization and Implementation of Dialysis Measures. Chronic kidney disease is an individual risk factor for cardiovascular diseases, which can lead to physical and cognitive impairment and also significantly reduce life expectancy. Despite general practitioner care, people with impaired kidney function are at risk of developing end-stage renal disease or specific complications. For these patients, kidney transplantation or lifelong renal replacement (dialysis) is often the only treatment option. Both treatments cause very high costs, with terminal renal failure being considered one of the most expensive chronic diseases. Projections show that in Germany, about 100,200 patients were permanently in need of dialysis in 2017 [41], a rate of 1 in 800 citizens. The average annual costs are between 43,000 € and 54,000 € per patient [41]. Of this, an average of between 6300 € and 9800 € is accounted for by the necessary travel costs. The total costs that burden just the statutory health insurance amount to about 4.73 billion € annually. Forecasts assume an increase in the number of patients in dialysis by 20 to 23% by 2040 [41]. This implies an increase in the affected patient group to 120,000 to 123,000. The most common dialysis methods are peritoneal and haemodialysis. While peritoneal dialysis can also be performed with mobile devices, the latter one usually has to be performed as a stationary procedure. Most machines for this are large and of-ten designed for use in a clinic [105]. For this reason, haemodialysis in Germany usually takes place as some kind of center dialysis [40, 41], yet it is the dominant form in Germany. The group of over 80-year-olds shows a particularly high prevalence; the needs-based care of this group must also be viewed critically from the aspect that they often have severely limited mobility [82].

However, according to analyses, the total annual costs, as far as the technical service part of the practice is concerned, are on average about 990,000 € per service contract. This does not include the costs for private patients. The *Standardized Assessment Scale* (EBM) is only based on costs of about 740,000 € [28]. This casts doubt on the economic efficiency of provision by low-frequency outpatient practices. In addition to the provision of outpatient care in dialysis centers, a large proportion of patients already receive their bloodwashing in hospitals. For MV, the *Klinikliste* 2023 of the internet platform Klinikradar refers to twenty-one clinics for dialysis in twenty cities. Therefor Klinikradar uses the quality reports of the hospitals of the *Joint Federal Committee* (G-BA). For the year 2020, 922 cases are indicated in the overview for Rostock, whereas the least frequented clinics each have less than 10 treatments to report.

In addition to the burden of high costs, there is an increasing shortage of specialists and expertise to secure adequate care for patients. A look at the development of the overall situation of nursing staff in the nephrology sector in relation to the increasing numbers of elderly people shows a clear discrepancy. At the same time, there are fewer and fewer classical nephrology nursing staff in relation to the patients to be cared for, also because of the now increasing retirement of veteran nursing staff [84]. As there will tend to be more and more patients requiring renal replacement therapy such as dialysis due to demographic change, nationwide care is a problem.

Radiological Methods of Treatment. According to the *German Radiology Network*, about 6,800 of the licensed physicians in Germany have completed training as specialists in radiology/diagnostic radiology and also work in this field. With about 2% of all licensed physicians, they form one of the smaller groups of specialists. Approximately 3,100 radiologists are active in the established sector, with further dovetailing between the outpatient and inpatient sectors. Looking at the different practice sizes, it becomes clear that the number of radiology individual practices is declining. Of the approximately 1,100 radiology centers in Germany, fewer than 300 are still run as individual practices. This is a significant decrease compared to the approximately 400 individual practices in 2016 [76], thus a trend toward the necessary centralization is evident here. The remainder are already group practices. Around 600 radiologists work in group practices with two partners and just under 900 radiologists are organized in group practices with 3–5 partners. With almost 350 radiologists, a not insignificant proportion is accounted for large group practices with six or more partners. Such large practices can be compared to medium-sized companies. They often have up to 50 employees and operate equipment worth well over 10 million euros in some cases. Private practice radiology is currently in a state of flux, and consolidation is taking place with the formation of large, supra-regional practice conglomerates [76].

Nationwide radiological care without teleradiology is already hard to implement today [69]. One of the main reasons for this success lies in the working methodology in the field of radiology. For example, an essential part of the work of radiologists is predominantly the interpretation of medical images, which are produced by medical-technical assistants and transmitted digitally by the equipment, be it conventional X-ray machines, CT or MRI devices, to be viewed and evaluated on a suitable monitor. Here it becomes clear that radiological care, in comparison to other medical disciplines, depends less on the universal availability of specialists, but rather on the availability of sufficiently trained (nursing) staff and the necessary technical equipment. Few radiological procedures, such as interventional radiology, conventional X-ray fluoroscopy or sonography, absolutely require the on-site presence of radiologists [69]. Since the number of radiological examinations in Germany is growing by about 10% annually, but only 2–3% of newly trained radiologists are coming on board [81], we already see modern approaches to solutions here. However, the basis for this is the provision of technical equipment both in the field of data collection as also in data processing and transmission. Another essential point is to ensure data security both for the transmission and the archiving of data. Combined with the growing need for medical-technical assistants [25], this form of universal care is facing problems.

For example, if one considers the imaging diagnostic procedures performed in MV alone, the extent of the demand becomes apparent. The *Federal Health Report* contains approx. 6,794,000 CT examinations and approx. 1,919,000 MRI examinations of full inpatients in hospitals for 2021. Compared to 2020, this is an increase of about 321,000 CT examinations and 50,000 MRI examinations in one year. This might hint that the importance of imaging diagnostics, especially CT examinations, has increased in Germany in the recent years. The path already taken towards partial centralization of radiological treatments in centers or larger practices offers the possibility of exploiting the synergies associated with the increasing size of the practices in terms of staff deployment, equipment procurement, service contracts, etc. [76].

Skin Cancer Detection. Malignant neoplasms of the skin (black skin cancer) are among the most common types of cancer worldwide. The frequency is increasing rapidly, but it is easily treatable if detected early [24]. Routine diagnostics for melanoma detection include full-body visual inspection, often supplemented by dermoscopy, which can significantly increase the diagnostic accuracy of experienced dermatologists [24]. A procedure that is additionally offered in some practices and clinics is *Total Body Digital Photography* (TBDP) in combination with digital dermoscopy. TBDP is also used in smartphone apps that serve the self-assessment of the skin by the user. The problem here is the lack of consistency in the image and light quality of the images used [65].

In recent decades, several non-invasive methods have been developed for the examination of suspicious pigmented lesions that have the potential to allow improved and, in some cases, automated assessment of these lesions. Currently, the most promising approach may be the analysis of routine macroscopic and dermoscopic images by AI [51]. In the classification of pigmented skin lesions based on macroscopic and dermoscopic images, AI, especially in the form of neural networks, has achieved diagnostic accuracy comparable to dermatologists in numerous experimental studies. Prerequisites for the transfer of such diagnostic systems into dermatological routine are the comprehensibility of the system decisions by the user as well as a uniformly high performance of the algorithms on image data from other clinics and practices.

As seen in recent studies, computer-aided diagnosis systems unfold the greatest benefit primarily as assistance systems [12, 101]. The physician/machine combination achieves the best results and AI-based diagnostic systems help to record morphological features quickly, quantitatively, objectively and reproducibly and could thus, in addition to medical experience, provide a more objective basis for analysis. Looking at the numbers delivered by the *National Association of Statutory Health Insurance Physicians* (KBV) from 2020 illustrates the problem. If one compares, for example, the density of dermatologists in the spatial planning regions of *Mecklenburgische-Seenplatte* (MS), *Mittleres Mecklenburg/Rostock* (MM), *Vorpommern* (VP), *Westmecklenburg* (WM) and Berlin, at first glance the picture is homogeneous; MS has 6.1 dermatologists per 100,000 inhabitants, MM 7.6, VP 7.4, WM 5.2 and Berlin 7.6. However, if one converts the physician density to the area, different ratios result. Berlin has 0.3125 dermatologists per km^2, while the region of MS has 0.0029 dermatologists per km^2 (MM 0.009; VP 0.0048; WM 0.0034). This means that, calculated on the area, dermatologist care in Berlin is 109 times higher than in the area of MS. This implies significantly longer journeys for the patients concerned, while mobility deficits are also evident here.

Ongoing Hospital Reform. In 2018, the G-BA defined minimum structural requirements for emergency care in three levels for the first time. This was an important first step towards a nationwide uniform definition of care structures and the creation of transparency. In December 2022 the *Government Commission for Modern and Needs-Based Hospital Care* has presented a reform proposal for hospital remuneration and a fixed definition of structural prerequisites in the sense of a minimum required hospital-wide structural quality [14]. The reform proposals of the government commission refer to inpatient and emergency care. Nevertheless, it also responds to problems, experiences and developments that can also be found in the outpatient sector. The politically forced restructuring of the hospital landscape, insofar as it is implemented, leads to a further centralization of hospital locations. The three examples described above are primarily long-term plannable and recurring treatments. Nevertheless, the coming structural change is an opportunity to further dovetail outpatient and inpatient care.

4.2 Concept of Area-Wide Hierarchically Structured Service

The implementation of a network with the objective of a comprehensive (hierarchically oriented) location structure for ensuring medical care for the population in rural areas is an essential and also necessary step within the framework of the realization of a targeted cohesion policy. The initial point is to consider central-location structures with a suitable differentiated scope of care [16, 23]. The essential condition in such location planning is the specification of the observance with a maximum (L_2 norm based) distance r (= radius), which is specified for the inhabitants to reach (potential) health care facilities. These are set covering problems [22, 106], where catchment areas are defined, i.e., from any location within a given area, the respective facilities must be accessible according to the specifications. Insofar as information is available regarding the road distances or travel times, the assignment to the locations can also be calculated on spatially aggregated settlement clusters [98, 106]. Outgoing from this an online-based management of medical care capacities can be established in a later phase, with respective planning of the necessary transport processes for the patients affected.

In the problem presented in this context, two specific framework conditions must be taken into account. For one thing, the location planning for the individual levels is carried out top down, whereby the locations of level i are set for the planning of level i-1, that means, the functions of a lower level are in case included in those above it ([16] 63–85). In addition, it must be taken into account that the area under consideration, the federal state of MV, is not spatially isolated, but is bordered by Schleswig-Holstein and Niedersachsen to the west and Brandenburg to the south. As a result, it may make sense that, to a certain extent, health care in the outlying areas can be provided from appropriate locations outside the borders of the region, also from the point of view of cost and distance. A possible three-tier structure with $r = 75$ km, $r = 40$ km and $r = 30$ is shown in Figs. 2, 3 and 4.

This approach shows that (largely) covering the area of the federal state can be ensured with the given radii on the three levels at $r = 75$ km with two sites, at $r =$

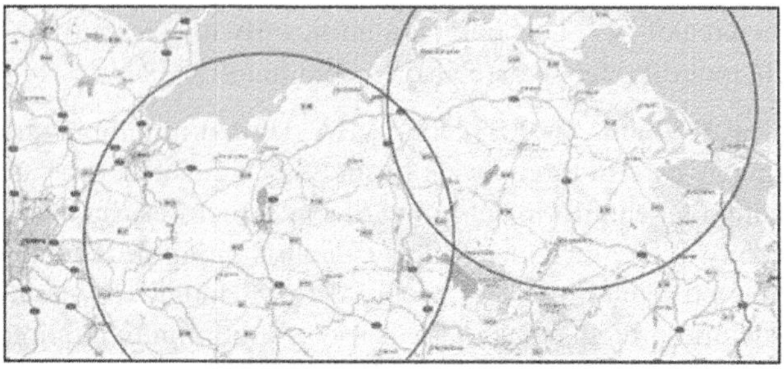

Fig. 2. Included locations at $r = 75$

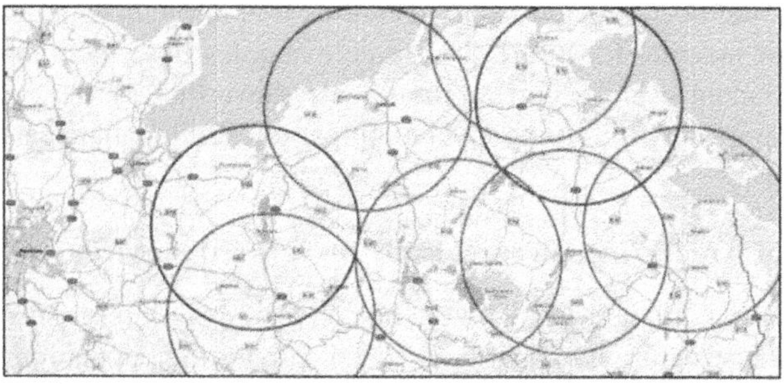

Fig. 3. Included locations at $r = 40$

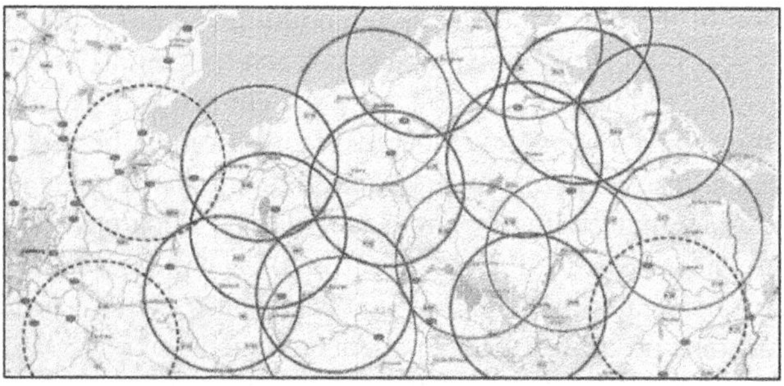

Fig. 4. Included locations at $r = 30$

40 km it is additionally six and at $r = 30$ km again nine more (see Table 1). Only in the western and southern peripheral areas are there smaller gaps, but these can be covered in cooperation with the neighboring federal states of Schleswig-Holstein (Lübeck) and Niedersachsen (Lüneburg) in the west and Brandenburg (Prenzlau) in the south. In the area of the Baltic Sea coast, on the other hand, complete coverage is required, due among other things to the geographic conditions, so that the Fischland-Darß-Zingst peninsula and the island of Rügen can be included in the coverage.

This solution does not include the existing settlement structures in detail, the distance-based accessibility of the locations within the existing transport networks and also

Table 1. Locations included at the respective central levels

Radius r	Included locations
75 km	Schwerin, Greifswald
40 km	Stralsund, Rostock, Torgelow, Neubrandenburg, Waren (Müritz), Ludwigslust
30 km	Wolgast, Bergen, Ribnitz-Damgarten, Wismar, Hagenow, Güstrow, Parchim, Neustrelitz, Demmin

(regional political) influences. In this respect, the outlined structure must be understood as an initial basis for discussion, which must be specified more precisely at the political level and the responsible technical levels.

4.3 Necessary Framework Conditions for the Implementation of Demand-Oriented Structures in Health Care in Rural Areas

Fundamental changes in health care as proposed in the outlined concept require (long-term) political decisions. The results must be implemented administratively and, what is often forgotten, also enforced (politically). The central basis is the necessary legal framework with clear regulation of responsibilities at the different administrative levels, as well as at the local authority level.

In this context, however, additional measures are required to create the necessary framework conditions. This may involve structural changes to the healthcare system and its long-term financing, the establishment and expansion of a suitable digital infrastructure for data management, and also communication between (potential) patients and healthcare institutions. It is also necessary to regulate the control and monitoring of transport processes in public transport in order to ensure the necessary (and also barrier-free) access to healthcare for all potential patients. It must also be taken into account that the structures to be developed will be influenced by ongoing adjustments due to changing framework conditions. In the foreground here are developments in population and settlement structures as well as in the demand structures (for example due to demographic factors). In addition, there are often (technical) developments in diagnostics and therapeutic methods that can have an impact on the care structures, that means, no static structure should be developed; instead, permanent further development must be ensured in the light of changing situations.

5 Expectations and Further Development

The main objective in connection with the introduction of autonomous driving as part of a redesign of mobility in rural areas is to improve living conditions of the local population and to increase the attractiveness and economic performance of these regions. A key point here is the health care service considered in this article, which, also in the view of demographic trends that are apparent, must be ensured for the coming years to the necessary extent and with the needed efficiency. In view of the EU's plans to regularly review the driving licenses of older citizens, the need for the availability of quasi-individual mobility as an alternative to private car use will increase significantly.

In addition, the above-mentioned changes in public transport must also be seen in terms of meeting the needs of rural areas in a wide variety of sectors. This concerns the accessibility of retail facilities and (commercial) services as well as public administration. In the field of education and access to cultural and leisure facilities, too, completely new opportunities arise for the inhabitants of rural areas. Substitution by online-based offerings, as has been propagated many times and is still being pushed today, cannot provide a sustainable solution here, since personal contact is of decisive importance in many situations. However, it can be achieved through the mobility services outlined above, resulting in substantial positive effects in terms of participation in social life in rural areas. In this way, an important step can also be taken toward ensuring equal living conditions, which has been called for over and over again.

References

1. Ainsalu, J., et al.: State of the art of automated buses. Sustainability **10**(9), 3118 (2018)
2. Arzt, C., Kleemann, S., Plappert, C., Rieke, R., Zelle, D.: Datenverarbeitung und Cybersicherheit in der Fahrzeugautomatisierung - Rechtliche und technische Anforderungen im Verbund. Zeitschrift für IT-Recht und Recht der Digitalisierung **25**(7), 593–614 (2022)
3. Asbach, L., Ortgiese, M.: Automatisierte Fahrzeuge in Europa sicher betreiben. Internationales Verkehrswesen **75**(1), 22–26 (2023)
4. Ayyasamy, S.: A comprehensive review on advanced driver assistance system. J. Soft Comput. Paradigm **4**(2), 69–81 (2022)
5. Avermann, N., Schlüter, J.: Determinants of customer satisfaction with a true door-to-door DRT service in rural Germany. Res. Transp. Bus. Manag. **32**, 100420 (2019)
6. Baba, L., Wilbert, K.: Soziale Stadt-und Ortsentwicklung in ländlichen Räumen. Bundesinstitut für Bau-, Stadt-und Raumforschung (BBSR) (2022)
7. Barillère-Scholz, M., Büttner, C., Becker, A.: Mobilität 4.0: Deutschlands erste autonome Buslinie in Bad Birnbach als Pionierleistung für neue Verkehrskonzepte. In: Riener, A., Appel, A., Dorner, W., Huber, T., Kolb, J.C., Wagner, H. (Hrsg.) Autonome Shuttlebusse im ÖPNV, pp. 15–22. Springer, Heidelberg (2020). https://doi.org/10.1007/978-3-662-59406-3_2
8. Bento, L.C., Parafita, R., Rakha, H.A., Nunes, U.J.: A study of the environmental impacts of intelligent automated vehicle control at intersections via V2V and V2I communications. J. Intell. Transp. Syst. **23**(1), 41–59 (2019)
9. Berg, J., Ihlström, J.: The importance of public transport for mobility and everyday activities among rural residents. Soc. Sci. **8**, 58 (2019)
10. Bernhard, C., Oberfeld, D., Hoffmann, C., Weismüller, D., Hecht, H.: User acceptance of automated public transport - valence of an autonomous minibus experience. Transp. Res. F **70**, 109–123 (2020)
11. Bissell, D., Birtchnell, T., Elliott, A., Hsu, E.L.: Autonomous automobilities - the social impacts of driverless vehicles. Curr. Sociol. **68**(1), 116–134 (2020)
12. Brinker, T.J., Schlager, G., French, L.E., et al.: Computerassistierte Hautkrebsdiagnose. Hautarzt **71**, 669–676 (2020)
13. Busse, R., Berger, E.: Vom planerischen Bestandsschutz zum bedarfsorientierten Krankenhausangebot. In: Klauber, J., Geraedts, M., Friedrich, J., Wasem, J. (Hrsg.) Krankenhaus-Report 2018 - Schwerpunkt Bedarf und Bedarfsgerechtigkeit, pp. 149–170. Schattauer, Stuttgart (2018)

14. Busse, R., Karagiannidis, C., Augurzky, B., Schmitt, J., Bschor, T.: Der Vorschlag der Regierungskommission für eine grundlegende Reform der Krankenhausvergütung. In: Klauber, J., Geraedts, M., Friedrich, J., Wasem, J. (Hrsg.) Krankenhaus-Report 2023 - Schwerpunkt - Personal, pp. 267–280. Springer, Heidelberg (2023). https://doi.org/10.1007/978-3-662-66881-8_17
15. Chen, X., Ouyang, Y., Arian, E., Yang, H., Ba, X.: Modeling and testing autonomous and shared multimodal mobility services for low-density rural areas. Civil Engineering Studies, Illinois Center for Transportation, Series No. 22-013 (2022)
16. Christaller, W.: Die zentralen Orte in Süddeutschland. Gustav Fischer, Jena (Neudruck 1968: Wissenschaftliche Buchgesellschaft, Darmstadt) (1933)
17. Coluccia, D.: The second industrial revolution (late 1800s and early 1900s). In: Zanda, G. (ed.) Corporate Management in a Knowledge-Based Economy, pp. 52–64. Palgrave Macmillan, London (2012)
18. Cramer, T.: Strafrechtsdogmatische Auflösung dilemmatischer Situationen beim autonomen Fahren - Entwicklung innovativer Leitlinien für die Programmierung von Notstandsalgorithmen in Lebensnotstandssituationen. Nomos, Baden-Baden (2022)
19. Crescenzi, R., Fratesi, U., Monastiriotis, V.: Back to the member states? Cohesion Policy and the national challenges to the European Union. Reg. Stud. **54**(1), 5–9 (2020)
20. Daduna, J.R.: Impacts of deregulation on planning processes and information management design in public transit. In: Voß, S., Daduna, J.R. (eds.) Computer-aided scheduling of public transport, pp. 429–441. Springer, Berlin (2001). https://doi.org/10.1007/978-3-642-56423-9_24
21. Daduna, J.R.: Evolution of public transport in rural areas - new technologies and digitization. In: Marcus, A., Rosenzweig, E. (eds.) HCII 2020. LNCS, vol. 12202, pp. 82–99. Springer, Cham (2020). https://doi.org/10.1007/978-3-030-49757-6_6
22. Daskin, M.S.: A maximum expected covering location model - formulation, properties and heuristic solution. Transp. Sci. **17**(1), 48–70 (1983)
23. Danielzyk, R., Priebs, A.: Die Sicherung der Daseinsvorsorge durch Klein-und Mittelstädte als Beitrag des zentralörtlichen Systems zu gleichwertigen Lebensverhältnissen. Europa Reg. **26**(3), 7–21 (2020)
24. de Buhr, Y., Bunde, H., Großmann, E., et al.: Prävention von Hautkrebs. Onkologe **28**, 49–54 (2022)
25. Deutscher Bundestag: Reformbedarf bei Medizinisch-Technischen Assistenten in Krankenhäusern und Arztpraxen. Drucksache 19/24629 (2020)
26. destatis - Statistisches Bundesamt: Verkehr - Verkehrsunfälle - Fachserie 8 Reihe 7 (2022)
27. Di Caro, P., Fratesi, U.: One policy, different effects - estimating the region-specific impacts of EU cohesion policy. J. Reg. Sci. **62**(1), 307–330 (2022)
28. Drabinski, T.: Nephrologische Versorgung in Deutschland - Bestandsaufnahme, Vergütung und Datengrundlage. Schmidt & Klaunig, Kiel (2014)
29. Eckhardt, J., Lauhkonen, A., Aapaoja, A.: Impact assessment of rural PPP MaaS pilots. Eur. Transp. Res. Rev. **12**(1), 1–14 (2020)
30. Einig, K., Zaspel-Heisters, B.: Das system Zentraler Orte in Deutschland. In: Greiving, S., Flex, F. (Hrsg.) Neuaufstellung des Zentrale-Orte-Konzepts in Nordrhein-Westfalen, pp. 3–19. Akademie für Raumforschung und Landesplanung (ARL) Hannover (2016)
31. Enoch, M.P.: How a rapid modal convergence into a universal automated taxi service could be the future for local passenger transport. Technol. Anal. Strateg. Manag. **27**(8), 910–924 (2015)
32. Enquete-Kommission Zukunft der medizinischen Versorgung in Mecklenburg-Vorpommern: Abschlussbericht. Stellungnahmen 7. Sitzung. Kommissionsdrucksache 7/46 (2021)

33. Farhan, J., Chen, T.D.: Impact of ridesharing on operational efficiency of shared autonomous electric vehicle fleet. Transp. Res. C **93**, 310–321 (2018)
34. Frank, J., Ryll, A.: Demographischer Wandel, Morbidität und Inanspruchnahme - Zur Projektion des ambulanten Leistungsvolumens. Gesundheitswesen **77**(12), 932–938 (2015)
35. Gail, M.M., Götz, G., Herold, D., et al.: Staatliche Eingriffe zur Erfüllung der Daseinsvorsorge - Der öffentliche Personennahverkehr. In: Gail, M.M., Götz, G., Klotz, P.A., et al. (Hrsg.) Staatliche Eingriffe in die Preisbildung - Darstellung, Erklärung und Wirkungsanalyse, pp. 49–66. Springer, Wiesbaden (2023). https://doi.org/10.1007/978-3-658-40674-5_5
36. Geissler, A., Wörz, M., Busse, R.: Deutsche Krankenhauskapazitäten im internationalen Vergleich. In: Klauber, J., Geraedts, M., Friedrich, J. (Hrsg.) Krankenhaus-Report 2010, pp. 25–40. Schattauer, Stuttgart (2010)
37. Gill, T.: Ethical dilemmas are really important to potential adopters of autonomous vehicles. Ethics Inf. Technol. **23**(4), 657–673 (2021). https://doi.org/10.1007/s10676-021-09605-y
38. Girdhar, M., Hong, J., Moore, J.: Cybersecurity of autonomous vehicles - a systematic literature review of adversarial attacks and defense models. IEEE Open J. Veh. Technol. (2023, in press)
39. Greiving, S., Flex, F., Terfrüchte, T.: Vergleichende Untersuchung der Zentrale-Orte-Konzepte in den Ländern und Empfehlungen zu ihrer Weiterentwicklung. Raumforsch. Raumordn. **73**(4), 285–297 (2015)
40. Haag-Weber, M.: Peritonealdialyse. Dialyse aktuell **21**(06), 290–295 (2017)
41. Häckl, D., Kossack, N., Schoenfelder, T.: Prävalenz, Kosten der Versorgung und Formen des dialysepflichtigen chronischen Nierenversagens in Deutschland - Vergleich der Dialyseversorgung innerhalb und außerhalb stationärer Pflegeeinrichtungen. Das Gesundheitswesen **83**(10), 818–828 (2021)
42. Hänsch, R., Hoelzmann, J., Mielke, S.: Flächendeckend Rufbusse? Eine Untersuchung zur Verbreitung alternativer Mobilitätskonzepte. Der Nahverkehr **37**(1+2), 39–43 (2019)
43. Hallewell, M., et al.: Deriving user experience design dimensions for future autonomous taxi interface design. J. Usability Stud. **17**(4), 140–163 (2022)
44. Hansson, S.O., Belin, M.Å., Lundgren, B.: Self-driving vehicles - an ethical overview. Philos. Technol. **34**, 1383–1408 (2021)
45. Hein, G.W.: Status, perspectives and trends of satellite navigation. Satell. Navig. **1**(1), 1–12 (2020). https://doi.org/10.1186/s43020-020-00023-x
46. Henning, F.W.: Handbuch der Wirtschafts-und Sozialgeschichte Deutschlands, Band 2, Deutsche Wirtschafts- und Sozialgeschichte im 19. Jahrhundert. Schöningh, Paderborn (1996)
47. Holzhüter, H., Bödewadt, J., Bayesteh, S., Aschinger, A., Blume, H.: Technical concepts of automotive LiDAR sensors - a review. Opt. Eng. **62**(3), 031213 (2023)
48. Hou, Z., Zhou, F.: Assessing the performance of precise point positioning (PPP) with the fully serviceable multi-GNSS constellations. Remote Sens. **15**, 807 (2023)
49. Illgen, S., Höck, M.: Establishing car sharing services in rural areas - a simulation-based fleet operations analysis. Transportation **47**(2), 811–826 (2020)
50. Jing, H., Gao, Y., Shahbeigi, S., Dianati, M.: Integrity monitoring of GNSS/INS based positioning systems for autonomous vehicles - state-of-the-art and open challenges. IEEE Trans. Intell. Transp. Syst. **23**(9), 14166–14187 (2022)
51. Jutzi, T., Krieghoff-Henning, E.I., Brinker, T.J.: Künstliche Intelligenz auf dem Vormarsch - Hohe Vorhersage-genauigkeit bei der Früherkennung pigmentierter Melanome. Laryngo-Rhino-Otologie 84–91 (2022)
52. Khan, M.A., Sayed, H.E., Malik, S., et al.: Level-5 autonomous driving - Are we there yet? A review of research literature. ACM Comput. Surv. (CSUR) **55**(2), 1–38 (2022)

53. Khan, S.K., Shiwakoti, N., Stasinopoulos, P., Warren, M.: Modelling cybersecurity regulations for automated vehicles. Accid. Anal. Prev. **186**, 107054 (2023)
54. Kiesewetter, H.: Industrielle Revolution in Deutschland - Regionen als Wachstumsmotoren. Franz Steiner, Stuttgart (2004)
55. Kim, S., Chang, J.J.E., Park, H.H., et al.: Autonomous taxi service design and user experience. Int. J. Hum.-Comput. Interact. **36**(5), 429–448 (2020)
56. Kleemann, S., Arzt, C.: Das Gesetz zum autonomen Fahren in Deutschland - Automatisiertes Fahren findet seinen Weg im StVG. RAW Recht-Automobil-Wirtschaft 99–195 (2021)
57. Knauff, M.: Verfassungs-, europa-und personenbeförderungsrechtliche Aspekte des Vorrangs der Eigenwirtschaftlichkeit. In: Knauff, M. (Hrsg.) Vorrang der Eigenwirtschaftlichkeit im ÖPNV, pp. 11–28. Nomos, Baden-Baden (2017)
58. Knierim, L., Schlüter, J.C.: The attitude of potentially less mobile people towards demand responsive transport in a rural area in central Germany. J. Transp. Geogr. **96**, 103202 (2021)
59. Kopper, C.: Der Durchbruch des PKW zum Massenkonsumgut 1950–1964. Jahrbuch für Wirtschaftsgeschichte **51**(1), 19–36 (2010)
60. López-Lambas, M.E., Alonso, A.: The driverless bus - an analysis of public perceptions and acceptability. Sustainability **11**(18), 4986 (2019)
61. Lucifora, C., Grasso, G.M., Perconti, P., Plebe, A.: Moral dilemmas in self-driving cars. Rivista Internazionale di Filosofia e Psicologia **11**(2), 238–250 (2020)
62. Lütge, C., Kriebitz, A., Max, R.: Ethische und rechtliche Herausforderungen des autonomen Fahrens. In: Mainzer, K. (Hrsg.) Philosophisches Handbuch Künstliche Intelligenz, pp. 1–18. Springer, Wiesbaden (2019). https://doi.org/10.1007/978-3-658-23715-8_30-1
63. Lutz, L.S.: Haftung am Beispiel automatisierter Fahrzeuge. In: Hartmann, M. (Hrsg.) KI & Recht kompakt, pp. 117–142. Springer, Berlin (2020). https://doi.org/10.1007/978-3-662-61700-7_3
64. Manik, D., Molkenthin, N.: Topology dependence of on-demand ride-sharing. Appl. Netw. Sci. **5**, 1–16 (2020)
65. Marek, A.J., Chu, E.Y., Ming, M., Khan, Z., Kovarik, C.L.: Impact of a smartphone application on skin self-examination rates in patients who are new to total body photography: a randomized controlled trial. J. Am. Acad. Dermatol. **79**(3), 564–567 (2018)
66. Meyer, M.: Bedarfsorientierte ÖPNV-Bedienung in der Fläche - Erfahrungen mit neuartigen Betriebsformen in der Bundesrepublik Deutschland und in den Niederlanden. Verkehr+Technik **41**(7), 280–289 (1988)
67. Michalik, D., Kohl, P., Krause, M., Kummert, A.: Virtueller Demonstrator zur Unterstützung der Einführung des autonomen Fahrens am Beispiel automatisierter Shuttlebusse. In: Proff, H. (Hrsg.) Transforming mobility - What next? - Technische und betriebswirtschaftliche Aspekte, pp. 399–418. Springer, Wiesbaden (2022). https://doi.org/10.1007/978-3-658-36430-4_24
68. Milakis, D., van Wee, B.: Implications of vehicle automation for accessibility and social inclusion of people on low income, people with physical and sensory disabilities, and older people. In: Antoniou, C., Efthymiou, D., Chaniotakis, E. (eds.) Demand for Emerging Transportation Systems, pp. 61–73. Elsevier, Amsterdam (2020)
69. Möller, T.B.: Teleradiologie in Deutschland. In: Fischer, F., Krämer, A. (Hrsg.) eHealth in Deutschland, pp. 295–305. Springer, Heidelberg (2016). https://doi.org/10.1007/978-3-662-49504-9_15
70. Nakoinz, O.: Zentralität - Theorie, Methoden und Fallbeispiele zur Analyse zentraler Orte. Edition Topoi, Berlin (2019)
71. Nanchen, B., Ramseyer, R., Grèzes, S., et al.: Perceptions of people with special needs regarding autonomous vehicles and implication on the design of Mobility as a Service to foster social inclusion. Front. Hum. Dyn. **3**, 751258 (2022)

72. Naveen, M.K., Lokesh, M., Varma, K.N.J.L., Teja, P.S.V.: A review on autonomous vehicles and its components. J. Pharm. Negative Results **13**(7), 6916–6922 (2022)
73. Neubauer, G., Beivers, A.: Zur Situation der stationären Versorgung: Optimierung unter schwierigen Rahmenbedingungen. In: Klauber, J., Geraedts, M., Friedrich, J. (Hrsg.) Krankenhaus-Report 2010: Schwerpunkt Krankenhausversorgung in der Krise?, pp. 3–11. Schattauer, Stuttgart (2010)
74. Ng, M.T., Mahmassani, H.S.: Autonomous minibus service with semi-on-demand routes in Grid Networks. Transp. Res. Rec. **2677**(1), 178–200 (2023)
75. Nobis, C., Kuhnimhof, T.: Mobilität in Deutschland - MiD Ergebnisbericht. (Bundesminister für Verkehr und digitale Infrastruktur) (FE-Nr. 70904/15) Bonn, Berlin (2018)
76. Notogamiprodjo, M., Remplik, P., Schricke, U.: Radiologische Praxis - Terra incognita. Radiologe **61**, 671–675 (2021)
77. Othman, K.: Public acceptance and perception of autonomous vehicles - a comprehensive review. AI Ethics **1**(3), 355–387 (2021)
78. Pangbourne, K.: Challenge, coordination, and collaboration for effective rural mobility solutions. In: Amaral, A.M., Barreto, L., Baltazar, S., Silva, J.P., Gonçalves, L. (eds.) Implications of Mobility as a Service (MaaS) in Urban and Rural Environments - Emerging Research and Opportunities, pp. 83–108. IGI Global, Hershey (2020)
79. Parekh, D., et al.: A review on autonomous vehicles - progress, methods and challenges. Electronics **11**(14), 2162 (2022)
80. Patoliya, J., Mewada, H., Hassaballah, M., Khan, M.A., Kadry, S.: A robust autonomous navigation and mapping system based on GPS and LiDAR data for unconstraint environment. Earth Sci. Inf. **15**, 2703–2715 (2022)
81. Quinsten, A.S., Bontke, B., Saur, A.: Radiologie im Wandel - Remote Scanning als Lösung gegen den Fachkräftemangel. Radiopraxis **15**(02), 62–71 (2022)
82. Rechel, B., Grundy, E., Robine, J.M., et al.: Ageing in the European Union. Lancet **381**(9874), 1312–1322 (2013)
83. Saxinger, A.: Genehmigungsvoraussetzungen und -wirkungen von Linienbedarfsverkehren. In: Knauff, M. (Hrsg.) Neuerungen im Rechtsrahmen für den ÖPNV, pp. 75–93. Nomos, Baden-Baden (2022)
84. Schäfer, C.: Werden alle Möglichkeiten genutzt? Dialyse aktuell **26**(9), 385 (2022)
85. Schäffner, V.: Wenn Ethik zum Programm wird - Eine risikoethische Analyse moralischer Dilemmata des autonomen Fahrens. Zeitschrift für Ethik und Moralphilosophie **3**(1), 27–49 (2020)
86. Schlüter, J., Bossert, A., Rössy, P., Kersting, M.: Impact assessment of autonomous demand responsive transport as a link between urban and rural areas. Res. Transp. Bus. Manag. **39**, 100613 (2021)
87. Schmidt-Seiwert, V., Binot, R., Kiel, L., et al.: Die Unterschiede bestimmen die Vielfalt in Europa - Ein Atlas ausgewählter Aspekte der räumlichen Strukturen und Entwicklungen. Bundesinstitut für Bau-, Stadt- und Raumforschung (BBSR), Bonn (2019)
88. Schreurs, M.A., Steuwer, S.D.: Autonomous driving - political, legal, social, and sustainability dimensions. In: Maurer, M., Gerdes, J.C., Lenz, B., Winner, H. (eds.) Autonomous Driving - Technical, Legal and Social Aspects, pp. 149–171. Springer, Heidelberg (2016). https://doi.org/10.1007/978-3-662-45854-9_8
89. Schreyögg, J.: Verbesserung der Personalallokation durch Strukturwandel. In: Klauber, J., Wasem, J., Beivers, A., Mostert, C. (Hrsg.) Krankenhaus-Report 2023 - Schwerpunkt Personal, pp. 197–211. Springer, Heidelberg (2023). https://doi.org/10.1007/978-3-662-66881-8_13
90. Shrestha, B.P., Millonig, A., Hounsell, N., McDonald, M.: Review of public transport needs of older people in European context. J. Popul. Ageing **10**, 343–361 (2017)

91. Sieber, L., Ruch, C., Hörl, S., Axhausen, K.W., Frazzoli, E.: Improved public transportation in rural areas with self-driving cars - a study on the operation of Swiss train lines. Transp. Res. A **134**, 35–51 (2020)
92. Siegel, J., Pappas, G.: Morals, ethics, and the technology capabilities and limitations of automated and self-driving vehicles. AI Soc. 1–14 (2021)
93. Simmler, M.: Maschinenethik und strafrechtliche Verantwortlichkeit. In: Bendel, O. (Hrsg.) Handbuch Maschinenethik, pp. 453–469. Springer, Wiesbaden (2019). https://doi.org/10.1007/978-3-658-17483-5_30
94. Sörensen, L., Bossert, A., Jokinen, J.P., Schlüter, J.: How much flexibility does rural public transport need? - Implications from a fully flexible DRT system. Transp. Policy **100**, 5–20 (2021)
95. Spindler, G.: Haftung für autonome Systeme. In: Arroyo Vendrell, T., Gsell, B., Kindl, J. (Hrsg.) Die Schadensersatzhaftung, pp. 139–184. Nomos, Baden-Baden (2022)
96. Stearns, P.N.: The Industrial Revolution in World History, 4th edn. Westview Press, Boulder, Co. (2020)
97. Südbeck, T.: Motorisierung, Verkehrsentwicklung und Verkehrspolitik in der Bundesrepublik Deutschland der 1950er Jahre. (Steiner) Stuttgart (1994)
98. Tansel, B.C., Francis, R.L., Lowe, T.J.: State of the art—location on networks: a survey. Part I: The p-center and p-median problems. Manag. Sci. **29**(4), 482–497 (1983). https://doi.org/10.1287/mnsc.29.4.482
99. Taylor, G.R.: The Transportation Revolution 1815–1860. Rinehart, New York (1951)
100. Thao, V.T., Imhof, S., von Arx, W.: Demand responsive transport - new insights from peri-urban experiences. Travel Behav. Soc. **31**, 141–150 (2023)
101. Tschandl, P., Codella, N., Akay, B.N., et al.: Comparison of the accuracy of human readers versus machine-learning algorithms for pigmented skin lesion classification - an open, web-based, international, diagnostic study. Lancet Oncol. **20**(7), 938–947 (2019)
102. van Suntum, U.: Verkehrspolitik. (Vahlen) München (1986)
103. Voigt, F.: Verkehr - Die Entwicklung des Verkehrssystems (Band 2, Teil 1). Duncker & Humblot, Berlin (1965)
104. Wachinger, L.: Mittel in Kooperationen und Verbünden. In: Knauff, M. (Hrsg.) Rechtsanwendung und Finanzierung im ÖPNV, pp. 193–204. Nomos, Baden-Baden (2020)
105. Wieringa, F.: Die Zukunft der Nierenersatztherapie. Nephrologie aktuell **27**(1), 26–30 (2023)
106. Ye, H., Kim, H.: Locating healthcare facilities using a network-based covering location problem. GeoJournal **81**, 875–890 (2016)
107. Ye, L., Yamamoto, T.: Evaluating the impact of connected and autonomous vehicles on traffic safety. Physica A **526**, 121009 (2019)
108. Zhou, J.: A review of LiDAR sensor technologies for perception in automated driving. Acad. J. Sci. Technol. **3**(3), 255–261 (2022)

Ridesharing in Rural Areas with Autonomous Electric Vehicles and Interrelated Trips

Marvin Soth, Lennart C. Johnsen, Sebastian Scholz(✉), and Frank Meisel

School of Economics and Business Management, Supply Chain Management, Kiel University, Olshausenstr. 40, 24098 Kiel, Germany
sebastian.scholz@bwl.uni-kiel.de

Abstract. Passenger cars are responsible for 44% of the greenhouse gas emissions within Europe's transportation sector. Especially rural areas are still fundamentally dependent on private motor vehicles, which is why in particular the younger and older population in such regions is limited in their mobility. The purpose of this paper is to determine the potential of shared, electric, autonomous vehicles to close the aforementioned mobility gap in an eco-friendly manner. It provides recommendations for the implementation of the associated transport services in terms of vehicle battery size and charging station infrastructure. For this purpose, we present a model for the electric autonomous dial-a-ride problem with interrelated trips (e-ADARP-IT), which is solved by a commercial solver and through a Variable Neighborhood Search heuristic. Computational experiments reveal the superior performance of the heuristic. It is shown that large shares of requested trips can be served efficiently at low operational cost. Results further indicate that expanding vehicle battery capacity seems more relevant than expanding the number of charging stations, even though both developments clearly have to go hand in hand.

Keywords: Dial-a-ride problem · electric autonomous vehicles · rural area · interrelated trips · variable neighborhood search

1 Introduction

The transport sector is responsible for more than a quarter of the EU's greenhouse gas emissions. 44% of its share is generated by passenger vehicles and, consequently, has a crucial impact on achieving the 1.5° C target of the Paris Climate Agreement [13]. The combination of the three innovations of electrification, autonomous driving, and shared mobility has the disruptive potential to significantly change the personal mobility sector [44]. Together they form the potential for *shared autonomous electric vehicles* (SAEVs). With the help of SAEVs, greenhouse gas emissions per kilometer can be reduced by over 90% and mobility cost reach 0.16–0.26 €/km, where both these performance measures lie significantly below those of private vehicles with combustion engines [4].

© The Author(s), under exclusive license to Springer Nature Switzerland AG 2023
J. R. Daduna et al. (Eds.): ICCL 2023, LNCS 14239, pp. 416–434, 2023.
https://doi.org/10.1007/978-3-031-43612-3_26

The route planning problem associated with SAEV services is the *dial-a-ride problem* (DARP), a combinatorial optimization problem. The DARP consists of customer requests for transportation from given origin locations to given destination locations, which have to be scheduled on a finite number of vehicles. The objective could be to maximize a service quality measure or to minimize transportation costs [5]. SAEV services as considered in this paper combine multiple DARP-variants within one problem: The dial-a-ride problem with interrelated trips (DARP-IT), which synchronizes customer requests that are related to each other by means of a common arrival time of multiple customers or a round trip with a desired stay time at a location [27], and the electric autonomous dial-a-ride problem (e-ADARP) that deals with electric and autonomous vehicles including battery management and recharging [5]. This article combines these two variants, resulting in the electric autonomous dial-a-ride problem with interrelated trips (e-ADARP-IT).

Most studies on DARPs for autonomous and electric vehicles focused on urban areas [4,5,30]. In contrast to this, [27] considered the DARP-IT for rural areas, where interrelated trips are of particular importance as customers also demand guaranteed return trips, synchronized arrivals for joint meetings, or other complex service patterns. The paper at hand also focuses on rural areas and interrelated trips. Mobility in such areas is characterized by relatively long transport distances and a very limited availability of public transport options. This effects that the population so far relies on privately owned vehicles, which heavily restricts those people that do not own or cannot operate a car on their own, such as young or elderly people, see [27]. We, therefore, explore the potential of SAEV in rural areas by combining the approaches of [27] for the ADARP-IT and of [5] for the e-ADARP within a holistic model and solution approach. The advances over [27] lie in the integration of battery management into the dial-a-ride problem with interrelated trips (ADARP-IT) and thus bridges the gap between these two research directions in the domain of dial-a-ride problems. A heuristic solution is adopted from [27] and compared to the solutions derived from solving the optimization model directly. In our experiments, we then focus on a rural area in the federal state of Schleswig-Holstein, Germany. The associated test instances vary in terms of the number of customer requests, the vehicles being available and their battery capacity, as well as the number of charging stations. The influence of the number of charging stations and the size of the battery capacity is then analyzed w.r.t. the service quality for the interrelated trips in this rural area setting.

Therefore, the implementation of an autonomous ridesharing system in rural areas can provide several advantages, for instance by offering mobility services to people that cannot operate a vehicle themselves, by avoiding operational limitations such as personnel costs and service time constraints of conventional mobility services, and by allowing for more efficient vehicle sharing as well as a provision of services during off-peak hours. As rural areas generally lack an offer of public transport options, such a system can close the gap between the demand for mobility and the supply of mobility services.

The remainder of this paper is organized as follows. Section 2 gives an overview of relevant SAEV literature. Section 3 formalizes the e-ADARP-IT planning problem and presents the corresponding optimization model. Computational experiments in Sect. 4 contrast the optimization model-based results with a heuristic solution approach, focusing on the effects of battery capacity and the number of available charging stations. Section 5 concludes the paper.

2 Literature Review

SAEV services combine features of electrification, autonomous driving, and shared mobility, where autonomous vehicles offer economic and service time advantages due to not having a driver [20]. This typically allows for uninterrupted service provision and greater flexibility in the deployment [5]. Thereby 'shared mobility' refers to the on-demand use of vehicles by multiple customers in contrast to privately owned vehicles that are exclusively used by their owners. Shared mobility can take various forms such as ridesharing, carsharing, or bike-sharing, and allows for cost savings, reduced greenhouse gas emissions, and less reliance on vehicle ownership [43].

The route planning problem of shared autonomous vehicles (SAVs) is treated within the DARP. The combinatorial optimization problem minimizes the transportation cost and/or maximizes the service quality [5].

[36] classify the literature on SAV research based on booking type and sharing system. The booking type divides into reservation-based and on-demand-based services. In the latter, the customer can book his/her trip in real-time, and those requests have to be integrated into the ongoing vehicle service process, see e.g. [25]. The use of priority rules has been established for this purpose by [15]. In contrast, in reservation-based services, customer requests are known before the vehicle routes are to be determined. This means that the DARP is solved using the data is available up to that time, which typically leads to a static perspective on this optimization problem, see [24] and [5]. Due to the longer distances and longer relocation times of vehicles in rural areas, reservation-based services appear suitable for mobility systems in such regions [27].

The mobility systems for SAVs can be divided into ridesharing, carsharing, and mixed systems based on the way vehicles are shared in the operations [36]. In carsharing, customers typically use a car one after the other, such that requests are serviced in a sequential manner. In ridesharing, several customers that demand transportation from/to similar locations might jointly use the same vehicle. In this context, [9] investigate how to identify suitable meeting points to which customers can walk over short distance from their actual origin location or desired destination location. They incorporate this feature into a DARP in order to reduce detouring of vehicles while offering attractive service routes to customers. In [29], the authors focus on the dial-a-ride problem in an urban road network with ride-sharing by autonomous taxis under consideration of traffic congestion. They propose a non-linear integer programming model embedded within a rolling horizon framework to optimize the routing of the taxis while maximizing the profit of the system. A mixed system is characterized by customers deciding whether to share the vehicle with other customers or use it on their own. The subdivision of SAVs described above also applies to SAEVs. Electric vehicles are more energy efficient and reduce CO_2 emissions compared to vehicles with internal combustion engines [14]. In the context of integrating electric vehicles into public transport, finding routes of minimal energy consumption, scheduling vehicle charging processes, and optimizing battery life have been identified as novel challenges [3]. Related issues for SAEVs are battery management and the provision of charging station infrastructure [30]. Aspects of electric vehicle battery management have been investigated in many studies on different vehicle routing problems. Examples include the electric and green vehicle routing problem, e.g. [11,19,41], the hybrid electric traveling salesman problem [1,12], and the vehicle routing problem with time windows and charging stations [2,22].

Also charging policies and charging functions have been investigated in detail for various routing problems. The charging policy determines the amount of battery capacity that can or must be restored at a charging station [35]. Established policies for the charging process include full charging [41], battery swapping [33], or partial charging [11,16]. Next to these charging policies, the assumption can be made that a charging process can be terminated prematurely when a new customer request arrives [4,30]. To deal with the large number of factors affecting the charging process, linear approximations of the charging function are often adopted in research [16,28,35]. Furthermore, the majority of approaches assume that the discharge of the battery occurs constantly over the travel time and that the corresponding discharge rate can be derived from an energy consumption model [17,19,39]. This assumption is typically valid if the vehicle load is negligible in comparison to the weight of the empty vehicle and if vehicles go at a quite constant speed [5,11,40]. Regarding the deployment of charging station infrastructure, different strategies exist, too. For example, [26] place charging stations at cab stands or other points of interest whereas [4] use an elimination strategy: charging stations are initially placed at all permissible locations and, then, those stations with the least impact on the system are eliminated in an iterative process. [31] proposes a two-stage solution approach, addressing the dynamic vehicle charging scheduling problem with the objective of minimizing the costs associated with daily charging operations for the fleet. The approach consists of two components: the scheduling of daily vehicle charging and the online assignment of vehicles to chargers. The above-mentioned elements of battery management are focused in [5] among others. The authors investigate the use of SAEVs in urban environments by modelling an e-ADARP and solving it through a branch-and-cut algorithm.

In our paper, we combine existing approaches from the literature. We investigate the e-ADARP-IT from the perspective of a mobility service provider, who uses autonomous e-vehicles for offering reservation-based ridesharing services in rural areas. We take up the modeling of battery management decisions of [5] and include it into the ADARP-IT of [27]. The ADARP-IT has been established to investigate SAV-services with interrelated trips in rural areas. Through the inclusion of aspects of electric vehicles management, we derive the e-ADARP-IT that closes the gap between these two directions of DARP-research.

In addition, the research conducted opens a potential link to existing publications in the area of demand-responsive transportation. While [10] investigate the benefits of meeting point usage for customer pick-up and drop-off, [23] evaluate the performance of a dial-a-ride service using simulation. With this, operators of transport systems can be provided with guidelines for designing their dial-a-ride services by identifying the parameters that significantly influence the evaluation criteria.

3 Modelling the E-ADARP-IT

In this section, we present the mathematical formulation for the e-ADARP-IT. Subsection 3.1 introduces the different types of customer requests that are to be considered. This is followed by introducing the used notation in Subsect. 3.2 and the presentation of the mixed-integer linear optimization model for the e-ADARP-IT in Subsect. 3.3.

3.1 Classification of Customer Requests

In DARPs, customers place requests for being transported from a specified starting point (pick-up location) to a specified destination point (drop-off location) [8]. In classical variants of the DARP, each customer is assumed to place one such request, without and interrelations among these requests existing, see [7]. We call such requests, *conventional requests.*

In our work, we also consider more complex trip request types, where two or more trips are interrelated with each other. Such complex customer requests were introduced by [27] and are distinguished into requests with serial relations and requests with parallel relations. *Serial relations* are characterized by an outbound and a return trip, combined with a stay time at the destination of the outbound trip. The drop-off location of the first trip and the pick-up location of the second trip are, thus, identical. Such trips play a role if a customer demands a guaranteed return trip, which is particularly relevant in urban area settings. The challenge in route planning is to schedule the drop-off of the first trip and the pick-up of the second trip such that the desired stay time is guaranteed. The second type of complex requests are those with *parallel relations*, which can be further subdivided into *parallel drop relations* and *parallel pick relations*. In this paper, only parallel drop relations are considered for reasons of brevity. A characteristic of such a parallel request is that two or more trips share the same drop-off location, for example as the involved customers want to meet there. The complexity of parallel drop requests results from the need to have customers arrive at the common drop-off location at approximately or exactly the same time. As is described by [27], these mentioned customer request types can be flexibly combined in a modular way, resulting in even more complex mobility request types.

Table 1. Notation

Sets	
$K = \{1, ..., m\}$	Set of vehicles
$O = \{o_1, ..., o_m\}$	Set of origin locations of vehicles
$R = \{1, ..., n\}$	Set of trips
$P = \{p_1, ..., p_n\}$	Set of pick-up locations
$D = \{d_1, ..., d_n\}$	Set of drop-off locations
$CS = \{cs_1, ..., cs_l\}$	Set of charging station locations
$V = O \cup P \cup D \cup CS$	Set of all locations
$S_i \subset R$	Set of trips that serially follow trip i
$G_i \subset R$	Set of trips with parallel drop-off relation with trip i
Parameters	
PC^k	Passenger capacity of vehicle $k \in K$
b_k	Energy storage capacity of vehicle $k's$ battery
o_k	Origin location of vehicle k
p_i	Pick-up location of trip $i \in R$
d_i	Drop-off location of trip i
q_i	Number of passengers boarding or disembarking at location $i \in V$
s_i	Service time for passenger boarding and disembarking at location i
e_i	Earliest starting time for the service at location i
l_i	Latest starting time for the service at location i
$\bar{u}_i$	Maximum travel time for trip i
$\delta_i^{min}, \delta_i^{max}$	Minimum / maximum stay time at drop-off location of serial related trip i
ω_i^{max}	Maximum waiting time for parallel related services of trip i
$t_{i,j}$	Vehicle travel time from location i to location j
$c_{i,j}$	Vehicle travel cost from location i to location j
$\beta_{i,j}$	Vehicle battery consumption for traveling from location i to j
α_{cs}	Charging rate at charging station $cs \in CS$ (in kWh per minute)
γ	Desired battery charging level
r	Objective weight for maximizing the number of fulfilled trips
Decision variables	
y_i	1 if trip $i \in R$ is served, 0 otherwise
$x_{i,j}^k$	1 if vehicle k drives directly from $i \in V$ to $j \in V$, 0 otherwise
z_i^k	1 if vehicle k ends its tour at location i, 0 otherwise
T_i^k	Arrival time of vehicle k at location i
L_i^k	Number of passengers on vehicle k after leaving location i
B_i^k	Battery charge level of vehicle k when arriving at location i
C_{cs}^k	Charging time of vehicle k at charging station cs

3.2 Notation

We use the following notation for modelling the e-ADARP-IT (see also summary in Table 1): The mobility service provider has a fleet of vehicles $K = \{1, ..., m\}$, where vehicle $k \in K$ has a passenger capacity PC^k, a battery capacity b_k, and starts its operations from the origin location o_k. These locations form set

$O = \{o_1, \ldots o_m\}$. Following the concept of a reservation-based service system, the relevant information about customer requests is known to the service provider at the time of the planning. More precisely, we denote by $R = \{1, ..., n\}$ a set of trip requests with corresponding pick-up location p_i and drop-off location d_i of trip $i \in R$. The pick-up and drop-off locations of all trips form sets $P = \{p_1, ..., p_n\}$ and $D = \{d_1, ..., d_n\}$, respectively. The set of available charging stations for the electric vehicles is denoted $CS = \{cs_1, ..., cs_l\}$. The set of all locations in a problem is denoted $V = O \cup P \cup D \cup CS$. Due to the ridesharing concept, a vehicle can serve different requests from multiple customers simultaneously. Each location $i \in V$ is thus characterized by a change in the number of customers q_i that occurs at this location. For pick-up locations p_i, q_{p_i} takes a positive value because customers are boarding. At drop-off locations d_i, customers leave the car which is reflected by a corresponding negative value $q_{d_i} = -q_{p_i}$. For all locations $i \in O \cup CS$, we set $q_i = 0$. In addition, service times s_i are incurred for customers boarding at pick-up location p_i and being dropped off at destination location d_i. Furthermore, we denote by e_i and s_i the earliest and latest time for starting service at a location i. Also, the overall travel time for a trip $i \in R$ is bounded to $\bar{u}_i$ time units in order to restrict the prolonged travel time that the customer might experience due to the detouring in the ridesharing system. For a serial-related outbound trip i, we state by $S_i \subset R$ the set of those trip(s) that have to follow on trip i subsequently. Furthermore, we denote by δ_i^{min} and δ_i^{max} the least and the maximum stay time of the customer at the drop-off location of trip i, respectively, before the subsequent trip(s) can be started. Finally, we denote by $G_i \subset R$ the set of those trips that have a parallel drop-off relation with trip i, i.e., that should arrive at the destination at similar time. For this, we denote by ω_i^{max} the maximum waiting time for the arrival of the customer(s) belonging to trip i and accordingly for the trips in G_i.

Each charging station $cs \in CS$ has a charging rate α_{cs}. This rate defines the electricity amount (in kWh per minute) that is taken up by a vehicle charging at cs. The charging time C_{cs}^k of vehicle k at station cs is a decision variable and determines the charged electricity quantity as $\alpha_{cs} \cdot C_{cs}^k$. Furthermore, we prescribe a target charging level γ that is not to be exceeded when charging a vehicle to proactively restrict long charging times if desired. Finally, $c_{i,j}, t_{i,j}$, and $\beta_{i,j}$ represent the travel cost, travel time, and battery consumption of a vehicle that goes directly from location i to location j. We assume that battery consumption $\beta_{i,j}$ depends linearly on the travel time $t_{i,j}$ and is not influenced by any further factors.

The decisions to be made are modeled through the following decision variables. The binary variable y_i equals 1 if request $i \in R$ is serviced, 0 otherwise. Variable x_{ij}^k equals 1 if vehicle $k \in K$ travels directly from location $i \in V$ to location $j \in V$, 0 otherwise. Variable z_i^k equals 1 if vehicle k ends its trip at location i, 0 otherwise. The continuous variable T_i^k expresses the arrival time of vehicle k at location i. The number of customers in vehicle k after leaving location i is expressed by variable L_i^k. While continuous variable B_i^k denotes the charge level of vehicle k's battery when arriving at location i, variable C^k_{cs} denotes the charging time of vehicle k at charging station $cs \in CS$.

3.3 Optimization Model for the E-ADARP-IT

The e-ADARP-IT is modeled through formulas (1) to (33). The objective function (1) primarily seeks to maximize the number of serviced requests, followed by the secondary objective of minimizing the operational service cost. Coefficient r serves as a weight in this combined objective function and ensures a hierarchy of the two goals if set to a sufficiently large value [27].

$$max\ Z = r\sum_{i \in R} y_i - \sum_{k \in K}\sum_{i \in V}\sum_{j \in V} x^k_{i,j} \cdot c_{i,j} \tag{1}$$

$$\sum_{j \in V} x^k_{o_k,j} = 1 \quad k \in K \tag{2}$$

$$\sum_{j \in V}\sum_{\substack{u \in K \\ u \neq k}} x^u_{o_k,j} = 0 \quad k \in K \tag{3}$$

$$\sum_{\substack{j \in V \\ j \neq i}} x^k_{j,i} - \sum_{\substack{j \in V \\ j \neq i}} x^k_{i,j} = 0 \quad k \in K, i \in P \tag{4}$$

$$\sum_{\substack{j \in V \\ j \neq i}} x^k_{j,i} - \sum_{\substack{j \in V \\ j \neq i}} x^k_{i,j} - z^k_i = 0 \quad k \in K, i \in D \cup CS \tag{5}$$

$$\sum_{i \in D \cup \{o_k\}} z^k_i = 1 \quad k \in K \tag{6}$$

$$\sum_{\substack{j \in V \\ j \neq p_i}} x^k_{p_i,j} - \sum_{\substack{j \in V \\ j \neq d_i}} x^k_{j,d_i} = 0 \quad k \in K, i \in R \tag{7}$$

$$\sum_{j \in V}\sum_{k \in K} x^k_{p_i,j} \geq y_i \quad i \in R \tag{8}$$

$$x^k_{i,i} = 0 \quad k \in K, i \in P \cup D \cup CS \tag{9}$$

$$T^k_j \geq T^k_i + s_i + t_{i,j} - M_{i,j}(1 - x^k_{i,j}) \quad k \in K, i, j \in V, i \neq j \tag{10}$$

$$T^k_{d_i} \geq T^k_{p_i} + s_{p_i} + t_{p_i,d_i} \quad k \in K, i \in R \tag{11}$$

$$e_i \leq T^k_i \leq l_i \quad k \in K, i \in V \tag{12}$$

$$\overline{u}_i \geq T^k_{d_i} - T^k_{p_i} - s_{p_i} \quad k \in K, i \in R \tag{13}$$

$$L^k_j \geq L^k_i + q_j - PC^k(1 - x^k_{i,j}) \quad k \in K, i, j \in V, i \neq j \tag{14}$$

$$L^k_j \leq L^k_i + q_j + PC^k(1 - x^k_{i,j}) \quad k \in K, i, j \in V, i \neq j \tag{15}$$

$$0 \leq L^k_i \leq PC^k \quad k \in K, i \in P \cup D \tag{16}$$

$$L^k_i = 0 \quad k \in K, i \in O \cup CS \tag{17}$$

$$y_i = y_j \quad i \in R, j \in S_i \cup G_i \tag{18}$$

$$T^u_{p_j} \geq T^k_{d_i} + \delta^{min}_i - M'_{d_i,p_j}(2 - \sum_{l \in V} x^k_{l,d_i} - \sum_{l \in V} x^u_{p_j,l}) \quad k,u \in K, i \in R, j \in S_i \quad (19)$$

$$T^u_{p_j} \leq T^k_{d_i} + \delta^{max}_i - M'_{d_i,p_j}(2 - \sum_{l \in V} x^k_{l,d_i} - \sum_{l \in V} x^u_{p_j,l}) \quad k,u \in K, i \in R, j \in S_i \quad (20)$$

$$T^u_{d_j} \leq T^k_{d_i} + \omega^{max}_i - M'_{d_i,d_j}(2 - \sum_{l \in V} x^k_{l,d_i} - \sum_{l \in V} x^u_{l,d_j}) \quad k,u \in K, i \in R, j \in G_i \quad (21)$$

$$0 \leq B^k_i \leq b_k \quad k \in K, i \in V \quad (22)$$

$$B^k_{o_k} = b_k \quad k \in K \quad (23)$$

$$B^k_j \leq B^k_i - \beta_{i,j} + b_k(1 - x^k_{i,j}) \quad k \in K, i \in V \backslash CS, j \in V \backslash \{o_k\}, i \neq j \quad (24)$$

$$B^k_j \geq B^k_i - \beta_{i,j} - b_k(1 - x^k_{i,j}) \quad k \in K, i \in V \backslash CS, j \in V \backslash \{o_k\}, i \neq j \quad (25)$$

$$B^k_j \leq B^k_{cs} + \alpha_{cs} \cdot C^k_{cs} - \beta_{cs,j} + b_k(1 - x^k_{cs,j}) \quad k \in K, j \in V, cs \in CS, j \neq cs \quad (26)$$

$$B^k_j \geq B^k_{cs} + \alpha_{cs} \cdot C^k_{cs} - \beta_{cs,j} - b_k(1 - x^k_{cs,j}) \quad k \in K, j \in V, cs \in CS, j \neq cs \quad (27)$$

$$C^k_{cs} \geq 0 \quad k \in K, cs \in CS \quad (28)$$

$$b_k \cdot \gamma \geq B^k_{cs} + \alpha_{cs} \cdot C^k_{cs} \quad k \in K, cs \in CS \quad (29)$$

$$T^k_i \leq T^k_{cs} + t_{cs,i} + C^k_{cs} + M^k_{cs,i}(1 - x^k_{cs,i}) \quad k \in K, cs \in CS, i \in D \cup P \cup CS \cup \{o_k\}, i \neq cs \quad (30)$$

$$T^k_i \geq T^k_{cs} + t_{cs,i} + C^k_{cs} - M^k_{cs,i}(1 - x^k_{cs,i}) \quad k \in K, cs \in CS, i \in D \cup P \cup CS \cup \{o_k\}, i \neq cs \quad (31)$$

$$x^k_{i,j}, z^k_i \in \{0,1\} \quad k \in K, i,j \in V \quad (32)$$

$$y_i \in \{0,1\} \quad i \in R \quad (33)$$

According to Constraints (2) and (3), each vehicle starts its tour at its own origin location o_k. Constraints (4) ensure the vehicle flow at pick-up locations. Constraints (5) define this for drop-off locations and charging stations. This constraint provides flexibility for the continuation of a route, as a vehicle k may continue its tour to some other location j ($x^k_{ij} = 1$) or end its tour at the current location i ($z^k_i = 1$). Constraints (6) then state that each vehicle route has a defined end location. This location can also be the origin location o_k if the vehicle did not move at all ($z^k_{o_k} = 1$). Constraints (7) ensure that both the pickup and the drop-off of a request are performed by one and the same vehicle. Constraints (8) ensure that a request is considered served, only if the pickup location has actually been visited by a vehicle. Constraints (9) avoid that this requirement is fulfilled via trivial sub-cycles.

Constraints (10) to (13) address the time components of the solution. Constraints (10) propagate the vehicle arrival time from one visited location to the next, where the value $M_{i,j}$ is set to $max(0, l_i + s_i + t_{ij} - e_i)$ as in [5]. Constraints (11) denote that a drop-off location d_i must be visited after the associated pick-up location p_i. Constraints (12) ensure the preset time windows for visiting the locations. With $i = o_k$ and a corresponding value for e_{o_k}, the time at which vehicle k becomes available for the service system can be considered in this constraint, too. The maximum travel duration of a trip is bounded by Constraints (13).

Capacity restrictions (14) and (15) derive the number of customers L_j^k onboard vehicle k after leaving a visited location j. Constraints (16) respect the vehicle capacity and Constraints (17) ensure that all vehicles are empty at their origin locations and while charging.

From Constraints (18), complex requests are always served completely or not at all, but never partially. More precisely, all interrelated trips $j \in S_i \cup G_i$ are served if trip i is served. Constraints (19) and (20) focus on serially related trips. They ensure the minimum and maximum customer stay times between drop-off and subsequent pick-up, where $M'_{d_i,p_j} = max(l_{d_i} + \delta_i^{min} - e_{p_j}, l_{p_j} - e_{d_i} - \delta_i^{max}, 0)$, see [27]. Note that the trips in a serial request can be served by different vehicles k and u ($k \neq u$). For example, vehicle k can drop off the customer at drop-off location d_i and another vehicle u can later collect the customer at pick-up location p_j for the subsequent trip. Constraints (21) focus on the second type of complex requests, the parallel related trips. The restriction synchronizes the arrival times of parallel related trips i and j at the drop-off locations, where $M'_{d_i,d_j} = max(l_{d_j} - e_{d_i} - w_i^{max}, 0)$. For this, trip $j \in G_i$ at the drop-off location $d_j = d_i$ must not occur later than w_i^{max} time units after trip i. By setting w_i^{max} and w_j^{max}, flexibility or strictness can be reflected for these trips. For example, if $w_i^{max} = w_j^{max} = 0$, the customers must arrive at the drop-off location at exactly the same time.

Constraints (22) to (31) are for battery management. According to Constraints (22), the battery level of a vehicle k must not be negative nor greater than the battery capacity b_k at any location i. Constraints (23) define that the battery of vehicle k is fully charged at the origin location o_k. The depletion of the battery level when going from some location i (which is not a charging station) to a subsequent location j is computed by Constraints (24) and (25). Constraints (26) and (27) calculate the battery status of a vehicle that just visited a charging station cs before going to a subsequent location j. These constraints take care of the charged quantity $\alpha_{cs} \cdot C_{cs}^k$. Charging times C_{cs}^k are non-negative according to Constraints (28). Additionally, through Constraint (29), charging of a vehicle can be restricted to not exceed a target level γ. This helps, for example, to proactively avoid increasing charging times when approaching the maximum battery level. Furthermore, the charging times of a vehicle at a station cs are included in the propagation of the arrival time at the subsequently visited location i through

Constraints (30) and (31), where $M^k_{i,s} = max(0, l_i + s_i + t_{i,s} - e_s)$. Eventually, Constraints (32) and (33) assure the binary character of variables $x^k_{i,j}$, z^k_i, and y_i.

The e-ADARP-IT model may be solved by any MIP-solver, provided that the instances are not too large. As an alternative solution approach, we have adopted the ADARP-IT VNS-heuristic of [27]. In general, VNS is a metaheuristic originally proposed by [21] that applies a systematic change of neighborhood structures within a local search scheme. In this paper, we take up the VNS of [27] and apply it to the e-ADARP-IT, by integrating battery management with the concept of a battery matrix derived from the matrix scheme proposed by [32]. This monitors chronologically the battery status of the vehicles and allows to include visits at charging stations suitably into the vehicle routes. The algorithm terminates after a predefined number of iterations without improvement of the current solution or after a prescribed number of fixed runs, whichever occurs first.

4 Computational Experiments

Section 4.1 describes the used test instances. Section 4.2 emphasizes a comparison of the solution approaches being available as well as the effects of battery capacity and charging station infrastructure on the solution quality.

4.1 Description of Test Instances

We use test instances from [27] for our computational experiments. These instances have been generated for the ADARP-IT and are supplemented here by data for an electric mobility system to use them for the e-ADARP-IT. The instances cover a rural area in the federal state of Schleswig-Holstein, Germany. In more detail, this rural area is located near the cities of Husum, Rendsburg, and Heide with the characteristic river Eider. This area is of a size of 45 × 25 km (approximately 1,125 km^2) and has an average population of 85 inhabitants per km^2 [37]. The map material of the test instances has been created with the help of OpenStreetMap [18]. Figure 1 presents a map of the studied region, where the areas in light gray indicate the low population density and its spread over the whole region.

The pick-up and drop-off locations of the test instances are derived from the distribution of households. Customer requests are, thus, based on population density. Travel times $t_{i,j}$ are calculated by the Open Source Routing Machine [38] for the fastest route between the involved locations. The test instances contain conventional and complex customer requests. For each conventional customer request, a conventional trip with a randomly selected drop-off time within the planning period is created. The associated time window $[e_{d_i}, l_{d_i}]$ is 15 min. For trips with parallel relations, it is assumed that each customer request consists of two trips from two customers. The customers will be picked up at their individual residences and dropped off at the same drop-off location. The customers'

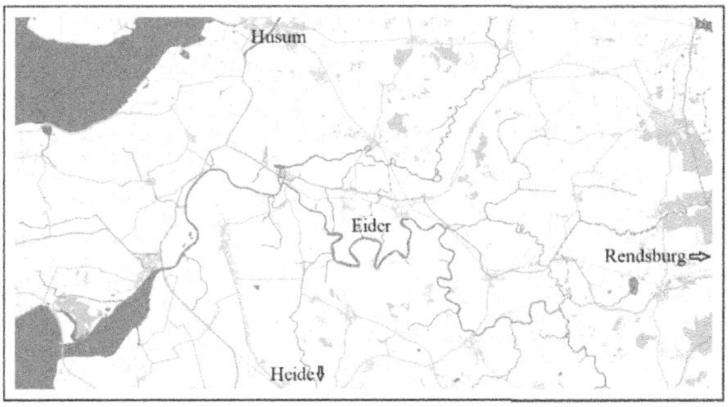

Fig. 1. Area under study.

maximum waiting time w_i^{max} for each other is randomly selected from the time interval U [1, 10] minutes. For trips with serial relations, it is assumed that each customer request consists of two trips, one outbound and one return trip, where the drop-off location of the outbound trip is identical to the pick-up location of the return trip. The trips are associated with a stay time at the destination. The least stay time δ_i^{min} is drawn from the distribution U [20, 60]. The maximum stay time δ_i^{max} is by 10 min greater than δ_i^{min}. The maximum travel time $\overline{u}_i$ for each trip i is 150% of the direct travel time. The examined planning period of each test instance comprises 12 h. It is assumed that customer requests are evenly distributed over the planning horizon.

We assume a homogeneous vehicle fleet. Each vehicle has a capacity of $\mathrm{PC}^k =$ 6 passengers, which is in line with ridesharing provider MOIA [42]. The vehicles' origin locations are randomly selected from the set of relevant locations within the considered area. The number of customers boarding or alighting at a location is $q_i = 1/\text{-}1$ for all requests. Customers can be picked up and dropped off within negligible time ($s_i = 0$). Each vehicle has a battery capacity of $b_k = 40$ kWh and is fully charged at the beginning of the planning horizon. The vehicles constantly consume 0.206 kWh per kilometer driven. All vehicles generate a travel cost of 0.1 monetary units per kilometer. The objective function primarily maximizes the number of served trips and secondarily minimizes the total cost. To ensure this, we set an objective weight of $r = 50$. Note that complex requests are only accepted if all involved trips can be served.

All charging stations support fast charging, meaning that a vehicle can be charged up to 80% within 40 min. This percentage value is also used for the target charge level γ in Constraint (29). During the charging process, the vehicles are supplied with a charging quantity of $\alpha_{cs} = 0.8$ kWh per minute at all stations.

The locations of the charging stations are determined using a grid heuristic [34]. Figure 2 illustrates the distribution of charging stations in the studied area for a total of 8 stations.

Using the above configurations, we employ eight sets of test instances for our experiment, each involving four individual instances. Table 2 provides an overview of these instance sets, illustrating that the number of trips per instance ranges

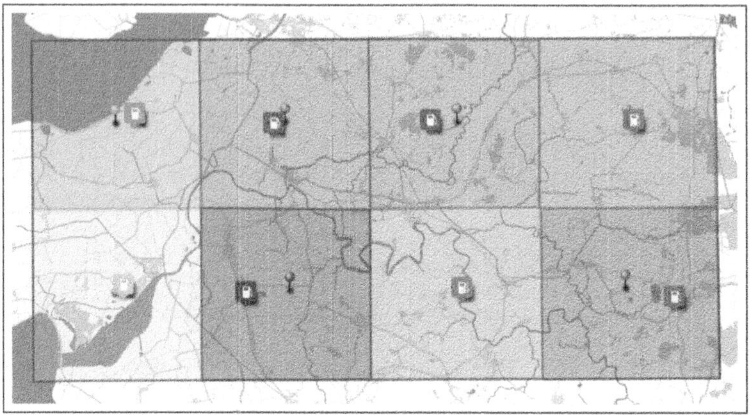

Fig. 2. Distribution of charging stations in the studied area.

from 10 to 50, with 2 to 5 vehicles, and 4 to 16 charging stations. The requests are a mix of conventional and complex requests. The abbreviations 'CLE' and 'MOI' that are added to the name of the last four instance sets refer to two mobility service providers operating in Germany, from which particular battery capacity values of vehicles have been taken as is described in the next subsection.

The VNS heuristic has been implemented in Python 3.7 and all computational experiments were performed on a computer with a 3.2 GHz CPU and 32 GB memory. For the exact solution of the optimization model, the MIP solver CPLEX 12.9 was applied with a maximum runtime per test instance of ten hours (36,000 s).

4.2 Influence of Battery Capacity and Charging Infrastructure on Solution Quality

The experiments first contrast the performance of VNS and CPLEX and afterwards address the impact of the number of charging stations as well as the

Table 2. Composition of the test instances.

Instance set	Trips	Vehicles	Charging stations
MIX10V2CS4	10	2	4
MIX25V5CS8	25	5	8
MIX40V5CS12	40	5	12
MIX50V5CS12	50	5	12
MIX50V5CS12CLE	50	5	12
MIX50V5CS16CLE	50	5	16
MIX50V5CS4MOI	50	5	4
MIX50V5CS8MOI	50	5	8

capacity of vehicle batteries. We first evaluate the performance of VNS and CPLEX for the first four instance sets with 10 to 50 trips, see Table 3. The results reported in a row are the averages over the four instances belonging to each set. The first column of the table identifies the instance set. Columns 2 to 6 report the results of the CPLEX solver and columns 7 to 11 the results of the VNS heuristic. Here, the abbreviation *Acc* denotes the percentage of accepted trips, i.e., those trips that are actually served in a solution, which refers to the primary goal of the objective function. The secondary objective, total transportation cost, is shown in column *Co*. *UB* represents the theoretic upper bound of the overall objective function value as determined by CPLEX. Performance measure $GAP = (obj - UB)/obj$ is the relative deviation of the actual objective function value *obj* of a solution to the upper bound. Value *obj* is not shown explicitly in the table but can be computed from the number of accepted requests and the objective weight $r = 50$ minus the operational cost. The calculation time is shown in column *CPU* in units of thousand seconds (k sec.). Columns 7, 8, and 11 (*Acc*, *Co*, *CPU*) of the VNS are analogous in meaning to the CPLEX columns. Furthermore, ΔAcc maps the difference in accepted trips *Acc* between the VNS solution and the CPLEX solution. In order to take into account the different acceptance rates $\Delta\overline{Co}$ represents the relative change in cost *per served trip* between CPLEX and VNS. Note that the *CPU* time of the VNS heuristic is composed of the total time of three runs with different initial solutions, which is why it may exceed the computation time limit set for CPLEX in rare cases.

Table 3. Results of the computational experiments for varied instance size.

Instance set	Solver					VNS				
	Acc [%]	*Co*	*UB*	*GAP* [%]	*CPU* [k sec.]	*Acc* [%]	*Co*	ΔAcc [%]	$\Delta\overline{Co}$ [%]	*CPU* [k sec.]
MIX10V2CS4	90.0	29.0	461	11.4	18	90.0	29.3	0.0	+1.7	0.14
MIX25V5CS8	96.0	71.8	1,221	8.4	36	99.0	70.7	+3.0	–4.8	1.1
MIX40V5CS12	53.0	88.6	1,963	105.8	36	72.5	89.5	+19.5	–22.2	6.5
MIX50V5CS12	37.0	80.8	2,462	203.3	36	84.0	132.0	+47.0	–27.3	22.5

The *GAP*s in Table 3 show that the CPLEX solver is hardly able to find optimal solutions. Actually, it only solves two out of the instances with 10 requests and one with 25 requests to optimality. Furthermore, even for the integer feasible solutions obtained for the other instances, the acceptance rate drops significantly the larger these instances are. The VNS algorithm produces comparable results for the very small instances but within negligible computation time. For the instances with 25 and more requests, it clearly outperforms CPLEX with much larger acceptance rates that increase by up to 47% points. At the same time, the operational costs per served trip are much lower (see column $\Delta\overline{Co}$), indicating that VNS not just manages to serve many more requests than CPLEX but also in a way more efficient fashion and within lower *CPU* times. Based on the VNS results, SAEVs can serve a large portion of the diverse mobility demands in rural areas, with an average acceptance rate of 86% over all considered test instances.

We next address the question of whether SAEV providers should prioritize a high-density charging infrastructure or vehicles with large battery capacities. Two strategies are developed for investigating this. The first strategy uses vehicles with a battery capacity of 40 kWh and a larger number of charging stations (12 and 16). The battery capacity is derived from the vehicles used by the ride-pooling provider CleverShuttle, which is why the test instances are marked with the abbreviation 'CLE' (MIX50V5CS12CLE and MIX50V5CS16CLE) [6]. For the setting with 12 charging stations, these instances are identical to the ones reported in the last row of Table 3. In contrast, the second strategy uses vehicles with a larger battery capacity of 86 kWh and fewer charging stations (4 and 8). The battery capacity is similar to those of vehicles used by ridesharing provider MOIA [42]. The corresponding test instances are, thus, identified by abbreviation 'MOI' (MIX50V5CS4MOI and MIX50V5CS8MOI).

Table 4 reveals the effects of battery capacity and charging infrastructure on solution quality. The CPLEX solver cannot reach optimality within the given runtime for any solution of these test instances. Its results all have low to moderate acceptance rates and very high *GAP*s. Best results with an acceptance rate of 59.0% and the only *GAP* below 100% are obtained for test instances MIX50V5CS4MOI, clearly indicating that the larger the number of charging stations gets, the more CPLEX struggles. If we consider the test instances in ascending order of the number of charging stations, the negative impact of this number on the performance of CPLEX becomes very clear. The average acceptance rate of 59.0% for MIX50V5CS4MOI strictly decreases to 47.5% (MIX50V5CS8MOI) to 37.0% (MIX50V5CS12CLE) and to 20.5% (MIX50V5CS16CLE). At the same time, the *GAP*s increase strictly from 85.9% up to 604.5%.

In contrast, the acceptance rates of the VNS solutions are above 80% for all test instances, even reaching 98% for instance set MIX50V5CS4MOI. At the same time, the cost per served trip is up to 42.8% below the cost of the CPLEX solutions, confirming the superior performance of VNS under all experimental settings investigated here. However, VNS also exhibits high computation times, especially for the CLE-instances with many charging stations. Based on the results of the VNS, it can be seen that the test instances of the vehicles with a

Table 4. Results of the computational experiments for varied charging infrastructure and battery capacities.

Instance set	Solver					VNS				
	Acc [%]	*Co*	*UB*	*GAP* [%]	*CPU* [k sec.]	*Acc* [%]	*Co*	ΔAcc [%]	$\Delta \overline{Co}$ [%]	*CPU* [k sec.]
MIX50V5CS12CLE	37.0	80.8	2,462	203.3	36	84.0	132.0	+47.0	-27.3	22.5
MIX50V5CS16CLE	20.5	49.9	2,466	604.5	36	83.0	118.7	+62.5	-42.8	60.2
MIX50V5CS4MOI	59.0	110.4	2,461	85.9	36	98.0	155.3	+39.0	-14.9	4.4
MIX50V5CS8MOI	47.5	83.8	2,461	126.5	36	97.5	145.9	+50.0	-11.9	3.3

higher battery capacity (MOI) provide results with better solution quality compared to the CLE-instances. The average acceptance rate of the MOI-instances is about 15% higher than for the CLE-instances. For the CLE-instances with the lower battery capacities, more charging processes (about 40) take place in the solutions (not shown in the table). For the MOI-instances MIX50V5CS4MOI and MIX50V5CS8MOI, just eight and two charging processes are required, respectively. Furthermore, for both strategies the number of charging processes decreases as the number of charging stations increases. From this, the average cost per trip served decreases for both strategies as the number of charging stations increases, which reveals the relevance of dense charging infrastructure.

In summary, it can be stated that the number of charging stations has no substantial impact on the acceptance rate but on the cost per served trip. The battery capacity, on the other hand, has a clear positive influence on the acceptance rate and, thus, a significant impact on the quality of the solutions. This finding is consistent with [30], who identified battery range as a critical component of SAEV service systems. Hence, based on the computational experiments, a strategy focusing on large battery capacity seems more advantageous with regards to the service rate of mobility requests, whereas additional charging stations can help reducing the operational cost of the system.

5 Conclusions

This paper has presented the electric autonomous dial-a-ride problem with interrelated trips (e-ADARP-IT). The associated mixed integer linear optimization model includes, in addition to the properties of the classical dial-a-ride problem, synchronization constraints on the interrelated trips and constraints on the battery charging management of electric, autonomous vehicles. A variable neighborhood search (VNS) algorithm has been applied for the efficient solution of larger instances of the e-ADARP-IT. For the computational experiments, test data from a rural area in the German federal state of Schleswig-Holstein was used. The results show that small test instances with ten requests can to some extent be solved optimally using CPLEX. With increasing problem size, the solution quality obtained by CPLEX decreases drastically, such that the share of served trips drops to 37% for instances with 50 requests. The limitations of the performance of CPLEX increase with a larger number of charging stations. In contrast, the VNS heuristic performs consistently good over all instance sets. It finds solutions that efficiently serve up to 99% of the trip requests at low operational cost. The experiments furthermore show that the battery capacity of vehicles is a crucial issue in SAEV service systems. Larger batteries allow to serve a much higher share of trip requests. Clearly, sufficient charging infrastructure needs to be available, too. Nevertheless, increasing the number of charging stations beyond that point merely reduced the operational service cost in our experiments but did not result in larger acceptance rates for the trip requests.

Altogether, this paper contributes to identifying the potential of electric autonomous vehicles for closing mobility gaps in rural areas. It also opens up opportunities for further research. The VNS has proven to be suitable for solving the e-ADARP-IT but it might be too slow for usage in large service systems. There are also further aspects at the operational level that require more research. As an example, if charging stations are occupied by other vehicles, it needs to be decided whether the SAEVs accept a waiting time or are rerouted to another charging station. A further area of future research could be to combine the ride sharing approach with public transport services. Here, an integration of school transport would be possible as well as an offer as feeder for rail commuter lines.

Acknowledgements. The authors gratefully acknowledge the financial support of this project through the German Research Foundation (DFG) under the reference number 418360126.

References

1. Arslan, O., Yildiz, B., Karaşan, O.E.: Minimum cost path problem for plug-in hybrid electric vehicles. Transp. Res. Part E Logist. Transp. Rev. **80**(1), 123–141 (2015)
2. Baldacci, R., Battarra, M., Vigo, D.: Valid inequalities for the fleet size and mix vehicle routing problem with fixed costs. Netw. Int. J. **54**(4), 178–189 (2009)
3. Barco, J., Guerra, A., Muñoz, L., Quijano, N.: Optimal routing and scheduling of charge for electric vehicles: a case study. Math. Probl. Eng. **2017**, 1–6 (2017)
4. Bauer, G.S., Greenblatt, J.B., Gerke, B.F.: Cost, energy, and environmental impact of automated electric taxi fleets in Manhattan. Environ. Sci. Technol. **52**(8), 4920–4928 (2018)
5. Bongiovanni, C., Kaspi, M., Geroliminis, N.: The electric autonomous dial-a-ride problem. Transp. Res. Part B Methodol. **122**, 436–456 (2019)
6. Clevershuttle: CleverShuttle fährt in Dresden On-Demand mit MOBIshuttle. https://www.clevershuttle.de/presse/clevershuttle-dresden-mobishuttle. Accessed 04 Apr 2023
7. Cordeau, J.F.: A branch-and-cut algorithm for the dial-a-ride problem. Oper. Res. **54**(3), 573–586 (2006)
8. Cordeau, J.F., Laporte, G.: The dial-a-ride problem (DARP): variants, modeling issues and algorithms. 4OR - Q. J. Belg. Fr. Ital. Oper. Res. Soc. **1**(2), 89–101 (2003)
9. Cortenbach, E.: The dial-a-ride problem with meeting points: a problem formulation for shared demand responsive transit. Master's thesis, University of Twente (2023). http://essay.utwente.nl/94545/. Accessed 25 June 2023
10. Czioska, P., Kutadinata, R., Trifunović, A., Winter, S., Sester, M., Friedrich, B.: Real-world meeting points for shared demand-responsive transportation systems. Public Transp. **11**, 341–377 (2019)
11. Desaulniers, G., Errico, F., Irnich, S., Schneider, M.: Exact algorithms for electric vehicle-routing problems with time windows. Oper. Res. **64**(6), 1388–1405 (2016)
12. Doppstadt, C., Koberstein, A., Vigo, D.: The hybrid electric vehicle - traveling salesman problem. Eur. J. Oper. Res. **253**(3), 825–842 (2016)
13. Earl, T.: Roadmap to decarbonising european cars (2018). https://www.transportenvironment.org/sites/te/files/publications/2050_strategy_cars_FINAL.pdf. Accessed 27 Mar 2023

14. Emadi, A.: Transportation 2.0. IEEE Power Energy Mag. **9**(4), 18–29 (2011)
15. Fagnant, D.J., Kockelman, K.M.: Dynamic ride-sharing and fleet sizing for a system of shared autonomous vehicles in Austin, Texas. Transportation **45**(1), 143–158 (2018)
16. Ángel Felipe, Ortuño, M.T., Righini, G., Tirado, G.: A heuristic approach for the green vehicle routing problem with multiple technologies and partial recharges. Transp. Res. Part E Logist. Transp. Rev. **71**, 111–128 (2014)
17. Genikomsakis, K., Mitrentsis, G.: A computationally efficient simulation model for estimating energy consumption of electric vehicles in the context of route planning applications. Transp. Res. Part D Transp. Environ. **50**, 98–118 (2017)
18. Geofabrik GmbH: Openstreetmap data extracts. https://download.geofabrik.de/. Accessed 04 Apr 2023
19. Goeke, D., Schneider, M.: Routing a mixed fleet of electric and conventional vehicles. Eur. J. Oper. Res. **245**(1), 81–99 (2015)
20. Greenblatt, J.B., Shaleen, S.: Automated vehicles, on-demand mobility, and environmental impacts. Current Sustain. Renew. Energy Rep. **2**(3), 74–81 (2015)
21. Hansen, P., Mladenović, N.: Variable neighborhood search. In: Glover, F., Kochenberger, G.A. (eds.) Handbook of Metaheuristics, pp. 145–184. Springer, US, Boston, MA (2003). https://doi.org/10.1007/0-306-48056-5_6
22. Hiermann, G., Puchinger, J., Ropke, S., Hartl, R.F.: The electric fleet size and mix vehicle routing problem with time windows and recharging stations. Eur. J. Oper. Res. **252**(3), 995–1018 (2016)
23. Häll, C.H., Lundgren, J.T., Voß, S.: Evaluating the performance of a dial-a-ride service using simulation. Public Transp. **7**, 139–157 (2015)
24. Hyland, M.F., Mahmassani, H.S.: Taxonomy of shared autonomous vehicle fleet management problems to inform future transportation mobility. Transp. Res. Rec. J. Transp. Res. Board **2653**(1), 26–34 (2017)
25. Hyland, M.F., Mahmassani, H.S.: Dynamic autonomous vehicle fleet operations: optimization-based strategies to assign AVs to immediate traveler demand requests. Transp. Res. Part C Emerg. Technol. **92**, 278–297 (2018)
26. Jäger, B., Agua, F.M.M., Lienkamp, M.: Agent-based simulation of a shared, autonomous and electric on-demand mobility solution. In: 2017 IEEE 20th International Conference on Intelligent Transportation Systems (ITSC), pp. 250–255 (2017)
27. Johnsen, L.C., Meisel, F.: Interrelated trips in the rural dial-a-ride problem with autonomous vehicles. Eur. J. Oper. Res. **303**(1), 201–219 (2022)
28. Keskin, M., Çatay, B.: Partial recharge strategies for the electric vehicle routing problem with time windows. Transp. Res. Part C Emerg. Technol. **65**, 111–127 (2016)
29. Liang, X., de Almeida Correia, G.H., An, K., van Arem, B.: Automated taxis' dial-a-ride problem with ride-sharing considering congestion-based dynamic travel times. Transp. Res. Part C Emerg. Technol. **112**, 260–281 (2020)
30. Loeb, B., Kockelman, K.M., Liu, L.: Shared autonomous electric vehicle (SAEV) operations across the Austin, Texas network with charging infrastructure decisions. Transp. Res. Part C Emerg. Technol. **89**(4), 222–233 (2018)
31. Ma, T.Y.: Two-stage battery recharge scheduling and vehicle-charger assignment policy for dynamic electric dial-a-ride services. PLoS ONE **16**(5), 1–27 (2021)
32. Mankowska, D.S., Meisel, F., Bierwirth, C.: The home health care routing and scheduling problem with interdependent services. Health Care Manag. Sci. **17**(1), 15–30 (2014)

33. Masmoudi, M.A., Hosny, M., Demir, E., Genikomsakis, K.N., Cheikhrouhou, N.: The dial-a-ride problem with electric vehicles and battery swapping stations. Transp. Res. Part E Logist. Transp. Rev. **118**, 392–420 (2018)
34. Mattfeld, D.C., Vahrenkamp, R.: Logistiknetzwerke: Modelle für Standortwahl und Tourenplanung, 2nd edn. Springer Gabler, Wiesbaden (2014). https://doi.org/10.1007/978-3-8349-6912-5
35. Montoya, A., Guéret, C., Mendoza, J.E., Villegas, J.G.: The electric vehicle routing problem with nonlinear charging functions. Transp. Res. Part B Methodol. **103**, 87–110 (2017)
36. Narayanan, S., Chaniotakis, E., Antoniou, C.: Shared autonomous vehicle services: a comprehensive review. Transp. Res. Part C Emerg. Technol. **111**, 255–293 (2020)
37. Nord, S.: Kreise und Städte in Schleswig-Holstein im Vergleich: Bevölkerung 2018 (2019). https://www.statistik-nord.de/fileadmin/Dokumente/NORD.regional/Schleswig-Holstein.regional/Band_1_-_Bevoelkerung/SH_regional_Band_1_2018.pdf. Accessed 04 Apr 2023
38. Open Source Routing Machine: OSRM (2020). https://project-osrm.org/. Accessed 04 Apr 2023
39. Pelletier, S., Jabali, O., Laporte, G.: Charge sheduling for electric freight vehicles. Transp. Res. Part B Methodol. **115**, 246–269 (2018)
40. Pelletier, S., Jabali, O., Laporte, G., Veneroni, M.: Battery degradation and behavour for electric vehicles: review and numerical analyses of several models. Transp. Res. Part B Methodol. **103**, 158–187 (2017)
41. Schneider, M., Stenger, A., Goeke, D.: The electric vehicle-routing problem with time windows and recharging stations. Transp. Sci. **48**(4), 500–520 (2014)
42. Schwarzer, C.M.: Volkswagen-Ridesharing: Moin, MOIA! MOIA startet im April den größten elektrischen Ridesharing-Dienst Europas (2019). https://www.electrive.net/2019/03/14/volkswagen-ridesharing-moin-moia/. Accessed 04 Apr 2023
43. Shaheen, S., Chan, N.: Mobility and the sharing economy: potential to facilitate the first- and last-mile public transit connections. Built Environ. **42**(4), 573–588 (2016)
44. Sprei, F.: Disrupting mobility. Energy Res. Soc. Sci. **37**, 238–242 (2018)

Combinatorial Optimization

Operational Integration of Supply Chain Activities with Earliness and Tardiness Considerations

Ece Yağmur(✉) and Saadettin Erhan Kesen

Konya Technical University, Konya, Turkey
{ecyagmur,sekesen}@ktun.edu.tr

Abstract. The operational integration of the production and distribution activities in a supply chain requires concurrent consideration of two major problems known as production scheduling and vehicle routing. While the production environment of the integrated problem under study consists of identical parallel machines, the distribution environment has a limited number of homogeneous vehicles that deliver completed orders to customers. The objective function is to minimize the sum of total earliness and tardiness according to the time windows specified by each customer. In this paper, we first describe the integrated problem as a Mixed Integer Programming (MIP) model and subsequently present an Iterated Local Search (ILS) algorithm to find optimal or near-optimal solutions in a reasonable time. The performance of the ILS is evaluated against the MIP-based solutions obtained by applying a standard solver like CPLEX. According to the computational findings, the suggested ILS can find optimal or near optimal solutions for randomly generated test instances in just a few seconds.

Keywords: parallel machine scheduling · vehicle routing · iterated local search · earliness · tardiness

1 Introduction

Today, the management of supply chain operations is a trending topic for many businesses where competition is of utmost importance. Thus, it is inevitable to provide effective coordination between the production and distribution phases of the supply chain. Fulfilling customer demands with the required quantity on time becomes an extremely difficult task, especially for companies which apply the zero-inventory model and make-to-order businesses. The integrated approach is also beneficial for time management of time-sensitive or perishable products. Considering all these aspects, operational integration for the two main stages is carried out by making decisions simultaneously for production scheduling and vehicle routing. According to the integrated approach, as the output of either does not affect the other, the decisions on production and distribution stages will not limit each other.

Recently, there has been a remarkable growth in the online shopping sector [2]. Due to the abundance of competitors in the market and the ease of communication between

© The Author(s), under exclusive license to Springer Nature Switzerland AG 2023
J. R. Daduna et al. (Eds.): ICCL 2023, LNCS 14239, pp. 437–449, 2023.
https://doi.org/10.1007/978-3-031-43612-3_27

customers and companies, firms are under increasing pressure to ensure customer satisfaction. For this reason, they have turned to customer-oriented performance measures rather than classical measures such as cost and profit. According to the current applications, customers know when they can receive the orders and even specify their own preferences regarding delivery time, which is often handled by time windows in the vehicle routing literature.

A current survey, which covers the enlarged literature on integrated production scheduling and outbound vehicle routing problems, can be found in [4]. In the survey, the literature is classified in terms of the number of operations, the number of vehicles, and the number of trips. According to this classification, the problem under study can be represented in a section of parallel machines, several vehicles, and single trips, as in the studies of [3, 5, 6, 11, 12, 18].

Although there are several criteria (i.e., objectives) identified by researchers, in general, objectives can be divided into two main groups: cost and service. In addition, sometimes multiple criteria can be handled simultaneously as a summation of objectives in a single form [5, 9, 21, 22] or multi-objective structure [7, 14, 23]. While many criteria that are related to the problem under study have been defined in the literature [4], the objective of this study can be expressed as minimizing the sum of total earliness and tardiness. Ullrich [18] considers a variant of the integrated problem with the objective of minimizing the total tardiness and proposes a genetic algorithm to produce optimal or near optimal solutions in a reasonable amount of time. Wu et al. [20] formulate a mathematical model for a production scheduling-based routing problem with time windows and setup times for minimizing total tardiness. Hou et al. [10] address an integrated problem where the production stage has multiple factories, and each factory has multiple machines based on the flow shop environment. For the objective of minimizing total weighted earliness and tardiness, they propose a swarm intelligence approach which is called brainstorm optimization algorithm.

In the integrated problem under investigation, the distribution phase has a homogeneous fleet that can only be utilized once, while the production environment consists of identical parallel machines and each job has a single operation that needs to be performed on any machines. It is very important for customer satisfaction to deliver orders according to the predefined time windows. In addition, vehicles that arrive earlier must wait idle until the lower time bound of any customer. So, the objective is to minimize the sum of total earliness and tardiness. After formulating the problem, we propose a metaheuristic approach, Iterated Local Search (ILS), to obtain good quality solutions in a reasonable time.

The contribution of the paper can be summarized as follows: (*i*) The sum of the total earliness and tardiness is studied simultaneously for the first time for the integrated problem at hand. (*ii*) A new mixed integer programming formulation is developed. (*iii*) A metaheuristic algorithm, Iterated Local Search (ILS), is presented, and a perturbation mechanism is proposed for the only production environment adapted for the integrated problem.

The remainder of the study is organized as follows: In Sect. 2, we define the MIP formulation for the integrated problem with an illustrative example. While in Sect. 3, the proposed ILS structure is given, in Sect. 4, computational experiments are discussed based on the different problem parameters. Finally, in Sect. 5, conclusions and future directions are discussed.

2 Problem Definition

This section is dedicated to two subsections including the MIP model and an illustrative example for visual presentation.

2.1 MIP Model

The assumptions of the problem can be summarized as follows: There is a single production facility in which a set of identical parallel machines is used to produce customer orders. After the production of a particular batch is completed, a limited number of vehicles is delivering the consolidated orders to associated customers by considering the time window of each customer. Vehicles can be used only once (i.e., multiple use is not allowed). Vehicle capacities are homogeneous, and the capacity of a vehicle is enough to serve all customers. As a result, there is no requirement to use all vehicles in the system. The sequence of production and distribution does not have to be identical. The objective is to minimize the sum of total earliness and tardiness penalties. The notations used in the MIP formulation are shown in Table 1.

Based on the formal definition and notations, we formulate an MIP model for the problem as follows:

$$minimize \sum_{j \in N_C} (E_j + T_j) \tag{1}$$

Subject to;

$$\sum_{j \in N_C} W_{jm} \leq 1 \qquad \forall m \in M \tag{2}$$

$$\sum_{i \in N_C} Z_{ji} + L_j = 1 \qquad \forall j \in N_C \tag{3}$$

$$\sum_{m \in M} W_{jm} + \sum_{i \in N_C} Z_{ij} = 1 \qquad \forall j \in N_C \tag{4}$$

$$C_j \geq p_j - H(1 - W_{jm}) \qquad \forall j \in N_C; m \in M \tag{5}$$

$$C_j \leq p_j + H(1 - W_{jm}) \qquad \forall j \in N_C; m \in M \tag{6}$$

$$C_i - C_j + HZ_{ij} + (H - p_i - p_j)Z_{ji} \leq H - p_j \qquad \forall i, j \in N_C; i \neq j \tag{7}$$

$$\sum_{j \in N_C} X_{0jk} \leq 1 \qquad \forall k \in K \tag{8}$$

Table 1. Notations used in the MIP model.

Notation	Definition
Indices:	
i, j, u	: Job (order, customer)
m	: Machine
k	: Vehicle
Sets:	
N_C	: Set of jobs (orders, customers)
N	: Set of nodes (including depot node)
M	: Set of machines
K	: Set of vehicles
Parameters:	
d_j	: Demand of customer j
p_j	: Processing time of order j
s_j	: Service time at customer j
t_{ij}	: Travel time between customers i and j
Q	: Capacity of any vehicle
H	: Sufficiently large number
a_j	: Lower bound of time windows for customer j
b_j	: Upper bound of time windows for customer j
Variables:	
Z_{ij}	: 1 if job i is processed just before job j, 0 otherwise.
X_{ijk}	: 1 if vehicle k goes directly from node i to node j, 0 otherwise.
W_{jm}	: 1 if job j is the first to be processed on machine m, 0 otherwise.
L_j	: 1 if job j is the last to be processed on any machine, 0 otherwise.
F_{ij}	: Total amount of load when a vehicle goes directly from node i to node j.
C_j	: Production completion time of order j.
V_k	: Service starting time of vehicle k from the depot.
Y_j	: Arrival time at customer j.
Y_j^*	: Service starting time at customer j.
E_j	: Earliness for customer j.
T_j	: Tardiness for customer j.
G_{ij}	: 1 if job i is processed before job j, 0 otherwise.
O_j	: 1 if earliness occurs for job j, 0 otherwise.
R_{jk}	: 1 if job j is served by the vehicle k, 0 otherwise.
$AX1_{ijk}$	$= R_{ik}R_{jk}$
$AX2_{ij}$	$= G_{ij}\sum_{k \in V} AX1_{ijk}$
$AX3_{ijk}$	$= R_{ik}AX2_{ij}$
$AX4_j$	$= Y_jO_j$

$$\sum_{k \in K}\sum_{i \in N} X_{ijk} = 1 \qquad \forall j \in N_C \tag{9}$$

$$\sum_{u \in N} X_{ujk} = \sum_{i \in N} X_{jik} \quad \forall j \in N; \forall k \in K \tag{10}$$

$$\sum_{u \in N} F_{uj} - \sum_{i \in N} F_{ji} = d_j \quad \forall j \in N_C \tag{11}$$

$$d_j \sum_{k \in K} X_{ijk} \le F_{ij} \quad \forall i, j \in N; i \ne j \tag{12}$$

$$Q - d_i + \sum_{k \in K} X_{ijk} \ge F_{ij} \quad \forall i, j \in N; i \ne j \tag{13}$$

$$R_{jk} = \left(\sum_{i \in N_C} X_{jik} \right) + X_{j0k} \quad \forall j \in N_C; \forall k \in K \tag{14}$$

$$C_i - C_j \le H\left(1 - G_{ij}\right) \quad \forall i, j \in N_C; i \ne j \tag{15}$$

$$C_j - C_i \le HG_{ij} \quad \forall i, j \in N_C; i \ne j \tag{16}$$

$$V_k \ge C_i - H\left(1 - X_{ijk}\right) \quad \forall i, j \in N; i \ne j; \forall k \in K \tag{17}$$

$$\begin{aligned} V_k \le C_j + H(1 - (R_{jk} - \textstyle\sum_{i \in N_C} AX3_{jik} \ \forall j \in N_C; \forall k \in K \\ + \textstyle\sum_{i \in N_C} (G_{ij} + G_{ji} - 1))) \end{aligned} \tag{18}$$

$$V_k - Y_j + s_0 + t_{0j} \le H\left(1 - X_{0jk}\right) \quad \forall j \in N_C; \forall k \in K \tag{19}$$

$$Y_j - V_k - s_0 - t_{0j} \le H\left(1 - X_{0jk}\right) \quad \forall j \in N_C; \forall k \in K \tag{20}$$

$$Y_i^* - Y_j + s_i + t_{ij} \le H\left(1 - \sum_{k \in K} X_{ijk}\right) \quad \forall i, j \in N_C; i \ne j \tag{21}$$

$$Y_j - Y_i^* - s_i - t_{ij} \le H\left(1 - \sum_{k \in K} X_{ijk}\right) \quad \forall i, j \in N_C; i \ne j \tag{22}$$

$$T_j \ge Y_j^* - b_j \quad \forall j \in N_C \tag{23}$$

$$E_j \ge a_j - Y_j \quad \forall j \in N_C \tag{24}$$

$$Y_j - a_j \le H\left(1 - O_j\right) \quad \forall j \in N_C \tag{25}$$

$$a_j - Y_j \le HO_j \quad \forall j \in N_C \tag{26}$$

$$Y_j^* = Y_j - AX4_j + a_jO_j \qquad \forall j \in N_C \tag{27}$$

The objective function minimizing the sum of total earliness and tardiness is given in (1). It is determined whether a job is the successor of any job on the same machine or the first/last job to be processed on any machine by Cons. (2)–(4). While Cons. (5) and (6) are used to determine the production completion time of the first jobs on each machine, Cons. (7) defines the production completion time for predecessor and successor jobs on each machine. Cons. (8) identifies the first customer on any tour. Cons. (9) and (10) guarantee that each customer must be visited exactly once, and the number of entering and leaving arcs must be the same for any node, respectively. Cons. (11)–(13) are based on a single-commodity flow formulation described by [8]. This set of constraints guarantee a connected tour. So, we define F_{ij} as a continuous variable indicating the amount of load flowing between nodes i and j. In order to assure subtour elimination in the formulation, we impose tight bounds on the flow variables F_{ij} in addition to a set of flow conservation constraints. Cons. (11) and (12) indicate that the total amount of load on any vehicle decreases as it delivers the order to the related customer. According to Cons (13), the total amount of load on any vehicle should not exceed its capacity. While Cons. (14) defines the variable of R_{jk}, , Cons. (15) and (16) define the variable of G_{ij}. . According to Cons. (17) and (18), each vehicle must wait in production facility until the production process of the batch assigned completes. Cons. (19) and (20) specify the arrival time to the first customer on any tour. Cons. (21) and (22) state the arrival time to the two consecutive customers on any tour. Cons. (23) and (24) calculate tardiness and earliness, respectively, if either of them occurs. Cons. (25) and (26) define the variable of O_j. . According to Cons. (27), the service starting time of any customer is equal to the maximum value of the lower bound of the time windows and arrival time for that customer.

As can be seen, the developed model is not linear because it consists of the product of two variables. So, while we use the Cons. (28)–(30) for $AX1_{ijk}$, $AX2_{ij}$ and $AX3_{ijk}$ where both x and y are binary variables, Cons. (31)–(33) are used for the linearization of $AX4_j$ where x is a binary variable and y is a non-negative continuous variable, and M is a sufficiently large number.

$$z \le x \tag{28}$$

$$z \le y \tag{29}$$

$$z \ge x + y - 1 \tag{30}$$

$$z \le xM \tag{31}$$

$$z \le y \tag{32}$$

$$z \ge y - (1 - x)M \tag{33}$$

2.2 Illustrative Example

Based on the formal definition given in the previous section, we present an illustrative problem for visualizing the integrated approach. In the example, whose parameters are listed in Table 2, there are nine customers, four identical parallel machines, and two homogenous vehicles with enough capacity to serve all customers. Table 1 contains the descriptions of parameters listed in the first row of Table 2.

Table 2. Parameters of an illustrative example

j	p_j	s_j	a_j	b_j	t_{ij}	*0*	*1*	*2*	*3*	*4*	*5*	*6*	*7*	*8*	*9*
0	–	19	–	–	*0*	0	3	13	5	18	10	12	22	18	10
1	39	1	69	75	*1*	3	0	13	7	19	12	10	23	16	9
2	20	9	55	61	*2*	13	13	0	14	30	19	22	11	19	5
3	91	5	128	138	*3*	5	7	14	0	18	7	15	21	23	12
4	52	2	199	201	*4*	18	19	30	18	0	14	13	38	31	27
5	85	14	114	135	*5*	10	12	19	7	14	0	16	26	27	18
6	13	9	108	126	*6*	12	10	22	15	13	16	0	33	18	18
7	18	9	61	106	*7*	22	23	11	21	38	26	33	0	29	16
8	2	15	54	81	*8*	18	16	19	23	31	27	18	29	0	15
9	71	6	132	139	*9*	10	9	5	12	27	18	18	16	15	0

A feasible solution for the given example is illustrated in Fig. 1. According to Fig. 1, jobs 7 and 5 are processed on the first machine. Jobs assigned to other machines are depicted similarly. While customers 2, 7, 8, and 6 are served by the first vehicle, the second vehicle delivers orders 1, 9, 3, 5, and 4, respectively. Shipping boxes show the service time spent on each customer. Vehicle one (v1) departs from the depot when the production process of the first batch completes at time 22, then goes directly from the depot to customer 2 at time 54. Based on the time window of customer 2, the vehicle must wait 1 min until the lower bound of the time window (i.e., 55). This process proceeds in the same way for other customers. Based on the following feasible solution, earliness occurs for customers 2 and 4, while tardiness occurs for customers 1, 3, 5, 6, and 8, as seen from Fig. 1. So, the objective value of the problem is equal to the 156 which is a summation of 6 earliness and 150 tardiness.

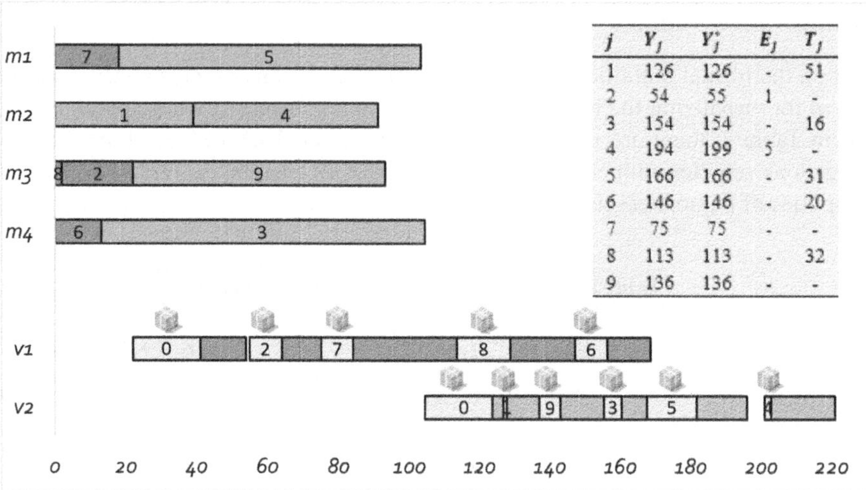

j	Y_j	Y_j^*	E_j	T_j
1	126	126	-	51
2	54	55	1	-
3	154	154	-	16
4	194	199	5	-
5	166	166	-	31
6	146	146	-	20
7	75	75	-	-
8	113	113	-	32
9	136	136	-	-

Fig. 1. A Gantt chart of a feasible solution (also optimal solution) for the illustrated example.

3 Iterated Local Search

The idea of Iterated Local Search (ILS) as an extension of the local search procedure was first introduced in [13]. Basically, ILS is formed by incorporating a perturbation mechanism into the local search process to avoid getting stuck in local optima. ILS has been used for many combinatorial optimization problems in the literature [15—17, 19]. The pseudo code of the proposed ILS is given in Fig. 2.

In the perturbation process, we use the regeneration operator proposed by [1]. In the selection process, parents are selected as the current local optimal solution and the neighbor solution with the best objective. The encoding scheme developed by Afralizad and Rezaeian [1] is also adapted to the integrated problem. According to the adapted chromosome, while the first and third rows represent the permutation of the jobs and customers, respectively, the second and fourth rows demonstrate the assignments of machines and vehicles for each job and customer in the corresponding position. The encoding scheme for the illustrated problem is depicted in Fig. 3. In the local search process, we use swap, insert, and 2-opt operators for both production and distribution phases so as to consider inter and intra machines and vehicles.

```
Algorithm 1: ILS
begin
    S ← Initial solution
    iter ← 0
    k ← 0
    while iter ≠ maxiter do
        S' ← Local search (S)
        if f(S') < f(S) then
            S ← S'
            k ← 0
        Else
            k ← k + 1
            if (k > 10) then
                S' ← Perturb (S)
                end if
            end if
        end if
        iter ← iter + 1
    end while
End
```

Fig. 2. The pseudocode of the proposed ILS.

Job order:	7	5	1	4	8	2	9	6	3
Machine assignment:	1	1	2	2	3	3	3	4	4
Customer order:	2	7	8	6	1	9	3	5	4
Vehicle assignment:	1	1	1	1	2	2	2	2	2

Fig. 3. The encoding scheme

4 Computational Results

For computational experiments, we generate a total of 486 instances randomly based on the number of customers, machines, and vehicles. While the number of customers includes six levels from 5 to 10, machines and vehicles are set to three levels covering 2, 3, and 4. In addition, for each factor level of the parameters, nine different random instances are generated.

The CPLEX solver embedded in GAMS is used as the MIP-solver. The maximum computational time for the CPLEX solver is set to 10800 s, and the stopping criterion for ILS is run $1000 \times N$ iterations, where N represents the number of customers.

Table 3 reports the comparative results of CPLEX and ILS based on the problem parameters. The column *Parameters* describes the level of problem parameters based on the number of customers, machines, and vehicles, respectively. In the *CPLEX* column, while *Obj.* Indicates the average objective value (i.e., upper bound), *LB* represents the lower bound found by CPLEX in a given time limit of 3 h. The number of optimal solutions found by CPLEX and ILS are given in column *#Opt.* Finally, the solution times in seconds for CPLEX and ILS are indicated by the *CPU* column. The deviation of objective values from each other (*DEV%*) is calculated by $\frac{Obj_{CPLEX}-Obj_{ILS}}{Obj_{CPLEX}} \times 100$ if the solution found by CPLEX is worse than ILS; otherwise, it is calculated by $\frac{Obj_{ILS}-Obj_{CPLEX}}{Obj_{ILS}} \times 100$.

We summarize the following remarks from Table 3: CPLEX can find all optimal solutions for all instances of six and seven customers. As the number of customers increases, the ability of CPLEX to find optimal solutions declines dramatically. For ten customers, CPLEX can only find seven optimal solutions out of 81 instances. Like the first remark, the CPU time also increases drastically when the number of customers increases from 5 to 10 and reaches to about 10,000 s for the level of 10 customers. In addition, when the effect of the number of machines and vehicles are examined, we reach the following results: As the number of machines increases, CPLEX's ability to find optimal solutions increases. This is a result of the reduction of the tardiness component in the objective function due to the simultaneous use of resources in the production phase. Similarly, as the number of vehicles increases, the average objective value decreases. However, the number of vehicles has not as much an effect as the number of machines in terms of the number of optimal solutions found and CPU times. As can be seen from Table 3, CPLEX is able to find the optimal solution in 331 instances out of 486 instances within 3 h. When the same instances are solved with ILS, it is seen to provide optimal solutions for 329 instances out of 331 instances whose optimality are proven by CPLEX. Especially in instances where the number of customers is set to 9 and 10, the solutions obtained by ILS are of higher quality, and the percent deviation of CPLEX from ILS (*DEV%*) reaches to 77%. As a result, ILS has shown superior performance in terms of both solution quality and solution time.

Table 3. The comparison of CPLEX and ILS based on the number of customers, machines, and vehicles.

	CPLEX					ILS			
N	***Obj.***	***LB***	***DEV%***	***#Opt.***	***CPU***	***Obj.***	***DEV%***	***#Opt.***	***CPU***
5	22.98	22.98	0	81/81	1.84	22.98	0	81/81	3.29
6	35.88	35.88	0	81/81	58.25	35.88	0	81/81	3.89
7	72.35	64.65	0	76/81	1594.47	72.35	0	76/76	4.57
8	117.43	39.76	18.45	50/81	4811.80	111.43	0	50/50	5.31
9	158.74	26.37	38.08	36/81	7047.14	140.07	0.10	35/36	6.11
10	293.09	9.66	77.34	7/81	9990.05	227.17	0.15	6/7	7.93
M	***Obj.***	***LB***	***DEV%***	***#Opt.***	***CPU***	***Obj.***	***DEV%***	***#Opt.***	***CPU***
2	230.29	46.94	35.09	81/162	5810.84	197.57	0.00	81/81	4.89
3	77.67	28.85	20.23	117/162	3594.04	67.88	0.05	116/117	5.14
4	42.28	23.86	11.62	133/162	2346.89	39.50	0.07	132/133	5.52
K	***Obj.***	***LB***	***DEV%***	***#Opt.***	***CPU***	***Obj.***	***DEV%***	***#Opt.***	***CPU***
2	153.83	51.50	20.91	113/162	3857.39	137.50	0.00	113/113	5.02
3	104.69	28.70	22.71	109/162	3916.62	88.55	0.07	108/109	5.14
4	91.71	19.45	23.31	109/162	3977.76	78.89	0.05	108/109	5.39
Avg.	***116.75***	***33.22***	***22.31***	***331/486***	***3917.26***	***101.65***	***0.04***	***329/331***	***5.18***

5 Final Remarks and Future Directions

In this study, we develop a new MIP model for a variant of the integrated production and distribution problem that consists of parallel machine scheduling and homogeneous vehicle routing problems with time windows. The objective of the model is formed by minimizing the sum of total earliness and tardiness. The performance of the exact method is found to be poor, even for only seven customers. We also examine the performance of CPLEX based on the number of customers, machines, and vehicles. According to the results, the increase in the number of customers reduces the performance of CPLEX dramatically. Especially for nine and ten customers, the exact method can no longer be considered a reasonable solution method for an operational-level problem. On the contrary, the increase in the number of machines positively affects the performance of CPLEX. The reason for this is that the departure times of the vehicles are moved earlier due to the simultaneous use of identical parallel machines in the production environment. Thus, the total tardiness in the objective function tends to decrease. When the number of vehicles increases, we see that the objective function value decreases, but there is no significant difference when CPU time and the number of optimal solutions found is examined. For a customer number of 10, CPLEX can only find optimality in 7 out of 81 instances in a given time limit of 10800 s, and the deviation between the upper and lower bounds found by CPLEX is calculated at 96.7%. Then, we propose the ILS algorithm for solving the integrated problem efficiently. According to the comparative results, the proposed ILS algorithm performs quite well in terms of both solution quality and time. The CPU time of ILS for a level of ten customers is about 8 s, even for 10000 iterations. In addition, ILS is found to produce 77% better solutions in terms of objective function value when compared to CPLEX for ten customers.

Future work may focus on larger instances, and the performance of ILS can be compared to other metaheuristics such as genetic algorithms, particle swarm optimization, etc. By considering specific situations of problem assumptions, such as heterogeneous vehicles, unrelated parallel machines, and sequence dependent set-up times, a new variant of an integrated problem can be handled. In addition, sustainable objectives such as energy-efficient strategies at both the production and distribution levels can be considered.

References

1. Afzalirad, M., Rezaeian, J.: Resource-constrained unrelated parallel machine scheduling problem with sequence dependent setup times, precedence constraints and machine eligibility restrictions. Comput. Ind. Eng. **98**, 40–52 (2016). https://doi.org/10.1016/j.cie.2016.05.020
2. Alzoubi, H., Alshurideh, M., Kurdi, B., Alhyasat, K., Ghazal, T.: The effect of e-payment and online shopping on sales growth: evidence from banking industry. Int. J. Data Netw. Sci. **6**(4), 1369–1380 (2022). https://doi.org/10.5267/j.ijdns.2022.5.014
3. Belo-Filho, M., Amorim, P., Almada-Lobo, B.: An adaptive large neighbourhood search for the operational integrated production and distribution problem of perishable products. Int. J. Prod. Res. **53**(20), 6040–6058 (2015). https://doi.org/10.1080/00207543.2015.1010744
4. Berghman, L., Kergosien, Y., Billaut, J.-C.: A review on integrated scheduling and outbound vehicle routing problems. Eur. J. Oper. Res. (2023). https://doi.org/10.1016/j.ejor.2022.12.036

5. Chang, Y.-C., Li, V.C., Chiang, C.-J.: An ant colony optimization heuristic for an integrated production and distribution scheduling problem. Eng. Optim. **46**(4), 503–520 (2014). https://doi.org/10.1080/0305215X.2013.786062
6. Farahani, P., Grunow, M., Günther, H.-O.: Integrated production and distribution planning for perishable food products. Flex. Serv. Manuf. J. **24**, 28–51 (2012). https://doi.org/10.1007/s10696-011-9125-0
7. Ganji, M., Kazemipoor, H., Molana, S.M.H., Sajadi, S.M.: A green multi-objective integrated scheduling of production and distribution with heterogeneous fleet vehicle routing and time windows. J. Clean. Prod. **259**, 120824 (2020). https://doi.org/10.1016/j.jclepro.2020.120824
8. Gavish, B., Graves, S.C.: The travelling salesman problem and related problems (1978). http://hdl.handle.net/1721.1/5363
9. He, P., Li, K., Kumar, P.R.: An enhanced branch-and-price algorithm for the integrated production and transportation scheduling problem. Int. J. Prod. Res. **60**(6), 1874–1889 (2022). https://doi.org/10.1080/00207543.2021.1876941
10. Hou, Y., Fu, Y., Gao, K., Zhang, H., Sadollah, A.: Modelling and optimization of integrated distributed flow shop scheduling and distribution problems with time windows. Expert Syst. Appl. **187**, 115827 (2022). https://doi.org/10.1016/j.eswa.2021.115827
11. Kesen, S.E., Bektaş, T.: Integrated production scheduling and distribution planning with time windows. Lean Green Supply Chain Manage: Optim. Models Algorithms, 231–252 (2019).https://doi.org/10.1007/978-3-319-97511-5_8
12. Liu, H., Guo, Z., Zhang, Z.: A hybrid multi-level optimisation framework for integrated production scheduling and vehicle routing with flexible departure time. Int. J. Prod. Res. **59**(21), 6615–6632 (2021). https://doi.org/10.1080/00207543.2020.1821927
13. Lourenço, H.R., Martin, O.C., Stützle, T., Iterated local search. In: Handbook of Metaheuristics, pp. 320–353. Springer, Cham (2003). https://doi.org/10.1007/0-306-48056-5_11
14. Mohammadi, S., Al-e-Hashem, S.M., Rekik, Y.: An integrated production scheduling and delivery route planning with multi-purpose machines: a case study from a furniture manufacturing company. Int. J. Prod. Econ. **219**, 347–359 (2020). https://doi.org/10.1016/j.ijpe.2019.05.017
15. Penna, P.H.V., Subramanian, A., Ochi, L.S.: An iterated local search heuristic for the heterogeneous fleet vehicle routing problem. J. Heuristics **19**(2), 201–232 (2013). https://doi.org/10.1007/s10732-011-9186-y
16. Stützle, T.: Applying iterated local search to the permutation flow shop problem. Technical Report AIDA-98–04, FG Intellektik, TU Darmstadt (1998)
17. Stützle, T.: Iterated local search for the quadratic assignment problem. Eur. J. Oper. Res. **174**(3), 1519–1539 (2006). https://doi.org/10.1016/j.ejor.2005.01.066
18. Ullrich, C.A.: Integrated machine scheduling and vehicle routing with time windows. Eur. J. Oper. Res. **227**(1), 152–165 (2013). https://doi.org/10.1016/j.ejor.2012.11.049
19. Vansteenwegen, P., Souffriau, W., Berghe, G.V., Van Oudheusden, D.: Iterated local search for the team orienteering problem with time windows. Comput. Oper. Res. **36**(12), 3281–3290 (2009). https://doi.org/10.1016/j.cor.2009.03.008
20. Wu, G.-H., Cheng, C.-Y., Pourhejazy, P., Fang, B.-L.: Variable neighborhood-based cuckoo search for production routing with time window and setup times. Appl. Soft. Comput. **125**, 109191 (2022). https://doi.org/10.1016/j.asoc.2022.109191
21. Yağmur, E., Kesen, S.E.: A memetic algorithm for joint production and distribution scheduling with due dates. Comput. Ind. Eng. **142**, 106342 (2020). https://doi.org/10.1016/j.cie.2020.106342

22. Yağmur, E., Kesen, S.E.: Multi-trip heterogeneous vehicle routing problem coordinated with production scheduling: memetic algorithm and simulated annealing approaches. Comput. Ind. Eng. **161**, 107649 (2021). https://doi.org/10.1016/j.cie.2021.107649
23. Yağmur, E., Kesen, S.E.: Bi-objective coordinated production and transportation scheduling problem with sustainability: formulation and solution approaches. Int. J. Prod. Res. **61**(3), 774–795 (2023). https://doi.org/10.1080/00207543.2021.2017054

Constrained Multi-agent Path Planning Problem

Ali Maktabifard[1(✉)], Dávid Földes[1], and Bendegúz Dezső Bak[2]

[1] Faculty of Transportation Engineering and Vehicle Engineering, Department of Transport Technology and Economics, Budapest University of Technology and Economics, Budapest, Hungary
a.maktabifard@edu.bme.hu, foldes.david@kjk.bme.hu
[2] Faculty of Mechanical Engineering, Department of Fluid Mechanics, Budapest University of Technology and Economics, Budapest, Hungary
bak.bendeguz@gpk.bme.hu

Abstract. Planning the most efficient routes in a cooperative manner is a challenge for many mobility and logistics service providers. In this paper, a new methodological approach is presented based on the Multi-Agent Path Planning (MAPP) problem which is a variant of the classical Multiple Traveling Salesmen Problem (MTSP). Given a team of m agents that must visit n targets, the optimal paths plan (a set of m paths) should be determined such that each target is visited only once. Minimizing the time of this cooperative operation is the optimization goal in this study. Thus, the plan is optimal, if the longest path in the plan is the shortest possible (Min-Max problem). In order to deal with more practical situations, two additional constraints are applied: the maximum number of targets each agent is allowed to visit, and the maximum range for each agent. Accordingly, a so-called Constrained Multi-Agent Path Planning (CMAPP) problem is elaborated in this paper. An easy to apply Genetic Algorithm (GA) is presented, which improves the paths using genetic-like operators and a heuristic method. The applicability of the approximate solution was tested in four random scenarios where it showed a decent performance. The developed method can be used for route planning of mobility and logistics services in which several destinations must be reached by a fleet of vehicles (e.g., group ride-sharing, last-mile delivery).

Keywords: Multi-Agent Planning Problem · Genetic Algorithm · Routing Problem · Optimization · Metaheuristic · MAPF · MTSP

1 Introduction

The importance of cooperative path planning for vehicle fleets has been demonstrated by various applications such as logistics and delivery services [19,26], ride-sharing services [13,25], and mission planning for autonomous/unmanned vehicles [4,28]. In general, a multi-agent planner is required for cooperative path

© The Author(s), under exclusive license to Springer Nature Switzerland AG 2023
J. R. Daduna et al. (Eds.): ICCL 2023, LNCS 14239, pp. 450–466, 2023.
https://doi.org/10.1007/978-3-031-43612-3_28

planning of vehicle fleets. This planning problem can be defined as finding a set of paths that allows a fleet of agents to reach a specified number of targets in the minimum amount of time. This problem is similar to the classical Multiple Traveling Salesmen Problem (MTSP) [1], and its variants such as the Multi-Agent Path Planning (MAPP) problem [16]. The classical MTSP is generally defined as follows. Given n cities (targets) and m salesmen (agents), the aim is to find m tours (closed paths) starting and ending at a depot (initial position of the agents) such that each target is visited only once and the total cost of visiting all targets is minimized. The cost metric can be expressed in terms of distance, time, etc., [1]. The MAPP problem is similar to the classical MTSP with two differences:

- Subtours (open paths) are considered in the MAPP problem, so each agent starts and ends its path at two distinct points.
- Agents can have different initial positions.

More practical situations can be modeled by applying additional restrictions to these combinatorial optimization problems. These restrictions affect the agents mostly by restricting their path length, workload, or operational range [13,19,25,26]. As a novelty, in this study the cooperative path planning for vehicle fleets is modeled as a so-called Constrained Multi-Agent Path Planning (CMAPP) problem. This problem is formed by applying two additional constraints to the MAPP problem: the maximum number of targets each agent is allowed to visit, and the maximum range for each agent. This paper presents a two-step solution method composed of an initial solution and a complex solution for this problem. The initial solution benefits from a new targets assignment algorithm. The complex solution uses a Genetic Algorithm (GA) to improve the result of the initial solution. The additional constraints are applied in both initial and complex solutions. The aim of this study is to show the applicability of the developed method.

The remainder of the paper is organized as follows. Section 2 reviews solution methods for similar problems. The CMAPP problem is described in detail in Sect. 3. The methodology of the proposed solution is described in Sect. 4; then results are presented and discussed in Sect. 5. Finally, conclusions are drawn in Sect. 6.

2 Review of Solution Methods

Solving the MTSP and the MAPP problem is difficult because of their complex combinatorial character (NP-hardness). In general, two types of approaches are used to tackle the MTSP [12]: *exact* and *heuristic-based* approaches.

The exact approaches are based on either the transformation of the MTSP to an equivalent Traveling Salesman Problem (TSP), or relaxing some constraints of the problem [1,12]. The problem is solved by applying exact methods such as Branch-and-Bound [6], Cutting Planes [20], and Integer Linear Programming

Table 1. Literature instances on the MTSP having similarities to the CMAPP problem considered in our study

Literature	Solution method	Multi-depot MTSP	Min-Max MTSP	Min. and Max. No. of targets for each agent
[17]	Integer linear programming formulations + new bounding and Subtour Elimination Constraints (SECs)	×		×
[18]	A heuristic approach based on an Evolution Strategy (ES)	×	×	
[8]	An ACO algorithm	×		×
[30]	Two variants of Parthenogenetic Algorithm (PGA)	×		Only Min.
[15]	An Ant Colony-Parthenogenetic Algorithm (AC-PGA)	×		×
[14]	A heuristic approach based on a graph simplification method and the 2-OPT algorithm	×		

Formulations [17]. The exact approaches are restricted to the MTSPs with reasonable sizes (Euclidean and Non-Euclidean problems up to 100 and 500 cities (targets), respectively [6]) because their performance is highly dependent on the size of the problem. Accordingly, the solution runtime encounters an exponential rise with increasing the problem size [1,12]. Additionally, transforming the MTSP to an equivalent TSP might result in an even more difficult problem to solve, especially using the exact approaches [6,20].

The heuristic-based approaches solve the problem by applying approximate heuristic methods such as Ant Colony Optimization (ACO) [8,12,15], Genetic Algorithm (GA) [12,15,29,30], Simulated Annealing [24], Neural Networks [23], and Tabu Search [22]. The heuristic-based approaches can achieve near-optimal solutions in a reasonable amount of time even for larger problems [12].

The problems tackled in several previous papers on the MTSP have some similarities to the CMAPP problem considered in our study (see Table 1). These similarities include considering multiple depots for the MTSP, minimizing the length (cost) of the longest tour (Min-Max MTSP), and applying additional constraints.

There are only a few studies on the variants of the MAPP problem. In [9], a GA was introduced to solve a so-called Subtour problem which is similar to the MAPP problem with one difference: there is only one agent. This method was developed for solving the MAPP problem in [10], and a similar method was proposed in [16] to address the MAPP problem. In [27], a heuristic approach based on a graph simplification method was presented to solve a multi-depot open tours MTSP which is basically the MAPP problem with Min-Sum optimization objective.

Concluding the literature review, the MTSP is a well-studied problem, while there are only a few studies on the MAPP problem. Furthermore, previous studies have not solved the MAPP problem with our additional constraints.

3 Constrained Multi-agent Path Planning Problem: General Terms and Notation

In this section, the required foundation from Graph theory, and the notations of the classical MTSP and the MAPP problem are presented. In addition, our additional constraints for the MAPP problem are defined.

According to Graph theory, a *graph* is an ordered pair $G = (V, E)$ consisting of: $V = \{v_1, ..., v_m\}$, a set of m *vertices* (nodes), and $E = \{(v_i, v_j) \mid v_i, v_j \in V,\ i \neq j\}$, a set of *edges* (links) connecting vertices v_i and v_j. This type of graph may be precisely referred to as *simple graph* which means multiple edges connecting the same two vertices are not allowed. In the context of the classical MTSP and the MAPP problem, the targets and the points where the agents begin their journey, are considered as vertices. In this study, only undirected graphs are taken into consideration. In an *undirected graph*, edges are comprised of unordered pairs of vertices where $(v_i, v_j) = (v_j, v_i)$. Moreover, if in a graph all vertices of V are connected to each other, the graph is a *complete graph* and it is designated by $K_m(V)$ where m is the number of vertices constituting the vertex set V.

A *path/cycle* is a sequence of edges connecting a sequence of vertices. If the sequence of vertices is composed of distinct vertices, a *simple path/cycle* is given with the exception that for simple cycle the starting and ending vertices are repeated. Here we only consider simple paths/cycles, so henceforth paths/cycles simply refer to simple paths/cycles. $P = (V_1, E_1)$ is a path in $G = (V, E)$ if: $V_1 = \{v_1, ..., v_k\} \subset V$, and $E_1 = \{(v_1, v_2), (v_2, v_3), ..., (v_{k-1}, v_k)\} \subset E$. This means a path consisting of k vertices is a sequence of $k - 1$ edges connecting these vertices in which each two consecutive edges share a vertex in common. Likewise, $C = (V_2, E_2)$ is a cycle in $G = (V, E)$ if: $V_2 = \{v_1, ..., v_k\} \subset V$, and $E_2 = \{(v_1, v_2), ..., (v_{k-1}, v_k), (v_k, v_1)\} \subset E$. In other words, a cycle comprising k vertices is a sequence of k edges connecting these vertices in which each two consecutive edges as well as the first and the last edge share a vertex in common. Hence, a cycle starts and ends at the same vertex (tour), while a path starts and ends at different vertices (subtour).

The number of edges in a path or cycle is called the length of that path or cycle. For $G = (V, E)$, the set of all paths and cycles with length k are designated by $\mathbb{P}_k(G)$ and $\mathbb{C}_k(G)$, respectively. A *weight* (cost) $w(v_i, v_j)$ can be assigned to an edge. If every edge of a graph has a weight, the graph is called a *weighted graph*. In a weighted graph if $w(v_i, v_j) = w(v_j, v_i)$ is valid for every edge, the weighted graph is called *symmetric*. In this study, for simplicity, the Euclidean distance between two vertices of each edge is assigned as the weight of that edge

$w(v_i, v_j) = w(v_j, v_i) = |\vec{r}(v_i) - \vec{r}(v_j)|$; note that the problems discussed here are not restricted to Euclidean distance, so any desired measure (e.g., rectilinear distance, actual driving distance) can be assigned as the weight of edges. For a path $P \in \mathbb{P}_k(G)$, the sum of its edges' weights is called the total cost of the path:

$$c(P) = \sum_{i=1}^{k} w(v_i, v_{i+1}) \tag{1}$$

Similarly, the total cost of a cycle $C \in \mathbb{C}_k(G)$ is:

$$c(C) = \sum_{i=1}^{k-1} w(v_i, v_{i+1}) + w(v_k, v_1) \tag{2}$$

If there is no associated weight to each edge, the total cost of a path or cycle is simply equal to the length of the path or cycle.

The classical MTSP and the MAPP problem can be formulated on the basis of the foundation from Graph theory described above. Consider $A = \{a_1, ..., a_m\}$ and $T = \{t_1, ..., t_n\}$ as the set of m agents and n targets, respectively. The agents and targets are located in Euclidean space. The location of the ith agent and the jth target is therefore determined by $\vec{r}(a_i)$ and $\vec{r}(t_j)$, respectively. The classical MTSP is formulated as follows. Consider a as the depot for all agents, so $\forall\, a_i = a$ and $\forall\, \vec{r}(a_i) = \vec{r}(a)$. The configuration space of the problem is the complete graph $K_{n+1}(V)$ with the vertex set $V = T \cup a$. Consider C_i as a cycle with length k_i that starts and ends at vertex a (the depot). Let $\mathbb{C} = \{C_1, ..., C_m\}$ be the set of m cycles C_i with length k_i. The aim is to determine $\mathbb{C}$ such that each target is visited only once (visitation only by one agent), and the total cost of $\mathbb{C}$ (Eq. (3)) is minimized (Min-Sum problem).

$$c(\mathbb{C}) = \sum_{i=1}^{m} c(C_i) \tag{3}$$

The total cost of $\mathbb{C}$ is the sum of the lengths (costs) of all m cycles C_i constituting $\mathbb{C}$ (see Eq. (3)).

Likewise, the MAPP problem is formulated as follows. For each agent, the configuration space of the problem is the complete graph $K_{n+1}(V_i)$ with the vertex set $V_i = T \cup a_i$. The Euclidean distance between two vertices of each edge (e.g., v_x and v_y) is assigned as the weight of that edge; $w(v_x, v_y) = w(v_y, v_x) = |\vec{r}(v_x) - \vec{r}(v_y)|$ where $v_x, v_y \in V_i$. As a result, $K_{n+1}(V_i)$ is a symmetric weighted graph. Consider P_i as a path with length k_i starting at vertex a_i. Let $\mathbb{P} = \{P_1, ..., P_m\}$ be the set of m paths P_i with length k_i that each pair of them do not have any vertex in common (except possible same position for starting points). The aim is to determine $\mathbb{P}$ such that each target is visited only once (visitation only by one agent), and the cost of the path with the largest cost in $\mathbb{P}$ (Eq. (4)) is minimized.

$$c_m(\mathbb{P}) = \max_{i=1}^{m} c(P_i) \tag{4}$$

Therefore, the MAPP problem is a Min-Max problem in which a team of m agents must visit n targets in the minimum amount of time. The whole team of agents should be used, so each agent must visit at least one target ($k_i \geq 1$). However, the number of targets visited by each agent can be different.

In this study, our additional constraints for the MAPP problem are applied independently of each other. These constraints are defined as follows. In the MAPP problem, if the maximum number of targets that can be assigned to each agent is limited, the solution would be affected since the maximum length of each agent's path is restricted. Accordingly, we introduced the maximum number of targets each agent is allowed to visit as the first additional constraint. Let $Q = \{q_1, ..., q_m\}$ be the set of the maximum number of targets for each agent, so the maximum number of targets that can be assigned to the ith agent is q_i. As a result, the length of each agent's path is limited to: $1 \leq k_i \leq q_i$. In the case of applying this additional constraint, if the sum of all elements of Q is less than the number of targets ($\sum_{i=1}^{m} q_i < n$), then the fleet of m agents cannot visit all n targets. Hereafter, this situation is referred to as the *lack-of-capacity issue*. Additionally, if the maximum number of targets for each agent is the same for all agents ($\forall\, q_i = q$), the fleet of agents is called a homogeneous capacity fleet. In this study, for solving the problem with the first additional constraint, a homogeneous capacity fleet was assumed.

Furthermore, we defined the maximum range of the ith agent as the maximum Euclidean distance from the position of a_i that can be accessed by the ith agent. This range is unlimited without applying any constraint on it, so each agent can access all targets regardless of their Euclidean distance from its position. However, if this range is limited, the only accessible targets for each agent are located within its maximum range. This not only impacts the assignment of targets to agents, but also can influence the total cost of each agent's path. Accordingly, we introduced the maximum range for each agent as the second additional constraint. Let $R = \{r_1, ..., r_m\}$ be the set of the maximum range for each agent, so the maximum range of the ith agent is r_i. Consequently, the jth target can be accessible for the ith agent only if: $|\vec{r}(a_i) - \vec{r}(t_j)| \leq r_i$. In the case of applying this additional constraint, if there would be at least one target that is not in the maximum range of any agent ($|\forall\, \vec{r}(a_i) - \vec{r}(t_j)| > r_i$), then the fleet of m agents cannot visit all n targets. Henceforth, this situation is referred to as the *out-of-range issue*. Moreover, if the maximum range for each agent is the same for all agents ($\forall\, r_i = r$), the fleet of agents is called a homogeneous range fleet. In this study, for solving the problem with the second additional constraint, a homogeneous range fleet was assumed.

4 Methodology of the Approximate Solution

In this study, a two-step solution based on the method developed in [16] is presented for the CMAPP problem. The solution method is composed of an initial solution and a complex solution. The complex solution improves the result of the initial solution using a GA that applies genetic-like operators and a heuristic method. A solution is a set of paths that is called *Plan* ($\mathbb{P}$) in this context. The Plan is optimal if the longest path in the Plan is the shortest possible (Min-Max problem). Thus, the solution algorithm is as follows:

- Step 1: a Plan $\mathbb{P}$ is generated by the initial solution.
- Step 2: the complex solution is applied to the Plan $\mathbb{P}$ to minimize the cost $c_m(\mathbb{P})$ (see Eq. (4)) and eventually obtain the near-optimal Plan.

4.1 Initial Solution

The initial solution generates the Initial Plan (a starting set of paths). Consider $A = \{a_1, ..., a_m\}$ and $T = \{t_1, ..., t_n\}$ as the set of m agents and n targets, respectively. A Plan is viable if each pair of paths do not have any vertex in common (except possible same starting points). For the order of planning, we assume that the targets are assigned to the agents in the following order: $a_1 \rightarrow a_2 \rightarrow \cdots \rightarrow a_m$. The targets assignment algorithm is as follows:

- Step 1: a target $t_{i_1} \in T_1 = T$ is selected and assigned to the first agent.
- Step 2: a target $t_{i_2} \in T_2 = T_1 - t_{i_1}$ is selected and assigned to the second agent.

  ⋮

- Step m: a target $t_{i_m} \in T_m = T_{m-1} - t_{i_{m-1}}$ is selected and assigned to the mth agent.

A viable Plan $\mathbb{P} = \{P_1, ..., P_m\}$ is generated by iterating this algorithm until all targets would be assigned to the agents.

However, a target selection approach is also required for selecting a target in every step of the targets assignment algorithm. Therefore, different initialization methods can be employed by adopting various target selection approaches. In this study, two initialization methods were employed:

1. *Greedy* initialization method:
   It selects targets on the basis of the nearest neighbor heuristic and assigns them to the agents. For each agent, the nearest unassigned target to the previously assigned target to that agent is selected in every iteration of the targets assignment algorithm. In order to select the first target for each agent, the nearest unassigned target to the position of that agent (a_i) is selected.
2. *Random* initialization method:
   It selects targets randomly and assigns them to the agents. For each agent, a random unassigned target is selected in every iteration of the targets assignment algorithm.

The solution for the non-constrained MAPP problem was also considered in order to enable us to evaluate the effect of applying our two additional constraints that were applied independently of each other. Hence, six different solution modes were analyzed in this study (see Table 2).

Table 2. Analyzed solution modes

Solution mode	Initialization method		Additional constraint	
	Greedy	*Random*	*Max. number of targets for each agent*	*Max. range for each agent*
1	×			
2	×		×	
3	×			×
4		×		
5		×	×	
6		×		×

4.2 Complex Solution

In order to evolve a Plan $\mathbb{P}$ towards a near-optimal Multi-Agent Plan, the complex solution is applied to the paths $P_i \in \mathbb{P}$. The complex solution uses a GA applying three genetic-like operators and another operator employing a heuristic method to minimize the cost $c_m(\mathbb{P})$ (see Eq. (4)). This reduces the length of the longest path in the Plan, and eventually the near-optimal Plan is obtained. The algorithm of the complex solution is the same as a classical GA [11] with one exception: there is only one Plan $\mathbb{P}$ generated by the initial solution to be evolved (the population size is 1).

In every evolutionary iteration, the developed operators are applied sequentially to a Plan $\mathbb{P}$ and generate a new Plan $\mathbb{P}^{'}$, then:

- If $c_m(\mathbb{P}^{'}) < c_m(\mathbb{P})$, Plan $\mathbb{P}^{'}$ is kept for the next evolutionary iteration and Plan $\mathbb{P}$ is discarded.
- If $c_m(\mathbb{P}^{'}) > c_m(\mathbb{P})$, Plan $\mathbb{P}$ is kept for the next evolutionary iteration and Plan $\mathbb{P}^{'}$ is discarded.

In every evolutionary iteration, the following operators are applied in the same order:

1. *Crossover* operator:
   It is stochastically applied with the probability of $\mathcal{P}_{crossover}$. It selects two paths stochastically either by the best-worst selection with the probability of $\mathcal{P}_{best-worst}$ or by random selection with the probability of $1 - \mathcal{P}_{best-worst}$, then each of them is randomly cleaved (cleaving position can be different for each of them) into two parts and the parts are swapped.
2. *Mutation* operator:
   It is stochastically applied with the probability of $\mathcal{P}_{mutation}$. It randomly selects two paths and swaps two randomly selected targets between them.
3. *Migration* operator:
   It is stochastically applied with the probability of $\mathcal{P}_{migration}$. It randomly selects two paths P_i and P_j, then it removes a randomly selected target from

P_i and adds it to P_j. Obviously, in this procedure the length of P_i reduces, while the length of P_j enlarges.

4. *Boosting* operator:
   It is stochastically applied with the probability of $\mathcal{P}_{boost}$. It enhances the quality of paths by applying the 2-OPT algorithm [2]. This algorithm examines whether the inequality (5) between each four targets v_i, v_{i+1}, v_j, v_{j+1} of a path is valid or not. If it is valid, edges (v_i, v_{i+1}) and (v_j, v_{j+1}) are substituted with edges (v_i, v_j) and (v_{i+1}, v_{j+1}), respectively. Applying this algorithm generates a shorter path.

$$c(v_i, v_{i+1}) + c(v_j, v_{j+1}) > c(v_i, v_j) + c(v_{i+1}, v_{j+1}) \tag{5}$$

5 Results and Discussion

In order to demonstrate the applicability of the developed solution, four *random scenarios* with 100 test cases for each one were considered (see Table 3). In all test cases, the agents and targets were spread out randomly in a dimensionless domain (*domain area* = 1 × 1). The cost reduction Δc_m was defined as the cost reduction of the Final Plan compared to the Initial Plan (see Eq. (6)). The following evaluation parameters were considered: $\overline{\Delta c_m}$ is the average Δc_m for 100 test cases; $\overline{c_m}(\mathbb{P}_{final})$ is the average final cost for 100 test cases; q_i is the maximum number of targets for each agent; $\overline{r_i}$ is the average maximum range for each agent for 100 test cases; and $\mathcal{T}_{100}$ is the runtime for 100 test cases.

$$\Delta c_m = \frac{c_m(\mathbb{P}_{Initial}) - c_m(\mathbb{P}_{Final})}{c_m(\mathbb{P}_{Initial})} \times 100\% \tag{6}$$

Table 3. Test scenarios

Scenario	Number of agents (m)	Number of targets (n)
1	10	100
2	9	100
3	20	200
4	10	200

In terms of the first additional constraint, in each test case the maximum number of targets for each agent was determined by $q_i = \lceil \frac{n}{m} \rceil$ to ensure that the lack-of-capacity issue would not occur. Regarding the second additional constraint, in each test case the developed solution numerically calculates the minimum value for the maximum range for each agent such that the out-of-range issue would not occur. As a result, here the maximum range for each agent is a case-sensitive variable.

The operators of the complex solution were applied with the probabilities of: $\mathcal{P}_{crossover} = 0.7$, $\mathcal{P}_{best-worst} = 0.5$, $\mathcal{P}_{mutation} = 0.4$, $\mathcal{P}_{migration} = 0.6$, and

$\mathcal{P}_{boost} = 0.3$. Simulations were run for 150000 evolutionary iterations for each test case by means of MATLAB R2021b. The hardware configuration of the PC used was as follows. CPU: AMD Ryzen^{TM} 5-5500U, RAM: 8 GB.

The computational results are shown in Table 4. Accordingly, if the maximum number of targets for each agent was restricted:

- in the case of employing Greedy initialization, the average final cost (except in scenario 1) and the runtime decreased, while the average cost reduction (except in scenario 1) increased compared to the non-constrained solution with Greedy initialization.
- in the case of employing Random initialization, the runtime (except in scenario 1) and the average cost reduction decreased, whereas the average final cost increased compared to the non-constrained solution with Random initialization.

Moreover, if the maximum range for each agent was limited:

- in the case of employing Greedy initialization, the average cost reduction and the average final cost decreased compared to the non-constrained solution with Greedy initialization. A general trend was not observed regarding the runtime.
- in the case of employing Random initialization, the average final cost in the scenarios with more targets (200) and the average cost reduction decreased, while the average final cost in the scenarios with fewer targets (100) increased compared to the non-constrained solution with Random initialization. A general trend was not observed regarding the runtime.

Additionally, in the absence of any additional constraints, Random initialization led to a smaller average final cost compared to Greedy initialization in scenarios with fewer targets (100). However, in the presence of additional constraints, Random initialization always led to a larger average final cost compared to Greedy initialization. An interesting result was that $\overline{r_i}$ was always less than 34% of the domain diameter ($\sqrt{1+1}$). Furthermore, if the number of agents and targets increased while $\frac{n}{m}$ remained constant, the average final cost decreased in the case of applying the additional constraints along with Greedy initialization. For 10 agents, when the number of targets increased by 100%, the average final cost experienced an increase averaging 47.4% and 59.6% across solution modes 1 to 3, and solution modes 4 to 6, respectively. For 100 targets, when the number of agents decreased by 10%, the average final cost underwent an increase averaging 5.4% across all solution modes. For 200 targets, when the number of agents decreased by 50%, the average final cost experienced an increase averaging 61% and 45.2% across solution modes 1 to 3, and solution modes 4 to 6, respectively.

In order to visualize some instances of the evolution accomplished by the approximate solution, Fig. 1 and Fig. 2 illustrate the Initial Plans and the Final Plans generated by three solution modes for two different test cases. In these figures, the yellow star is the initial position of the agent with the longest path; the green squares are the initial positions of other agents; the paths are shown

Table 4. Computational results

Scenario	Solution mode	$\overline{\Delta c_m}$ [%]	$\overline{c_m}(\mathbb{P}_{final})$	q_i	$\overline{r_i}$	$\mathcal{T}_{100}$ [s]
1	1	42.2161	1.1562			4275.8578
	2	39.5385	1.2115	10		3994.7323
	3	32.4922	1.1229		0.4466	4401.3488
	4	82.4312	1.1477			3702.8841
	5	80.3621	1.2843	10		4007.1264
	6	74.9173	1.1801		0.4466	4243.5765
2	1	41.7696	1.2622			4547.9586
	2	43.6597	1.2183	12		4446.8247
	3	32.6158	1.2054		0.4748	4146.6348
	4	83.0654	1.2370			4387.3790
	5	82.8877	1.2500	12		4157.2272
	6	76.1382	1.3021		0.4748	4302.6578
3	1	36.8756	1.1599			6314.7105
	2	38.3951	1.1295	10		6094.6654
	3	31.0760	0.9202		0.3416	6569.2436
	4	79.5629	1.3924			6533.8671
	5	77.7243	1.5373	10		6235.4490
	6	73.1099	1.0898		0.3416	6850.0604
4	1	31.1765	1.8080			7881.1427
	2	32.6695	1.7667	20		7332.4831
	3	28.0342	1.5705		0.4537	7552.6412
	4	85.0111	1.8575			7835.9091
	5	82.7509	2.1332	20		7334.5086
	6	80.2113	1.7799		0.4537	7824.6231

by solid lines and the longest path is highlighted in all illustrated Plans; and dashed-line circles depict the maximum range of the agents. Figure 1 shows the Plans obtained for a test case with 9 agents and 100 targets. In this test case the solution achieved the largest Δc_m (see Eq. (6)) among 100 test cases of scenario 2 in the case of applying Greedy initialization along with the constraint on the maximum number of targets for each agent. In the absence of any additional constraints, the cost $c_m(\mathbb{P})$ (see Eq. (4)) decreased from 3.16 in the Initial Plan (Fig. 1(a)) to 1.24 in the Final Plan (Fig. 1(b)). If the maximum number of targets for each agent was restricted to $q_i = 12$, the cost $c_m(\mathbb{P})$ reduced from 3.16 in the Initial Plan (Fig. 1(c)) to 1.17 in the Final Plan (Fig. 1(d)). Lastly, if the maximum range for each agent was limited to $r_i = 0.38$, the cost $c_m(\mathbb{P})$ dropped from 1.59 in the Initial Plan (Fig. 1(e)) to 1.17 in the Final Plan (Fig. 1(f)). Furthermore, the Plans generated for a test case with 10 agents and 200 targets

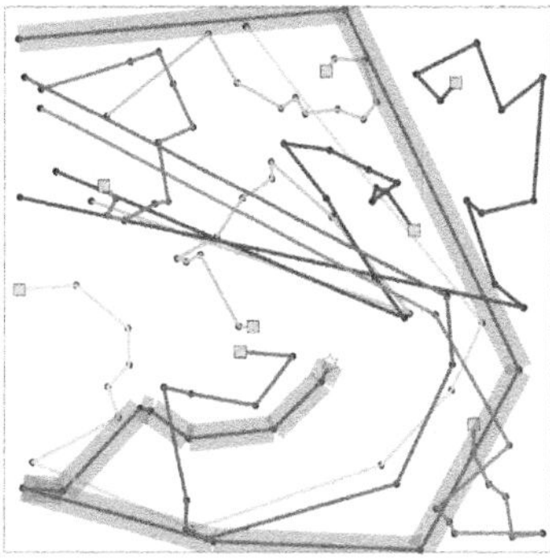

(a) Initial Plan, solution mode 1, scenario 2

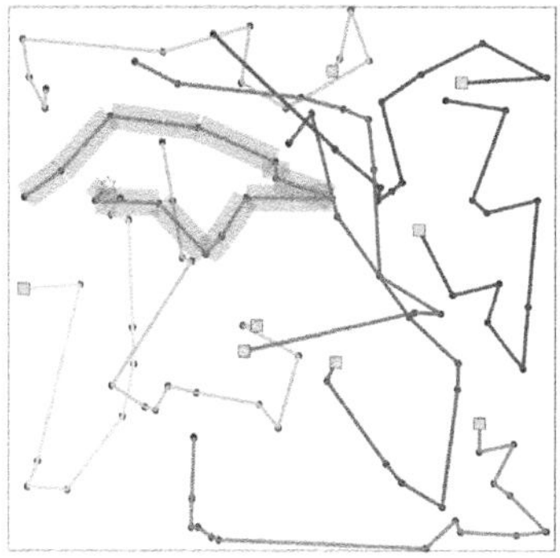

(b) Final Plan, solution mode 1, scenario 2

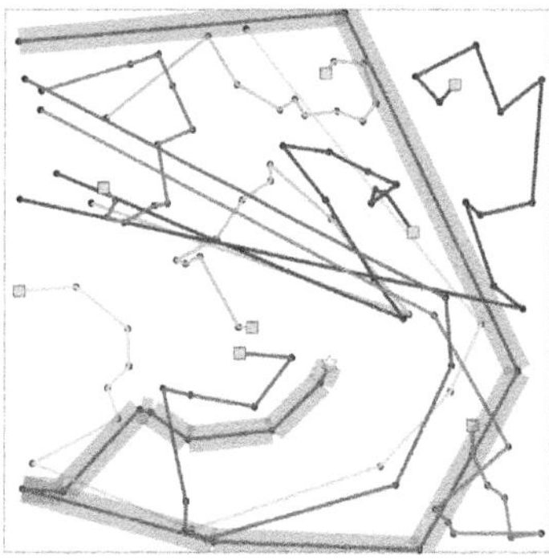

(c) Initial Plan, solution mode 2, scenario 2

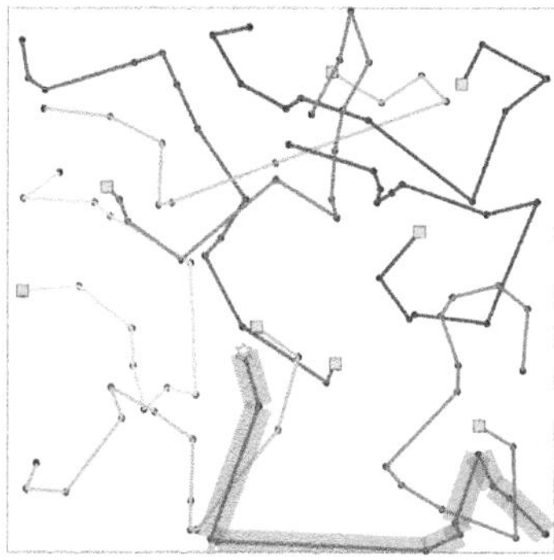

(d) Final Plan, solution mode 2, scenario 2

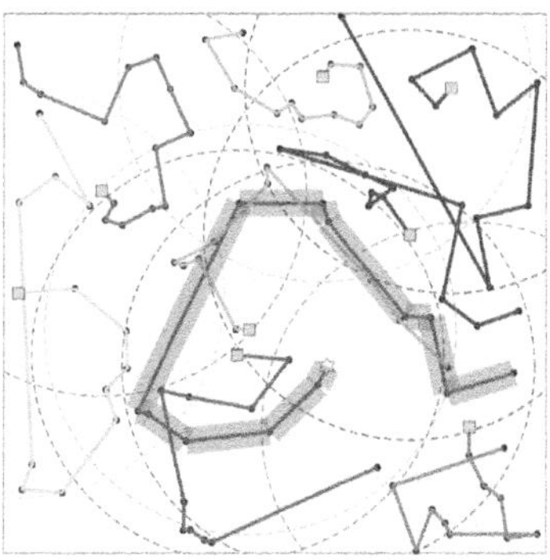

(e) Initial Plan, solution mode 3, scenario 2

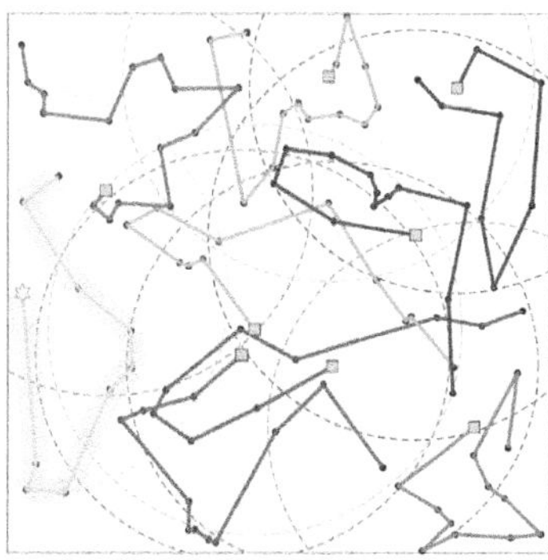

(f) Final Plan, solution mode 3, scenario 2

Fig. 1. Initial Plans (left) vs. Final Plans (right) generated by solution modes 1, 2 and 3; scenario 2; the test case in which the solution achieved the largest Δc_m in the case of applying Greedy initialization along with the constraint on the maximum number of targets for each agent. (Color figure online)

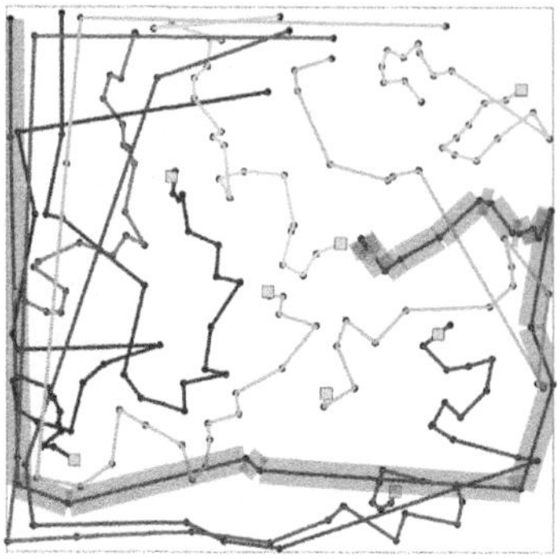

(a) Initial Plan, solution mode 1, scenario 4

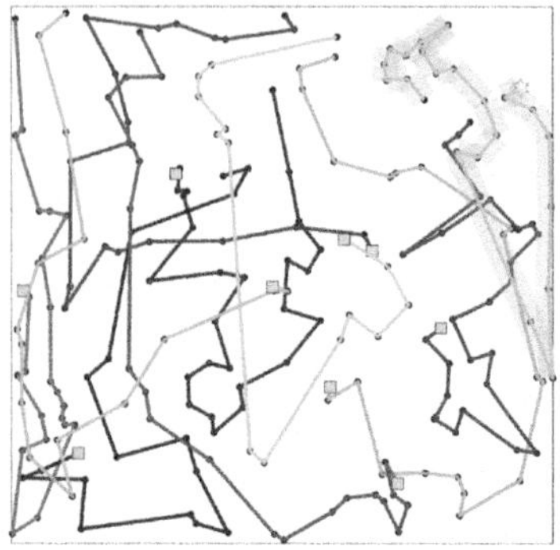

(b) Final Plan, solution mode 1, scenario 4

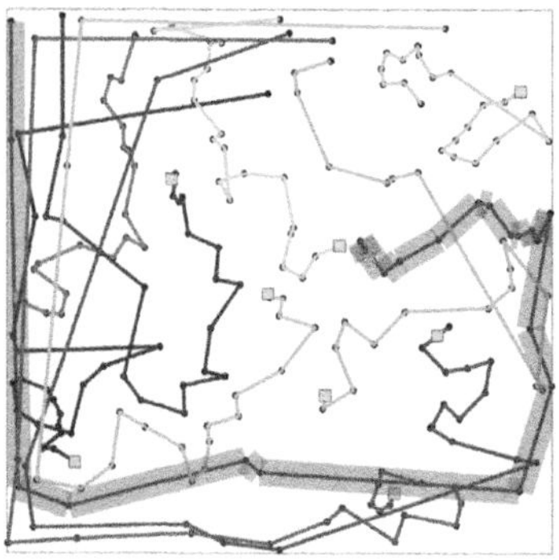

(c) Initial Plan, solution mode 2, scenario 4

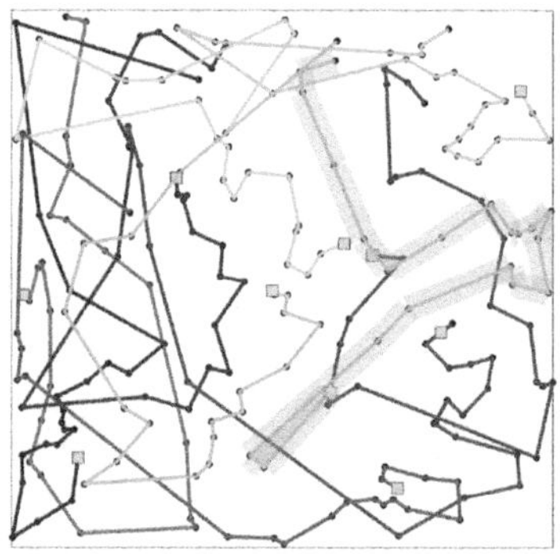

(d) Final Plan, solution mode 2, scenario 4

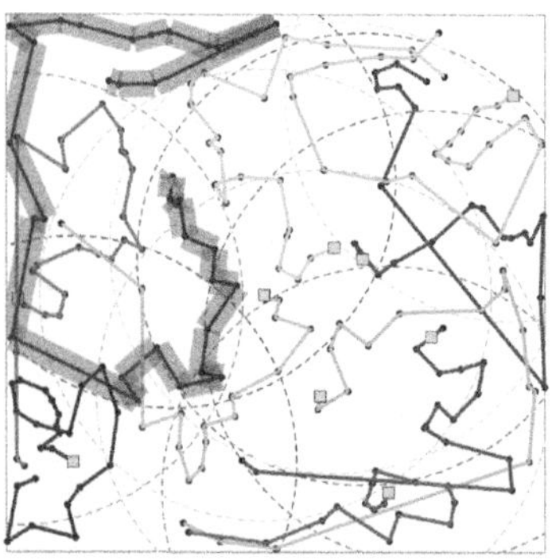

(e) Initial Plan, solution mode 3, scenario 4

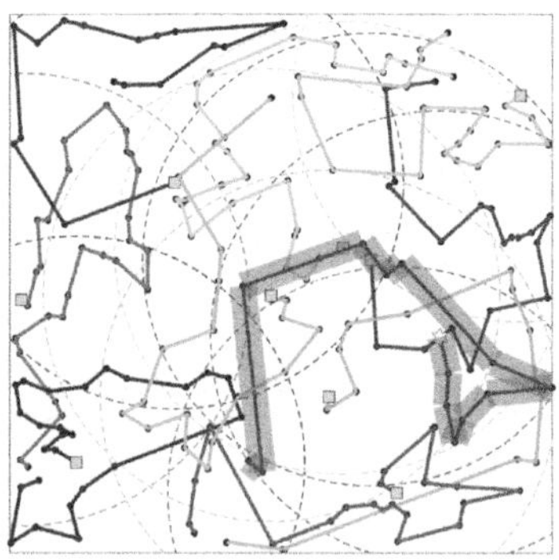

(f) Final Plan, solution mode 3, scenario 4

Fig. 2. Initial Plans (left) vs. Final Plans (right) generated by solution modes 1, 2 and 3; scenario 4; the test case in which the solution achieved the largest Δc_m in the case of applying Greedy initialization along with the constraint on the maximum range for each agent. (Color figure online)

are illustrated in Fig. 2. In this test case the solution attained the highest Δc_m among 100 test cases of scenario 4 if Greedy initialization was applied together with the constraint on the maximum range for each agent. In the absence of any additional constraints, the cost $c_m(\mathbb{P})$ reduced from 2.86 in the Initial Plan (Fig. 2(a)) to 1.74 in the Final Plan (Fig. 2(b)). If the maximum number of targets for each agent was limited to $q_i = 20$, the cost $c_m(\mathbb{P})$ dropped from 2.86 in the Initial Plan (Fig. 2(c)) to 1.95 in the Final Plan (Fig. 2(d)). Finally, if the maximum range for each agent was restricted to $r_i = 0.42$, the cost $c_m(\mathbb{P})$ decreased from 2.60 in the Initial Plan (Fig. 2(e)) to 1.52 in the Final Plan (Fig. 2(f)).

Comparing our developed method with previously proposed methods using a similar GA for the MAPP problem, our method is novel because despite the similarity in utilizing the mutation operator and the 2-OPT algorithm in [10], their initialization phase (initial solution) and crossover operator function differently. Moreover, our additional constraints were not applied in [16] and their initialization phase uses a different targets assignment algorithm. The presented method can be extended by applying other practical constraints realizing time windows and priorities [5,13,19,25], conflict-free paths [3,7], and multi-modal itinerary planning [21].

6 Conclusions

This paper presents a cooperative path planner based on the Multi-Agent Path Planning (MAPP) problem with additional constraints to model more practical situations. The proposed solution uses a Genetic Algorithm (GA) applying genetic-like operators and a heuristic method. It evolves an Initial Plan towards a near-optimal Multi-Agent Plan by minimizing the length of the longest path.

The applicability of the approximate solution was tested in four random scenarios. The computational results show that restricting the maximum number of targets for each agent can mostly improve the performance of the solution if the Initial Plan is generated by Greedy initialization. Furthermore, on average the cost of the Final Plan can be decreased by limiting the maximum range for each agent if the Initial Plan is generated by Greedy initialization. This trend is observed in the scenarios with more targets (200 in this study) even if the Initial Plan is generated by Random initialization. These results show that using a simple yet efficient initial solution, the developed method can potentially enhance the efficiency of route planning for a fleet of vehicles when the aim is to optimize open paths (subtours) in a cooperative manner, and the vehicles of the fleet have a limited operational range or a balance between their workload is desired. This situation can be observed in a variety of mobility and logistics services such as crowd-sourced delivery (e.g., TOURMIX), group ride-sharing, general home delivery, and airport shuttles.

The ultimate goal of this work is to simulate the challenges observed in cooperative path planning for vehicle fleets. Thus, it can be extended by applying other practical constraints like time windows and priorities. Our future work will focus on developing a Multi-Agent route planner for shared mobility services using the method presented here but by calculating the length of paths based on map data (i.e., actual driving distance).

References

1. Bektas, T.: The multiple traveling salesman problem: an overview of formulations and solution procedures. Omega **34**(3), 209–219 (2006). https://doi.org/10.1016/j.omega.2004.10.004
2. Bentley, J.L.: Experiments on traveling salesman heuristics. In: Proceedings of the First Annual ACM-SIAM Symposium on Discrete Algorithms (SODA 1990), USA, pp. 91–99. SIAM (1990)
3. Bose, J., Reiners, T., Steenken, D., Voss, S.: Vehicle dispatching at seaport container terminals using evolutionary algorithms. In: Proceedings of the 33rd Annual Hawaii International Conference on System Sciences (HICSS), USA, vol. 2, pp. 1–10. IEEE (2000). https://doi.org/10.1109/HICSS.2000.926669
4. Chen, J., Ling, F., Zhang, Y., You, T., Liu, Y., Du, X.: Coverage path planning of heterogeneous unmanned aerial vehicles based on ant colony system. Swarm Evol. Comput. **69**, 101005, 1–11 (2022). https://doi.org/10.1016/j.swevo.2021.101005
5. Fournier, S.M.R., Hülse, E.O., Pinheiro, É.V.: A*-guided heuristic for a multi-objective bus passenger Trip Planning Problem. Public Transp. **13**, 557–578 (2021). https://doi.org/10.1007/s12469-019-00204-1
6. Gavish, B., Srikanth, K.: An optimal solution method for large-scale multiple traveling salesmen problems. Oper. Res. **34**(5), 698–717 (1986). https://doi.org/10.1287/opre.34.5.698
7. Gawrilow, E., Köhler, E., Möhring, R.H., Stenzel, B.: Dynamic routing of automated guided vehicles in real-time. In: Krebs, H.-J., Jäger, W. (eds.) Mathematics - Key Technology for the Future, pp. 165–177. Springer, Heidelberg (2008). https://doi.org/10.1007/978-3-540-77203-3_12
8. Ghafurian, S., Javadian, N.: An ant colony algorithm for solving fixed destination multi-depot multiple traveling salesmen problems. Appl. Soft Comput. **11**(1), 1256–1262 (2011). https://doi.org/10.1016/j.asoc.2010.03.002
9. Giardini, G., Kalmár-Nagy, T.: Genetic algorithm for combinatorial path planning: the subtour problem. Math. Probl. Eng. **2011**, 483643, 1–31 (2011). https://doi.org/10.1155/2011/483643
10. Giardini, G., Kalmar-Nagy, T.: Genetic algorithm for multi-agent space exploration. In: Proceedings of AIAA Infotech@Aerospace 2007 Conference and Exhibit 2824, USA, pp. 1–15. AIAA (2007). https://doi.org/10.2514/6.2007-2824
11. Goldberg, D.E.: Genetic Algorithms in Search, Optimization, and Machine Learning. Addison-Wesley Publishing Company Inc., Boston (1989)
12. Harrath, Y., Salman, A.F., Alqaddoumi, A., Hasan, H., Radhi, A.: A novel hybrid approach for solving the multiple traveling salesmen problem. Arab J. Basic Appl. Sci. **26**(1), 103–112 (2019). https://doi.org/10.1080/25765299.2019.1565193
13. Herbawi, W., Weber, M.: The ridematching problem with time windows in dynamic ridesharing: a model and a genetic algorithm. In: Proceedings of 2012 IEEE Congress on Evolutionary Computation, USA, pp. 1–8. IEEE (2012). https://doi.org/10.1109/CEC.2012.6253001

14. Hou, M., Liu, D.: A novel method for solving the multiple traveling salesmen problem with multiple depots. Chin. Sci. Bull. **57**(15), 1886–1892 (2012). https://doi.org/10.1007/s11434-012-5162-7
15. Jiang, C., Wan, Z., Peng, Z.: A new efficient hybrid algorithm for large scale multiple traveling salesman problems. Expert Syst. Appl. **139**, 112867, 1–11 (2020). https://doi.org/10.1016/j.eswa.2019.112867
16. Kalmár-Nagy, T., Giardini, G., Bak, B.D.: The multiagent planning problem. Complexity **2017**, 3813912, 1–12 (2017). https://doi.org/10.1155/2017/3813912
17. Kara, I., Bektas, T.: Integer linear programming formulations of multiple salesman problems and its variations. Eur. J. Oper. Res. **174**(3), 1449–1458 (2006). https://doi.org/10.1016/j.ejor.2005.03.008
18. Karabulut, K., Öztop, H., Kandiller, L., Tasgetiren, M.F.: Modeling and optimization of multiple traveling salesmen problems: an evolution strategy approach. Comput. Oper. Res. **129**, 105192, 1–19 (2021). https://doi.org/10.1016/j.cor.2020.105192
19. Király, A., Abonyi, J.: Redesign of the supply of mobile mechanics based on a novel genetic optimization algorithm using Google Maps API. Eng. Appl. Artif. Intell. **38**, 122–130 (2015). https://doi.org/10.1016/j.engappai.2014.10.015
20. Laporte, G., Nobert, Y.: A cutting planes algorithm for the m-salesmen problem. J. Oper. Res. Soc. **31**(11), 1017–1023 (1980). https://doi.org/10.1057/jors.1980.188
21. Redmond, M., Campbell, A.M., Ehmke, J.F.: Data-driven planning of reliable itineraries in multi-modal transit networks. Public Transp. **12**, 171–205 (2020). https://doi.org/10.1007/s12469-019-00221-0
22. Ryan, J.L., Bailey, T.G., Moore, J.T., Carlton, W.B.: Reactive Tabu Search in unmanned aerial reconnaissance simulations. In: Proceedings of 1998 Winter Simulation Conference (Cat. No. 98CH36274), USA, vol. 1, pp. 873–879. IEEE (1998). https://doi.org/10.1109/WSC.1998.745084
23. Somhom, S., Modares, A., Enkawa, T.: Competition-based neural network for the multiple travelling salesmen problem with minmax objective. Comput. Oper. Res. **26**(4), 395–407 (1999). https://doi.org/10.1016/S0305-0548(98)00069-0
24. Song, C.-H., Lee, K., Lee, W.D.: Extended simulated annealing for augmented TSP and multi-salesmen TSP. In: Proceedings of the International Joint Conference on Neural Networks (IJCNN), USA, vol. 3, pp. 2340–2343. IEEE (2003). https://doi.org/10.1109/IJCNN.2003.1223777
25. Tong, Y., Zeng, Y., Zhou, Z., Chen, L., Ye, J., Xu, K.: A unified approach to route planning for shared mobility. Proc. VLDB Endow. **11**(11), 1633–1646 (2018). https://doi.org/10.14778/3236187.3236211
26. Torabbeigi, M., Lim, G.J., Kim, S.J.: Drone delivery scheduling optimization considering payload-induced battery consumption rates. J. Intell. Robot. Syst. **97**(3), 471–487 (2020). https://doi.org/10.1007/s10846-019-01034-w
27. Wang, X., Liu, D., Hou, M.: A novel method for multiple depot and open paths, multiple traveling salesmen problem. In: Proceedings of 2013 IEEE 11th International Symposium on Applied Machine Intelligence and Informatics (SAMI), USA, pp. 187–192. IEEE (2013). https://doi.org/10.1109/SAMI.2013.6480972
28. Yu, H., Meier, K., Argyle, M., Beard, R.W.: Cooperative path planning for target tracking in urban environments using unmanned air and ground vehicles. IEEE/ASME Trans. Mechatron. **20**(2), 541–552 (2015). https://doi.org/10.1109/TMECH.2014.2301459

29. Yuan, S., Skinner, B., Huang, S., Liu, D.: A new crossover approach for solving the multiple travelling salesmen problem using genetic algorithms. Eur. J. Oper. Res. **228**(1), 72–82 (2013). https://doi.org/10.1016/j.ejor.2013.01.043
30. Zhou, H., Song, M., Pedrycz, W.: A comparative study of improved GA and PSO in solving multiple traveling salesmen problem. Appl. Soft Comput. **64**, 564–580 (2018). https://doi.org/10.1016/j.asoc.2017.12.031

UAV Path Planning for Area Coverage and Energy Consumption in Oil and Gas Exploration Environment

Salim Sulaiman Maaji(✉) and Dario Landa-Silva

School of Computer Science, University of Nottingham, Nottingham NG8 1BB, UK
{salim.maaji2,dario.landasilva}@nottingham.ac.uk

Abstract. This paper proposes a model for unmanned aerial vehicles (UAV) grid-based coverage path planning, considering coverage completeness and energy consumption in complex environments with multiple obstacles. The work is inspired by the need for more efficient approaches to oil and gas exploration, but other application areas where UAVs can be used to explore unknown environments can also benefit from this work. An energy consumption model is proposed that considers acceleration, deceleration, and turning manoeuvres, as well as the distance to obstacles, to more accurately simulate the UAV's movement in different environments. Three different environments are modelled: desert, forest, and jungle. The energy-aware coverage path planning algorithm implemented seeks to reduce the energy consumption of a single drone while increasing coverage completeness. The model implementation and experiments were performed in the ROS/Gazebo simulation software. Obtained results show that the algorithm performs very well, with the drone able to manoeuvre itself in a combination of hills, valleys, rugged terrain, and steep topography while balancing coverage and energy consumption.

Keywords: UAV Path Planning · Drone Energy Optimisation · Coverage Path Planning · Multiple Obstacle Avoidance · Exploration in Unknown Environment

1 Introduction

Environmental concerns have brought challenges to the oil and gas industry, including pressure to reduce and stabilise costs for competitive advantage, improve its environmental blueprint, and optimise its performance. In recent years, the production of most onshore oil fields has declined [12] in part because, after a certain level of recovery, production costs do not justify further investment. Oil and gas exploration often takes place in difficult-to-reach environments where the use of robotic systems can be useful [37]. Petroleum deposits are generated by a natural process that commonly occurs at great depth and is often poorly understood and predicted by earth scientists. Hence large areas with significant oil and gas potential remain unexplored [25]. In 2015, Shell Oil decided to abandon efforts to find and develop hydrocarbon resources in the Chukchi Sea, despite having spent billions of dollars in exploration, which in the end turned out to be a dry

© The Author(s), under exclusive license to Springer Nature Switzerland AG 2023
J. R. Daduna et al. (Eds.): ICCL 2023, LNCS 14239, pp. 467–481, 2023.
https://doi.org/10.1007/978-3-031-43612-3_29

hole [38]. This type of risk cannot be eliminated, but it can be reduced through technological innovations. An example of such technology is magnetic exploration which measures variations in the earth's magnetic field to identify rocks containing hydrocarbon [1]. Aeromagnetic surveys are used to measure magnetic anomalies using low-flying aircraft carrying a high-precision magnetometer, a sensor for magnetic anomaly detection [2]. However, aeromagnetic surveying with low-flying aircraft brings challenges in terms of safety, terrain complexity, quality of data, and costs. An attractive alternative is to conduct magnetic exploration with UAVs [38]. UAVs can fly close to the surface at optimal speed with efficient coverage for gathering good-quality magnetic data [42]. UAVs are fast becoming an attractive solution for many scenarios like search and rescue [19], precision agriculture [31], and delivery systems [26].

Magnetic exploration with UAVs requires effective path planning in unknown environments and with possibly multiple obstacles (e.g., trees, large rocks, etc.). The robotic path planning problem can be divided into two main categories: motion path planning and coverage path planning. In motion path planning, there is a clear start point and an end point; the goal is to optimally cover the distance between the start to the endpoint at minimum cost while avoiding obstacles [35]. Coverage path planning (CPP) finds an optimal collision-free path that a robot must take to pass over each point in an area of interest in the given environment [10]. CPP is related to the covering salesman problem where an agent must travel a minimum-length tour covering the subsets of given cities or customers [46, 24]. CPP can be offline or online depending on the availability of a priori information about the area of interest [18], and several algorithms exist to tackle this problem [40]. In CPP, the area of interest can be decomposed into smaller regions or not at all. Simple and regular-shaped environments require no decomposition, and simple geometric patterns such as back-and-forth (BF), zigzag movement, or spiral patterns can be used to solve the problem [34]. When the exploration area is irregular-shaped and complex, decomposition can be done in different ways, like exact cellular decomposition [28], approximate cellular decomposition [8, 21], or grid-based decomposition [18]. For the scenarios investigated in this paper, grid-based decomposition was used to ensure that every cell within the area of interest is visited once. This method requires computational power to represent the cells at higher resolution grids [24]. After the grid is produced, a traveling salesman algorithm is applied to generate a sequence of nodes or subregions to visit [4]. The coverage path is generated by connecting these nodes in sequence using back-and-forth motion perpendicular to the sweep direction from the start to the goal region [9, 28].

Magnetic surveying with UAVs for oil/gas exploration requires complete coverage of the area of interest. Performing CPP with UAVs in an environment with multiple obstacles is energy-demanding due to the need for obstacle avoidance, and limited energy capacity is a feature of UAVs [20]. The approach in this paper minimised energy consumption by limiting accelerations, decelerations, and turning manoeuvres by the drone while at the same time maximising coverage. Aided by simultaneous localisation and mapping (SLAM), a model for coverage path-planning in a regular and irregular-shaped environment is developed in ROS/Gazebo platform. The regular-shaped environment has a perfect square-shaped setting with no mountains, hills, or valleys. In contrast, the irregular-shaped environment has a complex terrain with no specific shape. Experiments were conducted to study the tradeoff between area coverage and energy consumption. Section 2 outlines related research on coverage path planning. Section 3 describes the methodology and cost function. Section 4 presents the experimental result and discussions, and concluding remarks are presented in Sect. 5.

2 Related Research

Coverage path planning (CPP) has been extensively studied in the literature but is still an open problem in robotics [40]. Different approaches have been adopted to classify the problems into (i) increasing the coverage completeness, (ii) reducing the path overlapping, (ii) reducing the energy consumption, (iv) optimising the number of turns, and (v) reducing the time to completion. A randomised approach does not require sensors and algorithms for localisation, but such an approach is inefficient when dealing with large coverage areas requiring more energy and time to complete the coverage [14]. A distributed strategy and model for UAVs oil spill mapping used randomness and probabilistic guessing to avoid visiting all the cells and hence reduce the total distance travelled, but coverage completeness decreased [32]. Different geometric patterns and shapes for coverage patterns have been studied, including back-and-forth (BF), Hilbert curves, LMAT (chain of equilateral triangles), S curves, and spiral patterns [5]. An optimal line-sweep decomposition path planner to minimise the time required for covering the area with obstacles in an unknown environment was presented in [4]. The authors claimed that changing the sweep direction, as shown in Fig. 1, helps in minimising the number of turns and hence reducing the time to completion. Similarly, reducing the number of turns using optimal sweep direction and coverage pattern was considered in [3, 24] in a quest to reduce energy consumption. Energy-aware CPP is an active area of research aiming at minimum energy consumption and maximum area coverage. Some studies considered energy optimisation based on the UAV structure, aerodynamic properties, rotor efficiency, and energy consumed in onboard data processing and controls [17–44].

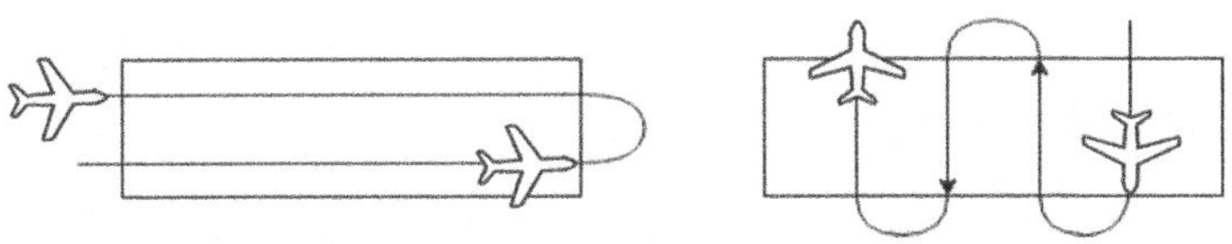

Fig. 1. Coverage path-planning with sweep direction changed to reduced turning angles.

Energy-aware coverage path planning algorithms with a high emphasis on trajectories that reduce power consumption during operations have been proposed [15, 36]. It has been found that the length of the trajectory, the UAV speed, and the way to make turns along the trajectory are the main energy sinks during the operation. In the literature, the performance index for energy consumption was to reduce the path length traveled during the coverage to minimise the energy consumption [45, 47], improve time-to-completion for both single and multi-robot coverage [13, 20, 30], and reduce the number of turns [11, 41]. An algorithm for single-robot coverage path planning under constrained energy was presented in [39]. The robot was aware of its energy limitation, and hence the total distance traveled to refueling was minimised. Boustrophedon cellular decomposition using back-and-forth or "ox-plow" motions and Dijkstra's algorithm were used. Although reducing the total distance to refueling is important, most of the energy is often consumed during the coverage and turning manoeuvres. Grid-based coverage path planning exhibits excellent performance in several robotic applications in irregular shapes and no fly-zones environments [5, 7]. In the work proposed by [43], the irregular-shaped area of interest was decomposed into regular cells of equal sizes, using an approximate cellular decomposition technique. The authors introduced a cost function to minimise the number of turning manoeuvres to save energy but did not take into account important factors like optimal energy and energy consumption due to accelerations and decelerations. The energy-aware algorithm proposed by [6] drastically reduced the energy consumption for the entire coverage. The model was based on optimising the turning manoeuvres, and avoiding sharp angles while reducing speed, acceleration, and deceleration at the turning angles. An improved cost function aimed at minimising energy consumption in an irregular shape was proposed in [7]. The model was good in energy saving, and it may scale well in a simplistic environment, especially those applications that do not require a high degree of coverage completeness. Only a single occlusion point was considered in their experiment, but multiple obstacles can have a significant effect on the coverage completeness.

Then, optimising the coverage completeness, energy consumption, and distance to obstacles in complex oil and gas environments with multiple occlusions is an interesting problem that has not been investigated to the best of our knowledge. The problem is unique because magnetic survey for oil/gas exploration requires near optimum line spacing and flight height, and the coverage completeness can be easily affected when trying to avoid obstacles. The environment is often mixed with regular and irregular settings of different terrains. In addressing this problem, the following question arises: Can an intelligent coverage path-planning algorithm that reduces the number of sharp turns for obstacle avoidance in a highly irregular-shaped environment reduce the amount of energy consumed by the UAV without reducing the coverage completeness?

3 Proposed Methodology

The proposed model was implemented in the ROS/Gazebo simulation software using a drone package hector quadrotor noetic [33]. As a proof of concept for the magnetometer, the drone is integrated with a magnetic sensor to read the magnetic field of the Gazebo environment. The modelled exploration environment is rugged terrain with steep topography, variations in the surface elevations, and thick vegetation cover, as illustrated in Fig. 2. The environment E is then partitioned into a grid with multiple cells of equal size $M_x \times M_y$ as illustrated in Fig. 3. Each cell (x, y) has an associated value $u(x, y, t) \in [0, 1]$ that represents the UAV's uncertainty about the target distribution in the cell at time interval t, for occupancy grid mapping, implemented using the slam_gmapping package provided in ROS [22]. The distance between each grid cell for cell-to-cell movement can be calculated using Eq. (1) where x_i, y_i are the target goal point [27].

$$d(x, y) = \sum_{i=1}^{m} |x_i - y_i| \quad (1)$$

Fig. 2. Example of forest environment modeled in the Gazebo simulation software for oil and gas exploration.

3.1 Energy Model

To derive the energy model, we first analysed energy consumption data obtained from real flights of a HEIFU drone [29] with a 22,000 mAh LiPo battery, and the nominal voltage and current were at 24 V and 60 A, respectively. The drone consumes around 23.5 V for hovering, 20.3 V for liner movement at a constant speed, 21.7 V when turning at a soft angle, and 22.6 V at a sharp bend. The nominal voltage drops drastically at around 35 min of flight from 25.2 V to 18.6 V; hence the drone has to come back for refueling. The drone's weight was 7.5 kg with maximum payload of 6 kg for a maximum take-off weight of 13.5 kg. To develop the energy cost function, we split the UAV path into a set of segments as in [7, 16]. The first segment consists of the path for constant speed (straight line movement), which does not consume much energy, compared to the second segment, the variable speed of the UVA, which includes hovering and angular movements for maneuvering and obstacle avoidance. The variable speed consumes energy due to the acceleration, deceleration, and point of discontinuity along the path. It is important to note that the energy model proposed by [43] and extended by [7] does not consider the effect of minimising the energy on coverage completeness, especially in multiple obstacle environments. Following the same idea, the cost function has been extended to consider coverage completeness and energy minimisation as two conflicting objective functions.

Figure 3 illustrates the concept of obstacle avoidance in coverage path planning. It shows a UAV flying at a fixed height h from the ground acquiring magnetic data from a cell in the grid. The field of view is the magnetometer's projected area of size 1×1

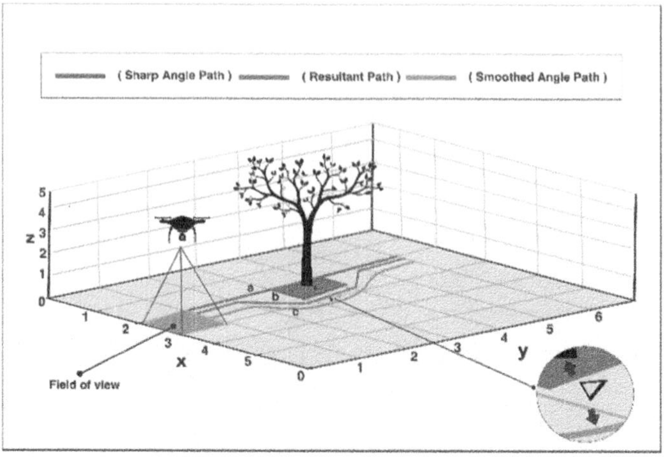

Fig. 3. Drone coverage path-planning with grid decomposition in an occluded environment.

square meter. An obstacle in the form of a tree is shown at the center of the exploration environment. Three possible waypoints are shown, marked as a, b, and c. Waypoint (a) maximises coverage in the occluded region but consumes more energy due to the sharp angles at the path. Waypoint (b) minimises energy consumption due to the reduced distance by the resultant vector but still consumes energy due to turning manoeuvres. Waypoint (c) consumes less energy because of the smoothed angle on the waypoint but with reduced coverage. The problem lies in optimising Delta Δ, the distance between the drone and the obstacle during the coverage as a constraint to be imposed for obstacle avoidance by the UAV. Minimising the delta increases the coverage, and maximising it reduces energy consumption.

Given an initial position (x_o, y_o) and target goal points (x_i, y_i), a collision-free path ensures that at no time should the UAV enter into the no-fly-zone region. The equation for collision avoidance is presented as follows:

$$\forall p \in [1 \ldots N], \forall i \in [0 \ldots \mathrm{T}]$$

$$\left| x_{ip} - x_k \right| \geq \Delta \tag{2}$$

$$\left| y_{ip} - y_k \right| \geq \Delta \tag{3}$$

In the Eqs. (2), (3) above, x_{ip}, y_{ip} are the drone position in the x and y axis at the T time instance, and x_k, y_k are the obstacle position at the x-axis and y-axis, respectively. Since most obstacles in the forest can be approximated to the shape of a sphere or circle in 2D, Eqs. (2) and (3) can be written as Eq. (4).

$$\left| x_{ip} - x_k \right| \sin \theta + \left| y_{ip} - y_k \right| \cos \theta \geq \Delta \tag{4}$$

The instantaneous power for the flight scenarios is calculated with Eq. (5), where V is an instantaneous voltage, and I is the instantaneous current consumed by the drone.

$$P = VI \tag{5}$$

The total energy consumption can be calculated by integrating the power over the period of the mission, as shown in the energy Eq. (6), where E is the energy consumed in joules, P is the instantaneous power consumed in watts, and t is the time interval for the flight mission.

$$E = \int_0^t Pdt = \int_0^t VIdt \tag{6}$$

The energy consumed when moving at a straight line to cover a distance d at constant speed v can be calculated with Eq. (7).

$$E_c = \int_0^{d/v} P_c dt = P_c \frac{d}{v} \tag{7}$$

The energy consumed for variable speed due to acceleration and deceleration can be calculated with Eq. (8).

$$E_{var} = \int_{d_o/v_o}^{d_i/v_i} P_{acc} dt = P_v(t_2 - t_1) + \int_{d_i/v_i}^{d_o/v_o} P_{decc} dt = P_v(t_2 - t_1) \tag{8}$$

The energy consumed for hovering is calculated using Eq. (9).

$$E_h = \int_0^{h/v_{climb}} P_h dt = P_h(t_2 - t_1) \tag{9}$$

In this work, the drone is restricted not to flying above trees for quality data collection as well as for manoeuvability. Hence the maximum height is set to 1 m as a constraint. Finally, the energy consumed during the rotation, maneuvering, and turning at a certain angle θ, with angular speed ω is calculated with Eq. (10).

$$E_{turn} = \int_{\Delta\theta o/\omega_o}^{\Delta\theta/\omega_i} P_{turn} dt = P_{turn} \frac{\Delta\theta}{\omega} \tag{10}$$

The cost function can be written by summing the total energy consumed in straight line movement, which also has sub-components of the constant speed and variable speed due to acceleration and deceleration, and the energy consumed in the rotational movement for turning and maneuvering in obstacle avoidance. The cost function is given by Eq. (11).

$$E_c = \sum\nolimits_{i=1}^{m} \left(\int_0^{v_i} P_{acc} dt + \int_{v_i}^{0} P_{dec} dt + \int_0^{d/v} P_c dt + \int_{\Delta\theta o/\omega_o}^{\Delta\theta/\omega_i} P_{turn} dt \right) \tag{11}$$

While the total energy needed for the coverage can be compud with Eq. (12).

$$E_{total} = \sum\nolimits_{i=1}^{m} \left(\int_0^{v_i} P_{acc} dt + \int_{v_i}^{0} P_{dec} dt + \int_0^{d/v} P_c dt + \int_0^{h/v_{climb}} P_h dt + \int_{\Delta\theta o/\omega_o}^{\Delta\theta/\omega_i} P_{turn} dt \right) \tag{12}$$

3.2 Coverage-Path Pseudocodes

Given the above energy model for the UAV, the coverage path planning shown below was implemented. The algorithm can be summarised in three sequential main steps: decomposition, planning, and execution. First, a cellular decomposition technique is applied over the irregular-shaped area to discretise the map to regular equal size cells. Second, a coverage path planning algorithm finds the nearest cell in back-and-forth movement based on the coverage goal received. The solution to the movement is according to the predefined cost function and obstacle avoidance constraint in the model. Finally, the resulting path is executed, and the coverage mission is completed.

```
BEGIN
    grid <= convertMaptoGrid(Map)
    initialPoint<=Origin(0,0)
    coverageGoal<=getCoverageGoal()
    EnergyCost <= 0
    path<=recursiveFunc(coverageGoal,EnergyCost)
    loop
    neighbors<= computeNeighbors(cells)
    if no neighbors
       return
    End if
    For each neighbors(i) do
      path<= path+ neighbors(i)
      cost<= $\sum_{i=1}^{m}\left(\int_{0}^{v_i} P_{acc}dt + \int_{v_i}^{0} P_{dec}dt + \int_{0}^{d/v} P_{c}dt + \int_{\Delta\theta o/\omega_o}^{\Delta\theta/\omega_i} P_{turn}dt\right)$
      Obstacle <= $|x_{ip} - x_k| \sin\theta + |y_{ip} - y_k| \cos\theta \geq \Delta$
      Cost<= +prevCost
      If cost < minCost
         Path <= recursiveFunc(coverageGoal,EnergyCost)
      Else:
        minCost <= cost
        minPath <= Path
      Endif
     End for
    End loop
```

The UAV energy model, environment model, and coverage path planning approach were all implemented in the ROS/Gazebo simulation software. Several experiments were conducted for various types of exploration scenarios. The scenarios consist of a perfect square regular-shaped environment and an irregular-shaped environment characterised by arbitrarily shaped obstacles. We investigated the tradeoff between coverage completeness and energy consumption in these environments.

4 Experimental Result

Three different environments usually seen in oil/gas exploration were modelled: a desert with low obstacles, including hills and valleys; a forest with a combination of hills, valleys, and moderate vegetation; and a jungle depicted rugged terrain and steep topography. A survey conducted by [48] shows that flying drones at varying altitudes of 0.5 m, 1.3 m, and 2.2 m above the ground with line spacing of 1 m provides a good result. The flight altitude was set to 1 m, and the speed was set to v = 2 m/s for the entire experiment. The experiment in a desert environment is considered a benchmark to evaluate the coverage quality, assuming the drone could successfully cover the cell with minimum energy consumption without obstacles.

4.1 Exploration Scenarios

First, an experiment was conducted in a rectangular-shaped environment, and three flights were performed to compare the algorithm's effectiveness in deserts, forests, and jungles. The environment is first decomposed into 20 cells of equal size (5 × 4) and delta set to 0.55 m. The obtained result shows that exploration in the desert consumes less energy and provides full coverage. The energy consumption doubled in the forest, and the coverage was 19 cells out of 20 target cells. The worst performance was recorded in the jungle exploration, in which the mean coverage was 11 cells out of 20 target cells, and the energy consumption was still high. A cross-section of the simulation result from the ROS-rviz software is shown in Fig. 4.

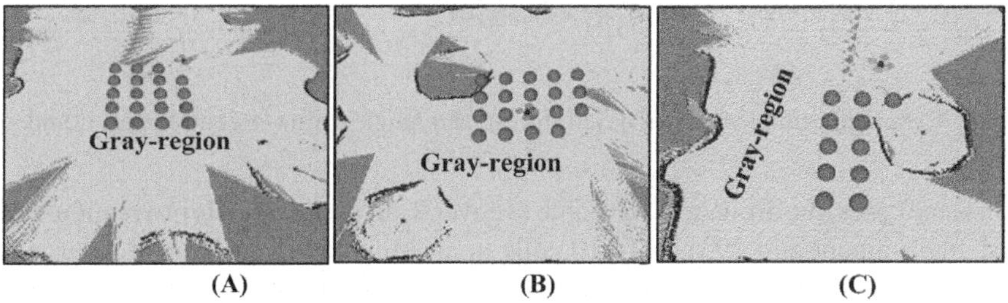

Fig. 4. The red dots represent the area in which the drone performs coverage path planning. The gray area represents a region in which the UAV is certain there is no obstacle, i.e., path-planning can be performed on it. The dark edges in the gray regions are obstacle or no-fly zones identified based on the principle of occupancy grid mapping, and the remaining part of the graph in light green represents the unexplored area.

To further assess the performance of the algorithm, another experiment was conducted using the same parameters but in a much bigger and irregular map illustrated in Fig. 5. The area was decomposed into 110 cells of equal size, and the algorithm scales well in the desert, and also performs well in the forest with few obstacles (Fig. 5b), as well as in the jungle with more obstacles (Fig. 5c). In the jungle exploration, the number of uncovered cells was 31 compared to 36 in the forest. In the second scenario, the delta was s et to 0.75 m, and an experiment was also conducted again in a regular-shaped environment, decomposed into 20 cells of equal size (5 × 4). It was also run in an irregular-shaped environment decomposed into 110 cells of equal size. Like the first scenario, three flights were performed to compare the algorithm's effectiveness in deserts, forests, and jungles. In the third scenario, the delta was set to 1.0 m, and the experiment was conducted similarly to scenarios one and two. The regular-shaped environment was decomposed into 20 cells of equal size (5 × 4). The irregular-shaped environment was decomposed into 110 cells of equal size. Three flights were performed to compare the algorithm's effectiveness in deserts, forests, and jungles. Setting the delta to 1.0 m makes the coverage very difficult in an obstacle environment. In most cases, the drone has to abandon the mission because it was trapped for over 8 min facing an obstacle, i.e., it cannot pass through a narrow path because the delta is too big. Hence, the energy consumed in the jungle was less than what was consumed in the forest. The trees in the forest along the way point were dense, and the drone was trapped hence abandoning the mission before completion.

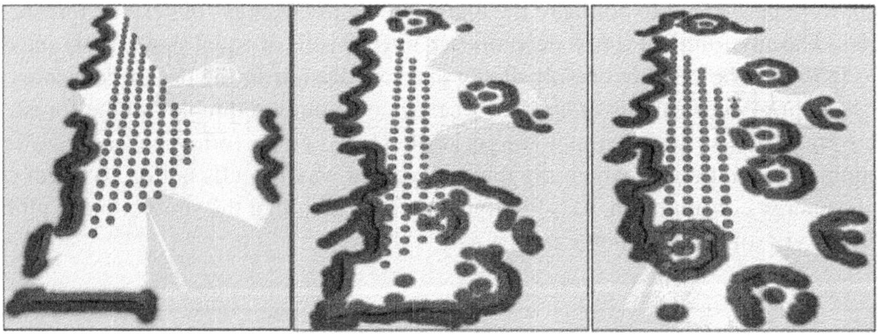

(A) (B) (C)

Fig. 5. Coverage path planning in desert, forest, and jungle for more complex environments.

In some cases, the drone was only able to cover 7 out of the 20 cells in a regular-shaped forest environment and 29 out of 110 cells in an irregular-shaped forest environment. Tables 1 and 2 show the average value of the energy consumption and coverage for the three flights performed in deserts, forests, and jungles.

Table 1. Mean energy (J) vs. Coverage (sq m) regular-shaped environment.

Environment	Delta = 0.55 m		Delta = 0.75 m		Delta = 1.0 m	
	Mean Energy	Mean Coverage	Mean Energy	Mean Coverage	Mean Energy	Mean Coverage
Desert	411.5	20	417.0	20	402.1	20
Forest	1120.9	19	393.5	19	724.7	7
Jungle	1198.2	11	523.6	11	259.2	4

Table 2. Mean energy (J) vs. Coverage (sq m) irregular-shaped environment.

Environment	Delta = 0.55 m		Delta = 0.75 m		Delta = 1.0 m	
	Mean Energy	Mean Coverage	Mean Energy	Mean Coverage	Mean Energy	Mean Coverage
Desert	2451.6	110	2388.8	110	2434.3	110
Forest	3462.7	73	942.7	26	2070.6	29
Jungle	2639.8	78	1380.5	28	1256.9	24

4.2 Evaluation of Experimental Results

The algorithm's performance was evaluated in terms of increased coverage and reduced energy consumption. The coverage results for regular-shaped and irregular-shaped environments are compared in Fig. 1 and Fig. 2, where the vertical axis is the number of cells covered, and the horizontal axis shows the various delta values for experiments in the desert, forest, and jungle. As can be seen, the algorithm achieved better coverage results in a regular-shaped environment when the delta was set to 0.55 m and 0.75 m, but the result for forest and jungle got worst when the delta was set to 1.0 m. The findings from these studies suggest that delta plays an important role and it has significance on energy consumption and coverage completeness. It allows the drone to maneuver freely out of the obstacle. That is, the higher the delta, the less energy consumption; the lower the delta, the more coverage completeness. As expected, there is a tradeoff between the number of cells covered and energy consumption in the occluded environment. Figure 6 and 7 compare energy consumption and coverage completeness for both regular and irregular-shaped environments.

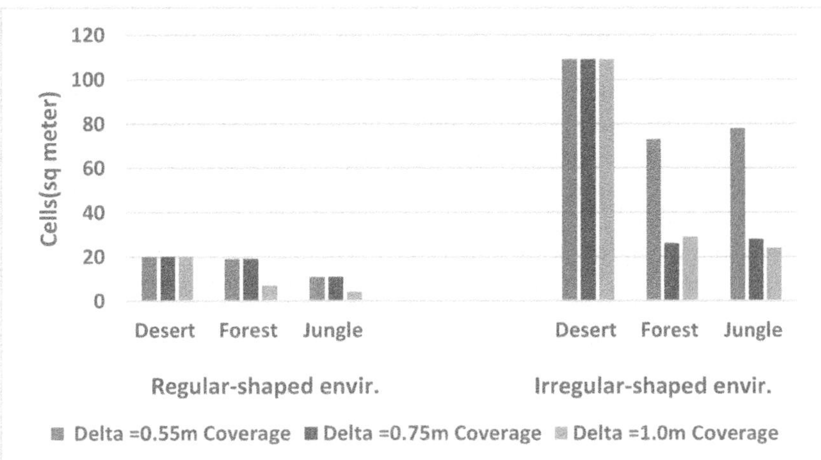

Fig. 6. Coverage completeness for regular-shaped and irregular-shaped environments.

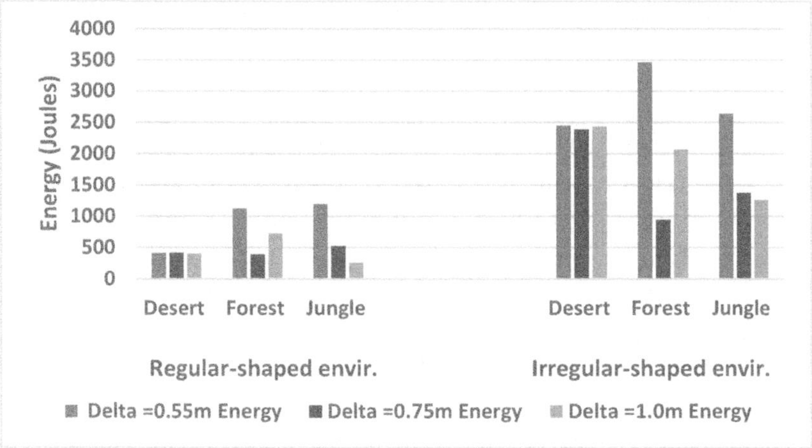

Fig. 7. Mean energy (J) in regular and irregular-shaped environments.

5 Conclusion

This paper described a model for UAV Path Planning considering the tradeoff between area coverage and energy consumption. The work is inspired by magnetic data surveying for oil/gas exploration, where environments are usually unknown and present multiple obstacles. Simulations were implemented in ROS/Gazebo for three environments: desert, forest, and jungle. A parameter delta is used to set the constraint for obstacle avoidance, and experiments with different values (0.5 m, 0.75 m, and 1.0 m) were conducted. Experimental results show that the drone effectively maneuvered itself in different environmental settings, achieving high coverage and moderate energy consumption when the delta was set to 0.5 m in a desert environment. As the complexity of the environment increases, energy consumption increases due to obstacle avoidance while the coverage optimality reduces. The overall best results were obtained when the delta was set to 0.5 m, skipping a few cells while performing coverage in forest and jungle but with added energy consumption compared to exploration in the desert. The worst coverage result was obtained when the delta was set to 1.0 m in the forest and the jungle. These results show that the delta value influences energy consumption and coverage completeness. The larger the delta value, the less energy consumption due to the smoothed angle and less acceleration and deceleration along the obstacle avoidance path. The lower the delta value, the more coverage completeness. There was a tradeoff between the number of cells covered and energy consumption in the occluded environment, and in some cases, the drone was trapped by the obstacles. Further work will look at more sophisticated path-planning algorithms and multiple drones.

References

1. Abubakar, R., et al.: Formation of magnetic minerals at hydrocarbon-generation conditions. Mar. Pet. Geol. **68**, 509–519 (2015). https://doi.org/10.1016/j.marpetgeo.2015.10.003
2. Aminzadeh, F., Dasgupta, S.: Geophysics for petroleum engineers: chapter 3. Fundamentals of Petroleum Geophysics, 1st edn, vol. 60, pp. 1–282. Elsevier Inc., UK (2013). ISBN: 978-0-444-50662-7
3. Araujo, J., Sujit, P., Sousa, J.: Multiple UAV area decomposition and coverage. In: 2013 IEEE Symposium on Computational Intelligence for Security and Defense Applications (CISDA), pp. 30–37 (2013). https://doi.org/10.1109/CISDA.2013.6595424
4. Bähnemann, R., Lawrance, N., Chung, J., Pantic, M., Siegwart, R., Nieto, J.: Revisiting boustrophedon coverage path planning as a generalized traveling salesman problem. In: Ishigami, G., Yoshida, K. (eds.) Field and Service Robotics. Springer Proceedings in Advanced Robotics, vol. 16, pp. 277–290. Springer, Singapore (2021). ISBN: 978-981-15-9459-5. https://doi.org/10.1007/978-981-15-9460-1_20
5. Cabreira, T.M., Brisolara, L.B., Paulo R, F.J.: Survey on coverage path planning with unmanned aerial vehicles. Drones **3**(1) (2019). https://doi.org/10.3390/drones3010004
6. Cabreira, T., Franco, C., Ferreira, P., Buttazzo, G.: Energy-aware spiral coverage path planning for UAV photogrammetric applications. IEEE Robot. Autom. Lett. **3**(4), 3662–3668 (2018). https://doi.org/10.1109/LRA.2018.2854967
7. Cabreira, T., Ferreira, P., Di Franco, G. Buttazzo, C.: Grid-based coverage path planning with minimum energy over irregular-shaped areas with UAVs. In: 2019 International Conference on Unmanned Aircraft Systems (ICUAS), pp. 758–767, (2019). https://doi.org/10.1109/ICUAS.2019.8797937
8. Cai, C., Ferrari, S.: Information-driven sensor path planning by approximate cell decomposition. IEEE Trans. Syst. Man Cybern. Part B **39**(3), 672–689 (2009). https://doi.org/10.1109/TSMCB.2008.2008561
9. Choset, H., Acar, E., Rizzi, A., Luntz, J.: Exact cellular decompositions in terms of critical points of Morse functions. In: Proceedings ICRA. Millennium Conference. IEEE International Conference on Robotics and Automation. Symposia Proceedings, vol. 3, pp. 2270–2277, USA (2000). https://doi.org/10.1109/ROBOT.2000.846365
10. Choset, H., Pignon, P.: Coverage path planning: the boustrophedon cellular decomposition. In: Field and Service Robotics, pp. 203–209 (1998). ISBN: 978-1-4471-1275-4
11. Choton, C., Prabhakar, P.: Optimal multi-robot coverage path planning for agricultural fields using motion dynamics. In: 2023 IEEE International Conference on Robotics and Automation(ICRA), pp. 11817–11823. IEEE (2023). https://doi.org/10.1109/ICRA48891.2023.10160265
12. Dou, L., et al.: Analysis of the world oil and gas exploration situation in 2021. Pet. Explor. Dev. **49**(5), 1195–1209 (2022). https://doi.org/10.1016/S1876-3804(22)60343-4
13. Duan, L., Wang, J. and Sun, Y.: Multi-robot online complete coverage based on collaboration. In: Yang, S., Islam, S. (eds.) Web and Big Data. APWeb-WAIM 2022 International Workshops. APWeb-WAIM 2022. CCIS, vol. 1784, pp. 219–231. Springer, Singapore (2023). https://doi.org/10.1007/978-981-99-1354-1_19
14. Engelsons, D., Tiger, M., Heintz, F.: Coverage path planning in large-scale multi-floor urban environments with applications to autonomous road sweeping, In: 2022 International Conference on Robotics and Automation (ICRA), pp. 3328–3334 (2022). "https://doi.org/10.1109/ICRA46639.2022.9811941"
15. Franco, C., Buttazzo, G.: Energy-aware coverage path planning of UAVs. In: 2015 IEEE International Conference on Autonomous Robot Systems and Competitions, pp. 111–117 (2015). https://doi.org/10.1109/ICARSC.2015.17

16. Franco, C., Buttazzo, G.: Coverage path planning for UAVs photogrammetry with energy and resolution constraints. J. Intell. Robot. Syst. **83**(3), 445–462 (2016). https://doi.org/10.1007/s10846-016-0348-x
17. Frew, E., Argrow, B., Houston, A., Weiss, C., Elston, J.: An energy-aware airborne dynamic data-driven application system for persistent sampling and surveillance. Procedia Comput. Sci. **18**, 2008–2017 (2013). https://doi.org/10.1016/j.procs.2013.05.370
18. Galceran, E., Carreras, M.: A survey on coverage path planning for robotics. Robot. Auton. Syst. **61**(12), 1258–1276 (2013). https://doi.org/10.1016/j.robot.2013.09.004
19. Gallego, A., Pertusa, A., Gil, P., Fisher, R.: Detection of bodies in maritime rescue operations using unmanned aerial vehicles with multispectral cameras. J. Field Robot. **36**(4), 782–796 (2019). https://doi.org/10.1002/rob.21849
20. Ghaddar, A., Merei, A., Natalizio, E.: PPS: energy-aware grid-based coverage path planning for UAVs using area partitioning in the presence of NFZs. Sensors **20**(13) (2020). https://doi.org/10.3390/s20133742
21. Guruprasad, K., Ranjitha, T.: CPC algorithm: exact area coverage by a mobile robot using approximate cellular decomposition. Robotica **39**(7), 1141–1162 (2021). https://doi.org/10.1017/S026357472000096X
22. GvdHoorn, slam_gmapping, gmapping, 2019. http://wiki.ros.org/gmapping. Accessed 07 Mar 2023
23. Jensen-Nau, K., Hermans, R, Leang, T., Leang, K.: Near-optimal area-coverage path planning of energy-constrained aerial robots with application in autonomous environmental monitoring. IEEE Trans. Autom. Sci. Eng. **18**(3), 1453–1468. IEEE (2020). https://doi.org/10.1109/TASE.2020.301627
24. John, R., Current, Schilling, D.: The covering salesman problem. Transp. Sci. **23**(3), 208–213 (1989). https://doi.org/10.1287/trsc.23.3.208
25. Jones, C.M.: The oil and gas industry must break the paradigm of the current exploration model. J. Pet. Explor. Prod. Technol. **8**(1), 131–142 (2017). https://doi.org/10.1007/s13202-017-0395-2
26. Kuru, K., Ansell, D., Khan, W., Yetgin, H.: Analysis and optimization of unmanned aerial vehicle swarms in logistics: an intelligent delivery platform. IEEE Access **7**, 15804–15831 (2019). https://doi.org/10.1109/ACCESS.2019.2892716
27. Kyaw, P., Paing, A., Thu, T., Mohan, R., Le, A., x Veerajagadheswar, A.: Coverage path planning for decomposition reconfigurable grid-maps using deep reinforcement learning based travelling salesman problem. IEEE Access **8**, 225945–225956 (2020). https://doi.org/10.1109/ACCESS.2020.3045027
28. Li, Y., Chen, H., Er, M., Wang, X.: Coverage path planning for UAVs based on enhanced exact cellular decomposition method. Mechatronics **21**(5), 876–885 (2011). https://doi.org/10.1016/j.mechatronics.2010.10.009
29. Merz, M., Pedro, D., Skliros. V., Bergenhem, C. Himanka, M.: Autonomous UAS-based agriculture applications: general overview and relevant European case studies, Drones. MDPI **6**(5), 128 (2022). https://doi.org/10.3390/drones6050128
30. Mukhamediev, R., et al.: Coverage path planning optimization of heterogeneous UAVs group for precision agriculture. IEEE Access **11**, 5789–5803 (2023). https://doi.org/10.1109/ACCESS.2023.3235207
31. Murugan, D., Garg, A., Singh, D.: Development of an adaptive approach for precision agriculture monitoring with drone and satellite data. IEEE J. Sel. Top. Appl. Earth Obs. Remote Sens. **10**(12), 5322–5328 (2017). https://doi.org/10.1109/JSTARS.2017.2746185
32. Odonkor, P., Ball, Z., Chowdhury, S.: Distributed operation of collaborating unmanned aerial vehicles for time-sensitive oil spill mapping, Swarm Evol. Comput. **46**, 52–68, (2019). https://doi.org/10.1016/j.swevo.2019.01.005

33. Rafalamao, hector-quadrotor-noetic. https://github.com/RAFALAMAO/hector-quadrotor-noetic. Accessed 7 Mar 2023
34. Rezazadeh, J., Moradi, M., Ismail, A., Dutkiewicz, E.: Impact of static trajectories on localization in wireless sensor networks. Wirel. Netw. **21**, 809–827. Springer (2015). https://doi.org/10.1007/s11276-014-0821-z
35. Sarvesh, A., Carroll, A., Gopalswamy, S.: Reshaping local path planner. IEEE Robot. Autom. Lett. **7**(3), 6534–6541 (2022). https://doi.org/10.1109/LRA.2022.3174366
36. Shivgan, R., Dong, Z.: Energy-efficient drone coverage path planning using genetic algorithm. In: 2020 IEEE 21st International Conference on High Performance Switching and Routing (HPSR), pp. 1–6 (2020). https://doi.org/10.1109/HPSR48589.2020.9098989"
37. Shukla, A., Karki, H.: Application of robotics in onshore oil and gas industry—a review Part I. Rob. Auton. Syst. **75**, 490–507 (2016). https://doi.org/10.1016/j.robot.2015.09.012
38. Shukla, A., Karki, H.: New Frontiers in Oil and Gas Exploration, 1st edn. Springer, Cham (2016). ISBN: 978-3-319-40122-5. https://doi.org/10.1007/978-3-319-40124-9
39. Strimel, G., Veloso, M., Coverage planning with finite resources. In: 2014 IEEE/RSJ International Conference on Intelligent Robots and Systems, pp. 2950–2956 (2014). https://doi.org/10.1109/IROS.2014.6942969
40. Tan, C., Mohd-Mokhtar, R., Arshad, M.: A comprehensive review of coverage path planning in robotics using classical and heuristic algorithms, IEEE Access (2021). https://doi.org/10.1109/ACCESS.2021.3108177
41. Torres, M., Pelta, D., Verdegay, J., x Torres, J.: Coverage path planning with unmanned aerial vehicles for 3D terrain reconstruction, Expert Syst. Appl. **55**, 441–451 (2016). https://doi.org/10.1016/j.eswa.2016.02.007
42. Vadim, T., Alexander, P., Vasily, A., Dmitry, K.: Unmanned airborne magnetic survey technologies: present and future. In: Nurgaliev, D., Shcherbakov, V., Kosterov, A., Spassov, S. (eds.) Recent Advances in Rock Magnetism, Environmental Magnetism and Paleomagnetism, pp. 523–534. Springer Geophysics. Springer, Cham (2019). ISBN:978-3-319-90436-8. https://doi.org/10.1007/978-3-319-90437-5_36
43. Valente, J., Sanz, D., Del Cerro, J., Barrientos, A., de Frutos, M.: Near-optimal coverage trajectories for image mosaicing using a mini quadrotor over irregular-shaped fields. Precis. Agric. **14**, 115–132 (2013). https://doi.org/10.1007/s11119-012-9287-0
44. Wenceslao, E., Shaw-Cortez, Frew, E.: Efficient trajectory development for small unmanned aircraft dynamic soaring applications. J. Guid. Control Dyn. **38**(3), 519–523 (2015). https://doi.org/10.2514/1.G000543s
45. Wu, C., Dai, C., Gong, X., Liu, Y., Wang, J., Gu, X., Wang, C.: Energy-efficient coverage path planning for general terrain surfaces. IEEE Robot. Autom. Lett. **4**(3), 2584–2591 (2019). https://doi.org/10.1109/LRA.2019.2899920
46. Xie, J., Carrillo, L., Jin, L.: An integrated traveling salesman and coverage path planning problem for unmanned aircraft systems. IEEE Control Syst. Lett. **3**(1), 67–72 (2018). https://doi.org/10.1109/LCSYS.2018.2851661
47. Xu, A., Viriyasuthee, C., Rekleitis, I.: Optimal complete terrain coverage using an unmanned aerial vehicle. In: 2011 IEEE International Conference on Robotics and Automation, pp. 2513–2519 (2011). https://doi.org/10.1109/ICRA.2011.5979707
48. Zheng, Y., Li, S., Xing, K., Zhang, X.: Unmanned aerial vehicles for magnetic surveys: a review on platform selection and interference suppression. Drones **5**(3), 93 (2021). https://doi.org/10.3390/drones5030093

Minimizing Peak Energy Demand in Flexible Job Shops

Michael Eley(✉)

Faculty of Engineering, TH Aschaffenburg, Aschaffenburg, Germany
michael.eley@th-ab.de

Abstract. In the flexible job shop scheduling problem under consideration a set of jobs consisting of different operations has to be scheduled. The operations can be processed on different machines that have different energy demands. The problem is formulated as a bi-objective optimization problem. A solution approach based on variable neighborhood search that minimizes peak energy demand for a given, minimal makespan is developed. Test results are presented based on modified benchmark problems from the literature. The results are compared with an alternative solution approach, where the problem is split up into the two subproblems, i.e. makespan minimization and peak energy demand minimization, that are solved sequentially to optimality. The results demonstrate that the proposed algorithm outperforms the benchmark approach.

Keywords: scheduling · flexible job shop · peak energy demand · variable neighborhood search

1 Introduction

In the flexible job shop problem (FJSP) a given set of jobs has to be scheduled. Each job consists of an ordered set of operations and for each operation a set of different machines is available to carry out the required processing. In most papers that address this classical version of the flexible job shop problem some given economic or production criteria like cost, total (weighted) tardiness or makespan have to be optimized while meeting some production constraints like adhering to the sequence of operations or preventing pre-emption.

In green scheduling this problem formulation is extended by considering additional aspects like energy cost, energy demand or carbon footprint. These additional aspects can be integrated by additional constraints or by adopting the objective function, for example in a multi-objective optimization approach. In this paper a hierarchical two-objective approach is pursued for a flexible job shop problem. This approach was motivated by a case study carried out at a mechanical engineering company. Besides the primary objective function that minimizes the makespan an additional secondary objective function that minimizes peak energy demand (peak load) is introduced. We assume that energy demand is determined

© The Author(s), under exclusive license to Springer Nature Switzerland AG 2023
J. R. Daduna et al. (Eds.): ICCL 2023, LNCS 14239, pp. 482–499, 2023.
https://doi.org/10.1007/978-3-031-43612-3_30

solely by electricity demand. Other forms of energy such as thermal energy or compressed air are not considered. As for the classical FJSP, the operations can be carried out on different machines, which, however, have different energy demands.

Obviously, the two objective functions are in conflict with one another. For example, in order to minimize peak energy demand, it could be advantageous not to use machines with high energy demand at the same time. However, this can lead to an increased makespan if machines with high energy demand are not used in parallel. In order to ensure high capacity utilization and adherence of delivery dates, makespan minimization is often the most important objective of a company.

The motivation for considering peak load minimization as the secondary objective is that in the German electricity market bulk consumers for energy like industrial companies are mainly charged according to their peak energy demand, as power providers have to guarantee that peak energy demand can be satisfied. Thus, minimizing peak demand results in lower energy costs for a company. Merely minimizing the peak energy demand makes no sense from an economic point of view since the proportion of energy costs in relation to total costs is low and, as described above, other criteria must also be considered in production planning.

The remainder of the paper is organized as follows. The relevant literature to the problem under consideration is reviewed in the next section. In the third section the problem is formulated as a non-linear integer programming problem. This problem formulation will later on be used to evaluate the performance of a solution approach that is presented in section four. The main focus of the proposed approach is to minimize the peak energy demand for a given makespan. The problem of minimizing the makespan in a flexible job shop is not addressed in this paper. We refer to the large number of articles in the literature addressing that problem (e.g. [1,2]). Results on comprehensive tests on extended benchmark problems taken from the literature are discussed in section five. The last section summarizes the main results and puts them into a perspective.

2 Literature Review

Below we review the literature on the flexible job shop problem with respect to papers dealing with energy aspects. In addition, we will also discuss the literature on minimizing peak energy demand. As the number of papers addressing this objective for the flexible job shop problem is rather limited, we will discuss peak load minimization for different variants of scheduling problems. A comprehensive survey on the literature on different types of green scheduling problems like single or parallel machine problems, job shop problems as well as flow shop problems can be found in the paper of [16].

2.1 Green Scheduling Approaches for Flexible Job Shops

The flexible job shop problem in which operations can be carried out on different machines, that also have different energy demands seems somehow predestined for the consideration of energy aspects. Thus, several authors have recently addressed green scheduling for different variants of the flexible job shop problem. Surveys on flexible job shop approaches can be found in the papers of [8] or of [23]. The latter one also includes green scheduling approaches. Besides makespan optimization or minimization of total tardiness in most approaches minimizing total energy demand (or total energy cost) is used as the secondary objective in a multi-objective optimization approach.

Many papers on green scheduling assume that energy demand at a given time depends on the state of the machine during that time. Therefore, states like idle, setup, loading, warm-up or processing are considered. For most of these states, the energy demand is known in advance and constant over time for each operation. Only total energy demand during idle times is not known in advance as the length of idle times depends on the result of the scheduling. Thus, in many approaches the objective of minimizing total energy demand can be reduced to minimizing idle energy demand or even idle times (cf. the approaches of [10,15,18,19,21,24,34,39,42–44]).

In some approaches the production speed for the operations is an additional decision variable, for example in the articles of [42] or [15]. With a higher production speed processing times for operations can be reduced, resulting for example in a lower makespan, but energy demand is increased.

2.2 Approaches Minimizing Peak Energy Demand

Peak energy demand aspects for different types of scheduling problems have recently been addressed by several authors. In these approaches, restricting peak energy demand can be imposed by a constraint that limits a given maximum value (threshold) for each single period or by the objective function that minimizes peak energy demand.

[4,27] as well as [36] addressed problems from the process industry. Single and parallel machine scheduling problems were discussed in the articles of [37] and [3] as well as [40], respectively. [14] as well as [25] addressed the general flow shop problem, whereas [6] and [12,13] focused on flexible flow shops. Peak energy demand minimization for job shop problems were discussed by several authors, e.g. [32,41,45] (reactive scheduling), [22] and [26].

As mentioned in Sect. 1, when peak energy demand aspects are considered, the energy demand of a machine must be modeled more precisely. The same applies if energy prices vary over time, e.g. for time-of-use tariffs. Therefore, [38] proposed using energy load profiles instead of average energy demand values particularly when considering peak energy demand. Furthermore, [35] recommended a discretization of the energy demand as it avoids the modelling of complex functions and thus reduces the problem's complexity.

Thus, it is interesting to see that in most papers energy demand solely depends on the factors like the operation, the machine, the machine load, the state of the machine or the chosen speed of the machine, but it is kept constant over the processing time (cf. [3,4,6,12–14,25,26,29,30,37,40]). Only a few authors consider fluctuating energy demand over time.

[27] were the first authors who examined variable energy demand (steam energy) in their simulation model for the process industry. [36] consider varying energy demand during processing a job for a batch production problem in the process industry. [45] and [22] divided each operation of their job shop scheduling problem into two parts. Energy demand is constant for both parts, but the energy demand for the first part is higher than for the second part. [32] model energy demand of machines by an integral of the energy during processing times. The authors address a reactive job shop scheduling problem for a flexible manufacturing system. [41] approximate the energy profile of a machine for a job shop problem by a mathematical power series.

In summary, it can be stated that the flexible job shop problem with different energy-oriented objectives and restrictions has been dealt with in the literature in recent years. The main focus, however, was on minimizing total energy consumption. There is also extensive literature on the topic of minimizing peak energy load, with various problems being discussed. In contrast, the intersection of the two subject areas green scheduling for the flexible job shop problem and minimization of peak energy load is hardly considered. Furthermore, if any, other optimization models than the problem presented in Sect. 1 are discussed. This is surprising insofar as it is precisely in this case that peak load minimization is promising if the machines that can carry out the processing of the operations have different energy demands, and if the energy demand also changes over the course of the processing.

Below we will introduce a new solution approach to the flexible job shop problem where we model the operation-dependent energy demand of the machines by step functions. In the objective functions we will consider minimization of the makespan and peak energy demand. We will implement a hierarchical approach minimizing in the first stage the time-based objective function and in the second stage peak energy demand. As far as the author is aware, this question has so far not been investigated for the flexible job shop problem. Similar optimization approaches have only been suggested for different scheduling problems. [6] proposed this hierarchical approach for the flow shop problem; [3] addressed it to the parallel machine problem.

3 Problem Formulation

The problem under consideration consists of n jobs that have to be scheduled on a set of m machines. We will pursue a hierarchical two-objective optimization approach. The primary objective function minimizes the makespan. Minimization of peak energy demand serves as a secondary objective. Each job j consists of h_j operations. For each operation $O_{j,h}$ a sub-set of the machines is permitted to carry out the operations. We assume that each operation can be processed by only one machine at a time and that each machine can only carry out one operation at a time. Pre-emption is not allowed.

Before stating the problem formally, we introduce some notation in Table 1. In the problem formulation used here, the use of time-indexed variables is dispensed with. The variables used instead lead to a non-linear constraint on the one hand. On the other hand, they increase the comprehensibility and make it clear how the sub-problems are separated from one another within the framework of the hierarchical solution approach. It should also be noted that the use of time-indexed variables does not improve the solvability of the problem since the number of variables increases with the number of periods. For example, in the test cases used in Sect. 5, this leads to a few million variables.

Table 1. Parameters and decision variables used

N	number of jobs
M	number of machines
h_j	number of operations for job j
l	maximal number of operations assigned to a machine
T	length of planning horizon
L	a large number
$a_{i,j,h}$	$= \begin{cases} 1 & \text{if operation } O_{j,h} \text{ can be performed on machine } i, \\ 0 & \text{otherwise} \end{cases}$
$p_{i,j,h}$	processing time of operation $O_{j,h}$ if performed on machine i
$E_{i,j,h}(d)$	energy demand (wattage) for processing operation $O_{j,h}$ on machine i after elapsing of $d = 1, ..., p_{i,j,h}$ periods
Γ	makespan
Π	peak energy demand
$t_{j,h}$	start time of the processing of operation $O_{j,h}$
$TM_{i,k}$	start working time of the k-th operation of machine i
$y_{i,j,h}$	$= \begin{cases} 1 & \text{if machine } i \text{ is selected for carrying out operation } O_{j,h}, \\ 0 & \text{otherwise} \end{cases}$
$x_{i,j,h,k}$	$= \begin{cases} 1 & \text{if operation } O_{j,h} \text{ is the } k\text{-th operation on machine } i, \\ 0 & \text{otherwise} \end{cases}$
$w_{i,k,r}$	$= \begin{cases} 1 & \text{if } r = TM_{i,k}, \\ 0 & \text{otherwise} \end{cases}$

$$min\ \Gamma \tag{1}$$

$$min\ \Pi \tag{2}$$

The two objective functions (1) and (2) minimize the makespan and the peak energy demand, respectively, subject to the following constraints.

$$\sum_{i=1}^{M} y_{i,j,h} = 1 \quad j = 1, ..., N; \quad h = 1, ..., h_j \tag{3}$$

$$y_{i,j,h} \leq a_{i,j,h} \quad i = 1, ..., M; \quad j = 1, ..., N; \quad h = 1, ..., h_j \tag{4}$$

$$\sum_{j=1}^{N}\sum_{h=1}^{h_j} x_{i,j,h,k} \leq 1 \quad i=1,...,M; \quad k=1,...,l \tag{5}$$

$$\sum_{j=1}^{N}\sum_{h=1}^{h_j} x_{i,j,h,k} \geq \sum_{j=1}^{N}\sum_{h=1}^{h_j} x_{i,j,h,k+1} \quad i=1,...,M; \quad k=1,...,l-1 \tag{6}$$

$$\sum_{k=1}^{l} x_{i,j,h,k} = y_{i,j,h} \quad i=1,...,M; \quad j=1,...,N; \quad h=1,...,h_j \tag{7}$$

Constraint (3) guarantees that each operation $O_{j,h}$ is assigned to exactly one machine. This assignment can only take place if the corresponding operation can be performed on the considered machine i. This is imposed by constraint (4). The following constraint (5) limits the number of operations that can be assigned on the k-th position of a machine to at most one. By constraint (6) the positions of a machine are assigned sequentially. Note, that this constraint is not required as one can always find an optimal solution that satisfies this constraint. Nevertheless, this constraint limits the number of possible assignments of operations to machine positions. Finally, each operation assigned to one machine must also be assigned to one position in the sequence of operations on that machine; cf. constraint (7).

$$t_{j,h} + \sum_{i=1}^{M} y_{i,j,h} \cdot p_{i,j,h} \leq t_{j,h+1} \quad j=1,...,N; \quad h=1,...,h_j-1 \tag{8}$$

$$\begin{gathered} TM_{i,k} \leq t_{j,h} + (1 - x_{i,j,h,k}) \cdot L \\ i=1,...,M; \quad j=1,...,N; \quad h=1,...,h_j; \quad k=1,...,l \end{gathered} \tag{9}$$

$$\begin{gathered} t_{j,h} \leq TM_{i,k} + (1 - x_{i,j,h,k}) \cdot L \\ i=1,...,M; \quad j=1,...,N; \quad h=1,...,h_j; \quad k=1,...,l \end{gathered} \tag{10}$$

$$\begin{gathered} TM_{i,k} + \sum_{j=1}^{N}\sum_{h=1}^{h_j} p_{i,j,h} \cdot x_{i,j,h,k} \leq TM_{i,k+1} \\ i=1,...,M; \quad k=1,...,l-1 \end{gathered} \tag{11}$$

Constraint (8) ensures that the available start time of operation $O_{j,h+1}$ is greater than or equal to the completion time of the previous operation of that job j. The following two constraints (9) and (10) guarantee the consistency of the time variables of operation $O_{j,h}$, i.e. $t_{j,h}$, with the time variables of machine i, i.e. $TM_{i,k}$. Both constraints are only restrictive in the event that the operation is carried out on the considered machine as the k-th operation, i.e. if $x_{i,j,h,k} = 1$. Finally, constraint (11) guarantees that the time span between the starting times of two consecutive operations on a machine are large enough to carry out the operation. Again, this constraint is only restrictive if operation $O_{j,h}$ is the k-th operation on machine i.

$$\sum_{i=1}^{M}\sum_{j=1}^{N}\sum_{h=1}^{h_j}\sum_{k=1}^{l}\sum_{d=1}^{p_{i,j,h}} x_{i,j,h,k}\cdot w_{i,k,t-d+1}\cdot E_{i,j,h}(d)\leq \Pi \qquad t=1,...,T \tag{12}$$

$$t_{j,h_j}+\sum_{i=1}^{M} y_{i,j,h_j}\cdot p_{i,j,h_j}\leq \Gamma \quad j=1,...,N \tag{13}$$

The non-linear constraint (12) imposes an upper bound on the energy demand for every single period of the planning horizon. If operation $O_{j,h}$ is assigned to the k-th position in the sequence of machine i, i.e. $x_{i,j,h,k}=1$, and the starting time of that operation was in period $t-d+1$, i.e. $w_{j,k,t-d+1}=1$, then an amount of $E_{i,j,h}(d)$ must be added to the total energy demand in period t. In addition, the makespan is restricted by the delivery dates of the jobs; c.f. constraint (13).

$$t_{j,h}\geq 0 \quad j=1,...,N; \quad h=1,...,h_j \tag{14}$$

$$TM_{i,k}\geq 0 \quad i=1,...,M; \quad k=1,...,l \tag{15}$$

$$y_{i,j,h}\in\{0,1\} \quad i=1,...,M; \quad j=1,...,N; \quad h=1,...,h_j \tag{16}$$

$$x_{i,j,h,k}\in\{0,1\} \quad i=1,...,M; \quad j=1,...,N; \quad h=1,...,h_j; \quad k=1,...,l \tag{17}$$

$$w_{i,k,r}\in\{0,1\} \quad i=1,...,M; \quad k=1,...,l; \quad r=0,...,T-1 \tag{18}$$

The remaining technical constraints (14) to (18) restrict the values of the decision variables.

Hereinafter we will focus on optimizing the problem with the secondary objective function, i.e. problem (2) to (18). Minimizing the first objective function corresponds to the classical FJSP, which is already an NP-hard combinatorial optimization problem. Several approaches have been proposed in the literature to approximately solve this problem. Instead of proposing a new solution algorithm for makespan minimization for the FJSP we refer to the comprehensive literature (cf. [8,23]).

The focus of our investigation is to examine the potential of peak energy demand minimization under a strict makespan restriction. This corresponds to the hierarchical optimization approach, where minimizing the makespan is the main objective.

4 Solution Approach

The solution approach pursued in this paper is based on the variable neighborhood search (VNS). VNS, originally proposed by [17,28], is a metaheuristic method for solving combinatorial optimizations problems. A pseudocode description of the solution approach is shown in Algorithm 1.

In a first step an initial solution is generated by solving a classical FJSP with respect to makespan minimization. For test runs carried out to assess the quality of the proposed approach we used known optimal solutions for test cases from the literature. It goes without saying that the proposed approach also works when the makespan is not set to its minimal value.

This starting solution is set as the incumbent solution s. Within the proposed approach a solution s is represented by a string that is a permutation of all operations supplemented by a feasible machine μ and a starting time $t_{j,h}$ for each operation $O_{j,h}$, i.e. $s_i(j, h, \mu, t_{j,h})$ for $i = 1 ... \sum_{j=1}^{N} h_j$. One should keep in mind that in order to reduce peak energy demand it is not sufficient to consider only active schedules where all operations are scheduled as early as possible. Therefore, the starting time of each operation must also be specified in the solution string. The transformation of a solution string into a solution is carried out by the local search procedures (cf. Sect. 4.2).

It should be noted that only permutations in which the specified sequence of operations is adhered to for all jobs represent feasible solutions.

In the VNS approach a predetermined number of iterations $i_{\max}$ is carried out, each of them consisting of a shaking procedure and a local search step. In every iteration, a random solution s' is generated in the current neighborhood $NH_g(s)$ of s (shaking). Therefore, a total of g_{max} neighborhoods are available. It starts in the first iteration with the first neighborhood, i.e. $g := 1$. Whenever a solution s is replaced by a new solution the value of g is reset to 1; otherwise g is increased by 1 in the subsequent iteration, i.e. $g := g + 1$. If g reaches a value bigger than a predetermined value g_{max} then g is set to 1.

A subsequent local search procedure is applied to s' transforming this solution to s''. If s'' is better than s with respect to a specific objective function $f(\cdot)$ or s'' meets another acceptance criterion then s'' replaces s. At the end of the VNS approach, the best solution s_{best} found during all iterations is returned as the final solution.

The implemented neighborhoods, the local search procedures as well as the acceptance criteria are presented in detail below.

4.1 Implemented Neighborhoods

Neighborhoods are used to generate new, potentially better solutions. As proposed by [33] two different types of neighborhoods are used within the approach. For both types the parameter n represents the neighborhood width.

The first type of neighborhood (NH1) changes the assignment of operations to machines. Each time this neighborhood is invoked, n operations are randomly

Algorithm 1. variable neighborhood search

generate initial solution s;
$s_{best} \Leftarrow s$, $g \Leftarrow 1$ and $iteration \Leftarrow 1$;
while $iteration \leq i_{\max}$ **do**
  shaking, i.e. rand. $s \Rightarrow s', s' \in NH_g(s)$;
  apply local search to $s' \Rightarrow s''$;
  if $f(s'') < f(s)$ or other criteria **then**
    $s \Leftarrow s''$ and $g \Leftarrow 0$;
  end if;
  if s'' is feasible and $f(s'') < f(s_{best})$ **then**
    $s_{best} \Leftarrow s''$;
  end if;
  $g \Leftarrow (g \text{ modulo } g_{max}) + 1$ and $iteration \Leftarrow iteration + 1$;
end while;
return s_{best};

selected from the set of operations that can be processed on at least two different machines and assigned to new machines. Thereby, all potential operations and all selectable machines for an operation have the same probability of being selected. After changing the machine assignment of n operations in the solution string, the starting times of all operations must be updated. This is done by the procedure presented in the next section.

The second type of neighborhood (NH2) changes the sequence of operations in the solution string. Whenever this neighborhood is invoked, up to n operations are shifted one after another. An operation $O_{j,h}$ is selected by roulette wheel selection, where probabilities for selecting an operation are calculated using values $\pi(j,h)$. When shifting operations to earlier or later periods in a classical FJSP while minimizing makespan there is always a direct relationship to the objective function value as the makespan is also measured in time periods. Unfortunately, there is no direct relationship between time and objective function value when minimizing peak energy demand is pursued. For this reason, we have to employ other mechanisms that detect which operations are difficult to plan and which are likely to cause high peak energy demands. This selection mechanism based on the π-values has been shown in test runs to be superior to neighborhoods in which the operations were selected according to their maximum energy demand. Variants in which operations were preferably selected that took place at peak times were also significantly worse. The $\pi(j,h)$ values are updated by the local search procedures (cf. explanation below). The new position of the operation to be shifted is selected randomly following a uniform distribution for all positions that do not violate the processing sequence of the corresponding job. After shifting one operation the local search procedure is started in order to update the starting time of all operations in the solution string.

Because of the high computing effort for the generation of solutions, we have restricted ourselves to inserting individual operations and have neglected more complex operators in which several operations swap positions. In addition, we had to restrict the neighborhood width n to at most 3. It turned out that larger values for n did not improve the solutions any more while just increasing required CPU times. Thus, the value of g_{max} was set to 6. The neighborhoods are applied in the following order: NH2/1, NH1/1, NH2/2, NH1/2, NH2/3, NH1/3, where the number after the slash represents the value of the neighborhood width n.

4.2 Local Search Procedures

A solution string can be transformed into a solution (Gantt chart) by scheduling the operations one by one starting with the first operation in the string. The optimal solution for minimizing the makespan always includes an active schedule in which all operations are scheduled as early as possible. To generate solutions with low makespan we limit ourselves to generating only active schedules when decoding a solution string into a solution. Therefore, each operation is scheduled as early as possible on the designated machine without any delays. It should be noted that an operation of a job can only be scheduled after the preceding operation of the job is completed. Additionally, scheduling an operation on a machine must not delay the beginning of another operation already scheduled on that machine.

In order to minimize the secondary objective function (peak energy demand) the following three different local search procedures have been implemented.

- Smoothing: Delaying the start of operations
- Shaving: Reducing energy demand in peak periods
- Updating machines: Changing the assignment of operations to machines

They are invoked in the displayed order. It should be noted that the first two procedures do not change the sequence of operations on the machines. With all three local search procedures shifts are carried out in such a way that makespan of a solution s' generated by shaking does not increase. As a result, optimization is no longer limited to only active schedules.

Smoothing. Starting from a given solution string where the sequence of operations is already given for every machine, this procedure tries to reduce peak energy demand by delaying the beginning of operations. Remember that every operation has been scheduled as early as possible when decoding a solution string. If, for example, a machine is not used after the completion of an operation, the start of processing that operation may be delayed in order to reduce peak energy demand. Figure 1 shows an illustrative example of this situation with three jobs. Each job consists of up to two operations that are denoted by $O_{j,h}$. The Gantt chart on the left shows the initial situation. Energy demand for the three jobs and total energy demand for all periods is shown in the table above the Gantt chart. The Gantt chart on the right shows the situation when the beginning of the first operation of job 1 on machine 2, i.e. operation $O_{1,1}$, is delayed by three periods. This shift results in a reduction of peak energy demand from 14 to 10.

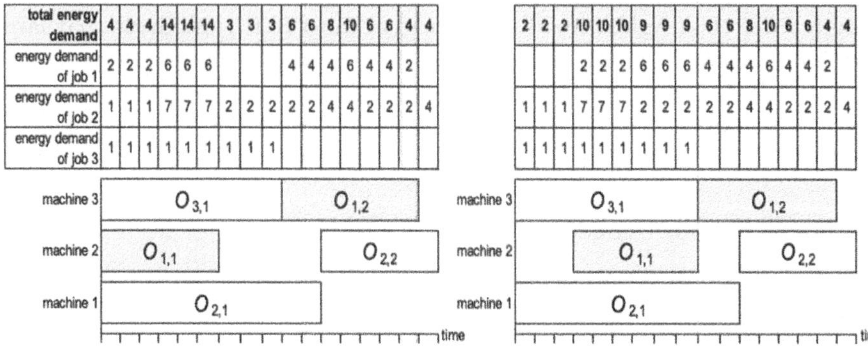

Fig. 1. Reducing peak energy demand from 14 (left) to 10 (right) by postponing the start of the first operation of job 1, i.e. operation $O_{1,1}$, on machine 2 by three periods

The procedure tries to shift operations one by one beginning with the operation that determines the makespan, i.e. the operation with the latest completion time. Thereafter, in every iteration of the smoothing procedure the operation with the latest completion time that has not yet been considered is identified and the beginning of that operation is delayed as long as makespan is not increased or the next operation scheduled on that machine had to be delayed.

Shaving. This local search procedure considers the whole planning horizon. Starting from the incumbent solution s' the procedure tries to shift operations that are processed during the peak period in order to reduce peak energy demand. At the same time, however, makespan must not be increased.

Let t'_{peak} denote the peak period of a solution s'. Energy demand for every period t of the planning horizon and therefore the peak period can be calculated by the left hand side of Eq. (12) as for a given solution s' the values of decision variables $x_{i,j,h,k}$ and $w_{j,k,t-d+1}$ are known.

Within the procedure the set P contains all operations that are carried out in solution s' during the peak period. In addition, let us define by $M(j,h)$ the machine an operation $O_{j,h}$ is assigned to. The operations from set P are examined one by one and the beginning of processing that operation is gradually increased by one period. Note that when shifting an operation, it might also be necessary to shift the succeeding operations belonging to the same job as well as operations of other jobs that are assigned in a later period to the same machine. These resulting shifts are also considered when examining the effects on peak energy demand. Whenever shifting an operation causes the completion of an operation (either that one or a different one) to be postponed beyond the end of the specified makespan, the examination of further shifting this operation is stopped and the starting period of that operation is set to its original period.

A second stopping criterion is a reduction in peak energy demand. In this case the incumbent solution is replaced by the newly generated solution, the value of the peak period as well as the set P are updated and the procedure starts again in trying to postpone the beginning of operations that are processed during the newly generated peak period. Eventually, the local search procedure terminates when all operations from set P have been checked without finding any further improvement.

During the execution of the shaving procedure values $\pi(i,j)$ for an operation $O_{j,h}$ that are used in the second type of neighborhood are updated. At the beginning of the VNS approach all values of $\pi(i,j)$ are initialized with 1. Whenever an increase of the peak energy demand is observed during a shift in the shavings procedure then we identify the operations that are processed in the peak period. For each of these operations it is compared how high the energy demand was at the peak period before and after the shift. In this way, we can identify the operations that contribute to the peak energy demand. For all contributing operations we increase the value $\pi(i,j)$ of that operation by 1. Thus, in the long run we can identify operations that are somehow critical and therefore should be considered during the shaking phase.

Updating Machines. A third local search procedure tries to reduce machine load by changing the assignment of operations to machines. Therefore, all operations are examined with respect to the feasible machines for each operation. Additionally, the smoothing and the shaving local search procedures are invoked for the newly generated assignment. Whenever an improvement in the objective function is found, the new assignment is realized and the search starts again from the beginning. The procedure terminates when all operations have been checked and no further improvement could be found.

4.3 Acceptance Criteria

To decide whether a newly generated solution s'' should be accepted, an objective function $f()$ that consists of two summands is employed. The first summand represents the peak energy demand of the solution. The second summand penalizes makespan violations of operations. Therefore, whenever an operation is not completed within the given makespan a penalty is incurred that is calculated by multiplying the length of the makespan violation with a penalty factor. This factor is initialized by 1 at the beginning. Whenever a new solution is accepted that has makespan violations then the penalty factor is increased by multiplying it with a factor randomly chosen from the interval $[1.05, 1.1]$. In contrast, when the newly accepted solution has no makespan violations then the penalty factor is decreased by dividing it again by a factor randomly chosen from the same interval. This type of acceptance criteria was first proposed by [9] for the dial-a-ride problem and has proven to be very effective in finding new feasible solutions for highly restricted optimization problems.

The newly generated solution s'' replaces the incumbent solution s if $f(s'')$ has a smaller value than $f(s)$. Additionally, also deteriorating solutions s'' may become incumbent solutions with probability $exp(-[f(s'') - f(s_{best})]/\tau)$. The initial temperature τ is then set such that if $f(s'')$ is 0.5% larger than $f(s_{best})$,

s'' is accepted with a probability of 0.2. Thereafter, τ is linearly decreased to 0 until the maximum number of iterations has been reached. Carrying out test runs it could be observed that after a strong reduction in the objective function value the temperature seemed to be too high, resulting in the acceptance of too many deteriorating solutions. Therefore, the temperature τ is additionally recalculated whenever a new best solution has been found based on this new solution. The temperature is again linearly decreased to 0 over the remaining number of periods.

5 Computational Results

The use of the proposed approach as part of the above-mentioned case study at the mechanical engineering company led to a reduction in peak energy demand of 23.6%. However, this result says little about the performance of the proposed approach in general. In order to enable a broader evaluation of the proposed approach, modified test cases from the literature were also used (cf. [31]). Therefore, the test cases were extended by adding randomly generated energy demands for all operations on their eligible machines. The profiles were generated in such a way that the difference between the machine with the lowest and the highest total energy demand for each operation is at most 20%.

5.1 Benchmark Approach

In order to assess the performance of the proposed approach from Sect. 4, we implemented the following benchmark approach. Therefore, the problem (2) to (18) is decomposed into two subproblems that are solved sequentially.

In the first subproblem the makespan is minimized subject to the classical FJSP constraints without considering energy demand aspects, i.e. this problem consists of the objective function (1) and constraints (3) to (11) and (13) to (18). We used the optimal solution as the starting point for minimizing the second subproblem that minimizes the objective function (2) subject to the constraints (3) to (18). With the solution of the first subproblem, the remaining problem can be simplified considerably.

This second subproblem could be solved for the test cases under consideration using the commercial solver CPLEX 12. In the following, this approach in which both subproblems are solved sequentially is referred to as the benchmark approach.

This benchmark approach corresponds to the procedure in many industrial companies where optimization is initially carried out subject to minimizing makespan. Only in the second step is an attempt made to minimize peak energy demand. Compared to the benchmark approach, the approach proposed in Sect. 4 possesses additional flexibility as operations might be rescheduled, processed in different orders on the machines or reassigned to other machines as long as makespan is not increased and the sequence of operations for each job is respected. The test results are intended to show whether or not this additional flexibility can be used to reduce peak energy demand.

Table 2. Aggregated results for the test cases of [5,7,11,20]

test case class	# problems	# VNS better	# ties	Min.	Avg.	Max.
[7]	21	18	0	0.719	0.814	0.902
[11]	7	4	3	0.801	0.841	0.892
[5]	9	8	1	0.719	0.814	0.902
edata set of [20]	51	39	1	0.744	0.863	0.972
rdata set of [20]	45	45	0	0.353	0.398	0.475
vdata set of [20]	40	40	0	0.214	0.242	0.289

5.2 Test Results

The proposed approach of Sect. 4 was coded in Delphi. Each test case was solved 20 times. The number of iterations was set to 20,000 in order to limit the computing effort.

Table 2 summarizes the aggregated results for the different classes of test cases. The values in columns two through four indicate the number of considered test cases. In addition, it is indicated how often the proposed approach achieved a better solution than the benchmark approach and how often both approaches led to the same results, respectively. In the remaining three columns the best, average and worst results are displayed that were obtained by applying the proposed solution approach. The given values represent the share in the objective function value achieved. For example, if the benchmark approach achieves an average objective function value of 1000 for all test problems of this class and the value in the column min is 0.95 then the average of the best objective function values obtained by the proposed approach was 950. Thus, values in columns 3 to 5 that are below 1 represent improvements obtained by the proposed solution approach over the benchmark.

The results can be summarized as follows. The proposed algorithm clearly outperformed the benchmark approach for most of the 173 test cases. With five test cases, namely three test cases of Dauzère-Pérès and Paulli and one test cases of Brandimarte and Hurink et al. respectively, both approaches achieved the same solution. For 14 test cases a better solution than the benchmark approach could not be found in any of the twenty test runs - these were three test cases of Chambers and Barnes and eleven test cases from the *edata* set of Hurink et al. In the remaining 159 test cases, however, almost consistently better results were achieved compared to the comparison method, in the majority of cases with a very clear difference based on the best or worst individual values as well as on the average values for all 20 test runs.

Of the test cases of [20] the *edata* test cases were the most difficult ones to solve. For the *rdata* and even more for the *vdata* test cases more machines are available to be chosen for the operations. Thus, this kind of flexibility can help to reduce peak energy demand considerably.

Finally, further experiments with the proposed approach were carried out to investigate whether and if so to what extent a relaxation of the strict limitation of the makespan has an impact on peak energy demand. Therefore, the optimal value of makespan, i.e. the value of Γ in Eq. (13), was increased in 1% steps from 1% to 15%. Test runs were carried out for 30 selected test cases from the *edata* set of Hurink et al., i.e. abz5 and abz6, la01 to la20, mt06, mt10 and mt20 and orb1 to orb10. Each test case was solved ten times for each step. With a larger makespan peak energy demand can be reduced considerably. The maximum decrease in peak energy demand is almost 20% if at the same time makespan is increased by 10%. Further reductions in peak energy demand could not be realized even with higher increases in makespan.

6 Conclusion

In this paper an approach to minimize peak energy demand in a flexible job shop considering narrow specifications for makespan was presented. In particular, the last results from Sect. 5.2 show that peak energy demand can be reduced if the makespan is increased. Obviously, there is a tradeoff between these two objectives. But, as the results of the test cases also show, there is even a strong potential for minimizing peak energy demand when the makespan is kept at its lowest value. The greater the number of alternative machines (with different energy requirements) available for the processing of individual operations, the greater this potential is.

Another finding from the computational tests is that a greater reduction in peak energy demand is possible if both objectives are considered at the same time. This becomes clear by comparing the results of the proposed algorithm with the benchmark approach. In the latter approach, the optimal solution for the objective of minimizing the makespan was first determined and then, based on this solution, peak energy demand was minimized in the second step. Although optimal solutions were generated for both subproblems, the approach presented in Sect. 4 outperformed the benchmark considerably. This is because the VNS approach can change the assignment of operations to machines, as well as the order of operations on the machines, provided that the makespan does not increase. And this additional flexibility is sufficient to reduce the peak energy demand significantly.

Apart from very energy-intensive industries, with today's energy prices, many companies do not view minimizing energy costs as a top priority. The proposed optimization approach could be of interest to these companies, especially if they want to cut down peak energy for environmental reasons or if energy prices rise. Another application would be in the context of a demand side management in which the local search procedures used in the article can also be used to smooth the demand.

Improvements would also be possible on the algorithmic side. Due to the very high computing times that are due to the optimization of the energy requirement, an obvious possibility would be to consider the parallelization of the calculation.

Acknowledgement. The research was funded by the Bavarian State Ministry for Economic Affairs, Regional Development and Energy as part of the R&D program "Information and communication technology" of the Free State of Bavaria, project title: KAnIS: Cooperative Autonomous Intralogistics Systems.

References

1. Amirghasemi, M.: An effective parallel evolutionary metaheuristic with its application to three optimization problems. Appl. Intell. **53**, 5887–5909 (2023). https://doi.org/10.1007/s10489-022-03599-w
2. Amirghasemi, M., Zamani, R.: An effective asexual genetic algorithm for solving the job shop scheduling problem. Comput. Ind. Eng. **83**, 123–138 (2015). https://doi.org/10.1016/j.cie.2015.02.011, https://www.sciencedirect.com/science/article/pii/S0360835215000686
3. Artigues, C., Lopez, P., Haït, A.: The energy scheduling problem: industrial case-study and constraint propagation techniques. Int. J. Prod. Econ. **143**(1), 13–23 (2013). https://doi.org/10.1016/j.ijpe.2010.09.030
4. Babu, C.A., Ashok, S.: Peak load management in electrolytic process industries. IEEE Trans. Power Syst. **23**, 399–405 (2008). https://doi.org/10.1109/TPWRS.2008.920732
5. Brandimarte, P.: Routing and scheduling in a flexible job shop by tabu search. Ann. Oper. Res. **41**(3), 157–183 (1993). https://doi.org/10.1007/BF02023073
6. Bruzzone, A., Anghinolfi, D., Paolucci, M., Tonelli, F.: Energy-aware scheduling for improving manufacturing process sustainability: a mathematical model for flexible flow shops. CIRP Ann. **61**(1), 459–462 (2012). https://doi.org/10.1016/j.cirp.2012.03.084
7. Chambers, J., Barnes, J.: Flexible job shop scheduling by tabu search. Technical report, The University of Texas, Austin, TX, Technical Report Series ORP96-09, Graduate Program in Operations Research and Industrial Engineering (1996)
8. Chaudhry, I., Khan, A.: A research survey: review of flexible job shop scheduling techniques. Int. Trans. Oper. Res. **23**, 551–591 (2016). https://doi.org/10.1111/itor.12199
9. Cordeau, J.F., Laporte, G.: A tabu search heuristic for the static multi-vehicle dial-a-ride problem. Transp. Res. Part B: Methodol. **37**, 579–594 (2003). https://doi.org/10.1016/S0191-2615(02)00045-0
10. Dai, M., Tang, D., Giret, A., Salido, M.: Multi-objective optimization for energy-efficient flexible job shop scheduling problem with transportation constraints. Robot. Comput.-Integr. Manuf. **59**, 143–157 (2019). https://doi.org/10.1016/j.rcim.2019.04.006
11. Dauzère-Pérès, S., Paulli, J.: An integrated approach for modeling and solving the general multiprocessor job-shop scheduling problem using tabu search. Ann. Oper. Res. **70**, 281–306 (1997). https://doi.org/10.1023/A:1018930406487
12. Fang, K., Uhan, N., Zhao, F., Sutherland, J.: A new approach to scheduling in manufacturing for power consumption and carbon footprint reduction. J. Manuf. Syst. **30**(4), 234–240 (2011). https://doi.org/10.1016/j.jmsy.2011.08.004
13. Fang, K., Uhan, N., Zhao, F., Sutherland, J.: A new shop scheduling approach in support of sustainable manufacturing. In: Hesselbach, J., Herrmann, C. (eds.) Glocalized Solutions for Sustainability in Manufacturing, pp. 305–310. Springer, Berlin (2011). https://doi.org/10.1007/978-3-642-19692-8_53

14. Fang, K., Uhan, N., Zhao, F., Sutherland, J.: Flow shop scheduling with peak power consumption constraints. Ann. Oper. Res. **206**(1), 115–145 (2013). https://doi.org/10.1007/s10479-012-1294-z
15. Gong, G., Deng, Q., Gong, X., Liu, W., Ren, Q.: A new double flexible job-shop scheduling problem integrating processing time, green production, and human factor indicators. J. Clean. Prod. **174**, 560–576 (2018). https://doi.org/10.1016/j.jclepro.2017.10.188
16. Grahm, C., Denz, F., Dirr, M., Tuma, A.: Energy efficient scheduling in manufacturing companies: a review and research framework. Eur. J. Oper. Res. **248**, 744–757 (2016). https://doi.org/10.1016/j.ejor.2015.07.017
17. Hansen, P., Mladenovic, N., Moreno-Perez, J.: Variable neighbourhood search: methods and applications. Ann. Oper. Res. **175**(1), 367–407 (2010). https://doi.org/10.1007/s10288-008-0089-1
18. He, Y., Li, Y., Wu, T., Sutherland, J.: An energy-responsive optimization method for machine tool selection and operation sequence in flexible machining job shops. J. Clean. Prod. **87**, 245–254 (2015). https://doi.org/10.1016/j.jclepro.2014.10.006
19. He, Y., Liu, B., Zhang, X., Gao, H., Liu, X.: A modeling method of task-oriented energy consumption for machining manufacturing system. J. Clean. Prod. **23**, 167–174 (2012). https://doi.org/10.1016/j.jclepro.2011.10.033
20. Hurink, J., Jurisch, B., Thole, M.: Tabu search for the job-shop scheduling problem with multi-purpose machines. OR Spektrum **15**(4), 205–215 (1994). https://doi.org/10.1007/BF01719451
21. Jin, L., Zhang, C., Fei, X.: Realizing energy savings in integrated process planning and scheduling. Processes **7**, 120 (2019). https://doi.org/10.3390/pr7030120
22. Kemmoe, S., Lamy, D., Tchernev, N.: Job-shop like manufacturing system with variable power threshold and operations with power requirements. Int. J. Prod. Res. **55**, 1–22 (2017). https://doi.org/10.1080/00207543.2017.1321801
23. Li, X., Xie, J., Peng, K., Li, H., Gao, L.: A review on flexible job shop scheduling. IET Collaborative Intell. Manuf. **1**(3), 63–77 (2019). https://doi.org/10.1049/iet-cim.2018.0009
24. Liu, Q., Chekem, F., Zhan, M., Shao, X., Ying, B., Sutherland, J.: A hybrid fruit fly algorithm for solving flexible job-shop scheduling to reduce manufacturing carbon footprint. J. Clean. Prod. **168**, 668–678 (2017). https://doi.org/10.1016/j.jclepro.2017.09.037
25. Luo, H., Du, B., Huang, G., Chen, H., Li, X.: Hybrid flow shop scheduling considering machine electricity consumption cost. Int. J. Prod. Econ. **146**, 423–439 (2013). https://doi.org/10.1016/j.ijpe.2013.01.028
26. Masmoudi, O., Delorme, X., Gianessi, P.: Job-shop scheduling problem with energy consideration. Int. J. Prod. Econ. **216**, 12–22 (2019). https://doi.org/10.1016/j.ijpe.2019.03.021
27. Mignon, D., Hermia, J.: Peak utility load reduction in batch processes operated periodically and under uncertainty. Comput. Chem. Eng. **20**(3), 249–263 (1996). https://doi.org/10.1016/0098-1354(95)00041-0
28. Mladenovic, N., Hansen, P.: A parallel iterated tabu search heuristic for vehicle routing problems. Comput. Oper. Res. **24**(11), 1097–1100 (1997). https://doi.org/10.1016/S0305-0548(97)00031-2
29. Mokhtari, H., Hasani, A.: An energy-efficient multi-objective optimization for flexible job-shop scheduling problem. Comput. Chem. Eng. **104**, 339–352 (2017). https://doi.org/10.1016/j.compchemeng.2017.05.004

30. Moon, J.Y., Park, J.: Smart production scheduling with time-dependent and machine-dependent electricity cost by considering distributed energy resources and energy storage. Int. J. Prod. Res. **52**, 3922–3939 (2014). https://doi.org/10.1080/00207543.2013.860251
31. OR library (2020). http://people.brunel.ac.uk/mastjjb/jeb/info.html
32. Pach, C., Berger, T., Sallez, Y., Bonte, T., Adam, E., Trentesaux, D.: Reactive and energy-aware scheduling of flexible manufacturing systems using potential fields. Comput. Ind. **65**, 434–448 (2014). https://doi.org/10.1016/j.compind.2013.11.008
33. Pezzella, F., Morganti, G., Ciaschetti, G.: A genetic algorithm for the flexible job-shop scheduling problem. Comput. Oper. Res. **35**(10), 3202–3212 (2008). https://doi.org/10.1016/j.cor.2007.02.014, https://www.sciencedirect.com/science/article/pii/S0305054807000524
34. Piroozfard, H., Wong, K.Y., Wong, W.P.: Minimizing total carbon footprint and total late work criterion in flexible job shop scheduling by using an improved multi-objective genetic algorithm. Res. Conserv. Recycl. **128**, 267–283 (2018). https://doi.org/10.1016/j.resconrec.2016.12.001
35. Rager, M., Gahm, C., Denz, F.: Energy-oriented scheduling based on evolutionary algorithms. Comput. Oper. Res. **54**, 218–231 (2015). https://doi.org/10.1016/j.cor.2014.05.002
36. Seid, E., Majozi, T.: Heat integration in multipurpose batch plants using a robust scheduling framework. Energy **71**, 302–320 (2014). https://doi.org/10.1016/j.energy.2014.04.058
37. Shrouf, F., Ordieres-Meré, J., García-Sánchez, A., Ortega-Mier, M.: Optimizing the production scheduling of a single machine to minimize total energy consumption costs. J. Clean. Prod. **67**, 197–207 (2014). https://doi.org/10.1016/j.jclepro.2013.12.024
38. Suwa, H., Samukawa, T.: A new framework of energy-efficient manufacturing systems based on energy load profiles. Procedia CIRP **41**, 313–317 (2016). https://doi.org/10.1016/j.procir.2015.10.011
39. Wang, H., Jiang, Z., Wang, Y., Zhang, H., Wang, Y.: A two-stage optimization method for energy-saving flexible job-shop scheduling based on energy dynamic characterization. J. Clean. Prod. **188**, 575–588 (2018). https://doi.org/10.1016/j.jclepro.2018.03.254
40. Wang, Y.C., Wang, M.J., Lin, S.C.: Selection of cutting conditions for power constrained parallel machine scheduling. Robot. Comput.-Integr. Manuf. **43**, 105–110 (2017). https://doi.org/10.1016/j.rcim.2015.10.010
41. Weinert, N., Chiotellis, S., Seliger, G.: Methodology for planning and operating energy-efficient production systems. CIRP Ann. **60**(1), 41–44 (2011). https://doi.org/10.1016/j.cirp.2011.03.015
42. Wu, X., Sun, Y.: A green scheduling algorithm for flexible job shop with energy-saving measures. J. Clean. Prod. **172**, 3249–3264 (2018). https://doi.org/10.1016/j.jclepro.2017.10.342
43. Zhang, L., Tang, Q., Wu, Z., Wang, F.: Mathematical modeling and evolutionary generation of rule sets for energy-efficient flexible job shops. Energy **138**, 210–227 (2017). https://doi.org/10.1016/j.energy.2017.07.005
44. Zhang, Z., Wu, L., Peng, T., Jia, S.: An improved scheduling approach for minimizing total energy consumption and makespan in a flexible job shop environment. Sustainability **11**(1) (2019). https://doi.org/10.3390/su11010179
45. Zheng, H.Y., Wang, L.: Reduction of carbon emissions and project makespan by a pareto-based estimation of distribution algorithm. Int. J. Prod. Econ. **164**, 421–432 (2014). https://doi.org/10.1016/j.ijpe.2014.12.010

Carbon-Aware Mine Planning with a Novel Multi-objective Framework

Nurul Asyikeen Binte Azhar[1,2(✉)], Aldy Gunawan[1], Shih-Fen Cheng[1], and Erwin Leonardi[2]

[1] School of Computing and Information Systems, Singapore Management University, 80 Stamford Road, 178902 Singapore, Singapore
{nurula.a.2020,aldygunawan,sfcheng}@smu.edu.sg

[2] Rio Tinto Ltd., Tower 3, 12 Marina Boulevard, Marina Bay Financial Centre, 018982 Singapore, Singapore
{asyikeen.azhar,erwin.leonardi}@riointo.com

Abstract. The logistical complication of long-term mine planning involves deciding the sequential extraction of materials from the mine pit and their subsequent processing steps based on geological, geometrical, and resource constraints. The net present value (NPV) of profit over the mine's lifespan usually forms the sole objective for this problem, which is considered as the NP-hard *precedence-constrained production scheduling problem* (PCPSP) as well. However, increased pressure for more sustainable and carbon-aware industries also calls for environmental indicators to be considered. In this paper, we enhance the generic PCPSP formulation into a multi-objective optimization (MOO) problem whereby carbon cost forms an additional objective. We apply the Non-Dominated Sorting Genetic Algorithm II (NSGA-II) to this formulation and experiment with variants to the solution generation. Our tailored application of the NSGA-II using a set of real-world inspired datasets can form an approximated Pareto front for planners to observe stipulated annual carbon emission targets. It also displays that tailored variants of the NSGA-II can produce diverse solutions that are close to the true Pareto front.

Keywords: Precedence-constraint production scheduling · Resource capacity optimization · Multi-objective evolutionary algorithm · Sustainability

1 Introduction

The five phases of mining present a number of logistical challenges (Fig. 1). During the planning, implementation, and production phases, logistics management must forecast, plan, and schedule tasks from strategic, tactical, and operational angles. During the planning phase, environmental concerns are addressed through the environmental impact assessment (EIA) and reclamation plan.

Supported by Enterprise Singapore.

© The Author(s), under exclusive license to Springer Nature Switzerland AG 2023
J. R. Daduna et al. (Eds.): ICCL 2023, LNCS 14239, pp. 500–516, 2023.
https://doi.org/10.1007/978-3-031-43612-3_31

These are submitted with the mining plan to the respective government authorities before the implementation phase [7]. As the mining phases mature, the mining plans, EIA, and reclamation plans are updated and can become progressively detailed. The reclamation plan is updated and reviewed periodically in certain jurisdictions such as Western Australia. However, regulatory rigor and intra-governmental coordination vary across jurisdictions and may be improved, such as integrating the EIA and reclamation plan processes [12]. These can be classified as the strategic perspective for mine planning.

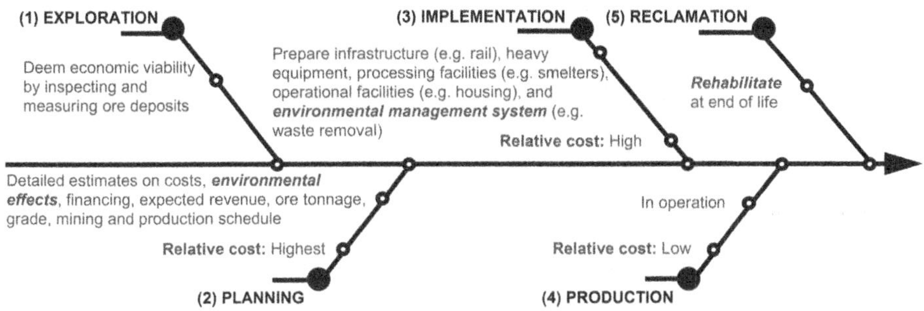

Fig. 1. Summary of activities for each mine phase and their influences on costs.

Similarly, the tactical and operational perspectives of mine planning are updated periodically and have the potential to incorporate environmental concerns. Planning from the tactical perspective [13] over the whole mine lifespan (decades) has been tackled as the *precedence-constrained* production scheduling problem (PCPSP) and acknowledged as NP-hard. The logistical challenge in the PCPSP involves the movement of extracted raw materials from the mine pit through the broad sequence of processing and refinement steps to obtain the desired products. To support these activities, there are various operational facilities for processing (e.g., crushing and grinding), refining (e.g., hydrometallurgy), storage (i.e., stockpile), and waste (e.g., tailings pond and dump). These facilities have their own set of resources and corresponding capacity constraints.

When modeling mines, planners discretize the buried materials into three-dimensional blocks to decide the sequence of extraction. Each block would have its own set of preceding blocks that require prior extraction due to the geology and geometry unique to each mine site. This is known as precedence constraints and is illustrated in Fig. 2. There are then diverse resource constraints for each block at the downstream processing and refining facilities. For the efficient and effective movement of extracted materials, these sequence and processing decisions are considered holistically with the approximate net present value (NPV) of profit throughout decades of the mine's lifespan.

Barring profit, environmental considerations and the push for net zero carbon emissions are reverberating within the mining industry due to its extensive processing and operations scale. Hence, the monitoring of carbon emissions

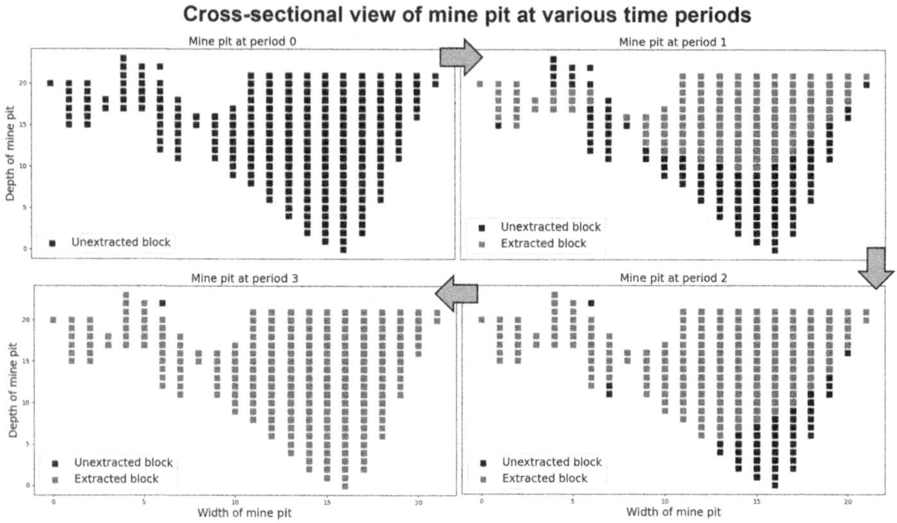

Fig. 2. Block extraction sequence example from year to year following precedence and resource constraints for MineLib's Newman1 instance [3]

throughout the value chain of the PCPSP is increasingly necessary and ties in with schemes such as the emission trading systems (ETS) and emission taxes. In this paper, we boost previous research on the PCPSP by enhancing the generic PCPSP formulation [6] with carbon cost. This allows planners to consider the NPV of carbon cost alongside profit.

Instead of solely maximizing the NPV of profit in the generic PCPSP formulation, we convert it into a multi-objective optimization (MOO) problem with another objective that minimizes the NPV of carbon cost. Next, we apply the NSGA-II [5] whereby components of the algorithm - initial solution generation, crossover and mutation - are tailored to the PCPSP. As far as we know, earlier works of evolutionary algorithms (EA) to the PCPSP did not propose similar frameworks. In fact, details on the initial solution generation, crossover, and mutation are quite lacking. Furthermore, earlier works for the PCPSP employed EA such as genetic algorithm [1] and differential evolution [8] for a single objective formulation problem whereas we use NSGA-II for an MOO problem. We then test variants of our approach with a real-world mine dataset from an operating mine and benchmark instances from Minelib [6]. It turns out that variants to the solution generation can improve results. Furthermore, we demonstrate how our approach can produce approximated Pareto fronts for planners to observe carbon emissions targets when deciding on mining plans.

2 Related Work

The angles of strategic, tactical, and operational issues are commonly used for research on the logistics of mining. Lately, qualitative and quantitative research on mine planning that incorporates sustainability elements has increased. However, quantitative research based on operations research, artificial intelligence, and machine learning trails behind qualitative research [21]. Furthermore, research that incorporates carbon emissions from a tactical angle remains sparse.

From the strategic angle, one of the research covers carbon emissions indirectly by increasing efficiency and thus minimizing haulage costs. The main focus of Rimélé, Dimitrakopoulos, and Gamache [14] is to minimize land disturbance by optimizing the order of ore extraction. To achieve this, they propose an in-pit waste disposal approach, which involves depositing unprofitable extracted ores in available areas within the pit instead of moving them to temporary dumps. Meanwhile, Xu et al. [20] model carbon emission cost directly as one of the undesirable environmental outputs. In their multi-objective approach, they aim to minimize undesirable environmental outputs while simultaneously maximizing both the NPV of profit and social benefits. It focuses solely on the pit limit, which determines whether or not to extract the ores while ignoring the sequencing and processing decisions thereafter.

From the operational angle, the objective is to explicitly decrease expenses associated with carbon emissions in operational facilities and transportation networks. Valderrama et al. [18] utilize a mixed integer programming (MIP) model to analyze carbon emissions from inter-facility transportation and operating facilities. Similarly, Attari and Torkayesh [2] employ a multi-objective MIP to examine carbon emissions in transportation between facilities and customers. In comparison, Canales-Bustos, Santibañez-González, and Candia-Véjar [4] develop a multi-objective hybrid particle swarm optimization algorithm to minimize investment costs, transportation costs, deviations between product quality and goals, and carbon emissions from facilities and vehicles. These operational angles ignore the tactical decisions of extraction and sequencing of blocks. Lastly, Wang et al. [19] indirectly model carbon emissions by comparing resource efficiency and the NPV of profit with an NSGA-II. Their formulation also pre-defines extraction decisions and focuses only on the processing of extracted ores.

Research from the tactical angle directly models carbon emission cost when examining trade-offs between profit and sustainability. Azhar et al. [3] consider extraction, sequencing, and processing decisions of ores as per the PCPSP. They enhance the generic PCPSP formulation with an additional constraint of carbon emission cost [20] to produce an approximated Pareto front.

Our research is based on the tactical angle of the PCPSP, focusing on decisions of block extraction, extraction sequence, and its processing steps [3]. We also directly model the trade-off between the NPV of profit and the carbon emission cost by adopting the carbon costing framework by Xu et al. [20]. However, we differ from Azhar et al. [3] by including the carbon emission cost as an additional objective function instead of a constraint.

3 The PCPSP Definition and Formulation

The PCPSP determines the entire mining process, including extraction and processing decisions for valuable mineral ores, and provides investors with an estimate of a mine's value [7]. The mine consists of several components, such as the pit, dump, stockpiles, processing plants, and heavy machinery. In the pit, mineral ore deposits are divided into blocks of the same size for modeling purposes. Each block has a unique value and a set of precedence constraints based on geology, which affects the overall extraction sequence over time and how the ore is processed, as illustrated in Fig. 2. After extraction, the block is transported to processing facilities where it undergoes various treatments, such as crushing, grinding, and screening, to reduce it according to the requirements. Then, the material is refined to improve its quality and obtain various desired end products. Unfortunately, this value chain consumes significant raw materials (e.g., energy, water, gases) and generates harmful by-products (e.g., water and air pollution, chemical waste).

3.1 Carbon Costing Formulation

Our main aim is to augment the PCPSP formulation with carbon costing. To measure carbon emissions, we use the metric by Xu et al. [20], which defines the cost of carbon emissions $\mathcal{C}_{i,e}$ from energy consumption. This cost reflects the amount of carbon dioxide that is absorbed during ore excavation, processing, and refining. The formula includes two key quantities: the amount of ore extracted from the pit and sent for further processing $\mathcal{Q}_{i,o}$, and the amount of waste material extracted and treated $\mathcal{Q}_{i,w}$. These quantities are multiplied by the energy consumed using coal to extract one unit tonne of material (either ore or waste) from the pit e_m, and the energy consumed to process one unit tonne of ore e_p. These values are then multiplied by the carbon factor of coal f_c, the conversion coefficient of carbon dioxide from carbon f_a, and the absorption cost of carbon dioxide $\mathcal{C}_c$.

$$\mathcal{C} = \frac{(\mathcal{Q}_{i,o} + \mathcal{Q}_{i,w})e_m + \mathcal{Q}_{i,o}e_p}{1000} f_c f_a \mathcal{C}_c \tag{1}$$

3.2 Enhanced Multi-objective PCPSP Formulation

The PCPSP is a problem in scheduling mining activities that aims to maximize the NPV of profit while satisfying several requirements related to mineral ore grade, equipment availability, and processing plant capacity [6]. This requires expertise in multiple domains such as geology, chemistry, engineering, economics, and customer relations. Firstly, geologists provide information on the ore components and grades based on multiple drill samples and the structure of the surrounding materials. Secondly, mining engineers use this information to assess the structure, methods, and equipment needed to access the ore. Next, geologists and chemists determine the type of processing and refining required for different ores, which can result in varying products. Then, economists estimate the economic value of each block based on demand and supply worldwide. Lastly, customer relations evaluate the demand of current and potential customers. All these considerations make mine scheduling a complex task.

Mine scheduling research usually relies on real-world case studies because mining operations are unique and shaped by geo-metallurgical factors [13]. However, this approach leads to solution techniques that cannot be directly compared with others. The MineLib library [6] provides a set of generalized mathematical formulations and instances for three problem variants, including the PCPSP, which is the most complex problem. By adopting the PCPSP formulation, our work enables other researchers to build upon it.

The generic formulation for the PCPSP [6] defines $\mathcal{B}$ as the set of blocks, $\mathcal{B}_b$ as the subset of predecessors for block $b \in \mathcal{B}$, and $\mathcal{D}$ as the set of destinations. The profit $\tilde{p}_{bdt}$ is obtained by extracting a block b and processing it at a destination d during a specific period, using q_{bdr} units of operational resource $r \in \mathcal{R}$. A binary decision variable x_{bt} is used to indicate whether block b is extracted during period t. A continuous decision variable y_{bdt} represents portions of block b delegated to destination d during period t. The augmented multi-objective PCPSP has two objective functions. The first objective maximizes the NPV of profit for periods $\mathcal{T}$, while the second objective minimizes the carbon emission cost pegged to the extraction and processing of mineral ores.

The first objective function derives the profit $\tilde{p}_{bdt}$ for a given period $t \in \mathcal{T}$ with $\frac{p_{bd}}{(1+\alpha)^t}$, where α denotes the discount factor. The estimated value of a block is determined by geologists using its ore composition and grade. The summation of the NPV of profit throughout the mine's lifespan emphasizes the significance of extracting blocks with higher value earlier.

$$\textbf{(Objective function 1)} \quad \mathcal{Z}_1 = \max \sum_{b \in \mathcal{B}} \sum_{d \in \mathcal{D}} \sum_{t \in \mathcal{T}} \tilde{p}_{bdt} y_{bdt} \tag{2}$$

The second objective function calculates the discounted carbon cost $\tilde{c}_{bdrt}$ from using operational resource $r \in \mathcal{R}$ to extract or process block b at destination $d \in \mathcal{D}$ during period $t \in \mathcal{T}$. It is derived using $\frac{c_{bdr}}{(1+\alpha)^t}$. Practically, this function can be crucial within the framework of carbon credit trading, a market-based instrument aimed at reducing carbon dioxide emissions. Under this system, economies that exceed their allocated emissions can purchase credits from those that have reduced their emissions below their carbon emission permits.

$$\textbf{(Objective function 2)} \quad \mathcal{Z}_2 = \min \sum_{b \in \mathcal{B}} \sum_{d \in \mathcal{D}} \sum_{r \in \mathcal{R}} \sum_{t \in \mathcal{T}} \tilde{c}_{bdrt} y_{bdt} \tag{3}$$

Constraint (4) sets conditions for the order in which blocks can be extracted, and it applies to all blocks and periods. It states that block b' must be extracted in the same or an earlier period than block b, as b' is a predecessor of b. This constraint is decided by mining engineers based on the materials surrounding the ore, including sand, silt, and clay, as well as the ore's type and composition. The latter is determined by geologists.

$$\sum_{\tau \leq t} x_{b\tau} \leq \sum_{\tau \leq t} x_{b'\tau} \quad \forall b \in \mathcal{B},\, b' \in \mathcal{B}_b,\, t \in \mathcal{T} \tag{4}$$

Constraint (5) specifies that a block should be completely dispatched to one or multiple destinations if it is mined. Otherwise, it should not be sent to any destination. The selection of destination is influenced by the ore's grade and composition, as well as the demands of customers.

$$x_{bt} = \sum_{d \in \mathcal{D}} y_{bdt} \quad \forall b \in \mathcal{B},\ t \in \mathcal{T} \tag{5}$$

Constraint (6) limits block extraction to only once during the mine's lifespan.

$$\sum_{t \in \mathcal{T}} x_{bt} \leq 1 \quad \forall b \in \mathcal{B} \tag{6}$$

Constraint (7) guarantees that for each time period t, the use of every operational resource r is within the limits of minimum $\underline{\mathcal{R}}_{rt}$ and maximum $\bar{\mathcal{R}}_{rt}$. These resources are managed by mining engineers and technicians, and they include diggers, haulage trucks, grinders, and processing plants.

$$\underline{\mathcal{R}}_{rt} \leq \sum_{b \in \mathcal{B}} \sum_{d \in \mathcal{D}} q_{bdr} y_{bdt} \leq \bar{\mathcal{R}}_{rt} \quad \forall r \in \mathcal{R},\ t \in \mathcal{T} \tag{7}$$

Constraint (8) represents side constraints with lower bound $\underline{a}$ and upper bound $\bar{a}$. It can represent various mining situations, including grade constraints.

$$\underline{a} \leq \mathcal{A} y \leq \bar{a} \tag{8}$$

Finally, constraints (9) and (10) reflect the range of values.

$$x_{bt} \in \{0, 1\} \quad \forall b \in \mathcal{B}, t \in \mathcal{T}, \tag{9}$$

$$y_{bdt} \in [0, 1] \quad \forall b \in \mathcal{B}, d \in \mathcal{D}, t \in \mathcal{T}. \tag{10}$$

4 NSGA-II for the Augmented Multi-objective PCPSP

Diverse techniques are available for MOO problems with their own advantages and disadvantages [11]. Due to the NP-hard nature of the PCPSP, exact methods such as the MIP and constraint programming [15], are found to be efficient for smaller instances but become intractable as the instance size increases. Hence, alternatives have to be explored. One of them is the extension of the genetic algorithm framework. Genetic algorithms use a population of randomly generated solutions that are evaluated for improvement at each iteration, making it possible to converge on the entire Pareto set in one run. Multi-objective evolutionary algorithms (MOEAs) belong to the class of genetic algorithms used for MOO problems. They utilize additional advanced methods to maintain a varied population of Pareto optimal solutions throughout the iterations. The MOEAs are differentiated by their fitness assignment, diversity mechanism, elitism, and the use of external population [9].

We utilize NSGA-II [5] as it remains a popular choice due to its effective mechanisms of non-domination sorting, crowding distance sorting, and elitism, which contribute to a diverse Pareto optimal set and accelerated convergence. Its wide application across other industries, including medicine [10] and manufacturing [17], further demonstrates its strength. Our implementation of the NSGA-II for the augmented multi-objective PCPSP is summarized in Fig. 3.

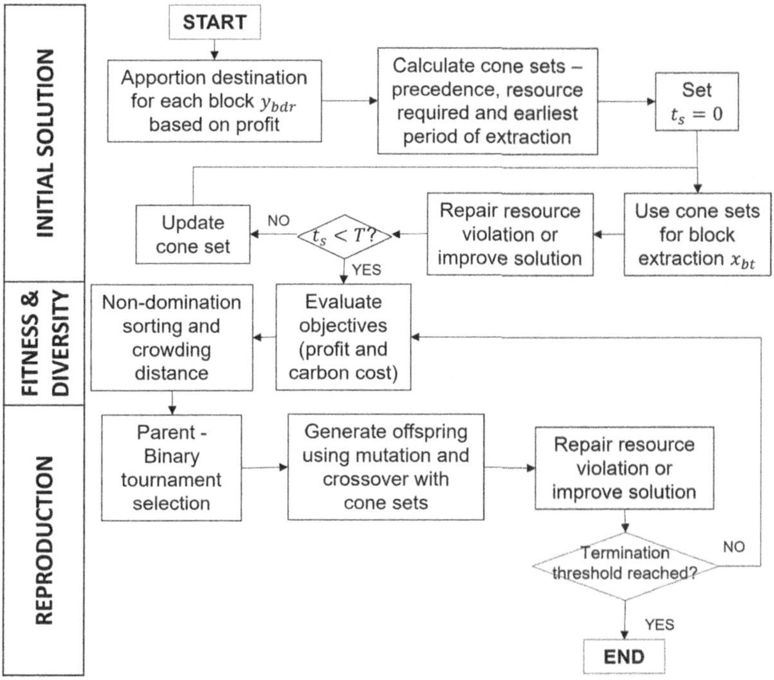

Fig. 3. Overview of NSGA-II implementation.

4.1 Initial Population of Solutions with Cone Sets

The repair of precedence constraint violation is computationally intensive and hence, it should be prevented as much as possible. To do so, we compute the complete set of preceding blocks that need to be extracted before the current block of interest with a directed acyclic graph (DAG). The shape of this set, together with the block of interest, can be described as a cone set, illustrated in Fig. 4. For each cone set, we compute the resources required, the profit, and the earliest period the cone set can be extracted based on the cumulative resource capacity for each period t. The apportionment of blocks to destinations at each time period, y_{bdt} is determined by the profit associated with each destination; we utilize `argmax` and `softmax` (details in Sect. 5). These components form the heuristic for the initial solution, shown in Algorithm 1.

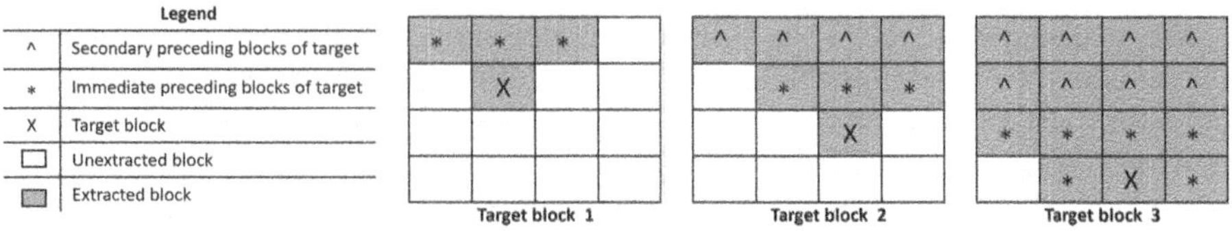

Fig. 4. Cross-sectional view of mine pit when excavating different target blocks.

Algorithm 1 produces a population of solutions Ω_j where each solution j is the set of blocks extracted at each time period x_{bt}. Each solution is processed progressively through each time period $t \in \mathcal{T}$ (line 6). At each time period, blocks are pre-selected based on the earliest period of extraction (line 9) with allowance for resource violation (line 15) using an upper bound resource multiplier ρ. The resource multiplier is randomly generated where $\rho \in [0, 1]$ (line 5). This allows variants amongst solutions in the population set Ω_j. Then, the resources required for the solution are checked against the upper bound of resources for the time period t. If there are no violations, a local improvement heuristic is run (line 20). Otherwise, a repair operator is invoked (line 22).

Both the improvement heuristic and the repair operator rely on finding fringe blocks. These are blocks situated at the periphery of the solution that may prevent major disruptions to the current solution when added or removed. If there is no resource violation, the priority is to add more profitable blocks. Otherwise, blocks that consume the least resources are added. Conversely when removing blocks, blocks that are least profitable are prioritized. Finally, the solutions are ranked based on the two objective functions with non-domination sorting and crowding distance [5].

4.2 Reproduction

The reproduction of offspring from the initial solution or parent solution consists of the binary tournament operator, mutation, and crossover. Once offspring solutions are produced, they are again ranked based on the two objective functions with non-domination sorting, and crowding distance. This reproduction step is run till the maximum number of generations (i.e., the termination threshold).

The binary tournament operator randomly selects two individuals (or solutions) from a population and chooses the best (based on the rank function of NSGA-II) for the next generation. This procedure is repeated until the desired number of individuals for the next generation is obtained. The set of parent solutions from this step then leads to the crossover operator.

Crossover facilitates the creation of new offspring solutions by combining genetic material from two parent solutions. The process involves selecting a crossover point in the parents' genetic code and exchanging genetic information beyond that point to generate two new offspring solutions. The crossover rate parameter η determines whether this step occurs for the parent pair. A high

Algorithm 1. Generation of the population of initial solutions.

Input: Block model $\mathcal{B}$, destinations $\mathcal{D}$, predecessor edges $\mathcal{E}$, time periods $\mathcal{T}$, resource types $\mathcal{R}$, resource capacity required per block at each destination and resource type q_{bdr}, resource bounds for each resource type $\bar{\mathcal{R}}_{rt}$, profit of block when sent to destination $\tilde{p}_{bd}$, apportionment of the block to each destination y_{bdt} upper bound resource multiplier ρ, population size Ω
Output: Population of solutions Ω_j where each solution is block extracted at each time period x_{bt}

$G \leftarrow ConstructDAG(\mathcal{B}, \mathcal{E})$
$\theta \leftarrow ConeSetComputaions(G, \mathcal{D}, \mathcal{T}, \mathcal{R}, q_{bdr}, \bar{\mathcal{R}}_{rt}, \tilde{p}_{bd}$
$\Omega_j \leftarrow \emptyset$
for j in Ω **do**
    $\rho \leftarrow RANDOM(0, 1)$
    for t in $\mathcal{T}$ **do**
        $\hat{\mathcal{B}} \leftarrow \emptyset$
        for b in θ **do**
            if b earliest extraction period $= t$ **then**
                $\hat{\mathcal{B}} \leftarrow \hat{\mathcal{B}} \cup b$
            end if
        end for
        for b in $\hat{\mathcal{B}}$ **do**
            $\hat{\mathcal{I}} \leftarrow \emptyset$
            if $\sum_{b \in \hat{\mathcal{B}}} \sum_{d \in \mathcal{D}} q_{bdr} y_{bdt} \leq \bar{\mathcal{R}}_{rt} * \rho$ **then**
                $\hat{\mathcal{I}} \leftarrow \hat{\mathcal{I}} \cup b$
            end if
        end for
        if $\sum_{b \in \hat{\mathcal{I}}} \sum_{d \in \mathcal{D}} q_{bdr} y_{bdt} < \bar{\mathcal{R}}_{rt}$ **then**
            $x_{btj} \leftarrow ImproveSolution(G, q_{bdr}, \tilde{p}_{bd}, \hat{\mathcal{I}})$
        else if $\sum_{b \in \hat{\mathcal{I}}} \sum_{d \in \mathcal{D}} q_{bdr} y_{bdt} > \bar{\mathcal{R}}_{rt}$ **then**
            $x_{btj} \leftarrow RepairResourceViolation(G, q_{bdr}, \tilde{p}_{bd}, \hat{\mathcal{I}})$
        end if
    end for
    $\Omega_j \leftarrow \Omega_j \cup x_{bt\omega}$
end for
return Ω_j

crossover rate reflects a higher chance that crossover occurs. Due to the multi-period structure of the PCPSP, we design an interdependent-period single-point crossover that accounts for the entire mine lifespan. It combines two parent solutions by exchanging portions of their periodic components. We use a crossover cut $\zeta \in [0, 1]$, drawn randomly, to determine the crossover index using $\zeta * \sum_{t \in \mathcal{T}} x_{bt}$. This index can fall in any time period. Figure 5 illustrates a crossover between two feasible solutions. The last step in this illustration is an immediate fix to prevent block extraction across multiple periods.

Subsequently, mutation introduces a small random alteration to the genetic code of an individual. In the mutation step, we choose blocks for extraction (i.e., $x_b t = 1$) with no precedence blocks. The current time period t' is mutated randomly to another time period $t \in \{\mathcal{T} \setminus t'\}$. The mutation step occurs for all parent pairs, but we used the mutation rate γ to select the percentage of blocks with no precedence $|\{\hat{b}\}|$ to mutate. The subset of blocks with no precedence is selected uniformly using $SAMPLE(RANDOM(0, \gamma) * |\{\hat{b}\}|, \{\hat{b}\})$.

Solutions may become infeasible after crossover and mutation. The crossover step may result in precedence violation whereas the mutation step may result in resource violation. Hence, the repair operator is invoked. It uses the pre-computed cone sets that are akin to the initial solution generation.

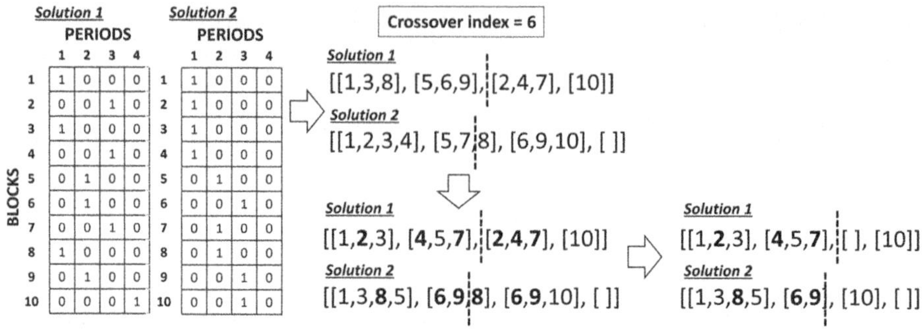

Fig. 5. Crossover between two feasible solutions.

5 Experiments

We utilize a small-sized real-world inspired dataset from an operating copper and gold mine, Wilma1. It was adapted for the generic formulation and mocked up. We complemented it with benchmark instances from MineLib - Newman1 and Kd. Newman1 is small-sized whilst Kd is medium-sized (Kd is a copper mine in North America). Table 1 informs the number of blocks $|\mathcal{B}|$, precedence $|\mathcal{B}_b|$, time periods $|\mathcal{T}|$, destinations $|\mathcal{D}|$ and operational resource constraints $|\mathcal{R}|$.

Table 1. Key characteristics of the dataset.

Name	Block	Precedence	Periods	Destinations	Resources
Newman1	1,060	3,922	6	2	2
Wilma1	1,960	7,112	4	3	3
Kd	14,153	219,778	12	2	2

5.1 Experimental Setup

There are two NSGA-II variants - based on the `argmax` and `softmax` functions – for the portions of block b delegated to destination d during period t, $y_{bdt} \in [0, 1]$. This directly affects Objective Function 1. The first variant, using the `argmax` function, apportions a block fully to the destination with the most profit. Meanwhile, the `softmax` function variant, apportions a block across all destinations with a multiplier λ on the profit of that block when sent to each destination, p_{bd}:

$$\text{softmax} = \frac{e^{\lambda p_{bd}}}{\sum_{d=1}^{\mathcal{D}} e^{\lambda p_{bd}}} \tag{11}$$

We run the two variants three times, each with 100 solutions in a population and generations ranging from eight to ten. From the six populations of solution sets, we derive the true Pareto front of non-dominated solutions. Then, the solution sets from each population are compared using the ratio of non-dominated individuals (RNI) [16], distance, and diversity metrics [5]. Firstly, the RNI metric yields the proportion of best-known solutions ϕ (i.e., solutions that form part of the Pareto front) that exist in a population Ω_j with $\mathcal{N}$ solutions:

$$\text{Ratio of non-dominated individuals (RNI)} = \frac{|\phi_j|}{\mathcal{N}} \tag{12}$$

Secondly, the distance metric assesses how closely a solution j in population Ω_j converges to the true Pareto front. Initially, the metric calculates the minimum Euclidean distance between a solution from population Ω_j and all solutions k from the true front Ω_k. This is then averaged across all $\mathcal{N}$ solutions. A value close to zero is desired.

$$\text{Distance metric} = \frac{\sum_{j=1}^{\mathcal{N}} \min d_{jk}}{\mathcal{N}} \tag{13}$$

Finally, the diversity metric evaluates the even spread of solutions over the true Pareto front using the Euclidean distance. It considers the distance between successive solutions d_i, the average distance $\bar{d}$ of all d_i, distances between extreme solutions of the true Pareto-optimal front d_k, and distances between extreme solutions in a population set d_j. A value close to one indicates better diversity.

$$\text{Diversity metric} = \frac{d_k + d_j + \sum_{i=1}^{\mathcal{N}-1} |d_i - \bar{d}|}{d_k + d_j + (\mathcal{N} - 1)\bar{d}} \tag{14}$$

The NSGA-II model for the augmented multi-objective PCPSP was built using Python. The algorithm was executed on a Linux operating system with 3.5 GHz 3rd generation Intel Xeon Scalable processor, 128 vCPUs and 128 Gb memory. The initial solution was produced with the upper bound resource multiplier ρ of 1.2. In the reproduction, the mutation γ and crossover η rates were set to 0.2 and 0.6, respectively. Lastly, the softmax multiplier λ was 4.

5.2 Results

The performance metrics of RNI, distance, and diversity for the argmax and softmax variants are summarized in Table 2. Overall for Newman1 and Wilma1 instances, the `argmax` variants, compared to the `softmax` variants, generate *sets of solutions* that are closer to the true Pareto front (distance metric), but with less assortment (diversity metric) and lesser *individual solutions* that form part of the true Pareto front (RNI). For Newman1, the `argmax` and `softmax` average distance metrics are 0.290 and 0.304, respectively, while for Wilma1, their values are 0.056 (argmax) and 0.074 (softmax). Next, the diversity metric averages 0.753 (argmax) and 0.830 (softmax) for Newman1, and 0.863 (argmax) and 1.017 (softmax) for Wilma1. Finally, the RNI averages 0.003 (argmax) and 0.007 (softmax) for Newman1, and 0.007 (argmax) and 0.037 (softmax) for Wilma1.

Table 2. Performance metrics of experiment variants across datasets.

Experiment	Softmax			Argmax		
Generation	RNI	Distance	Diversity	RNI	Distance	Diversity
Newman1						
8	0	0.264	**0.862**	0	**0.254**	0.780
9	0	0.332	0.820	0	0.295	0.767
10	**0.02**	0.317	0.807	0.01	0.321	0.713
Average	0.007	0.304	0.830	0.003	0.290	0.753
Wilma1						
8	**0.09**	0.082	1.037	0.01	**0.039**	0.803
9	0.01	0.078	0.977	0	0.070	0.875
10	0.01	0.063	**1.038**	0.01	0.058	0.911
Average	0.037	0.074	1.017	0.007	0.056	0.863
Kd						
8	0	0.332	0.749	**0.03**	0.322	**0.946**
9	0	0.251	0.684	0	0.324	0.905
10	0	**0.236**	0.685	0.01	0.333	0.925
Average	0	0.273	0.706	0.01	0.326	0.925

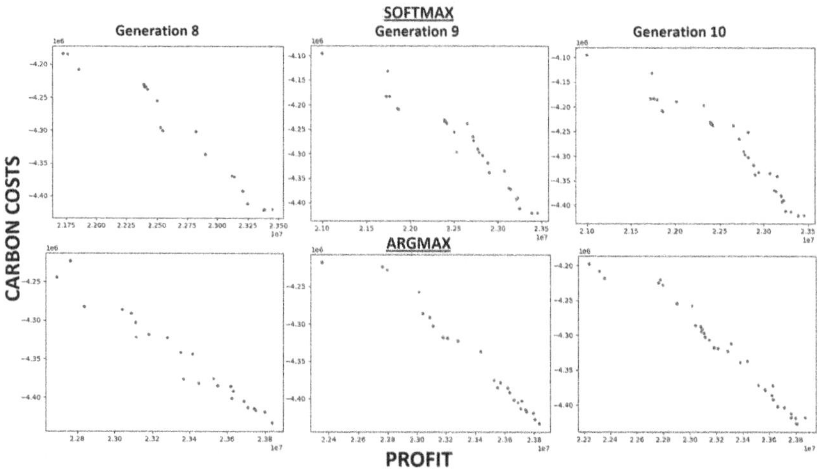

Fig. 6. Newman1 Pareto front across generations for two NSGA-II variants.

Meanwhile for the medium-sized instance of Kd, these observations between the `argmax` and `softmax` variants are reversed. The `softmax` variants, compared to the `argmax` variants, generate *sets of solutions* that are closer to the true Pareto front (distance metric), but with less assortment (diversity metric) and lesser *individual solutions* that form part of the true Pareto front (RNI). The average values are found in Table 2.

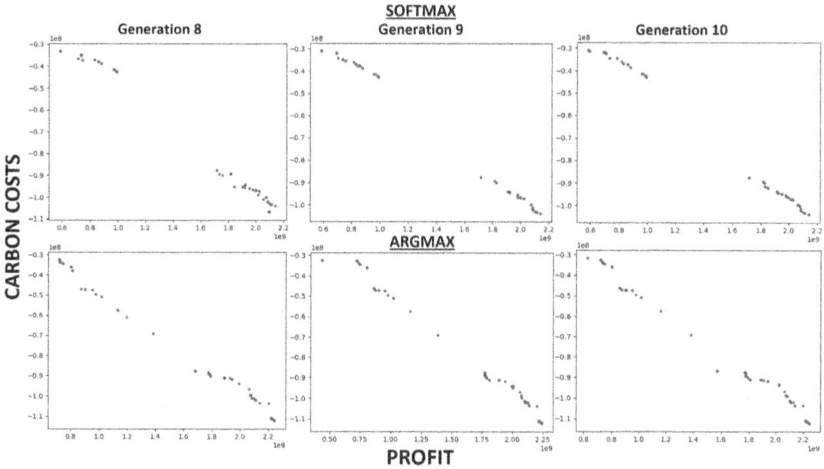

Fig. 7. Wilma1 Pareto front across generations for two NSGA-II variants.

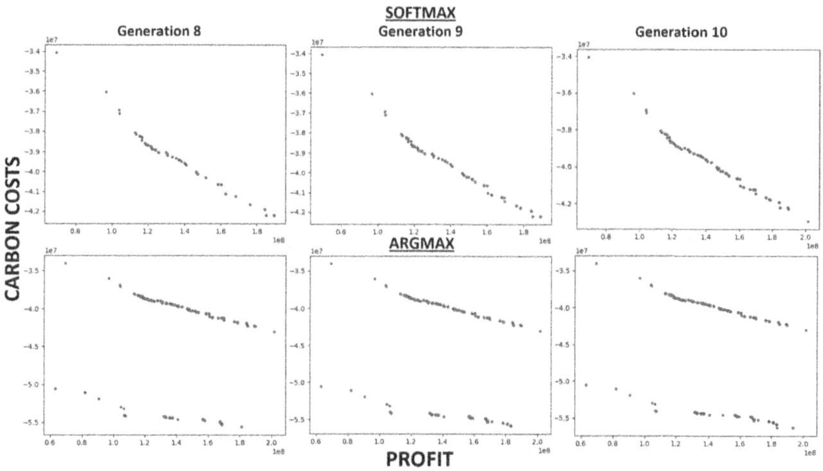

Fig. 8. Kd Pareto front across generations for two NSGA-II variants.

A Pareto optimal front is also produced for each population variant. This visual aid allows mine planners to appreciate the trade-off between the NPV of profit and carbon cost for decision making. Figure 6, Fig. 7 and Fig. 8 display the Pareto front of the population variants across generations for Newman1, Wilma1, and Kd respectively. The computation time for each population variant was less than an hour for Newman1. However, when the model is applied to larger datasets, the computation time increases. Hence, the traversal of the search space may be improved for this framework to be applied to much larger instances.

6 Conclusion

In this paper, we implement the NSGA-II model to balance the NPV of profit with carbon emissions when managing the movement of ores from the mine pit to the production facilities. Our framework for the open pit mine addresses sustainability concerns by augmenting the generic PCPSP into a multi-objective problem that can be catered to diverse environmental concerns. It is applied to real-world instances of an operating mine and MineLib that have been extended for carbon emission considerations. Our approach demonstrates the effective formation of Pareto fronts with profit and carbon cost axes so that mine planners can consider both aspects concurrently.

Previous work has used the generic PCPSP for carbon emissions trade-off but through an additional constraint. To the best of our knowledge, this is the first reformulation into a MOO problem. Future work can focus on improving the computation time to extend this proof of concept to larger datasets. Additionally, other MOEAs can be evaluated against the NSGA-II model and the objective functions can be further expanded for other environmental concerns.

Acknowledgements. This work is supported by Enterprise Singapore under the grant 20-IPPII-T-001-B-1 and Rio Tinto Ltd.

References

1. Alipour, A., khodaiari, A.A., Jafari, A., Tavakkoli-Moghaddam, R.: A genetic algorithm approach for open-pit mine production scheduling. Int. J. Mining Geo Eng. **51**(1), 47–52 (2017). https://doi.org/10.22059/ijmge.2017.62152
2. Attari, M.Y.N., Torkayesh, A.E.: Developing benders decomposition algorithm for a green supply chain network of mine industry: case of Iranian mine industry. Oper. Res. Perspect. **5**, 371–382 (2018). https://doi.org/10.1016/j.orp.2018.11.002
3. Azhar, N.A.B., Gunawan, A., Cheng, S.F., Leonardi, E.: A carbon-aware planning framework for production scheduling in mining. In: Computational Logistics: 13th International Conference, ICCL 2022, Barcelona, Spain, 21–23 September 2022, Proceedings, pp. 441–456. Springer, Heidelberg (2022). https://doi.org/10.1007/978-3-031-16579-5_30
4. Canales-Bustos, L., Santibañez-González, E., Candia-Véjar, A.: A multi-objective optimization model for the design of an effective decarbonized supply chain in mining. Int. J. Prod. Econ. **193**, 449–464 (2017). https://doi.org/10.1016/j.ijpe.2017.08.012
5. Deb, K., Agrawal, S., Pratap, A., Meyarivan, T.: A fast elitist non-dominated sorting genetic algorithm for multi-objective optimization: NSGA-II. In: Schoenauer, M., et al. (eds.) PPSN 2000. LNCS, vol. 1917, pp. 849–858. Springer, Heidelberg (2000). https://doi.org/10.1007/3-540-45356-3_83
6. Espinoza, D., Goycoolea, M., Moreno, E., Newman, A.: MineLib: a library of open pit mining problems. Ann. Oper. Res. **206**(1), 93–114 (2012). https://doi.org/10.1007/s10479-012-1258-3
7. Hustrulid, W.A., Kuchta, M., Martin, R.K.: Open Pit Mine Planning and Design, Two Volume Set & CD-ROM Pack. CRC Press, Boca Raton (2013)

8. Khan, A., Niemann-Delius, C.: A differential evolution based approach for the production scheduling of open pit mines with or without the condition of grade uncertainty. Appl. Soft Comput. **66**, 428–437 (2018). https://doi.org/10.1016/j.asoc.2018.02.010
9. Konak, A., Coit, D.W., Smith, A.E.: Multi-objective optimization using genetic algorithms: a tutorial. Reliabil. Eng. Syst. Saf. **91**(9), 992–1007 (2006). https://doi.org/10.1016/j.ress.2005.11.018
10. Luong, N.H., Alderliesten, T., Bel, A., Niatsetski, Y., Bosman, P.A.: Application and benchmarking of multi-objective evolutionary algorithms on high-dose-rate brachytherapy planning for prostate cancer treatment. Swarm Evol. Comput. **40**, 37–52 (2018). https://doi.org/10.1016/j.swevo.2017.12.003
11. Marler, R.T., Arora, J.S.: Survey of multi-objective optimization methods for engineering. Struct. Multidisc. Optim. **26**(6), 369–395 (2004). https://doi.org/10.1007/s00158-003-0368-6
12. Morrison-Saunders, A., McHenry, M.P., Sequeira, A.R., Gorey, P., Mtegha, H., Doepel, D.: Integrating mine closure planning with environmental impact assessment: challenges and opportunities drawn from african and australian practice. Impact Assess, Project Apprais. **34**(2), 117–128 (2016). https://doi.org/10.1080/14615517.2016.1176407
13. Newman, A.M., Rubio, E., Caro, R., Weintraub, A., Eurek, K.: A review of operations research in mine planning. Interfaces **40**(3), 222–245 (2010). https://doi.org/10.1287/inte.1090.0492
14. Rimélé, M.A., Dimitrakopoulos, R., Gamache, M.: A stochastic optimization method with in-pit waste and tailings disposal for open pit life-of-mine production planning. Res. Policy **57**, 112–121 (2018). https://doi.org/10.1016/j.resourpol.2018.02.006
15. Soto, R., Crawford, B., Almonacid, B., Johnson, F., Olguín, E.: Solving open-pit long-term production planning problems with constraint programming a performance evaluation. In: 2014 9th International Conference on Software Engineering and Applications (ICSOFT-EA), pp. 70–77. IEEE (2014). https://doi.org/10.5220/0005093900700077
16. Tan, K.C., Lee, T.H., Khor, E.F.: Evolutionary algorithms for multi-objective optimization: performance assessments and comparisons. Artif. Intell. Rev. **17**(4), 251–290 (2002). https://doi.org/10.1023/a:1015516501242
17. Touzout, F.A., Benyoucef, L.: Multi-objective multi-unit process plan generation in a reconfigurable manufacturing environment: a comparative study of three hybrid metaheuristics. Int. J. Prod. Res. **57**(24), 7520–7535 (2019). https://doi.org/10.1080/00207543.2019.1635277
18. Valderrama, C.V., Santibanez-González, E., Pimentel, B., Candia-Vejar, A., Canales-Bustos, L.: Designing an environmental supply chain network in the mining industry to reduce carbon emissions. J. Clean. Prod. **254**, 119688 (2020). https://doi.org/10.1016/j.jclepro.2019.119688
19. Wang, X., Gu, X., Liu, Z., Wang, Q., Xu, X., Zheng, M.: Production process optimization of metal mines considering economic benefit and resource efficiency using an NSGA-II model. Processes **6**(11), 228 (2018). https://doi.org/10.3390/pr6110228

20. Xu, X.C., Gu, X.W., Qing, W., Zhao, Y.Q., Wang, Z.K.: Open pit limit optimization considering economic profit, ecological costs and social benefits. Trans, Nonferrous Metals Soc. China **31**(12), 3847–3861 (2021). https://doi.org/10.1016/s1003-6326(21)65769-2
21. Zeng, L., Liu, S.Q., Kozan, E., Corry, P., Masoud, M.: A comprehensive interdisciplinary review of mine supply chain management. Res. Policy **74**, 102274 (2021). https://doi.org/10.1016/j.resourpol.2021.102274

Multi-product Lot-Sizing Problem with Remanufacturing, Lost Sales and Sequence-Dependent Changeover Cost

Lucas Gana[1], Sebastián Dávila-Gálvez[1,2], and Franco Quezada[1,2(✉)]

[1] Faculty of Engineering, Industrial Engineering Department, University of Santiago of Chile (USACH), Santiago, Chile
{lucas.gana,sebastian.davila,franco.quezada}@usach.cl

[2] Faculty of Engineering, Program for the Development of Sustainable Production Systems (PDSPS), University of Santiago of Chile (USACH), Santiago, Chile

Abstract. This work studies a lot-sizing problem motivated by a textile remanufacturing company in Chile. In particular, we investigate a multi-product lot-sizing with remanufacturing, lost sales, and sequence-dependent changeover costs. The problem is first formulated as a mixed-integer linear program. Then, we adapted a known family of valid inequalities and proposed a new exponential family of valid inequalities taking advantage of the problem structure. We use them in a branch-and-cut algorithm to solve the problem. The preliminary numerical results show the proposed inequalities' usefulness in strengthening the proposed formulation's linear relaxation and show that the method outperforms the generic branch-and-cut algorithm embedded in a stand-alone mathematical solver.

Keywords: Lot-sizing and Scheduling · Remanufacturing · Changeover cost · Valid inequalities · Branch-and-Cut algorithm

1 Introduction

The alarming rise of environmental issues and climate change has shifted how things are done. Industrial companies, which share partial responsibility for the current environmental crisis, face pressure from governments and consumers alike to adopt more eco-friendly practices. In Chile, a public law known as The Extended Liability of the Producer (ERP) has been promoting waste management since 2016 to create a circular production model that retains the utility and worth of products and their components. One way to achieve this is through remanufacturing, which involves transforming waste materials into like-new products, materials, or substances for the original or other purposes [15].

This research was partially supported by Dicyt projects 062217QV and 062217DG, Vicerrectoría de Investigación, Desarrollo e Innovación, Universidad de Santiago de Chile.

© The Author(s), under exclusive license to Springer Nature Switzerland AG 2023
J. R. Daduna et al. (Eds.): ICCL 2023, LNCS 14239, pp. 517–532, 2023.
https://doi.org/10.1007/978-3-031-43612-3_32

Remanufacturing can effectively reduce pollution emissions and natural resource consumption by reusing embedded materials and components in used products, making production processes more environmentally friendly.

This work focuses on a remanufacturing system in which end-of-life products are collected, sorted by material, and transformed into raw materials to create new products. We aim to optimize production planning for this system over a multi-period horizon while meeting customer demand for remanufactured products most cost-effectively. This problem is motivated by a Chilean textile remanufacturing company called ECOCITEX, which specializes in producing high-quality recycled cotton yarn. The company's main objective is to contribute to developing a circular economy by reusing textile waste that would otherwise end up in landfills. ECOCITEX's remanufacturing process involves collecting textile waste from various sources, including used clothing, industrial scraps, and post-consumer waste. The collected waste is then sorted, cleaned, and processed into high-quality recycled cotton yarn that can be used for various applications, including textiles, clothing, and other products. One of the key benefits of ECOCITEX's remanufacturing process is that it significantly reduces the environmental impact of textile production by minimizing the use of water, energy, and other natural resources. The company's products are also free from harmful chemicals and toxins, making them a safe and sustainable choice for consumers.

We are studying a scenario where each finished product is made from a unique bill-of-material of end-of-life products, and the production process takes place on a single production line of machinery. As a result, whenever the production line needs to switch from producing one finished product to another, there are setup costs for cleaning the machinery during product changeovers. These operations consume both time and financial resources, impacting the profitability and production capacity of the system. Naively, reducing setup costs is best achieved by running large lot sizes. However, this approach leads to desynchronized patterns between customer demand and production plans, resulting in costly high inventory levels. Lot-sizing models thus aim at reaching the best possible trade-off between minimizing the setup costs and the inventory holding costs, taking into account both the customers' demand satisfaction and the practical limitations of the system. Finally, as the system's production is implicitly limited by the quantity of returned end-of-life products by customers, we consider an additional lost sales cost to be paid when the customers' demand is not satisfied on time. We thus investigate a multi-product lot-sizing problem with remanufacturing, lost sales, and sequence-dependent changeover costs.

Only a few works have addressed multi-product lot-sizing production systems with remanufacturing and sequence-dependent changeover setups. Heuristic solution approaches lot sizing problem with sequence-dependent setups ,and setup carry-over in a closed-loop supply chain is investigated in [16]. Similarly, Roshani et al. [14] investigate a MIP heuristic for an integrated lot sizing and single machine scheduling problem considering sequence-dependent setup time and costs in a closed-loop supply chain network with an energy-efficient objective function. However, these authors investigate a hybrid manufacturing/remanufacturing system, where finished products can be manufactured from raw materials or remanufactured from end-of-life products, and focus on developing heuristic solution approaches to solve the problem. In contrast, we investigate exact solution methods for a multi-product lot-sizing within a pure remanufacturing production system with sequence-dependent changeover costs. Exact solution approaches for a multi-echelon lot-sizing problem with remanufacturing and lost sales have been addressed, for example, in [12] and [11]. They propose to solve the problem through a branch-and-cut algorithm based on the new valid inequalities that explicitly take into account the impact of a limited returns quantity on the production system. Nonetheless, they consider a single type of product and do not take into account sequence-dependent or changeover setup costs. In contrast, we consider a multi-product remanufacturing production system, where each finished product is composed of a different bill-of-material of end-of-life products, and we take into account the changeover setup cost incurring each time switches are made between products in the production line.

To the best of our knowledge, the multi-product lot-sizing for a pure remanufacturing system with lost sales and sequence-dependent changeover cost has not yet been studied in the literature. The present work aims at partially closing this gap by investigating solution approaches for this problem. Our contributions are twofold. First, we propose a mixed-integer linear programming formulation for a practical lot-sizing problem with remanufacturing motivated by a Chilean textile remanufacturing company. Second, we adopt a well-known family of valid inequalities to solve this problem. Then, we propose a new family of single-product valid inequalities that aim to better take into account the fact that the production quantity that can be processed on a resource is limited by the availability of its input product. Finally, we develop branch-and-cut algorithms based on these valid inequalities and assess their computational performance by comparing them with the one of a stand-alone mathematical programming solver. The preliminary numerical results show the proposed inequalities' usefulness in strengthening the proposed formulation's linear relaxation and show that the method outperforms the generic branch-and-cut algorithm embedded in a stand-alone mathematical solver.

The remainder of this paper is organized as follows. We first provide a brief overview of the related literature in Sect. 2. The problem description and its MILP formulation are provided in Sect. 3. We then present the proposed families of valid inequalities in Sect. 4 and discuss their corresponding separation algorithms. Computational results are summarized in Sect. 5. Finally, Sect. 6 gives a conclusion and some research perspectives.

2 Related Works

In the past decade, various efforts have been made to enhance the MILP formulation of single-echelon lot-sizing problems that involve remanufacturing. This has been achieved through the development of extended reformulations and valid inequalities in the literature.

Helmrich et al. [13] discussed several MILP formulations of the uncapacitated single-item single-echelon lot-sizing problem with remanufacturing and introduced new valid inequalities by adapting the previously known (l, S, WW) proposed by [10] to their problem. Similarly, [5] proposed a multi-commodity reformulation and a new set of valid inequalities for this problem. In particular, they further strengthened the (l, S, WW) inequalities presented in [13] by considering that the amount of finished products remanufactured in a given period t is limited by the cumulative quantity of returned products brought back up to t. Ali et al. [3] enriched the previous works by highlighting a theoretical property about the equivalence of the shortest path and facility location reformulations. They also carried out a polyhedral analysis of a related sub-problem based on the single-node fixed-charge network problem, proving the validity of several flow cover inequalities and their facet-defining conditions. Akartunali and Arulselvan [2] studied the uncapacitated and capacitated variants of this single-item single-echelon lot-sizing problem. They showed that the uncapacitated problem could not have a fully polynomial time approximation scheme (FPTAS) and provided a pseudo-polynomial algorithm to solve the problem. They also provided valid inequalities based on the flow-cover inequalities for the problem with a limited production capacity. Authors of [1] studied a capacitated lot sizing problem in a hybrid system. They incorporated three families of valid inequalities to strengthen the formulation and performed a computational test to demonstrate that these valid inequalities improved upon the original formulation. In addition, valid inequalities for a multi-echelon lot-sizing problem with remanufacturing were investigated in [11,12]. Quezada et al. [12] propose to extend previously known valid inequalities to a stochastic setting by exploiting the underlying structure of the stochastic process. In contrast, Quezada et al. [11] introduced new valid inequalities that explicitly consider the impact of a limited returns quantity on the production system. Other related works are the ones that deal with defective items that may result from an imperfect production system and the need for reworking. Recent works on these production systems can be found, for example, in [7] and [6]. One main distinction between rework and remanufacturing lies in the nature of the flows involved. Rework focuses on internal flows within the production process, whereas remanufacturing involves external flows through the return of products. Finally, we refer the reader to [4] for a recent survey on single-item lot-sizing problems with remanufacturing.

Most of the works mentioned above focus on single-item, single-echelon problems in hybrid manufacturing/remanufacturing production systems. They assume that, due to an uncapacitated manufacturing system, it will always be possible to satisfy the demand for finished products on time or consider explicit capacity constraints that can be directly included in formulating valid inequalities. In contrast, our investigation focuses on a pure remanufacturing system. It considers that the demand will be lost if the quantity and/or quality of the returned products is insufficient to meet it on time. As a result, most of the inequalities introduced in the literature need to be more directly valid for our problem. Finally, to our knowledge, no current work investigates valid inequalities and exact solution approaches for a multi-product lot-sizing problem over a remanufacturing production system with sequence-dependent changeover setup costs and lost sales.

3 Problem Description and Modeling

In this section, we provide a description of the production system and mathematical definitions to formulate a mixed-integer linear program for the problem.

3.1 Production System

We consider a remanufacturing system where a set of end-of-life products are transformed into a different set of like-new products (or materials). Thus, the system involves a set $\mathcal{J}$ of end-of-life type of products and a set $\mathcal{I}$ of finished products. Each finished product is composed of different types of end-of-life products. The production system is assumed to be uncapacitated. However, the system might not be able to satisfy the customer demand on time due to part shortages if customers do not return enough end-of-life products. In this situation, the corresponding demand is lost, incurring a penalty cost to account for the loss of customer goodwill. In addition, we consider the case of the production process involving changeover setup cost, i.e., the cost associated with the time and resources required to switch a production process from producing one product to another. It includes cleaning the equipment, changing the tools and machinery, and adjusting the production line for the new product. These activities are necessary to ensure the quality and consistency of the new product and represent a cost for the company, as they consume resources and reduce production capacity.

The time-dependent input parameters of the problem are introduced as follows. For each period $t \in \mathcal{T} := \{1, \ldots, T\}$,

- r_t^j denotes the quantity collected of the end-of-life product $j \in \mathcal{J}$.
- d_t^i denotes the customers' demand for finished product $i \in \mathcal{I}$,
- f_t^i denotes the setup cost for processing a product $i \in \mathcal{I}$ on the machine,
- g_t^i, denotes the unit production cost for the finished product $i \in \mathcal{I}$,
- $h(s)_t^i$ denotes the unit inventory cost for finished product $i \in \mathcal{I}$,
- $h(r)_t^j$ denotes the unit inventory cost for end-of-life product $j \in \mathcal{J}$,
- cs_t^i denotes the unit lost-sales penalty cost for finished product $i \in \mathcal{I}$.

On the other hand, the time-invariant input parameters are defined as follows:

- α^{ij} denotes the quantity of the end-of-life product j required for the finished product i.

3.2 Mixed-Integer Linear Programming Formulation

In order to build a mathematical model for the problem, we introduce the following decision variables for time period $t \in \mathcal{T}$:

- X_t^i defines the quantity of finished products $i \in \mathcal{I}$,
- $Y_t^i \in \{0,1\}$ represents the setup variable for finished products $i \in \mathcal{I}$,
- $I(r)_t^j$ denotes the inventory level of the end-of-life products $j \in \mathcal{J}$,
- $I(s)_t^i$ denotes the inventory level of the finished products $i \in \mathcal{I}$,
- $W_t^{ii'} \in \{0,1\}$ represents the changeover variable from product i to product i', with $i, i' \in \mathcal{I}$, $i \neq i'$,
- L_t^i defines the lost sales variables for finished product $i \in \mathcal{I}$.

We thus introduce the following MILP formulation for the multi-product lot-sizing problem with remanufacturing and lost sales to minimize the total cost of production:

$$\min \sum_{t\in\mathcal{T}} \sum_{i\in\mathcal{I}} \left(\left(f_t^i Y_t^i + g_t^i X_t^i + h(s)_t^i I(s)_t^i + cs_t^i L_t^i + \sum_{j\in\mathcal{I}:j\neq i} c_t^{ij} W_t^{ij} \right) + \sum_{j\in\mathcal{J}} h(r)_t^j I(r)_t^j \right) \tag{1a}$$

$$s.t. \quad I(r)_t^j = I(r)_{t-1}^j + r_t^j - \sum_{i\in\mathcal{I}} \alpha^{ij} X_t^i \qquad \forall t \in \mathcal{T}, \forall j \in \mathcal{J} \tag{1b}$$

$$I(s)_t^i = I(s)_{t-1}^i + X_t^i - d_t^i + L_t^i \qquad \forall t \in \mathcal{T}, \forall i \in \mathcal{I}, \tag{1c}$$

$$X_t^i \leq M_t^i Y_t^i \qquad \forall t \in \mathcal{T}, \forall i \in \mathcal{I}, \tag{1d}$$

$$L_t^i \leq d_t^i \qquad \forall t \in \mathcal{T}, \forall i \in \mathcal{I}, \tag{1e}$$

$$W_t^{ii'} \geq Y_{t-1}^i + Y_t^{i'} - 1 \qquad \forall t \in \mathcal{T}, \forall i, i' \in \mathcal{I} : i \neq i', \tag{1f}$$

$$\sum_{i\in\mathcal{I}} Y_t^i \leq 1 \qquad \forall t \in \mathcal{T}, \tag{1g}$$

$$Y_t^i, W_t^{ii'} \in \{0,1\} \qquad \forall t \in \mathcal{T}, \forall i, i' \in \mathcal{I}, \tag{1h}$$

$$X_t^i, L_t^i, I(s)_t^i \geq 0 \qquad \forall t \in \mathcal{T}, \forall i \in \mathcal{I}, \tag{1i}$$

$$I(r)_t^j \geq 0 \qquad \forall t \in \mathcal{T}, \forall j \in \mathcal{J}. \tag{1j}$$

The objective function (1a) minimizes the total production cost over the whole planning horizon, i.e., the sum of the setup, production, inventory holding, lost sales, and changeover costs. Constraints (1b)–(1c) are the inventory balance constraints. More specifically, constraints (1b) ensure that any remanufactured/finished product is either used to satisfy the demand or kept in stock. if there are not enough remanufactured products to satisfy the demand, the unsatisfied demand is lost. Constraints (1c) ensure that end-of-life product are re-manufactured or kept in stock. Constraints (1d) link the production quantity variables to the setup variables. Constraints (1e) restrict the quantity of lost sales. Constraints (1f) link the setup variable with the changeover variable, indicating if a transition occurs in production from one product to another. Constraints (1g) ensure that a maximum of one product per time period is produced in the production line. Without loss of generality, we assume that the initial inventory, $I(r)_0^j$ and $I(s)_0^i$ for each $j \in \mathcal{J}$ and $i \in \mathcal{I}$, is set to 0. Finally, Constraints (1h)–(1j) provide the domain of the decision variables.

In order to set the value of each constant M_t^i using an upper bound on the quantity that can be processed of each product i at each time period t, this quantity is limited by two elements: the availability of the end-of-life products already returned by customers and the future demand for finished products. We thus define the value of M_t^i, for each period t and product i, as follows:

$$M_t^i = \min \left\{ \min_{j \in \mathcal{J}} \left\{ \sum_{1 \leq k \leq t} \alpha^{ij^{-1}} r_k^j \right\}, \sum_{t \leq k \leq T} d_k^i \right\}$$

4 Valid Inequalities

We now seek to adapt the single-echelon single-item (k, U) inequalities introduced in [9] and further investigated in [12] for the case of stochastic demand and [11] for the case of the remanufacturing system by considering the limited quantity of returned products available at each time period.

We first recall that a single-echelon single-item (k, U) is defined as follows:

Proposition 1. *Let* $1 \leq k \leq T$ *be a time period of the planning horizon. Let* $U \subseteq \{k, ..., T\}$ *be a subset of periods and* $t^* = \max\{\tau : \tau \in U\}$ *be the last time period belonging to* U*. Then, the following inequalities are valid for Problem* (1a)–(1j)*:*

$$I(s)_{k-1}^i + \sum_{k \leq t \leq t^*} \left(\sum_{l \in U : t \leq l} d_l^i \right) Y_t^i \geq \sum_{t \in U} (d_t^i - L_t^i) \qquad \forall i \in \mathcal{I} \tag{2}$$

Proof. There is a simple proof to show the validity of the inequalities (2) for Problem (1a)–(1j). Let us start by summing up constraints (1c) from period k to period T for any product $i \in \mathcal{I}$, obtaining the subsequent inequality:

$$I(s)_T^i = I(s)_{k-1}^i + \sum_{t \leq k \leq T} X_t^i + \sum_{t \leq k \leq T} (-d_t^i + L_t^i) \tag{3}$$

Then, by the non-negativity of variables $I(s)_t^i$, we have:

$$I(s)_{k-1}^i + \sum_{t \leq k \leq T} X_t^i \geq \sum_{t \leq k \leq T} (d_t^i - L_t^i) \tag{4}$$

Replacing X_t^i by its upper bound provided by constraints (1d), we have:

$$I(s)_{k-1}^i + \sum_{t \leq k \leq T} \left(\sum_{l \leq t \leq T} d_l^i \right) Y_t^i \geq \sum_{t \leq k \leq T} \left(d_t^i - L_t^i \right). \tag{5}$$

Finally, taking any set $U \subseteq \{k, \ldots, T\}$, we can replace $\sum_{t=k}^{T} (d_t^i - L_t^i)$ by $\sum_{t \in U} (d_t^i - L_t^i)$ in the right-hand side of inequality (5) as the former is always greater of equal to the latter due to the non-negativity of variables L_t^i. On the other hand, we can replace $\sum_{t=k}^{T} (\sum_{l=t}^{T} d_l^i) Y_t^i$ by $\sum_{t=k}^{T} (\sum_{l \in U : l \geq t} d_l^i) Y_t^i$ on the left-hand as we must now satisfy the demand in time periods $t \in U$. □

Note that inequalities (2) can be strengthened by taking into account that the production of each product i is limited by the minimum availability among all end-of-life products j returned from period one until period t, i.e., we replace $\sum_{l=t}^{T} d_l^i$ by

$$\phi_t^i = \min\left\{\min\left\{j\in\mathcal{J} \sum_{1\leq l\leq t} {\alpha^{ij}}^{-1} r_l^j\right\}, \sum_{l\in U:t\leq l} d_l^i\right\}. \tag{6}$$

Proposition 2. *Let $1 \leq \ell < k \leq T$ be two periods of the planning horizon. Let $U \subseteq \{k, ..., T\}$ be a subset of periods and $t^* = \max\{\tau : \tau \in U\}$ be the last time period belonging to U. Then, $\forall i \in \mathcal{I}, \forall j \in \mathcal{J}$ the following inequalities are valid for Problem* (1a)–(1j)*:*

$${\alpha^{ij}}^{-1} I(r)_{\ell-1}^j + I(s)_{k-1}^i + \sum_{k\leq t\leq t^*} \min\left\{\sum_{\ell\leq l\leq t} {\alpha^{ij}}^{-1} r_l^j, \sum_{l\in U:t\leq l} d_l^i\right\} Y_t^i \geq \sum_{t\in U}(d_t^i - L_t^i) \tag{7}$$

Note that the proposed inequalities (7) correspond to a simple adaptation of the single-echelon (ℓ, k, U) inequalities introduced in [11], and its validity can be proved directly by following the proof in [11].

We now investigate a family of new single-echelon inequalities which seek to better take into account the fact that the production quantity that can be processed on a resource is limited by the availability of its input product. More precisely, the quantity that can be processed in period t is limited by the amount of used products which has been returned up to period t but not yet processed in this period. We thus introduce a set of valid inequalities stating that the total quantity processed over a given time interval $[\ell, t]$ is limited by the sum of the number of used products already returned and not yet transformed at the end of the period $\ell - 1$ and of the amount of used products returned during interval $[\ell, t]$.

Proposition 3. *Let $1 \leq \ell \leq T$ be a time period of the planning horizon and $S \subseteq \{\ell, ..., T\}$ be a subset of periods. The following inequalities are valid for Problem* (1a)–(1j)*:*

$$I(r)_{\ell-1}^j + \sum_{t\in S}\left(\sum_{\ell\leq l\leq t} r_l^j\right) Y_t^i \geq \alpha^{ij} \sum_{t\in S} X_t^i \qquad \forall i \in \mathcal{I}, \forall j \in \mathcal{J} \tag{8}$$

Proof. Let $(\mathbf{X}, \mathbf{Y}, \mathbf{I(r)}, \mathbf{I(s)}, \mathbf{W}, \mathbf{L})$ be a feasible solution of Problem (1a)–(1j). We show that this solution complies with inequalities (8) for any period ℓ and any subset $S \subseteq \{\ell, ..., T\}$. This is done by induction on the index of the last period t that may belong to subset S.

Base step: Set $t = \ell$ and $S \subseteq \{\ell\}$.

We consider two cases:

- $S = \emptyset$. In this case, $\sum_{\tau \in S} X_\tau^i = 0$ whereas $I(r)_{\ell-1}^j + \sum_{\tau \in S} \phi_\tau^j Y_\tau^i \geq I(r)_{\ell-1}^j \geq 0$. Inequality (8) is trivially respected.
- $S = \{\ell\}$. If $Y_\ell^j = 0$. There is no production in period ℓ so that $\sum_{\tau \in S} X_\tau^i = X_\ell^i = 0$ whereas $I(r)_{\ell-1}^j + \sum_{\tau \in S} \phi_\tau^j Y_\tau^i \geq I(r)_{\ell-1}^i \geq 0$. Inequality (8) is trivially respected. If $Y_\ell^i = 1$. In this case, the inventory balance constraint (1c) for period ℓ gives:

$$I(r)_{\ell-1}^j + r_\ell^j - X_\ell^i \geq 0 \qquad \text{by non-negativity of variables } I(r)_\ell^j.$$

By noting that, under the current assumptions, $\phi_\ell^j Y_\ell^i = r_\ell^j$, we have:

$$I(r)_{\ell-1}^j + \phi^\ell Y_\ell^i \geq X_\ell^i,$$

which corresponds to the expression of inequality (8) for $S = \{\ell\}$. Therefore, inequality (8) is thus valid for any $S \subseteq \{\ell\}$.

Induction step: Assume that inequality (8) is valid for any $S \subset \{1, ..., t\}$. We show that, under this assumption, inequality (8) is valid for any $S \subset \{1, ..., t+1\}$. We again consider two cases:

- $t+1 \notin S$. Using the induction hypothesis, inequality (8) is valid for S.
- $t+1 \in S$. If $Y_{t+1}^i = 0$. There is no production in period $t+1$ so that $\sum_{\tau \in S} X_\tau^i = \sum_{\tau \in S \setminus \{t+1\}} X_\tau^i$ whereas $I(r)_{\ell-1}^j + \sum_{\tau \in S} \phi_\tau^j Y_\tau^i = I(r)_{\ell-1}^j + \sum_{\tau \in S \setminus \{t+1\}} \phi_\tau^j Y_\tau^i$. Using the induction hypothesis, we have: $I(r)_{\ell-1}^j + \sum_{\tau \in S \setminus \{t+1\}} \phi_\tau^j Y_\tau^i \geq \sum_{\tau \in S \setminus \{t+1\}} X_\tau^i$ so that inequality (8) holds.

  If $Y_{t+1}^i = 1$. Summing up the inventory balance constraints (1c) over periods ℓ to $t+1$ and using the non-negativity of variables $I(r)_\ell^j$ and X_τ^i gives:

$$I(r)_{\ell-1}^j + \sum_{\tau=\ell}^{t+1} r_\tau^j - \sum_{\tau=\ell}^{t+1} X_\tau^i \geq 0$$
$$I(r)_{\ell-1}^j + \sum_{\tau=\ell}^{t+1} r_\tau^j - \sum_{\tau \in S} X_\tau^i \geq 0.$$

  By noting that under the current assumption, $\phi_{t+1}^j Y_{t+1}^i = \sum_{\tau=\ell}^{t+1} r_\tau^j$ and adding the non-negative terms $\sum_{\tau \in S \setminus \{t+1\}} \phi_\tau^j Y_\tau^i$ to the left-hand side of the previous inequality, we obtain:

$$I(r)_{\ell-1}^j + \sum_{\tau \in S} \phi_\tau^j Y_\tau^i - \sum_{\tau \in S} X_\tau^i \geq 0.$$

This shows that if Inequality (8) is valid for any $S \subset \{1, ..., t\}$, it is also valid for any $S \subset \{1, ..., t+1\}$, which concludes the proof. □

4.1 Separation Algorithms

We now briefly discuss the resolution of the separation problem for each proposed valid inequality. We first recall that this problem consists in finding an inequality violated by a given solution $(\tilde{\mathbf{X}}, \tilde{\mathbf{Y}}, \tilde{\mathbf{I}(\mathbf{r})}, \tilde{\mathbf{I}(\mathbf{s})}, \tilde{\mathbf{L}}, \tilde{\mathbf{W}})$ of the linear relaxation of Problem (1a)–(1j) or prove that no such inequality exists.

In the case of the simple (k, U) inequalities in Proposition 1, an exact separation algorithm is known to find the most violated inequality that runs in $\mathcal{O}(T^2)$. For each period $k = 1, ..., T$, the algorithm finds the set U of time periods by inspection. See [9] for further details on the separation algorithm.

Then, for the case of valid inequalities in Proposition 2, the separation is not trivial as is mentioned in [11], in particular, because the value of each coefficient ϕ_t^j simultaneously depends on U and ℓ. We thus consider a heuristic separation algorithm in our computational experiments as is proposed in [11], which consists of finding the set U as is done for inequalities in Proposition 1 and then computing the coefficient ϕ_t^j for each given period ℓ. The algorithm has a time complexity of $\mathcal{O}(T^2)$.

Finally, we note that inequalities in Proposition 3 form an exponential class of valid inequalities, i.e., their number grows exponentially fast with the number of time periods T. However, the corresponding separation problem is polynomially solvable by inspection in $\mathcal{O}(T^2)$. Namely, to find the most violated valid inequalities (8) by the current linear relaxation, we need to find, for each period $\ell \in \mathcal{T}$, the subset U minimizing the difference between the left and the right-hand side of inequality (8). This amounts to finding the subset S minimizing $\sum_{t \in S} \phi_t^j \tilde{Y}_t^i - \sum_{t \in S} \tilde{X}_p^t$. This can be done by inspection of each period $t \in \{\ell, \dots, T\}$ and adding the time period t to the set S if $\phi_t^j \tilde{Y}_t^i - \tilde{X}_t^i \leq 0$.

We briefly summarize the proposed valid inequalities and their related features in Table 1. Column `Class` indicates whether the number of valid inequalities in the family grows linearly or exponentially fast concerning the number of periods in the planning horizon. Column `Complexity` reports the difficulty of the corresponding separation problem. Column `Sep. alg.` then indicates whether the proposed separation problem is solved by an exact or a heuristic algorithm in our numerical experiments. Column `Time` reports the asymptotic time complexity of the implemented separation algorithm, and Column `Total #` reports the total possible number of valid inequalities that can be generated. Note that all these features significantly impact the numerical tractability and efficiency of a class of valid inequalities.

Table 1. Class and complexity of valid inequalities

Inequalities	Class	Complexity	Sep. alg.	Time	Total #
Proposition 1	Exponential	Polynomial	Exact	$\mathcal{O}(\lvert\mathcal{T}\rvert^2)$	$2^{\lvert\mathcal{T}\rvert}\lvert\mathcal{I}\rvert$
Proposition 2	Exponential	unknown	Heuristic	$\mathcal{O}(\lvert\mathcal{T}\rvert^2)$	$2^{\lvert\mathcal{T}\rvert}\lvert\mathcal{T}\rvert\lvert\mathcal{I}\rvert\lvert\mathcal{J}\rvert$
Proposition 3	Exponential	Polynomial	Exact	$\mathcal{O}(\lvert\mathcal{T}\rvert^2)$	$2^{\lvert\mathcal{T}\rvert}\lvert\mathcal{I}\rvert\lvert\mathcal{J}\rvert$

5 Computational Experiments

In this section, we focus on assessing the performance of the proposed valid inequalities when used within a branch-and-cut algorithm. We compare the performance of this algorithm with one of the generic branch-and-cut algorithms embedded in a mathematical programming solver.

5.1 Instance Generation

We considered two sets of instances: Set 1 instances involve $|\mathcal{T}| = 25$ periods and $|\mathcal{I}| = |\mathcal{J}| = 5$ finished/end-of-life products, whereas instances from Set 2 involve $|\mathcal{T}| = 25$ periods and $|\mathcal{I}| = |\mathcal{J}| = 10$ finished/end-of-life products. The instances were randomly generated within each set by adapting the procedure presented in [8] and extended in [11]. More precisely, we consider one value of the setup-holding cost ratio $f/h \in \{1000\}$, two values for the production-holding cost ratio $g/h \in \{2, 4\}$ and three values of the returns-demand quantity ratio $r/d \in \{1, 2, 3\}$. For each set and each possible combination of f/h, g/h, and r/d, ten random instances were generated, resulting in a total of 120 instances.

For each instance, the value of each problem parameter was set as follows. Demand d^t was uniformly distributed in the interval $[0, 100]$ and the returns quantity r^t was uniformly distributed in the interval $[0.8(r/d)\bar{d}, 1.2(r/d)\bar{d}]$, where $\bar{d} = \frac{\sum d^t}{|\mathcal{T}|}$ is the average demand per period. The bill-of-materials coefficients α^{ij} were randomly generated following a discrete uniform distribution over interval $[1, 6]$ for each $i \in \mathcal{I}, j \in \mathcal{J}$. The holding cost $h(r)^j_t$ for each end-of-life product $j \in \mathcal{J}$ was randomly generated following a discrete uniform distribution over interval $[2, 7]$ and the holding cost $h(s)^i_t$ for each finished product $i \in \mathcal{I}$ was randomly generated following a discrete uniform distribution over interval $[7, 12]$. The production cost g^i_t was uniformly distributed in the interval $[0.8(g/h)\bar{h}^i$, $1.2(g/h)\bar{h}]$, where $\bar{h}^i = \frac{\sum_{t \in \mathcal{T}} \sum h(s)^i_t}{|\mathcal{T}|}$ is the average holding cost for finished product $i \in \mathcal{I}$. The setup f^i_t and changeover setup $c^{i,j}_t$ cost were uniformly distributed in the interval $[0.8(f/h)\bar{h}, 1.2(f/h)\bar{h}]$. The unit penalty cost for lost sales, cs^i_t, was fixed at 200 per unit. grhttps://github.com/LucasGana/ICCL.

5.2 Results

We carried out extensive numerical experiments in order to assess the computational performance of the proposed valid inequalities. This was achieved by solving each considered instance using three alternative branch-and-cut algorithms:

- *GRB*: the generic branch-and-cut algorithm embedded in GUROBI 9.5.2 using the formulation (1a)–(1j).
- *P*1: a branch-and-cut algorithm using the (k, U) inequalities in Proposition 1 with coefficient ϕ proposed in (6) to strengthen the formulation (1a)–(1j).

Table 2. Performance of GUROBI and branch-and-cut methods over instance in Set 1.

r/d	Method	R.LP$_{gap}$	R.MIP$_{gap}$	MIP$_{gap}$	C.Time	R.Time	T.Time	# Cuts
1	*GRB*	2.4	1.2	0.2	0.0	0.2	237.9	–
	*P*1	2.2	0.8	0.2	0.6	0.7	240.4	295
	*P*2	1.8	0.8	0.3	10.0	16.3	243.9	10628
	*P*3	1.8	0.8	0.3	1.3	2.6	240.8	254
	*P*1+*P*3	1.9	0.8	0.2	1.5	2.5	235.3	488
	*P*2+*P*3	1.5	0.0	0.0	10.0	14.3	242.6	9919
2	*GRB*	3.6	2.1	0.5	0.0	0.0	240.3	–
	*P*1	3.1	1.3	0.5	0.8	0.8	240.4	359
	*P*2	2.5	1.3	0.6	9.2	13.9	242.2	11063
	*P*3	2.8	1.4	0.5	1.3	2.0	240.9	218
	*P*1+*P*3	2.9	1.4	0.5	1.4	2.6	240.8	487
	*P*2+*P*3	2.3	0.0	0.0	10.1	17.1	242.3	11002
3	*GRB*	4.4	2.6	0.5	0.0	0.0	225.6	–
	*P*1	3.6	1.7	0.5	0.9	1.3	223.2	401
	*P*2	3.0	1.7	0.5	9.2	12.6	220.1	12041
	*P*3	3.6	1.7	0.5	1.1	1.8	205.4	179
	*P*1+*P*3	3.4	1.7	0.5	1.3	2.8	206.0	485
	*P*2+*P*3	2.7	0.0	0.0	11.3	18.9	232.2	11735

- $P2$: a branch-and-cut algorithm using the (ℓ, k, U) inequalities in Proposition 2 to strengthen the formulation (1a)–(1j).
- $P3$: a branch-and-cut algorithm using the newly introduced (ℓ, S) inequalities in Proposition 3 to strengthen the formulation (1a)–(1j).
- $P1 + P3$: a branch-and-cut algorithm using valid inequalities in Proposition 1 and 3 to strengthen the formulation (1a)–(1j).
- $P2 + P3$: a branch-and-cut algorithm using valid inequalities in Proposition 2 and 3 to strengthen the formulation (1a)–(1j).

Each algorithm is based on the solver GUROBI 9.5.2, and it generates corresponding inequalities through a cutting-plane generation algorithm at the root node and at intermediate nodes of the branch-and-bound search tree using the user Callbacks provided by the solver.

All related linear programs and mixed-integer linear programs were solved using GUROBI 9.5.2 with the solver default settings. The algorithms were implemented in Python 3.9. All tests were run on the computing infrastructure consisting of an Intel(R) Core(TM) i5-10.300H, 2.50 GHz, and 8 GB RAM to solve each instance. We imposed a time limit of 300 s to find an optimal solution for each instance.

The corresponding results are displayed in Table 2 for Set 1 instances and Table 3 for Set 2 instances. Column `Method` indicates the branch-and-cut

Table 3. Performance of GUROBI and branch-and-cut methods over instance in Set 2.

r/d	Method	R.LP$_{gap}$	R.MIP$_{gap}$	MIP$_{gap}$	C.Time	R.Time	T.Time	# Cuts
1	*GRB*	2.2	1.7	0.9	0.0	0.0	300.1	–
	*P*1	2.1	1.1	0.9	1.1	2.8	300.1	569
	*P*2	1.9	1.2	1.0	37.9	63.8	300.1	37273
	*P*3	1.7	1.1	0.9	6.4	12.0	300.0	691
	*P*1+*P*3	1.8	1.1	0.9	7.3	15.7	300.3	1159
	*P*2+*P*3	1.7	0.0	0.0	53.2	51.4	300.2	36025
2	*GRB*	2.9	2.5	1.2	0.0	0.0	300.1	–
	*P*1	2.7	1.5	1.2	1.5	4.1	300.0	822
	*P*2	2.4	1.6	1.3	34.5	64.3	300.0	42574
	*P*3	2.4	1.5	1.2	5.2	14.4	300.1	579
	*P*1+*P*3	2.5	1.5	1.2	4.7	15.1	300.3	1221
	*P*2+*P*3	2.2	0.0	0.0	184.4	98.4	300.1	40734
3	*GRB*	3.6	2.6	1.3	0.0	0.3	300.0	–
	*P*1	3.2	1.9	1.5	1.7	6.2	300.2	952
	*P*2	2.9	2.0	1.6	32.2	97.3	300.1	45887
	*P*3	3.1	1.9	1.5	5.0	11.0	300.0	470
	*P*1+*P*3	3.1	1.8	1.4	4.2	14.4	300.1	1251
	*P*2+*P*3	2.8	0.0	0.0	43.5	187.2	300.0	43018

algorithm used to solve the instances. Column `R.LP`$_{gap}$ reports the gap between the value of the linear relaxation strengthened by the corresponding valid inequalities and the best feasible solution found through the branch-and-bound search. The GRB method reports the gap between the value of the initial linear relaxation and the best feasible solution found through the branch-and-bound search. Column `R.MIP`$_{gap}$ reports the gap between the lower bound at the root node (after the generation of GUROBI generic cutting planes) and the best feasible solution found through the branch-and-bound search. Column `MIP`$_{gap}$ reports the gap between the best lower bound and the best feasible solution found through the branch-and-bound search. The average CPU time in seconds for the cutting-plane generation of each method is reported in column `C.Time`, the CPU time in seconds spent at the root node in column `R.Time` and the average total CPU time in seconds in column `T.Time`. Finally, column # `Cuts` reports the number of cuts generated by each method. Note that each line corresponds to the average value of the corresponding 10 instances.

In general, we observe that the customized branch-and-cut algorithms based on valid inequalities in Proposition 2 and 3 ($P2 + P3$) outperforms the method GRB and the other methods, providing solutions of better quality with similar computation times for all group of tested instances. Specifically, the method $P2 + P3$ is able to almost close the optimality gap at the root node of the branch-and-bound tree (see column $\texttt{R.MIP}_{gap}$) in shorter computation times (see column $\texttt{R.Time}$).

Regarding the relative performance of the methods $P1$ and $P2$, the results suggest that the branch-and-cut algorithm based on the valid inequalities in Proposition 2 always provides a better linear relaxation strengthening than the valid inequalities in Proposition 1 (see column $\texttt{R.LP}_{gap}$); however, this improvement is not exhibited by the performance of the branch-and-cut algorithm based on the same valid inequalities (see column $\texttt{MIP}_{gap}$ and column $\texttt{T.Time}$). This might be explained by the large number of valid inequalities generated through the cutting generation process, which can deteriorate the global performance of the algorithm. Regarding the method $P3$, we observe that the method can usually provide better linear relaxation strengthening than the methods $P1$ and $P2$. However, its performance deteriorates for the instances with the largest demand-return ratio. This might be explained by the fact that the corresponding instances involve a large amount of returned products as compared to the demand so that the availability of the returned products does not necessarily limit the quantity processed on most periods. Thus, method $P2$ seems to provide a better trade-off for this case.

6 Conclusion and Perspectives

We consider a multi-product lot-sizing problem to plan production activities and determine the product sequence for a remanufacturing system. The problem is formulated as a mixed-integer linear program ,and we focused on strengthening this formulation in order to be able to provide optimal or near-optimal solutions for the problem. Besides the formulation of a new practical lot-sizing and scheduling problem, our main contribution is the adaptation and the development of a new family of valid inequalities which take into account the limitations of the production system given by the limited availability of end-of-life products. Computational experiments show that valid inequalities perform well at strengthening the linear relaxation of the formulation, and the proposed branch-and-cut algorithm performs well as compared to the generic branch-and-cut algorithm of the GUROBI 9.5 solver and other studied methods.

The first research direction is to develop a more effective cutting plane generation algorithm for better selecting valid inequalities to be added in the branch-and-cut algorithm and acceleration techniques that further improve their performance. Additional computational experiments are also needed to assess the size of the largest instances that may be solved with the proposed exact solution approach. On a longer perspective, we could extend the proposed valid inequalities to lot-sizing problems with returns involving complicating features such as changeover setups, a limited capacity, or backlogging.

In terms of modeling, an interesting research direction will be to extend the model to a multi-echelon or small-bucket formulation to become closer to a more realistic and practical problem. In general, assuming that all information is certain leads to formulations that might deviate from reality. However, these models often serve as a starting point for future research. In our case, the proposed deterministic approach opens up an interesting discussion about the returned flows in the textile industry. In a favorable scenario where the returns are significantly higher than the demand, the deterministic assumption does not highly impact the production plan since there are enough returned products to carry out the production plan. Otherwise, as the amount of end-of-life products available restricts the ability to comply with the planning, it might incur new costs and lost sales to adjust the production plan. Hence, extending the model to a stochastic setting is also worth investigating, as demand and end-of-life product quantities are usually difficult to predict accurately.

References

1. Aishah, S., Ali, S., Ali, F., Talib, M.L., Rozita, W., Din, W.: Valid inequalities for the capacitated lot-sizing problem in a hybrid manufacturing and remanufacturing system (2021)
2. Akartunalı, K., Arulselvan, A.: Economic lot-sizing problem with remanufacturing option: complexity and algorithms. In: Pardalos, P.M., Conca, P., Giuffrida, G., Nicosia, G. (eds.) MOD 2016. LNCS, vol. 10122, pp. 132–143. Springer, Cham (2016). https://doi.org/10.1007/978-3-319-51469-7_11
3. Ali, S.A.S., Doostmohammadi, M., Akartunalı, K., van der Meer, R.: A theoretical and computational analysis of lot-sizing in remanufacturing with separate setups. Int. J. Prod. Econ. **203**, 276–285 (2018)
4. Brahimi, N., Absi, N., Dauzère-Pérès, S., Nordli, A.: Single-item dynamic lot-sizing problems: an updated survey. Eur. J. Oper. Res. **263**(3), 838–863 (2017)
5. Cunha, J.O., Konstantaras, I., Melo, R.A., Sifaleras, A.: On multi-item economic lot-sizing with remanufacturing and uncapacitated production. Appl. Math. Model. **50**, 772–780 (2017)
6. Goerler, A., Lalla-Ruiz, E., Voß, S.: Late acceptance hill-climbing matheuristic for the general lot sizing and scheduling problem with rich constraints. Algorithms **13**(6), 138 (2020)
7. Goerler, A., Voß, S.: Dynamic lot-sizing with rework of defective items and minimum lot-size constraints. Int. J. Prod. Res. **54**(8), 2284–2297 (2016)
8. Guan, Y., Ahmed, S., Nemhauser, G.L.: Cutting planes for multistage stochastic integer programs. Oper. Res. **57**(2), 287–298 (2009)
9. Loparic, M., Pochet, Y., Wolsey, L.A.: The uncapacitated lot-sizing problem with sales and safety stocks. Math. Program. **89**(3), 487–504 (2001)
10. Pochet, Y., Wolsey, L.A.: Polyhedra for lot-sizing with wagner-whitin costs. Math. Program. **67**(1), 297–323 (1994)
11. Quezada, F., Gicquel, C., Kedad-Sidhoum, S.: New valid inequalities for a multi-echelon multi-item lot-sizing problem with returns and lost sales. In: Mes, M., Lalla-Ruiz, E., Voß, S. (eds.) ICCL 2021. LNCS, vol. 13004, pp. 192–207. Springer, Cham (2021). https://doi.org/10.1007/978-3-030-87672-2_13
12. Quezada, F., Gicquel, C., Kedad-Sidhoum, S., Vu, D.Q.: A multi-stage stochastic integer programming approach for a multi-echelon lot-sizing problem with returns and lost sales. Comput. Oper. Res. **116**, 104865 (2020)
13. Retel Helmrich, M.J., Jans, R., van den Heuvel, W., Wagelmans, A.P.: Economic lot-sizing with remanufacturing: complexity and efficient formulations. IIE Trans. **46**(1), 67–86 (2014)

14. Roshani, A., Paolucci, M., Giglio, D., Demartini, M., Tonelli, F., Dulebenets, M.A.: The capacitated lot-sizing and energy efficient single machine scheduling problem with sequence dependent setup times and costs in a closed-loop supply chain network. Ann. Oper. Res. **321**(1–2), 469–505 (2023)
15. Suzanne, E., Absi, N., Borodin, V.: Towards circular economy in production planning: challenges and opportunities. Eur. J. Oper. Res. **287**(1), 168–190 (2020)
16. Torkaman, S., Ghomi, S.F., Karimi, B.: Multi-stage multi-product multi-period production planning with sequence-dependent setups in closed-loop supply chain. Comput. Ind. Eng. **113**, 602–613 (2017)

A Radius-Based Approach for the Bi-Objective p-Center and p-Dispersion Problem

Niels De Walsche, Carlo S. Sartori(✉), and Hatice Çalık

Department of Computer Science, KU Leuven, Ghent, Belgium
niels.dewalsche@student.kuleuven.be,
{carlo.sartori,hatice.calik}@kuleuven.be

Abstract. Facility location is a well-known class of problems which come with a variety of objective functions. In applications such as emergency facility location where human life is at stake, service quality, which is measured by distance or time to reach facilities, and fairness become priority over cost. A certain level of service quality is often achieved through coverage constraints or *minimax* type of objective functions as it is the case in the p-center problem. In some other applications such as location of military bases and franchise stores, in addition to minimizing maximum service distance it may be desirable also to keep the facilities as distant as possible for competitiveness or security reasons. A problem of this sort corresponds to the bi-objective p-center and p-dispersion problem which requires locating p centers to serve a set of demand points. The p-center and p-dispersion problems are rather well-studied independently with efficient approximation algorithms, mathematical models and exact algorithms. This paper investigates effectiveness of radius-based formulations, approximation algorithms and matrix reduction rules for solving the complex optimization problem where these two objectives must be simultaneously optimized. We develop an exact algorithm to produce a set of efficient solutions for this problem by employing a mathematical formulation based on state-of-the-art models for both independent p-center and p-dispersion problems. Our algorithm creates a Pareto set with multiple solutions presenting different tradeoffs between the two objectives. A computational study with large-scale instances demonstrates the improved performance of our method compared to a previous approach from the literature.

Keywords: Facility location · p-center · p-dispersion · Bi-objective optimization

1 Introduction

The p-center problem (pC) is an NP-Hard [13] facility location problem (FLP) that requires location of p centers on a given network such that the maximum

© The Author(s), under exclusive license to Springer Nature Switzerland AG 2023
J. R. Daduna et al. (Eds.): ICCL 2023, LNCS 14239, pp. 533–549, 2023.
https://doi.org/10.1007/978-3-031-43612-3_33

distance between demand nodes and centers is minimized. The problem arises in emergency logistics for locating ambulances, fire stations, police patrol units and shelters; military logistics as well as districting. Similar to pC, the p-dispersion problem (pD) is also NP-hard [9] and requires locating p facilities on a given network. Unlike pC, the goal is to maximize the minimum distance between the selected facilities. The optimal solutions to these two problems could be significantly different as it can be observed in an OR-Library instance in Fig. 1. In the pC solution of Fig. 1(a), the facilities are more centralized in their clusters and in the entire network. The pD facilities in Fig. 1(b), however, are more dispersed and located at the extremes of the network. It is therefore worthwhile investigating bi-objective approaches if one wishes to maintain a certain level of balance between the two objectives.

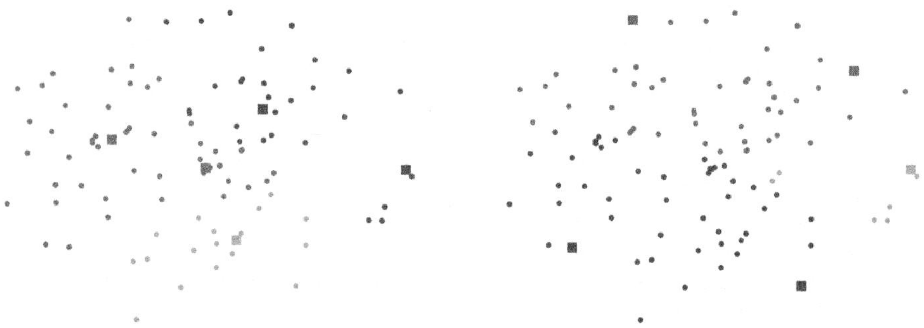

(a) Optimal pC solution. (b) Optimal pD solution.

Fig. 1. Optimal solutions for instance `pmed1` from OR-Library ($p = 5$). Square nodes indicate facilities and circles indicate demand points clustered with the color of their closest open facility.

In this paper we consider the *Bi-objective p-center and p-dispersion problem* (BpCD) which has been introduced by [20]. The BpCD requires locating p centers on a given network while simultaneously minimizing the maximum distance between demand points and centers (pC objective) and maximizing the minimum distance between centers (pD objective).

A notable application of BpCD is the location of franchises. Kuby [15] notes that pD is useful to reduce intra-chain competition, which arises when stores from the same franchise are located too close to each other. When they are close, their profit margins are reduced. However, Kuby also mentions that pD could be used in a multi-objective scenario alongside objectives such as the p-center. In such a case, we would like not only to minimize intra-chain competition, but also maximize customer reach by means of the p-center objective.

Similarly, one may find applications of BpCD in the positioning of military bases. On the one hand, we would like to ensure short distance ranges for the defense of strategic areas (pC). On the other hand, we want to maintain a safe distance between bases so as to avoid catastrophic results in case of enemy attacks (pD). Tutunchi and Fathi [20] also refer to applications in the positioning of traffic sensors in road networks. The objective is to monitor similar road segments using a few sensors (pC), while simultaneously diversifying the types of road segments for the remaining sensors (pD). It is clear therefore that there are many practical applications for the BpCD which motivated us to study new solution methods to solve this problem.

The contributions of this paper are twofold. First, we develop a method to quickly solve BpCD employing state-of-the-art mathematical formulations for p-center and pD. This includes exploiting the problem structure to develop a special-purpose algorithm based on decomposition into simpler subproblems instead of relying solely on general-purpose mathematical programming solvers. To speed up the methods, we employ effective lower and upper bounds as well as matrix reduction rules inspired by the well-established p-center literature. Second, we demonstrate by means of a comprehensive computational study the improvements obtained with our method, which is capable of solving far larger problems than previous approaches in the literature. We conclude this paper with a discussion over our results and directions for future research.

2 Literature Review

The seminal paper by [12] introduces the 1-center problem for the purpose of locating a police station on a given network so that the maximum distance from this station is minimum. Both absolute and vertex-restricted 1-center problems are discussed. An absolute center can be placed anywhere on the network whereas a vertex center has to be located at a vertex. Minieka [16] extends the problem to the case where $p > 1$ and provides an exact algorithm solving *set covering problems* for a finite number of *radius* (distance) values. This method has inspired the most efficient *radius formulations* and set covering-based algorithms for solving various p-center variants which have been reviewed by [2]. As [16] proves that there exists a finite set of points in the given graph which contains an optimal set of p centers for the absolute p-center problem and [10] provides a method for generating this finite set, it has been possible to develop mathematical formulations which can tackle both absolute and vertex p-center variants without further adaptations ([3,6,8] and [14] are a few examples). Although recently most p-center studies consider only vertex-restricted problems, absolute variants remain valid for many real-world applications.

A critical and careful review of the pC literature reveals two main categories of compact mathematical formulations: (1) Mixed-Integer Linear Programming (MILP) models based on the classical formulation with two-index allocation variables first provided by [6]. (2) Radius-based Integer Linear Programming (ILP) formulations which exploit the finite set of distinct distance values between the centers and the demand nodes. Radius formulations typically utilize either a telescopic sum of radius values [8] or enforce selection of exactly one radius value [3]. When the radius set is large, solving these formulations may require a substantial amount of computational resources. One may therefore resort to rather solving a set covering problem for each radius value, as done by [16], or within a more efficient binary search framework like [8]. The special structure of the formulations provided by [3] inspires many efficient search strategies solving the formulations for a subset of radius values at each iteration. Among them, the strategies considering two radius values at each iteration (double bound - DB), enable faster convergence in the presence of high quality upper bounds. The DB methods can easily be adapted to favor instances with high quality lower bounds. The computational study by [3] on data sets from the OR-Library [1] indicates that the formulations introduced by [3] are the most efficient pC formulations. One model by [3] provides the tightest known lower bound equivalent to that of [8]. The DB methods successfully solve instances with up to 3038 nodes from the TSPLIB (with 3 h time limit per model) while this number was restricted to 1817 previously. The efficiency of the DB methods for solving problem instances at this scale is also confirmed through the recent study by [5] whose algorithm solves problems with up to a million nodes, with relatively small p values that are not observed to be very challenging in previous studies.

In addition to the classical pC problems, many variants inspired by real-world applications have been investigated. We refer to [2] for further reading on several other pC variants and focus on the pD and BpCD in what follows.

The first discrete FLP with a pD objective can be traced back to [15]. Kuby [15] introduced MILP formulation for the problem using one-index variables. He also performed initial computational experiments with small instances and even considered a limited form of multi-objective optimization with a lexicographic evaluation where pD was first optimized and then an alternative objective was considered after fixing pD to its maximum value. Erkut [9] employed an IP formulation and both branch-and-bound and heuristic methods to solve the pD. Ravi et al. [17] presented a polynomial time 1/2-approximation algorithm for the pD, which is based on the same principles as of the 2-approximation algorithm for the pC [11].

Sayah and Irnich [19] introduced a new formulation for the pD which uses radius-based variables similarly to the formulation of [8] for the pC. They also discussed other models to solve the pD, including non-linear formulations. They performed a computational study using large p-median instances from the OR-Library and compared the performance of these different models. Results clearly demonstrated that the new formulation could solve more instances to optimality compared to other models within a time limit of 1800 s. Nevertheless, the formulation proposed by Sayah and Irnich [19] was not able to solve all `pmed` instances from the OR-Library to optimality. Contardo [4] further expanded on the research of [19] by employing a decomposition approach for solving the radius-based formulation instead of directly utilizing a general-purpose solver. He proposed to solve the problem by iteratively clustering locations, solving the pD and refining the clusters. This enabled reducing the model size and solve instances with up to 100,000 nodes under a time limit of 20h. For smaller instances the speedup compared to [19] was significant, thereby demonstrating the importance of not only employing an efficient formulation (the radius-based one), but also of using an efficient decomposition procedure to solve the problem.

The BpCD is first addressed by [20] who provided IP models for both the bi- and single-objective problems. As a solution approach, [20] introduced an incremental algorithm which is similar to the ϵ-constraint method. They used the pC model as base and added a constraint to ensure a minimum dispersion level in the optimal solution. By doing so, [20] obtained optimal values of pC at different dispersion levels, thereby creating a set of efficient solutions (Pareto front) for the bi-objective problem. Tutunchi and Fathi ensure additional computational efficiency by solving the pC formulation using a binary search approach where each subproblem is a set cover problem.

Table 1 provides a summary of the relevant literature. Column *Prob.* specifies the problem class. Columns *Ref.*, *Model and alg.* and *Notes* present information about each of the main references relevant to our research. Here, we make a distinction between approaches which use radius-based formulations and those that use some other form of (M)ILP model, including formulations with one- and two-index variables. The terms *LB* and *UB* denote that the approach makes use of lower- and upper-bound information during the optimization process. The term *VI* stands for Valid Inequalities, while *DR* stands for Dominance Rules, which can reduce the size of the formulation. The last two columns, n and p, indicate respectively the largest number of nodes and the largest number of facilities to be located in the instances tested by the associated reference.

Table 1. Summary of relevant literature.

Prob	Ref	Model and alg	Notes	n	p
pC	Daskin [6]	MILP, bisection search		900	200
	Elloumi et al. [8]	Radius, binary search	LB,UB	1817	150
	Çalık and Tansel [3]	Radius, DB	LB,UB,DR	3038	500
	Contardo et al. [5]	Row generation alg	LB,UB,DR	1,000,000	30
pD	Kuby [15]	MILP		25	10
	Erkut [9]	MILP, branch-and-bound	LB,UB	40	16
	Sayah and Irnich [19]	Radius	LB,UB,VI	900	200
	Contardo [4]	Radius, decomposition alg	LB,UB	100,000	20
BpCD	Tutunchi and Fathi [20]	MILP, incremental alg	LB,UB,VI	600	30
	This work	Radius, incremental alg	LB,UB,DR	2500	200

It becomes clear from Table 1 that developments for both pC and pD are a lot more advanced than those for BpCD, which is still a relatively recent problem. While researchers have been able to solve instances with up to a million nodes for pC and a hundred thousand nodes for pD, for BpCD only instances with up to 600 nodes could be solved until now. Table 1 also demonstrates that successful approaches for pC and pD make use of radius-based formulations. Finally, most methods make use of lower- and upper-bound information to at least some extent. However, only a few approaches use valid inequalities or dominance rules, techniques which can sometimes speed up the solution process.

Based on the information from the relevant literature, it is surprising that Tutunchi and Fathi [20] did not experiment with radius-based formulations to solve BpCD. It is our main hypothesis that addressing the BpCD by means of radius-based formulations allows us to increase the size of the problems that can be efficiently solved. Indeed, we will demonstrate that employing a suitable mathematical formulation allows us to solve instances which are 3–4 times larger than those solved using classic two-index MILP formulation.

3 Mathematical Model

Let G be a given undirected network with $I = \{1, \dots, n\}$ being the set of demand nodes and $J = \{1, \dots, m\}$ being the set of potential centers. The BpCD requires selecting a subset $X \subset J$ such that $|X| = p$ under two objective functions: (1) minimize the maximum distance between the centers and demand points and (2) maximize the minimum distance between the centers. Let us define d_{ij} as the shortest path distance between points i and j. Let $D^c = [d_{ij}]$ denote the $n \times m$ distance matrix between demand nodes and potential centers and $D^d = [d_{hj}]$ denote the $m \times m$ distance matrix between potential centers. The pC can then be formalized as $\min\limits_{X \subset J:|X|=p} \max\limits_{i \in I} \min\limits_{j \in X} d_{ij}$ whereas pD can be formalized as $\max\limits_{X \subset J:|X|=p} \min\limits_{h,j \in X:h \neq j} d_{hj}$. It is easy to observe that the optimal values of pC and pD will be equal to one of the entries in D^c and D^d, respectively. Consider two ordered sets $R = \{r_1, \dots, r_K\}$ and $Q = \{q_1, \dots, q_L\}$ of distinct distance values in D^c and D^d, respectively, and let R^I and Q^I be the corresponding index sets. Recalling the pC formulations of [3], it is then intuitive to associate a binary variable for each radius value in each set as follows.

$u_k = 1$ if $r_k, k \in R^I$ is the value of pC objective for BpCD, $u_k = 0$ otherwise.

$v_l = 1$ if $q_l, l \in Q^I$ is the value of pD objective for BpCD, $v_l = 0$ otherwise.

We may then formulate the BpCD as follows:

$$\min\ f_1 = \sum_{k \in R^I} r_k u_k \tag{1}$$

$$\max\ f_2 = \sum_{l \in Q^I} q_l v_l \tag{2}$$

$$\text{s.t.} \sum_{j \in J} y_j = p \tag{3}$$

$$\sum_{j \in J: d_{ij} \leq r_k} y_j \geq u_k, \qquad \forall\, i \in I,\ k \in R^I \tag{4}$$

$$\sum_{k \in R^I} u_k = 1 \tag{5}$$

$$y_h + y_j \leq 1 + \sum_{l \in Q^I: d_{hj} \geq q_l} v_l, \qquad \forall\, h, j \in J \tag{6}$$

$$\sum_{l \in Q^I} v_l = 1 \tag{7}$$

$$u_k \in \{0,1\}, \qquad \forall\, k \in R^I \tag{8}$$

$$v_l \in \{0,1\}, \qquad \forall\, l \in Q^I \tag{9}$$

$$y_j \in \{0,1\}, \qquad \forall\, j \in J \tag{10}$$

Functions (1) and (2) determine the objective values for pC and pD selected by Constraints (5) and (7) from R and Q, respectively. Constraints (4) ensure that each demand point is covered by a center within the selected pC radius. For any open center pair, Constraints (6) guarantee that the distance between them is greater than or equal to the selected pD value. Constraints (3) select exactly p centers and Constraints (8)-(10) are binary restrictions.

However, this BpCD formulation cannot be directly solved by general-purpose mathematical programming solvers. The existence of two competing objective functions requires more sophisticated solution techniques and, more importantly, it requires that we clarify what a good solution is. In this paper, we will use a terminology based on the work of Erghot et al. [7]. Let us begin by defining S as the set of all feasible solutions to BpCD and $s \in S$ is a solution (an assignment of facilities). Let us further denote objective value for pC by $f_1(s)$ and objective value for pD by $f_2(s)$ for solution s. A solution $s \in S$ *dominates* another solution $s' \in S$ if one of the following two conditions is true:

$$f_1(s) < f_1(s') \text{ and } f_2(s) \geq f_2(s') \tag{11}$$

$$f_1(s) \leq f_1(s') \text{ and } f_2(s) > f_2(s') \tag{12}$$

A solution s *strictly dominates* s' if

$$f_1(s) < f_1(s') \text{ and } f_2(s) > f_2(s') \tag{13}$$

Furthermore, a solution $s' \in S$ is called *weakly efficient* if there is no other solution $s \in S$ which strictly dominates s'. Meanwhile, a solution s' is called *efficient* if there is no other solution s which dominates s'. If we project solutions onto an x-y plane where the x-axis refers to f_1 and the y-axis to f_2, the resulting point of a (weakly) efficient solution is called a *(weakly) non-dominated* point. The goal of solving a bi-objective problem is typically that of producing the set of all (weakly) efficient solutions for which the set of all points in the plane is called the (weakly) non-dominated frontier. This frontier shows the tradeoffs between the two objective functions while the resulting set of solutions provides decision makers a number of options to choose from, rather than a single solution which is often the case for single-objective problems. The next section describes an algorithm to produce the set of weakly efficient solutions.

4 A Radius-Based Incremental Algorithm

The proposed *Radius-based Incremental Algorithm* (RIA) is based on the incremental algorithm from Tutunchi and Fathi [20]. The main difference between these two methods lies on how we approached the solution of subproblems. Algorithm 1 provides an overview of RIA.

In lines 1–2, the pC and pD associated with the BpCD instance are solved to optimality. This is done by employing the algorithms described in Sects. 4.1 and 4.2, respectively. Their results provide 2 sets of bounds for the subsequent incremental algorithm. Bound $[c^{min}, c^{max}]$ on pC objective, and bound $[l^{min}, l^{max}]$ on pD objective. Note that c^{min} is the optimal pC objective and l^{max} the optimal pD objective. Meanwhile, c^{max} is the center value obtained from the optimal pD solution. Similarly, l^{min} is the dispersion value obtained from the optimal pC solution. In other words: the optimal solutions of *pC* and *pD* form the extreme points in our (weakly) non-dominated frontier.

After these extreme points are obtained, RIA continues to the main loop spanning lines 4–7. In each iteration of this loop, another (weakly) efficient solution is generated in line 5. The MCD-Algorithm is used to solve a pC formulation with an added constraint on the minimum dispersion required in the optimal solution. This dispersion is defined by means of parameter l, which changes in each iteration of the loop. A full description of the MCD-Algorithm can be found in Sect. 4.3. The algorithm returns both the optimal pC objective given a minimum dispersion l, denoted by $CenterVal$ as well as the dispersion $DispVal$ associated with this solution. Note that $DispVal \geq l$. In line 6, the minimum center bound c^{min} is updated to speed up subsequent MCD-Algorithm executions. The dispersion level l is updated in line 7 with the minimum value in Q that is larger than $DispVal$. The main loop is executed as long as $l \leq l^{max}$.

Algorithm 1. Radius-based Incremental Algorithm

Require: Network $G = (N, E)$, distance matrix D^c and D^d, and parameter p
1: $c^{min}, l^{min} \leftarrow$ MC-Algorithm(G, D^c, p)
2: $c^{max}, l^{max} \leftarrow$ MD-Algorithm(G, D^d, p)
3: $l \leftarrow l^{min}$
4: **while** $l \leq l^{max}$ **do**
5: $\quad CenterVal, DispVal \leftarrow$ MCD-Algorithm$(G, D^c, D^d, p, l, c^{min}, c^{max})$
6: $\quad c^{min} \leftarrow CenterVal$
7: $\quad l \leftarrow \min q \in Q : q > DispVal$

4.1 MC-Algorithm

In order to solve the pC problem, we use formulation MC which is defined as

$$\begin{aligned} &\min\ (1) \\ &\text{s.t. } (3) - (5), (8), (10) \end{aligned}$$

Optimal solutions for MC are obtained by means of the *double bound algorithm* DBR2 [3], which decomposes pC into a series of restrictive feasibility subproblems. It then simply searches for the smallest radius with an associated feasible solution. To speedup solving pC even further, we utilize the quick approximation algorithms from [3] to obtain lower- and upper-bounds for pC. This in turn can potentially reduce the number of radii that must be considered by DBR2.

4.2 MD-Algorithm

For solving the pD problem, we utilize model MD which is defined as

$$\begin{aligned} &\max \ (2) \\ &\text{s.t. } (3), (6), (7), (9), (10) \end{aligned}$$

We again exploit the structure of the problem to solve pD as a series of restrictive feasibility subproblems by means of DBR2. Here, we employ the 1/2-approximation algorithm introduced by Ravi et al. [17] for pD. This provides us with lower- and upper-bound for the problem in a similar fashion as for the pC [3], which speeds up the solving time. Finally, we make the necessary modifications to the DBR2 for solving a maximization problem.

4.3 MCD-Algorithm

The MCD-Algorithm aims solving model MCD which is defined as follows

$$\begin{aligned} &\min \ (1) \\ &\text{s.t. } (3) - (5), (8), (10) \\ &y_i + y_j \leq 1 \qquad\qquad \forall\, i, j \in J : d_{ij} < l, i < j \qquad (14) \end{aligned}$$

where l is a parameter representing the minimum level of dispersion required in the optimal solution of pC. By varying l and solving different MCDs, we can successfully produce (weakly) efficient solutions for each dispersion level.

Unlike MC- and MD-Algorithm, DBR2 is not used to solve the MCD model. Instead we devise a similar algorithm which exploits the fact that the pC objective value will likely be close to the pC value found in a previous execution of the MCD-Algorithm. The rationale is simple. Suppose that during an iteration of RIA an objective value of c is found. If the solution is weakly efficient then the objective value of the next iteration is likely c as well. Since we do not know whether the solution found is efficient, it makes sense to first consider that the optimal solution for the model at an increased dispersion level is also c. Once we start solving model MCD by decomposition to a set cover problem, we first check whether c leads to a feasible set cover. If so, we can stop the search prematurely and save significant computational effort.

Based on these observations, we developed an alternative decomposition algorithm which proved to be more efficient for use within the MCD phase in RIA. This algorithm employs an ordered list of radii T containing all radius values between c^{min} and c^{max}. In this ordering, a radius value $r_k \in T$ is optimal for MCD with dispersion level l if r_{k-1} is an infeasible radius. It is therefore easy to see how we can quickly obtain an optimal solution by employing binary search, DBR2 or similar methods. With that in mind, our decomposition algorithm can be defined with three simple steps.

Step 1 - Find a Feasible Solution. We begin by searching for a radius which leads to a feasible MCD solution for the given dispersion l. This is achieved by starting with an index $k = 0$ and then repeatedly trying other radius values from the ordered list T until a feasible one is found. Note that $k = 0$ is associated with the optimal radius from the previous RIA iteration (current c^{min} value). Whenever the k-th radius fails to provide a feasible solution, we increase k by $k \leftarrow k + \alpha$. Value α denotes the step size. After each k update, we also update the step size as $\alpha \leftarrow 2\alpha$ (initially we set $\alpha = 4$). Step 1 terminates as soon as a feasible radius $r_k \in T$ is found. We will denote by k' the last k before we found a feasible solution (if $k = 0$ then $k' = 0$).

Step 2 - Reduce Range of Bounds. Once we have determined a feasible radius r_k for the current dispersion level, we try to find a small range of radii within which the optimal solution exists. This is done by means of a straightforward binary search over T. In the binary search, we use two indices: $a = k'$ and $b = k$. We then proceed by trying the middle point $m = \lfloor (a + b)/2 \rfloor$ and updating either a or b accordingly. This is done so long as $a - b > 4$.

Step 3 - Find Optimal Value. Finally, we search for the optimal value, which we know lies within the (index) range $[a, b]$. Note that $r_a \in T$ is infeasible from Steps 1 and 2. Therefore, if we try r_{a+1} and it turns out to be feasible, we may quickly end the search (r_{a+1} is optimal). Otherwise, we try r_{b-1} and if it is infeasible, we can also stop the search (r_b is optimal). If neither of the previous situations applies, we check r_{a+2}. If feasible, then the optimal solution is r_{a+2}, otherwise it must be r_{b-1} (recall that the range $[a, b]$ has at most five values because of Step 2).

4.4 Matrix Reduction Rules

In order to speed up RIA, we employ matrix reduction rules which can reduce the size of the models. This is done whenever we solve a feasibility subproblem to verify whether a given radius is feasible, for example when employing DBR2, or our special procedure from Sect. 4.3.

Consider an arbitrary iteration of the MC- or MCD-Algorithm where we are solving a feasibility problem for radius value r_k to verify whether it is a feasible pC objective. Recall that I denotes the set of demand nodes and J the set of potential facilities. We construct a matrix A^0 as follows.

$$A^0 = [a^0_{ij}] \text{ where } a^0_{ij} = 1 \text{ if } d_{ij} \leq r_k \text{ for } i \in I \text{ and } j \in J \tag{15}$$

This implies that matrix A^0 has a row corresponding to each demand point and a column corresponding to each potential facility.

Consider an arbitrary iteration of the MD- or MCD-Algorithm, where the radius value is equal to l for the pD objective. We construct a matrix B^0 as follows.

$$B^0 = [b^0_{jm}] \text{ where } b^0_{jm} = 1 \text{ if } d_{jm} \geq l \text{ for } j, m \in J \tag{16}$$

This implies that matrix B^0 has a row and column corresponding to each potential facility. Assuming that D^d is symmetric, B^0 will also be symmetric.

With the matrices defined, we can employ the following reduction rules sequentially and repetitively, where relevant and potentially beneficial. One of the consequences of these rules is removing potential facility locations. Suppose we know that node m can be excluded, we then update J as $J\backslash\{m\}$ which reduces the number of y variables. Where applicable, this change can be reflected in the matrices as follows. Column m from matrix A^h can be removed to obtain A^{h+1} and both row and column m from matrix B^h can be removed to obtain B^{h+1}.

Rule 1 - Center Fixing. Applicable to solve MC and MCD. Suppose for any row $i \in I$ and center matrix A^h the following condition holds:

$$\sum_{j \in J} a_{ij}^h = 1 \tag{17}$$

This implies that demand node i can only be covered by a single facility j^1 within the given radius r_k. Therefore, j^1 should be selected as facility location in every feasible solution of the problem with radius r_k. This can be ensured by setting $y_{j^1} = 1$. In BpCD it also implies that any facility $m \in J$ for which $b_{j^1 m}^h = 0$ holds should be excluded. Stated differently, because facility j^1 has to be selected, any facility m within the dispersion threshold l can not be selected.

Rule 2 - Coverage Feasibility. Applicable to solve MC and MCD. Suppose for any row $i \in I$ and center matrix A^h the following condition holds:

$$\sum_{j \in J} a_{ij}^h = 0 \tag{18}$$

This implies that demand node i cannot be covered by any facility within a given radius value r_k. Therefore, the problem is not feasible for that radius value (r_k) and will have to be increased. In BpCD facility coverage is not only dependant on r_k but also on the dispersion threshold l, consequently feasibility can be recovered by increasing r_k or lowering l.

Rule 3 - Dispersion Suitability. Applicable to solve MD and MCD. Suppose for some $j \in J$ the following condition holds:

$$\sum_{m \in M} b_{jm} < p - 1 \tag{19}$$

This implies that selecting j as a facility will make the problem infeasible for the given dispersion value (q_l) since it will not be possible to select $p-1$ other centers that are distant enough from j. Therefore, one can safely exclude j from J.

Rule 4 - Dominance. Applicable to solve MC and MCD. Suppose for any column pair j, $m \in J$ the following condition holds:

$$\text{For each } i \in I,\ a_{ij}^h \geq a_{im}^h \tag{20}$$

The condition implies that j can serve every demand point that m can and maybe more. Therefore, one can safely exclude m from the set of potential facilities since every solution that includes m can instead include j.

For MD and MCD we can similarly state the following. Suppose for any column pair j, $m \in J$ with $b_{jm} = 0$ the following conditions hold:

$$\text{For each } i \in J \setminus \{j, m\},\ b_{ij} \geq b_{im} \tag{21}$$

The condition implies that any potential facility respecting the dispersion threshold when m is selected will remain a potential facility if j is selected instead. Therefore, one can safely exclude m from J.

While Condition (20) can be applied to MC, and Condition (21) to MD, both conditions must be simultaneously verified to exclude m when solving MCD.

5 Computational Study

In this section we evaluate the performance of RIA to solve BpCD using instances from both the OR-Library [1] and the TSPLIB [18]. We implemented RIA in Java (OpenJDK 19) using CPLEX 22.1 to solve the mathematical programming formulations. All experiments were conducted in a computer with an AMD Ryzen 7 5800X processor at 3.8GHz with 8 cores, 16 GB of RAM and Windows 10 operating system. Furthermore, we have imposed a time limit of 2h per instance following the settings of Tutunchi and Fathi [20].

Table 2 reports results over the 40 `pmed` instances from the OR-Library. Column *Instance* provides the name of the instance, while columns $|N|$ and p contain the number of nodes in the input graph and the number of facilities that should be placed, respectively. Columns T_C and T_D report the execution time, in seconds, required to solve the first pC and pD, which provide bounds for the subsequent incremental algorithm. Finally, columns *Iter.* and T_{Total} report the number of iterations of the incremental algorithm and the total execution time in seconds to solve the BpCD defined by the given instance. Note that the number of iterations corresponds to the number of weakly efficient solutions. In other words: it corresponds to the size of the final pareto front.

The first observation we can make from Table 2 is that RIA was able to solve every OR-Library instance within less than 1600 s seconds of execution time. Although a precise comparison is not possible due to technological differences, this brings a great contrast to the results of Tutunchi and Fathi [20] where instances with $|N| = 300$ required 1600 s seconds on average to be solved. Furthermore, solving the initial pC and pD problems never required more than 30 s. Indeed, most of the time is spent in MCD-Algorithm executions where some dispersion limits l lead to difficult subproblems. For example, RIA solved the initial pC and pD for instance `pmed40` in 23 s, while the 19 iterations of the incremental algorithm required, in total, 1500 s seconds.

Let us now turn our attention to larger instances from TSPLIB to verify the scalability of RIA. Table 3 reports the results for a set of selected TSPLIB instances which are instances frequently utilized in the pC and pD literature. The Euclidean distance values are rounded up to the nearest integer. All of the selected instances contain $|N| > 1000$ locations. We solved each instance for $p \in \{5, 10, 20, 40, 100, 200\}$. The selection of p values was based on the results

Table 2. Results for `pmed` instances from OR-Library.

Instance	$\|N\|$	p	T_C	T_D	Iter.	T_{Total}
pmed1	100	5	0.2	<0.1	22	3.32
pmed2	100	10	0.1	<0.1	31	3.57
pmed3	100	10	<0.1	0.3	27	3.37
pmed4	100	20	<0.1	<0.1	31	1.20
pmed5	100	33	<0.1	<0.1	21	0.49
pmed6	200	5	0.4	<0.1	36	22.28
pmed7	200	10	0.1	0.2	40	24.42
pmed8	200	20	<0.1	0.5	38	19.15
pmed9	200	40	<0.1	0.2	31	3.23
pmed10	200	67	<0.1	<0.1	17	0.63
pmed11	300	5	<0.1	<0.1	33	28.63
pmed12	300	10	0.2	<0.1	43	62.11
pmed13	300	30	0.1	0.3	47	44.68
pmed14	300	60	<0.1	0.3	26	5.79
pmed15	300	100	<0.1	<0.1	20	0.75
pmed16	400	5	0.1	<0.1	39	47.40
pmed17	400	10	0.4	<0.1	47	119.30
pmed18	400	40	0.2	3.7	37	90.33
pmed19	400	80	0.1	0.5	25	7.15
pmed20	400	133	<0.1	<0.1	14	1.23
pmed21	500	5	0.6	<0.1	37	91.71
pmed22	500	10	1.3	0.1	35	144.36
pmed23	500	50	0.3	13.3	28	145.09
pmed24	500	100	0.2	1.1	21	6.91
pmed25	500	167	0.1	<0.1	13	1.62
pmed26	600	5	0.5	<0.1	27	115.97
pmed27	600	10	0.7	<0.1	44	240.65
pmed28	600	60	0.3	6.6	25	105.39
pmed29	600	120	0.2	1.1	21	16.09
pmed30	600	200	0.2	0.1	14	3.05
pmed31	700	5	1.3	<0.1	31	217.85
pmed32	700	10	3.0	<0.1	35	408.70
pmed33	700	70	0.6	11.5	23	316.41
pmed34	700	140	0.4	1.8	15	17.79
pmed35	800	5	0.3	<0.1	28	188.42
pmed36	800	10	2.4	<0.1	37	549.71
pmed37	800	80	0.6	7.4	22	631.15
pmed38	900	5	0.5	<0.1	17	122.80
pmed39	900	10	1.5	<0.1	28	516.80
pmed40	900	90	0.7	22.3	19	1516.84

of [3] so that we have different degrees of difficulty when solving BpCD. It is known that extreme values of p (too small or large) have a tendency of being easy to solve for pC and pD, while values in-between typically make the instance much harder to solve. Entries with a – denote cases for which RIA reached the 2h time limit and full execution could not be completed. Best lower- and upper-bounds obtained are reported for those instances under columns C_{LB}, C_{UB} and D_{LB}, D_{UB} for pC and pD, respectively.

Table 3. Results for selected TSPLIB instances.

Instance	$\|N\|$	p	C_{LB}	C_{UB}	T_C	D_{LB}	D_{UB}	T_D	Iter.	T_{Total}
u1060	1060	5	3456	3456	2.8	6862	6862	1.2	33	1235.69
u1060	1060	10	2273	2273	3.5	4478	4478	1.0	56	763.94
u1060	1060	20	1581	1581	7.0	2865	2865	1.8	56	434.30
u1060	1060	40	1021	1021	2.5	1758	1758	6.9	68	595.76
u1060	1060	100	570	570	1.3	944	944	2.2	59	55.74
u1060	1060	200	360	360	1.2	566	566	1.0	33	7.58
rl1323	1323	5	4543	4543	6.0	9719	9719	2.2	65	4509.53
rl1323	1323	10	3077	3077	8.4	5865	5865	2.4	58	2332.50
rl1323	1323	20	2016	2016	5.8	3612	3612	8.4	70	2159.99
rl1323	1323	40	1352	1352	9.9	2352	2352	34.5	86	3460.95
rl1323	1323	100	787	787	3.8	1270	1270	8.4	115	328.94
rl1323	1323	200	518	518	2.5	783	783	1.1	118	37.58
u1817	1817	5	715	715	7.6	1535	1535	3.4	76	–
u1817	1817	10	458	458	16.0	881	881	5.5	62	–
u1817	1817	20	309	309	97.1	559	559	167.2	40	5319.61
u1817	1817	40	209	209	503.6	364	364	516.8	16	–
u1817	1817	100	127	127	2.1	205	205	16.5	28	3449.97
u1817	1817	200	80	80	3.0	130	130	17.6	16	71.54
pr2392	2392	5	3827	3827	18.7	8086	8086	7.6	32	–
pr2392	2392	10	2581	2581	60.2	4976	4976	11.7	44	–
pr2392	2392	20	1736	1736	1693.1	3150	3150	1176.7	4	–
pr2392	2392	40	1173	1193	–	–	–	–	–	–
pr2392	2392	100	708	708	4069.6	1204	963	–	–	–
pr2392	2392	200	481	481	49.7	781	781	2059.7	90	–
d15112-modif-2500	2500	5	5856	5856	27.8	12217	12217	11.2	40	–
d15112-modif-2500	2500	10	3705	3705	27.8	7132	7132	5.0	62	–
d15112-modif-2500	2500	20	2573	2573	237.5	4773	4773	125.4	11	–
d15112-modif-2500	2500	40	1713	1726	–	–	–	–	–	–
d15112-modif-2500	2500	100	1050	1090	–	–	–	–	–	–
d15112-modif-2500	2500	200	723	723	2472.8	1146	1119	–	–	–

The increased size of the TSPLIB instances poses a challenge to our method. It is clear from Table 3 that solving the BpCD takes much longer for these instances, even if the times required to solve the initial pC and pD are still relatively short (most times are under 60 s). Total execution times grow significantly and in some cases they are close to, or exceed, 1h. These TSPLIB instances also have larger sets of weakly efficient solutions (*Iter.*) compared to OR-Library instances with differences as high as five times. However, this does not seem to be the cause of increased computation times since larger *Iter.* values are not necessarily correlated to longer total execution times.

Another interesting observation from Table 3 is that while solving instances for $p \in \{5, 10, 20, 40\}$ is difficult, the time to solve the same instance with $p \in \{100, 200\}$ is often much shorter. This corroborates what Çalık and Tansel [3] observed for pC, but here we notice the same behavior in the pD and BpCD. However, while pC and pD can be quickly solved for $p \in \{5, 10\}$, the same is not observed when solving BpCD. Indeed, for instance `u1817`, RIA could not finish execution for $p \in \{5, 10\}$ while it finished for $p = 20$. The reason being that some executions of the MCD-Algorithm took longer for these values of p and certain dispersion levels, leading RIA to exceed the time limit of 2h.

The positive contribution of the strong lower- and upper-bounds to improve the efficiency of the radius-based algorithms were confirmed in our computational study. We also observed a significant speed gain by utilizing the matrix reduction rules. More specifically, for MCD-Algorithm itself, these rules provided an average improvement of 22 s and a maximum improvement of 186 s when solving `pmed` instances. Employing a list of bitsets for the matrices instead of lists of Boolean variables played a very important role in this significant improvement with up to 100 times speed improvement.

6 Conclusion

This study reinforced the efficiency of radius-based formulations and exact decomposition algorithms based on their restrictive subproblems for solving a bi-objective location problem where the two objectives have *minimax* and *maximin* structures (BpCD). The efficient approximation algorithm available for the p-center (pC) and p-dispersion (pD) problems proved effective in largely reducing the search spaces for the decomposition algorithms for each individual problem. Another important improvement component which can be utilized in methods for solving similar pC and pD variants consists of the matrix reduction rules which were effectively employed in multiple steps of our radius-based incremental algorithm (RIA).

Despite our improvements, there are still limitations concerning the size of BpCD instances which can be effectively solved within a short computation time. The state-of-the-art methods for both pC and pD can tackle instances with tens of thousands of nodes. Meanwhile, RIA is the first approach to successfully breach the one thousand nodes threshold for BpCD, which indicates that there is a lot of room for additional research in trying to further reduce the gap between the single- and the bi-objective problems.

Possible options for future research include exploring a change in the main formulation within the incremental algorithm. While both our RIA and Tutunchi and Fathi [20] employed the pC formulation with an additional dispersion constraint, how would the performance be impacted if we employed the pD formulation with additional center constraints? Are there instances for which one formulation outperforms the other? Another open question refers to a capacitated version of BpCD where facilities have an associated maximum capacity. Although the radius-based formulations are still valid, they require additional allocation variables which increases the size of the models. Hence, a natural question appears: can medium- and large-scale instances still be solved exactly when facilities have capacities?

Acknowledgments. The authors acknowledge the support by Internal Funds KU Leuven and the Research Foundation Flanders (FWO) through the Strategic Basic Research project Data-driven logistics (S007318N).

References

1. Beasley, J.E.: OR-Library: distributing test problems by electronic mail. J. Oper. Res. Soc. **41**(11), 1069–1072 (1990). https://doi.org/10.2307/2582903
2. Çalık, H., Labbé, M., Yaman, H.: p-center problems. Location Sci. 51–65 (2019). https://doi.org/10.1007/978-3-319-13111-5_4
3. Çalık, H., Tansel, B.C.: Double bound method for solving the p-center location problem. Comput. Oper. Res. **40**(12), 2991–2999 (2013). https://doi.org/10.1016/j.cor.2013.07.011
4. Contardo, C.: Decremental clustering for the solution of p-dispersion problems to proven optimality. INFORMS J. Optim. **2**(2), 134–144 (2020). https://doi.org/10.1287/ijoo.2019.0027
5. Contardo, C., Iori, M., Kramer, R.: A scalable exact algorithm for the vertex p-center problem. Comput. Oper. Res. **103**, 211–220 (2019). https://doi.org/10.1016/j.cor.2018.11.006
6. Daskin, M.: Network and Discrete Location: Models, Algorithms and Applications, 2nd edn. Taylor & Francis, Milton Park (2013)
7. Ehrgott, M., Gandibleux, X., Przybylski, A.: Exact methods for multi-objective combinatorial optimisation. In: Greco, S., Ehrgott, M., Figueira, J.R. (eds.) Multiple Criteria Decision Analysis. ISORMS, vol. 233, pp. 817–850. Springer, New York (2016). https://doi.org/10.1007/978-1-4939-3094-4_19
8. Elloumi, S., Labbé, M., Pochet, Y.: A new formulation and resolution method for the p-center problem. INFORMS J. Comput. **16**(1), 84–94 (2004). https://doi.org/10.1287/ijoc.1030.0028
9. Erkut, E.: The discrete p-dispersion problem. Eur. J. Oper. Res. **46**(1), 48–60 (1990). https://doi.org/10.1016/0377-2217(90)90297-O
10. Garfinkel, R.S., Neebe, A.W., Rao, M.R.: The m-center problem: minimax facility location. Manage. Sci. **23**(10), 1133–1142 (1977). https://doi.org/10.1287/mnsc.23.10.1133
11. Gonzalez, T.F.: Clustering to minimize the maximum intercluster distance. Theor. Comput. Sci. **38**, 293–306 (1985). https://doi.org/10.1016/0304-3975(85)90224-5

12. Hakimi, S.L.: Optimum locations of switching centers and the absolute centers and medians of a graph. Oper. Res. **12**(3), 450–459 (1964). https://doi.org/10.1287/opre.12.3.450
13. D Kariv, O., Hakimi, S.L.: An algorithmic approach to network location problems. Part I: the p-centers. SIAM J. Appl. Math. **37**(3), 513–538 (1979). https://doi.org/10.1137/0137040
14. Kramer, R., Iori, M., Vidal, T.: Mathematical models and search algorithms for the capacitated p-center problem. INFORMS J. Comput. **32**(2), 444–460 (2020). https://doi.org/10.1287/ijoc.2019.0889
15. Kuby, M.J.: Programming models for facility dispersion: the p-dispersion and maxisum dispersion problems. Geogr. Anal. **19**(4), 315–329 (1987). https://doi.org/10.1111/j.1538-4632.1987.tb00133.x
16. Minieka, E.: The m-center problem. SIAM Rev. **12**(1), 138–139 (1970). https://doi.org/10.1137/1012016
17. Ravi, S.S., Rosenkrantz, D.J., Tayi, G.K.: Heuristic and special case algorithms for dispersion problems. Oper. Res. **42**(2), 299–310 (1994). https://doi.org/10.1287/opre.42.2.299
18. Reinelt, G.: TSPLIB-A traveling salesman problem library. ORSA J. Comput. **3**(4), 376–384 (1991). https://doi.org/10.1287/ijoc.3.4.376
19. Sayah, D., Irnich, S.: A new compact formulation for the discrete p-dispersion problem. Eur. J. Oper. Res. **256**(1), 62–67 (2017). https://doi.org/10.1016/j.ejor.2016.06.036
20. Tutunchi, G.K., Fathi, Y.: Effective methods for solving the bi-criteria p-center and p-dispersion problem. Comput. Oper. Res. **101**, 43–54 (2019). https://doi.org/10.1016/j.cor.2018.08.009

Author Index

© The Editor(s) (if applicable) and The Author(s), under exclusive license
to Springer Nature Switzerland AG 2023

J. R. Daduna et al. (Eds.): ICCL 2023, LNCS 14239, pp. 551–552, 2023.
https://doi.org/10.1007/978-3-031-43612-3

The manufacturer's authorised representative in the EU is Springer
Nature Customer Service Centre GmbH, Europaplatz 3, 69115 Heidelberg,
Germany. If you have any concerns regarding our products, please
contact ProductSafety@springernature.com

Printed and bound by CPI Group (UK) Ltd, Croydon, CR0 4YY
28/09/2026
02224064-0005